Texts in Philosophy
Volume 27

Unorthodox Analytic Philosophy

Volume 18
Contemporary Problems of Epistemology in the Light of Phenomenology. Temporal Consciousness and the Limits of Formal Theories
Stathis Livadas

Volume 19
History and Philosophy of Physics in South Cone
Roberto A. Martins, Guillermo Boido, and Víctor Rodríguez, eds.

Volume 20
History and Philosophy of Life Sciences in South Cone
Pablo Lorenzano, Lilian Al-Chueyr Pereira Martins, and Anna Carolina K. P. Regner, eds.

Volume 21
The Road Not Taken. On Husserl's Philosophy of Logic and Mathematics
Claire Ortiz Hill and Jairo José da Silva

Volume 22
The Good, the Right & the Fair – an introduction to ethics
Mickey Gjerris, Morten Ebbe Juul Nielsen, and Peter Sandøe

Volume 23
The Normative Structure of Responsibility. Law, Language, Ethics
Federico Faroldi

Volume 24
Karl Popper. A Centenary Assessment. Volume I. Life and Times, and Values in a World of Facts
Ian Jarvie, Karl Milford and David Miller, eds

Volume 25
Karl Popper. A Centenary Assessment. Volume II. Metaphysics and Epistemology
Ian Jarvie, Karl Milford and David Miller, eds

Volume 26
Karl Popper. A Centenary Assessment. Volume III Science
Ian Jarvie, Karl Milford and David Miller, eds

Volume 27
Unorthodox Analytic Philosophy
Guillermo E. Rosado Haddock

Texts in Philosophy Series Editors
Vincent F. Hendriks   vincent@hum.ku.dk
John Symons   jsymons@utep.edu
Dov Gabbay   dov.gabbay@kcl.ac.uk

Unorthodox Analytic Philosophy

Guillermo E. Rosado Haddock

© Individual authors and College Publications 2018.
All rights reserved.

ISBN 978-1-84890-273-2

College Publications
Scientific Director: Dov Gabbay
Managing Director: Jane Spurr

http://www.collegepublications.co.uk

Original cover design by Laraine Welch

Printed by Lightning Source, Milton Keynes, UK

All rights reserved. No part of this publication may be reproduced, stored in a retrieval system or transmitted in any form, or by any means, electronic, mechanical, photocopying, recording or otherwise without prior permission, in writing, from the publisher.

For Tinna,
for her love and emotional support

Table of Contents

Preface	ix
Acknowledgements	xiii
Introduction	1

(I) Some Fundamental Issues

1.	'The Interplay between Logic, Mathematics and Philosophy'	13
2.	'The Fine Structure of Sense-Referent Semantics'	31
3.	'On Analytic *a posteriori* Statements: are they Possible?'	57
4.	'On Analyticity *a posteriori* and Syntheticity *a priori*'	71
5.	'Some Heterodox Analytic Philosophy'	83
6.	'Intuitions, Concepts and Wholes'	105

(II) Husserl and other Philosophers

7.	'Husserl and Kant: voilà la différence'	115
8.	'Husserl as Analytic Philosopher'	143
9.	'The Old Husserl and the Young Carnap'	167
10.	'Husserl and Riemann'	199
11.	'Idealization in Mathematics: Husserl and Beyond'	221

(III) Doing Rigorous Philosophy: Critical Studies and Critical Reviews

12. Critical Study of Matthias Schirn (ed.), *Studien zu Freges Logik*	235
13. Essay Review of Matthias Schirn (ed.), *Frege: Importance and Legacy*	267
14. Critical Study of Oswaldo Chateaubiand's *Logical Forms*	297
15. Rereading the Young Carnap: Critical Study of *Der Raum*	327
16. 'Carnap's Relevance': Critical Study of Ramón Cirera, Andoni Ibarra and Thomas Mormann (eds.), *El Programa de Carnap*	359
17. Critical Review of Elisabeth Schuhmann (ed.), Edmund Husserl, *Alte und neue Logik: Vorlesung 1908/09*	391
18. Critical Review of Anastasio Alemán's, *Lógica, Matemáticas y Realidad*	403
19. 'The Other Philosophers of Mathematics': Critical Study of Jaakko Hintikka (ed.), *From Dedekind to Gödel*	419
20. Frege and the Fregeans: Critical Review of Dirk Greimann's, *Essays on Frege's Conception of Truth*	445
21. 'Critical Footnotes to Kanitscheider's Paper on Naturalism'	461

Bibliography 471
Name Index 487
Subject Index 495

Preface

The present book, *Unorthodox Analytic Philosophy*, is the third book I publish since my retirement from the University of Puerto Rico at Río Piedras in December 2010 and my sixth book since 2000. As happened with my books of 2000, 2012 and 2016, it is a book of essays, and like my book of 2012, *Against the Current*, all the essays are mine. The present book, however, combines two sorts of writings, since besides papers, most of them relatively recent –and three of them published here for the first time-, it contains some critical studies, most of them written earlier, even one of them almost at the beginning of my career. But critical studies have been especially helpful in polishing and developing my views, and I consider them as valuable for the philosopher as the exercises and practices in the gym for the athletes. I hope that some of the critical studies can serve as models for much younger philosophers to follow.

As all my previous writings, the present book is written from the perspective of someone who, though doing rigorous philosophy, clearly rejects the, in the best of cases, simplistic division of philosophy in analytic versus continental philosophy. But to reject such a grotesque simplification of the history of philosophy does not mean that we are opening the doors to all sorts of irrationalisms and obscurantisms. It means, among other things, that we do not want to be deprived of the rigorous study of the great philosophers of the past, like Plato or Aristotle, Leibniz, Kant or Husserl, in case some or all of their views cannot be forced into the rigid schemes of the ideological empiricism prevalent in the Anglo-American world, for which Ockam's razor is the first commandment of philosophy. Thus, it is not enough to go "*against the current*", but one has to clearly trace the boundaries between orthodox ideologically blinded empiricist analytic philosophy and "*unorthodox analytic philosophy*". It does not seem pointless to emphasize here, however, that ideological empiricism should be clearly distinguished from empiricism as a philosophical trend, as it flourished in the seventeen and eighteen centuries especially in Great Britain. By the way, I could very well have added David Hume to the above list of philosophers, and that because of two reasons, firstly, because Hume is also one of the really great philosophers in the history of mankind and, secondly, because his distinction between knowledge of matters of fact and that of relations of ideas –to which would belong logical and mathematical knowledge- would no doubt awake the ire of the Quineans and their ideological siblings.

***

Having been born and raised in Puerto Rico, the smallest Latin American country and the only one that has never obtained its independence, I, nonetheless, benefitted from the glory days of the University of Puerto Rico at Río Piedras, where I began my university studies at the age of sixteen in August of 1962, and where I obtained my BA in philosophy in 1966 and my MA in philosophy in 1968. The university had especially benefitted from the exiles after the Spanish Civil War and the Second World War, as well as from the dictatorships in different Latin American countries. Thus, the university combined North American, Latin American and European traditions, being the latter probably the strongest at the Philosophy Department. The Department of Philosophy had been founded in the early 1950s by an Austrian professor and a Chilean professor, and in my courses there all but one professor were either European or Latin American. There was also an emphasis in the study of languages, and in reading philosophers in the original and not via translations –and I followed that tradition. A solid knowledge of Kant's theoretical philosophy was probably the center of our formation, though already in my MA studies I developed a brief interest in Whitehead's and then a life long interest in Husserl's philosophy, but from a different perspective than phenomenologists.

As was natural in view of my philosophical education, immediately after obtaining my MA, I went to Germany for my doctoral studies. I studied in Göttingen, mostly philosophy of science, Tarski, Frege and traditional (empiricist) analytic philosophy, and in Bonn especially logic and some Husserl. Of course, since in Germany you had to be examined in three disciplines, I studied some mathematics and a little bit of linguistics, though I did not need the latter. After finishing my doctor studies at the Department of Logic of the University of Bonn under the guidance of Gisbert Hasenjaeger with a thesis on Husserl's philosophy of logic and mathematics, I returned to the University of Puerto Rico, which had financed my doctoral studies, and to the Department of Philosophy, where I had already taught an introductory course from 1967 to 1968. The commitment to the philosophical education and development of younger compatriots prevailed over the more egoistic decision of remaining in Europe and doing philosophy in a place with much more philosophical tradition. But in that moment I could not even envisage that I would write so much in philosophy and for so long. And, in fact, in my first years after my return to Puerto Rico I mostly taught and barely wrote. Indeed, it was already in the early 1980s that I began to publish mostly papers and critical studies, sometimes in our local philosophy journal, others – in a crescent rhythm- in international journals or collections of papers.

Nonetheless, the philosophical journey was not an easy one. Being an independent thinker and with a strong personality, I did not find much sympathy either in some colleagues or in the crescent strong bureaucracy of the university administration, and needed to waste much time and energy just trying to survive at the university. And in fact, since my interests and views were so strange even for colleagues at the department, my work was mostly done in isolation and with very little understanding or approval by the university authorities. In some sense, only the increasing international contacts –both by publishing in international journals and by taking part in international conferences- helped me prevent the complete isolation. On the other hand, although from the very beginning as university professor I was usually surrounded by the very best philosophy students –what certainly also helped generate jealousy in some colleagues-, times had changed, the university had begun, probably since about 1975, a long process of intellectual deterioration, and the selection of the very best students to help them financially in their doctoral studies completely disappeared. In a brief period at the end of the 1980s, in which I was chairman of the Department of Philosophy, I created a system of assistantships – usually an assistant in the Introduction to Logic course and a second one- to help some of the very best MA students finance their MA studies. But the process of deterioration of the university was already really underway, having had a quantum jump in the first decade of this century, and a complete academic deterioration after my retirement at the end of 2010. The Department of Philosophy exists now only nominally, having been almost completely dismantled. Thus, my individual success, which has certainly accelerated in this century, cannot make disappear the dark shadow of the deterioration of a university that was one of the best in Latin America in the 1960s to one of the worst in these days–with only a few bright spots in the natural sciences.

***

Most of the present book has been, therefore, written in an even more radical isolation than the previous ones. Only my life long friend Rafael González Rodríguez has set aside momentarily his obsessive interest in number theory to inquire about my papers, very especially about 'On Analytic *a posteriori* Statements: are they Possible?'. The preparation of this book would not have been possible without the emotional support and the technical aid of my wife, Tinna, to whom I dedicate the book. I have also benefitted from the technical advice and great patience of Jane Spurr of College Publications, as well as the technical advice of my friend Joel Donato, Director of the LabCAD of the general library of the University of Puerto Rico at Río Piedras. To both of them I am especially grateful.

Acknowledgements

The following eighteen of the twenty-one items (papers and critical studies) are published here with the kind permission of the original publishers, namely:
South-American Journal of Logic for item (1) 'The Interplay between Logic, Mathematics and Philosophy'
Logique et Analyse for item (3) 'On Analytic *a posteriori* Statements: are they Possible?
Principia for items (5) 'Some Heterodox Analytic Philosophy' and (16) "Carnap's Relevance': Critical Study of R. Cirera et al. (eds.), *El Programa de Carnap*'
Notae Philosophicae Scientia Formalis for item (6) 'Intuitions, Concepts and Wholes'
Walter de Gruyter for items (8) 'Husserl as Analytic Philosopher' and (9) 'The Old Husserl and the Young Carnap'
Springer Science for items (10) 'Husserl and Riemann', (17) 'Critical Review of Elisabeth Schuhmann (ed), Edmund Husserl, *Alte und neue Logik, Vorlesungen 1908/09*' and (19) 'The Other Philosophers of Mathematics: Critical Study of Jaakko Hintikka (ed.), *From Dedekind to Gödel*'
Brill-Rodopi for item (11) 'Idealization in Mathematics'
Diálogos for item (12) 'Critical Study of Matthias Schirn (ed.), *Studien zu Freges Logik*'
Taylor and Francis for item (13) 'Essay Review of Matthias Schirn (ed.), *Frege: Importance and Legacy*'
Manuscrito for items (14) 'Critical Study of Oswaldo Chateaubriand's *Logical Forms* and (15) 'Rereading the Young Carnap: Critical Study of *Der Raum*'
Oxford University Press for item (18) 'Critical Review of Anastasio Alemán's, *Lógica, Matemáticas y Realidad*'
Philosophisches Jahrbuch for item (20) 'Frege and the Fregeans: Critical Review of Dirk Greimann's, *Essays on Frege's Conception of Truth*
Prof. Dr. Werner Loh, former editor of the now defunct journal *Erwägen, Wissen, Ethik* for 'Critical Footnotes to Kanitscheider's Paper on Naturalism'
Items (2), (4) and (7) have never been published before.

Introduction

If Karl Popper had not baptized his philosophy with the name 'critical rationalism', I would have used that expression to name my philosophical endeavours since the 1970s up to this date. Thus, I have called those endeavours 'unorthodox analytic philosophy', trying to point out both that I am perfectly conscious that you cannot do serious philosophy without taking in account the development at least of the three more exact sciences, namely, logic, mathematics and physics, but without committing to or presupposing in any sense the giant meta-dogma of empiricist ideology. The empiricist ideology operates, mostly in Anglo American philosophy as a presupposition of most of the academic discussion –not very different from historical and so-called dialectical materialism in the former Soviet Union-, and even the insurmountable difficulties confronted by the relatively moderate logical empiricism with the testing (verification or falsification) of physical laws has not deterred empiricists from their ideology. On the contrary, instead of considering more adequate non-empiricist approaches to the philosophy of physical science, after the demise of logical empiricism many have found a presumed salvation in a more radical form of empiricism, namely, that of Quine and its followers, with its 'bugs epistemology' –as I call it in one of the papers- and its totally unfounded holism, which has been unsoundly baptized as the 'Duhem-Quine thesis', doing a great injustice to the certainly non-empiricist Duhem and a great undeserved honour to Quine. By the way, it was precisely Duhem, as well as Husserl in his brief but very profound analysis of physical laws at the beginning of the last chapter of the first volume of *Logische Untersuchungen*, and, on the other hand, Poincaré, who showed the way for a more adequate and more rational analysis of physical science.

My concerns, however, both here and elsewhere have been more with the other two most exact disciplines, logic and mathematics, and only somewhat marginally with physics. And in mathematics, empiricism has its ideological cousin, namely, nominalism, which has permeated for many decades in the Anglo American world the central discussion in the philosophy of mathematics. Thus, nominalist philosophers of mathematics have built all sorts of fairy tales to avoid accepting abstract entities, and once more another of Quine's incorrect theses, namely, that 'to be is to be the value of a variable' has served many nominalist analytic philosophers to find illusory comfort in first-order logic. But if they accept the semantics of classical first-order logic, that is classical model theory, there is no way out of Platonism, since one is dealing with full blown mathematical structures. After many frustrations, some empiricist analytic philosophers have evolved to what they call "indispensabilism", according to which mathematical entities exist if they are applied to the natural sciences, especially to physics and, moreover, their existence is similar to that of physical entities. But besides arbitrarily dividing the family of mathematical entities in those that exist –for example, real-valued functions- and those that do not exist –for example, the fifth infinite cardinal, ultraproducts and the category of topological spaces-, it is a consequence of such a bizarre conception that some mathematical entities can be born, as happened with tensors, which luckily had general relativity as midwife –or Hilbert spaces, with quantum mechanics as midwife-, and that some could even die, if with the evolution of physics its applications to that discipline disappear.

Leaving orthodox (empiricist) analytic philosophy and its difficulties aside, let us now consider, on a more positive note, unorthodox analytic philosophy. Besides taking seriously the development of the three more exact sciences and even using some of its results to refute rival philosophical views, unorthodox analytic philosophy is essentially a contemporary version of rigorous philosophy in its most genuine sense. Leaving aside the great rigorous philosophers of antiquity and the modern period, the best-known analytic philosopher who certainly has nothing to do with orthodox (=empiricist) analytic philosophy is Gottlob Frege. The great logician and also very important philosopher was almost the antithesis of an empiricist. Though in comparison with other important philosophers of the past Frege's choice of philosophical issues was rather scarce, he was not only a staunch Platonist in mathematics, but also a logicist, believing that all non-geometrical mathematics was derivable from logic. But since he was both a logicist and a mathematical (ontological, not structuralist) Platonist, he felt compelled to postulate

Introduction

the existence of logical objects, being for him truth-values the quintessential logical objects. Though Frege did not discuss traditional metaphysical issues and almost nothing about physical science, it should be clear that he was as strongly rationalist and anti-empiricist as any philosopher in the last two centuries. And though orthodox analytic philosophers, not being able to render Frege as an empiricist, have tried to render him at least as a Kantian, even that rendering has no solid basis in Frege's writings. Besides very general and irrelevant points that so many post-Kantian philosophers have shared with the great Kant and that do not make one a Kantian, the only two substantial coincidences of Frege with Kant are (i) on the synthetic *a priori* nature of geometrical knowledge as discussed in Frege's philosophical masterpiece, *Die Grundlagen der Arithmetik*, though Frege's argumentation on behalf of the synthetic *a priori* nature of geometrical statements is different from that of Kant; and (ii) his classification of our cognitive faculties, present without any further discussion only in some sketches of papers of 1924-1925 –the last two years of Frege's life. Of course, Frege also coincided with Kant in his faith in Euclidean geometry, but so did almost all philosophers before Einstein's general theory of relativity in 1915, being Husserl the only notable exception, having adopted Riemann's views on geometry both with respect to geometrical multiplicities as to physical space since 1892, as attested by a letter to Franz Brentano at the end of that year.

Husserl, one of the really great philosophers in the history of mankind, is also one of the most misunderstood philosophers, misunderstood by his detractors, most of them among orthodox analytic philosophers who have not studied him, and misunderstood also by many of his followers who see in him only the founder of transcendental phenomenology. Both parties miss completely that part of Husserl's endeavours that make him without any doubt an unorthodox analytic philosopher. Besides his more transcendental phenomenological writings, the student of Kronecker and both student and assistant of Weierstrass, the colleague and friend of Cantor and later colleague and friend of Hilbert, Klein and Zermelo, and professor and later friend of Weyl and Born was intensively concerned from his youth work, *Philosophie der Arithmetik* of 1891 to the work he was organizing for publication with the help of his former assistant

Ludwig Landgrebe at the end of his life, *Erfahrung und Urteil* (1939), with central issues of analytic philosophy. Husserl's masterpiece, *Logische Untersuchungen* (1900-1901) is mostly concerned with problems central to analytic philosophy, as also is his *Formale und transzendentale Logik* (1929). Moreover, other books of Husserl concerned with logic, mathematics and language –three of the preferred areas of analytic philosophers- were published only posthumously, among them *Vorlesungen über Bedeutungslehre*, *Einleitung in die Logik und Erkenntnistheorie*, *Logik und allgemeine Wissenschaftstheorie* and *Vorlesungen über alte und neue Logik*, to name just a few. All of these works and others are especially relevant to the issues usually treated in analytic philosophy. Without entering in the details, since *Logische Untersuchungen* Husserl presented a program for mathematics that rivalled that of Frege. Husserl was a structuralist Platonist in mathematics, and not a logicist, though conceived logic and mathematics as sister disciplines, the second one clearly ontological –a formal ontology-, the first one more syntactic-semantic. Mathematics was for Husserl a theory of structures, with its fundamental disciplines built on what he called "formal-ontological categories", being the remaining mathematical structures obtained either by combination of some of the fundamental ones, or by specialization or a combination of both. If that sounds familiar is because the Bourbaki school adopted basically the same program even in the details, except for two points, namely, Husserl included a mereology among the fundamental disciplines and, more importantly, contrary to the Bourbaki school, Husserl did not consider the notion of set as the fundamental notion of mathematics, but only as one of the formal-ontological categories, together with those of part and whole, relation and others. One does not need to say too loud that this Husserlian program, with its synthesis of logic and mathematics in a *mathesis universalis*, has been much more successful than Frege's logicism even if the completeness of all formal systems in the *mathesis universalis* will remain forever as a Kantian idea. Frege's attempts to establish logicism in *Grundgesetze der Arithmetik* failed with the discovery of the Zermelo-Russell paradox –as it should be called-, and the later attempt by Whitehead and Russell in *Principia Mathematica* failed because (i) the Multiplicative Axiom is an equivalent of Zermelo's Axiom of Choice and, thus, is a non-logical mathematical statement, (ii) the Axiom of Reducibility seems arbitrary and of a non-logical nature, and (iii) the Axiom of Infinity, which also seems arbitrary and is not even a mathematical statement. Recent work by the so-called "neo-logicists" has not only been unsuccessful, but after the development of mathematics more or less along the lines of the Bourbaki school and that of category-theorists, the neo-logicist or neo-Fregean program is nothing other than an anachronistic remnant of nineteenth century mathematical reductionism, which played an important role in the rigorization and arithmetization of analysis by Weierstrass and Dedekind, but has been surpassed by twentieth century more abstract mathematics. If there were some doubt about the failure of the neo-Fregean program, I urge the neo-Fregeans to show where in the deductive chain beginning with purely logical axioms are theorems of category theory and general topology derived.

Karl Popper and even Alfred North Whitehead can also be considered unorthodox analytic philosophers, since both were very conscious of the importance and results of the three most exact sciences and developed philosophies that were consonant with such results. The case of Popper is clearer and we do not need to emphasize it. In the case of Whitehead, one should not forget his *Concept of Nature* and his *An Enquiry Concerning the Principles of Natural Knowledge*, which developed philosophical views taking serious account of General Relativity. But even his more metaphysical *Process and Reality* did not ignore the development of physics and, in particular, his theory of the extensive continuum contains interesting sketches of mereological nature –developed with independence of Husserl's sketches in the third of the *Logical Investigations* and of the much more elaborated mereology of Stanislaw Lesniewski.

Without doubt, many recent analytic philosophers in different countries are not orthodox but unorthodox analytic philosophers, since they in no way accept the meta-dogma of the empiricist ideology. The late Jaakko Hintikka would be a good example, as also the late Bob Hale, the German Gottfried Gabriel and other German Frege scholars, the Italian Roberto Poli, the Argentinean Mario Bunge, the Brazilian

Oswaldo Chateaubriand and many other Latin American analytic philosophers.

***

But let us say now a little about the papers and critical studies included in this book. The present collection consists of eleven mostly relatively recent papers and ten, sometimes longer and mostly older critical studies. I learned very early in my rather long career that writing detailed critical studies of books is an excellent way to sharpen your ideas, and I did it mostly with studies on Frege and on Husserl, which were the philosophers I was mostly concerned with. (In the case of Husserl I do not dare to say that I am a specialist, since he wrote so much –and a substantial part still awaits publication- that in a strict sense no one masters everything or almost everything written by the great philosopher.) I had originally a solid formation in Kant's theoretical philosophy and in Whitehead's philosophy –having studied the three above mentioned books when I was twenty to twenty-one years old-, but abandoned Whitehead completely, while only in two papers of the present book do I examine briefly some views of the great Kant.

The present book is divided into three parts, the first part – under the heading *Some Fundamental Issues*- consists of six papers concerned not with philosophers but with philosophical problems. The first one discusses interrelations between logic, mathematics and philosophy, offering examples of one of them being relevant to or even applied to another. Precisely the second paper -one of the three papers published here for the first time- is concerned with the application of the Frege-Husserl distinction between sense and referent, in the Husserlian version, since the Fregean version is sterile, to mathematical theories. (That distinction has been erroneously and unjustly attributed by scholars in the North American philosophical world –Church, Føllesdal et alia- only to Frege, though Husserl had it already in his paper 'Zur Logik der Zeichen', written in 1890 and in his review of Schröder's *Vorlesungen über die Algebra der Logik I* of 1891, which was in press when Frege's 'Funktion und Begriff' was

Introduction

published in January of 1891 and, moreover, since Frege himself acknowledges Husserl's independent discovery in a letter to Husserl of 24 May 1891.) The paper is in some sense the fulfilment of a promise to myself made after finishing my 'Remarks on Sense and Reference in Frege and Husserl', originally published in *Kant-Studien* in 1982 and then in my joint book with Claire Ortiz Hill included in the references. The third paper is the most ambitious. It contains a new definition of analyticity that survives all criticisms made to Kant's, Frege's and Carnap's definitions of analyticity, and even to the critique the present author had made to Husserl's definition of analyticity. By the way, I had already tried to define analyticity, for example, in the papers 'Husserl on Analyticity and Beyond' and 'Some Uses of Logic in Rigorous Philosophy', reprinted in my book of essays *Against the Current*, but needed to add an extra (third) condition to close a gap. My paper 'On Analytic *a posteriori* Statements: are they possible?' offers my definitive definition of analyticity. And with respect to the question made in the title of the paper, the answer is in a strict sense 'no'. Nonetheless, there exist instantiations of analytic laws, that is, what Husserl called "analytic necessities", that are *a posteriori*. Such instantiations of analytic laws, however, do not satisfy the third new clause of the definition of analyticity. The fourth paper, which is published here for the first time, is a sort of less rigorous presentation of the results in the former paper. The fifth paper of the first group deals with different issues in unorthodox analytic philosophy, in particular, presents my argument, already touched in the first paper, that Robinson's Model-Completeness test in classical (that is, first-order) model theory can be used to refute nominalism. The last paper of this first group serves as a sort of transition to the second group, since it touches an issue treated also in the first paper of the second group, namely, a critique of one of Kant's argumentations in the Transcendental Aesthetic to show that space (and time also) is not a concept but an intuition. Reference to Riemann's views is later made, and finally some remarks on Frege's and Husserl's divergent attitudes towards the notion of whole are discussed.

The second part –under the heading *Husserl and other Philosophers*-is concerned mostly, though not exclusively, with

Husserl's views and those of other philosophers or, in one case, with those of a mathematician with philosophical interests. The first paper is concerned with Husserl and Kant, a philosopher from whose views Husserl's views are sometimes not clearly distinguished by superficial readers or non-readers. The second paper in this second group is concerned with the many reasons why Husserl should be considered also an analytic philosopher, though clearly not an orthodox one. The third paper is concerned with Husserl's influence on Carnap, an issue on which I wrote a whole book, namely, *The Young Carnap's Unknown Master*, a critical study of Carnap's dissertation –which is included in the third part of this book- and another paper, namely, 'On the Interpretation of the Young Carnap's Philosophy', included in *Against the Current*. This is a delicate issue, since the unacknowledged strong influence of Husserl, especially in *Der logische Aufbau der Welt* but not only there is a clear example of intellectual dishonesty of Carnap. I know of this issue of Carnap's appropriation of Husserl's ideas since I was writing my MA thesis in 1967-1968 with respect to Carnap's distinction in *Logische Syntax* between formation rules and transformation rules and of the constitution of the heteropsychological in Carnap's *Aufbau* since 1968-1969 when I was beginning my doctoral studies in Germany, but only wrote about this, for my purely intellectual interests a relatively marginal issue, at the beginning of this century. In any case, though I studied Carnap very intensively during my doctoral studies, I always considered him a second fiddle philosopher. He needed someone to take the lead, first Husserl, who rejected him, then Wittgenstein who seemed not to like him, then Gödel up to the publication of *Logische Syntax* and finally Tarski after 1935. The fourth paper of the second part is a paper on the influence of the great German mathematician Bernhard Riemann on Husserl, a very important issue in order to understand the origin of Husserl's views on mathematics as a formal ontology, as a theory of formal structures or formal multiplicities. But Riemann also influenced Husserl on his views on physical space, as attested by letters of 1892 to Brentano –as mentioned above-, and of 1897 and 1901 to the Neo-Kantian Paul Natorp. Finally, the fifth and last paper in this section is concerned with idealization in mathematics, and more specifically, with Husserl's epistemology of mathematics.

The third part of the book –under the heading *Doing Rigorous Philosophy*- contains nine critical studies of books and a critical commentary of a long paper by the late Bernulf Kanitscheider. The first two very extensive critical studies, one of them by far the oldest piece in this book, are on books edited by one of the foremost –if not the foremost- Fregean scholar nowadays, Matthias Schirn. As a Fregean scholar myself, I used the occasions to point out my coincidences and differences with other Fregean scholars, and in this way also sharpen my views. I confess that in the later years I have felt disappointed with the popularity that some erroneous and sometimes almost crazy- interpretations of Frege have had in the Anglo American world, not to say with the incapacity of some so-called Anglo-American Fregean scholars to read Frege's writings in their original German. (By the way, Frege's, writings as well as Wittgenstein's *Tractatus* are written in the most simple German possible, especially if one contrasts it with the immeasurably more complicated German of Kant, Husserl or Hegel, to name only a few.) The third critical study is concerned with Oswaldo Chateaubriand's *Logical Forms*, a two-volumes Latin American masterpiece of philosophical analysis that deserves to be much better known. The fourth critical study concerns Carnap's not well known and not well understood dissertation, *Der Raum*, in which it is clearly seen –for those that want to see- the great influence of Husserl on that work, and which served me as a point of departure for my later writings on Husserl's influence on Carnap and on the attempts of the latter to cover them up. The fifth critical study is concerned with a book of essays on Carnap. As I did in the two books of essays on Frege mentioned above, I critically assessed the different renderings of Carnap while sharpening my own. The sixth critical study concerns a recent publication by Elisabeth Schuhmann of lectures of Husserl on old and new logic. In those lectures of 1908-1909, that is, after his transcendental turn, Husserl stresses that (philosophical) logic is *first philosophy*, contrary to what one would expect of the father of transcendental phenomenology. (I deal with this issue in more detail in my 'Husserl and Kant' paper.) Moreover, in these lectures Husserl answers critically to Frege's confusion in his letters to Husserl of 1906 of identifying having the same sense with being logically equivalent. Husserl had probably answered in letters to Frege of the same year, but they are missing from Frege's posthumous writings, apparently lost, together with Löwenheim's letters to Frege, during the so-called second-world war. The seventh critical study is of the book *Lógica, Matemáticas y Realidad* of the distinguished Spanish philosopher Anastasio Alemán. The eight rather long critical study, under the title 'The Other Philosophers of Mathematics' critically assesses the book edited by the late Jaakko Hintikka, *From Dedekind to Gödel*. The term 'other' in the title of the critical study is used in the sense of 'non-Frege'. The last of the critical studies of books is a critical assessment of a book of essays edited by the Fregean scholar Dirk Greimann on Frege's views on truth. Finally, the last piece of the book is a commentary to a long paper by the late Bernulf Kanitscheider, in a now extinct journal that used a format somewhat similar to that of The Library of Living Philosophers. In this case, a philosopher wrote a long paper, some twenty scholars criticized him and the original author responded to their criticisms. I felt especially honoured for being invited with Hintikka, Dummett, Bunge and others to assess Kanitscheider's paper.

I

Some Fundamental Issues

The Interplay between Logic, Mathematics and Philosophy

> In my opinion, mathematics, physics and philosophy form an interconnected scientific system, and I have always seen it a part of my life's work especially to cultivate the relationship between mathematics and philosophy.
> David Hilbert, Letter to the Undersecretary of the Ministry of Culture of 30 July 1918, quoted in Ortiz Hill and da Silva, *The Road Not Taken*, p. 391

Abstract

Applications of logic to mathematics are well known, as are also those of elementary logic in the refutation of the various empiricist criteria of cognitive significance and of Riemann's conception of n-extended magnitudes in the refutation of Kant's conception of space. However, the interplay between the three disciplines is much richer, and not only philosophy can serve to the conceptual clarification in the other two disciplines, but model theory can be used to refute views in the philosophy of logic and the philosophy of mathematics

§0 Introduction *et alia*

Probably the most important contribution of so-called analytic philosophy to philosophy is the application of logical tools to the study of philosophical problems. The development of logic in the last one hundred fifty years has been simply extraordinary, though usually only some of its most elementary parts have found application in philosophy. An example thereof was the refutation of the different proposals of cognitive significance by the logical empiricists and their associates in the 1930s. On the other hand, mathematics has also been applied during that same period to elucidate central philosophical problems, like that of the nature of physical space and time. As is well known, the development of non-Euclidean geometries helped refute the well-entrenched Kantian theory of space and time as *a priori* forms of our intuition. Though there was a staunch resistance by some philosophers, Riemann's view of the empirical nature of physical space and time finally triumphed after the development of general relativity.

In this paper we will be concerned not only with some applications of logic and mathematics to philosophy, and applications of logic to mathematics and of mathematics to logic, but also with the application of philosophy to logic and mathematics, something that at first sight looks as unreal.

As a sort of footnote to this Introduction, let us consider a very elementary application of a mathematical theory to philosophy, namely, to a philosophical assertion by Georg Wilhelm Friedrich Hegel that certainly has irritated more than one philosopher with some knowledge of post-Cantorian mathematics. In his book *Wissenschaft der Logik*[1], in English: *The Science of Logic* –though the book is neither about science nor about logic, but a metaphysical treatise-, Hegel asserts that there are two sorts of infinite, namely, an infinite that opposes the finite and that he calls "false infinite", and an infinite that synthesizes the finite and the so-called false infinite, which is supposed to be the "true infinite". However, as is now well known from the rudiments of set theory, adding finite to any sort of infinite leaves us with the same infinite. To put it more precisely: for any infinite cardinal κ and any finite n, $\kappa+n=\kappa=n+\kappa$. In fact, the following is true: $\kappa+\kappa=\kappa$, for any infinite κ. Of course, Hegel preceded the birth of set theory and, thus, one should not be too hard on him for the blooper. Nonetheless, it should serve as a reminder for any serious philosopher not to ignore the results of the most exact sciences: logic and mathematics (and also physics!). Let us consider in what follows less trivial and more interesting cases of the interplay between logic, mathematics and philosophy.

---

[1] *Wissenschaft der Logik* 1812-1813, second revised edition 1834, reprint, Felix Meiner, Hamburg 1967-1969. See volume I, Chapter II, Part C(c), pp. 132ff., especially p. 133.

§1 On the Application of Group Theory to Semantic Theories

The best-known semantic theory of sense and referent is that of Gottlob Frege[2], and many authors either consider that it is the only one, or prefer not to consider any alternative. Two expressions have the same sense if they are essentially synonymous. Hence, expressions in different languages that are perfect translations of each other are said to have the same sense. The same happens in the rare occasions in which two expressions of the same language are perfectly synonymous. Thus, 'The morning star is a planet' and 'Der Morgenstern ist ein Planet' are statements expressing the same sense, in one case in English, in the other one in German. On the other hand, different expressions can have different senses but refer to the same entity. Thus, for example, 'the least prime number', 'the least even number' and 'the only number that is both even and prime' are expressions referring uniquely to the number 2, though expressing different senses. On the other hand, the expression 'die kleinste Primzahl' has the same sense as the expression 'the least prime number'. But let us confine ourselves to only one language. The statements (i) 'the least even number is smaller than 3' and (ii) 'the least prime number is smaller than 3' express different senses. According to Frege, the referents of statements are truth-values, of which there are only two, namely, truth and falsity. Statements (i) and (ii), though having different senses, refer both to the truth. However, (iii) 'Paris is the capital of France on the 1st of January 2014; and (iv) 'The morning star is a planet' are also true statements and, thus, also refer to the truth.

A mapping from an English language statement to another can be called a transformation. One can consider a set of transformations in this mathematical sense of English statements to English statements in such a way that true statements are always assigned to true statements and false statements are always assigned to false ones, thus, dividing the set of statements into two equivalence classes. It can be easily seen

---

[2] See his classic paper 'Über Sinn und Bedeutung' 1892, reprint in Gottlob Frege, *Kleine Schriften*, edited by I. Angelelli, 1967, second edition, 1990, pp. 143-162, as well as, among others, *Grundgesetze der Arithmetik I*, 1893, reprint 1962.

that such a set of transformations is a group in the precise mathematical sense, since (a) any transformation has an inverse transformation, (b) there is the identical transformation assigning each statement to itself, and (c) the composition of transformations is associative. This group can very well be called "the Fregean Group".

However, if we examine statements (i)-(iv) above, we immediately observe that statements (i) and (ii) seem to be much nearly related to each other than to statements (iii) and (iv). An alternative semantic theory of sense and referent was propounded by Husserl in 1900 in the First Logical Investigation.[3] Husserl had already obtained the distinction between sense and referent in 1890[4] and made use of it in his review of Schröder's *Vorlesungen über die Algebra der Logik I*[5], as Frege himself acknowledged in a letter to Husserl dated 24 May 1891.[6] However, only in *Logische Untersuchungen* did Husserl's semantic theory with respect to statements reach its complete maturity. As Frege, Husserl distinguished between the sense and the referent of expressions, but besides a general agreement, radically differed both on the sense and referent of what Frege called 'conceptual words' and, more importantly for our present purpose, on the issue of the referents of statements. For Husserl, statements (i) and (ii) above have much more in common than with (iii) and (iv), namely, they refer to the same state of affairs, whereas (iii) and (iv) refer to completely different states of affairs. Thus, for Husserl, not truth-values, but states of affairs are the referents of statements. Both sentences (i) and (ii) refer to the mathematical fact that the number 2 is smaller than the number 3. There should be no doubt that Husserl's choice of a referent for statements is by far more informative than Frege's.

Nonetheless, in the First Logical Investigation Husserl had still not distinguished between his preferred candidate for the referent of

---

[3] *Logische Untersuchungen II* 1901, Hua XIX(1) 1984.
[4] In the posthumously published paper 'Zur Logik der Zeichen (Semiotik)', published as appendix to the Husserliana edition of *Philosophie der Arithmetik* 1891, Hua XII 1970, pp. 340-373.
[5] 'Besprechung von Ernst Schröders *Vorlesungen über die Algebra der Logik I*', reprint in *Aufsätze und Rezensionen 1890-1910*, Hua XXII, pp. 3-43.
[6] See Frege's *Wissenschaftlicher Briefwechsel* 1974, pp. 94-98.

statements and its supporting referential basis, namely, what from the Sixth Logical Investigation[7] on he called "the situation of affairs". Let us consider the following inequalities: (v) 5+2<7+1' and (vi) '7+1>5+2'. Contrary to the difference existing between (i) and (ii) above or between '5+2<7+1' and (vii) '4+3<6+2', which is a mere semantic difference, referring to the same states of affairs by means of expressions with different senses, the distinction between (v) and (vi) has a more ontological nature. Nonetheless, there is a common ontological basis for both inequalities, namely, that the number 8 occurs later in the natural number sequence –is, hence, a larger number- than the number 7. This Husserlian distinction between state of affairs and situation of affairs seems to be mostly limited to mathematical contexts, though a colloquial language case could be the following. Consider the following pairs of statements: (a) 'My neighbour, the car merchant Joe, has sold an expensive car' and (b) 'My childhood friend Peter has bought an expensive car'. Though I am not aware of it, it could very well be the case that statements (a) and (b), that clearly refer to different states of affairs, have the same situation of affairs as referential basis, in case Peter bought the car from Joe.[8]

Both the sameness of state of affairs and the sameness of situation of affairs give rise to groups of transformations between statements, as also does the sameness of sense. Hence, we now have four different groups of transformations of the statements of a natural language, as we sketched in an old paper a long time ago.[9] This is a clear case of the application of the mathematical theory of groups of transformations to philosophical semantics. Moreover, since states of affairs can be seen as equivalence classes of senses, situations of

---

[7] *Logische Untersuchungen II*, Hua XIX(2), 1984, §48. See also his *Vorlesungen über Bedeutungslehre*, Hua XXVI, 1987 §7.
[8] I obtained this example when I was nineteen and had my first acquaintance with the sense-referent distinction in Husserl's states of affairs version, only to learn some three years later that Husserl had obtained the distinction at least some sixty-five years before me.
[9] 'Remarks on Sense and Reference in Frege and Husserl' 1982, reprint in Claire Ortiz Hill & Guillermo E. Rosado Haddock, *Husserl or Frege?: Meaning, Objectivity and Mathematics* 2000, paperback edition, 2003, pp. 23-40. For the groups of transformations, see especially pp. 36-37.

affairs as equivalence classes of states of affairs, and truth-values as equivalence classes of situations of affairs, the groups of transformations determined by the sameness of truth-value, of situation of affairs, of state of affairs and that determined by the sameness of sense are clearly formally related. Nonetheless, only the groups of transformations determined by sameness of state of affairs and by sameness of situation of affairs are non-trivial, since the group of transformations determined by truth-value allows only for two equivalence classes, whereas the group of transformations determined by sameness of sense allows for as many equivalence classes as there are statements in the language, in fact, countably many. The group determined by sameness of state of affairs and the group determined by sameness of situation of affairs can be called the Husserlian Group I and the Husserlian Group II, respectively.

§2 The Application of Husserlian Philosophical Semantics to Logic

Though analytic philosophers and philosophical logicians are usually so fond of Fregean semantics, the fact of the matter is that only in propositional logic does Fregean semantics seem to be useful. As is well known, in that very elementary part of logic in some sense all differences between statements seem to be reduced to the sameness of truth-value.

The situation is certainly much different when we move up to first order logic, not to mention more complicated systems. Already in the intuitive and informal interpretation of first-order formulas and statements, what is referred to is not a truth-value, but a state of affairs. This is still clearer when we consider first-order semantics, namely classical model theory. Statements are interpreted by states of affairs or classes of states of affairs in the different models, not simply by truth-values.

Nonetheless, situations of affairs –although less conspicuously than states of affairs- also admit an important application to first order semantics. As already mentioned, situations of affairs can be seen as equivalence classes of states of affairs. Now, in classical model theory there are metatheorems establishing the equivalence between statements that seem at first sight not to be related, since they talk about very different states of affairs. Nonetheless the statements are equivalent. A foremost example of this issue is Abraham Robinson's Model-Completeness Test, of which we will say much more below. The necessary and sufficient conditions for model-completeness made explicit in the formulation of that important result in classical model theory, though equivalent, clearly refer to different states of affairs. On the other hand, such statements are more strongly related with each other than with statements with which they only share the same truth-value. It seems pertinent to say that the necessary and sufficient conditions for model–completeness mentioned in the Model-Completeness Test have in common the same situation of affairs.

§3 The Application of Husserlian Philosophical Semantics to Mathematics

In his *Vorlesungen über Bedeutungslehre*[10] the mathematician turned philosopher Edmund Husserl considered –though did not elaborate- the possibility of applying his distinction between states of affairs and situations of affairs to physics. So far as we know, he did not envisage its application to mathematics –as the present author has done in some older papers.[11] In any case, as we mentioned above, equivalences between statements in classical model theory can be fruitfully rendered as sameness of situation of affairs. On the other hand, not only in logic, but also in mathematics, statements seem to refer to states of affairs. And as happens with meta-statements in model theory about equivalences between statements, meta-statements in mathematics can very well be interpreted as saying that two or more equivalent statements have the same situation of affairs as referential basis. In earlier papers we have argued that one can fruitfully use the notion of situation of affairs to render both what dual statements in mathematics -like the Prime Ideal Theorem and the Ultrafilter

---

[10] *Vorlesungen über Bedeutungslehre*, Hua XXVI, 1987, §30 (b), pp. 101-102.
[11] See on this issue our 'On Husserl's Distinction between State of Affairs (Sachverhalt) and Situation of Affairs (Sachlage)', 'Interderivability of Seemingly Unrelated Mathematical Statements' and 'Platonism, Phenomenology and Interderivability', all included in the references.

Theorem- have in common and, more generally, what statements like the Axiom of Choice and its many equivalents in different areas of mathematics have in common. Thus, for example, the Axiom of Choice, Zorn's Lemma and Tychonoff's Theorem talk about very different things, that is, they refer to different states of affairs. But they have much more in common than any of them with the also true statement that 'Paris is the capital of France the 1st of January of 2014' or with '2+2=4'. What the Axiom of Choice, Zorn's Lemma and Tychonoff's Theorem have in common is the situation of affairs.[12]

§4 Logic Applied to Mathematics and Mathematics Applied to Logic

The application of one of the sister disciplines to the other is a much better known fact than the already mentioned. Among the many instances of application of logic to mathematics one can mention the applications of recursive function theory to applied mathematics and, more specifically, to computer science. One can also mention the multiple applications of classical model theory to algebra, a field that is especially alive and fruitful. Since one can consult almost any book on model theory to find multiple examples of those applications, it is unnecessary to dwell on this issue.[13]

A less studied case is that of the applications of mathematics to logic. Probably, the logicist prejudice that mathematics is derivable from logic -which, by the way, is not the case- has prevented logicians to explicitly discuss this issue. The fact of the matter is that mathematics makes possible the establishment of many metatheorems of logic. Both mathematical induction and its variant complete induction are of a mathematical nature, but they are used extensively in

---

[12] As pointed out in 'On Frege's Two Notions of Sense', we do not exclude the possibility of finer semantic distinctions in mathematics or elsewhere. In some sense, the semantic scheme of statement ↦ proposition ↦state of affairs ↦ situation of affairs ↦ truth-value should be seen as minimal.

[13] We have just recently learnt that there are applications of model theory by Jean-Louis Krivine and others to functional analysis. See José Iovino's *Applications of Model Theory to Functional Analysis*.

the proof of logical metatheorems. Hence, it was Husserl –and also Hilbert-, not Frege, who was right with respect to the relation between logic and mathematics. If mathematics were derivable from logic, one could not make use of mathematical theorems to prove logical theorems or metatheorems.

§5 Excursus on a non-logical Refutation of Kantian Constructivism

Before considering the application of logic to philosophical issues, specifically, issues in the philosophy of mathematics and the philosophy of logic, let us consider arguments not originating in logic that can be used to refute one of the most popular views in the philosophy of mathematics, namely, Kantian constructivism.

As is well known, there seem to be as many constructivisms as there are constructivists. Thus, the first problem with constructivism is that people like Kant, Brouwer, Markov, Bishop, Griss and others do not understand the same thing under mathematical constructivism. Moreover, in any of its versions constructivism has difficulties dealing with uncountable cardinalities. But even for the application of mathematics to physics you have to deal with real numbers and with functions on real numbers, thus, you have to admit at least two uncountable cardinalities, namely, the cardinality of the set of real numbers and the cardinality of the set of functions on real numbers.

Now, the origin of constructivism as a serious philosophy of mathematics is due mostly to the groundwork of Immanuel Kant, and his extraordinary influence on philosophy in the last two centuries. Nonetheless, as many others, Kant was a child of his century's theoretical limitations. Not only had alternative geometries not been seriously considered in Kant's times, but Kant was also limited by the philosophical tradition. As we have shown in our paper 'Intuitions, Concepts and Wholes'[14], Kant's arguments in the Transcendental Aesthetic on the intuitive nature of space and time, and on which the whole constructivist conception of Kant is built -according to which

---

[14] 'Intuitions, Concepts and Wholes', in *Notae Philosophicae Scientia Formalis 2 (1)*, 2013, pp. 45-53.

we construct mathematical entities in pure intuition-, is based on an exceptionally narrow view of concepts, a view entrenched in the philosophical tradition almost until the twentieth century. According to Kant, pure space (and also pure time) is an intuition because it is given to us as a unity such that all possible partial spaces are seen as delimitations of the one space, whereas concepts are given to us as contained in each of its presumed parts, for example, as the concept of a horse is contained in any representation of a concrete horse, or the concept of number is in some sense contained in the representation of any of the natural numbers. Nonetheless, it should be clear that Kant is presupposing that concepts are concerned only with discrete objects, each of which is a sort of instantiation of the concept. That is exactly what happens with discrete collections of objects, be they empirical and also finite, as that of horses, or non-empirical and also infinite, as that of natural numbers. Since partial spaces and partial times are not discrete instantiations of a general concept, but delimitations of the unique space or time, respectively, obtained by means of division –a division that can be iterated indefinitely and we always obtain smaller and smaller spaces (or times)-, space and time cannot be concepts, but intuitions.

However, since at least Bernhard Riemann's epoch-making monograph *Über die Hypothesen, welche der Geometrie zugrunde liegen*[15], in which the great mathematician, among many other things, subsumed Euclidean and non-Euclidean geometries with zero, respectively, negative or positive curvature under a general concept of an n-fold extended magnitude and then subsumed the concept of an n-fold extended continuous magnitude under the more general concept of a continuous manifold, contrasting this notion with that of a discrete manifold, while operating only with concepts and without referring to any sort of intuition, the ground for Kant's mathematical constructivism disappeared. There is no need to refer to intuition when considering the different geometric manifolds. Space and time are simply continuous manifolds, whereas the set of natural numbers is a

---

[15] *Über die Hypothesen welche der Geometrie zugrunde liegen* 1867, reprint, 1923, 1960.

manifold of discrete entities as is that of the set of horses. In fact, the development of mathematics in the nineteenth century, and not only that of geometry, helped expand considerably our notion of concept, and now the mathematician talks about the concept of group or the concept of topological space[16], though such concepts have little to do with concepts as understood by the philosophical tradition, including the great Kant.

§6 Classical Model Theory versus Constructivism

According to a well-known Quinean dogma[17], a logic's ontological commitment is determined by the application of the quantifiers: to be is to be a possible value of a quantifier. Hence, since second- and higher-order logics quantify over properties and relations, they are committed to abstract entities. On the contrary, since first-order logic only quantifies over individuals, it is not committed to the existence of abstract entities, and is safe for nominalists and other sorts of anti-Platonists. Carnap basically, though not in the details, agrees with Quine –of course, Carnap wrote it first- when, after postulating his Principle of Tolerance in *Logische Syntax der Sprache*[18], he discusses both an example of a restricted logic presumably without commitment to abstract entities, and a more liberal logic with such commitments. And as his Principle of Tolerance puts it, it is a matter of choice or taste to choose between logical languages with different commitments. In the present and the next section we will show that both Quine's and Carnap's assertions are false. In both cases we will be dealing with a first-order language with its classical semantics, that is, with what is usually called 'classical model theory'.

---

[16] A topological space is a family $\mathcal{T}$ of sets such that both $\mathcal{T}$ and the empty set $\emptyset$ are members of the family, as are also arbitrary unions and finite intersections of members of the family.

[17] See 'On what there is', 1948, reprinted in his *From a Logical Point of View*, pp. 1-19.

[18] *Logische Syntax der Sprache* 1934, enlarged English edition, *Logical Syntax of Language* 1937, §17, pp. 51-52.

In a philosophical paper of dubious quality[19] published in *The Journal of Symbolic Logic* when he was presiding over the *Association for Symbolic Logic*, Hilary Putnam defended a sort of mild constructivism for mathematics. He seemed not to be aware that the moment one accepts classical model theory one has to abandon any sort of constructivism. As stated by Wilfrid Hodges[20] and also by the present author[21], there are multiple theorems in model theory that directly belie any sort of constructivism. The best-known and probably most dramatic example is Tarski's Upward Löwenheim-Skolem Theorem, according to which, if a first-order theory has an infinite model of cardinality α, it has models of any infinite cardinality $\beta \geq \alpha$. In combination with the usual Löwenheim-Skolem Theorem, that means that when a first order theory has an infinite model, it has models of any infinite cardinality. Such results –and many others- in classical model theory clearly belie any idea of constructing models. They are simply forced on us the moment we accept classical, that is, first-order model theory.

As mentioned above, there are many other theorems in model theory that counter any attempt to interpret model theory constructively. An example is the famous theorem of Morley, according to which any (deductively) complete first-order theory with infinite models in a countable language that is α-categorical for a non-countable α is also β-categorical for any non-countable β. This surprising powerful result is also a slap in the face of any constructivism in mathematics.

§7 Classical Model Theory versus Nominalism and Conventionalism

If nominalism in mathematics were true, any existential statement about mathematical entities would be false. Moreover, if

---

[19] 'Models and Reality' 1980, reprinted in P. Benacerraf and H. Putnam (eds.), *Philosophy of Mathematics*, revised edition, pp. 421-444.
[20] See his 'Elementary Logic', in D. Gabbay and F. Guenthner (eds.), *Handbook of Philosophical Logic I*, p. 34.
[21] In 'Why and How Platonism?', *JIGPAL 15 (5/6)*, 2007, pp. 185-218.

nominalism were true, any universal statement about mathematical entities would be vacuously true. On the other hand, if conventionalism in mathematics were true, the truth or falsity of a mathematical statement, be it existential, universal or whatever, would not depend on how things are in the mathematical universe, but on our arbitrary conventions. We will show that classical model theory is incompatible both with nominalism and with conventionalism, refuting once and for all mathematical nominalism and mathematical conventionalism, and showing, by the way, that Quine's contention that first-order logic is only committed to the existence of individuals is false, and that, contrary to Carnap's Principle of Tolerance, one cannot arbitrarily choose a logic free of ontological commitments –of course, except when you renounce completely to classical model theory, depriving logic of any talk about mathematics.

Let us first fix some terminology. Let £ be a first-order language and $\mathcal{T}$ a theory –set of closed formulas- in that language. Let $\mathcal{M}$ and $\mathcal{M}^*$ be two models of the theory $\mathcal{T}$. The structure $\mathcal{M}$ is an elementary substructure of the structure $\mathcal{M}^*$ if and only if the universe M of $\mathcal{M}$ is a subset of the universe M* of $\mathcal{M}^*$, in symbols M⊆M*, and for any well-formed formula φ∈£ in the variables $x_1,…,x_n$ and any $d_1,…,d_n$∈M, $\models_{\mathcal{M}}\varphi[d_1,…,d_n]$ if and only if $\models_{\mathcal{M}^*}\varphi[d_1,…,d_n]$. $\mathcal{M}$ is only a substructure of $\mathcal{M}^*$ if the above is valid only for atomic φ (and its Boolean combinations, that is, its quantifier-free combinations). Moreover, a theory $\mathcal{T}$ in a first-order language £ is model-complete if for any two models $\mathcal{M}$ and $\mathcal{M}^*$ of $\mathcal{T}$, if $\mathcal{M}$ is a substructure of $\mathcal{M}^*$, then $\mathcal{M}$ is an elementary substructure of $\mathcal{M}^*$. Abraham Robinson's Model-Completeness Test then says, among other things, that a consistent first-order theory $\mathcal{T}$ in the language £ is model-complete if and only if for any existential sentence φ in £, there exists a universal sentence ψ in £ such that $\mathcal{T}\models\varphi\leftrightarrow\psi$, that is, on the basis of $\mathcal{T}$, φ and ψ are logically equivalent.

Now let us suppose, for the sake of the argument, that we have a nominalist first-order language, that is, one in which any existential statements are false and any universal statements are vacuously true. However, an immediate consequence of Robinson's Model-Completeness Test is precisely that not all existential statements in a first-order language can be false or all universal statements true. For any (presumably false) existential statement in the language, there is a universal one logically equivalent to it, and thus, false. Hence, not all universal statements can be true. But their negations are also logically equivalent though true, and are also logically equivalent to a universal, respectively, to an existential statement. Thus, not all existential statements can be false. Hence, nominalism has been refuted. Moreover, since we cannot make all existential statements false, or all of them true, or all universal statements true, or all of them false, conventionalism is also false. It is also false that first-order logic does not have an ontological commitment to abstract entities. Thus, Quine's contention about ontological commitment of logical languages is false. Moreover, it is also false that we can freely choose between an ontologically loaded and an ontologically virgin quantifier language. Hence, Carnap's Principle of Tolerance is also false.

§8 Abstract Model Theory and the First-Order versus Second-Order Issue

Mostly motivated by their nominalist prejudices some philosophers of logic have tried more or less to disqualify second-order logic, arguing that since it is semantically incomplete, that is, there is not a complete adequacy between truth and theoremhood, it lacks a very important and desirable metalogical property of logical systems. However, their selection of semantic completeness –a property had by first-order and propositional logic-, as playing such a decisive role as to make logical systems lacking that property as affected by a plague, seems unwarranted. There are other desirable metalogical properties of logical systems under whose test first-order logic does not fare well. Take for example the property of decidability, namely, that there is a mechanical decision procedure to determine whether any given statement of the logic's language is a theorem or not. That metalogical property is had by propositional logic and by the first-order monadic fragment of first-order logic, but not by full first-order logic. Full first-order logic is as undecidable as second-order logic. On the other hand, there is the very important metalogical and metamathematical property of categoricity, that is, a theory $\mathcal{T}$ is categorical when all its models are isomorphic. With regard to this property, it is first-order logic, when compared to second-order logic that fares badly. There are mathematical theories known to be categorical, which when expressed in the language of first-order logic are not categorical, but when expressed in the language of second-order logic are categorical. The best-known example of such theories is Dedekind-Peano arithmetic: first-order Dedekind-Peano arithmetic is non-categorical –in virtue both of the Löwenheim-Skolem theorems and of Skolem's non-standard countable model (and its uncountable elementary extensions)-, whereas second-order Dedekind-Peano arithmetic is categorical. Of course, the expressive poverty of first-order languages has resulted in an extraordinary richness of its semantics. Non-categoricity, the Löwenheim-Skolem theorems and the Compactness theorem have made possible the unsuspected richness of classical model theory, whereas the categoricity of second-order theories, together with the failure both of the Löwenheim-Skolem theorems and the Compactness theorem do not allow for an interesting model theory of second-order logic.

In any case, the fact of the matter is that philosophers of logic have argued against second-order logic and on behalf of first-order logic adducing that second-order logic, besides not being semantically complete, does not have a unique semantics. They have argued that, besides full second-order semantics, in whose models there are as many relations and functions as there can possibly be, there are two other semantics for second-order logic, namely, Henkin's semantics and multi-sorted semantics. In multi-sorted semantics there are multiple non-hierarchisized domains, whereas in some models of Henkin's semantics there are not as many relations and functions as they can possibly be, for example, there are models with countable domain and also countable sets of functions and relations.

However, the fact of the matter is that one can prove that multi-sorted semantics and Henkin's semantics are equivalent, what reduces the number of possible semantics to two. Let us then leave multi-sorted semantics aside and examine Henkin's semantics. Henkin built his deviant second-order semantics in order to make possible the obtainment of a sort of Weak-Semantic Completeness Theorem for second-order logic. However, from this Weak Semantic Completeness Theorem follow as corollaries both a Compactness theorem for second-order logic as well as a sort of Löwenheim-Skolem theorem, thus, precisely the two fundamental metatheorems which second-order logic with its usual full semantics lacks. It was the great Swedish logician Per Lindström who offered a correct explanation for this presumed incongruence in the first and most important of his characterization theorems of first-order logic in contrast to any of its extensions.[22] The First Characterization theorem says that any extension of first-order logic –second-order logic is its most natural one- for which both the Compactness theorem and the Löwenheim-Skolem theorem are valid is equivalent to first-order logic. Hence, what Henkin really did when building a deviant semantics for second-order logic and then proving a Weak Semantic Completeness Theorem for second-order logic based on that semantics was really a reduction of second-order logic to first-order logic. Second-order logic with Henkin's semantics is no second-order logic at all, but a version of first-order logic. Therefore, the argument of the plurality of semantics used against second-order logic has been deflated. Second-order logic has only one semantics, namely, its classical full semantics for which neither semantic completeness, compactness nor the Löwenheim-Skolem theorem are valid. Thus, once more, logic has helped to solve a philosophical problem, this time in the philosophy of logic, not in the philosophy of mathematics, as in the previous section.

References

Carnap, Rudolf – *Logische Syntax der Sprache* 1934, enlarged English edition, *The Logical Syntax of Language*, Routledge, London 1937

---

[22] See, for example, his 'On Characterizing Elementary Logic', in Sören Stenlud (ed.), *Logical Theory and Semantic Analysis*, Reidel, Dordrecht 1974, pp. 129-146.

Frege, Gottlob – 'Über Sinn und Bedeutung' 1892, reprinted in Gottlob Frege *Kleine Schriften*, edited by Ignacio Angelelli, 1967, second revised edition, 1990, pp. 143-162

Frege, Gottlob – *Grundgesetze der Arithmetik I* 1893, *II* 1903, reprint in one volume, Georg Olms, Hildesheim 1962

Frege, Gottlob – *Kleine Schriften*, edited by Ignacio Angelelli, 1967, revised second edition, Georg Olms, Hildesheim 1990

Frege, Gottlob – *Wissenschaftlicher Briefwechsel*, Felix Meiner, Hamburg 1974

Frege, Gottlob – 'Brief an Husserl vom 24ten Mai 1891', in *Wissenschaftlicher Briefwechsel*, pp. 94-98

Hartimo, Mirja (ed.) – *Phenomenology and Mathematics*, Springer, Dordrecht et al. 2010

Hegel, Georg W.F. – *Wissenschaft der Logik* 1812(I)-1813(II), second edition, 1834, reprint, Felix Meiner, Hamburg 1967(I) and 1969(II)

Hill, Claire O. & Rosado Haddock, Guillermo E. – *Husserl or Frege: Meaning, Objectivity and Mathematics*, Open Court, Chicago et al. 2000, 2003

Hodges, Wilfrid – 'Elementary Logic', in D. Gabbay & F. Guenther (eds.), *Handbook of Philosophical Logic I*, Kluwer, Dordrecht 1983, pp. 1-131

Husserl, Edmund – 'Besprechung von E. Schröders *Vorlesungen über die Algebra der Logik I*' 1891, reprinted in Edmund Husserl, *Aufsätze und Rezensionen 1890-1910*, Hua XXII, Martinus Nijhoff 1979, pp. 3-43

Husserl, Edmund – *Logische Untersuchungen I* 1900 & *II* 1901, Hua XVIII 1975 & XIX 1984, Martinus Nijhoff, The Hague

Husserl, Edmund – 'Zur Logik der Zeichen' (1890), Appendix B(I) to *Philosophie der Arithmetik*, Hua XI 1970, pp. 340-373

Husserl, Edmund – *Vorlesungen über Bedeutungslehre*, Hua XXVI, Martinus Nijhoff 1987

Iovino, José – *Applications of Model Theory to Functional Analysis*, Dover, Mineola, N. Y. 2014

Lindström, Per – 'On Characterizing Elementary Logic', in Sören Stenlund (ed.), *Logical Theory and Semantic Analysis*, Reidel, Dordrecht 1974, pp. 129-146

Putnam, Hilary – 'Models and Reality', in *Journal of Symbolic Logic 45*, 1980 reprinted in P. Benacerraf & H. Putnam (eds.), *Philosophy of Mathematics*, revised edition, Cambridge University Press 1983, pp. 421-444

Quine, Willard van Orman – 'On what there is' 1948, reprinted in *From a Logical Point of View* 1953, pp. 1-19

Riemann, Bernhard – *Über die Hypothesen welche der Geometrie zugrunde liegen* 1867, third edition, Berlin 1923, reprint, Chelsea, New York 1960

Rosado Haddock, Guillermo E. – 'Remarks on Sense and Reference in Frege and Husserl' *Kant Studien* 1982, reprinted in Claire Ortiz Hill and Guillermo E. Rosado Haddock, pp. 23-40

Rosado Haddock, Guillermo E. – 'On Frege's Two Notions of Sense', *History and Philosophy of Logic 7 (1)* 1986, reprinted in Claire O. Hill and Guillermo E. Rosado Haddock, pp. 53-66

Rosado Haddock, Guillermo E. – 'On Husserl's Distinction between State of Affairs (Sachverhalt) and Situation of Affairs (Sachlage)', in Føllesdal, D., Mohanty, J. N. & Seebohm, Th. (eds.), *Phenomenology and the Formal Sciences*, Kluwer, Dordrecht 1991, pp. 35-48, reprinted in Claire O. Hill and Guillermo E. Rosado Haddock, pp. 253-262

Rosado Haddock, Guillermo E. – 'Interderivability of Seemingly Unrelated Mathematical Statements and the Philosophy of Mathematucs' *Diálogos 59* 1992, reprinted in Claire O. Hill and Guillermo E. Rosado Haddock, pp. 241-252

Rosado Haddock, Guillermo E. – 'Platonism, Phenomenology and Interderivability', in Mirja Hartimo (ed.), *Phenomenology and Mathematics*, Springer, Dordrecht et al. 2010, pp. 23-46, reprinted in *Against the Current*, Ontos Verlag 2012, pp. 235-259

Rosado Haddock, Guillermo E. – 'Why and How Platonism?', in *Journal of the Interest Group in Pure and Applied Logic 15 (5/6)*, 2007, pp. 621-636, reprinted in *Against the Current*, pp. 341-364

Rosado Haddock, Guillermo E. – *Against the Current*, Ontos Verlag, Frankfurt 2012

The Fine Structure of Sense-Referent Semantics (An Excursus into Semantic and Mathematical Platonism)

§1 Brief Historical Introduction

Around 1890 two seminal philosophers, namely, Husserl and Frege, arrived almost simultaneously and independently of each other to the semantic distinction between sense and referent. In fact, the also seminal philosopher and mathematician Bernard Bolzano almost arrived at the same distinction some half a century earlier.[1]

In any case, the distinction made famous by Frege's well known paper 'Über Sinn und Bedeutung'[2] of 1892 was present already in his also famous paper 'Funktion und Begriff'[3], which appeared in January of 1891. There is no earlier reference to the distinction in Frege's works, but one can suspect that he obtained it around 1889 to 1890. When 'Funktion und Begriff' was published, Husserl's review of Ernst Schröder's *Vorlesungen über die Algebra der Logik I*[4], which already contained the semantic distinction, had already been sent to the publisher, and appeared in March of 1891. Of course, as is well-known, the not so well-informed analytic philosophers usually attribute the distinction solely to Frege –and on this point they are easily rebutted by their same admired Frege, who in a letter to Husserl of 24 May 1891[5], acknowledged that the latter had arrived independently of him to the general distinction, though correctly suspected that they differed in the details.

---

[1] See his *Wissenschaft der Logik* 1812-1813, second revised edition 1834, Felix Meiner 1967-1969, volume I, Chapter II, Part C(c), pp. 132ff., especially p.133.
[2] 'Über Sinn und Bedeutung' 1892, reprinted in Frege's, *Kleine Schriften*, edited by Ignacio Angelleli, 1967, second edition, 1990, pp. 143-162.
[3] 'Funktion und Begriff' 1891, reprinted also in Frege's *Kleine Schriften*, edited by Ignacio Angelleli, pp. 125-142.
[4] 'Besprechung von Ernst Schröders *Vorlesungen über die Algebra der Logik I*' 1891, reprinted in *Aufsätze und Rezensionen 1890-1910*, Hua XXII, pp. 3-43.
[5] On this point, see Frege's *Wissenschatlicher Briefwechsel* 1974, pp. 94-98.

As a matter of fact, Husserl's earliest paper containing the distinction, 'Zur Logik der Zeichen (Semiotik)'[6] dates from 1890, though it was published only posthumously as an appendix to the Husserliana edition of *Philosophie der Arithmetik*. And certainly, Frege's suspicion was correct. Husserl differed from him in the details, having Frege also correctly mentioned that whereas for him the referent of a conceptual word (Frege's terminology) was the concept, for Husserl it was the extension of the concept, the concept being for the more than ten years younger of the two mathematicians turned (great) philosophers the sense of the conceptual word. By the way, Frege never clarified what the sense of a conceptual word is and how it can be distinguished both from the conceptual word itself and from the concept, that is, Frege never showed that many conceptual words express the same sense, which is (presumably) not the concept, nor how many of these mysterious senses "refer" to the same concept. He did not show that those relations were many-one relations, thus, that the presumed sense of conceptual words did not collapse either in the conceptual word itself or in the concept, which for him was supposed to be the referent of the conceptual word.

However, we are not interested here in the sense or referent of conceptual words, but in the referents of statements, and on this point Husserl also diverged clearly from Frege.

§2 Frege and Husserl on the Referents of Statements

As is well known, in Frege's sense-referent scheme the referent of a statement is a truth-value. But for Frege –and we are here, with Frege, presupposing classical logic- there are only two truth-values: the True and the False. Hence, the most diverse true statements, be it of

---

[6] 'Zur Logik der Zeichen (Semiotik)' was published as an appendix to the Husserliana edition of *Philosophie der Arithmetik*, Hua XI 1970, pp. 340-373.

logic or mathematics, of empirical science or of ordinary life, have the same referent, the True, and their negations have all the same referent, namely, the False. Thus, (1) The product of two compact topological spaces is a compact topological space; (2) 2+2=4; (3) Tigers are felines; (4) Bonn was the capital of Germany in 1973; and (5) The author of this paper is Guillermo Ernesto Rosado Haddock, all have the same referent, namely: the True; whereas their negations all refer to the False. Certainly, by putting all true statements in the same basket and all false ones in another complementary basket, Fregean semantics has reached a great simplicity very dear to simple-minded orthodox analytic philosophers, fearful of abstract entities and faithful to Ockam's Razor, the First Commandment of orthodox analytic ideology. Things, however, are not so simple, and throwing all statements expressible in natural language as well as those in the more exact languages of logic and mathematics in one of two baskets obscures obvious important distinctions. Moreover, the fact of the matter is that Fregean sense-referent semantics is useless in almost all logical-mathematical contexts. Solely in the case of propositional logic, where only the truth-value counts, could one argue that Fregean semantics is fruitful.

Husserl did not arrive to complete clarity on the referents of statements until the publication of his *opus magnum, Logische Untersuchungen*[7], and even in the First Logical Investigation the distinction between the two Husserlian alternatives –the 'Sachverhalt', usually translated as 'state of affairs' and the 'Sachlage', which we usually translate as 'situation of affairs', though maybe 'situation' would be sufficient- was not completely clear, and thus he states that the referents of statements are states of affairs but his examples correspond better to the notion of situation of affairs. Only in the Sixth Logical Investigation is the distinction between the two Husserlian candidates for referents of statements neatly established.[8] Let us consider first the notion of state of affairs.

Consider the following statements: (a) 'The morning star is a planet'; (b) 'The evening star is a planet'; (c) 'Berlin is the capital of

---

[7] See *Logische Untersuchungen* 1900-1901, U. I, Hua XIX(1) 1984.
[8] See *Logische Untersuchungen*, U. VI, §48.

Germany in September of 2016'; (d) '2+2<5'; and (e) '3+1<5'. According to Husserl, sentences (a) and (b) refer to the same state of affairs, namely, to the fact that Venus is a planet, whereas sentences (c), (d) and (e) do not refer to that state of affairs but to other states of affairs. But statements (d) and (e) also refer to the same state of affairs, namely to the mathematical fact that the number 4 precedes the number 5 in the natural number series. Statement (c) refers to a completely different state of affairs as (a) and (b), and also as (d) and (e).

Let us consider now the notion of a situation of affairs, the second Husserlian candidate for the referent of a statement, although in Husserlian semantics properly situations of affairs are really a sort of referential basis for states of affairs, which are the primary referents of statements. The following statements are certainly related: (i) '4+4>5+2'; (ii) '9-1>5+2'; and (iii) '5+2<9-1'. Statements (i) and (ii) differ in the same way as statements (a) and (b), or (d) and (e) above, namely, they express different senses, but refer to the same state of affairs, or, in other words, though they refer to the same state of affairs, namely, to the fact that the number 8 succeeds the number 7 in the natural number series, the reference is done by means of expressions that are not only different but express different senses. On the other hand, the difference between (ii) and (iii) is not one of two expressions having different senses but referring to the same state of affairs. The difference between (ii) and (iii) is not a difference of expressions diverging in meaning, but is more ontologically anchored. (iii) does not refer to the same relation as (ii), though by other expressive means, but to the inverse relation of the referent of (ii). They do not have the same state of affairs in common but the sort of proto-relation on which the relation '<' between natural numbers and its inverse '>' are based, a sort of abstract relation, or as Husserl used to say, a pre-predicative relation that serves as basis for the two states of affairs.

Though the distinction between states of affairs and situations of affairs seems to be more fruitful in logical-mathematical contexts, with which we will be mostly concerned here, that does not mean that it is not present also in natural languages. Firstly, it should be pointed out that pairs of sentences like 'John gives a rose to Mary' and 'Mary receives a rose from John', that is, pairs of sentences consisting of a sentence in which the verb 'to give' occurs and the corresponding sentence with the verb 'to receive', are very simple examples of two statements referring to different states of affairs with the same situation of affairs as referential basis. Other trivial examples are sentences in the active mode and their corresponding sentences in the passive mode. A less trivial example reads as follows. Let us consider the following two statements: 'My neighbour Peter, who is a salesman, has sold a luxurious car' and 'My childhood's friend John has bought a luxurious car'. Certainly, the two statements refer to two clearly different states of affairs, though as I could learn much later, those two different states of affairs had the same situation of affairs in common, in case Peter had sold the luxurious car to John.

That is enough for natural languages, and from now on we will be concerned exclusively with logic and mathematics. Before going into deeper waters, let us fix some important formal concepts.

§3 Some Preliminary Formal Considerations

At the end of our paper 'Remarks on Sense and Reference in Frege and Husserl'[9] we made some observations of a formal nature, some of which we will briefly mention here. We can consider the different sense-referent theories from a formal standpoint as objects associated to some group of transformations, since each corresponding set of transformations contains the identity transformation -id(s)=s for any statement s-, for any transformation tr in the set, its inverse tr^{-1} also belongs to the set, and the transformations obey the associative law. Moreover, the group of transformations associated to Fregean

---

[9]Originally published in *Kant-Studien 73 (4)*, pp. 425-439, 1982, and reprinted as Chapter 2 of Claire Ortiz Hill and Guillermo E. Rosado Haddock, *Husserl or Frege?*, Open Court 2000, 2003, pp. 23-40.

semantics, that is, transformations that preserve truth-value, is clearly the largest group of transformations, and divides the set of all statements of a language into two equivalence classes. With the two Husserlian alternatives that we have considered there are associated smaller groups of transformations, the larger one determined by the invariance of the situation of affairs, the smaller one determined by the invariance of the state of affairs. Both of them determine corresponding equivalence classes. In the case of the larger group, to an equivalence class belong all statements having the same situation of affairs as referential basis. In the case of the smaller group of transformations, to an equivalence class belong all statements referring to the same state of affairs. Finally, there is still the trivial group of transformations determined by sameness of sense. To the same equivalence class determined by sameness of sense belong only statements that are perfect synonyms, in case such statements exist in the language, thus, in this trivial uninteresting case equivalence classes will usually be unit classes.

One can also define a notion of depth of a semantic theory of sense and referent as follows: the depth of a sense-referent semantic theory is the number of semantic levels between the sense of a statement and its truth-value. In virtue of that definition, it follows that Frege's choice of a sense-referent theory has depth 0, whereas a semantic theory that has states of affairs as the referents of statements, but does not take into consideration the situations of affairs, has depth 1, and a theory like Husserl's, that considers both states of affairs and situations of affairs as intermediate levels between the level of senses and that of truth-values has depth 2. For semantic theories of natural languages that seems certainly enough. Let us now sketchily examine how some of the ideas introduced above could be used in other realms.

§4 What about Logic?

The semantics of a logical language –leaving aside the triviality of the truth-tables for propositional logic- is its model theory, and when we say 'model theory', we have to especially consider the model theory of first-order classical logic. The model theory of all extensions of classical first-order logic have the handicap established by Per Lindström's First Characterization Theorem[10], namely: Any extension of first-order (classical) logic for which both the Compactness Theorem and the Löwenheim-Skolem Theorem are true is equivalent to first-order logic; that is, it collapses into first-order logic and is, thus, no proper extension of it. Hence, any genuine extension of first-order logic lacks either the Compactness Theorem or the Löwenheim-Skolem Theorem, or –as in the case of second-order logic- both, and since precisely both theorems play a decisive role in the richness of classical model theory, the model theory of genuine extensions of first-order logic is essentially poorer than its first-order counterpart. Nonetheless, such a limitation does not concern us here, since for our present purpose and perspective -which are not those of the model-theorist but of the philosopher acquainted with that beautiful part of science- classical (first-order) model theory is enough.

Thus, let us consider a first-order language with its corresponding semantics, that is, model theory. Our purpose here is to sketchily examine the layers of semantic levels. Consider first a quantifier-free statement, that is, a well-formed-formula without quantifiers or free variables, for example, a statement of the form '$H(c_1,c_2)$', which states that the individuals (objects) a_1 and a_2 denoted by c_1 and c_2, respectively, and belonging to the universe of a structure $\mathcal{M}$ are in the relation R_H that interprets the dyadic predicate H in that structure. The referent of the statement '$H(c_1,c_2)$' is, hence, a state of affairs in the structure $\mathcal{M}$ -thus, certainly not a truth-value. In the same way, a Boolean combination of statements, for example, '$H(c_1,c_2) \vee G(c_2,c_3)$' has also a state of affairs as referent, though a

---

[10] See his paper 'On Characterizing Elementary Logic', in Sören Stenlund, ed., *Logical Theory and Semantic Analysis*, pp.129-146.

complex one. Of course, in other possible interpretations, the quantifier free statements refer to other states of affairs.

In the case of so-called propositional functions of first-order logic, that is, schemes of statements having free variables, they, of course, do not refer to any particular state of affairs, though we can here, correspondingly, speak of schemes of states of affairs.

Much more interesting is the case of statements containing quantifiers, be it the universal or the existential one, or both. Statements containing quantifiers certainly refer in the different models that serve as their interpretations, but their referents are not particular states of affairs, as in the case of quantifier-free statements. Statements containing quantifiers refer, in any interpretation, to sets of states of affairs, namely, of all states of affairs that would result if we were to delete all quantifiers, fix the referents of the predicate letters and simultaneously replace all the individual variables in the matrix of the propositional function by names of members of the universe of the interpretation. But since there are indefinitely (most surely infinitely) many models in which the quantified statement is true, the referent of the quantified statement is not a set of states of affairs but a sort of set of sets of states of affairs.[11] We will call such referents of quantified statements abstract states of affairs. And when two quantified statements of first-order logic are logically equivalent they have the same set of sets of states of affairs, thus, the same abstract state of affairs as referent.

Things would get a little more complicated if we were to abandon first-order logic and enter the realm of its most natural extension: second-order logic. Then we would have to take into account the predicate variables and, hence, richer and more

---

[11] For simplicity's sake, we ignore here the distinction made in Bernays-von Neumann-Gödel set theory between sets and classes (very big sets), thus, implicitly presupposing a Zermelo-Fraenkel set theory.

complicated sets of sets of states of affairs. Nonetheless, we can still say that the referents of second-order quantified statements are also sets of sets of states of affairs, that is, abstract states of affairs. A more significant difference appears when we move not higher in the hierarchy of object languages but to the metalogical level. But before entering in metalogical considerations, let us say a few words about logic's sister discipline.

§5 What about Mathematics?

We have already considered in an informal way some arithmetical equalities and inequalities, and have argued that they refer to states of affairs. And, in general, such concrete arithmetical statements having one of the forms 'n=m', 'n>m' or 'n<m', where n and m are numbers (natural or whatever) refer to states of affairs.

However, modern mathematics is concerned mostly not with such concrete cases, but with more general ones involving variables, theorems that are valid for a complete realm of objects and not for particular objects. Let us now consider some examples from contemporary mathematics, two from (abstract) algebra and two from general (or point-set) topology.

(A) Let S and T be similar relational systems, and let $\varphi \in \text{Hom}(S,T)$. Then φ is an isomorphism if and only if there exists $\psi \in \text{Hom}(T,S)$ such that $\varphi \circ \psi = I_T$ and $\psi \circ \varphi = I_S$.

(B) Let G be a set with a binary operation $\circ$, which is associative. Then the following conditions are equivalent:
(i) G is a group[12].
(ii) G is not empty and for all $a, b \in G$, the equations $b \circ x = a$ and $y \circ b = a$ each have a solution.
(C) The following properties are equivalent:
(i) The topological space T is connected[13].

---

[12] A set G is a group if and only if: (i) G has a binary operation $\circ$ defined on it; (ii) the operation $\circ$ is associative, that is, $(x \circ y) \circ z = x \circ (y \circ z)$, for all $x, y, z \in G$; (iii) G has a neutral element 1 such that $1 \circ x = x = x \circ 1$; and (iv) every element $x \in G$ has an inverse x^{-1} such that $x \circ x^{-1} = 1 = x^{-1} \circ x$.

(ii) The only subsets of T that are both open and closed are ∅ and T itself.

(D) A topological space T is a Hausdorff space[14] if and only if for all x∈T, the intersection of the closures of open neighbourhoods of x is the unit set {x} of x.

In all four examples it is asserted that two statements are equivalent. But these statements do not simply refer to states of affairs. They refer to a set of states of affairs. And what the theorems essentially say is that the sets of states of affairs referred to by the two equivalent statements are the same. As in the examples from first-order logic discussed above, the referents of the four theorems are abstract states of affairs.

Up to now we have not needed to introduce the notion of a situation of affairs in our semantic reassessment of logical and mathematical theories. In the following we will consider equivalences of a different sort, and for such cases we will need to introduce that additional tool. Some of such cases are certainly more profound that all those already examined. Nonetheless, the first case to be examined is the most obvious one, namely, that of dualism in logic and mathematics, and some examples of dualism are extremely simple.

§6 A Brief Excursus into Dualism

In logic and mathematics it is common to speak of dualism and of dual statements. There are certainly pairs of concepts that admit of parallel corresponding theorems. For example, in propositional logic the logical connectives '∧' and '∨' admit some parallel treatments,

---

[13] A topological space T is connected if it is not the union of two non-empty disjoint open sets.

[14] A topological space is a Hausdorff space if and only if for any two distinct elements x and y of the space, there exist neighbourhoods N_x of x and N_y of y such that their intersection is empty, in symbols: $N_x \cap N_y = \emptyset$.

especially in combination with the negation sign '¬' A simple example of that treatment are the De Morgan's laws, namely: (i) ¬(p∨q)↔(¬p∧¬q), (ii) ¬(p∧q)↔(¬p∨¬q).

A more interesting case of dualism originates with the notions of 'ideal' and 'filter'. By the way, although ideals and filters are related by a sort of dualism, they can, nevertheless, be studied for their own sake and, in fact, the notions were not developed simultaneously. Let us fix the concepts a little. Given a set S, an ideal is a family $\mathcal{F}$ of subsets of S such that (i) the union of any two members of the family is also a member of the family, that is, if $\mathcal{B}\in\mathcal{F}$ and $\mathcal{C}\in\mathcal{F}$, then $\mathcal{B}\cup\mathcal{C}\in\mathcal{F}$; and (ii) subsets of members of the family are members of the family, that is, if $\mathcal{B}\in\mathcal{F}$ and $\mathcal{C}\subseteq\mathcal{B}$, then $\mathcal{C}\in\mathcal{F}$. A filter, on the other hand, is a family $\mathcal{F}$ of subsets of a set S such that (i) the intersection of any two members of the family is a member of the family, that is, if $\mathcal{B}\in\mathcal{F}$ and $\mathcal{C}\in\mathcal{F}$, then $\mathcal{B}\cap\mathcal{C}\in\mathcal{F}$, and (ii) supersets of members of the family are members of the family, that is, if $\mathcal{B}\in\mathcal{F}$ and $\mathcal{B}\subseteq\mathcal{C}$, then $\mathcal{C}\in\mathcal{F}$.

The most famous results in both theories, namely, the Maximal Ideal Theorem and Tarski's Ultrafilter Theorem are dual statements. Once more, let us fix the concepts a little. A maximal ideal is one that cannot be extended by (is not a subideal of) any other ideal. An ultrafilter is its dual notion, namely, a maximal filter. The Maximal Ideal Theorem says that any ideal can be extended to a maximal ideal, whereas the Ultrafilter Theorem says that any filter can be extended to an ultrafilter. Certainly, those two important theorems are dual to each other. Though they refer to different states of affairs, they seem to have something in common, something that is not even pointed to in their formulations. The notion of a situation of affairs seems pertinent to characterize what the two dual theorems have in common. But there are without doubt more interesting cases.

§7 Some Metalogical Considerations

When you want to assess from our present standpoint metalogical results, especially non-trivial ones, in model theory, then you are constrained by the meta-logical facts to introduce new tools. We will consider the content of some very important model-theoretic results, namely:

(A) Robinson's Model-Completeness Test: Given a theory T in a first-order language $\mathcal{L}$, the following conditions are equivalent:

(i) T is model-complete[15].

(ii) For any model $\mathcal{M}$ of T, the theory $T \cup \Delta(\mathcal{M})$ is (syntactically) complete[16] in the language $\mathcal{L}_\mathcal{M}$, where $\Delta(\mathcal{M})$ is the diagram of $\mathcal{M}$[17].

(iii) If $\mathcal{M}$ and $\mathcal{M}^*$ are models of T and $\mathcal{M} \subseteq \mathcal{M}^*$, then an existential closed formula true in $\mathcal{M}^*_\mathcal{M}$ is true in $\mathcal{M}_\mathcal{M}$.

(iv) For any existential closed formula φ there exists a universal closed formula ψ such that $T \models \varphi \leftrightarrow \psi$.

---

[15] A theory T in a first-order language $\mathcal{L}$ is model-complete if given any two models $\mathcal{M}$ and $\mathcal{M}^*$ of T, if $\mathcal{M} \subseteq \mathcal{M}^*$, then $\mathcal{M} \prec \mathcal{M}^*$, that is, if $\mathcal{M}$ is a substructure of $\mathcal{M}^*$, then $\mathcal{M}$ is an elementary substructure of $\mathcal{M}^*$.

[16] A theory T in a first-order language $\mathcal{L}$ is syntactically complete if and only if for any statement (closed formula) σ in $\mathcal{L}$, either $T \vdash \sigma$ or $T \vdash \neg \sigma$.

[17] The diagram $\Delta(\mathcal{M})$ of a structure $\mathcal{M}$ for the first-order language $\mathcal{L}$ is the union of the set of all atomic closed formulas of $\mathcal{L}_\mathcal{M}$ (expansion of $\mathcal{L}$) true in $\mathcal{M}_\mathcal{M}$ with that of all negations of atomic closed formulas of $\mathcal{L}_\mathcal{M}$ true in $\mathcal{M}_\mathcal{M}$. (If $\mathcal{M}$ is a model of a first-order theory T in a language $\mathcal{L}$, then $\mathcal{L}_\mathcal{M}$, the expansion of $\mathcal{L}$, results by adding constants c_{a_i} to $\mathcal{L}$ for each $a_i \in M$, that is, of the universe of $\mathcal{M}$. Then the model $\mathcal{M}_\mathcal{M}$, which has the same universe as $\mathcal{M}$, though it is clearly more determined by the constants in $\mathcal{L}_\mathcal{M}$ naming the elements of M, is also called an expansion of $\mathcal{M}$.)

(B) Eklof-Sabbagh Theorem: Let $\mathcal{T}^*$ be a model companion[18] of $\mathcal{T}$ and let $\mathcal{T} \subseteq \mathcal{T}^*$. The following conditions are equivalent:

(i) $\mathcal{T}^*$ is a model completion[19] of $\mathcal{T}$.

(ii) $\mathcal{T}$ has the amalgamation property[20].

(C) Keisler-Shelah Theorem: Let $\mathcal{L}$ be a first-order language, $\mathcal{M}$ and $\mathcal{M}^*$ structures for $\mathcal{L}$. Then the following are equivalent:

(i) $\mathcal{M} \equiv \mathcal{M}^*$ (that is, M and $\mathcal{M}^*$ are elementarily equivalent[21]).

(ii) There are a set I of indices and an ultrafilter U, such that $\mathcal{M}^I/U \cong \mathcal{M}^{*I}/U$ (that is, the ultrapowers of $\mathcal{M}$ and $\mathcal{M}^*$ over the ultrafilter U are isomorphic).[22]

---

[18] A theory $\mathcal{T}^*$ ia a model companion of a theory $\mathcal{T}$ if: (i) $\mathcal{T}$ and $\mathcal{T}^*$ are mutually model-consistent, and (ii) $\mathcal{T}^*$ is model-complete. A theory $\mathcal{T}^*$ is model-consistent relative to a theory $\mathcal{T}$ if any model of $\mathcal{T}$ is contained in a model of $\mathcal{T}^*$; and $\mathcal{T}$ and $\mathcal{T}^*$ are mutually model-consistent if each is model-consistent relative to the other.

[19] A theory $\mathcal{T}^*$ is a model completion of a theory $\mathcal{T}$ if it is a model companion of $\mathcal{T}$ and if $\mathcal{M}$ is a model of $\mathcal{T}$, then $\mathcal{T}^* \cup \Delta(\mathcal{M})$ is syntactically complete.

[20] $\mathcal{T}$, or better, its class of models $\mathcal{K}_\mathcal{T}$ possesses the amalgamation property if whenever $\mathcal{B}, \mathcal{C}, \mathcal{D} \in \mathcal{K}_\mathcal{T}$ and there are embeddings f, g such that $f:\mathcal{B} \longrightarrow \mathcal{C}, g:\mathcal{B} \longrightarrow \mathcal{D}$, there exists a structure $\mathcal{A} \in \mathcal{K}_\mathcal{T}$ and embeddings h, j such that $h:\mathcal{C} \longrightarrow \mathcal{A}$ and $j:\mathcal{D} \longrightarrow \mathcal{A}$.

[21] Two structures $\mathcal{M}$ and $\mathcal{M}^*$ for a first-order language $\mathcal{L}$ are elementarily equivalent if and only if any closed formula σ of $\mathcal{L}$ is true in $\mathcal{M}$ if and only if it is true in $\mathcal{M}^*$

[22] In the same way in which, given a family of sets $A_i, i \in I$, we can build the Cartesian product $A_{i1} \times \ldots A_{in} \times \ldots$ (and if for all $i,j \in I$, $A_i = A_j$, the Cartesian power), given a set of structures $\mathcal{A}_i$ and a set of indices I, we can build the direct product of such structures. And in the same way in which, given an algebraic structure, for example, a group, we can build a corresponding quotient structure, given a direct product of structures, we can use a filter as congruence base to build a reduced product of structures. If the filter is an ultrafilter, we obtain an ultraproduct. Finally, if for all $i,j \in I$ the components $\mathcal{A}_i/\mathcal{F} = \mathcal{A}_j/\mathcal{F}$, we have a reduced power, and if the filter is an ultrafilter, we have an ultrapower. (Please, excuse the "constructive jargon" of this footnote, but the precise definitions would make the footnote too extensive!)

(D) Morley's Categoricity Theorem: Let $\mathcal{T}$ be a (syntactically) complete theory in a countable first-order language $\mathcal{L}$. Then the following statements are equivalent:
(i) $\mathcal{T}$ is κ-categorical for some uncountable κ.
(ii) $\mathcal{T}$ is λ-categorical for any uncountable λ.[23]

We have chosen those four theorems, three ((A), (C) and (D)) of which are of great importance, especially because the equivalences are not trivial and, thus, serve better to illustrate our point.[24] In fact, they are not even related by a relation like that of dualism discussed above. Hence, it should be perfectly clear that these equivalences are of a much deeper nature than those between quantified statements in the object language that referred to abstract states of affairs, and even deeper than the equivalences between dual statements, and, thus, we need new semantic tools to assess those equivalences. The equivalence between (i)-(iv) of (A), or between (i) and (ii) of (B) above are much better described by saying that though the statements (i)-(iv) of (A), as well as the statements (i) and (ii) of (B) –and the same in the corresponding cases of theorems (C) and (D)-, refer to different states of affairs, they have a sort of very deep unity, which we could describe by saying that they have the same abstract situation of affairs in common.

---

[23] A theory $\mathcal{T}$ is κ-categorical, for κ an infinite cardinality, if and only if $\mathcal{T}$ has models of cardinality κ and all models of $\mathcal{T}$ of cardinality κ are isomorphic.

[24] In the case of (D), it is not usually formulated as an equivalence, since (ii)⇒(i) is an utmost triviality, but we formulated it as an equivalence to emphasize what we are trying to convey.

§8 The Top of the Ladder

The most general and surprising sort of equivalence in mathematics occurs between statements belonging to different areas of mathematics and seemingly totally disconnected from another. The most blatant example of such a phenomenon is that of the Axiom of Choice and its many equivalents in very different areas of mathematics. A second example is that of the Ultrafilter Theorem already mentioned above, which besides being equivalent to its dual, the Maximal Ideal Theorem, is also equivalent to other statements in different areas of mathematics. For our purpose here a few examples seem more than enough.

(A) The Axiom of Choice and a few of its Equivalents:

(0) Axiom of Choice: Given any family $\mathcal{F}$ of non-empty sets, there is a function f which assigns to each member S of $\mathcal{F}$ an element $f(S)$ of S.[25]

(1) Trichotomy of Cardinals: For any cardinal numbers n, m, either m<n or m=n or m>n.

(2) Tychonoff's (Compactness) Theorem: The product of any family of compact topological spaces is a compact topological space.[26]

(3) Every lattice with a unit and at least one other element has a maximal ideal.

(4) If $\mathcal{V}$ is a real vector space, then for every subspace W there is a subspace W^* such that $W \cap W^* = \emptyset$ and $W \cup W^*$ generates $\mathcal{V}$.

(5) Every function f includes a one-to-one function f^* with the same range as f.

---

[25] The problem with the acceptance of the Axiom of Choice by mathematicians originated in the fact that there is no restriction to the cardinality of the sets in the family. For infinite sets, the axiom was postulating a choice function that arbitrarily (or mysteriously) selected a member of each of the infinitely many sets in the family. But after being shown to be equivalent to or imply so many well-established statements in so different areas of mathematics, it seems quite unreasonable to reject the Axiom of Choice. For more on the Axiom of Choice, see Gregory H. Moore's monumental *Equivalents of the Axiom of Choice*, on which we have relied in this section.

[26] A topological space $\mathcal{T}$ is compact if any cover of it has a finite subcover.

(6) Every relation $\mathcal{R}$ includes a function f with the same domain as $\mathcal{R}$.

The above six equivalents of the Axiom of Choice come from different areas of mathematics, for example, lattice theory, general topology or the theory of vector spaces, and vary greatly in complexity. Example (1), which belongs to the same area as the Axiom of Choice, namely, set theory, expresses something that seems intuitively clear, as also examples (5) and (6), and, nonetheless, they are equivalent to the much less intuitive Axiom of Choice. (2) and (4) belong to areas of mathematics clearly distinct from set theory, and in the case of (4) it seems concerned with much less abstract mathematical entities as those of set theory. Nonetheless, both (4) and (2) are equivalent to the Axiom of Choice.

In the case of the Ultrafilter Theorem, which, by the way, is implied by the Axiom of Choice, besides the Maximal Ideal Theorem mentioned above, for example, the following statements are its equivalents:

(1) Tychonoff's Theorem for Hausdorff Spaces: The product of any family of compact Hausdorff spaces is a compact Hasudorf space.
(2) On each infinite set there is a two-valued additive measure such that each singleton {x} has measure zero.[27]
(3) Stone's Representation Theorem: Every Boolean ring is isomorphic to a ring of sets, that is, a family of sets with symmetric difference as addition and intersection as multiplication.

Once more, we have equivalent statements talking about completely different issues, but that, nonetheless, are equivalent to each other. (1) belongs to general topology, (2) to measure theory, and

---

[27] A measure is an extended real-valued, non-negative and countably additive set function defined on a ring of sets, such that its value when applied to the empty set is zero. See on this point, p. 30 of the classic Halmos' *Measure Theory* for the definition and those of the familiar concepts used in its definition.

(3) to the theory of Boolean algebras, whereas the Ultrafilter Theorem is a central theorem of the Theory of Ultrafilters.[28]

As shown with the help of both sets of examples, we are dealing here with fairly thematically unrelated mathematical statements, some clearly belonging to very different areas of mathematics, which nonetheless can be derived from each other. If we follow Bourbaki (Dieudonné et alia) in considering topological structures, algebraic structures and order structures as the three major families of mathematical structures, the three mother structures, we can find statements from areas falling under the three mother structures that are mathematically equivalent. They have in common some very abstract equivalence, more abstract than any considered before, a sort of ultra abstract situation of affairs.

In fact, though the case of the equivalence between the Axiom of Choice and its many mathematical equivalents, as well as the case of the Ultrafilter Theorem and its equivalents, build a sort of limit to relations of equivalence in the logical-mathematical disciplines, we certainly in no way pretend to have covered all the intermediate cases. Thus, we cannot establish the depth of most equivalence relations considered. Only in very elementary cases, like the equivalence of two quantified statements of first-order logic can we say that between their sense and their truth value there are the states of affairs referred to by their instances, the set of states of affairs referred by the quantified statements and the set of sets of states of affairs corresponding to their equivalence, thus, the depth in such cases is =3.

Things can get much more complicated, if we also consider the results of so-called 'reverse mathematics'. In this relatively new and

---

[28] In the long list of (presumed) equivalents of the Axiom of Choice and of the Maximal Ideal Theorem offered by Gregory H. Moore in his *Zermelo's Axiom of Choice* he includes some presumed logical equivalents, namely, the Downward Löwenheim-Skolem Theorem and the Löwenheim-Skolem-Tarski Theorem for the Axiom of Choice, and the Completeness Theorem for First-Order Logic and the Compactness Theorem for First-Order Logic for the Ultrafilter Theorem. However, such equivalences depend on the choice of First-Order Logic as "the Logic". If we take, for example, second-order logic as basis for our discussion, all those results are false and, thus, not equivalent to the Axiom of Choice. By the way, elsewhere I have shown the fragility of the arguments on behalf of first-order logic against second-order logic. See the references.

very active branch of the foundations of mathematics one considers as basis systems weaker than Zermelo-Fraenkel with Choice (ZFC) or Bernays-von Neumann-Gödel, and studies the interderivability or mathematical equivalence of mathematical statements belonging to very different areas of mathematics, relative to the system chosen. A favourite candidate for such studies is second order arithmetic Z_2 and, especially some of its subsystems, and the very interesting results obtained in some sense mimic the interderivability results on the basis of full axiomatic set theory.[29] Such results in reverse mathematics would certainly require an extension of the application of the semantic tools here discussed by means of a relativisation to such weaker deductive systems. The prospects look very bright, but we cannot discuss such extension here.

On the other hand, all levels of states of affairs, abstract states of affairs, situations of affairs, abstract situations of affairs or whatever that we have considered in our examination of the semantic levels of logical and mathematical theories originate groups of transformations similar to those of the natural languages. Consider, for example the group of transformations generated by the Axiom of Choice and its mathematical equivalents. It is easy to see that there is an identity transformation of a statement into itself, that for any transformation in the set, there is an inverse transformation, and that the associative law is valid for such transformations. The same happens with the model-theoretic metalogical theorems considered above (as well as with the other cases examined). The set of transformations between any set of

---

[29] For a sort of brief survey of the results of reverse mathematics, see Stephen G. Simpson's 'The Gödel Hierarchy and Reverse Mathematics', in Charles Parsons, Solomon Feferman and Stephen G. Simpson (eds.), *Kurt Gödel: essays for his Centennial*, CUP 2010, pp. 109-127.

such equivalent statements as displayed, for example, in the Model Completeness Test, builds a group.[30]

Since in this paper we have relied so much on mathematical structures and facts, it is not necessary to ask about the commitments of the paper to Platonic entities: it has been written from a Platonist perspective. Thus, as a sort of appendix to the discussion of the application of neo-Husserlian semantics of sense and referent to logical and mathematical contexts, it seems not completely unwarranted to make here a brief defence of mathematical Platonism inspired by some of the material we have considered.[31]

§9 A Sort of Platonist Dessert for a Semantic Menu

In Anglo-American orthodox analytic ideology not only is Ockam's razor the first commandment, but empiricism in the philosophy of physical science and nominalism in the philosophy of mathematics are exactly what the ideological physician ordered. However, life has not been too kind to staunch empiricists, and even the more moderate reconstruction of physical science by the logical empiricists and their sympathizers were doomed from the very beginning. In the philosophy of mathematics, all nominalist attempts to get rid of mathematical entities have faced insurmountable difficulties, and their more moderate cousins, namely, constructivists, conventionalists and even the more liberal empiricists in their recent indispensabilist clothes à la Quine or Putnam have not fared much better.

By the way, there was a second reason why we chose some of the four model-theoretic metatheorems, namely to use them in the definitive refutation of nominalism and its more moderate cousins. Besides Robinson's Model Completeness Test and Morley's Theorem,

---

[30] Relativisations to weaker systems, for example, to subsystems of second order arithmetic, as mentioned in the preceding paragraph, would also give rise to transformation groups of statements.
[31] Since we have made use of so many logical and mathematical concepts, besides the books already referred to, we will include in the references other books consulted, though such definitions can be found in most textbooks of the corresponding areas.

we want the reader to have in mind also the content of the following two theorems, namely:

(A) Löwenheim-Skolem-Tarski Theorem: If a first-order theory T has an infinite model, then it has models of any infinite cardinality.

(B) Skolem's Theorem on Non-Standard Models: First-order Dedekind-Peano Arithmetic has a countable model not isomorphic to the standard arithmetic model.

Let us begin considering nominalism, a philosophical theory that denies the existence of abstract entities. If one pays tribute to Quine's big dogma, namely, that the ontological commitment of a theory is determined by the type of quantifiers present in the theory, thus, that second-order logic is committed to abstract entities but first-order logic is not, one could try to work in first-order logic thinking that it is safe from abstract mathematical entities. However, first-order logic is no shelter for nominalists or conventionalists, since the whole classical first-order model theory is completely committed to abstract entities, namely, to sets, structures, relations between structures, cardinalities, and so on. Moreover, if you accept model theory, there is precisely one model-theoretic metatheorem, that refutes nominalism, namely, Robinson's Model Completeness Test. Since if nominalism were true, there would not be any mathematical entities. Thus, all existential statements talking about mathematical entities would be false and all universal ones would be vacuously true and, thus, would have the opposite truth-value as their existential counterparts. However, according to the Model Completeness Test –see (i) and (iv)- a theory is model-complete if and only if for any existential statement in the language of the theory, there is a universal statement logically equivalent to it. Hence, for any presumably false mathematical existential statement expressed in a first-order language, there exists an also false mathematical universal statement expressed in the same language, which is logically equivalent to it; and, since statements logically equivalent to the negations of logically equivalent statements are logically equivalent, for any true mathematical universal statement in a first-order language, there exists a true mathematical existential statement expressed in the same language, which is logically equivalent to it. Thus, there are both false mathematical universal statements and true mathematical existential statements. Hence, there exist mathematical entities, and nominalism has been refuted. By the way, it follows as a corollary that we cannot conventionally decide to make all existential mathematical statements false, nor true, and hence, conventionalism is no way out here for those who abhor abstract mathematical entities.

With respect to constructivism, the first thing to be stressed is that constructivism is a mess, because there are almost as many constructivisms as constructivists. Moreover, no constructivism, no matter how liberal, is adequate to account for higher mathematical cardinalities - $\aleph_1$, $\aleph_2$, $\aleph_3$ etc.- and, hence, cannot do justice to mathematical analysis, with its real and complex numbers, and functions on real or complex numbers, and to its applications in physical science. But in any case, the remaining model-theoretic metatheorems already mentioned disclaim any attempt to defend constructivism in mathematics. Already the very distinguished model-theorist Wilfrid Hodges has stressed[32] that the Löwenheim-Skolem-Tarski Theorem is incompatible with the constructivist thesis. But the same could be said about Morley's Theorem, about Skolem's Theorem on Non-standard Models of Arithmetic or the Keisler-Shelah Theorem. Let us consider only the first two as a sort of examples. The Löwnheim-Skolem-Tarski Theorem says that if a theory has an infinite model, then it has models of any infinite cardinality —and there are infinitely many infinite cardinalities. There simply are no rules for "constructing" models of infinitely many infinite cardinalities. Something very similar occurs with Morley's especially deep theorem. Under certain unproblematic presuppositions about the language $\mathcal{L}$ and the theory $\mathcal{T}$, categoricity in any uncountable domain is basically reduced to categoricity in an uncountable domain: if κ is an

---

[32] See his 'Elementary Logic', in D. Gabbay and F. Guenthner (eds.), *Handbook of Philosophical Logic I*, pp.1-131, specifically p.34.

uncountable cardinal number and a (syntactically complete) theory $\mathcal{T}$ (in a countable language) has a model of cardinality κ and is κ-categorical, then it is λ-categorical for any uncountable λ. And putting κ=$\aleph_1$, categoricity in any uncountable domain is reduced to $\aleph_1$-categoricity. Once more there is absolutely no trace of even the possibility of a rule of construction here. Model theory not only refutes nominalism and conventionalism, it also shows the falsehood of any constructivist thesis concerning mathematical entities.

With regard to Quine's, Putnam's and others' versions of so-called indispensabilism, we will not waste much energy in such a hopeless attempt to save naturalism.[33] Put briefly, (i) indispensabilists acknowledge a sort of existence of those mathematical entities that are applicable in the empirical sciences, in particular, in physics, and (ii) pretend that there is a sort of continuity or similarity between (existence of) physical objects and (that of) mathematical entities. The first problem with respect to (i) is that if the existence of mathematical entities depends on their applicability to physics and other empirical sciences, some mathematical entities would exist while many others would not. Moreover, some of them would be born in the moment in which one finds them a physical application, and if a mathematical theory is not used anymore in physical science, then the entities about which such a mathematical theory presumes to talk would pass away. Thus, triangles with positive curvature, as well as spaces with variable curvature, were probably born the day Riemannian geometry found application in general relativity, whereas poor triangles with negative curvature –so far as we know- are still trying to legitimize their birth certificates, while very large cardinals, as well as Skolem's non-standard models of arithmetic of any infinite cardinality –obtained by combining Skolem's theorem on a countable non-standard model of

---

[33] For more detailed criticism, we refer the reader to our 'Why and How Platonism?', included in the references.

arithmetic with the Löwenheim-Skolem-Tarski theorem- will most surely never be born. All those consequences of the indispensabilist thesis –which would make mathematical entities have humanlike properties, like the Greek gods in Mount Olympus- are nonsense, and the thesis itself is also nonsensical. Furthermore, with respect to (ii), we can add that those who seek some continuity beginning with the statements of ordinary life –for example, 'Immanuel Kant lived all his life in Königsberg'-, then going to the statements of the so-called social sciences, to those of the biological sciences, to those of the physical sciences up to the logical-mathematical statements, better take into account that the methods of proof in logic and mathematics are essentially different from those of even the mostly theoretic physical science[34], and that the objects studied by logic and mathematics are of a completely different sort from those of even physical science. Is there any physical property had by a neutrino or an electron, not to say by a tiger, that is also a property of topological spaces or of groups? Or is there any hope of finding an ultraproduct of a family of mathematical structures in some other galaxy or in the quantum world, not to say in Quine's favourite primitive pseudoscience of behaviourism? To put it somewhat colourfully: logical-mathematical entities are some uncountable cardinality far away from the objects studied by the empirical sciences, even from those studied by the much more theoretical than empirical physical science. There is an essential difference between the logical-mathematical formal sciences, on the one hand, and the empirical sciences, on the other, and there is no way to bridge that enormous gap between them, since theorems of the Löwenheim-Skolem-Tarski sort (or of the Morley sort) are forever inexistent in the empirical sciences, even in the most theoretic and abstract areas of physical science.

---

[34] There is no point of comparison, for example, between the proof of the mathematical "fact" that there exist non-standard models of first-order arithmetic of any infinite cardinality, on the one hand, and the discovery of a new star or of a new subatomic particle -except perhaps that they are all discoveries, though of objectualities [in Husserl's German: Gegenständlichkeiten] of completely different sorts.

References

Bolzano, Bernard – *Grundlegung der Logik*, selected sections from volumes 1 and 2 of his *Wissenschaftslehre*, Felix Meiner, Hamburg 1963, revised edition 1978

Bourbaki, N. – 'The Architecture of Mathematics', *American Mathematical Monthly 57*, 1950, pp. 221-232

Bourbaki, Nicholas – 'Foundations of Mathematics for the Working Mathematician', *Journal of Symbolic Logic 14 (4)*, 1949, pp. 1-8

Chang, C. C. and Keisler, H. J. – *Model Theory*, North Holland, Amsterdam 1974, revised edition 1990

Confort, W. W. and Negrepontis, S. – The Theory of Ultrafilters, Springer, New York et al. 1978

Dugundji, James – *Topology*, Allyn and Bacon, Boston 1966, ninth printing 1974

Frege, Gottlob – 'Funktion und Begriff' 1891, reprinted in *Kleine Schriften*, pp. 125-142

Frege, Gottlob – 'Über Sinn und Bedeutung' 1892, reprinted in *Kleine Schriften*, pp. 143-162

Frege, Gottlob – 'Brief an Husserl vom 24-ten Mai 1891', reprinted in *Wissenschftlicher Briefwechsel*, pp. 94-98

Frege, Gottlob – *Kleine Schriften*, edited by Ignacio Angelleli, Georg Olms, Hildesheim et al. 1967, revised edition 1990

Frege, Gottlob – *Wissenschftlicher Briefwechsel*, Felix Meiner, Hamburg 1974

Gabbay, D. and Guenthner, F (eds.) – *Handbook of Philosophical Logic I*, Kluwer, Dordrecht 1983

Grätzer, George – *Universal Algebra* 1968, revised edition, Springer, New York et al. 1978

Halmos, Paul – *Measure Theory* 1950, reprint, Springer, New York et al. 1974

Hill, Claire O. and Rosado Haddock, Guillermo E. – *Husserl or Frege?: Meaning, Objectivity and Mathematics*, Open Court, Chicago et al. 2000, 2003

Hodges, Wilfrid – 'Elementary Logic', in D. Gabbay and F. Guenthner (eds.), *Handbook of Philosophical Logic I*, pp.1-131

Husserl, Edmund – *Philosophie der Arithmetik* 1891, Hua XI, M. Nijhoff, Den Haag 1970

Husserl, Edmund – 'Besprechung von Ernst Schröders *Vorlesungen über die Algebra der Logik I*' 1891, reprinted in *Aufsätze und Rezensionen (1890-1910)*, Hua XXII, Den Haag, pp. 3-43

Husserl, Edmund – *Logische Untersuchungen* (two volumes) 1900-1901, Hua XVIII, 1975, and XIX 1984, M. Nijhoff, den Haag

Husserl, Edmund – 'Zur Logik der Zeichen (Semiotik)', printed as Appendix B(I) in *Philosophie der Arithmetik* 1970, pp. 340-373

Husserl, Edmund – *Aufsätze und Rezensionen (1890-1910)*, Hua XXII, M. Nijhoff, Den Haag 1979

Lindström, Per – 'On Characterizing Elementary Logic', in S. Stenlund (ed.), *Logical Theory and Semantic Analysis*, pp. 129-146

Moore, Gregory H. –*Zermelo's Axiom of Choice*, Springer, New York et al. 1982

Pierce, Richard S. *Introduction to the Theory of Abstract Algebras* 1968, reprint, Dover, New York 2014

Rosado Haddock, Guillermo E. – 'Remarks on Sense and Reference in Frege and Husserl', *Kant-Studien 73 (4)* 1982, pp. 425-439, reprinted in Claire O. Hill and Guillermo E. Rosado Haddock, *Husserl or Frege?*, pp. 23-40

Rosado Haddock, Guillermo E. – 'Why and How Platonism?', JIGPAL 2007, reprinted in *Against the Current*, pp. 341-364

Rosado Haddock, Guillermo E. – 'On First- and Second-Order Logic', in *Against the Current*, pp. 385-398

Rosado Haddock, Guillermo E. – *Against the Current*, Ontos Verlag, Frankfurt am Main 2012

Simpson, Stephen G. – 'The Gödel Hierarchy and Reverse Mathematics', in Charles Parsons, Solomon Feferman and Stephen G. Simpson (eds.), *Kurt Gödel: Essays for his Centennial*, Cambridge University Press 2010, pp. 109-127

Stenlund, Sören (ed) – *Logical Theory and Semantic Analysis*, Reidel, Dordrecht 1974

Thron, Wolfgang J. – *Topological Structures*, Holt, Rinehart and Winston, New York et al. 1966

On Analytic *a posteriori* Statements: are they Possible?

Abstract
Traditionally, the notions of analyticity, aprioricity and necessity have been considered coextensive, and also their counterparts, namely, syntheticity, aposterioricity and contingency. Such coextensiveness has been questioned by philosophers like Kant and Husserl who, on the basis of very different definitions of analyticity, postulated the existence of synthetic *a priori* statements and, on the other hand, by Kripke, who argued for the existence of contingent *a priori* and necessary *a posteriori* statements. In this paper, on the basis of a new definition of analyticity that can be seen as a refinement of Husserl's, it is argued for the existence of analytic *a posteriori* instantiations of analytic laws.

§1 Preliminaries

Traditionally, the notions of necessity and aprioricity, on the one hand, and the notions of contingency and aposterioricity, on the other, were considered to have the same extension. In his seminal papers 'Naming and Necessity'[1] and 'Identity and Necessity'[2] Saul Kripke challenged the received view and distinguished between the metaphysical notions of necessity and contingency, on the one hand, and the epistemological notions of *a priori* and *a posteriori*, on the other. Kripke attempted to offer examples both of contingent *a priori* and of necessary *a posteriori* statements, in the last case basing his examples on the questionable contention that strict proper names are rigid designators.

---

[1] 'Naming and Necessity' 1972, enlarged edition, Blackwell, Oxford 1980.
[2] 'Identity and Necessity', in Stephen P. Schwartz (ed.), *Naming, Necessity and Natural Kinds*, Cornell University Press. 1977, pp. 66-101.

Notwithstanding the fragility of Kripke's examples, the fact of the matter is that the distinction between the two pairs of notions retains its importance irrespectively.

A third pair of related notions has traditionally been related to the two former ones, namely, that of analyticity and syntheticity. It has usually been considered that the notion of analyticity has the same extension as that of aprioricity and, thus, *a fortiori* of that of necessity. And though three of the greatest philosophers ever, namely, Kant, Frege and Husserl have questioned the identification of syntheticity with contingency and aposterioricity, arguing for the existence of synthetic *a priori* statements, especially in empiricist circles the three notions have been considered as being at least extensionally equivalent. But the notions of analyticity and syntheticity are neither epistemological nor metaphysical, but semantic. Hence, an argument needs to be offered to establish the extensional equivalence of the semantic notions be it with the metaphysical or with the epistemological notions. In this paper, however, it will be shown that the semantic notions of analyticity and syntheticity are extensionally equivalent neither to the metaphysical notions of necessity and contingency nor to the epistemological notions of aprioricity and aposterioricity.

§2 On Analyticity

The task of defining analyticity has been a very hard one. Since Kant characterized a statement as analytic when the concept of its predicate is included in the concept of its subject,[3] but in the same work later characterized analytic statements as those derivable from the Principle of Non-Contradiction,[4] and, thus, really offered two non-equivalent characterizations of analyticity, there have been multiple attempts to define that elusive notion, as attested by the list of more than

---

[3] *Kritik der reinen Vernunft*, A7-8, B11-12.
[4] Ibid., A150-153, B190-193.

sixty enumerated by Jan Wolenski in his 'Analytic vs. Synthetic and A Priori vs. A Posteriori'[5].

In any case, the two definitions of analyticity best known in analytic circles are those of Frege and Carnap, both of which are refinements of Kant's two different notions of analyticity. Carnap's characterization of analytic statements as those whose truth could be known by the mere analysis of the concepts involved[6] is inspired by Kant's first characterization, and seems vulnerable both with respect to Quine's objections in his famous 'Two Dogmas of Empiricism'[7] and to the objection that the truth of statements like 'All bachelors are not married' is dependent on the historical and, thus, empirical evolution of language. Frege's characterization of analyticity in *Die Grundlagen der Arithmetik*,[8] according to which a statement is analytic if it can be derived from the logical principles and definitions is clearly a refinement of Kant's second characterization and, though it is immune to Quine's criticism, it faces the difficulties resulting from the collapse of logicism, namely, that since arithmetic and the whole analysis cannot be derived exclusively from logical laws and definitions, on the basis of Frege's notion of analyticity, arithmetical statements and statements of mathematical analysis would have to be considered as synthetic.

A less known but more solid definition of analyticity is that of Husserl, according to which a statement is analytic if it is true and its truth can be completely formalized *salva veritate*, that is, without its truth being affected. Husserl's definition is immune both to Quine's criticism and to the demise of logicism. Nonetheless, it seems more adequate as a

---

[5] In I. Niniluoto et al. (eds.), *Handbook of Epistemology*, Kluwer, Dordrecht 2004, pp. 781-839.

[6] See Carnap's *Meaning and Necessity*, University of Chicago Press 1947, enlarged edition 1956, and, especially, his paper 'Meaning Postulates' of 1952, included as Appendix B in the enlarged edition.

[7] 'Two Dogmas of Empiricism' 1951, reprint in *From a Logical Point of View*, Harvard University Press, Cambridge, Ma. 1953, pp. 20-46.

[8] *Die Grundlagen der Arithmetik* 1884, Centenarausgabe, Felix Meiner, Hamburg 1986, §3.

definition of logical truth[9] and would face the problem that concrete number-theoretic truths, like $1^3+2^3+3^3+4^3=100$ or even more trivial ones like '2 is both even and prime' would turn out to be non-analytic, since they cannot be completely formalized *salva veritate*. In any case, though Husserl's definition based on logical form is on the right track, it seems to be a syntactical definition of a semantic notion. Thus, the task is to offer a definition of analyticity based not on syntactical but on semantic form. In my papers 'Husserl on Analyticity and Beyond'[10] and 'Some Uses of Logic in Rigorous Philosophy'[11] I have offered a new definition of analyticity based on the semantic form of statements, in fact a model-theoretical definition, namely: A statement is analytic if it is true in a model M and when true in a model M, it is true in any model M^* isomorphic to M. In other words, a statement σ is analytic whenever (i) {σ} has a model and (ii) if {σ} has a model M, then any structure M^* isomorphic to M is also a model of {σ}, that is MOD{σ} is closed under isomorphisms. Such a definition was intended to capture a semantic property of mathematical (and also logical) statements, not shared with any other sort of statement. However, I now acknowledge that the definition is too wide and would admit as analytic statements like, e.g. 'Two colours cannot cover the same surface at the same time', which clearly have material content, though they seem to be true in any physical world. Moreover, one could also argue that the laws of physics are supposed to be invariant under isomorphisms, though they are certainly not true in any physical world. In any case, it seems pertinent to introduce an additional clause that can serve to exclude exactly those two sorts of

---

[9] In the second volume of his masterful *Logical Forms* Oswaldo Chateaubriand characterized logical truth in a similar way to Husserl's definition of analyticity. I side with Chateaubriand against Husserl on this point.
[10] In *Husserl Studies 24*, 2008, reprinted in *Against the Current*, pp. 327-339.
[11] In *Axiomathes 20 (2-3)*, 2012, reprinted in *Against the Current*, pp. 365-383. See also my brief treatment of the definition of analyticity in 'Issues in the Philosophy of Logic: a Heterodox Approach', in *Principia 11 (1)*, 2007, reprinted in *Against the Current*, pp. 305-325.

statements without excluding any mathematical statement.[12] One could try to add a third clause excluding analytic statements from having empirical content. Such a restriction would certainly exclude physical laws of low-level and at most physical laws of higher level –what Husserl called[13] *hypotheses cum fundamento in re*, like the law of gravitation in classical mechanics-, whose relation to experience is somewhat tenuous, though their explanatory power and their role in systematization of our empirical knowledge is fundamental. However, with such an additional clause, the definition would still be too wide, since statements with material content true in any physical world –statements like those Husserl considered synthetic *a priori*[14]- would still be considered analytic. On the other hand, one could try to add a clause excluding the occurrence of any constants in analytic statements. Such an additional clause, however, would not only exclude all statements about any physical world, but will also exclude arithmetical statements from being analytic. In fact, it would make the definition essentially equivalent to Husserl's. Hence, the definition would be too narrow. Thus, one has to find a clause intermediate in strength between those two. The clause should read as follows: (iii) σ, or better {σ} should not imply or presuppose the existence either of a physical world or of a world of consciousness. Therefore, the definition should now read as follows: A statement σ is analytic if and only if: (i) {σ} has a model, (ii) if {σ} has a model M, then any structure M^* isomorphic to M is also a model of {σ}, and (iii) {σ} does not imply or presuppose the existence either of a physical world or of a world of consciousness. This

---

[12] In my previous papers touching on this issue I have considered only mathematical statements and seem to have tacitly assumed that analytic statements do not have any sort of material content, since that is what is meant when one says that they are true in virtue of their semantic form. An objection to the former version of the definition made by Jairo da Silva, in the sense that the definition was too wide, made me reconsider it and make the assumption explicit.

[13] See, for example *Logische Untersuchungen I*, Chapter IV, §23 as well as Chapter XI, §§62-66 for a more thorough discussion of Husserl's views on explanatory versus descriptive sciences.

[14] See *Logische Untersuchungen II*, U. III, §12.

new definition, however, forces us to make some additional distinctions. There are essentially two sorts of analytic statements, namely, those that contain mathematical constants –like the two number-theoretic examples mentioned above- and those that do not contain any constants and could appropriately be called "analytic laws". Let us, following Husserl[15], call a statement an "analytic necessity" if it is obtained from an analytic law by instantiation (or exemplification), that is, by the usual method of replacement of occurrences of a variable by a constant (and the corresponding deletion of the corresponding quantifier –in our case, a universal quantifier). Since such constants do not need to be mathematical constants, it is clear that analytic necessities, in general, do not satisfy the third clause of the definition of analyticity.

§3 Some Conceptual Elucidations

The present definition –even in its now abandoned original version- is certainly immune to the three objections brought against the other three attempts to define analyticity already mentioned. Moreover, the resulting notion of analyticity does not coincide with that of categoricity, since {σ} can very well be analytic but have models that are not isomorphic. In fact, under this definition, not only all number-theoretic theorems turn out to be analytic, but also statements like the commutative law for groups, true only in all Abelian groups but not in all groups, and Skolem's statement asserting that there is a number larger than any natural number, a statement true only in non-standard models of first-order arithmetic, including their elementary extensions, which can have any infinite cardinality. Hence, the notion of analyticity does not coincide either with that of categoricity or with that of necessity, that is, of truth in

---

[15] Ibid. It should be pointed out that our use of the expresion "analytic necessity" is just a "façon de parler" for the instantiations of analytic laws, and should be clearly distinguished from my use of the concept of mathematical necessity in the next §. See also Chateaubriand's *Logical Forms II*, Chapter 18 for a distinction parallel to Husserl's but concerning logical truth.

any possible world (or in any possible world in which the objects referred to by designators in the statement exist).[16] The commutative law for Abelian groups is certainly not necessary, since it is not true in a world populated by all groups, and Skolem's existence statement for a number larger than all natural numbers is not necessary, since it is not true in the standard model of first-order arithmetic and certainly not true in any model of second-order arithmetic.

A similar example of an analytic but not necessary statement can be obtained from general topology.[17] All Hausdorff spaces are topological spaces, but not all topological spaces are Hausdorff spaces. In order for a topological space to be Hausdorff, it has to satisfy the following condition ©: any two distinct points α and β have non-intersecting neighbourhoods, that is, in the topological space there exist open sets A and B such that $\alpha \in A$, $\beta \in B$ and $A \cap B = \emptyset$, briefly, disjoint points have disjoint neighbourhoods. If a topological space T satisfies condition ©, then all spaces T^* isomorphic to T satisfy ©. Moreover, as any genuine mathematical statement, it does not presuppose or imply the existence of any physical world or world of consciousness. Hence, © is an analytic statement, according to the above definition. Nonetheless, it is not necessary for all topological spaces to satisfy condition ©. Therefore, © is an analytic but not necessary statement.

In order to avoid some misunderstandings, the following should be stressed before continuing. Firstly, since analyticity and necessity have been shown to be different, there is nothing abnormal when an analytic statement σ is true in a structure M and its negation, namely $\neg \sigma$, is true in other structures not isomorphic to the structure M. In fact, mathematical

---

[16] When dealing with abstract mathematical entities Leibniz's characterization of necessity would be sufficient. Nonetheless, the notion of mathematical necessity used below is neither Kripkean nor even Leibnizian in a strict sense, but a sort of analogue of the latter adapted to mathematical structures.

[17] See any good book on general topology, e.g., Wolfgang J. Thron's, *Topological Structures*, Holt, Rinehart and Winston, New York et al. 1966, or John L. Kelley, *General Topology*, D. Van Nostrand, Princeton, New Jersey 1955.

statements usually are true only in families of structures, not in all structures, and are either not defined or not true in structures not isomorphic to those in which they are true. I have defined analyticity to capture precisely that "truth in virtue of its semantic form" that presumably distinguishes mathematical from empirical and, in general, synthetic statements, whereas logical truths, which are supposed to be true in any model, are simply a limiting case of analyticity. In fact, logical truths are not only necessary –as is the case of axioms defining general mathematical structures-, but are also true in any possible circumstance, under any interpretation. In fact, we can distinguish here three different concepts corresponding to three different levels of conceptual generality[18], namely, from the more general to the less general: (i) a logically true statement is a statement true in any possible model; (ii) a mathematical necessary statement is a statement true in any model of the axioms of a mathematical theory, for example, true in any topological spaces, in any groups, in any rings, etc.[19]; (iii) an analytic statement is a statement true in at least one model as well as in any model isomorphic to a model of the statement, and such that it does not imply or presuppose the existence of any physical world or world of consciousness, thus, it does not have any content besides mathematical content.

Secondly, it should be stressed that although our definition of analyticity is clothed in model-theoretic vocabulary, that does not mean that we are in any sense bound to classical first-order model theory. In fact, "isomorphism" is not a first-order notion, like its first-order approximation "elementary equivalence", and the notion of model is also

---

[18] Of course, the extensions of the concepts are in reverse order, being the extension of the concept of analyticity the widest of the three concepts.

[19] We are perfectly conscious that this distinction makes the concept of mathematical necessity have a somewhat fuzzy extension, since what has been called "mathematically necessary" at one moment in history could be 'degraded' to being 'merely' analytic by the consideration of more abstract structures. Hence, the extension of the concept of analyticity could augment -though not diminish-, whereas its meaning remains fixed once and for all.

not limited to first-order theories. Hence, the definition of analyticity is in no way bound to first-order languages.

However, since the notions of aprioricity and aposterioricity are epistemological, whereas the notions of analyticity and syntheticity are semantic, it still needs to be examined whether there exist statements that are analytic, but are not *a priori*. Since it has already been shown that analyticity and necessity do not coincide, we will examine a collection of statements that are *a posteriori*, but seem to be necessary and even analytic. In fact, it will be shown that though the clause added above prevents analytic laws and other strictly analytic statements from being *a posteriori*, some instantiations of analytic laws, that is, some analytic necessities can be *a posteriori*.

§4 On Analytic Necessities that are *a posteriori*

It is said that the great Gauß once conceived the possibility of measuring the angles of a triangle formed by three mountains with the hope of definitely establishing whether space was Euclidean or non-Euclidean. After the advent of non-Euclidean geometries and, especially, of general relativity the belief in the empirical nature of physical space has been widely accepted. Thus, on the one hand, there are the geometrical multiplicities, the n-extended magnitudes of which the great Riemann spoke, some of them three-dimensional, some four-dimensional and, in general, for every natural number n, n-dimensional manifolds, some of them Euclidean, others Riemannian[20] and others Lobachevskian. On the other hand, there is physical space, whose dimensionality and structure are, contrary to our old friends Kant and Frege's views, to be empirically determined. Thus, let us suppose that physicists are able to measure the structure, not of the space between the three mountains near Göttingen, as Gauß hoped, but of a big chunk of intergalactic space. Let us suppose that the result of such measurement is that the sum of the angles of the triangle

---

[20] In this paper we only use the term "Riemanian" in the restricted sense of geometrical manifolds with positive curvature.

is less than (or greater than) 180 degrees. Hence, the structure of space is Lobachevskian (respectively, Riemannian). Therefore, the theorems of three-dimensional Lobachevskian (respectively, Riemannian) geometry are all true for physical space.[21] Moreover, such theorems of Lobachevskian (respectively, Riemannian) geometry are true not only for physical space, but for any structure isomorphic to physical space. Thus, if as a result of the measurements we conclude that space (or space-time) is Lobachevskian, the following three statements are true in our physical world and in any world isomorphic to our physical world: (i) rectangles do not exist, and all triangles have angle sum less than 180 degrees; (ii) it is impossible to magnify or shrink a triangle without distortion; (iii) if l and l^* are any distinct parallel lines, then any set of points in l equidistant from l^* has at most two points in it.[22] According to the first two clauses of our definition of analyticity –that is, to the older now abandoned version of the definition-, those three statements, as all other theorems of Lobachevskian geometry, would be analytic. On the other hand, our knowledge of the truth of those theorems in physical space was empirically obtained and could not be obtained otherwise. Thus, our knowledge of them is *a posteriori*.

However, if one takes into account –as one should do- the third clause of our definition of analyticity finer distinctions are required. What was empirically obtained was not a pure statement of Lobachevskian geometry but one of its instantiations, namely, the statement: 'In our physical universe the sum of the angles of a triangle are less than 180^0'. That statement, and the other similar statements, for example, 'In our physical universe if l and l^* are two distinct parallel lines, then any set of points in l equidistant from l^* has at most two points in it', though not only true in our physical world, but also in any other physical world

---

[21] For simplicity, we speak here of 'space', not of '(four-dimensional) space-time', but nothing in our argument would change if we did.
[22] For those three statements, see, e.g., Marvin Jay Greenberg's *Euclidean and Non-Euclidean Geometries*, W. H. Freeman, San Francisco 1973, pp. 150-152.

isomorphic to ours[23], express structural features of our physical world and certainly presuppose the existence of that physical world. They should be clearly distinguished from the corresponding statements of Lobachevskian geometry, which are pure mathematical statements, do not refer to any world, and are clearly both *a priori* and analytic on the basis of my definition of analyticity. Contrary to the latter, the above quoted statements are not analytic laws of three-dimensional geometric manifolds with negative curvature, since though they satisfy the first two of the three clauses of our definition of analyticity they are not free of all material content and cannot satisfy the third clause. Thus, such statements are really instantiations of analytic laws, that is, they are analytic necessities. Hence, one can conclude that there exist statements that are analytic necessities and are, nonetheless *a posteriori*.[24]

References

---

[23] We are here presupposing that an isomorphism between physical structures does not present any difficulties. Nonetheless, one would need to fix the individuals that are members of the universe, which could very well be either mass points or space-time points, and somehow presuppose that there is a bijection between the individuals of our physical world and the individuals of those other possible physical worlds, as well as that the structure of our physical world is completely given by its physical laws –which could very well not be the currently accepted ones. Thus, there is a lot of idealization when one speaks about isomorphisms between our physical world and other possible physical worlds.

[24] A former version of this paper was presented in the XVI Conesul Congress in Santa María, Brazil on 8 November 2012. The author is grateful especially to Jairo da Silva, but also to Max Fernández, José Ferreiros, Abel Lasalle, Marco Ruffino and Wagner Sanz for their critical remarks, which not only helped me sharpen the conceptual distinctions but, as mentioned in footnote 12 above, forced me to revise the definition of analyticity and also to refine its ensuing consequences. The author is also grateful to Prof. David Miller for some critical comments in private communications of the earlier version of the definition.

Carnap, Rudolf – *Meaning and Necessity*, The University of Chicago Press, Chicago 1947, enlarged edition 1956

Chateaubriand, Oswaldo – *Logical Forms* (two vols.), Centro de Lógica, Epistemologia e Historia da Ciência, Campinas (I) 2001 and (II) 2005

Frege, Gottlob – *Die Grundlagen der Arithmetik* 1884, Centenarausgabe, F. Meiner, Hamburg 1986

Greenberg, Marvin Jay – *Euclidean and Non-Euclidean Geometries*, W. H. Freeman, San Francisco 1973

Husserl, Edmund – *Logische Untersuchungen* (two vols.)1900-1901, Hua XVIII and XIX, M. Nijhoff, Den Haag 1975 & 1984

Kant, Immanuel – *Kritik der reinen Vernunft* 1781, revised edition 1787, reprint of both editions, F. Meiner, Hamburg 1930, third edition 1990

Kelley, John L. – *General Topology*, D. Van Nostrand, Princeton, New Jersey 1955

Kripke, Saul – 'Naming and Necessity', in D. Davidson and G. H. Harman (eds.), *Semantics of Natural Language*, Reidel, Dordrecht 1972, enlarged edition, Blackwell, Oxford 1980

Kripke, Saul – 'Identity and Necessity', in Stephen P. Schwartz (ed.), *Naming, Necessity and Natural Kinds*, Cornell University Press 1977, pp. 66-101

Quine, Willard v. O. – 'Two Dogmas of Empiricism' 1951, reprinted in *From a Logical Point of View*, Harvard University Press 1953, pp. 20-46

Riemann, Bernhard – 'Uber die Hypothesen, welche der Geometrie zugrunde liegen' 1867, third edition, Berlin 1923, reprint, Chelsea, New York 1973

Rosado Haddock, Guillermo E. – 'Necessità *a posteriori* e Contingenze *a priori* in Kripke: alcune Note Critiche', *Nominazione 2* 1981 (in Italian), revised English version in *Against the Current*, Ontos Verlag, Frankfurt 2012, pp. 285-301

Rosado Haddock, Guillermo E. – 'Issues in the Philosophy of Logic: a Heterodox Approach', *Principia 11 (1)*, 2007, reprinted in *Against the Current*, Ontos Verlag, Frankfurt 2012, pp. 305-325

Rosado Haddock, Guillermo E. – 'Husserl on Analyticity and Beyond', *Husserl Studies 24*, 2008, reprinted in *Against the Current*, Ontos Verlag, Frankfurt 2012, pp. 327-339

Rosado Haddock, Guillermo E. – 'Some Uses of Logic in Rigorous Philosophy', *Axiomathes 20 (2-3,)* 2010, reprinted in *Against the Current*, Ontos Verlag, Frankfurt 2012, pp. 365-383

Rosado Haddock, Guillermo E. – *Against the Current*, Ontos Verlag, Frankfurt 2012

Thron, Wolfgang J. – *Topological Structures*, Holt, Rinehart and Winston, New York et al. 1966

Wolenski, Jan – 'Analytic vs. Synthetic and A Priori vs. A Posteriori', in I. Niniluoto, M. Sintonen and J. Wolenski (eds.), *Handbook of Epistemology*, Kluwer, Dordrecht 2004, pp. 781-839

On Analyticity *a posteriori* and Syntheticity *a priori*

§1 Introduction

As is well known, Carnap's notion of analyticity is based on the meaning of statements[1], and is a sort of heir to Kant's notion of analyticity introduced at the very beginning of the latter's *Kritik der reinen Vernunft*.[2] Kant, however, had a second non-equivalent notion of analyticity, according to which a statement is analytic if it can be derived from the Principle of Non-Contradiction.[3] Frege's definition of analyticity at the beginning of his *Die Grundlagen der Arithmetik*[4], according to which a statement is analytic if it can be derived solely from logical axioms with the help of definitions, is a refinement of Kant's second notion of analyticity. Husserl's definition[5] in the Third Logical Investigation, according to which a statement is analytic if it is true and does not cease to be true when it is completely formalized, is not inspired by Kant but by Bolzano.

In three recent papers, namely, in 'Husserl on Analyticity and Beyond'[6], 'Some Uses of Logic in Rigorous Philosophy'[7] and, very briefly, in 'Issues in the Philosophy of Logic'[8] we have considered the possibility of a new definition of analyticity that does survive to the objections levelled by Quine to Carnap's definition of analyticity[9], to

---

[1] See his *Meaning and Necessity* 1947, revised edition 1956, as well as his 'Meaning Postulates' 1952, reprinted as an Appendix to the enlarged edition of the book.
[2] *Kritik der reinen Vernunft* A7-8, B11-12.
[3] Ibid., A150-153, B190-193.
[4] *Die Grundlagen der Arithmetik* 1884, Centenarausgabe, Felix Meiner, Hamburg 1986, §3
[5] *Logische Untersuchungen II*, U. III, §13.
[6] 'Husserl on Analyticity and Beyond', *Husserl Studies 24*, 2008, reprinted in *Against the Current*, Ontos Verlag, Frankfurt 2012, pp. 327-339
[7] 'Some Uses of Logic in Rigorous Philosophy', *Axiomathes 20 (2-3)*, 2010, reprinted in *Against the Current*, Ontos Verlag, Frankfurt 2012, pp. 365-383..
[8] 'Issues in the Philosophy of Logic: an Heterodox Approach', *Principia 11 (1)*, 2007, reprinted in *Against the Current*, Ontos Verlag, Frankfurt 2012.
[9] See his 'Two Dogmas of Empiricism' 1951, reprinted in *From a Logical Point of View*, Harvard University Press, Cambridge, Ma. 1953.

the demise of logicism, which destroys Frege's definition of analyticity by making most mathematical statements synthetic, and to the objection to Husserl's definition of analyticity of being too restrictive, since arithmetical statements containing constants essentially –like '2 is an even prime number' or '$1^3+2^3+3^3+4^3 = 100$'- turn out to be synthetic under that definition. Our definition, which attempts to delimit exactly what distinguishes mathematical statements from other statements originally read as follows: A statement σ is analytic if and only if (i) $\{\sigma\}$ has a model, and (ii) if $\{\sigma\}$ has a model M, then any structure M^* isomorphic to M is also a model of $\{\sigma\}$. At the end of 'Husserl on Analyticity and Beyond' we have also given a definition of syntheticity *a priori*, though we have not discussed it elsewhere. Thus, a statement σ is synthetic *a priori* if (i) σ is true in some physical world and (ii) if σ is true in a physical world W, then it is true in any physical world W^*.

§2 Revised Definition

In our recent paper 'On Analytic *a posteriori* Statements: are they Possible?'[10] we have corrected our definition of analyticity by adding a third clause that was taken for granted in the earlier versions of the definition, but if not explicitly included, the definition would be too wide. In fact, it could be inferred from both definitions that synthetic *a priori* statements –and probably also general physical laws- should be considered analytic, not only obliterating any distinction between mathematical and non-mathematical statements, but as well destroying the purpose of such definitions.[11] Thus we added the tacitly

---

[10] In *Logique et Analyse 229*, 2015, pp. 25-33, a special number in honour of the late Paul Gochet.

[11] It should be pointed out, however, that although we did not explicitly include the third clause, it was certainly tacitly included, not only because in all those papers we considered as examples of analytic statements only mathematical statements, as mentioned already in 'On Analytic *a posteriori* Statements: are they Possible?, but more importantly, because in 'Husserl on Analyticity and Beyond', we explicitly stated that synthetic *a priori* statements in Husserl's sense –whose extension would include that of our corresponding notion- presupposed the existence of a physical

assumed third clause to our definition of analyticity, namely: (iii) the statement σ can neither imply nor presuppose the existence either of a physical world or of a world of consciousness. In this way, we exclude exactly what we wanted to exclude, namely, all physical laws and all purportedly synthetic *a priori* statements of the Husserlian sort -of the Kantian sort there are none.[12] In that recent paper, we also examined other alternative third clauses, but they were either too wide or too restrictive. For example, if we only excluded empirical statements, the definition would be too wide, and the extension of the concept of analyticity would include purportedly synthetic *a priori* statements in the sense of Husserl's and also of our definition. On the other hand, if we were to exclude all constants from analytic statements, i.e. if the presence of constants in any analytic statement were always inessential, then we could replace all constants by variables, but the definition would be too restrictive, since it would exclude some arithmetical statements, like those mentioned at the end of §1. In fact, such a purported definition would most surely be co-extensive with Husserl's definition.

§3 General Considerations

In some of those papers, and especially in the last one, we have emphasized that our notion of analyticity does not coincide with the well known notion of categoricity, that is, the property of a statement or set of statements, whose class of models is constituted exclusively by isomorphic structures. On this point, we have discussed the case of first-order arithmetic –let us call it DP_1, for Dedekind-Peano in first-order logic. That theory is not categorical, since in virtue of Tarski' Upward Löwenheim-Skolem Theorem there exist models of DP_1 of any infinite cardinality. Nonetheless, the DP_1 axioms are all analytic

---

world and that such presupposition is completely foreign to our notion of analyticity. See *Against the Current*, pp. 342-343.

[12] Kant's conception of so-called synthetic *a priori* statements is based on his conception of space and time as intuitions and not concepts. However, as we have shown in our 'Intuitions, Concepts and Wholes', Kant's notion of 'concept' was too restrictive. Current use of 'concept' in mathematics –at least since Riemann- deflates Kant's arguments in the Transcendental Aesthetic.

both in the sense of the first and of the corrected version of our definition of analyticity. Moreover, DP_1 is not even $\aleph_0$-categorical, since it admits Skolem's non-standard model and, once more, all its elementary extensions of any infinite cardinality – hence, it is not α-categorical for any infinite cardinal α. Interestingly enough, Skolem's first-order non-standard arithmetic, that is, DP_1 + Skolem's Axiom is closed under isomorphisms and, hence, its axioms are all analytic in our new sense of analyticity. Another similar example is that of geometric manifolds. The class of models of three-dimensional Euclidean geometry is closed under isomorphisms, and its axioms are analytic in our usage of that term. But the class of models of three-dimensional Lobachevskian manifolds is also closed under isomorphisms and, hence, its axioms are also analytic on the basis of our original or our corrected version of analyticity. In fact, our notion of analyticity is moulded to apprehend exactly the class of mathematical (including logical) statements, which are statements whose class of models is closed under isomorphisms but, nonetheless, are true only in a restricted class of models. Logical statements, which are true in any model, are, hence, a limiting case of mathematical statements.

The refinement of our definition of analyticity mentioned above -and introduced for the first time in 'On Analytic *a posteriori* Statements: are they Possible?- prompts us to make a small revision of our definition of syntheticity *a priori* as well. As already mentioned above in 'Husserl on Analyticity and Beyond' we defined a synthetic *a priori* statement σ as (i) one which is true in a physical world W, and (ii) if it is true in a physical world W, then it is true in any possible physical world W^*. Thus, here we do not limit the range of application of syntheticity *a priori* to physical worlds isomorphic to a world W in which such a statement is true, but simply to all physical worlds.[13]

---

[13] By the way, although it is intuitively perfectly clear that physical laws true in our world should be true in any other world isomorphic to ours and, moreover, the intuitive idea of such an isomorphism between physical worlds seems at first sight simple, for example, by considering first the physical laws of our present universe and then all physical worlds with the same number of particles and same "structure", things are not so simple. In fact, to obtain a precise generally acceptable definition of

Nonetheless, it seems pertinent now to make a slight alteration of that definition of syntheticity *a priori* in order to adjust it to the revised definition of analyticity, in whose third clause we exclude reference not only to a physical world but to any consciousness. Hence, the definition should now read as follows: A statement σ is synthetic *a priori* if (i) it presupposes or entails the existence of a physical world or a world of conciousness, (ii) it is true in a physical world W or for a world of consciousness $\mathcal{B}$ and (iii) if it is true in a physical world W, then it is true in any physical world W^*, and if it is true for a world of consciousness $\mathcal{B}$, then it is true for any world of consciousness $\mathcal{B}^*$.

§4 On Synthetic *a priori* Statements

In the above mentioned papers, but especially in the last one, we have made it clear that analyticity and syntheticity are semantic notions, whereas –as Kripke pointed out in two seminal papers, the notions of *a priori* and *a posteriori* are of an epistemological nature. Kripke stressed that if the notions of aprioricity and aposterioricity were to be coextensive with the metaphysical notions of necessity, respectively, contingency, it would have to be shown and not taken for granted. In fact, he tried to show that the respective notions are not coextensive. Leaving Kripke aside, we have argued[14] that the semantic notion of analyticity is not coextensive either with that of necessity in a metaphysical sense, or with a notion of mathematical necessity, nor with the notion of aprioricity, whereas the notion of syntheticity is not coextensive either with that of aposterioricity or with that of contingency. But if those notions are not coextensive, then one can ask about the possibility not only of synthetic *a priori* statements, but even about the possibility of analytic *a posteriori* statements.

---

isomorphism between physical worlds is not an easy task, at least among other things (i) because it is by no means clear what is meant by having the same "structure" as our physical world –does it mean having the same physical laws, or also the same chemical laws, or also some sort of more plebeian laws like the biological ones?-, and (ii) because there is still no complete certainty as to which are the physical laws true of our physical world.

[14] In 'On Analytic *a posteriori* Statements: are they Possible?'.

On synthetic *a priori* statements we have little to say. In the Third Logical Investigation Husserl offered some examples of possible synthetic *a priori* statements, for example, that 'any colour presupposes a surface of which it is the colour', or that 'two colours cannot cover the same surface completely at the same time'. Those two statements would certainly also fall under our definition of syntheticity *a priori*. Another possible example concerns the intentionality of consciousness, namely 'any conscience is conscience of something'. Probably very general statements relating to the spatial and temporal structure of any physical world, for example, 'there is no physical world without spatial structure' or 'any physical world has at least one spatial dimension' will also fall under our definition of syntheticity *a priori*.

§5 Analyticity and *Aposterioricity*

The issue of mixing analyticity with *aposterioricity* seems certainly the most bizarre, and almost any philosopher would consider it a non-issue: there are no statements of that sort. Nonetheless, since aposterioricity is an epistemological notion and analyticity a semantic one, an argument has to be given to show that they exclude each other. In our recent paper, we have argued that there exist sentences obtained from analytic laws by the method of instantiation, which are, nonetheless, *a posteriori*. First of all let us recall the definition of analytic statements, characterized by the three clauses, namely, (i) $\{\sigma\}$ has (at least) one model, (ii) if $\{\sigma\}$ has a model $\mathcal{M}$, then any structure $\mathcal{M}^*$ isomorphic to $\mathcal{M}$ is also a model of $\{\sigma\}$, that is, $\{\sigma\}$ is closed under isomorphisms, and (iii) $\{\sigma\}$ neither implies nor presupposes the existence either of a physical world or of a world of consciousness. Hence, analytic statements are such that they either do not contain any constants or contain only mathematical constants, for example, arithmetical constants. Let us now distinguish between analytic statements and their instantiations, which we will call, following Husserl, analytic necessities. Thus, $1+2 = 3$ and $n+m = m+n$ are analytic statements, whereas 1 orange + 2 oranges = 3 oranges and 2 apples + 3 apples = 3 apples + 2 apples are analytic necessities. You cannot require of such analytic necessities that they do not imply or presuppose any physical world, since they are precisely physical instantiations of analytic statements, in the case of the second example, of an analytic law. Thus, analytic necessities do not satisfy the third clause of our definition of analyticity, hence, they are not analytic statements in our strict sense. Analytic necessities are instantiations of analytic statements and satisfy only the first two clauses of the definition of analyticity. Moreover, the examples of analytic necessities given above are true in virtue of being instantiations of analytic statements. Therefore, they are certainly *a priori*.

However, those are not the only sorts of examples of analytic necessities. Let us consider the situation of some physicists that want to determine once and for all the curvature of physical space in our universe. As known at least since Riemann (or even since Gauß), such a determination cannot be obtained *a priori*, but only *a posteriori*. Thus, they design an experiment and finally measure the curvature of physical space. To the surprise of physicists, let us suppose that the result of the measurement is that the curvature is negative. Hence, our physical space is Lobachevskian: the sum of the angles of a triangle is less than 180 degrees. Then all theorems of Bolyai-Lovachevsky geometry are true in our physical space. But since the theorems of that geometry, as of any mathematical structure, are closed under isomorphisms, they are true in any structure isomorphic to our physical world. In fact the abstract theory of Bolyai-Lobachevkian geometries of any dimension is composed solely of analytic statements- as happens with the corresponding Euclidean and Riemannian theories. The statements valid of our physical world are simply analytic necessities obtained by instantiation from the theory of four-dimensional Bolyai-Lovachevsky manifolds. Nonetheless, contrary to the analytic necessities of arithmetical statements mentioned above, we could not know *a priori* that such analytic necessities were valid of our physical world. We obtained that important knowledge *a posteriori* and we could not obtain it otherwise. Therefore, there exist statements, namely, analytic necessities, that is, instantiations of analytic laws, which are *a posteriori*.

This result is probably modest, especially in comparison with the definition of analyticity itself, as certainly also is the existence of synthetic *a priori* statements. Nonetheless, at least it is interesting to know that being (an instantiation of) an analytic statement and being *a priori* are not coextensive, and that being synthetic and being *a posteriori* are not coextensive either. By the way, as a sort of corollary to the above discussion, we may have finally made precise an elusive intuition had by many researchers since antiquity concerning a fundamental difference between arithmetic and geometry, according to which arithmetic is more abstract or less related to the physical world than geometry, namely: while all instantiations of arithmetical laws (that is, in Husserlian terminology, arithmetical analytic necessities) are known *a priori*, some instantiations of geometrical laws (that is, some geometrical analytic necessities) can be known only *a posteriori*.

References

Carnap, Rudolf – *Meaning and Necessity*, University of Chicago Press, Chicago 1947, enlarged edition 1956
Carnap, Rudolf – 'Meaning Postulates' 1952, reprinted as Appendix B in the enlarged edition of *Meaning and Necessity*, pp. 222-229
Frege, Gottlob – *Die Grundlagen der Arithmetik* 1884, Centenarausgabe, Felix Meiner, Hamburg 1986
Husserl, Edmund – *Logische Untersuchungen* (2 vols.) 1900-1901, Hua XVIII & XIX, Martinus Nijhoff, Den Haag 1975 & 1984
Kant, Immanuel – *Kritik der reinen Vernunft* 1781, revised edition, 1787, reprint of both editions, Felix Meiner, Hamburg 1930, third edition 1990
Kripke, Saul – 'Naming and Necessity', in D. Davidson and G. H. Harman (eds.), *Semantics of Natural Language*, Reidel, Dordrecht 1972, enlarged edition in book form, Blackwell, Oxford 1980
Kripke, Saul – 'Identity and Necessity', in Stephen P. Schwartz (ed.), *Naming, Necessity and Natural Kinds*, Cornell University Press 1977, pp. 66-101
Riemann, Bernhard – 'Über die Hypothesen, welche der Geometrie zugrunde liegen' 1867, third edition, Berlin 1923, reprint, Chelsea, New York 1973

Rosado Haddock, Guillermo E. – 'Issues in the Philosophy of Logic: a Heterodox Approach', in *Principia 11 (1)*, 2007, reprinted in *Against the Current*, pp. 305-325

Rosado Haddock, Guillermo E. – 'Husserl on Analyticity and Beyond', *Husserl Studies 24*, 2008, reprinted in *Against the Current*, Ontos Verlag, Frankfurt 2012, pp. 327-339

Rosado Haddock, Guillermo E. – 'Some Uses of Logic in Rigorous Philosophy', *Axiomathes 20 (2-3)*, 2010, reprinted in *Against the Current*, Ontos Verlag, Frankfurt 2012, pp. 365-383

Rosado Haddock, Guillermo E. – *Against the Current*, Ontos Verlag, Frankfurt 2012

Rosado Haddock, Guillermo E. – 'On Analytic *a posteriori* Statements: are they Possible?', *Logique et Analyse 229*, 2015, pp. 25-33

Appendix (added April 2018)

In my 'On Analytic *a posteriori* Statements: are they possible? We presented a new definition of analyticity, which was a correction to a definition given in earlier papers included in our book *Against the Current*. The definition is as follows, and the correction consisted in adding the third clause to the original attempt.

Def. A statement σ is analytic if and only if (i) $\{\sigma\}$ has a model [that is, σ is not contradictory]; (ii) if $\{\sigma\}$ has a model M, then any structure M^* isomorphic to M is also a model of $\{\sigma\}$ [that is, σ is closed under isomorphisms], and (iii) $\{\sigma\}$ does not imply or presuppose the existence either of a physical world or of a world of consciousness.

Up to now there is no reason to abandon such a definition, whose principal objective was to exclude Husserlian synthetic *a priori* statements and probably the most general laws of physics from falling in the extension of our concept of analyticity. But clause (iii) seems to be of a complete different nature than clauses (i) and (ii), which certainly are model-theoretic. Thus, even if the above definition does exactly the job it is supposed to do, namely, of fixing an adequate concept of analyticity, the definition could be charged of lacking 'elegance'. We will presently consider the possibility of replacing clause (iii) by one of a model-theoretic nature.

Firstly, let us remember that Husserl's definition of analyticity is too narrow, since it excludes mathematical, specifically, number-theoretic statements containing constants in an essential way, that is, which cannot be eliminated. Examples of those statements are (α) 'The number 2 is the only natural number that is both even and prime', (β) '$1^3+2^3+3^3+4^3=100$'. Since those statements are true only of the numbers referred to by the above constants, but false of any other numbers, we cannot replace the constants by other constants with different referents and, hence, cannot replace the constants by variables and prefix the propositional function with universal quantifiers for each variable.

What we need is to somehow fix the referents of the constants in any possible interpretation. However, such fixing of the referents cannot be done in Kripke's way, postulating that proper names are rigid designators, since there are no proper names, in fact, no constants that are rigid designators. The sign '2' in the examples refers to the second positive integer, that is, to the third natural number in the natural number series, but we could very well use the sign '2' to refer to the Pope or to the president of a given country. And we could very well use the Roman numeral 'II' to refer to the second positive integer, as the Romans did many centuries ago. Hence, it is not a matter of so-called rigid designators but of the senses of constants fixing their referents. It is the sense expressed by the constant '2' which fixes the referent of that constant in a given interpretation. Now we can try to formulate an alternative definition of analyticity.

Def. a statement σ is analytic if and only if (i) {σ} has a model, (ii) if {σ} has a model M, then any structure M^* isomorphic to M is also a model of {σ}, and (iii*) either σ contains no constant essentially or, if it contains constants essentially, then the respective senses of the constants fix the same respective referents of the constants in any model of σ. Hence, in any model of the statement '$1^3+2^3+3^3+4^3=100$', the constant '2^3' refers to the natural number 8 –and not to a cardinal of the catholic church or to the vice-president of any country.

However, though the first two clauses of the definitions are identical, clause (iii*) seems weaker than clause (iii). (iii*) certainly guarantees that number-theoretic statements containing constants in an essential way are analytic -since it is tailor-made for such statements-, while excluding physical constants, like 'the velocity of light', which need not have the same referent in all possible interpretations. Husserlian synthetic *a priori* statements, however, contain no constants essentially and (iii*) alone seems not to exclude them. Hence, clause (iii) of the original definition seems irreplaceable.

The two definitions are attempts at finally capturing the elusive notion of analyticity. If our original and seemingly more adequate definition has not attained its goal it is very near, certainly much nearer than Kant's two attempts, or Frege's or Carnap's ever were, and even nearer than Husserl's. Of course, one sees better when one sits on the shoulders of giants like Husserl, Kant or Frege.

Some Heterodox Analytic Philosophy

§1 Introduction

Analytic philosophy has been without any doubt the most influential philosophical movement in 20th century philosophy. In fact, it has most surely contributed like no other movement in the history of philosophy to the elucidation and demarcation of philosophical problems. Certainly, the self-imposed rigour of most analytic philosophy –with the exception of the English ordinary language philosophers, of which here nothing else will be said- and the use of logical tools in philosophy has without doubt elevated the discussion of philosophical problems in many areas of philosophy.

Nonetheless, the use of the word "analytic" in analytic philosophy is not uniformly applied. Analytic philosophy is usually traced back to Frege's views both on the philosophy of logic and mathematics, and to his semantic insights. Russell, Carnap, Quine and many leading figures of what could be called "orthodox analytic philosophy" see themselves as continuators of the same tradition inaugurated by Frege. However, such predominant trend in so-called analytic philosophy is permeated by a commitment to one or another sort of empiricism –and even nominalism-, which are totally foreign to Frege's views. In fact, the so-called Ockam's Razor, according to which one should not postulate the existence of entities that are not strictly indispensable, has been considered since Russell as the first commandment of orthodox analytic philosophy. Thus, in order to see Frege as their grandfather, empiricist philosophers had the extremely difficult task of trying to accommodate Frege's views to their ideology. Moreover, they felt compelled to reject any other philosopher or philosophical trend that could not be accommodated to their empiricist ideology. Hence, they both neglected valuable work that was not done by members of the empiricist church, while transforming, or better, deforming the philosophical work of others in order to make it presentable to an empiricist audience. So was born the dichotomy between analytic and continental philosophy, the latter a sort of wastebasket in which the most dissimilar philosophical trends found their "final destination". In this sense, empiricists in philosophy are very similar to Marxist-leninists in the political arena: non-empiricist philosophers should not be read and if possible ostracized, very especially those concerned with similar issues, but under different presuppositions.

Such an attitude against other philosophical trends has both served orthodox analytic philosophers to give completely inadequate and even biased renderings of recent philosophers –even of those they consider their own-, and to propound conceptions that are clearly non-starters and that could very well had been prevented had they taken seriously philosophers they have preferred to ignore or to see through blinkers.

§2 Some Examples of Historical Distortions

Let us begin with the so-called Duhem-Quine thesis. The first thing to be said about that thesis is that it lacks a referent. There is no such thing as the Duhem-Quine thesis. There is a very reasonable thesis of Duhem about the impossibility of isolating hypotheses in physics, with the immediate consequence of the non-existence of crucial experiments in physics.[1] That thesis concerns exclusively physics, not even the other natural sciences, and, of course, does not concern logic or mathematics. It is based on the fact that to submit a physical hypothesis to experimentation and possible refutation the physicist needs to make use of instruments designed on the basis of physical laws. No matter how well established those laws are, it is not excluded that one of them is false and that the negative outcome of the experiment is due not to the hypothesis under scrutiny but to that law. In contrast with what happens in physics, in the

---

[1] See on this issue Duhem's paper 'Some Reflections on the Subject of Experimental Physics', in the English translation of his papers *Essays in the History and Philosophy of Science*, edited by Roger Ariew and Peter Baker, pp. 75-111, especially pp. 81-88, as well as his book *La Théorie Physique: son Objet, sa Structure*, 1914, English translation 1955, 1991.

other natural sciences one makes use of instruments not belonging to the same discipline but to physics and, thus, the biologist or physiologist makes an act of faith with regard to physics and is able to isolate the biological or physiological hypothesis from any law of the same discipline.

On the other hand, there is a completely unfounded thesis of Quine[2] about the connection of all our beliefs in a so-called web of belief, according to which all statements, from the most trivial logical or arithmetical statements to statements such as that Newton had a toothache when he discovered the law of gravitation are connected, none of them is either analytic or *a priori*, thus, any of them can be refuted by experience, though we on purely pragmatic grounds prefer to save from refutation the logical and mathematical statements in the centre of our web of belief, while making those in the periphery responsible for any anomalies. Such an ungrounded thesis, instead of clarifying anything, serves only to add confusion. In fact, its origin is already doubtful, since it is based on Quine's so-called refutation of analyticity, which is basically restricted to the certainly very questionable Carnapian examples of presumed analytic statements like "All bachelors are not married". In fact, Quine's criticism of analyticity applies only to Carnap's definition of analyticity and, more specifically, to Carnap's unwarranted extension of his notion of analyticity to statements as the above, not to logical statements, and certainly not to Frege's, Husserl's or others' definitions of analyticity. We cannot dwell, however, on this issue here. It should be pointed out, nonetheless, that Quine's thesis under discussion has indirectly served to give life support to recent irrationalism in the form of post-modernism. Thus, it can be said that Quine is the grandfather or great-grandfather of post-modernism from the mother's side, while Nietzsche is the great-grandfather and Heidegger the grandfather of that sort of irrationalism from the father's side.

Our second example of a historical distortion is the common belief of analytic philosophers, based on assertions by E. W. Beth, Dagfinn

---

[2] See his 'Two Dogmas of Empiricism' 1951, reprinted in *From a Logical Point of View*, pp. 20-46.

Føllesdal³ and others that: (i) Husserl abandoned psychologism as a result of Frege's criticism, (ii) that in his *Logische Untersuchungen* he adhered to Frege's conception of logic, (iii) that Husserl learnt the sense-referent distinction from Frege, and (iv) that Husserl's notion of "noema" is a generalization of Frege's notion of sense. Since analytic philosophers usually do not read Husserl, they believe as religious fanatics the words of their prophets. The fact of the matter, however, is completely different. First of all, it should be stressed that Husserl did not obtain the sense-referent distinction present in *Logische Untersuchungen* from Frege. In fact, he had obtained that distinction in a paper written in 1890 and published only in 1970 as the second appendix to the Husserliana edition of his youth work *Philosophie der Arithmetik* under the title 'Zur Logik der Zeichen (Semiotik)'.⁴ Frege's first public mention of that distinction was in 'Funktion und Begriff'⁵, which appeared in January of 1891, when both *Philosophie der Arithmetik* and Husserl's review of the first volume of Schröder's book on the algebra of logic were in press.⁶ In that review, which appeared with the book in March of 1891 the distinction between sense and referent (in its Husserlian version) is also present. Husserl sent immediately copies of the two writings to Frege, and Frege himself acknowledged that Husserl had obtained the distinction independently of him in a letter to Husserl of May of the same year⁷, in which he discusses one of their differences, namely, that for Frege concepts were referents of

---

³ Certainly, the objective of Føllesdal, a renowned Husserl scholar who has certainly contributed to making Husserl known to analytic philosophers, were very different from those of other scholars trying to dismiss or disqualify Husserl. By the way, it should be pointed out that both Føllesdal's and Beth's contentions precede the publication in 1970 and 1975 of two writings of Husserl of decisive importance in this controversy -see footnotes 4 and 9 below.
⁴ 'Zur Logik der Zeichen (Semiotik)', in *Philosophie der Arithmetik*, Hua XII, pp. 340-373.
⁵ 'Funktion und Begriff' 1891, reprint in Gottlob Frege, *Kleine Schriften* 1967, revised edition 1990.
⁶ 'Besprechung von E. Schröders *Vorlesungen über die Algebra der Logik I*, reprinted in *Aufsätze und Rezensionen (1890-1910)*, Hua XXII, 1983, pp. 3-43.
⁷ See his *Wissenschaftlicher Briefwechsel* 1974, pp. 94-98.

conceptual words, whereas for Husserl they were senses of conceptual words (using Frege's better known terminology). There was another more important difference with respect to the referent of statements, but that does not concern us here.

Philosophie der Arithmetik was in some sense a dead born child. It was an extension of Husserl's professorship's thesis of 1887, and represented Husserl's views probably up to 1889. Nonetheless, that youth book is not guilty of many of the exaggerations attributed to it by Frege in his late review of 1894. It contained a mild Brentanian psychologism that was supposed to be counterbalanced by a planned second volume concerned with logical foundations of arithmetic. The project of a second volume was abandoned probably a little after the publication of the first volume. If you examine Husserl's writings of that period, some important ones published only posthumously, as is the case of his *Studien zur Arithmetik und Geometrie*[8], you observe a constant evolution.[9] In fact, already by 1894 –the year of Frege's infamous review- Husserl arrived at his mature view of logic and mathematics presented for the first time in his *Logische Untersuchungen* and since then maintained by him all his life.[10] To say it very briefly, for him logic and mathematics were related not as mother and daughter but as sisters. Mathematics is not derived from logic, as in Frege's views, and logic is not ontological as is mathematics. Logic is a discipline in the realm of senses, that in its first level protects against nonsense, in its second level protects against countersense or contradiction, and in its third level is concerned with the notion of truth and similar semantic concepts, whereas mathematics is a formal ontology, a theory of structures with its mother structures as in the Bourbaki school, being the other mathematical structures either specializations of the most

---

[8] *Studien zur Arithmetik und Geometrie*, Hua XXI, 1983.
[9] For the intellectual development of Husserl from *Philosophie der Arithmetik* to *Logische Untersuchungen* see Husserl's *Introduction to the Logical Investigations* 1975.
[10] See *Logische Untersuchungen* 1900-1901, Hua XVIII, Chapter XI, as well as his *Formale und transzendentale Logik* 1929, Hua XVII, where the semantic level is neatly demarcated from the logical-syntactic level, to use Carnap's later terminology, and the posthumously published *Einleitung in die Logik und Erkenntnistheorie*, Hua XXIV.

general structures, or combinations of them, or combinations of their specializations. Moreover, that ontological mathematics merges with logic in Husserl's version of the *mathesis universalis*, then crowning the edifice by a sort of theory of all possible theories. Such a conception of logic and mathematics -the latter a generalization of Riemann's views[11] and a forerunner of Bourbaki's[12]- has nothing to do with the much simpler Fregean conception.

A third case of historical distortion is the interpretation of Frege by Anglo-American scholars. According to the main trend in Fregean scholarship in English speaking countries, Frege was after all a Kantian or neo-Kantian, and primarily an epistemologist.[13] Such a rendering is based almost exclusively on the fact that Frege coincided with Kant with respect to his conception of geometry as a synthetic *a priori* science based on intuition. However, there end the coincidences. Even the arguments brought by Frege on behalf of his view of geometry are different from Kant's. Moreover, Frege forcefully rejects Kant's conception of arithmetic as synthetic *a priori*, and the central part of his work is concerned precisely with showing that his logicist views on arithmetic are correct and, hence, Kant's are false.[14] Moreover, in multiple passages of his *Die Grundlagen der Arithmetik* and elsewhere Frege –who was primarily a philosopher of mathematics- makes it clear that he is a rationalist and Platonist in the best Leibnizian tradition.[15] Kant's mathematical constructivism, and the grounding of non-geometrical mathematics on the

---

[11] See his classic monograph 'Über die Hypothesen, welche der Geometrie zugrunde liegen' 1867, third edition, Berlin 1923, reprint Chelsea, New York 1973

[12] See his 'The Architecture of Mathematics', *American Mathematical Monthly 57*, 1950, pp. 221-232.

[13] For a critical assessment of the thesis –not discussed here- that Frege was an epistemologist, see the present author's paper 'On the Interpretation of Frege's Philosophy' in *Against the Current*, pp. 21-62.

[14] For Frege's views on arithmetic and geometry see his *Die Grundlagen der Arithmetik*, especially the first part. See also §2 of the present author's 'On the Interpretation of Frege's Philosophy', in *Against the Current*, pp. 21-62.

[15] See op.cit., as well as 'Der Gedanke' 1918, reprinted in *Kleine Schriften*, pp. 342-362.

forms of sensibility of the human subject[16] are completely foreign to Frege.

But a still more alienated rendering of Frege is that of Jamie Tappenden[17], who conceives the history of mathematics in Germany in the nineteenth century as a cowboys versus Indians film. On the one hand, there are the cowboys –the good ones- of the Göttingen school founded by Gauß and presumably solidified by Riemann. On the other hand, there are the bad guys, the Indians, from the Berlin school of Weierstraß and Kronecker. Hence, since Frege studied in Göttingen (and also in Jena), he has to be somehow a Riemannian. Nonetheless, the fact of the matter is not only that Frege never referred to Riemann in his writings –and there is no evidence that Frege ever read Riemann's revolutionary monograph *Über die Hypothesen, welche der Geometrie zugrude liegen*-, and, moreover, Frege not only rejected non-Euclidean geometry in *Die Grundlagen der Arithmetik* for its lack of intuitivity, but in a posthumously published paper[18] compared non-Euclidean geometry to alchemy and astrology, and wanted it ostracized from the scientific realm. On the other side of the coin were the poor Indians, Cantor, Husserl and Minkowski, who had the "misfortune" of having studied with Kronecker and very especially with chief Weierstraß. The case of Husserl is even worst, since he was also Weierstraß' assistant. Nonetheless, it was the Indian Husserl who was strongly influenced by Riemann, not only, as already mentioned, by developing a conception of mathematics as a generalization of Riemann's views, but by accepting already by the end of 1892 Riemann's conception of physical space as empirical, distinguishing with Riemann between the formal study of geometrical manifolds of any

---

[16] See Kant's *Kritik der reinen Vernunft*, especially the Transcedental Aesthetic and the first part of the Doctrine of Method.

[17] See his papers 'Geometry and Generality in Frege's Philosophy of Arithmetic', *Synthese 102 (3)*, 1995, pp. 319-361, and 'The Riemannian Background of Frege's Philosophy', in José Ferreiros and Jeremy Gray (eds.), *The Architecture of Mathematics*, pp. 97-132.

[18] See his paper 'Über Euklidische Geometrie', in his *Nachgelassene Schriften* 1969, revised edition 1983, pp. 182-184.

number of dimensions and curvature, and the investigations on the nature of physical space, which are and have to be empirical.[19] Hence, Husserl rejected already in 1892 Kant's aprioricity of both the three-dimensionality and the Euclidicity of space.

A last example of a historical distortion we want to discuss here is the case of the interpretations of Carnap's *Der logische Aufbau der Welt*, from now on *Aufbau*[20], and Husserl's influence on that book. The case of the young Carnap is certainly the most complex and delicate, since already in *Aufbau* and during the rest of his life Carnap himself deliberately tried to mask Husserl's influence. Only in his dissertation, *Der Raum*[21], published in 1922 is Husserl's influence perfectly acknowledged. In that small book Husserl is referred to many times and always positively. In fact, *Der Raum* was written by someone who, not only had a very good knowledge of Husserl's views, but by someone that at that moment considered himself Husserl's disciple. Nonetheless, in his so-called Intellectual Autobiography of 1963[22], Carnap says that it were Kant and the neo-Kantians, especially Natorp and Cassirer who exerted a decisive philosophical influence on *Der Raum*. It was Adolf Grünbaum, in his commentary on *Der Raum* in the same volume[23], who mentioned Husserl's influence on that small book and forced Carnap to accept in his 'Reply to Grünbaum'[24] that besides Kant, Husserl also influenced his conception of intuitive space in *Der Raum*. But even that presumed acknowledgement was far from sufficient. As pointed out first by Sahotra Sarkar and then by the present author, Husserl was clearly the main philosophical influence on *Der Raum* and, moreover, though Kant is mentioned many times in the book, it is not always mentioned positively –

---

[19] See Husserl's letter to Brentano of 29 December 1892 in *Briefwechsel I*, pp. 8-11, as well as his letters to Natorp of 29 March 1897 and of 7 September 1901, also in *Briefwechsel I*, pp. 59-64 and 80-86, respectively.
[20] *Der logische Aufbau der Welt* 1928, second edition, 1961.
[21] *Der Raum* 1922, reprint 1991.
[22] In Paul A. Schilpp, *The Philosophy of Rudolf Carnap*, 1963, pp. 3-84.
[23] 'Carnap's Views on the Foundations of Geometry', ibid., pp. 599-684.
[24] See his 'Replies and Systematic Expositions', especially, pp. 952-958.

as Husserl is- and sometimes seems to have been mentioned in order to appease Carnap's thesis director, the neo-Kantian Bruno Bauch, who probably was not especially fond of Husserl. On the other hand, the reference to Natorp and Cassirer is simply grotesque.[25] They are barely mentioned, and when mentioned, together with Russell, on p. 81 of *Der Raum*, only as philosophers that erroneously believed that the notions of Euclidean space and of homogeneous space are extensionally equivalent. Nonetheless, most Anglo-American Carnapian scholars still think that Kant and the neo-Kantians were the main influences on *Der Raum*.

With respect to *Aufbau*, in his Intellectual Autobiography Carnap says that the main influences were Frege and Russell –see p. 12-, the Gestalt psychology of Wertheimer and Köhler –see pp. 16-17-, Ernst Mach, Richard Avenarius, Richard von Schubert-Soldern and Wilhelm Schuppe –see p. 18-, once more Mach and Russell –see p. 50-, and Mach, Russell and Wittgenstein –see p. 57. Once more, Husserl is not even mentioned. In his commentary, Robert Cohen mentions Husserl's influence on *Aufbau*[26], but this time in his 'Reply to Cohen'[27] Carnap completely ignores Cohen's remark. Moreover, on p. 50 and on p. 57 Carnap tries to make us believe that in *Aufbau* he took Ernst Mach's sense data as the basis of the system. This certainly contradicts what he said two years before on p. XII of the Preface to the second edition of *Aufbau*, namely, that he had taken the 'Erlebnisse' as the basis of his system and that if he had to write the book at that moment, that is, in 1961, he would have used instead a Machian basis, thus, clearly acknowledging that he did not use a Machian basis in *Aufbau*. In fact, he used a Husserlian basis, the elementary experiences of consciousness, the "Erlebnisse" in their

---

[25] In 1911 Husserl was by far the first candidate to occupy a position of full professor at the University of Jena, but for still unclear reasons the full professorship was given to the clearly inferior Bauch instead of to the author of *Logische Untersuchungen*, who in 1913 published his *Ideen zu einer reinen Phänomenologie und phänomenologischen Philosophie I* and in 1916 succeeded Bauch's teacher Rickert in Freiburg.

[26] See his 'Dialectical Materialism and Carnap's Logical Empiricism' in Schilpp's, *The Philosophy of Rudolf Carnap*, pp. 99-158.

[27] See his 'Replies and Systematic Expositions', ibid., especially, pp. 863-867.

constant flow in the stream of consciousness, in German: "Erlebnisstrom"[28], though on pp. 16-17, in which he acknowledged the fact that he used Erlebnisse as basis –by the way contradicting his later assertions in the same 'Intellectual Autobiography'- he attributed the influence not to Husserl but to a paper of Wertheimer of 1925 and to one of Köhler of 1922.[29] Moreover, Carnap not only based his constitutional system on a Husserlian basis, but (i) he used Husserl's argument –that Machian sense data are not given in experience but abstracted from what is given- to reject any Machian or Russellian basis, (ii) his notions of constitution and of grounding, in German: "Fundierung", are those of Husserl, (iii) his constitutional system is structured as a mirror image of Husserl's in the second volume of *Ideen zu einer reinen Phänomenologie und einer phänomenologischen Philosophie*, abbreviated: *Ideen II*[30], (iv) he committed himself to Husserl's phenomenological reduction, understood as in Husserl, as a methodological device, (v) his constitution of the heteropsychological is a mirror image of Husserl's attempt to solve the problem of intersubjectivity in *Ideen II*, in his *Cartesianische Meditationen*[31] and in his three volume posthumous work *Zur Phänomenologie der Intersubjektivität*.[32] We could have mentioned other minor points of Husserl's influence on Carnap's *Aufbau*, but those six fundamental points are enough to prove that also in *Aufbau* Husserl was the main philosophical influence. Nonetheless, it should be pointed out that already in *Aufbau* Carnap consciously tries to mask Husserl's

---

[28] On this and other points below see Husserl's *Ideen zu einer reinen Phänomenologie und phänomenologischen Philosophie I* 1913, Hua III.

[29] It is simply ridiculous to attribute such an influence to a paper published in 1925, when *Aufbau* was been finished, and even to one of 1922, after having referred to Husserl's *Ideen I* in *Der Raum*. The fact of the matter is that Gestalt psychologists –like Wertheimer and Köhler- most probably also obtained those concepts from Husserl.

[30] *Ideen zu einer reinen Phänomenologie und phänomenologischen Philosophie II*, Hua IV.

[31] *Cartesianische Meditationen* 1928, Hua I.

[32] *Zur Phänomenologie der Intersubjektivität* (three volumes), Hua XIII-XV.

influence by usually referring to many different authors that barely have to do with *Aufbau* and including Husserl as one of the last in the list.

Once more Anglo-American Carnapian scholars have opted to ignore Husserl's influence on *Aufbau*, and tried either to argue that Mach and Russell were the most important influences on that book or, as has happened most recently, that Kant and the neo-Kantians were the main influences.[33] The ignorance of Husserl's views, as well as some incredible blindness are the only grounds for such renderings, especially when there are passages in *Aufbau* in which Carnap explicitly rejects both empiricist-positivist views as well as neo-Kantian ones. We have already mentioned both that Carnap rejects a Machian-Russellian basis, and that he criticizes their views following Husserl's prior criticism of positivism. With respect to neo-Kantians, there is a very interesting passage[34] in which Carnap includes neo-Kantians in a group of philosophers that –contrary to Carnap himself, Husserl and others- reject the autopsychological basis. He does not mention Kant, but even a very superficial examination of the latter's *Kritik der reinen Vernunft* should convince the sceptics that Kant's system has a heteropsychological basis, hence, one that was considered by Carnap a constitutional and epistemological non-starter. Furthermore, it should be mentioned that though Kant also uses the term 'constitution', he uses it precisely in the opposite sense of Husserl's and Carnap's usage in this context, namely, from the top to the bottom, not from the bottom to the top. Finally, the most decisive divergence between Husserl and Carnap, on the one side, and Kant, on the other, lies in the necessity of constituting the heteropsychological. For Kant that problem does not exist, since he presupposes the existence of other similarly endowed human beings. For Husserl and Carnap –as for Descartes- the allegiance to methodological solipsism forces them to tackle the problem of intersubjectivity (or heteropsychologicality), and their solution is the same.

In fact, Carnap's attitude towards Husserl not only borders on plagiarism, but is a clear case of dishonesty. Even the distinction between

---

[33] See Friedman's and Richardson's books included in the references.
[34] See *Aufbau*, p. 87.

formation rules and transformation rules in *Logische Syntax der Sprache* was taken from Husserl, in this case from his *opus magnum Logische Untersuchungen* –see volume I, Chapter XI-, as was also the distinction made in 'Überwindung der Metaphysik durch logische Analyse der Sprache' between two different types of nonsense –see volume II, Fourth Investigation. Moreover, it is not simply casual that Carnap was so strongly influenced by Husserl in his younger years. In fact, Carnap was Husserl's student, even if he was not honest enough to accept it. At least during three crucial semesters between 1924 and 1925 in which he was writing *Aufbau* the young doctor Carnap studied in Husserl's "Oberseminare", that is, seminars for doctor students and young doctors.[35] He was in especially friendly terms with the ten years younger Ludwig Landgrebe[36], who was Husserl's assistant during those years and worked precisely on the manuscripts that now constitute *Ideen II*. Moreover, there is the strong suspicion that Carnap had already met Husserl and probably visited Husserl's seminars while writing *Der Raum*, since while writing his dissertation (and also after his doctorate) he lived in Buchenbach in the outskirts of Freiburg, where Husserl was professor since 1916. Nonetheless, Carnap never publicly mentioned having studied with Husserl. Even in his Intellectual Autobiography he did not mention it, though he mentioned that he visited three of Frege's lecture courses. But anyone that knows something about the traditional German university system knows that when you visited a lecture course you did not have the least contact with the professor, you could not even ask a question, that is, your role was totally passive. On the other hand, it is in the seminars, especially in the "Oberseminare", that professors and students got acquainted with each other.

---

[35] See on this issue, Karl Schuhmann's *Husserl-Chronik*, p. 281, where he refers to a letter of 6 August 1976 sent to him by Ludwig Landgrebe, in which the latter mentions that Carnap took part in Husserl's seminars from the summer semester of 1924 to the summer semester of 1925.

[36] See Landgrebe's letter to Husserl of 11 November 1932 in Husserl's *Briefwechsel IV*, p. 298.

§3 Ignorance and Prejudice

After 1926 when he went to Vienna Carnap seemed to have developed some sort of intellectual amnesia, not only with respect to Husserl's influence but also with respect to philosophical knowledge. Thus, he forgot Husserl's and his' criticism of Machian-Russellian positivist-empiricist views, and took active part in the discussion on protocol sentences, in which presumably one wanted the simple facts to speak for themselves be it in its physicalist or in its phenomenalist version. On the other hand, if Carnap and others had studied the non-empiricist Duhem carefully they would have not engaged in such a discussion about protocol sentences. As Duhem puts it[37], in physical science there are certainly experiments, but they are not as simple and naive as the logical-positivists and, before them, for example, Claude Bernard, as mentioned by Duhem, believed. Even the simplest physical experiences in laboratory are theory-laden. What the physicist (or chemist) 'sees' in the laboratory is not what the layman casually invited to the laboratory observes. Such 'observations' are automatically interpreted by the specialist on the basis of theoretical knowledge serving as basis even in the design of the experiment. Such is the basis of the empirical knowledge used in the physical sciences, not the so-called protocol sentences, be it in their physicalist or in its phenomenalist version. The whole debate on protocol sentences was a complete waste of time.

Logical-positivists hoped that on the basis of the so-called protocol sentences they could obtain physical laws by induction, and in this way the verification of physical laws could be reduced to the direct verification of protocol sentences. It is unnecessary to mention here how trivial logical arguments destroyed the logical-positivists' program, as well as their

---

[37] See, for example, Duhem's 'Some Reflections on the Subject of Experimental Physics' 1894, reprinted in the English translation of his papers, *Essays in the History and Philosophy of Science*, edited by Roger Ariew and Peter Baker, pp. 75-111, especially pp. 78-81.

variants using falsification or confirmation instead of verification, and even the more sophisticated Carnapian program of the observational and theoretical languages did not survive. In fact, already the design of the whole logical-positivist program, based on empiricist prejudices, was a non-starter, though the empiricist blinkers did not allow them to see it. A careful study precisely of Duhem's views on physical theories would probably have helped them discover their error.[38] But what Duhem said about the theoretical nature of physical laws was not as clear and terse as what Husserl briefly said in Chapter IV and, especially, in Chapter XI of *Logische Untersuchungen I*.[39] For Husserl, physics is an explanatory science and is a theoretical endeavour similar to mathematics, in which contrary to sciences like history, the decisive nexus is that of truths. Husserl clearly distinguishes between laws of low level, obtained more or less by some sort of induction, and genuine physical laws, which are of a theoretical nature and are called by Husserl "*hypotheses cum fundamento in re*". Husserl's preferred example of a *hypothesis cum fundamento in re* is Newton's law of gravitation. Such theoretical laws –in contrast to logical and mathematical laws, which are free of any link to experience– are linked, though only tenuously, to experience. They are not obtained by induction, but are introduced in order to explain the laws of low level originating in experience. By the way, Husserl obtained the deductive-nomological model for the explanation of laws of low level many years before Popper and Hempel. Such theoretical laws of higher level are not only tenuously linked to experience, but are in no way uniquely determined by the low level laws they are supposed to explain. There exists an indefinite number of possible *hypotheses cum fundamento in re* that could also explain the same low level law, that is, for example, *hypotheses cum fundamento in re* that are empirically equivalent to the law of gravitation but theoretically different from it. Thus, the laws of higher level are underdetermined by experience. Hence, Husserl obtained the underdetermination of physical theories –sometimes attributed to

---

[38] See ibid., pp. 90-91.
[39] *Logische Untersuchungen I*, Chapter IV, §23 and Chapter XI, §§62-66.

Quine- many decades before its introduction by analytic philosophers in the discussion of empirical theories. Once more, if logical-empiricists and other empiricist analytic philosophers had read Husserl carefully they would have avoided much effort that resulted in nothing fruitful.

§4 Empiricism, Nominalism and Logic

We have already mentioned that very simple logic helped defeat the verificationism and its variants of logical positivism. But logical positivism was after all one of the most liberal versions of empiricism. One can very well suspect that other more radical forms of empiricism, for example Quine's or Mill's are non-starters in the philosophy of science and, generally, in philosophy. But paradoxically empiricists seem to be unable to learn from experience. Some of them have seen the Platonist demons in higher-order logic, and have tried to limit logic to first-order logic. They have found some comfort in adopting Quine's *dictum* that to be is to be the value of a quantified variable. Thus, since first-order logic quantifies only over individuals, you can continue being an empiricist and be a nominalist. In fact, empiricism and nominalism are near cousins.

Things, however, are not so smooth as nominalists and Quineans would like. First-order logic has by far the most developed semantics of any logic, and that semantics consists of structures and families of structures of all infinite cardinalities in virtue of Tarski's so-called Upward Löwenheim-Skolem Theorem. You do not quantify over them, but your whole first-order semantics presupposes their existence. By the way, Quine abandoned the nominalism of his younger years and accepted a sort of moderate realism for mathematical entities, according to which you have to acknowledge the existence of those mathematical entities postulated by mathematical theories applicable to physical science. Thus, the entities postulated by the remaining non-applied mathematics do not exist. Such a moderate physicalist realism of mathematical entities based on the so-called "indispensability argument" has, however, some difficulties. It has as a consequence that mathematical entities have properties very similar to living creatures, namely, they are born at a determinate temporal point and could very well die. Thus, tensors were born when Einstein and Hilbert independently of each other discovered the general theory of relativity. Other mathematical entities, for example, some abstract ones postulated by universal algebra or category theory have still not been born, though one can still hope that they will finally be born. For the moment, however, at least parts of those areas of mathematics are no more than a game similar to chess. On the other hand, if a mathematical theory ceases to be applied in physical science, the entities postulated by that theory would die. I consider all those consequences of Quine's moderate realism absurd enough, so that the theory itself does not merit further consideration.

But certainly among empiricists there are more consistent and staunch nominalists that would not accept even Quine's moderate realism. However, if you are a true nominalist and do not accept the existence of mathematical entities, then you have to consider any existential statement purporting to talk about mathematical entities as false and universal statements purporting to talk about mathematical entities as vacuously true. Nonetheless, there is an important theorem in classical first-order model theory, namely, Robinson's Model-Completeness Test, which states, among other things, that a theory is model-complete –that is, substructures of models of the theory are always elementary substructures- if and only if for any existential statement in the language of the theory, there exists a universal statement in the same language that is equivalent to it. Hence, if an existential statement is false, then there is a universal one equivalent to it and, thus, false, and, conversely, their negations, which are respectively equivalent to a universal and to an existential statement, are true. Thus, there are true existential statements. Therefore, in virtue of the Model-Completeness Test, nominalism is false. Moreover, once more in virtue of the Model-Completeness Test, conventionalism in mathematics is also false, since one cannot make all existential statements false and all universal statements true, or the other way around. As a corollary, one can also conclude that Carnap's Principle of Tolerance, according to which, among other things, you are in complete liberty to choose a Platonist or a nominalist language, is also refuted. Classical (first-order) model theory is incompatible with the Principle of Tolerance.

Finally, among empiricists there have been some that have tried to argue on behalf of first-order logic and against second- and higher-order logic by referring to some desirable properties of first-order logic and contrasting the latter with the lack of such properties in higher-order logic. Let us examine some of those arguments. They certainly cannot reasonably refer to the fact that first-order logic has a very rich model theory, because that model theory consists precisely of abstract structures of any infinite cardinality. They can, however, refer to semantic completeness, the fact that first-order syntax is capable of properly covering first-order semantics, whereas that is not the case with classical – I would say "genuine"- second-order logic. Nonetheless, decidability and categoricity are also very desirable meta-mathematical properties, but first-order logic –except for its small monadic segment- is not decidable, whereas mathematical theories that are usually categorical are not categorical when expressed in the language of first-order logic. Those theories are, however, categorical when expressed in second-order logic. No matter what the defenders of first-order logic say, that is a clear sign of the inadequacy to express mathematical theories in first-order logic. Hence, one has to balance the positive and negative aspects of both logics without blinkers when comparing them and should not be in any hurry to condemn second-order logic.

Another popular argument wielded by defenders of first-order logic against second-order logic is that the former has only one semantics, whereas the latter has multiple semantics. Presumably, second-order logic allows besides its classical semantics a multi-sorted semantics and Henkin's semantics, which admits truncated models and served him to obtain a Weak Semantic Completeness Theorem. Nonetheless[40], once more one should not hurry to conclusions and interpret such presumed

---

[40] For a detailed treatment of this theorem see Chapter V of Alonzo Church's *Introduction to Mathematical Logic*, Princeton University Press, Princeton 1944, enlarged edition, 1956.

facts as a clear victory for first-order logic. In fact, there is no victory at all. Many-sorted second-order semantics is equivalent to Henkin's deviant semantics[41], thus, reducing the number of semantics for second-order logic to two. Moreover, Henkin's semantics for second-order logic was introduced in order to prove the Weak Semantic Completeness Theorem. But once you have semantic completeness, you can obtain, as corollaries both the Compactnes Theorem and the Downward Löwenheim-Skolem Theorem. There is, however, an extremely important result in abstract model theory, namely, Lindström's First Characterization Theorem[42], which states that any extension of first-order logic for which both the Compactness Theorem and the Downward Löwenheim-Skolem Theorem are valid is equivalent to first-order logic. Hence, what Henkin's Weak Semantic Completeness Theorem accomplishes is a reduction of second-order logic to first-order logic. Therefore, it is not the case that second-order logic properly has a diversity of semantics. The argument against second-order logic based on the multiplicity of semantics has been refuted.

References

Beth, E. W. – *The Foundations of Mathematics*, North Holland, Amsterdam 1965
Bourbaki, Nicholas – 'The Architecture of Mathematics', *American Mathematical Monthly 57*, 1950, pp. 221-232
Carnap, Rudolf – *Der Raum* 1922, reprint, Topos Verlag, Vaduz 1991
Carnap, Rudolf – *Der logische Aufbau der Welt* 1928, second edition, Felix Meiner, Hamburg 1961
Carnap, Rudolf – 'Überwindung der Metaphysik durch logische Analyse der Sprache' 1932, reprinted in *Scheinprobleme in der Philosophie und*

---

[41] See, for example, María Manzano's book *Extensions of First Order Logic* 1996.
[42] See, for example, Lindström's paper 'On Characterizing Elementary Logic', in Sören Stenlund (ed.), *Logical Theory and Semantic Analysis* 1974, pp. 129-146.

andere metaphysikkritische Aufsätze, Felix Meiner, Hamburg 2004, pp. 81-109

Carnap, Rudolf – *Logische Syntax der Sprache* 1934, enlarged English edition, Routledge, London 1937

Carnap, Rudolf – 'Intellectual Autobiography', in Paul A. Schilpp (ed.), *The Philosophy of Rudolf Carnap*, pp. 3-84

Carnap, Rudolf – 'Replies and Systematic Expositions', in Paul A. Schilpp (ed.), *The Philosophy of Rudolf Carnap*, pp. 859-1013

Church, Alonzo – *Introduction to Mathematical Logic*, Princeton University Press, Princeton 1944, enlarged edition 1956

Cohen, Robert – 'Dialectical Materialism and Carnap's Logical Empiricism', in Paul A. Schilpp (ed.), *The Philosophy of Rudolf Carnap*, pp. 99-158

Duhem, Pierre – *La Théorie Physique, son Objet, sa Structure* 1914, English translation, *The Aim and Structure of Physical Theory*, Princeton University Press, Princeton 1955, 1991

Duhem, Pierre – 'Some Reflections on the Subject of Experimental Physics', French original, 1894, translated in his *Essays in the History and Philosophy of Science*, pp. 75-111

Duhem, Pierre – *Essays in the History and Philosophy of Science*, edited by Roger Ariew and Peter Baker, Hackett, Indianapolis 1996

Field, Hartry – *Science without Numbers*, B. H. Blackwell, Oxford 1980

Field, Hartry – 'Realism and Antirealism about Mathematics', in H. Field, *Realism, Mathematics and Modality*, B. H. Blackwell, Oxford 1989

Føllesdal, Dagfinn – *Husserl und Frege, ein Beitrag zur Beleuchtung der phänomenologischen Philosophie* 1958, English translation in L. Haaparanta (ed.), *Mind, Meaning and Mathematics*, Kluwer, Dordrecht 1994, pp. 3-47

Føllesdal, Dagfinn – 'Husserl's Concept of Noema', *Journal of Philosophy 66 (20)*, 1969, pp. 680-697

Frege, Gottlob – *Die Grundlagen der Arithmetik* 1884, Centenary edition, Felix Meiner, Hamburg 1986

Frege, Gottlob – 'Funktion und Begriff' 1891, reprinted in *Kleine Schriften*, pp. 125-142

Frege, Gottlob – Rezension von: E. G. Husserl, *Philosophie der Arithmetk I*, 1894, reprinted in *Kleine Schriften*, pp. 179-192

Frege, Gottlob – 'Der Gedanke' 1918, reprinted in *Kleine Schriften*, pp. 342-362

Frege, Gottlob – *Kleine Schriften* 1967, revised edition, Felix Meiner, Hamburg 1990

Frege, Gottlob – 'Über Euklidische Geometrie', in *Nachgelassene Schriften*, pp. 182-184

Frege, Gottlob – *Nachgelassene Schriften* 1969, revised edition, Felix Meiner, Hamburg 1983

Frege, Gottlob – 'Brief an Husserl vom 24ten Mai 1891', in *Wissenschftlicher Briefwechsel*, pp. 94-98

Frege, Gottlob – *Wissenschaftlicher Briefwechsel*, Felix Meiner, Hamburg 1974

Friedman, Michael – *Reconsidering Logical Positivism*, Cambridge University Press, Cambridge 1999

Grünbaum, Adolf – 'Carnap's Views on the Foundations of Geometry', in Paul A. Schilpp (ed.), *The Philosophy of Rudolf Carnap*, pp. 599-684

Husserl, Edmund – *Über den Begriff der Zahl* 1887, reprint as Appendix A in Hua XII, pp. 289-339

Husserl, Edmund – *Philosophie der Arithmetik* 1891, Hua XII, Martinus Nijhoff 1970

Husserl, Edmund – 'Zur Logik der Zeichen (Semiotik)', in Hua XII, pp. 340-373

Husserl, Edmund – 'Beschprechung von E. Schröders *Vorlesungen über die Algebra der Logik I*' 1891, reprinted in *Aufsätze und Rezensionen (1890-1910)*, Hua XXII, Martinus Nijhoff, Den Haag, pp. 3-43

Husserl, Edmund – *Logische Untersuchungen* (2 vols.) 1900-1901, Hua XVIII and Hua XIX, Martinus Nijhoff, Den Haag 1975 & 1984

Husserl, Edmund – *Ideen zu einer reinen Phänomenologie und phänomenologischen Philosophie I* 1913, Hua III, 1950, revised edition, Martinus Nijhoff, Den Haag 1976

Husserl, Edmund – *Cartesianische Meditationen* 1928, Hua I, Martinus Nijhoff, Den Haag 1950

Husserl, Edmund – *Formale und transzendentale Logik* 1929, Hua XVII, Martinus Nijhoff, Den Haag 1974

Husserl, Edmund – *Ideen zu einer reinen Phänomenologie und phänomenologischen Philosophie II*, Hua IV, Martinus Nijhoff, Den Haag 1952

Husserl, Edmund – *Zur Phänomenologie der Intersubjektivität* (3 vols.), Hua XIII-XV, Martinus Nijhoff, Den Haag 1973

Husserl, Edmund – *Introduction to the Logical Investigations*, Martinus Nijhoff, Den Haag 1975

Husserl, Edmund – *Studien zur Arithmetik und Geometrie*, Hua XXI, Martinus Nijhoff, Den Haag 1983

Husserl, Edmund – *Einleitung in die Logik und Erkenntnistheorie*, Hua XXIV, Martinus Nijhoff, Den Haag 1984

Kant, Immanuel – *Kritik der reinen Vernunft* 1781, revised edition 1787, reprint of both versions, edited by R. Schmidt, Felix Meiner, Hamburg 1930, third edition 1990

Lindström, Per – 'On Characterizing Elementary Logic' in Sören Stenlund (ed.), *Logical Theory and Semantic Analysis*, Reidel, Dordrecht 1974, pp. 129-146

Manzano, María – *Extensions of First Order Logic*, Cambridge University Press, Cambridge 1996

Richardson, Alan – *Carnap's Construction of the World*, Cambridge University Press, Cambridge 1998

Rosado Haddock, Guillermo E. – *A Critical Introduction to the Philosophy of Gottlob Frege*, Ashgate, Aldershot 2006

Rosado Haddock, Guillermo E. – *The Young Carnap's Unknown Master*, Ashgate, Aldershot 2008

Rosado Haddock, Guillermo E. – 'On the Interpretation of Frege's Philosophy', in *Against the Current*, pp. 21-62

Rosado Haddock, Guillermo E. – *Against the Current*, Ontos Verlag, Frankfurt 2012

Schilpp, Paul A. (ed.) – *The Philosophy of Rudolf Carnap*, Open Court, La Salle et al. 1963

Schuhmann, Karl – *Husserl-Chronik*, Martinus Nijhoff, Den Haag 1977

Tappenden, Jamie – 'Geometry and Generality in Frege's Philosophy of Arithmetic', *Synthese 102 (3)*, 1995, pp. 319-361

Tappenden, Jamie – 'The Riemannian Background of Frege's Philosophy', in José Ferreiros and Jeremy Gray (eds.), *The Architecture of Modern Mathematics*, Oxford University Press, Oxford 2006, pp. 97-132

Intuitions, Concepts and Wholes

Abstract

Kant's conception of mathematics as constructible in pure intuition is based on his arguments in the Transcendental Aesthetic on behalf of the intuitive nature of space and time. It is here shown that Kant's conclusion is completely unfounded, since one can reproduce those arguments on the basis both of the concept of a continuous manifold in Riemann's sense and of that of an extensive whole in Husserl's sense.

§1 Introduction

In the *Kritik der reinen Vernunft* and very especially in the first part of the Doctrine of Method[1] Immanuel Kant argued for the constructibility of mathematical objects in pure intuition. According to Kant[2], philosophical knowledge is supposed to be rational knowledge from concepts, whereas mathematical knowledge is rational knowledge from the construction of concepts in pure intuition. Since intuitions are always singular, mathematical knowledge considers the general in the particular. Kant's conception of intuition had already been elucidated in the first part of the Critique, namely, in the Transcendental Aesthetic, especially in the Metaphysical Exposition, where he argued on behalf both of the *a priori* nature of space and of its intuitive nature.[3] We are not concerned here with the very questionable *a priori* nature of space, against which so much has been said and can be said, but with its intuitive nature. On this presumably intuitive nature of space (and of time) is based Kant's contention already mentioned that we construct mathematics in our pure intuition of space and time. In what follows we will first expose Kant's argumentation in his terms and then later show that the argumentation does not establish what Kant thinks it does.

---

[1] *Kritik der reinen Vernunft*, A713f., B741f.
[2] Ibid., A713, B741.
[3] For our purposes, see especially arguments 3 and 4, A25, B39-40.

§2 Kant's Arguments

In the third and fourth of the four arguments offered by Kant in the Metaphysical Exposition on behalf of the nature of space in the second edition of the *Kritik der reinen Vernunft* – which correspond to the fourth and fifth arguments of the first edition - Kant wants to establish that space is not a discursive concept but an intuition. According to the first of the two arguments, one can only have a representation of a single space, and when one considers different spaces, one is solely considering parts of one and the same space. Moreover, such partial spaces cannot precede the unique space of which they are partial components, since they can only be considered as parts of the unique space, as sorts of internal delimitations of the unique whole space. Any concept of space would then be derivative, based on the *a priori* unique intuition of space.

The second of the two arguments with which we are concerned contrasts our representation of space as that of a unique magnitude containing infinitely many parts with that of a concept, which is a representation that seems contained in a possibly infinite number of single representations – like the concept of horse in any single horse -, not one which contains an infinite number of partial representations, as is the case of space.

The distinction envisioned by Kant in the two related arguments is made clear when one considers the traditional view of concepts, which Kant certainly presupposes. An empirical concept, like that of being a horse, is a representation present in an indefinite number of representations of concrete horses, not a representation that contains representations of different horses as parts obtained by delimitation or restriction of the representation of the concept of a horse. The same happens with non-empirical traditional concepts, like that of a natural number. The concept of natural number is not such that it contains the representations of the different natural numbers as restrictions or delimitations of the general representation of a natural number, as parts of this latter representation, but is in some sense contained in each representation of a single natural number in the same way in which the concept of a horse is contained in the representation of any singular horse.

§3 A Few Remarks on Concepts and Manifolds

Notwithstanding his genius, Kant was limited by a philosophical and scientific tradition that was soon to collapse. The nineteenth century saw revolutions (i) in physics with the advent of electromagnetism, (ii) in mathematics with the rigourization and arithmetization of analysis, the origins of abstract algebraic systems and, more importantly for our discussion, the advent of non-Euclidian geometries, a fact that severely questions the relevance of intuition in mathematics, and finally (iii) in logic, a revolution that began with the work of George Boole and culminated in the epoch-making contributions to logic of Gottlob Frege. Most importantly for our purposes, our present conception of concepts has little to do with the very restricted traditional view presupposed by Kant. Thus, we now speak of the mathematical concepts of a group or of a topological space, though they have little to do with traditional concepts as that of horse.

In fact, already in the mid-nineteenth century one of the most distinguished mathematicians ever propounded the eradication of intuition from mathematics and its replacement by a broader understanding of the notion of concept. In his epoch-making monograph *Über die Hypothesen, welche der Geometrie zugrunde liegen*[4] the great Bernhard Riemann, without mentioning Kant by name but certainly having him in mind, questioned the traditional views on space in a most radical fashion. Not only did he consider physical space as just a particular case of the much more general concept of an n-fold extended magnitude, but made it perfectly clear that as to the determination of the exact nature of physical space no *a priori* considerations are available, but only empirical ones. Moreover, he neglected sensible intuition any role in geometrical considerations, obtaining the notion of an n-fold extended magnitude from a more

---

[4] *Über die Hypothesen, welche der Geometrie zugrunde liegen*. See already p. 1.

general notion of manifold. In fact, he drew[5] a very general division between the concept of a discrete manifold and that of a continuous one. He called[6] "quanta" the particular portions of a manifold, "elements" the quanta of discrete manifolds, and "points" those of the continuous ones. Moreover, he stressed that in the case of discrete manifolds, the quantitative comparison of quanta is obtained by counting, whereas in the case of continuous manifolds, the quantitative comparison of its quanta is obtained by measuring, which involves the superposition of portions of the manifold and, thus, presupposes the possibility of transporting a quantity used as a standard for the remaining quantities. Under that general purely conceptual division, the set of natural numbers would certainly be a discrete manifold – as well as the set of all horses. Space (as well as time), be it physical, intuitive or whatever, would certainly seem to be a continuous manifold.[7]

Thus, the difference made by Kant in his argumentation on behalf of the intuitive nature of space (and time) can now be very easily explained using Riemann's distinction by pointing out that space is a continuous manifold, not a discrete one, and such that portions of space are obtained by division of the continuous manifold, and all parts and parts of parts of a continuous manifold are of exactly the same nature as the manifold. In contrast, in discrete manifolds, in which the comparison of different quanta is obtained by counting, there is no subdivision in parts homogeneous to the whole discrete manifold. Contrary to Kant's views, there is nothing intuitive about space, just a sort of general concept different from the more traditional concepts dealing with discrete manifolds. More generally, there is no such construction of mathematical objects in the pure intuition of space (and of time), as alleged by Kant: there is no ground for mathematical intuitionisms and constructivisms.

---

[5] Ibid., p. 3.
[6] Ibid.
[7] Nonetheless, the great Riemann admits the possibility that in the infinitesimally small things could be different, not excluding the possibility that at the microcosmic level physical space could be discrete. See ibid, p. 20.

§4 Brief Remarks on Sets and Wholes

With the development of set theory in the second half of the nineteenth century and the beginning of the twentieth century, and its decisive role as the sole foundation of classical mathematics, in some sense the distinction between discrete and continuous manifolds lost some of its importance. Thus, one frequently spoke both of the set of real numbers, to which the number π belongs as a member, and of the continuum of real numbers, to which π is also supposed to belong. The double-duty is most clearly present in general topology. A topology T is a family (i.e., a set or collection) of sets, usually called "open sets". For any point in a topological space one can consider multiple neighbourhoods, namely, open sets containing the point. But this containment is ambiguous. The neighbourhood can be rendered as a collection of points or as a sort of region of which the point is an extremely small part. Moreover, open sets usually have accumulation points, and the set of all accumulation points of an open set O constitute what is sometimes called the derived set D of that open set. Together an open set and its derived set build what is usually called a closed set O^c, which is the closure of the open set O. But the derived set can be rendered either as the set of its accumulation points or as a whole composed of all its accumulation points as parts. In some sense, the distinction between member of a set and part of a whole is washed out.

Of course, one could counter-argue that the notion of continuity, though a topological notion, is not needed when considering only one topological space. However, when it is introduced, the notion of continuity does not change anything in the ambiguity present in general topology between discrete and continuous. The distinction pointed out by Riemann between discrete and continuous manifolds seems to have its roots much higher than the topological concept of continuity. Maybe we should look at the distinction between set and whole for some help.

We are not going to discuss this issue in any detail. But it should be pointed out that some of Cantor's contemporaries seem to have quarrelled a little with the distinction between those two notions.

Both Husserl[8] and more forcefully Frege[9] in their respective critical reviews of Ernst Schröder's *Vorlesungen über die Algebra der Logik I* accused Schröder of confusing the notions of set and whole. While Frege did not see any mathematical future for the notion of a whole, his younger rival dedicated the whole Third Logical Investigation to a very general discussion of a theory of parts and wholes. Of course, in that Investigation there is a lot that does not fit under a mathematical treatment of wholes, being concerned mostly with what Husserl considered as belonging to the synthetic *a priori*, Nonetheless, besides such considerations and the definition of synthetic *a priori*, there is also a treatment of more formal analytic aspects of wholes, including – in §12 - Husserl's definitions of analyticity and of analytic necessity. More importantly for our purposes, in his philosophy of mathematics from approximately 1894 or 1895 on Husserl not only clearly distinguished between set and whole, but considered that a theory of parts and wholes had to be developed as one of the, to use some Bourbakian nomenclature, mother structures of the whole of mathematics on the same level as set theory and number theory. One should note that Husserl, though a structural Platonist, was no reductionist at all, and that set theory did not have for him any privileged status among the most fundamental mathematical disciplines. It should be mentioned here that the great Polish logician Stanislaw Lesniewski, certainly under some Husserlian influence, developed a theory of wholes and parts, which he called "mereology", though, probably due to his nominalist leanings, as a sort of logical theory that would replace the presumably more ontologically committed set theory, not as another part of formal ontology at the side of and with equal rights as set theory, as conceived by Husserl.

As a sort of final note, let us remember that in the Third Logical Investigation Husserl briefly discussed a less general but still very general theory of wholes, namely, the theory of extensive

---

[8] See Husserl's 'Besprechung von E. Schröder, *Vorlesungen über die Algebra der Logik I*', 1891, reprint in *Aufsätze und Rezensionen (1890-1910)*, Hua XXII, 1983, pp. 3-43, especially pp. 13-14.
[9] See Frege's 'Kritische Beleuchtung einiger Punkte in E. Schröders *Vorlesungen über die Algebra der Logik*', 1895, reprint in *Kleine Schriften*, revised edition 1990, pp. 193-210, especially pp. 196, 198 and 210.

wholes,[10] which are such that the subdivision of the whole in parts can follow indefinitely without there being a determined hierarchy of parts of parts being nearer or farther from the whole or, in other words, a part of ... a part of a part of a whole does not need to be the result of an iterated division of the whole but could very well be the result of a first division. Interestingly enough, Husserl mentioned spatial and temporal lines as examples of extensive wholes.[11] It would be a routine exercise for someone interested to show that Kant's arguments on behalf of the intuitive nature of space (and time) can also be easily expressed in the language of extensive wholes without any trace of reference to anything intuitive, simply by pointing out that space and time are extensive wholes, not sets in the restricted but precise sense in which sets are sets of discrete objects. A more general and bold enterprise, which I envisioned during my student days but never undertook, and which would require much fresher knowledge of mathematics and more spiritual strength than I presently have, is to develop mathematical analysis as exclusively based on the notion of extensive whole.

References

Cantor, G. – *Abhandlungen mathematischen und philosophischen Inhalts*, Georg Olms, Hildesheim 1966

Frege, G. – *Die Grundlagen der Arithmetik* 1884, Centenarausgabe, with an Introduction by Christian Thiel, Felix Meiner, Hamburg 1986

Frege, G. – 'Kritische Beleuchtung einiger Punkte in E. Schröders *Vorlesungen über die Algebra der Logik*', 1895, reprint in *Kleine Schriften*, Georg Olms, Hildesheim 1967, revised edition 1990, pp. 193-210

Husserl, E. – 'Besprechung von E. Schröder, *Vorlesungen über die Algebra der Logik I*', 1891, reprint in Hua XXII, M. Nijhoff, Den Haag 1979, pp. 3-43

Husserl, E. – *Logische Untersuchungen* 1900-1901, Hua XVIII & XIX, Martinus Nijhoff, The Hague 1975 & 1984

---

[10] *Logische Untersuchungen*, U. III, §17
[11] Ibid.

Kant, I. – *Kritik der reinen Vernunft* 1781, revised edition 1787, reprint of both editions, Felix Meiner, Hamburg 1930, third edition 1990
Lesniewski, S. – *Collected Works I*, Kluwer, Dordrecht et al. 1992
Riemann, B. – 'Über die Hypothesen, welche der Geometrie zugrunde liegen' 1867, third edition, Berlin 1923, reprint in *Das Kontinuum und andere Monographien*, Chelsea, New York 1973

II

Husserl and Other Philosophers

Husserl and Kant: voilà la différence

Abstract

Kant's transcendental philosophy and Husserl's transcendental phenomenology have often and rightly been compared, especially since Husserl was a contemporary of the Neo-Kantian movement. Nonetheless, there are noticeable divergences between the two great philosophers. In this paper some of the most important of those divergences are considered, mostly by contrasting many of Husserl's seminal contributions to foundational philosophical issues with the more traditionally bounded views of Kant.

§1 Introduction

Kant's and Husserl's philosophies have been frequently compared, and their similarities stressed, to the point that, since Husserl was a contemporary of most Neo-Kantians, scholars that have never studied Husserl seriously[1], cannot distinguish Husserl's views from those of the Neo-Kantians and, in some cases, from those of Kant himself. The purpose of the present paper is precisely the opposite, namely, without disregarding the general similarities between the two great philosophers, to point out the many important differences.

Certainly both Kant and Husserl called their respective philosophies 'transcendental', namely 'transcendental philosophy' the former, and, for his post *Logische Untersuchungen*[2] period, 'transcendental phenomenology' the latter. And that was not a pure terminological coincidence, but based on a common interest in putting the 'transcendental subject' at the centre stage of philosophical research and examining the conditions of possibility of having (scientific) knowledge. In some sense, placing the theory of knowledge at the centre stage of philosophy was not a task of any of

---

[1] Almost any Anglo-American scholar in the analytic tradition could serve here as an example, but probably the so-called Carnap specialists are the most glaring examples.
[2] *Logische Untersuchungen I-II*, 1900-1901, *Husserliana XVIII* (1975), *XIX* (1984).

them, but of Descartes[3], and permeates also the great British empiricist philosophers of the seventeenth and eighteenth centuries, namely, Locke, Berkeley and Hume. As is well known, since Aristotle, the discipline that philosophers use to call 'metaphysics' was the fundamental philosophical discipline, in the strict and genuine sense of the term[4]: first philosophy. With Descartes' revolution in philosophy the theory of knowledge replaced metaphysics as the genuine first philosophy. After some failed attempts by metaphysicians, like Hegel and the other German idealists to restore the hegemony of metaphysics, the theory of knowledge prevailed, only to be replaced at the beginning of the twentieth century by what we will carefully designate as 'philosophical logic', understanding by this term –for simplicity's sake[5]- not only the fundamental propositional and first-order logic, but also the logical analysis of concepts and of language, and even those parts of more advanced contemporary logic with philosophical implications.

Kant and Husserl were heirs of Descartes, but in different senses. For Kant most surely the theory of knowledge was first philosophy, though he was probably more strongly influenced by Hume, and the former's philosophy could be seen as a reaction to that of the latter. Husserl's transcendental phenomenology was without doubt strongly influenced by Descartes, but he was also influenced by Hume in ways unforeseen by most scholars.[6] As a matter of fact, the mathematician turned philosopher, whose *opus magnum*, *Logische*

---

[3] See his *Meditationes de Prima Philosophia* 1642, reprint, with parallel German translation, 1959.

[4] That is, the founding (or fundamental) philosophy, the *philosophia prima*; which should clearly be distinguished from other recent uses of the expression 'first philosophy', probably ignorant of the already historically compromised use of that expression.

[5] Of course, in a strict sense, propositional logic and first-order logic are not philosophy, but the most elementary parts of the formal science of logic, while both the logical analysis of concepts as well as the use of logic to solve philosophical problems, thus, the purely philosophical-logical considerations, belong to philosophy but are grounded in logic.

[6] Hume, together with Leibniz, Bolzano and Lotze, influenced Husserl's abandonment of the mild Brentanian psychologism of his first book, *Philosophie der Arithmetik* in the early 1890s.

Untersuchungen, does not belong to the school of transcendental phenomenology, which he originated in 1905-1907, is much more difficult to encapsulate in the traditional philosophical categories. His transcendental phenomenology is clearly immersed in the tradition of the theory of knowledge as *philosophia prima* founded by Descartes, and, due to his transcendental reduction, is certainly nearer to Descartes than any philosopher of the modern period. But at the same time, not only did Husserl ever abandon his fundamental views of *Logische Untersuchungen*, but developed some of them further in the first part of *Formale und transzendentale Logik*[7] and in the book he was working on when he died in 1938, *Erfahrung und Urteil*[8]. Moreover, in his course on old and new logic[9], from 1908-1909, thus, after the transcendental turn, he emphasized that it is philosophical logic, which deserves the name of first philosophy, in some sense anticipating what would soon be the trend, especially, among so-called 'analytic philosophers'.

§2 Kant's Theoretical Philosophy I: Revolution and Tradition

Descartes' revolution in philosophy is certainly more radical than Kant's. It consisted first and foremost, in the replacement of metaphysics with the theory of knowledge as first, that is, as fundamental, philosophy. But Descartes went a step further, by introducing his methodological doubt, which left him only with his conscience and its *cogitationes* as the secure basis of his philosophy.[10] From that sole basis, the task of his philosophy was to obtain secure knowledge of God, the world and the other consciousnesses. In more recent Husserlian terminology, he had to *constitute* all those different levels of reality from that meagre autopsychological basis –to use Carnap's *Aufbau*[11] nomenclature. As we know, Descartes' attempt was a complete failure, and it was not taken seriously until the surge of Husserl's transcendental phenomenology.

---

[7] *Formale und transzendentale Logik* 1929, *Husserliana XVII*, 1974.
[8] *Erfahrung und Urteil*, 1939.
[9] *Vorlesungen über Alte und Neue Logik (1908-1909)*, 2003.
[10] See Descartes, op. cit., *Meditatio I* and *Meditatio II*.
[11] Rudolf Carnap, *Der logische Aufbau der Welt* 1928, second edition, 1961.

The British empiricists of the seventeenth and eighteenth centuries followed Descartes in the shift from metaphysics to the theory of knowledge as first philosophy, though they did not follow him in his methodological radical doubt, but, on the contrary, reacted against it; while the great rationalists, Spinoza and Leibniz, did not make the turn completely, though the great Leibniz' rich but disorganized philosophy has both components that point backwards to metaphysics and forwards even to contemporary philosophy.[12] Kant, on the other hand made the turn completely, though only in the less radical sense of the British empiricists, not on Descartes' more radical terms. As a matter of fact, Kant's philosophy was a reaction mostly to Hume, though also, on the other side, to some followers of Leibniz, and in the case of Hume, it was not always Kant who was nearer to the rationalists.[13] Although Hume was an empiricist, he is probably the less radical of classical empiricists –logical empiricists included. For him logical and mathematical knowledge was concerned with relations of ideas and was, hence, independent of experience, that is, *a priori*, and what is usually called 'analytic'.

Kant's theoretical philosophy[14] is said to have consisted in a Copernican revolution; and certainly his work, as an attempt to combine the positive aspects of both rationalism and empiricism, can also be considered a sort of bridge from modern philosophy, extending over the deep waters of German idealism, to late nineteenth century German philosophy, especially to the Neo-Kantian movement, though not exclusively to it.[15] He tried to avoid the excesses both of a rationalism that pretended to derive everything from pure concepts,

---

[12] On Leibniz, see his *Allgemeine Untersuchungen über die Analyse der Begriffe und Wahrheiten*, bilingual edition Latin-German, edited by Franz Schupp 1982.

[13] As explained immediately below, Hume's views on logical and mathematical propositions coincided with those of the rationalists, while Kant's did not. See the former's *Enquiry Concerning Human Understanding*, 1777, third revised edition, 1975, section IV, p. 25.

[14] With respect to Kant, we will consider here almost exclusively his *opus magnum*, *Kritik der reinen Vernunft* 1781, second revised edition 1787, and, in case there is some difference between the two editions, we will refer to the first edition, as is usual, with 'A' and to the second edition with 'B'.

[15] Besides the affinities with Husserl, there were also affinities with Frege, though not so strong ones as some Fregean scholars would like us to believe.

without the intervention of experience, and of an empiricism that was blind to the contributions of our mind in the assessment and organization of what is given in experience. Hence, Kant's famous motto that concepts without sensibility are empty and sensibility without concepts is blind.

Kant's task, therefore, was to examine the contributions of our capacities to our knowledge of the world. And by 'our capacities' what is meant are the capacities had in common by human beings. Thus, Kant distinguished four human cognitive faculties, namely, sensibility, imagination, understanding and reason, the first and the third being the fundamental ones, the faculties of intuitions and concepts, respectively, whereas the second is a sort of intermediary between the first and the third, and the fourth is a sort of uncontrolled use of the third one; uncontrolled in the sense that its application is not restricted by the first two faculties. The two most important faculties are discussed in great detail[16], and their description helps us see that Kant, the revolutionary components of his philosophy notwithstanding, was more attached to and limited by tradition than is usually accepted. As is well known by every serious student of philosophy, the faculty of sensibility consisted of two forms of sensibility, space and time, which are not given in experience but, on the contrary, make possible that the matter of experience is given to us in an organized way and not as a chaotic sequence of sensations. On the other hand, the faculty of understanding is endowed with twelve categories, that is, twelve very general concepts not obtained from experience, thus being *a* priori, divided into four different groups, and which are applied to the material given in experience, this application being possible by the mediation of the imagination. Since Kant had a very restricted notion of analyticity –in fact, he had two different notions, both very restricted of analyticity, namely, 'a statement is analytic if the concept of its predicate is included in the concept of its subject'[17] and 'derivable from the Principle of Non-Contradiction'[18]-,

---

[16] As every student of philosophy should know, sensibility is discussed in the part of the *Kritik* called 'Aesthetics' and understanding in the part called 'Analytics'.
[17] See the Introduction to the second edition of *Kritik der reinen Vernunft*, Section IV, pp. 45-48.

in the best of cases, only the statements from traditional logic would be analytic. Hence, all of mathematics, as well as the general principles of physics should be both synthetic and *a priori*, since their unrestricted generality does not allow them to be empirical.

Kant's official definition of analyticity -as being such that the concept of the predicate is included in the concept of the subject- already points to a very narrow conception of the notion of a statement, as being basically of the form 'S is P'. But that would seem to exclude statements of a relational form –very frequent in geometry and arithmetic-, which would seem to be forced to be non-analytic. And the other, unofficial definition, used in the section titled 'About the Highest Principle of all Analytic Judgements' –being meant the Principle of Non-Contradiction- has its own serious problems, since from the Principle of Non-Contradiction –even with the help of the Principle of Identity and that of the Excluded Middle- one cannot derive almost anything.

But leaving such an issue aside, one should point out that Kant's twelve categories are obtained –with slight modifications- from the usual classification of judgements in traditional Aristotelian logic. Thus, on this point also Kant looks to the past, in fact, to the remote past of a discipline that had stagnated for more than two thousand years, but less than a century after Kant's death began to experience an accelerated growth that has very few parallels in the history of mankind. Nonetheless, one can be somewhat generous with Kant while correctly arguing that what is important are not the specific concepts selected as categories of the understanding, but the acknowledgement of the existence of general concepts –or categories- of the understanding, which do not derive from experience, but serve instead to understand such experience.

However, Kant's roots in the tradition went deeper, and concerned the same notion of concept. While arguing in the so-called 'metaphysical exposition' of the Aesthetics that space –and similarly time- are intuitions and not concepts, he states in arguments three and

---

[18] See ibid., p. 207 (A 151, B 190), under the heading 'Von dem obersten Grundsatze aller analytischen Urteile'.

four of the second edition[19] of the *Kritik der reinen Vernunft* that space (and time also) is an intuition because it is a sort of totality given before its parts, and such that those parts are obtained by indefinite division of the one space, whereas in the case of concepts we do not have such a totality, but simply the indefinite plurality of objects falling under the concept is given and in each of those single objects the representation of the concept is also given. The latter is the case of the concept of a horse, which is in some sense contained in the representation of each single horse; and the case of the concept of natural number, which in some sense is given in the representation of each single natural number. In fact, Kant seems rather to point out confusedly to the distinction between countable manifolds, like those of all horses or all natural numbers, and manifolds with the cardinality of the continuum, like space and time. Nonetheless, also on this issue Kant is attached to tradition. His notion of a concept is that of the tradition, that of a discrete manifold of objects, and of each individual of the discrete manifold one predicates the concept. Nowadays, however, one has a much broader notion of concept, and one speaks without any qualm of the concept of a group[20] or of the concept of a topological space[21], though the definitions of such and other more complicated mathematical concepts are completely differently structured than those of the traditional concepts.

§3 Kant's Theoretical Philosophy II: Intuition and its Limitations

We pointed out above that Kant's arguments to prove that space and time are intuitions and not concepts are fallacious, since based on an unduly restricted traditional notion of concept. But that is not the only problem with intuition. As already pointed out, Kant

---

[19] For arguments 3 and 4, see A25, B39-40.
[20] A group G is a set of objects, together with a binary operation ×, such that (i) the operation × is associative, (ii) there is a unit member e, such that for any $g \in G$, $g \times e = g = e \times g$, and for any $g \in G$, there is a g^{-1} such that $g \times g^{-1} = g^{-1} \times g = e$.
[21] Given a set T, a topological space is a family $\mathcal{T}$ of sets such that $T \in \mathcal{T}$, the empty set $\emptyset \in \mathcal{T}$, the union of any members of $\mathcal{T}$ is also a member of $\mathcal{T}$, and the finite intersection of any members of $\mathcal{T}$ is also a member of $\mathcal{T}$.

conceived the faculty of sensibility, that is, the faculty of intuitions, as providing us with two *a priori* forms of intuition, space and time, which organize the material given in perceptions. But they can operate without sensory material being given in perceptions, and in such a case make possible our *a priori*, though not purely analytic, but synthetic knowledge of the axioms and theorems of geometry. A similar, though much less elaborated conception was supposed to apply also, in Kant's view, to the remaining parts of mathematics, in those days, arithmetic, school algebra, analytic geometry and elementary (non-rigorous) analysis, for which the temporal form of intuition would play a decisive role. Geometry, of course, meant for Kant Euclidean geometry. Thus, his philosophy offered a sort of transcendental validation of Euclidean geometry. Mathematical entities and theorems were constructed in the spatial, temporal, or both spatial and temporal forms of intuition, and thanks to such constructions the truth of at least the axioms, but also even of theorems, was "seen" by the transcendental subject.

This transcendental subject was not endowed with any other sort of intuition, except sensible intuition, with its a *priori* forms of space and time, which operated by construction of the objects of all of mathematics. Contrary to rationalist philosophers that had preceded Kant, and which conceived of a sort of "intellectual" intuition that gave us immediate knowledge of fundamental truths, for example, axioms, Kant rejected such sort of immediate knowledge by intuition, and more than once in the *Kritik der reinen Vernunft* contrasted our meagre intellectual capacities with those presumably had by God, precisely by stressing that whereas God possessed a sort of immediate intellectual intuition[22], Kant's transcendental subjects, which were simply we, human beings, were only endowed with the mediate forms of sensible intuition, space and time, which allow us to construct mathematical entities and, thus, see the truth of mathematical theorems. The fundamental laws of physics also had this synthetic *a priori* nature, though we will not dwell on this issue here

Kant's transcendental subjects are, as already mentioned, we, human beings; that is, not the isolated transcendental subject of

---

[22] See, for example, op. cit., B72.

Descartes, who had the difficult task, among others, of demonstrating the existence of other human beings, taking only his conscience as basis. For Kant such a problem of intersubjectivity, posed by Descartes, taken as fundamental by Husserl's constitutional system, usually called "transcendental phenomenology", and, following Husserl, also by Rudolf Carnap in his *Logische Aufbau der Welt*, did not exist. Only in the Third Paralogism of the *Kritik der reinen Vernunft* did Kant momentarily smell the problem.[23] But in the rest of his *opus magnum* and in his other writings Kant did not see the problem. It is, therefore incomprehensible that some Carnapian scholars, some of them presumably being also Kantian scholars[24], have argued that Kant was the primary influence on Carnap's *Logische Aufbau der Welt*. The *Aufbau*, as we will briefly say, is a constitutional system in Husserl's sense –see *Ideen zu einer reinen Phänomenologie und phänomenologischen Philosophie*[25]-, in which from a solid basis –in Husserl's and Carnap's sense the autopsychological basis of consciousness-, one constitutes the other spheres of entities. By the way, Kant also uses the term "constitution", but in a completely different and, directionally opposite sense, downwards and not upwards.[26] Much more importantly, if one were to classify the *Kritik der reinen Vernunft* as a constitutional system – which it certainly is not- it would be a sort of heteropsychological constitutional system, that is, one based on a plurality of similar consciousnesses, something that Carnap totally rejected in *Aufbau*, acknowledging only physicalist and autopsychological constitutional systems.[27] As Husserl, and distancing himself explicitly from the Neo-

---

[23] See ibid., pp. 390a-395a, especially, p. 391a.
[24] For example, Michael Friedman. See his *Reconsidering Logical Positivism* of 1999.
[25] See the first two volumes of that work, especially the second, whose subtitle is *Phänomenologische Untersuchungen zur Konstitution*.
[26] See,. Herbert J. Paton's *Kant's Metaphysics of Experience*, second volume, p. 179, as well as Michael Friedman's *Kant and the Exact Sciences*, p. 51. Hence, the same Michael Friedman has explicitly accepted this point, though certainly not its relevance for the rendering of Carnap's *Aufbau*, while other Carnapian scholars probably have not even seen this fundamental difference.
[27] On this issue, see *Der logische Aufbau der Welt*, §§50-54.

Kantians and from Mach[28], Carnap chose an autopsychological basis, in fact, exactly the same, even in details as Husserl. By the way, the constitutional system in *Aufbau* is a copy of that of the second volume of Husserl's *Ideen zu einer reinen Phänomenologie und phänomenologischen Philosophie*, and, in particular, the construction of the heteropsychological sphere is even in details that of Husserl.[29]

Leaving Carnap and his deeds aside, and returning once more to Kant, it is especially important for the present discussion that for Kant the transcendental subjects were the human beings, all of us, and that the only sort of intuition he accepted was sensible intuition, while the only non-sensible intuition he had in mind and rejected was a sort of intellectual immediate intuition he attributed to God.

More importantly, it should be emphasized here that such sensible intuition in which we construct mathematical objects is completely incapable of doing justice to our mathematical knowledge. As a matter of fact, constructivist conceptions of mathematics, be it Kant's, Brouwer's, Markov's, Bishop's, or whoever's, not only cannot assess the vast richness of pure mathematics, but probably not even that of the mathematics applicable in theoretical physics.[30]

§4 Introducing Husserl

Husserl is certainly much more difficult to assess than Kant. The former mathematician turned philosopher, who had been Weierstrass' and Kronecker's student, and also Weierstrass' assistant –certainly, not a small honour- turned to philosophy already in his professorship's thesis *Über den Begriff der Zahl* of 1887[31], expanded

---

[28] See ibid., pp. 86-88 for the connection with Husserl and for the disconnection from the Neo-Kantians and Mach. Kant is, by the way, not even mentioned, although the issue under consideration, that is, that of the constitutional basis, is fundamental for understanding the *Aufbau*.

[29] Contrast Friedman's book mentioned in footnote 24 with our analysis in *The Young Carnap's Unknown Master*.

[30] Since one considers functions on real (and complex) numbers, that is, entities of the second uncountable cardinality $\aleph_2$.

[31] *Über den Begriff der Zahl*, published only as an appendix to the *Husserliana* edition of *Philosophie der Arithmetik*, pp. 289-339.

considerably in his first publication, *Philosophie der Arithmetik*[32] of 1891, a book that was supposed to be the first of two volumes, but that was already old immediately after its publication. As shown by his posthumously published *Studien zur Arithmetik und Geometrie*[33], his *Briefwechsel*[34] and the Appendices to the *Husserliana* edition of *Philosophie der Arithmetik*[35], already by the end of 1892 Husserl was on the way to essentially different and important views. The mild Brentanian psychologism of his first published work was soon to be abandoned –which certainly was one of the main reasons why he never published, nor even wrote, the promised second volume of that work. In 1890, in the posthumously published 'Zur Logik der Zeichen'[36] Husserl introduced the distinction, made famous by Frege, between sense and referent. Husserl first mentioned that distinction in print in his review of the first volume of Ernst Schröder's *Vorlesungen über die Algebra der Logik*[37]. The review, which was in print when Frege's 'Funktion und Begriff'[38] was published in January of 1891, in which the distinction –which can be traced to Bolzano- was first explicitly mentioned in print, appeared in March of 1891, and in a letter of Frege to Husserl of May 1891[39], the former acknowledged that they had arrived independently of each other to the same fundamental distinction.

But also contrary to Frege, to Poincaré and other late nineteenth century philosophers, already in a letter of December 1892 to his former professor Brentano, Husserl accepted Riemann's conception of space, both by conceiving the different mathematical n-dimensional spaces, be it of positive, zero or negative curvature, as mathematical manifolds, and by rejecting Kant's conception of the

---

[32] *Philosophie der Arithmetik* 1891, *Husserliana* edition, 1970.
[33] *Studien zur Arithmetik und Geometrie*, Husserliana XXI, 1983.
[34] *Briefwechsel*, ten volumes, 1994.
[35] *Philosophie der Arithmetik*, from p. 340 onwards.
[36] Published as Appendix B.I to the Husserliana edition of *Philosophie der Arithmetik*.
[37] 'Besprechung von E. Schröders *Vorlesungen über die Algebra der Logik I*' 1891, reprint in *Aufsätze und Rezensionen (1890-1910)*, Husserliana XXII, pp. 3-43.
[38] 'Funktion und Begriff' 1891, reprinted in Gottlob Frege, *Kleine Schriften*, pp. 125-142.
[39] See Gottlob Frege, *Wissenschaftlicher Briefwechsel*, 1976, p. 98.

aprioricity of the three-dimensionality and Euclidicity of physical space. In letters of 1897 and 1902 to the Neo-Kantian Paul Natorp Husserl reiterated such views[40], and in the second part of his *Studien zur Arithmetik und Geometrie* one can trace the evolution of the young Husserl's views on that issue.[41]

In the first nine chapters of the first volume of his *opus magnum*, *Logische Untersuchungen*, Husserl offered the most devastating critique of psychologism ever to appear in print, and the critique included some criticism of what he called Kant's "transcendental psychologism".[42] Without entering in the extraordinary richness of the second volume, namely, the six logical investigations, it is difficult to understand how could Husserl had committed to psychologism in that second volume, as some scholars[43] have stated. Certainly, the fifth and sixth logical investigations deal with epistemological issues, but that does not mean –and could not possibly mean, unless Husserl were a sort of schizophrenic- a fall into psychologism.

As a matter of fact, as already briefly mentioned, even after his transcendental turn, in his course on old and new logic of 1908-1909, the epistemologist Husserl stressed that philosophical logic was first philosophy. But, of course, from the standpoint of transcendental phenomenology, it should be the theory of knowledge, not logic, the one deserving the name of 'first philosophy'. The fact of the matter is that in Husserl's extremely rich philosophy, one can consider without contradiction both philosophical logic and the theory of knowledge as first philosophy –but, of course, from different standpoints. Neither the theory of knowledge nor any other part of philosophy or of science can violate the most basic parts of logic. In this sense is logic first philosophy. But from the radical epistemological point of view of Husserl's transcendental phenomenology, with its phenomenological

---

[40] See Husserl's *Briefwechsel I*, pp. 8-11 for the letter to Brentano, and *Briefwechsel V*, pp. 59-64 and 80-86 for the two letters to Natorp.
[41] See the second part of Husserl's *Studien zur Arithmetik und Geometrie*, therein beginning with his lectures of 1889-1890 titled 'Geschichtlicher Überblick über die Grundlagen der Geometrie' on.
[42] See *Logische Untersuchungen I*, §38.
[43] See, for example Evert W. Beth in his The Foundations of Mathematics, p. 353.

reduction[44], that is, for the radicalization of Descartes' methodological doubt, in which only consciousness with its *cogitationes* and its intentional objects remain, the theory of knowledge is the most fundamental discipline, the first philosophy, while logic, mathematics and the other disciplines need to be constituted. But as seeing in *Formale und transzendentale Logik*, the logic and mathematics constituted by the transcendental consciousness is not one constructed or invented arbitrarily, but the same undistorted logic and the same undistorted mathematics already discussed in Chapter XI of the first volume of *Logische Untersuchungen*, only seen from a deeper standpoint. And the special intuition that allows us to constitute mathematical objects, introduced in the Sixth Logical Investigation, was once more at centre stage in Husserl's *Erfahrung und Urteil*, the work that, as mentioned above, Husserl was working on, together with his former assistant Ludwig Landgrebe, when he died. This shows clearly that Husserl's transcendental turn did not mean any abandonment of his *Logische Untersuchungen* views, but a restatement and deepening of them from the perspective of transcendental phenomenology, a perspective that also allowed (and sometimes forced) Husserl to tackle other problems not considered in his *opus magnum*.[45] A few words about some fundamental issues seem pertinent.

§5 On Husserl on Logic and Mathematics

After having accepted Riemann's views on manifolds at least as early as the end of 1892, and having obtained the distinction between sense and referent already in 1890 on the shoulders of Bolzano, the terrain was fertile, and certainly the renewed study of Leibniz, Bolzano, Lotze and Hume contributed to the development –

---

[44] See *Ideen I*, §§31-32.
[45] The most clear example of a problem forced upon Husserl by the transcendental turn is the problem of intersubjectivity, what Carnap called the problem of the constitution of the heteropsychological, to which Husserl dedicated the last of the *Cartesianische Meditationen*, a considerable part of the second volume of *Ideen*, and the three tick volumes –more than 1,500 pages- of his posthumously published *Studien zur Intersubjektivität*.

around 1894[46] - of Husserl's mature views on logic, mathematics and their relation. As a preliminary to the presentation of Husserl's views, it should be pointed out from the very beginning that although Husserl conceived logic and mathematics as very strongly related, he never accepted Lotze's or Frege's logicism, in fact, he did not ever accept set-theoretical reductionism either. Husserl was, in fact, no reductionist. Nonetheless, as Frege and Hilbert, Husserl is also a heir of the great Leibniz, though the three intellectual grandsons of Leibniz extracted related but not similar views from the latter's *mathesis universalis*. Instead of a mother-daughter relationship between logic and (non-geometrical) mathematics, as in Frege, Husserl conceived logic and mathematics (including geometry) as sister disciplines. The main difference between the sister disciplines consisted in mathematics being a formal ontology, thus, rich in ontological commitments, while logic remained a purely syntactic and semantic enterprise.[47]

At the foundation of Husserl's conception of logic and mathematics there are, on the logic side, some basic meaning categories, on the mathematics side some formal-ontological categories. Continuing with the logic side, those meaning categories are accompanied by some logical-grammatical laws that serve to build sentences and especially complex sentences from simpler ones, and which Husserl called "laws that protect against nonsense", putting emphasis on the exclusion of non-well formed sentences. Expressing it positively, such logical-grammatical laws allow us to form well-formed sentences of any degree of complexity by their iterative application. One does not need to be especially knowledgeable of logic to recognize under this laws that protect against nonsense the "formation rules" introduced by Carnap –without mentioning Husserl-

---

[46] See his *Introduction to the Logical Investigations*, pp. 35-38, as well as Karl Schuhmann's *Husserl-Chronik*, 1977, p. 26.

[47] See on this whole issue Chapter XI of *Logische Untersuchungen I*, the first part of *Formale und transzendentale Logik*, as well as the posthumously published *Einleitung in die Logik und Erkenntnistheorie* and *Logik und allgemeine Wissenschaftstheorie*.

in his *Logische Syntax der Sprache*[48], and since then accepted and presented in any rigorous introductory book on mathematical logic. Hence, this first floor of the logic building is not due to Carnap, nor to Frege, Russell or Whitehead, or anyone else not named Edmund Husserl.

The next floor is that of logic proper, and Husserl characterized it once more negatively as that of the laws that protect against formal countersense, that is, against contradiction, or, but this time positively as "the logic of formal consequence", that is, the laws of formal inference and derivation, thus, the level called by Carnap in *Logische Syntax der Sprache* –once more ignoring Husserl- of the "transformation rules". Although in *Logische Untersuchungen* there is no clear distinction between what we now call "(logical) syntax" and "semantics", in *Formale und transzendentale Logik*[49] Husserl distinguished a third level of logic, which was obtained from the "logic of formal consequence" by addition of the notion of truth and of related semantic notions. By the way, though *Formale und transzendentale Logik* was published immediately before the epoch-making work of Gödel[50] and Tarski[51], one should not forget that the

---

[48] *Logische Syntax der Sprache* 1934. See already pp. 2 and 4. It is interesting that no book of Husserl, particularly *Logische Untersuchungen*, is included in the references, while they are included in the references of both Carnap's earlier *Der Raum* and *Aufbau*, though *Logische Untersuchungen I* seems more relevant to *Logische Syntax der Sprache* than to those two previous books.

[49] Ibid.

[50] 'Über formal unentscheidbare Sätze der *Principia Mathematica* und verwandter Systeme' 1931, reprinted in Kurt Gödel, *Collected Works I* (followed by English translation), pp. 144-195.

[51] 'Der Wahrheitsbegriff in den formalisierten Sprachen' (expanded –questioned- version of the Polish original), English –even more questioned- translation of the German version, 'The Concept of Truth in Formalized Languages', in Tarski's *Logic, Semantics, Metamathematics*, pp.152-278. Certainly at least the title of the German and English versions is not a correct translation of the original Polish, which reads 'Pojecie prawdy w jezykach nauk dedukcyjnych', that is, 'The Concept of Truth in the Languages of the Deductive Sciences'. Another interesting point is the conscious attempt both in the German and English translations to avoid translating the Polish word "intuicijny" literally as "anschaulich" or "intuitiv" in German, as "intuitive" in English. See Monika Gruber's recent book, *Alfred Tarski and the "Concept of Truth in Formalized Languages"*, for some other cases of incorrect

manuscripts on which such a book was based were written much earlier and, hence, Husserl's views on this issue can be seen in some sense as a forerunner of Tarski's extraordinary work on the concept of truth in the deductive sciences of the early 1930s. But Husserl's anticipation of the prevailing conception of contemporary mathematics is by far more amazing.

In some sense, Husserl's conception of mathematics as a formal ontology, which is basically a conception of mathematics as a theory of structures, can be seen as a generalization of Riemann's conception of mathematics as a theory of manifolds. Firstly, it should be pointed out, that since Husserl was no reductionist, for him there was no single fundamental mathematical concept. He acknowledged a plurality of fundamental concepts, which he called 'formal ontological categories'. Different presentations of his views on the nature of mathematics diverged a little on the list of formal-ontological categories, though that is nothing substantial. Certainly, the notions of set, whole and relation were usually included, accompanied by notions like that of combination, or of ordinal and cardinal number. But what is important is how Husserl conceived such formal-ontological categories. Each of the formal-ontological categories gave rise to a foundational mathematical disciplines, whose axioms made explicit the corresponding category. Thus, would the basic mathematical areas be constituted, set theory, number theory, the theory of wholes and parts usually called 'mereology', following the later usage by Lesniewski[52], etc. The remaining mathematical disciplines were then obtained either (i) by combination of two or more fundamental mathematical disciplines, or (ii) by specialization of one of those

---

translations in that monograph, though in the case of "intuicijny"-see her commentaries on pp. 117-119- she failed to emphasize that in the empiricist German speaking and English speaking circles in which Tarski's monograph would be studied the word "intuicijny" was not, to use an adequate German expression, "salonfähig" (or in Spanish: "presentable en sociedad").

[52] Husserl influenced Lesniewski with respect to the latter's mereology and with respect to his theory of semantic categories, as well as Ajdukiewicz paper 'Syntactic Connexion'. Since that influence has been clearly acknowledged, it is unnecessary to dwell on it here. Nonetheless, it should be pointed out that whereas for Lesniewski mereology was a part of logic, for Husserl it was a part of formal ontology, that is, of mathematics.

fundamental mathematical disciplines, or (iii) by combining the procedures described in (i) and (ii), that is, by combination of different specializations of the fundamental mathematical disciplines.

Before continuing with the exposition of the constitution of the whole mathematical building, it should be pointed out that the aforementioned description of the whole of mathematics as a theory of mathematical structures of more or less generality and more or less complexity is, with some change of characters, essentially the same as was later developed –some forty years after *Logische Untersuchungen*- by the French school of mathematicians, Jean Dieudonné, Henri Cartan, André Weil *et alia*, using the general pseudonym of Nicholas Bourbaki.[53] The basic difference is that for them the notion of set was the most fundamental mathematical concept. Mathematics was conceived as a sort of theory of structures, with topological structures, algebraic structures and order structures playing the role of the three ground (or mother) structures. Then the remaining mathematical structures were once more, either (i) a combination of two of those fundamental structures –think about topological groups-, or (ii) a specialization of one of those fundamental structures –for example, metric spaces, rings or total orders, or (iii) a combination of specializations –for example, the structure of the real number system, or Banach spaces.

But Husserl went much further. Inspired by Leibniz, Husserl conceived of a higher level, a *mathesis universalis*, in which logic and mathematics would come together in a single discipline. This was Husserl's response to the logicism of Frege, and certainly Husserl's views are much more consonant than Frege's with the development of mathematics since the late 1890s. It seems pertinent to compare a little the views of both mathematicians turned philosophers. Frege's objective is supposed to have been to derive the whole of non-geometrical mathematics from logical axioms, a task in which he certainly failed, but even if he had succeeded, it would not had satisfied the requirements of the new mathematics. Basically, Frege's plan was to, firstly, derive arithmetic from logic, and then the theories of rational, real and complex numbers. But mathematics had already

---

[53] See Bourbaki's papers in the references.

developed in many directions completely ignored by Frege. Not only was mathematics to follow Riemann in considering abstract geometrical manifolds independently of their application to physical space —something completely alien to Frege[54]-, but there had been generalizations and abstractions in other important areas. Algebraic structures obtained their independence from the concrete numerical theories already in the second half of the nineteenth century, a process that would continue generalizing until the development of universal algebra in the twentieth century. On the other hand, already at the end of the nineteenth and the beginning of the twentieth century topology surged as a fundamental area of mathematics. And in the middle of the twentieth century category theory surged as a foundational mathematical theory rivalling with set theory. Neither Frege nor his later epigones from Russell to the contemporary neo-logicists have shown the place where the theorems of disciplines like group theory, general topology, universal algebra or category theory should be obtained on the exclusive basis of logical axioms. Up to now they have done nothing of this sort, and simply cannot be taken seriously. They all remain prisoners of (a limited understanding of) nineteenth century mathematics, since the logicism of Frege and Dedekind was just the culmination of the process of rigorous foundation of analysis originated by Cauchy, Bolzano and others, and going through Weierstraß' arithmetization of analysis.

Husserl was certainly better equipped to assess the development of mathematics than Frege, even though Frege was all his life a mathematics professor, though a marginal one at a lesser known university than Husserl. Besides having been Weierstraß' student and later assistant, while at Halle Husserl was a very near friend of Georg Cantor, who was at the forefront of mathematical research, and at Göttingen he was from the very beginning in 1901 in

---

[54] Besides Frege's arguments in *Die Grundlagen der Arithmetik* on behalf of the presumed synthetic *a priori* nature of geometric —of course, Euclidean-geometric- statements, it seems pertinent to consult his posthumous paper 'Über Euklidische Geometrie', in *Nachgelassene Schriften*, pp. 182-184, a paper written between 1899 and 1906, in which Frege not only asserts that there is only one true geometry, but dares —what a beauty!- to put non-Euclidean geometries at the level of alchemy and even of astrology.

friendly terms and academic contact with Felix Klein, Ernst Zermelo and very especially with David Hilbert, and the best mathematics (and physics) students in those years in Göttingen –for example, Max Born and Hermann Weyl- were usually also Husserl's students in philosophy courses.

As a matter of fact, Husserl's conception of logic and mathematics as sister disciplines, and mathematics as a theory of structures allow both for geometric structures and for all those more recent developments in mathematics to find a home. And their union in the *mathesis universalis* is both more natural and realistic than Frege's logicism. But Husserl did not finish his building of the formal sciences with the *mathesis universalis*. On top of the logical-mathematical building, Husserl conceived a sort of theory of all possible theories, a sort of abstract meta-logical-mathematical discipline that would consider the forms of all possible theories and the relations between them with the utmost generality. It has been a matter of discussion, whether the incompleteness theorems set a limit to what can be done in this very abstract theory of all possible theories. But even if that is the case –as the present author believes-, that does not mean that all considerations of such an extremely general (and beautiful) enterprise are futile.[55] The theory of all possible theories can be seen as an unattainable Kantian idea towards which the efforts of mathematicians should converge, Once more, the Bourbaki project, as well as the more recent theory of categories, remain as partial realizations of this marvellous enterprise.

§6 Husserl's Two New Forms of Intuition: some Brief Notes

In order to round up our discussion, it seems pertinent to contrast Husserl and Kant's views of intuition. As already mentioned, Kant believed that we are only capable of a sort of sensible intuition in which the objects of experience are given to us and in which, without that such objects be given, we can construct mathematical objects in it. Moreover, the only sort of non-sensible intuition whose existence

---

[55] See, for example, Husserl's *Einleitung in die Logik und Erkenntnistheorie*, pp. 86-87 for an illustration of the considerations in the theory of all possible theories.

Kant acknowledged was a sort of mysterious intellectual immediate intuition had by God.[56]

Husserl, on the other hand acknowledged two sorts of non-sensible intuition with which we are endowed, namely, the much commented but little understood "eidetic intuition", or intuition of essences, and the often ignored categorial intuition. Husserl sometimes saw one as a special case of the other, though it is not clear which was a special case of which. In §48 of the Sixth Logical Investigation[57], while discussing categorial intuition, he mentions eidetic intuition as a sort of special case of the former. But in *Ideen I*, when discussing material essences, he mentions "formal essences" as if they were a special case of the former.[58] And though they are certainly not unrelated, we do not consider that any of them is a special case of the other, since they differ both in their objects of study, as well as in their procedure. In what follows, we will be concerned almost exclusively with the by far less known categorial intuition. Husserl discussed and applied eidetic intuition, whose primary[59] objective –though neither its procedure nor its result- is similar to Kant's, namely, to obtain a sort of synthetic *a priori* knowledge, much more frequently than categorial intuition, and a treatment of the former –adequate or inadequate- can be found in many expository works on Husserl.[60]

---

[56] See footnote 21 above.
[57] *Logische Untersuchungen II*, Sixth Logical Investigation, §48. By the way, the fact that eidetic intuition is also present in *Logische Untersuchungen* should help avoid a possible misunderstanding of Husserl, incorrectly identifying eidetic intuition with the period after the transcendental turn.
[58] See *Ideen zu einer reinen Phänomenologie und phänomenologischen Philosophie I*, §§7-11.
[59] We are certainly stricter than Husserl on this point, since he seems to have acknowledged a role for eidetic variation also in the formal sciences. Nonetheless, it is important to clearly differentiate between eidetic intuition and categorial intuition, as well as between eidetic variation and categorial abstraction –see below.
[60] We especially recommend the excellent exposition of Husserl's eidetic intuition in Jairo da Silva's recent book, *Mathematics and its Applications*. See also the already classic studies of Husserl by J. N. Mohanty and David Woodruff Smith included in the bibliography.

Thus, with respect to eidetic intuition we would only like to emphasize a few points. Firstly, that it is not a sensible intuition in the sense of Kant, though it can (but not need to) begin with the empirical perception of an object –it can also begin with an act of the imagination-, and is concerned with the material or synthetic *a priori*. Secondly, that it is not a sort of mysterious immediate intuition, like that attributed by Kant to God, but a mediated one. Thirdly, that eidetic intuition is based on what Husserl called "eidetic variation", that is, in order to obtain the material essence, there is a process of indefinite –in principle, infinite- (imaginative) variation of the object perceived or imagined, until the "essence" of the concept instantiated in the original object is apprehended.

Empiricist philosophers of different sorts all agree in believing that what is given in experience are either sense data or sensations, or something equally primitive, no matter with what name it is referred to, and then we combine somehow those primitive components to form an empirical object. The best example of that epistemology of bugs is Quine's primitive behaviouristic pseudoscientific analysis in *Word and Object*[61]. The fact of the matter, however, is that what we experience are not pure sensations or sense data, but at least objects or, more exactly, not only objects but states of affairs, and only later, by means of a sort of abstraction, are we able to concentrate on the redness of the cover of the book seen.[62] At this point, our knowing process is exactly opposite to the bugs' process described by Quine and others. Here lies the basic point of divergence between Husserl's phenomenology and all sorts of empiricist and positivist schools, and here lies also the reason for Husserl's claim in *Ideen I* that the true positivists are the phenomenologists, since only the latter go directly to the things themselves, whereas the empiricists and presumed positivists take as given what is the result of abstractions.[63]

Moreover, as Husserl emphasizes in the Sixth Logical Investigation, we not only perceive objects, we perceive states of

---

[61] *Word and Object* 1960.
[62] See *Logische Untersuchungen II*, U. VI, second part.
[63] See *Ideen zu einer reinen Phänomenologie und phänomenologischen Philosophie I*, §20.

affairs.[64] We do not only see the book, the table and the pencil, we see the book and the pencil on the table, and also the pencil at the side of the book. We do not see Peter, see Charles and see the door, but see Peter and Charles at the door. And we also see that Charles is taller than Peter. In those two cases what we perceive are states of affairs, namely: (I.1) the state of affairs that the book is on the table, (I.2) the state of affairs that the pencil is on the table, (I.3) the state of affairs that the pencil is at the side of the book, and (I.4) the complex state of affairs that the book and the pencil are on the table side by side; while in the other example we perceive (II.1) the state of affairs that Charles is at the door, (II.2) the state of affairs that Peter is at the door, (II.3) the complex state of affairs that Peter and Charles are together, (II.4) the even more complex state of affairs that Peter and Charles are together at the door, and (II.5) the one level higher complex state of affairs that Charles is taller than Peter.

We have correctly used the word 'perceive' in all those cases, though what we perceive is not the object of pure (sensible) perception. When we perceive states of affairs, we perceive components that do not have a sensible correlate. Though there is something sensible, material corresponding to 'book' to 'table' and to 'pencil', and surely something sensible corresponding to 'door', to 'Peter' and to 'Charles', there is nothing sensible corresponding to 'on', to 'at the side of', to 'and', to 'at' or to 'taller than'.[65] Those are all categorial components of perception. And when we say that we see a group –in mathematical jargon 'set'- of persons in the room, we sensibly perceive each person individually, but we do not sensibly perceive the collection (group or set). The latter is also a categorial component of perception. Hence, even in our most simple 'sensible' perceptions there are categorial components, namely, states of affairs, relations, sets, etc. This is the ground and the origin of what Husserl called 'categorial intuition'.

But we do not need to stay at the ground level. Given two collections in perception, we can relate the two collections, for example, we can bring the members of the two collections together,

---

[64] See footnote 59.
[65] See once more *Logische Untersuchungen II*, U. VI, second part.

thus, building a bigger collection, or we can try to establish a one-to-one correlation between the collections, for example, of the students in one class and the students in another class, and conclude that one collection is bigger than the other. Moreover, we can also consider relations of sets of relations, or sets of relations between sets of relations, and continue up the ladder constituting –to use Husserl's terminology- each time more complex categorial objectualities up to any finite level. Thus, we obtain an infinite hierarchy of categorial objectualities based on sense perception by indefinite iteration of the operations 'set of' and 'relation between'.[66] There is nothing mysterious or esoteric in this procedure, but simply the iteration of a simple procedure based on the unavoidable, since inherent, categorial components of sensible perception, and the objectualities, no matter how high in the hierarchy, are rooted in sensible perception and are not independent of their sensible origin.

But we are especially interested in knowledge of pure mathematics. In order to obtain mathematical objectualities, that is, mathematical entities and states of affairs, which are completely free of any sensible trait, a second procedure is indispensable, namely, the procedure of categorial abstraction in Husserl's terminology, or simply formalization, in more common terminology. This procedure, which should not be confused with eidetic variation, can intervene at any stage in the hierarchy of categorial objectualities. For example, given the state of affairs that Charles is taller than Peter, we can replace the names 'Charles' and 'Peter' with variables and the relation of 'being taller than' with the sign '>', obtaining an expression of the form '$x>y$', which is completely free of any sensibility and has the same order properties as the relation of being taller than. We can also replace the concrete objects in a set with variables, and do the same with the concrete members of another set, and then compare the two 'formalized' sets as to their cardinalities. Hence, the presumably 'mysterious' mathematical intuition is nothing else than (Husserlian) categorial intuition + formalization. Thus, it was not simply casual that Gödel recommended logicians to read Husserl's Sixth Logical

---

[66] For our expository purposes, it is unnecessary to consider any other formal-ontological category.

Investigation.[67] But presumed philosophers of mathematics should study it also, and maybe we will finally be freed of so many artificially built nominalistic sand castles of nonsense.

But Husserl was perfectly conscious that mathematical intuition was just part of the arsenal available to the classical mathematician. Certainly, definitions, axiomatization, more formalization and different levels of generalization –plus deduction, of course- have also played important roles in the edification of contemporary mathematics. His generalization of Riemann's conception of geometrical manifolds to a general theory of structures –since that is what Husserl's formal ontology consists in-, his conceptions of a *mathesis universalis* and of a theory of all formal theories, as well as his conception of mathematical intuition, are the best testament to the relevance for the philosophy of mathematics of the views on mathematics, logic and their epistemology of one of the greatest philosophers ever.

References

Beth, Evert W. – *The Foundations of Mathematics*, revised edition, North Holland 1965
Bourbaki, Nicholas – 'Foundations of Mathematics for the Working Mathematician', *The Journal of Symbolic Logic 14 (4)*, 1949, pp. 1-8
Bourbaki, Nicholas – 'The Architecture of Mathematics', *American Mathematical Monthly 57*, 1950, pp. 221-232
Carnap, Rudolf – *Der logische Aufbau der Welt* 1928, second edition, Felix Meiner, Hamburg 1961
Carnap, Rudolf – 'Die Überwindung der Metaphysik durch logische Analyse der Sprache' 1932, reprint
Carnap, Rudolf – *Logische Syntax der Sprache* 1934, expanded English version, Routledge, London 1937, reprint, Open Court, Chicago et al. 2003

---

[67] On this point, see Hao Wang's *A Logical Journey*, 1996, p. 164. Before reading Husserl, however, Gödel seems to have envisaged mathematical intuition as a sort of immediate intuition, in the mould of traditional Leibnizian rationalism. See references.

Da Silva, Jairo – *Mathematics and its Applications*, Springer, Dordecht 2017

Descartes, Réné – *Meditationes de prima philosophia 1641,* reprinted with parallel German translation, Felix Meiner, Hamburg 1959, English translation, Hackett, Indianapolis 1951

Frege, Gottlob – 'Funktion und Begriff' 1891, reprinted in *Kleine Schriften*, pp. 125-142

Frege, Gottlob – 'Über Sinn und Bedeutung' 1892, reprinted in *Kleine Schriften*, pp. 143-162

Frege, Gottlob – 'Letter to Husserl of 24 May 1891', in *Wissenschftlicher Briefwechsel*, pp. 94-98

Frege, Gottlob – *Kleine Schriften*, edited by Ignacio Angelelli, 1967, revised edition, Georg Olms 1990

Frege Gottlob – *Nachgelassene Schriften*, Felix Meiner, Hamburg 1969, revised edition 1983

Frege, Gottlob – 'Über Euklidische Geometrie', in *Nachgelassene Schriften*, pp. 182-184

Frege, Gottlob – *Wissenschaftlicher Briefwechsel*, Felix Meiner, Hamburg 1974

Friedman, Michael – *Kant and the Exact Sciences*, Harvard University Press, Cambridge, Ma. 1992

Friedman, Michael – *Reconsidering Logical Positivism*, Cambridge University Press, Cambridge 1999

Gödel, Kurt – 'Über formal unentscheidbare Sätze der *Principia Mathematica* und verwandter Systeme' 1931, reprinted with English translation in Kurt Gödel, *Collected Works I*, Oxford University Press, Oxford 1986, pp. 144-195

Gödel, Kurt – 'Russell's mathematical logic', in Kurt Gödel, *Collected Works II*, pp. 119-141

Gödel, Kurt – 'Some basic theorems on the foundations of mathematics and its implications', in Kurt Gödel, *Collected Works III*, pp. 304-323

Gödel, Kurt – 'Is mathematics syntax of language?', in Kurt Gödel, *Collected Works III*, pp. 334-356 (version III), 356-362 (version V)

Gödel, Kurt – *Collected Works* (5 vols.), Oxford University Press, Oxford 1986-2003

Gruber, Monika – *Alfred Tarski and the 'Concept of Truth in Formalized Languages'*, Springer, Switzerland 2016

Hume, David – *An Enquiry Concerning Human Understanding* 1777, third revised edition, Oxford University Press, Oxford 1975

Husserl, Edmund - 'Über den Begriff der Zahl' 1887, reprinted as appendix A in Husserliana XII, pp. 289-339

Husserl, Edmund – *Philosophie der Arithmetik* 1891, Husserliana XII, M. Nijhoff, Den Haag 1970

Husserl, Edmund - 'Zur Logik der Zeichen', Appendix B(I) of Husserliana XII, pp. 340-373

Husserl, Edmund – 'Besprechung von E. Schröders *Vorlesungen über die Algebra der Logik I*' 1891, reprinted in *Aufsätze und Rezensionen (1890-1910)*, Husserliana XXII, pp. 3-43

Husserl, Edmund – *Logische Untersuchungen* 1900-1901, Husserliana XVIII & XIX, M. Nijhoff, Den Haag 1975 and 1984

Husserl, Edmund – *Ideen zu einer reinen Phänomenologie und phänomenologischen Philosophie I*, 1913, Husserliana III, 1950, revised edition, M. Nijhoff, Den Haag 1976

Husserl, Edmund – *Cartesianische Meditationen* 1928 (French Version), Husserliana I, Den Haag 1950

Husserl Edmund – *Formale und transzendentale Logik* 1929, Husserliana XVII, Martinus Nijhoff, Den Haag 1974

Husserl, Edmund – *Erfahrung und Urteil* 1939, sixth edition, Felix Meiner, Hamburg 1985

Husserl, Edmund – *Ideen zu einer reinen Phänomenologie und phänomenologischer Philosophie II*, Husserliana IV, M. Nijhoff, Den Haag 1952

Husserl, Edmund – *Zur Phänomenologie der Intersubjektivität* (3 vols.), Husserliana XIII-XV, M.Nijhoff, Den Haag 1973

Husserl, Edmund – *Introduction to the Logical Investigations*, M. Nijhoff, Den Haag 1975

Husserl, Edmund – *Aufsätze und* Rezensionen *(1890-1910)*, Husserliana XXII, M. Nijhoff, Den Haag 1979

Husserl, Edmund – *Studien zur Arithmetik und Geometrie*, Husserliana XXI, M. Nijhoff, Den Haag 1983

Husserl, Edmund – *Einleitung in die Logik und Erkenntnistheorie*, Husserliana XXIV, M. Nijhoff, Den Haag 1984

Husserl, Edmund – *Vorlesungen über Bedeutungslehre*, Husserliana XXVI, M. Nijhoff, Den Haag 1987

Husserl, Edmund – *Briefwechsel* (10 vols.), Kluwer, Dordrecht 1994

Husserl, Edmund – *Logik und allgemeine Wissenschaftstheorie*, Hua XXX, Kluwer, Dordrecht 1996

Husserl, Edmund – *Alte und neue Logik: Vorlesungen 1908/09*, edited by Elisabeth Schuhmann, Kluwer, Dordrecht 2003

Kant, Immanuel – *Kritik der reinen Vernunft* 1781, revised edition, 1787, reprint of both versions, Felix Meiner, Hamburg 1930, third edition, 1990

Leibniz, Gottfried W. – *Allgemeine Untersuchungen über die Analyse der Begriffe und Wahrheiten*, bilingual edition Latin-German, edited by Franz Schupp, Felix Meiner, Hamburg 1982

Mohanty, J. N. – *The Philosophy of Edmund Husserl* (2 vols.), Yale University Press, New Haven 2008 (I) and 2011(II)

Paton, Herbert J. – *Kant's Metaphysics of Experience* (2 vols.), Allen and Unwin, London 1936

Quine, Willard van Orman – *Word and Object*, MIT Press, Cambridge, Ma. 1960

Riemann, Bernhard – 'Über die Hypothesen, welche der Geometrie zugrunde liegen' 1867, third edition, Berlin 1923, reprint, Chelsea, New York 1973

Rosado Haddock, Guillermo E. – *The Young Carnap's Unknown Master*, Ashgate, Aldershot 2008

Rosado Haddock, Guillermo E. – *Against the Current* Ontos Verlag, Frankfurt 2012

Schuhmann, Karl – *Husserl-Chronik*, Martinus Nijhoff, Den Haag 1977

Smith, David W. – *Husserl*, Routledge, London 2007

Tarski, Alfred – 'Der Wahrheitsbegriff in den formalisierten Sprachen' (expanded version of the Polish 1933 original), English translation from the German version, 'The Concept of Truth in Formalized Languages', in Alfred Tarski, *Logic, Semantics, Metamathematics* 1956, second edition, Hackett, Indianapolis 1983

Wang, Hao – *A Logical Journey*, MIT Press, Cambridge, Ma. 1996

Husserl as Analytic Philosopher

Abstract

Analytic philosophers tend to ostracize Husserl without ever having read him. In fact, very few scholars know that in a text from 1908-09 Husserl stated that analysis was the method of philosophy and that logic was 'first philosophy'. In fact, as Frege himself acknowledged, Husserl obtained the sense-reference distinction independently of him. The rest of the paper is concerned with Husserl's many contributions, ignored by analytic philosophers, to the philosophy of logic and mathematics, the philosophy of language, the epistemology of mathematics and even the philosophy of physical science.

§1 Introduction

Consider the following quotations:

> Introduction in this philosophical logic means at the same time introduction to philosophy properly. Since philosophical logic is the introductory discipline of philosophy, it is the first one in view of its nature in the series of philosophical disciplines, it is presupposition and foundation for all the other disciplines that can be called philosophical in a genuine sense. In order to use an Aristotelian expression…: it is "first philosophy", and by the way first philosophy in the most rigorous and authentic sense.[1]

> Our procedure will be purely analytic. We proceed from what is near to us, from what is evident to the beginner.[2]

> Our path being analytic proceeds from the composite and near to us to what is simple…. Every science grounds, and analytic grounding laws ought to belong in common to all sciences. Thus, let us go on analytically.[3]

---

[1] "Einführung in diese philosophische Logik bedeutet zugleich Einführung in die Philosophie selbst. Denn die philosophische Logik ist die Eingangsdisziplin der Philosophie, sie ist in der Reihe der philosophischen Disziplinen die ihrer Natur nach erste, sie ist Voraussetzung und Fundament für alle anderen Disziplinen, die im echten Sinn philosophisch heißen können. Um einen artistotelischen Ausdruck zu gebrauchen…: sie ist „Erste Philosophie", und zwar die Erste Philosophie im strengsten und eigentlichsten Sinn." *Alte und Neue Logik: Vorlesungen 1908/1909*, p. 3

[2] "Unser Verfahren soll rein analytisch sein. Wir gehen von dem Nächstliegenden, von dem dem Anfänger Selbstverständlichen." *Alte und Neue Logik: Vorlesungen 1908/09*, p 8.

The above quotations are certainly not from Frege or from any acknowledged analytic philosopher. Nonetheless, they put logic –or philosophical logic- as the most fundamental philosophical discipline, as first philosophy, and analysis as the method of first philosophy. The quotations are from a little known text of Husserl, namely, his 1908-1909 lectures on ancient and new logic. The fact of the matter is that even that relatively late Husserl was concerned with some of the problems that concerned Gottlob Frege, the so-called 'father of analytic philosophy'. Thus, Husserl could very well have been considered one of the founding fathers of analytic philosophy. Of course, orthodox historians of analytic philosophy would immediately object that Husserl was no empiricist, though Frege himself had nothing to do with empiricism, being clearly a Platonist in the philosophy of mathematics and a rationalist all his life. Thus, if on the basis of not being a sort of empiricist or even nominalist you want to exclude Husserl from having been a sort of analytic philosopher, you would also have to exclude Frege.

In any case, it is interesting that the course on ancient and new logic from which those quotations were taken is from the winter semester of 1908-1909, thus, it was given more than one year after his course on "the idea of phenomenology", which is usually considered the official date of Husserl's transcendental phenomenological turn, and three years after his course on the phenomenology of internal time consciousness, which already dealt with issues central to his transcendental phenomenology. Those two sets of lectures, certainly, can be seen as a return to epistemology as first philosophy, and in its most radical Cartesian sense. Nonetheless, the fact of the matter is that the transcendental turn did not bring with it any essential changes either in Husserl's views on the nature and foundational role of logic or of mathematics, or in his explanation in the Sixth Logical Investigation of how we have access to logical and mathematical entities and truths. No discipline, not even epistemology, can violate the laws of logic or mathematics, though it can very well try to explain

---

[3] "Unser Weg als analytischer geht ja überhaupt vom Zusammengesetzten und Näherliegenden zum Einfachen.... Alle Wissenschaft begründet, und analytische Begründungsgesetze müssen zu aller Wissenschaft gemeinsam gehören. Nun gehen wir analytisch weiter." *Alte und Neue Logik: Vorlesungen 1908/1909*, p. 40.

how we have access to such laws. In fact, in Husserl's philosophy there are two very different senses in which one can legitimately say – of course, without contradiction- that logic is first philosophy and that epistemology is also first philosophy. Leaving that issue aside, let us consider other Husserlian texts that can serve to confirm our thesis that Husserl can very well be considered, besides a phenomenologist, also an analytic philosopher.

§2 Frege and Husserl on Sense and Referent

The best-known contribution of Gottlob Frege to analytic philosophy is the semantic distinction between sense and referent introduced by Frege for the first time in his 1891 paper "Funktion und Begriff"[4] and discussed extensively in his classic paper of analytic philosophy "Über Sinn und Bedeutung"[5] of 1892. However, there is a posthumously published text of Husserl, dating from 1890, in which the distinction between sense and referent is also made. Moreover, in his 1891 critical review of Ernst Schröder's *Vorlesungen über die Algebra der Logik I*[6], published in March of 1891, thus, two months after the publication of Frege's "Funktion und Begriff" –but sent to the publisher already in January-, Husserl makes use of that semantic distinction. Furthermore, in a letter to Husserl of May 1891 Frege acknowledges what hard-core analytic philosophers would never acknowledge, namely, that Husserl obtained the distinction independently of Frege. In fact, a few decades earlier Bolzano had almost obtained the fundamental semantic distinction.[7] But leaving the great Bolzano aside, it seems pertinent to quote Husserl once more.

> In the case of indirect signs it is necessary to distinguish that which the sign means from that which it designates. In the case of direct signs the two are the same. The meaning of a proper name, for example, consists precisely in that it names this determinate object. In the case of indirect signs, however,

---

[4] 'Funktion und Begriff' 1891, reprinted in his *Kleine Schriften*, edited by I. Angelelli 1967, revised edition 1990, pp.125-142.
[5] 'Über Sinn und Bedeutung' 1892, reprinted in *Kleine Schriften*, edited by I. Angelelli, revised edition, pp. 143-162.
[6] 'Besprechung von E. Schröders *Vorlesungen über die Algebra der Logik I*' 1891, reprinted in *Aufsätze und Rezensionen 1890-1910*, pp. 3-43.
[7] See *Wissenschaftslehre I*, §25.

there are intermediaries between sign and thing, and the sign designates exactly by means of these intermediaries, and precisely because of this [fact] constitute the meaning.[8]

Two signs are equivalent in case they designate in different manner the same object or objects of the same contour, be it by means of external or conceptual means, for example, a pair of names with the same meaning, like king and rex; William the third=the present German emperor, 2+3=7-2=$\sqrt{25}$.[9]

Meanwhile...the author identifies the meaning of a name with the representation of the object named by the name.... Moreover, he uses the term meaning equivocally, and [does] this in an already unacceptable level. In the above quotation, the incompatible and confusing explanations aside, what is pointed out to is the usual sense. But in another occasion what is really meant is the object named by the name.[10]

With the unclearness about the concept of meaning is, moreover, connected [the fact] that Schröder puts names of the sort of "round square" as 'senseless" together with those with one or more meanings. Obviously, he confuses two different questions, namely, 1) whether a name has a meaning (a "sense"); and 2) whether an object corresponding to it exists or does not exist. Senseless names in a strict sense are names without meaning,

---

[8] "Bei indirekten Zeichen ist es notwendig zu trennen dasjenige, was das Zeichen bedeutet und das, was es bezeichnet. Bei direkten Zeichen fällt beides zusammen. Die Bedeutung eines Eigennamens z. B. besteht darin, daß er eben diesen bestimmten Gegenstand benennt. Bei indirekten Zeichen hingegen bestehen Vermittlungen zwischen Zeichen und Sache, und das Zeichen bezeichnet die Sache gerade durch diese Vermittlungen, und eben darum machen sie die Bedeutung aus." 'Zur Logik der Zeichen', p. 343.

[9] "Zwei Zeichen sind äquivalent, sofern sie denselben Gegenstand bzw. die Gegenstände eines und desselben Umkreises von Gegenständen in verschiedener Weise bezeichnen, sei es durch verschiedene äußerliche oder begriffliche Mittel, z. B. ein Paar gleichbedeutender Namen wie König und rex; Wilhelm III=gegenwärtiger deutscher Kaiser; 2+3=7-2= $\sqrt{25}$." 'Zur Logik der Zeichen', p. 344

[10] "Indessen...identifiziert der Verfasser die Bedeutung des Namens mit der Vorstellung des durch den Namen gennanten Gegenstandes.... Überdies gebraucht er den Terminus Bedeutung selbst äquivok, und dies in einem schon unerträglichen Grade. Im obigen Zitat ist trotz der engegengesetzten und irrigen Erklärungen auf den gewöhnlichen Sinn abgezielt. Ein andermal aber ist wirklich gemeint der durch den Namen genannten Gegenstand" 'Besprechung von E. Schröders *Vorlesungen über die Algebra der Logik I*', p.11

pseudonames like Abracadabra. "Round square", however, is a univocal general name to which, nonetheless, nothing really corresponds.[11]

Although one could add here a pair of additional passages from 'Zur Logik der Zeichen' to make *ad nauseam* clear that Husserl obtained the sense-referent distinction independently of Frege, we prefer to include another quotation from Husserl's review of Schröder's book because it also serves to make clear that already in 1891, hence three years before Frege's late review of his *Philosophie der Arithmetik,* Husserl had already abandoned the mild psychologism of his youth book, and clearly distinguished the logical content of a statement –its meaning- from any psychological sort of content.

> That is why also Schröder's distinction between 'logical" and "psychological" content of a judgement, or more exactly: of a statement, is unacceptable. The truly logical content of a statement is the judgement content, hence, that what it states.[12]

Interestingly enough, though orthodox analytic philosophers have never accepted that the discovery of the sense-referent distinction was independently made not only by their dear but never understood Frege but also by Husserl, the conscious founder of the phenomenological school, as already mentioned above, it was Frege himself who, after having received copies of Husserl's *Philosophie der Arithmetik* and of his critical review of Schröder, acknowledged in a letter dated 24 May 1891 that Husserl had arrived at the distinction

---

[11] "Mit der Unklarheit über den Begriff der Bedeutung hängt es ferner zusammen, daß Schröder Namen der Art "rundes Viereck" als "unsinnige" den ein- und mehrsinnigen an die Seite stellt. Offenbar vermengt er hier zwei verschiedene Fragen, nämlich 1) ob einem Namen eine Bedeutung (ein "Sinn") zukomme; und 2) ob einem Namen entsprechend ein Gegenstand existiere oder nicht. Unsinnige Namen, in exaktem Sinne sind Namen ohne Bedeutung, Scheinnamen wie Abracadabra. "Rundes Viereck" aber ist ein univoker Gemeinname, dem jedoch in Wahrheit nichts entsprechen kann." 'Besprechung von E. Schröders *Vorlesungen über die Algebra der Logik I*', p. 12. In this last quotation one can see that Husserl's terminology differed from Frege's, using 'Gegenstand' as the referent, but 'Sinn' and 'Bedeutung' as synonyms, as is usual in German.

[12] "Demgemäß ist auch die Schrödersche Unterscheidung zwischen "logischem" und "psychologischem" Gehalt eines Urteils, oder genauer: einer Aussage, nicht zu billigen. Der wahrhaft logische Gehalt einer Aussage ist ihr Urteilsgehalt, also das, was sie behauptet.' 'Besprechung von E. Schröders *Vorlesungen über die Algebra der Logik I*', p. 25

independently of him.¹³ In that letter, Frege discusses an important difference in the details, namely, that for him the referent of what he called a 'conceptual word' was the concept, whereas it seemed to him –and he was right- that for Husserl the referent of the conceptual word was the extension of the concept, whereas the concept itself was the sense of the conceptual word. Husserl could have asked Frege what was then the sense of the conceptual word and how can one distinguish it, on the one hand, from the concept and, on the other, from the conceptual word. Frege never answered that hypothetical question.

A much more important difference, not mentioned by Frege, concerns the referents of statements. As is well known, for Frege the referents of statements are truth-values, as discussed in great detail in his duly famous 'Über Sinn und Bedeutung'.¹⁴ Although already at that moment Husserl would have rejected Frege's identification of the referents of statements with truth-values and would probably had identified the referents of statements somewhat vaguely with states of affairs, it took him almost a decade to gain complete clarity on this issue. In fact, even in the First Logical Investigation, in which he discusses these issues thoroughly and makes clear that statements refer to states of affairs¹⁵, there is some inadequacy in the examples, which will disappear only in the Sixth Logical Investigation¹⁶ with the introduction of the important and useful semantic distinction between states of affairs (the referents of statements) and situations of affairs (the foundations -or bases- of the states of affairs).¹⁷ To understand this important distinction, let us consider the following inequalities: (i) 5+2<9-1, (ii) 4+3<9-1 and (iii) 9-1>4+3. According both to Frege and Husserl, the inequalities (i) and (ii) express different senses, though have the same truth-value. For Frege, that is all that counts, since he

---

[13] See his *Wissenschaftlicher Briefwechsel* 1974, pp. 94-98, especially p. 98.
[14] 'Über Sinn und Bedeutung' 1892, reprinted in I. Angelelli (ed.), *Kleine Schriften* 1967, revised edition 1990, pp. 143-162.
[15] See *Logische Untersuchungen II*, U. I, §12. See also U. IV, §12.
[16] Ibid. U. VI, §48.
[17] Husserl certainly had been dealing with this distinction without obtaining complete clarity for many years. See on this issue, e.g. his *Logik Vorlesungen 1896*, edited by Elisabeth Schuhmann, p. 95.

considers that the referents of statements are truth-values. For Husserl, however, though those statements have the same truth-value, they have much more in common than the truth-value: they refer to the same state of affairs, namely, that the number '7' is smaller than the number '8'. In fact, the statements (iv) '2 is a prime number', and (v) 'Paris is the capital of France in January 2015' have the same truth-value as (i), (ii) and (iii), but intuitively seem far less related to (i), to (ii) and even to (iii) than any of these three from each other. Leaving (iii) aside for a moment, one can say of (i) and (ii) that they have different senses, but refer to the same state of affairs, whereas (iv) and (v) refer to very different states of affairs, respectively, to the mathematical fact that the number '2' is a prime number and to the contingent fact that a certain city named 'Paris' is the capital in January 2015 of a certain country named 'France'.

The difference between (i) and (ii), on the one hand, and (iii) is more subtle. Let us consider the distinction between (ii) and (iii). They are certainly also very nearly related, but not in the same way that (i) and (ii). They are not obtained from each other by replacing a name with a different name having the same referent, as is the case not only of (i) and (ii), but also of Frege's well-known example (vi) 'The morning star is a planet' and (vii) 'The evening star is a planet'. Hence, contrary to what happens with the pairs of statements {(i), (ii)} and {(vi), (vii)}, (ii) and (iii) refer to different states of affairs, namely, in one case to the state of affairs that the number '7' is smaller than the number '8' and in the other case to the state of affairs that the number '8' is larger than the number '7'. Nonetheless, they are also very nearly related. Both inequalities have in common a sort of non-categorial proto-relation that serves as their base. That proto-relation is what Husserl called 'the situation of affairs'. In the same way in which states of affairs can be seen as equivalence classes of statements having different senses but referring to the same state of affairs, situations of affairs can be seen as equivalence classes of states of affairs. The statements (i), (ii) and (iii) have the same situation of affairs as referential basis and, thus, the state of affairs referred to by

(i) and (ii) and the state of affairs referred to by (iii) belong to the same equivalence class of states of affairs.[18]

It is certainly surprising how much valuable semantic analysis was hidden under the carpet by the founding father of so-called analytic philosophy and of contemporary logic, and even more astonishing how such a procedure was uncritically accepted by orthodox analytic philosophy. Nonetheless, the fact of the matter – acknowledged or not- is that only in propositional logic does one work with such a semantics like Frege's, for which the referents of statements are truth-values, and that is all that counts. Certainly that is not the case in first-order logic with its extremely rich semantics (classical model theory), nor in its extensions, or in philosophical logic or in any mathematical theory.

§3 On *Logische Untersuchungen*

The prejudices of orthodox analytic philosophers notwithstanding, Husserl's *opus* magnum, Logische *Untersuchungen*, has much more to say to analytic philosophy than to transcendental phenomenologists. For example, Husserl's refutation of psychologism in logic in the first nine chapters of the first volume of that work does not presuppose any phenomenological thesis, and is far superior to Frege's refutation of psychologism in logic in the Preface to the first volume of his *Grundgesetze der Arithmetik*[19] and to his earlier refutation of psychologism in mathematics in his *Die Grundlagen der Arithmetik*.[20] Not only is Husserl's refutation more detailed and better organized than Frege's, but it also contains a criticism of earlier antipsychologistic conceptions of logic, like Kant's, who conceived logic as a normative discipline. Though Frege coincided with Husserl in

---

[18] Of course, in a very trivial sense, truth-values can be seen as equivalence classes of situations of affairs. See on this issue, the present author's paper 'Remarks on Sense and Reference in Frege and Husserl', published in 1982 in *Kant-Studien*, and reprinted in the joint collection of papers with Claire Ortiz Hill, *Husserl or Frege?*, Open Court 2000, 2003.

[19] See the Preface to *Grundgesetze der Arithmetik I* 1893, pp. XIV-XXV.

[20] *Die Grundlagen der Arithmetik* 1884, Centenary Edition 1986. See parts I through III.

conceiving logic as a theoretical science, his distancing from the normative conception was not as neat as Husserl's. In fact, some prominent Fregean scholars –like Hans Sluga[21]- have erroneously thought that Frege conceived logic as a normative discipline. Moreover, whereas Frege did not distinguish between the specific relativism of logical psychologism and individual relativism, and both in his critique of mathematical psychologism in his philosophical masterpiece as of logical psychologism in the first volume of his logical treatise he passed from a sober criticism of the specific relativism of his adversaries to the construction of a caricature of such adversaries, ascribing to them a subjectivism –according to which each of us would be speaking about his subjective representations of numbers or of logical laws- that none of them had ever sustained.

The last chapter of the first volume of *Logische Untersuchungen* contains –besides very interesting views on scientific theories and, especially, on physical theories in its first sections-, beginning on §67, Husserl's mature philosophy of logic and mathematics, which Husserl conceived already in 1894-1895[22] and which survived any changes in his philosophical conceptions on other issues. Husserl's conception of logic and mathematics as being formal disciplines running parallel to one another, being logic basically syntactic and semantic, whereas mathematics is a sort of formal ontology, more specifically, a theory of manifolds, a sort of generalization of Riemann's conception of mathematical manifolds[23], and such that there are some (more than one) fundamental mathematical disciplines, being the remaining mathematical disciplines combinations of the fundamental disciplines, specializations of those disciplines or combinations of their specializations, is a clear anticipation of the conception of

---

[21] See, e.g. his *Gottlob Frege* 1980, as well as, for example, his paper 'Frege as a Rationalist', in M. Schirn (ed.) *Studien zu Frege I*, pp. 27-47.
[22] See Husserl's *The Idea of Phenomenology*, M. Nijhoff 1975 pp. 35-36.
[23] See Riemann's duly famous monograph *Über die Hypothesen, welche der Geometrie zugrunde liegen* 1867, third edition, 1923, reprint, Chelsea 1973.

mathematics of the mid-twentieth century French school of mathematicians usually known as the Bourbaki school.[24]

Of the six 'logical investigations' of the second volume the first one is concerned with problems of semantics and philosophy of language, the second mostly with the traditional problem of universals, the third with problems of philosophical logic and ontology, including, among many other issues the first steps towards a formal theory of wholes and parts –a mereology, in later parlance-, and definitions of analyticity, syntheticity *a priori* and related notions, whereas the fourth one is concerned with logical grammar and linguistic universals. Only the last two investigations are of an epistemological flavor but, nonetheless, references to intuitions of essences are not frequent: the treatment is that of an analysis of knowledge. In the second part of the Sixth Logical Investigation – titled not casually 'Sensibility and Understanding'- Husserl's categorial intuition, which should be clearly distinguished from intuition of essence, is introduced as a clear alternative to Kant's conception of mathematical knowledge. Mathematical intuition is then conceived as categorial intuition plus formalization. It would take us too long to explain this almost completely ignored but extremely interesting Husserlian theory of categorial intuition and mathematical knowledge.[25]

A few words, however, should be said about some of the most interesting issues for analytic philosophers treated in *Logische Untersuchungen*.

§4 On Physical Theories

Husserl did not write much on physical theories, at least in comparison with other areas of knowledge. Nonetheless, his remarks on physical theories both in Chapter IV and, especially, in Chapter XI of the first volume of *Logische Untersuchungen* go so deep into the

---

[24] See Nicholas Bourbaki, 'The Architecture of Mathematics', *American Mathematical Monthly 57* 1950, pp. 221-232.
[25] On this issue see the present author's paper 'Husserl's Epistemology of Mathematics and the Foundation of Platonism in Mathematics' 1987, reprinted in Hill & Rosado Haddock, *Husserl or Frege*, pp.121-139.

nature of physical theories that had many later authors read him carefully, they would not have wasted their time trying to develop a positivist approach to the philosophy of science. We cannot deal here with Husserl's views in detail and refer the reader to our paper 'Husserl's Conception of Physical Theories and Physical Geometry in the Time of the Prolegomena: A Comparison with Duhem's and Poincaré's Views'.[26] Thus, we can only mention here a few salient points.

Husserl distinguishes three sorts of nexus that are present in scientific activity.[27] Firstly, there is the subjective nexus of the mental activities of the scientist, a nexus that properly does not interest us much here, but which should be clearly differentiated from the two more important objective nexus. Secondly, in every science there is an objective ontological nexus. We do not have different sciences to study lions, dogs and elephants, but a single science, zoology, which studies all sorts of animals. Similarly, we do not have a discipline studying the history of countries below the equator and one studying the history of countries above the equator –or one studying world history before Christ and one studying world history after Christ-, but a single discipline, history, to study the history of each and every country, and as far into the past as feasible. In this same sense, physics –or its best-known subdiscipline: classical mechanics- is concerned with masses, forces, velocities and accelerations, not a special discipline (or subdiscipline) for each physical concept. There is, thus, an ontological connection between objects (or concepts) that is objective and serves as a base for the building of even the most primitive sciences. In fact, this ontological nexus is sufficient for the building of a science, and many sciences –e.g. history- have no other foundation than that given to them by the ontological nexus. Nonetheless, there is still a very different objective nexus, namely, the nexus of truths present only in the most developed sciences, especially, in those called by Husserl explanatory sciences, like logic, mathematics and (theoretical) physics. Thus, Newton's second law

---

[26] Originally published in *Axiomathes* in 2012 and immediately thereafter as Chapter 6 of the authors' collection of papers *Against the Current*.
[27] See §62.

tells us that force equals mass times acceleration, establishing a perfectly definite relation between such concepts that, as already mentioned, are ontologically related and deserve to be treated by the same discipline. Other physical theories could have envisaged other sorts of definite relations, other presumed nexus of truths, between such same ontologically related concepts.

It should be clear that the nexus of truths is the most perfect of the three nexus, though it is present only in the more advanced sciences, like logic, mathematics and physical science. In these three disciplines, truths are obtained from other more fundamental truths by deduction, and Husserl calls those disciplines "explanatory sciences".[28] But whereas logic and mathematics are purely deductive and formal disciplines, the situation in the case of physical science is more complicated, since physical science is, after all, a science of (the most general aspects of) our physical world. Certainly, in physics as in other empirical sciences, like biology, there are low-level laws, more or less obtained from experience by some sort of induction. But that does not characterize physical science. Physical theories go far above the realm of induction by introducing –and that is what makes them special- *hypotheses cum fundamento in re*.[29] These are theoretical high-level laws thinly based on experience and introduced to explain the low-level laws obtained by a sort of induction, though they themselves are not obtained by any induction. In fact, as Husserl –and, less neatly though almost at the same time, Duhem- has emphatically argued, there exists an indefinite number of other possible *hypotheses cum fundamento in re* that could also do the same task of serving to derive the low-level law. This derivation of the low-level laws from the higher-level laws follows the path of the deductive-nomological or the probabilistic-nomological schemes of explanation of low-level laws.[30] Husserl obtained such schemes a few decades before their rediscovery by Hempel, Popper and others. Moreover, if the logical empiricists and even Popper had studied Husserl carefully, they would not have wasted their time discussing the empirical verification or

---

[28] See §64.
[29] See Chapter IV, §23 and Chapter XI, especially §§65-66.
[30] See Chapter XI, §§65-66 and 72.

falsification of hypotheses. They would have learned that although in the last instance physical theories have to respond to experience, it is not the case that there is such a direct relation between experience and the higher-level laws of physics as the logical empiricists envisaged. Carnap, in particular, who was so strongly influenced by Husserl's *Ideen zu einer reinen Phänomenologie und phänomenologischen Philosophie*[31] both in *Der Raum*[32] and in *Der logische Aufbau der Welt*[33], and –as mentioned in the next §- by Husserl's *Logische Untersuchungen* both when distinguishing two sorts of nonsense in 'Überwindung der Metaphysik durch logische Analyse der Sprache'[34] and when distinguishing between formation rules and transformation rules in *Logische Syntax der Sprache*[35], failed to learn from Husserl about the nature of physical theories.

§5 On Protecting against Nonsense

In §67 of the first volume of *Logische Untersuchungen* Husserl begins the exposition of his conception of logic, mathematics and their relationship. The theoretical building begins with a discussion of the meaning categories ("Bedeutungskategorien") and the formation of more and more complicated statements on the basis of the simpler ones by the iterative use of the propositional connectives. Husserl calls such laws of formation of complex statements by the iterated use of logical connectives "laws that protect against nonsense". In all further

---

[31] *Ideen zu einer reinen Phänomenologie und phänomenologischen Philosophie I* 1913, Hua. III, 1950, revised edition, edited by Karl Schuhmann 1976.
[32] *Der Raum* 1922, reprint 1991.
[33] *Der logische Aufbau der Welt* 1928, second edition, 1961. See our book *The Young Carnap's Unknown Master* 2008, as well as our papers 'On the Interpretation of the Young Carnap's Philosophy', in *Against the Current* 2012, pp. 261-284, and 'The Old Husserl and the Young Carnap'.
[34] 'Überwindung der Metaphysik durch logische Analyse der Sprache' 1932, reprint in his *Scheinprobleme in der Philosophie und andere metaphysikkritische Abhandlungen* 2004, pp. 81-109.
[35] *Logische Syntax der Sprache* 1934, expanded English version 1937.

expositions of his views on logic and mathematics[36] these logical-grammatical laws constitute the basis of the system, and Husserl makes it perfectly clear that the level in which appear the logical laws properly, that is, the level of the laws that "protect against formal countersense" or contradiction and govern formal deduction is necessarily based on the logical-grammatical level. Briefly: the distinction between formally coherent sense and countersense is already a distinction in the realm of sense. In the Fourth Logical Investigation Husserl discusses once more the issue of the meaning categories and the laws protecting against nonsense.

This important distinction between the laws that protect against nonsense and the logical laws was not present in Frege. In fact, this distinction, which is now part of the logical folklore and is present in every rigorous textbook in logic, was introduced for the first time in the literature read by most analytic philosophers in Carnap's 1934 *Logische Syntax der Sprache* as the distinction between formation rules and transformation rules. But Carnap not only does not mention that Husserl had made the distinction thirty-four years before, but does not even include Husserl's *Logische Untersuchungen* in the bibliography. However, Carnap not only had studied with Husserl from 1924 to 1925[37], but he had also included *Logische Untersuchungen* in the bibliographies of his dissertation, *Der Raum*, and of *Der logische Aufbau der Welt*. Thus, one can assume that Carnap had read Husserl's *Logische Untersuchungen* and had learned the distinction between formation rules and transformation rules from Husserl. Furthermore, the distinction between two different sorts of nonsense discussed in Carnap's 'Die Überwindung der Metaphysik durch logische Analyse der Sprache', namely, (i) that a statement is devoid of sense because it contains a word devoid of sense, and (ii) that a statement is devoid of sense because it combines words with sense in a way not allowed by the rules of logical grammar, is also

---

[36] See his 1929 *Formale und transzendentale Logik*, as well as his posthumously published *Einleitung in die Logik und Erkenntnistheorie: Vorlesungen 1906/1907* and *Logik und allgemeine Wissenschaftstheorie: Vorlesungen 1917/1918*.

[37] See on this important historical issue both Karl Schuhmann's *Husserl-Chronik* 1977, p. 281, and Ludwig Landgrebe's letter to Husserl in the latter's *Briefwechsel IV*, p. 298.

present in Husserl's Fourth Logical Investigation, though once more Carnap does not give credit to Husserl in his 1932 paper, and does not even include *Logische Untersuchungen* in its bibliography.

§6 On Logic and Mathematics

In the exceptionally important Chapter XI of *Logische Untersuchungen I* Husserl also expounds for the first time his mature conception of logic and mathematics, arrived at about 1894-1895, a conception that –as already mentioned- will not suffer any essential transformation either with his transcendental phenomenological turn or with any other change of emphasis in his later philosophy. For Husserl, logic and mathematics are intimately related, though none of the two can be derived from the other, as Frege and the logicists believed. Logic is essentially a syntactic-semantic discipline, whereas mathematics is more ontologically committed. As already mentioned in §5, Husserl conceives logic as based on a logical-grammatical foundation constituted by what he called 'meaning categories' [Bedeutungskategorien], among them the concept of (an elementary) statement, together with rules for forming elementary statements and, more importantly, rules –he calls them 'laws'- for forming complex statements by the iterative composition of statements by means of the logical connectives. As mentioned above, Husserl calls these rules that guarantee the formation of well-formed complex statements of any degree of complexity on the basis of well-formed elementary statements 'laws that protect against nonsense'.

Once this sort of logical-grammatical grounding of logic is fixed, on a second level logic proper is constituted. It is constituted firstly as a syntactic theory, as the formal theory of deduction, a theory of formal consequence or, to put it negatively –as Husserl liked to do-, the theory of the laws that protect against formal countersense (or contradiction). In *Logische Untersuchungen* and some posthumously published works the distinction between this syntactic level and a semantic one are not clearly demarcated.[38] Nonetheless, in his definitive exposition of his logical views in *Formale und transzendentale Logik*[39], this second level of the logical building is extended by a semantic level obtained by the addition to the syntactic level of the concept of truth and related concepts. Any similarity with Carnap's distinction between syntax (and its rules of formation), logical syntax (and its rules of transformation) and semantics (with the introduction of the concept of truth and related concepts) is not a pure coincidence.

On the other hand, the building blocks of mathematics are what Husserl called the 'formal-ontological categories', that is, the fundamental mathematical concepts. Husserl, who not only was not a logicist but also not a set-theoreticist, considered that the notion of set was only one of the formal-ontological categories. Relations, parts and wholes, cardinal[*] and ordinal numbers, and possibly others seem to have been considered by Husserl also as formal-ontological categories.[40] Such formal-ontological categories are the basis on which the fundamental theories of mathematics are built, as groups of axioms characterizing the different formal-ontological categories. The rest of the mathematical theories are obtained, (i) either by combination of the basic ones, (ii) or by specialization of one of the basic ones, (iii) or by combinations of specializations of the basic ones. The similarity with the Bourbakian conception of mathematics is obvious, though up to now the line of influence from Husserl to Bourbaki has not been traced.[41]

Husserl conceived mathematical theories as formal manifolds, and mathematics, in general, as a theory of manifolds. This theory of

---

[38] See *Einleitung in die Logik und Erkenntnistheorie*, based on lectures of 1906-1907, and his *Logik und allgemeine Wissenschaftstheorie*, based on lectures of 1917-1918.

[39] *Formale und transzendentale Logik* 1929.

[*] [Inadvertently omitted in the original!]

[40] See Husserl's different expositions of his views on logic and mathematics in *Logische Untersuchungen* and in his writings mentioned in the previous two footnotes.

[41] It is, however, very probable that French mathematicians of the Bourbaki group heard about Husserl's theories from Jean Cavaillès or from some other French scholar interested in Husserl's views on logic and mathematics.

manifolds combined with logic –as the theory of formal deduction- to form a sort of Husserlian *mathesis universalis*. Thus, this *mathesis universalis* would include the whole domain of what can be formally studied, that is, the totality of the logical-mathematical. Finally, Husserl's conception is crowned by what Husserl called a 'theory of all formal theories', which from a sort of metamathematical perspective was supposed to be able to *a priori* apprehend all possible formal theories. This upper level of Husserl's conception of formal theories was perhaps somewhat ambitious, and Husserl seemed to postulate a sort of completeness of this theory of all theories though[42], as was common before Gödel and Tarski, he did not seem to clearly distinguish between semantic and syntactic completeness. In any case, Husserl's assertions have prompted a discussion among Husserlian scholars on whether Gödel's incompleteness results apply or not to Husserl's theory of all theories.[43] But even if it were not feasible in all its strength, that is, even if some of the tasks of its upper level remain as a sort of Kantian idea, already Husserl's conceptions both of logic and, especially of mathematics as a theory of manifolds, and its union in the Husserlian *mathesis universalis* represent a great contribution to our understanding of the realm of formal theories.

§7 Husserl's Response to Frege's Letters of 1906

It seems pertinent to conclude this paper with an issue barely discussed even by Husserlian scholars. As is known from Frege's correspondence, Husserl and Frege exchanged letters in 1891 and fifteen years later in 1906. Of the letters exchanged in 1906 only Frege's letters are included in his *Wissenschaftlicher Briefwechsel*[44].

---

[42] See *Formale und transzendentale Logik*, pp.101-102.
[43] For some of the most recent discussions on this issue see Ulrich Majer, 'Husserl and Hilbert on Completeness', *Synthese 110*, 1997, pp. 37-56, Jairo da Silva's papers 'The Many Senses of Completeness', *Manuscrito 23(2)*, 2000, pp. 41-60 and 'Husserl's Two Notions of Completeness, Husserl and Hilbert on Completeness and Imaginary Elements', *Synthese 120*, pp. 417-438, both reprinted in Claire Ortiz Hill and Jairo José da Silva, *The Road Not Taken*, College Publications 2013, and Stefania Centrone's *Logic and Philosophy of Mathematics in the Early Husserl*, Springer 2010.
[44] Gottlob Frege, *Wissenschaftlicher Briefwechsel*, pp.101-107.

Husserl's letters seem to have been destroyed by bombings in the Second World War. Thus, the reader has only one side of the debate. However, precisely in his lectures on *Alte und Neue Logik*, dating from 1908-1909, Husserl returns to the issue of the 1906 exchange and clearly shows why he could not accept Frege's analyses.

In his letters to Husserl of 1906 Frege argued that logical equivalence is identical to having the same sense. Though Fregean scholars have not thought through what such unfortunate assertions of Frege mean, let us firstly point out that such an identification is incompatible with Frege's conception of having the same sense both in 'Über Sinn und Bedeutung' and in *Grundgesetze der Arithmetik I*. In this last work Frege underscores that statements like (a) '2+2=4' and (b) '2×2=4' do not express the same thought, since '2+2' and '2×2' do not have the same sense. Nonetheless, equations (a) and (b) are mathematically equivalent and, in virtue of Frege's logicism, they are also logically equivalent. In fact, according to Frege's official notion of sense, present in those two fundamental Fregean writings, only synonymous expressions, be it in the same language or in different ones, can be considered as having the same sense. Hence, the identification of logical equivalence with sameness of sense would make logical equivalence a rather uninteresting and unfruitful trivial notion. However, as we have emphasized in earlier writings[45], in the 1906 letters and in a passage of 'Der Gedanke'[46] Frege's notion of sense is certainly different and non-equivalent to the official one, in fact, it seems to approach his notion of conceptual content from his *Begriffsschrift*.[47] But Frege's notion of conceptual content is a forerunner of Husserl's notion of a situation of affairs. Thus, it seems

---

[45] See, for example, our paper 'On Frege's Two Notions of Sense' 1986, reprint in Claire O. Hill and Guillermo E. Rosado Haddock, *Husserl or Frege* 2000, 2003, pp. 53-66.

[46] 'Der Gedanke' 1918, reprint in *Kleine Schriften*, edited by I. Angelelli, pp. 342-362.

[47] See *Begriffsschrift* 1879, §3. In the preceding §2 he had already introduced the notion of judgeable content, which is a forerunner of his later official notion of thought, that is, the sense of statements. It should be clear to anyone not blind that the notions of conceptual content and of judgeable content are completely different.

pertinent to examine what Husserl had to say about Frege's identification of logical equivalence with sameness of sense.

As Husserl puts it on p. 111 of his *Alte und Neue Logik*, it is an error to identify the sameness of meaning of two judgements with their being immediately derivable from each other. As Husserl puts it on p. 163 and elsewhere, having the same sense and being interderivable are not the same thing. In general, two statements can be interderivable without –in Frege's official terminology- expressing the same thought. In fact, on p. 272 Husserl characterizes logical equivalence similarly to one of Frege's not easily reconcilable characterizations of conceptual content in *Begriffsschrift*, while at the same time reiterating that logical equivalence does not coincide with sameness of sense. Husserl says[48]:

> Thus, with respect to the same collection of fundamental truths and the same terms, M ought to follow, that is, be demonstrable, from N and N from M. Of course, M and N do not need to have the same terms.

Furthermore, on pp. 273-274 Husserl distinguished two sorts of logical equivalence both different from Frege's 1906 characterization –if we insist in understanding Frege's 'sense' as 'official sense'-, namely, one corresponding to the identity of state of affairs referred to by two statements expressing different thoughts, and which Husserl calls 'specifically logical equivalence', and a second one, which he calls 'content equivalence' –better: 'content logical equivalence'- of two statements expressing different thoughts and referring to different states of affairs, but having the same situation of affairs as referential basis. It is most surely the second of these two concepts, which is characterized in the quotation from p. 272 and which is more important for logic and mathematics.

It should finally be pointed out that in these lectures Husserl also goes on to reject –see p. 72- Frege's Context Principle of *Die Grundlagen der Arithmetik* with respect to the referents[49], and

---

[48] "Also mit Beziehung auf denselben Inbegriff von Grundwahrheiten und dieselben Termini soll M aus N und N aus M folgen bzw. beweisbar sein. Natürlich brauchen dabei M und N nicht dieselben Termini zu haben." *Alte und Neue Logik: Vorlesungen 1908/1909*, p. 272.

[49] In his later philosophy, both in 'Über Sinn und Bedeutung' and in *Grundgesetze der Arithmetik*, Frege also seems to clearly reject the Context Principle for the

throughout the whole lectures a very important issue treated briefly in *Logische Untersuchungen*, namely Husserl's definitions of analyticity and syntheticity *a priori*, receives its due consideration. Husserl's definition of an analytic statement as one that can be completely formalized *salva veritate* is a refinement of Bolzano's, in contrast to those of Frege and Carnap, which are both refinements of Kant's two non-equivalent definitions of analyticity.[50]

§8 Appendix: Two Words on Husserl's *Philosophie der Arithmetik*

It is customary among analytic philosophers not to read Husserl and especially to completely ignore his youth work *Philosophie der Arithmetik I*, so strongly criticized by Frege in his very late review of 1894. The fact of the matter was that in his youth work –which was supposed to be only the first volume of a two volume work, of which the never completed second would be concerned with logical foundations of arithmetic- Husserl incurred in a mild psychologism, one that had little to do with Frege's exaggerations in his critical assessment. Thus, analytic philosophers did not benefit from reading Husserl's criticisms, among them, those of Frege's attempt to define the concept of number.

Much more importantly, analytic philosophers and logicians missed the opportunity of getting acquainted with Husserl's studies on arithmetical operations and, by the way, his anticipation by almost half a century of recursive function theory. Just recently Stefania Centrone, in an especially deep study of Husserl's early investigations on logic, arithmetic and the philosophy of mathematics[51] unearthed this important contribution to the history of logic. Of course, Frege missed the point completely, but many later authors sympathetic to Husserl, as the present author, also missed it. We cannot discuss even briefly this issue here and refer the reader to Centrone's book.

---

referents –if not also tacitly for the senses. See on this issue the discussion in the present author's book *A Critical Introduction to the Philosophy of Gottlob Frege* and the references therein to Frege's texts.
[50] See Kant's *Kritik der reinen Vernunft*, A7-8, B11-12, and A150-153, B190-193.
[51] *Logic and Philosophy of Mathematics in the Early Husserl* 2010, §§1.16-1.18.2.

References

Bolzano, Bernard – *Grundlegung der Logik*, selected sections from volumes 1 and 2 of his *Wissenschaftslehre*, Felix Meiner 1963, revised edition 1978

Bourbaki, Nicholas – 'The Architecture of Mathematics', *American Mathematical Monthly 57* 1950, pp. 221-232

Carnap, Rudolf – *Der Raum* 1922, reprint, Topos Verlag, Vaduz 1991

Carnap, Rudolf – *Der logische Aufbau der Welt* 1928, second edition, Felix Meiner, Hamburg 1961

Carnap, Rudolf – 'Überwindung der Metaphysik durch logische Analyse der Sprache' 1932, reprint in Rudolf Carnap, *Scheinprobleme in der Philosophie und andere metaphysikkritische Schriften*, edited by Thomas Mormann, Felix Meiner, Hamburg 2004, pp. 81-109

Carnap, Rudolf – *Logische Syntax der Sprache* 1934, English revised edition, Routledge, London 1937

Centrone, Stefania – *Logic and Philosophy of Mathematics in the Early Husserl*, Springer 2010

da Silva, Jairo J. – 'The Many Senses of Completeness', *Manuscrito 23(2)*, 2000, pp. 41-60, reprinted in Hill & da Silva, *The Road Not Taken*, pp. 137-150

da Silva, Jairo J. – 'Husserl's Two Notions of Completeness, Husserl and Hilbert on Completeness and Imaginary Elements', *Synthese 120*, 2010, pp. 417-438, reprinted in Hill & da Silva, *The Road Not Taken*, pp. 115-136

Frege, Gottlob – *Begriffsschrift* 1879, reprint, Georg Olms, Hildesheim 1964

Frege, Gottlob – *Die Grundlagen der Arithmetik* 1884, Centenary edition, edited and with an Introduction by Christian Thiel, Felix Meiner, Hamburg 1986

Frege, Gottlob – 'Funktion und Begriff' 1891, reprint in Gottlob Frege, *Kleine Schriften*, edited by I. Angelelli, second edition 1990, pp. 125-142

Frege, Gottlob – 'Über Sinn und Bedeutung' 1892, reprint in Gottlob Frege, *Kleine Schriften*, edited by I. Angelelli, second edition 1990, pp. 143-162

Frege, Gottlob – *Grundgesetze der Arithmetik I* 1893, reprint of the two volumes in one, Georg Olms, Hildesheim 1962
Frege, Gottlob – 'Der Gedanke' 1918, reprint in *Kleine Schriften*, edited by I. Angelelli, second edition 1990, pp. 342-362
Frege, Gottlob – *Kleine Schriften*, edited by I. Angelelli, 1967, second edition 1990
Frege, Gottlob – *Wissenschaftlicher Briefwechsel*, Felix Meiner, Hamburg 1974
Hill, Claire O. & Rosado Haddock, Guillermo E. – *Husserl or Frege: Meaning, Objectivity and Mathematics*, Open Court 2000, 2003
Hill, Claire O. & Da Silva, Jairo J. – *The Road Not Taken*, College Publications, London 2013
Husserl, Edmund – *Philosophie der Arithmetik I* 1891, Hua XII, M. Nijhoff 1970
Husserl, Edmund – 'Besprechung von E. Schröders *Vorlesungen über die Algebra der Logik I*' 1891, reprint in Edmund Husserl, *Aufsätze und Rezensionen 1890-1910*, pp. 3- 43
Husserl, Edmund – *Logische Untersuchungen* (2 vols.) 1900-1901, reprint, Hua XVIII 1975 & XIX 1984
Husserl, Edmund – *Ideen zu einer reinen Phänomenologie und phänomenologischen Philosophie* 1913, Hua III, 1950, revised edition, M. Nijhoff, Den Haag 1976
Husserl, Edmund – *Formale und transzendentale Logik* 1929, Hua. XVIII, M. Nijhoff, Den Haag 1974
Husserl, Edmund – 'Zur Logik der Zeichen', Appendix B.I to Husserliana edition of *Philosophie der Arithmetik*, Hua XII, 1970, pp. 340-373
Husserl, Edmund – *Introduction to the Logical Investigations*, M. Nijhoff, Den Haag 1975
Husserl, Edmund – *Aufsätze und Rezensionen (1890-1910)*, Hua XXII, M. Nijhoff, Den Haag 1979
Husserl, Edmund – *Einleitung in die Logik und Erkenntnistheorie*, Hua XXIV, M. Nijhoff, Den Haag 1984
Husserl, Edmund – *Vorlesungen über Bedeutungslehre*, Hua XXVI, M. Nijhoff, Den Haag 1987
Husserl, Edmund – *Briefwechsel* (ten vols.), Kluwer, Dordrecht 1994

Husserl, Edmund – *Logik und allgemeine Wissenschaftstheorie*, Hua XXX, Kluwer, Dordrecht 1996
Husserl, Edmund – *Logik Vorlesung 1896*, edited by Elisabeth Schuhmann, Kluwer, Dordrecht 2001
Husserl, Edmund – *Alte und Neue Logik: Vorlesung 1908/09*, edited by Elisabeth Schuhmann, Kluwer, Dordrecht 2003
Kant, Immanuel – *Kritik der reinen Vernunft* 1781, revised second edition 1787, reprint of both editions, edited by R. Schmidt, Felix Meiner, Hamburg 1930, third edition 1990
Majer, Ulrich – 'Husserl and Hilbert on Completeness: A Neglected Chapter in Early Twentieth Century Foundation of Mathematics', *Synthese 110*, 1997, pp. 37-56
Riemann, Bernhard – 'Über die Hypothesen, welche der Geometrie zugrunde liegen' 1867, third edition, Berlin 1923, reprint, Chelsea, New York 1973
Rosado Haddock, Guillermo E. – 'Remarks on Sense and Reference in Frege and Husserl' *Kant-Studien 73(4)* 1982, reprint in Hill & Rosado Haddock, pp. 23-40
Rosado Haddock, Guillermo E. – 'On Frege's Two Notions of Sense' *History and Philosophy of Logic 7(1)* 1986, reprint in Hill & Rosado Haddock, pp. 53-66
Rosado Haddock, Guillermo E. – 'Husserl's Epistemology of Mathematics and the Foundation of Platonism in Mathematics', *Husserl Studies 4(2)* 1987, reprint in Hill & Rosado Haddock, pp. 121-139
Rosado Haddock, Guillermo E. – *A Critical Introduction to the Philosophy of Gottlob Frege*, Ashgate, Aldershot 2006
Rosado Haddock, Guillermo E. – 'Husserl's Conception of Physical Theories and Physical Geometry in the Time of the Prolegomena' *Axiomathes 22* 2012, reprint in *Against the Current*, pp. 183-214
Rosado Haddock, Guillermo E. – 'On the Interpretation of the Young Carnap's Philosophy', in *Against the Current*, pp. 261-284
Rosado Haddock, Guillermo E. – *Against the Current*, Ontos Verlag, Frankfurt 2012
Rosado Haddock, Guillermo E. – 'The Old Husserl and the Young Carnap', first published in Guillermo E. Rosado Haddock (ed.),

Husserl and Analytic Philosophy, Walter de Gruyter, Berlin 2016, pp. 261-286

Schirn, Matthias (ed.) – *Studien zu Frege* (3 vols.), Fromann-Holzboog, Stuttgart-Bad Canstatt 1976

Schuhmann, Karl – *Husserl-Chronik*, M. Nijhoff, Den Haag 1977

Sluga, Hans – 'Frege as a Rationalist', in M. Schirn (ed.), *Studien zu Frege I*, Fromann-Holzboog, Stuttgart-Bad Canstatt 1976, pp. 27-47

Sluga, Hans – *Gottlob Frege*, Routledge, London 1980

The Old Husserl and the Young Carnap

Abstract

Carnap, whose dissertation, *Der Raum*, had the imprint of Husserl's phenomenology, was also decisively influenced by Husserl in *Aufbau*, and to a lesser degree in *Logische Syntax*. Nonetheless, he tried to mask that influence, what resulted in incoherent and even incompatible explanations in his *Autobiography* of the influences on his 1922 and 1928 books. In this paper it is shown that not only the empiricist-positivist interpretation of *Aufbau* is unsustainable, but also that the Kantian or Neo-Kantian rendering is untenable, whereas Husserl's masked influence emerges as the strongest.

§1 Introduction[1]

The relation between Edmund Husserl and Rudolf Carnap is without doubt one of the less known and most problematic in the history of philosophy. However, if we take into account only what Carnap says in his 1963 sort of 'Intellectual Autobiography'[2] there never existed any relation between the two philosophers at all. Husserl is mentioned only twice, on pp. 20 and 40, of the 'Intellectual Autobiography', and in both cases Husserl is related to other philosophers, namely, to Felix Kaufmann and to some unnamed American philosophers. When Carnap refers to his dissertation, *Der Raum*[3], on pp. 11-12 he mentions that, with regard to intuitive space, Kant and the neo-Kantians, especially Natorp and Cassirer exerted a decisive influence. And when he refers to influences in *Der logische Aufbau der Welt*[4], he mentions Frege and Russell (p. 12), the Gestalt psychology of Wertheimer and Köhler (pp. 16-17), Ernst Mach, Richard Avenarius, Richard von Schubert-Soldern and Wilhelm Schuppe (p. 18), once more Mach and Russell (p. 50) and, finally, Mach, Russell and Wittgenstein (p. 57).

---

[1] All translations in this paper were done by the present author.
[2] In Paul A. Schilpp (ed.), *The Philosophy of Rudolf Carnap*, Open Court, La Salle et al., pp. 3-84
[3] *Der Raum* 1922, reprint, Topos Verlag, Vaduz 1991.
[4] *Der logische Aufbau der Welt* 1928, second edition, F. Meiner, Hamburg 1961.

It were Adolf Grünbaum and Robert Cohen in their respective commentaries[5] on aspects of Carnap's philosophy that refer to Husserl's influence on Carnap's early writings, namely, Grünbaum on p. 666 on *Der Raum* and Cohen on p. 146 on *Der logische Aufbau der Welt*. Grünbaum's comment forces Carnap to reply (p. 957)[6] that in his conception of intuitive space in *Der Raum* he had followed Kant and Husserl. With respect to Cohen's remark nothing similar occurs.

Moreover, on pp. 50 and 57 Carnap tries to make us believe that in *Aufbau* –as we will call *Der logische Aufbau der Welt* from now on- the basis of the system consisted of Ernst Mach's sense data. This clearly contrasts with his remarks two years earlier on page XII of the Preface to the second edition of *Aufbau*, in which he said that the basic elements of his constitutional system were the 'Elementarerlebnisse' but that if he were to write that book in 1961 he would take Ernst Mach's sense data as the basis. Hence, he had acknowledged two years before the publication of his 'Intellectual Autobiography' that he had not taken Mach's sense data as the basis of the system. In fact, in the same 'Intellectual Autobiography' he had written on pp. 16-17 that, following the Gestalt psychologists –presumably Köhler and Wertheimer-, he used the instantaneous whole experiences (Elementarerlebnisse) as the basis of his *Aufbau*. At first sight, such a remark concerning the basis of his *Aufbau* system seems more nearer to the truth than those referring to Mach, Avenarius *et alia* or to Russell. However, the fact of the matter is that the writings of Köhler and Wertheimer included in the references of *Aufbau* are from 1922 and 1925, respectively, whereas Husserl's *Ideen I*, in which "Erlebnisse" and "Erlebnisstrom" are central grounding notions, was published in 1913 and, as will be shown below, already when he wrote *Der Raum* Carnap was very well acquainted with that central work of Husserl's phenomenology. By the way, one can wonder how a paper published by Wertheimer in 1925 could have influenced Carnap in

---

[5] Adolf Grünbaum, 'Carnap's Views on the Foundations of Geometry', and Robert S. Cohen, 'Dialectical Materialism and Carnap's Logical Empiricism', in Paul A. Schilpp (ed.), *The Philosophy of Rudolf Carnap*, pp. 599-684 and 99-158, respectively.
[6] 'Replies and Systematic Expositions', in Paul A. Schilpp (ed.), *The Philosophy of Rudolf Carnap*, pp. 859-1013.

choosing the basis of his system, since at that time he had already written a substantial part of the book. Hence, it should by now be perfectly clear that, with regard to Husserl, Carnap's *Intellectual Autobiography* turned to be a glaring case of intellectual dishonesty. It will be shown below that such signs of dishonesty began much earlier.

§2 The Truth about *Der Raum*

An examination of Carnap's dissertation easily refutes Carnap's commentaries on it in his 'Intellectual Autobiography'. First of all, Cassirer and Natorp are barely mentioned, though included in the references. Moreover, when mentioned, as happens on p. 81 in the notes at the end of the small book, it is not precisely in a favourable way. On that page, Carnap refers to Natorp and Cassirer, as well as to Russell and others, as examples of philosophers that erroneously considered the notions of Euclidean space and of homogeneous space as extensionally equivalent.

With respect to Husserl's influence, it is true that Grünbaum's remarks referred to above 'refreshed Carnap's memory' and made him 'acknowledge' that his conception of intuitive space in *Der Raum* was influenced by 'Kant and Husserl'. In fact, so much has been already accepted by some of the best known Carnapian scholars, among them Michael Friedman[7] in his 'Carnap and Weyl on the Foundations of Geometry and Relativity Theory'. However, things are not exactly as Carnap put it in his answer to Grünbaum. Husserl's influence on Carnap's *Der Raum* is by far greater than that of Kant.[8] In fact, the influence of Hans Driesch seems to be stronger than that of Kant, from whose specific views on space Carnap clearly disassociates. Thus, a more exact phrasing of the situation would have been that 'with respect

---

[7] See the above mentioned paper in U. Majer and H. J. Schmidt (eds.), *Reflections on Spacetime*, Kluwer, Dordrecht et al. 1995.
[8] Besides Grünbaum's brief remark already referred to, for a detailed discussion of Husserl's influence on *Der Raum* see Sahotra Sarkar's paper 'Husserl's Role in Carnap's *Der Raum*', in Thomas Bonk (ed.), *Language, Truth and Logic*, Kluwer, Dordrecht 2003, pp. 179-190, and especially the present author's by far more detailed treatment in his book *The Young Carnap's Unknown Master*, Ashgate, Aldershot 2008.

to intuitive space Carnap was strongly influenced by Husserl, in a lesser degree by Driesch and in an even lesser one by Kant'. Let us now quote some of the passages of *Der Raum*, in which Carnap refers to Husserl or explicitly uses Husserl's terminology.

> By intuitive space, on the other hand, is understood the structure of relations between "spatial" figures in the usual sense…whose particularity we apprehend by means of perception or mere representation. One is still not concerned there with spatial facts present in empirical reality, but only with the "essence" of those figures, which can be recognized in any representative of the species. [*Der Raum*, pp. 5-6][9]

Anyone familiar with Husserl's philosophy, especially with Husserl's 1913 *Ideen zu einer reinen Phänomenologie und phänomenologischen Philosophie I*[10] –from now on *Ideen I*- will recognize that Carnap is assuming Husserl's conception of the contemplation of essences. But there is much more, and the following two passages should leave little doubt that they were written by someone who at that moment considered himself a disciple of Husserl in philosophical matters.

> Since here one is not concerned, as Husserl has shown, with facts in the sense of empirical reality, but with the essence ("Eidos") of certain given objectualities [Gegebenheiten], which being as they are, can be apprehended by means of [their] being given [Gegebensein] only once. [*Der Raum*, p. 22][11]

---

[9] "Unter Anschauungsraum dagegen wird das Gefüge der Beziehungen zwischen den im üblichen Sinne "räumlichen" Gebilden verstanden, also den Linien-, Flächen- und Raumstücken, deren bestimmte Eigenheit wir bei Gelegenheit sinnlicher Wahrnehmung oder auch bloßer Vorstellung erfassen. Dabei handelt es sich aber noch nicht um die der Erfahrungswirklichkeit vorliegenden räumlichen Tatsachen, sondern nur um das "Wesen" jener Gebilde selbst, das an irgendwelchen Artvertretern erkannt werden kann."

[10] *Ideen zu einer reinen Phänomenologie und phänomenologischen Philosophie I* 1913, Hua III M. Nijhoff, Den Haag, 1950, revised edition 1976.

[11] Denn es handelt sich hier, wie Husserl gezeigt hat, gar nicht um Tatsachen im Sinne der Erfahrungswirklichkeit, sondern um das Wesen ("Eidos") gewisser Gegebenheiten, das in seinem besonderen Sosein schon durch einmaliges Gegebensein erfaßt werden kann."

Since we refer here not to the isolated fact..., but to the non-temporal species, its "essence", it can be important to distinguish this mode of experience from intuition in the strict sense, which refers to the fact itself, by means of the designation "contemplation of essences [Wesenserschauung]" (Husserl), where there could seem to be [some] confusion. But, in general, it can be the case that the expression intuition also includes the contemplation of essences, since in this wide sense is also used by Kant. [*Der Raum*, pp. 22-23][12]

The reference to Kant at the end of the last passage, after a clear acknowledgment of the author of *Der Raum* of his allegiance to Husserl's phenomenology, is certainly unnecessary, regardless of whether Kant's notion of intuition could be rendered in some sense as a forerunner of the contemplation of essences. In any case it seems like a wart on the corpus of the passage. The reason for this unnecessary addition is certainly an attempt to please and appease his dissertation's director, the neo-Kantian Bruno Bauch. A little bit of history should make things clearer.

In 1911 Husserl was by far the first candidate to occupy a vacancy as full professor of philosophy at the University of Jena, the university where Frege was associate professor of mathematics. Because of still unclear reasons, at the last moment the faculty decided to give the chair to Bruno Bauch instead of Husserl. Uwe Dathe has tried to explain this decision in a very superficial way by referring to Husserl's presumed tendency to acknowledge only one sort of dialogue, namely monologues in which Husserl spoke and the other person heard.[13] More plausible explanations are that Frege intervened with Rudolf Eucken to block Husserl's appointment and that Husserl's

---

[12] "Weil wir hierbei nicht auf die einzelhafte Tatsache eingestellt sind...sondern nur um seine zeitlose Art, sein "Wesen", kann es von Wichtigkeit sein, diese Erfahrungsweise von der Anschauung im engeren Sinne, die auf die Tatsache selbst geht, durch die Benennung "Wesenserschauung" (Husserl) zu unterscheiden, wo Verwechslung möglich erscheint. Im Allgemeinen mag aber der Ausdruck Anschauung auch die Wesenserschauung mit umfassen, da er in diesem Sinne auch schon von Kant her gebräulich ist."

[13] Uwe Dathe, 'Eine Ergänzung zur Biographie Edmund Husserls', in Werner Stelzner (ed.), *Philosophie und Logik*, Walter de Gruyter, Berlin 1993, pp. 160-166.

Jewish origin played a decisive role in the faculty's decision. Those two explanations can very well be complementary. The fact of the matter is that Bruno Bauch, a neo-Kantian and an incomparably inferior philosopher was appointed to the vacant chair of philosophy, and precisely the same year of 1911 in which Carnap entered the university. By the way, all that occurred a decade after the publication of Husserl's *Logische Untersuchungen*, one of the really great books in the history of philosophy.

It seems pertinent here to quote two additional passages from *Der Raum*, which should leave no doubt about Husserl being the primary philosophical influence in *Der Raum* and of the cautious rejection of specific Kantian theses, while agreeing with Kant "in principle".

> Here [in intuitive space] we have distinguished between the principles in the strict sense and the requirements. Those build the result of a determined sort of "contemplation of essences" [Wesenserschauung] (in Husserl's sense) and as such, like all knowledge from this source, do not need of the accumulation of empirical facts, [and] as such are not to be referred to as empirical knowledge, but also are not independent of every experience, since they are obtained from any representative of the kind of objects concerned. Requirements, on the other hand, are not knowledge but stipulations that have to be made in order to obtain a total structure "space" from such knowledge, which in virtue of their own nature [ihrem Wesen nach] seem limited to an incomplete region. Topological space presents [darstellt] what is common to all [those possibilities] and on this ground ought to be seen as the form of the spatial apprehensible in the contemplation of essences. Intuitive metric spaces, on the contrary, also depend on the choice of the stipulations, and as such lack the property of unlimited validity, which possess [both] intuitive topological space and all knowledge originating in this source. [*Der Raum*, pp. 62-63][14]

---

[14] "Hier haben wir unterschieden zwischen den Grundsätzen im engeren Sinne und den Forderungen. Jene bilden den Befund einer bestimmten Art der "Wesenserschauung" (im Husserlschen Sinne) und sind daher wie alle Erkentnisse dieser Quelle nicht auf Häufung von Erfahrungstatsachen angewiesen, daher nicht als

The principles of intuitive space are equally *a* priori. According to the well-known distinction of Kant between " to originate [Entspringen] in experience" and "to begin [Anheben] with experience", this does not mean apprehensible without experience, but "independent of the quantity of experience" (Driesch) and on this ground does not contradict that for the contemplation of essences is required what is given in experience, be it immediately [given] in perception or mediately in representation. In these principles of intuitive space we have before us the synthetic a priori propositions asserted by Kant. But the same is not valid of the theorems derived from them, except to the point in which they concern only topological space, since those [theorems] that refer us to metric spaces are dependent not only on the principles, but also on the requirements, on whose base the complete structure of intuitive space is obtained, thus, on determinations that are not a priori knowledge, since they are not knowledge, but stipulations. Kant's assertion is, thus, indeed correct, but is not valid for the whole domain of those propositions to which he referred. [*Der Raum*, pp. 63-64][15]

Erfahrungserkenntnisse zu bezeichnen, aber auch nicht unabhängig von jeder Erfahrung, insofern als sie an irgendwelchen Vertretern der betrefflichen Art von Gegenständen gewonnen werden. Die Forderungen dagegen sind nicht Erkentnisse, sondern Festsetzungen, die getroffen werden, um ein geschlossenes Gesamtgefüge "Raum" aus jenen Erkentnissen zu gewinnen, die ihrem Wesen nach auf ein nicht vollständiges Gebiet beschränkt erscheinen. Für diese Erweiterungen zum vollständigen Gefüge zeigten sich verschiedene Möglichkeiten. Der topologische Raum stellt das ihnen allen gemeinsame dar und ist deshalb als Form in der Wesenserschauung des Räumlichen faßbar anzusehen. Die metrischen Anschauungsräumen dagegen sind noch von der Wahl jener Festsetzungen abhängig; daher fehlt ihnen die dem topologischen Anschauungsraum wie allen dieser Quelle entstammenden Erkenntnisse zukommende Eigenschaft der unbedingten Gültigkeit."
[15] "Die Grundsätze des Anschauungsraumes sind gleichfalls *a priori*. Nach der bekannten Unterscheidung Kants zwischen dem "der Erfahrung Entspringen" und dem "Anheben mit der Erfahrung" bedeutet dies ja nicht: ohne Erfahrung erfaßbar, sondern "unabhängig von der Menge der Erfahrung" (Driesch) und steht deshalb nicht im Widerspruch dazu, daß zu der Wesenserschauung des Gegebenseins von Erfahrung entweder unmittelbar in der Wahrnehmung oder mittelbar in der Vorstellung, erforderlich ist. In diesen Grundsätzen des Anschauungsraumes haben

The references to Kant in the last passage should not make us believe that Carnap was endorsing any fundamental specific concrete thesis. What Carnap says in the two passages amounts to the following: there is a sort of synthetic *a priori* knowledge in the topological level of intuitive space, and this knowledge is obtained by means of Husserl's method of the contemplation of essences. On the other hand, Kant's specific metric theses about the synthetic *a priori* character of the three-dimensionality and Euclidicity of space are false.

Furthermore, on pp. 64-65, where Carnap makes a very interesting classification of our geometrical knowledge of the different sorts of spaces, and in which he uses the abbreviation 'W' for 'contemplation of essences', 'S' for 'freely chosen stipulation' and 'T' for 'factual knowledge', while referring to Husserl, he mentions that 'W' is present in all cases, though with respect to formal topological space –be it three- or n-dimensional-, the application is of a formal nature, since those formal spaces belong to what Husserl had called since the last chapter of the Prolegomena 'formal ontology'. In fact, Carnap seems to be echoing Husserl's distinction, already present in the Sixth Logical Investigation and especially underscored in *Ideen I* between formal essences and the more familiar for phenomenologists material essences.

Finally, it seems pertinent to mention that in Appendix II of Carnap's first book there are many –always positive- references to Husserl, including one on p. 85 in which Carnap correctly observes that the distinction between formal, intuitive and physical space, which is central to the book, is just a special case of Husserl's distinction between formal ontology, regional ontology and factual science. If there still were some doubt, that remark on p. 85 is a clear

---

wir die von Kant behaupteten synthetischen Sätze *a priori* vor uns. Dasselbe gilt aber nicht für die aus ihnen abgeleiteten Lehrsätze, sondern nur, soweit sie den topologischen Raum betreffen; denn diejenigen, die sich auf einen der metrischen Räume beziehen, sind nicht nur von den Grundsätzen, sondern auch von den Forderungen abhängig, auf Grund deren das vollständige Gefüge des Anschauungsraumes sich ergibt, also von Bestimmungen, die nicht Erkenntnisse *a priori* sind, weil überhaupt nicht Erkenntnisse, sondern Festsetzungen. Kants Behauptung ist also zwar richtig, aber nicht für den ganzen Bereich derjenigen Sätze gültig, auf die er selbst sie bezog."

acknowledgement of Carnap that what he has done in *Der Raum* is a clarification of the relation between formal, intuitive and physical space embedded in the philosophical views of Edmund Husserl.

§3 The Unknown Relation between Husserl and Carnap

Notwithstanding Husserl's decisive influence on Carnap's dissertation, as already pointed out above, Husserl is barely mentioned in Carnap's 'Intellectual Autobiography'. In fact, neither the 'Intellectual Autobiography' nor any of Carnap's writings can serve to arouse the suspicion that there was a personal relation between Husserl and Carnap. Let us now mention a few facts about the young Carnap.

Carnap began his studies of philosophy and physics in Jena in 1911 and also studied in Freiburg, where he attended courses by Rickert, who had been Bruno Bauch's teacher. After the war he returned to Jena and first considered writing a thesis at the physics department, but his proposal was too philosophical and was sent to the philosophy department. Thus, he ended writing a dissertation under the direction of Bruno Bauch, though there does not seem to exist any ground to make us believe that Carnap was a near student of Bauch. Interestingly enough, during the two years from 1919 to 1921, in which Carnap was working in his dissertation, he lived in Buchenbach, a town in the outskirts of Freiburg, where Husserl had replaced Rickert as full professor since 1916. It is not completely clear whether Carnap met Husserl during those two years in which he was at most a half hour by train from Freiburg, but the odds are by far in favour of having met the great philosopher. The reader can imagine himself writing a dissertation, let us say, in the 1970s mostly influenced by Quine and living for two years in the outskirts of Boston, but without having the temptation to meet the admired philosopher. That is an extremely improbable situation, as is Carnap's not having met Husserl during those two years. In any case, the fact of the matter is that after obtaining his doctor's degree in Jena, Carnap returned to Buchenbach and then took part in four of Husserl's seminars during the years 1923-1925, that is, precisely when he was writing the *Aufbau* and, according to mainstream interpretations, was either under the influence of Mach's phenomenalism and Russell's empiricism or under the influence of

Kant and the neo-Kantians. Though Carnap never mentioned in his writings that he was Husserl's student, the latter's assistant during those years, the ten years younger than Carnap Ludwig Landgrebe informed Prof. Karl Schuhmann in a letter dated 6 August 1976, referred to on p. 281 of Schuhmann's *Husserl-Chronik*[16] that Carnap was in three of Husserl's seminars during those days. Moreover, in a letter of Landgrebe to Husserl of 1932 he not only reminds Husserl of the fact that Carnap visited his seminars almost a decade earlier, but especially that he and Carnap were then in friendly terms and used to discuss philosophical matters.[17] By the way, in those days Landgrebe was organizing the material that much later –in fact, after Husserl's death- was published as the second volume of *Ideen*.[18] Before we say something about the other partner of such mysterious relation, let us mention some facts about traditional university studies in Germany that are particularly relevant to what Carnap said in his 'Intellectual Autobiography' about his relation to Frege and what he did not say about his relation to Husserl.

At German universities the academic hierarchy has traditionally been much more rigid than, for example, in the USA, and the lack of relationship between professors and students is remarkable. Full professors (ordentliche Professoren) are by far at the top of the hierarchy, whereas associate professors (außerordentliche Professoren) received by far less respect. At the bottom of the hierarchy are the auxiliary professors (Privatdozenten) that traditionally were not even paid by the university, even though, after obtaining their doctor's degree, they had to write a professor's dissertation (Habilitationsschrift) and give a public (inaugural) lecture in order to obtain the *venia legendi*, that is, the right to teach at the university

---

[16] *Husserl Chronik*, M. Nijhoff, Den Haag 1977. Landgrebe speaks of three semesters from the summer semester of 1924 to the summer semester of 1925, but Carnap also attended Husserl's seminar during the winter semester of 1923-24, as attested by the Carnap Diaries. By the way, Carnap mentions there that on that same first day that he attended Husserl's seminar Husserl invited him to his house to drink tea in the evening, what makes extremely probable that Carnap and Husserl were already acquainted.

[17] Landgrebe's letter is of 11 November 1932. See *Briefwechsel IV*, p. 298.

[18] *Ideen zu einer reinen Phänomenologie und phänomenologischen Philosophie II*, Hua IV, M. Nijhoff, Den Haag 1952.

level. Courses were basically divided in lecture courses for a general public and seminars for more specialized students, including the Oberseminare for doctoral students and young doctors. In the lecture courses no questions were asked, the role of students being totally passive, and the professor sometimes did not even dare to look at the students during a whole semester and probably would not recognize them if they were to cross paths in the street. Thus, it is by no means strange that Carnap heard three of Frege's lectures, but never dared to talk to him. The opportunity to get acquainted with the professor and, especially, for the professor to acknowledge the student's existence was in the seminars, particularly in those destined for doctoral students and young doctors. It was precisely in four of those elitist courses of Husserl that Carnap took part between 1923 and 1925. Hence, even in the improbable case that Carnap had not visited other of Husserl's seminars or at least met him before obtaining his doctor's degree, he had four semesters in which he certainly had the opportunity of getting to know Husserl both as a teacher and as a person. Thus, Carnap's acquaintance with Husserl was by far greater than his acquaintance with Frege -which simply consisted in having visited three of his lecture courses, without even asking him any question. Hence, there should be no doubt that in his Autobiography Carnap intentionally omitted any reference to his relation with Husserl and, of course, any reference to Husserl's influence on him. Even in the case of *Der Raum*, where Husserl was without doubt the greatest philosophical influence, he intentionally tried to distort the facts by referring not only to Kant's influence but also to the presumed influence of Natorp and Cassirer. Let us turn now to Husserl.

As attested by his *Briefwechsel* (10 volumes), in his relation with his students Husserl was a sort of atypical professor of German universities. There is a massive correspondence with students from his Göttingen years, with students from München –where Husserl never taught- and with students of his Freiburg years. The correspondence is not only philosophical but also personal, be it asking a former student to send him tobacco from München[19], serving as a sort of private

---

[19] See Husserl's four letters to Johannes Dauben of 27 and 29 October, 11 and 18 November 1906.

advisor to depressed former students[20], or accepting a former Canadian student's offer to send him money, though not for himself but for Heidegger, who was having economic difficulties in post-war Germany.[21] With some of his former students Husserl developed a friendship that lasted until his death, among them probably the best known are Roman Ingarden, Hermann and Helene Weyl, and Max Born. Of all Husserl's students mentioned in the *Briefwechsel*, only in the case of a student of his Göttingen years who had tried to plagiarize Husserl, of Hugo Dingler, who took part, together with Max Born and Helene Weyl, in a seminar of Husserl's on the philosophy of mathematics, and of Carnap did Husserl show lack of sympathy. In the case of Dingler, Husserl's answers to Dingler's letters are evasive.[22] In the case of Carnap, it is interesting that Heinrich Scholz once asked Husserl how he would classify three of his former students who were candidates for a professorship, namely, Oskar Becker, Moritz Geiger and Rudolf Carnap, and –contrary to what would be an almost unanimous opinion nowadays- he put them in exactly that order, with Carnap way back last.[23] Moreover, after Husserl gave a lecture in 1935 in Prague, Husserl's wife, Malvine, wrote Husserl's former student and long time friend Roman Ingarden that she was pleased that Husserl was able to avoid the painful situation of having to say hello to Carnap.[24] We can ask ourselves whether Carnap had fallen so low in Husserl's eyes just by abandoning phenomenology and adhering to logical empiricism, or whether there was a still stronger reason for not

---

[20] See his correspondence with Manke, and even some of his correspondence with Landgrebe when the latter was desperate looking for a university at which to present his professorship's thesis and be able to teach as a "Privatdozent".
[21] See Husserl's letter to Winthrop Pickard Bell of 18 September 1921, in *Briefwechsel III*, especially p. 21.
[22] See *Briefwechsel III*, pp. 59-76
[23] See letter of Husserl to Heidegger of 9 May 1928 in *Briefwechsel IV*, pp. 157-158, in which Husserl informs Heidegger of a letter of Heinrich Scholz, who was looking for a replacement in Kiel, since he had accepted a professorship in Münster. Husserl recommends Oskar Becker clearly over the other two, with Geiger in the second place and Carnap far behind, in Husserl's words: "…was aber Carnap anbelangt, so stehe er doch gar zu weit zurück" ("…with respect to Carnap, he remains by far behind").
[24] See *Briefwechsel III*, p. 305. The letter is dated 14 January 1936.

even wanting to see him. In the following we will show that there could have been a stronger reason for Husserl's attitude towards Carnap, namely, the latter's attempt to mask Husserl's influence on *Aufbau*. Though Husserl most surely did not read Carnap's book, it is not excluded that some assistant or former student of Husserl had read it and informed Husserl of the content.

§4 Husserl's Influence on *Aufbau*

Carnap wrote the bulk of the *Aufbau* in 1924 to 1925, that is, precisely when he was attending Husserl's seminars. Thus, it should not be surprising if the footprints of Husserl's views are present in that work. Nonetheless, very few authors seem to have detected those footprints, probably the most notable has being Verena Mayer, who in two important papers in the early 1990s[25] stressed the influence of Husserl on Carnap's *Aufbau*. In fact, as the present author has shown in his book *The Young Carnap's Unknown Master*[26] the influence is not only larger than expected but intentionally masked.

Thus, in 1926, the 35 years old Carnap went to Vienna with the whole manuscript of *Aufbau* and showed it to Moritz Schlick and Otto Neurath, who made some criticisms and forced Carnap to make some changes in the manuscript. The book that was finally published in 1928 is still very strongly influenced by Husserl but for whatever reason that influence is intentionally masked. The general strategy is to refer to two or more authors, sometimes even to seven or eight authors, one of the last of which usually is Husserl. However, when you examine the text you see that Husserl's influence is by far the strongest.

Carnap's objective in the *Aufbau* is to build a constitutional system of objects (or concepts), where constitution, contrary to Kant's notion of constitution but in perfect agreement with Husserl's usage,

---

[25] 'Die Konstruktion der Erfahrungswelt: Carnap und Husserl', in W. Spohn (ed.), *Erkenntnis Orientated* 1991, pp. 287-303, and 'Carnap und Husserl', in D. Bell and W. Vossenkuhl (eds.), *Wissenschaft und Subjektivität* 1992, pp. 181-205. See also Mayer's definitive paper 'Der *Logische Aufbau* als Plagiat', in Guillermo E. Rosado Haddock (ed.), *Husserl and Analytic Philosophy*, Walter de Gruyter, Berlin et al., pp.175-260.
[26] *The Young Carnap's Unknown Master*, Ashgate 2008.

goes from the bottom up. In fact, the notion of constitution, in the same sense in which Carnap used it, is the basis of Husserl's phenomenology. As Carnap stresses, only an autopsychological or a physicalist basis make sense, though from an epistemological standpoint an autopsychological basis is preferable.[27] Thus, on an autopsychological basis Carnap is to constitute the physicalist world, then the heteropsychological, that is, the existence of other human subjects, and finally the cultural or spiritual world. Before continuing, it should be pointed out that Carnap's constitutional system's structure is basically the same of Husserl's manuscripts on which Landgrebe was working when he was befriended with Carnap and used to have philosophical discussions with him. In *Ideen II* –published only posthumously-, whose subtitle is *Phänomenologische Untersuchungen zur Konstitution* (*Phenomenological Investigations on Constitution*)[28], Husserl proceeds from an autopsychological basis that is exactly the one chosen by Carnap, namely, the pure subject with its internal experiences of consciousness (*Erlebnisse*) flowing in the stream of the internal time of consciousness, to the physical world, and from there to the heteropsychological world, and from there to the cultural or spiritual world. Furthermore, it should already be pointed out that the transit from the physical world to the heteropsychological proceeds in both authors exactly alike.

With respect to the basis, it seems pertinent to quote a passage that exemplifies Carnap's masking strategy. Thus, on p. 4 of *Aufbau* Carnap states:

> The most important motivations for the solution of the problem [of] how the scientific concepts are to be reduced to the "given" were given by Mach and Avenarius. Points of contact are also

---

[27] See *Aufbau*, p. 81.
[28] By the way, *Ideen II* is divided in three main Parts, namely, (i) Die Konstitution der Materiellen Natur (The Constitution of Material Nature), (ii) Die Konstitution der Animalischen Natur (The Constitution of Animal Nature) and (iii) Die Konstitution der Geistigen Welt (The Constitution of the Spiritual World). Moroever, the third and fourth chapters of part two are titled: (i) Die Konstitution der Seelischen Realität durch den Leib (The Constitution of the Reality of the Soul by means of the Body) and (ii) Die Konstitution der Seelischen Realität in der Einfühlung (The Constitution of the Reality of the Soul in Empathy).

present with Husserl's indicated objective of a "mathesis of experiences of consciousness".[29]

Certainly that passage contrasts with what Carnap stated in 1961 in the Preface to the second edition of *Aufbau*, namely, that he had taken the 'Elementarerlebnisse' as the basic elements of his system in *Aufbau* but that if he were to write the book at that moment -1961- he would follow Mach in taking sense data as basis. It is clearly implicit that he did not do that in 1928. In fact, as he repeatedly states in the book, he did not follow Mach or Avenarius.

> Our use of such a form of a system [with an autopsychological basis] by no means signifies that we are presupposing a sensualistic or positivistic conception. [*Aufbau*, p. 82][30]

After the autopsychological was chosen as basic domain, thus, the processes of consciousness or experiences of consciousness of the I, it must still be determined which formations of this region are going to serve as basic elements. One could, let us say, consider taking as basic elements the ultimate constituent parts obtained by means of psychological and phenomenological analysis of the experiences of consciousness, thus, let us say, the simplest sensory sensations (as Mach), or more generally: psychic elements of different forms, from which the experiences of consciousness are formed. On a closer examination, however, we must acknowledge that in this case not the given itself, but abstractions from it, thus, something epistemologically secondary, has been taken as basic elements.... Since we, however, wanted also to require from our constitutional system the consideration of the epistemological order of the objects, we shall, thus, start from what is epistemologically primary to everything else, from "[the] given", and those are the

---

[29] "Die wichtigsten Anregungen für die Lösung des Problems, wie die wissenschaftlichen Begriffe auf das "Gegebene" zurückzuführen sind, haben Mach und Avenarius gegeben. Berührungspukte liegen ferner auch vor mit dem von Husserl als "mathesis der Erlebnisse" angedeuteten Ziel."

[30] Unsere Anwendung einer solchen Systemform [mit psychischer Basis] bedeutet aber keineswegs, daß wir eine sensualistische oder positivistische Anschauung zugrunde legen."

experiences of consciousness themselves in their totality and closed unity.... To the chosen basic elements, those experiences of consciousness of the I as unities... we refer as "elementary experiences of consciousness". [*Aufbau*, pp. 91-92][31]

The elementary experiences of consciousness shall be the basic elements of our constitutional system. On this basis shall be constituted all other objects of our pre-scientific and scientific knowledge, including also the objects that one is accustomed to refer to as the constituent parts of the experiences of consciousness or as components of the psychic process, and which are obtained as result of the psychological analysis. [*Aufbau*, p. 93][32]

Another passage from p. 130 can be referred to in this context, and we have quoted it in the book. Nonetheless, the three passages quoted should be conclusive evidence that Carnap's constitutional system in the *Aufbau* does not have any Machian sense data basis, but a Husserlian one. Hence, the passage of p. 4 quoted above only serves to

---

[31] "Nachdem als Basisgebiet das eigenpsychische gewählt ist, also die Bewußtseinsvorgänge oder Erlebnisse des Ich, muß noch festgelegt werden welche Gebilde dieses Gebietes als Grundelemente dienen sollen. Man könnte etwa daran denken die letzten Bestandteile, die sich bei psychologischer und phänomenologischer Analyse der Erlebnisse ergeben, als Grundelemente nehmen, also etwa einfachste Sinnenempfindungen (wie Mach), oder allgemeiner: psychische Elemente verschiedener Arten, aus denen die Erlebnisse aufgebaut werden könnten. Bei näherer Betrachtung müssen wir jedoch erkennen, daß in diesem Falle nicht das Gegebene selbst, sondern Abstraktionen daraus, also etwas erkenntnismäßig Sekundäres, als Grundelemente genommen werden.... Da wir jedoch von unserem Konstitutionssystem auch die Berücksichtigung der erkenntnismäßigen Ordnung der Gegenstände verlangen wollten, so müssen wir von dem ausgehen, was zu allem anderen erkenntnismäßig primär ist, vom "Gegebenem", und das sind die Erlebnisse selbst in ihrer Totalität und geschlossenen Einheit.... Die gewählten Grundelemente, jene Erlebnisse des Ich als Einheiten... bezeichnen wir als "Elementarerlebnisse"."

[32] "Die Elementarerlebnisse sollen die Grundelemente unseres Konstitutionssystems sein. Auf dieser Basis sollen alle anderen Gegenstände der vorwissenschatlichen und wissenschaftlichen Erkenntnis konstituiert werden, somit auch die Gegenstände, die man als Bestandteile der Erlebnisse oder als Komponenten der psychischen Vorgänge zu bezeichnen pflegt, und die als Ergebnis der psychologischen Analyse gefunden werden.

mask the fact of the matter about the influences on the *Aufbau*. By the way, in an extensive remark on pp. 163-165 of *Aufbau*, Carnap rejects on similar terms Russell's choice of an epistemological basis in *Our Knowledge of the External World*.[33] For the Carnap of *Aufbau*, as for Husserl, neither sense data nor sensations, nor any presumed minimal component of experience is really experienced, but abstracted from what is really given.[34]

It seems pertinent to quote now an extremely important passage of the *Aufbau*, important because of at least two completely different reasons. Firstly, it shows an explicit and most decisive commitment of Carnap to the core of Husserl's transcendental phenomenology, the so-called "εποχη". Secondly, it gives a correct rendering of the role of that phenomenological reduction, seldom understood by hard-core phenomenologists.

---

[33] See especially p. 164 of *Aufbau*.

[34] There is, nonetheless, a later passage in *Aufbau* on p. 105 that seems both to support the positivist interpretation of that book and could also make happy the Kantian and neo-Kantian interpreters. We quote this time in German and then translate into English: "Das Verdienst der Aufdeckung der nowendigen Basis des Konstitutionssystems kommt somit zwei ganz verschiedenen und häufig einander feindlichen, philosophischen Richtungen zu. Der Positivismus hat hervorgehoben, daß das einzige Material der Erkenntnis im unverarbeiteten, erlebnismäßigen Gegebenen liegt; dort sind die Grundelemente des Konstitutionssystems zu suchen. Der transzendentale Idealismus insbesondere neukantischer Richtung (Rickert, Casirer, Bauch) hat aber mit Recht betont, daß diese Elemente nicht genügen; es müssen Ordnungssetzungen hinzukommen, unsere „Grundrelationen"." That is: The merit of having discovered the necessary basis of the constitutional system belongs to two very different and frequently adversative philosophical tendencies. Positivism has emphasized that the stuff for knowledge is the unadulterated given in experiences of consciousness; it is there that one has to look for the basic elements of the constitutional system. But transcendental idealism, particularly of the neo-Kantian variety (Rickert, Cassirer, Bauch), has correctly stressed that those elements are not enough; one has to add some order arrangement, our „basic relations"." The fact of the matter is that the stressed Carnap could have been more coherent if he had just mentioned the basis of his system, namely Husserl's "Erlebnisse" in the "Erlebnisstrom" and remembered that his basic relation of similarity between "Erlebnisse" was made possible precisely by the stream of consciousness, as emphasized *ad nauseam* by Husserl in *Ideen I*. Once more, Carnap attempts to mask Husserl's influence on him, though this time in a more grotesque fashion.

The distinction between actually real and not actually real is not present at the beginning of the constitutional system. For the basis no differentiation will be made between the experiences of consciousness, which on the basis of later constitution will be differentiated as perceptions, hallucinations, dreams, and so forth. This distinction and with it that between actually real and not actually real objects appears for the first time in a sufficiently high constitutional level. At the beginning of the system the experiences of consciousness are to be taken as they are given; the postulations (or determinations) of reality and the postulations (or determinations) of unreality present in them will not be included, but "put in parenthesis"; thus, the phenomenological suspension ("εποχη") in Husserl's sense [is] exercised. [*Aufbau*, p. 86][35]

By the way, the correctness of Carnap's rendering of the phenomenological reduction not only serves to understand the fact that after the 1907 so-called "transcendental phenomenological turn" Husserl's conception of logic and mathematics, expounded in Chapter XI of his *opus magnum*, *Logische Untersuchungen*[36] did not suffer any essential change –just the clearer distinction in *Formale und transzendentale Logik*[37] between apophantic logic (syntax) and logic of truth (semantics)-, but also is confirmed by the following passage of Husserl's in *Ideen I*:

---

[35] "Die Unterscheidung zwischen wirklichen und nichtwirklichen steht nicht am Beginn des Konstitutionssystems. Für die Basis wird kein Unterschied gemacht zwischen den Erlebnissen, die auf Grund späterer Konstitution als Wahrnehmung, Halluzination, Traum usw. unterschieden werden. Diese Unterscheidung und damit die zwischen wirklichen und nichtwirklichen Gegenständen tritt erst auf einer ziemlich hohen Konstitutionsstufe auf. Zu Beginn des Systems sind die Erlebnisse einfach so hinzunehmen, wie es sich geben; die in ihnen vorkommenden Realsetzungen und Nichtrealsetzungen werden nicht mitgemacht, sondern "eingeklammert"; es wird also die phänomenologische "Enthaltung" (εποχη) im Husserlschen Sinne gemacht."

[36] *Logische Untersuchungen* (2 vols.) 1900-1901, Hua XVIII and XIX, M. Nijhoff, Den Haag 1975 and 1984.

[37] *Formale und transzendentale Logik* 1929, Hua. XVII, M. Nijhoff, Den Haag 1974.

We adhere here, but immediately stress, that the attempt at a universal doubt shall serve us only as a methodological aid, to emphasize certain points.... [*Ideen I*, p. 64][38]

With respect to consciousness and the stream of consciousness, it seems pertinent to insert here a passage of Aufbau followed by three passages of Husserl's *Ideen I*.

... the basic domain lies only in consciousness (in the wider sense): to it belong all experiences of consciousness, no matter whether they are immediately or afterwards reflected upon. We speak therefore preferably of "stream of consciousness". [*Aufbau*, p. 86][39]

By experiences of consciousness in the broadest sense we understand everything present in the stream of consciousness, thus, not only the intentional experiences of consciousness, the actual and the potential cogitations, [and] these taken in their complete concretion, but whatever of real moments is present in this stream and its concrete parts. [*Ideen I*, p. 80][40]

A unity determined purely by the proper essence of the experiences of consciousness itself is exclusively the unity of the stream of consciousness... [*Ideen I*, p. 86][41]

The stream of consciousness is an infinite unity, and the form of a stream is a form embracing necessarily all experiences of consciousness of a pure I.... [*Ideen I*, p. 200][42]

---

[38] "Wir knüpfen hier an, betonen aber sogleich, daß der universelle Zweifelsversuch uns nur als methodischer Behelf dienen soll, um gewisse Punkte hervorzuheben...."

[39] ".... das Grundgebiet liegt nur im Bewußtsein (im weiteren Sinne): zu ihm gehören alle Erlebnisse, ob gleichzeitig oder nachträglich auf sie reflektiert wird oder nicht. Wir sprechen deshalb lieber vom "Erlebnisstrom"."

[40] "Unter Erlebnissen im weitesten Sinne verstehen wir alles und jedes im Erlebnisstrom vorfindliche, also nicht nur die intentionalen Erlebnisse, die aktuellen und potentiellen cogitationen, dieselben in ihrer vollen Konkretion genommen, sondern was irgend an reellen momenten in diesem Strom und seinen konkreten Teilen vorfindlich ist."

[41] "Eine rein durch die eigenen singulären Wesen der Erlebnisse selbst bestimmte Einheit ist ausschließlich die Einheit des Erlebnisstromes."

[42] "Der Erlebnisstrom ist eine unendliche Einheit, und die Stromform ist eine alle Erlebnisse eines reinen ich umspannende Form ...."

Hence, for both Husserl and Carnap the basic domain on which all other domains of objects are going to be constituted, the autopsychological basis, in Carnap's terminology, is that of consciousness, more specifically, of the stream of consciousness with its elementary experiences [Erlebnisse]. And the term "reflection" used by Carnap in the passage of p. 86 of *Aufbau* quoted above is also a technical Husserlian term, as attested by passages on pp. 180, 181 and 184 of *Ideen I* quoted on p. 54 of the present author's book *The Young Carnap's Unknown Master*.[43]

It seems appropriate to insert here some passages both of Carnap and Husserl, which show, firstly, that Carnap's and Husserl's views on constitution are very similar and, secondly, that in Carnap's constitutional system there is no such thing as an ontological reduction of the objects of higher levels to those of lower levels. The reduction amounts to an epistemological grounding of our knowledge of objects of higher level on those of lower level and ultimately on the autopsychological basis. On this point the author of *Aufbau* is once more in accord with Husserl, not with his later self as a logical empiricist, as attested by the following passages of both authors.

> By a "constitutional system" we understand a hierarchical order such that the objects of each level are constituted from those of the lower levels. In view of the transitivity of the reducibility, all objects of the constitutional system will in this way be constituted from the objects of the first level; the basic objects form the basis of the system. [*Aufbau*, p. 2][44]
>
> ...the constitution of an object on the basis of other determined objects not only does not mean that the object is of a similar kind as the others, but, on the contrary, if the constitution (as it frequently happens with the spiritual objects, particularly those of the higher levels) leads to the formation of new logical

---

[43] See footnote 7.
[44] "Unter einem "Konstitutionssystem" verstehen wir eine stufenweise Ordnung der Gegenstände derart, daß die Gegenstände einer jeden Stufe aus denen der niederen Stufen konstituiert werden. Wegen der Transitivität der Zurückführbarkeit werden dadurch indirekt alle Gegenstände des Konstitutionssystems aus den Gegenständen der ersten Stufe konstituiert; diese "Grundgegenstände" bilden die "Basis" des Systems."

levels, then the constituted objects belong to a different kind of being, more precisely: to a new sphere of objects. Thus, in my kind of constitution of the spiritual objects no psychologism is present. [*Aufbau*, pp. 202-203][45]

Now let us also quote some passages of Husserl from both *Ideen I* and *Ideen II*.

Clearly, in the case of all these forms of constitution of objects we will be brought back to objects, which do not remit to already given objects of the sort that are originated by means of some theoretical, value-giving or practical spontaneity....then we eventually arrive in a series of steps to grounding objectualities.... [*Ideen II*, p. 17][46]

We know that objects, no matter how constituted (objects of completely arbitrary region, completely arbitrary genus and species), can be substrata precisely for categorial syntheses, can enter as constitutive elements in "categorial" formations of higher level. [*Ideen II*, p. 18][47]

But seen free of prejudices and phenomenologically brought back to its sources, the grounded unities are both grounded and novel, the new that can be constituted with them, can ... never

---

[45] ".... die Konstitution eines Gegenstandes auf Grund bestimmter anderen Gegenständen nicht nur nicht besagt, daß der Gegenstand mit den anderen gleichartig sei, sondern im Gegenteil wenn die Konstitution (wie es bei den geistigen Gegenständen besonders der höheren Stufen in hohem Grade der Fall ist) zur Bildung neuer logischen Stufen führt, so gehören die konstituierten Gegenstände einer anderen Seinsart, genauer: einer neuen Gegenstandssphäre an. In unserer Art der Konstitution der geistigen Gegenstände liegt also kein Psychologismus."

[46] "Offenbar werden wir bei allen diesen Formen der Konstitution von Gegenständen zurückgeführt auf Gegenstände, welche nicht mehr auf vorgegebene Gegenstände der Art zurückweisen, die ursprünglich durch irgend welche theoretischen, wertenden oder praktischen Spontaneitäten entsprungen sind ..., so kommen wir ev. in einer Reihe von Schritten, auf fundierende Gegenständlichkeiten ...."

[47] "Wir wissen, daß wie immer konstituierte Gegenstände (Gegenstände ganz beliebiger Region, ganz beliebigen Gattungen und Arten) Substrate für gerade kategoriale Synthesen sein können, als konstitutive Elementen in "kategoriale" Bildungen von Gegenständen höherer Stufe eintreten können."

and nevermore be reduced to mere sums of other realities." [*Ideen I*, §152, p. 355][48, 49]

§5 On the Kantian- neo-Kantian Rendering of Aufbau

We have already shown that the positivist-sensualist Machian rendering of *Aufbau* is untenable. The only other rendering that deserves attention, not because of its presumed tenability but because it is widely spread in English speaking countries, is the Kantian or neo-Kantian rendering of Carnap's *Aufbau*. Like the parallel rendering of Frege as a Kantian or neo-Kantian, instead of what he evidently was, namely, a rationalist and Platonist, the Kantian rendering of Carnap's *Aufbau* is based on superficialities. In any case, if any of the Kantianizers of the *Aufbau* wants to prove his case, I want him to produce passages of Kant or of any neo-Kantian that run parallel to some passages of *Aufbau*, as I have done in my book already mentioned and to a lesser extent in my paper 'On the Interpretation of the Young Carnap's Philosophy' and in this paper. In fact, the last passages quoted in the preceding section should leave no doubt that when Carnap is speaking of constitution he is using the term in the same way as Husserl, and that constitution in Carnap's sense and constitution in Kant's sense are completely different notions that even go in opposite directions: from the bottom up (Husserl and Carnap), from top to bottom (Kant).

Moreover, it should be mentioned that immediately after the passage on pp. 86-87 in which Carnap declares his allegiance to methodological solipsism, he mentions eight philosophers, among them Husserl, that he considers methodological solipsists. Neither Kant nor any of the neo-Kantians, Cohen or Rickert, Natorp, Cassirer or

---

[48] "Aber vorurteilsfrei angesehen und phänomenologisch auf seine Quellen zurückgeführt, sind die fundierten Einheiten eben fundierte und neuartige; das Neue, das sich mit ihnen konstituiert, kann .. nie und niemmer auf bloße Summen von anderen Realitäten reduziert werden."

[49] Both in *The Young Carnap's Unknown Master* as in this paper's first appearance in Guillermo E. Rosado Haddock (ed.), *Husserl and Analytic Philosophy*, the page number indicated, namely, p. 375, corresponds to the first non-revised Husserliana edition of *Ideen I*. The §152 is, however, the same.

Bauch appears in that list. On the contrary, he includes the neo-Kantians Cassirer, Natorp and Rickert, as well as Mach, in a complementary list of philosophers that explicitly rejected the methodological solipsism of his autopsychological basis. He does not mention Kant, though he could have done it, since Kant's system is clearly not autopsychological. It is also not physicalist, but heteropsychological, since it presupposes from the very beginning that all men are similarly endowed with the same faculties of sensibility, understanding and reason, with the same two forms of pure intuition and the same twelve neo-Aristotelian categories. Hence, the problem faced by Descartes and Husserl of trying to obtain secure knowledge of the existence of other human subjects was not even a problem for Kant. Furthermore, for the Carnap of *Aufbau* only a physicalist and an autopsychological basis were possible, and, as already mentioned, he opted for the latter on epistemological grounds. Thus, for Carnap, Kant's system based on a tacit acceptance of a heteropsychological basis was no alternative at all.

But the most decisive argument against the Kantian or neo-Kantian rendering of Carnap's *Aufbau* is precisely the fact that Carnap followed in the footsteps of Descartes and most significantly of Husserl in trying to solve the problem called by Husserl of "intersubjectivity" and by Carnap of the "heteropsychological", whereas for Kant that problem was non-existent. Leaving Descartes and his attempted "solution" aside, we can concentrate on Husserl and Carnap. In fact, Husserl's and Carnap's solutions are basically the same. It would take us too long to discuss this delicate matter in some detail here. We have done it in the whole Chapter 3 of our book on Carnap and prefer to refer the reader to that chapter, in which we compare passages of the *Aufbau* with passages of Husserl's *Ideen II*, *Cartesianische Meditationen* and the three enormous volumes of *Zur Phänomenologie der Intersubjektivität*, the first of which is based on manuscripts from 1913 up to 1920, the second on manuscripts from 1921 to 1928 and the third on manuscripts from 1929 to 1935. In any case, we give here a brief survey of the Husserl-Carnap solution, or better, the Husserl solution used by Carnap without referring to Husserl.

As already mentioned, the so-called autopsychological basis consists of a consciousness –Husserl would also say transcendental *ego*- with its experiences of consciousness (*Erlebnisse*) in the flow of internal time, that is, the stream of consciousness. In the process of constituting the external world, the physicalist level, consciousness constitutes a peculiar physical object, which accompanies consciousness everywhere and moves according to the designs of consciousness. Thus is constituted the body of consciousness. Later on, consciousness will constitute other bodies, among them some that seem to be moving on their own, that is, that do not need to be pushed by the body of consciousness. Moreover, some of those bodies seem to express emotions of joy or fear, and even emit some sort of sounds, including utterances or verbal expressions. Then consciousness will assign by a sort of analogy a sort of consciousness to those bodies moving on their own and emitting utterances. In this way intersubjectivity is reached and the level of the heteropsychological is constituted.

In my book I have tried to correct Husserl's solution, adopted by Carnap, on the basis that to recognize the existence of other embodied consciousness, voluntary movements of a body accompanied by expressions of joy or fear, and sounds is not enough. Verbal expressions of the language understood by the so-called transcendental ego play the decisive role in acknowledging that the other is an embodied consciousness like myself. In such a way the social character of language is forced unto him and he acknowledges the existence of other similar embodied transcendental egos. I am not going to say anything more about this issue here, though in my book I used my modified solution of the problem of constituting the heteropsychological to try to found a sort of revised Kantian ethics that could serve as an ethical grounding for an equalitarian society as that in which I have believed since my student years.

Finally, I just want to mention that Husserl's influence on Carnap continued beyond 1928. Carnap's distinction in 'Überwindung der Metaphysik durch logische Analyse der Sprache' between two sorts of nonsensical pseudo-sentences, in one case because they contain a nonsensical word, in the other because they violate the laws for the correct grammatical construction of sentences, is Husserl's.[50] Moreover, the distinction in *Logische Syntax der Sprache* between rules of formation and rules of transformation is also Husserl's. Once more Carnap does not have the moral courage to acknowledge that he learned both distinctions from Husserl. On those issues, see Chapter XI of *Logische Untersuchungen I* and, especially, *Logische Untersuchungen II*, Fourth Investigation.

§6 Final Comments: Some Medicine for Empiricist Blindness

The case of the young Carnap should serve in many ways as an example of the dangers of empiricism. First of all, as shown in this paper, almost all scholars, especially those formed in the Anglo-American empiricist tradition, failed to correctly render Carnap's *Aufbau* as a book strongly influenced by Husserl, in which the still young Carnap basically tried to reshape with the help of logical-linguistic tools the Husserlian program of constitution from the autopsychological basis of the transcendental *ego* to the physical world, the heteropsychological and, finally, the cultural and spiritual world. But the positivist-empiricist dogma had an even much deeper effect on Carnap himself. Probably acquainted with the lack of sympathy that Moritz Schlick had for Husserl and also conscious of Neurath's Marxist fanaticism, Carnap masked Husserl's influence on the *Aufbau* and beyond, making him appear dishonest to the eyes of someone acquainted enough both with Husserl and Carnap. Nonetheless, when Carnap wrote his 'Intellectual Autobiography' Moritz Schlick and Otto Neurath had been dead for many years, but the author of *Aufbau* did not have the moral courage to accept Husserl's overwhelming influence in *Der Raum*, in *Aufbau* and in a lesser degree elsewhere.[51]

---

[50] On Husserl's influence on this famous paper, see also Thomas Mormann's overview of Carnap's philosophy in his book *Rudolf Carnap*, C.H. Beck, München 2000. By the way, the distinction between two sorts of nonsense is already present in *Aufbau*, p. 254.

[51] Besides 'Überwindung der Metaphysik durch logische Analyse der Sprache' and *Logische Syntax der Sprache* of the early 1930s, as late as in his 1950 *Logical Foundations of Probability* Carnap tries to mask Husserl's influence using once more

But if Carnap and other logical empiricists had reflected on some of Husserl's and other non-empiricist philosophers, for example, Pierre Duhem's, writings, then they would have avoided the blind alley to which their empiricism forced them. Already in the first volume of *Logische Untersuchungen* Husserl observed[52] that the most general physical laws, like the law of gravitation, are not obtained from experience by any sort of induction, but are what Husserl called *hypotheses cum fundamento in re*, that is, hypotheses with some tenuous contact with reality. Such hypotheses, or laws of higher level, serve to explain laws of lower level, and, hence, there is already in Husserl the deductive-nomological scheme of explanation, particularly, for explaining laws of lower level, and, thus, not only that of pure deductive explanation, but especially the approximate explanation scheme. In fact, Husserl stressed most forcefully, that there are other possible hypotheses that could also serve to explain the laws of lower level or, more succinctly, that there are many non-equivalent hypotheses that, nonetheless, can explain the same laws of lower level and are, therefore, empirically equivalent. Hence, such laws of higher level, such *hypotheses cum fundamento in re* are empirically underdetermined. Thus, many of the most interesting issues discussed later by logical empiricists and the Quineans, as well as their difficulties had already been briefly but pointedly discussed by Husserl, and a study of Chapter XI of *Logische Untersuchungen I* would have helped the logical empiricists avoid wasting their time and energy looking for a criterion of verification or falsification and for the so-called protocol sentences, be it in their phenomenalist or in their physicalist version.

---

the strategy of mentioning other authors before Husserl –this time Langford and Kant-, whereas the decisive influence seems to come from Husserl. See p. 3, as well as Michael Beaney's paper 'Carnap's Conception of Explication: from Frege to Husserl', in Steve Awodey and Carsten Klein (eds.), *Carnap Brought Home*, Open Court, Chicago et al. 2004, pp. 117-150.

[52] See *Logische Untersuchungen I*, Chapter IV, §23 and very especially Chapter XI, §§62-66, especially, §§63 and 64, as well as §72.

On the other hand, if you look at Duhem's work[53], you also find enough reasons to reject the later empiricism. In a less clear way than Husserl, Duhem also saw the problem of the underdetermination of physical laws.[54] Moreover, he also stressed the fact that even in the most simple of physical experiments there are already many implicit assumptions of a physical-theoretical nature, even in the instruments used in the experiments.[55] That is the reason why he postulated the impossibility of isolating physical hypotheses, a very sound thesis that in Anglo-American empiricist circles has been muddled with something completely different and much more questionable, namely, Quine's thesis[56] that all our beliefs, from the logical truths to the most accidental empirical statements are connected in a sort of web of belief and, hence, according to Quine, there is no fundamental difference, but only one of degree between the law of commutativity of the sum in arithmetic and the proposition that says that Newton had a toothache when he discovered his law of gravitation.

Appendix I

Some Husserlian Technical Terms used in Carnap's *Aufbau* From Register of Elisabeth Ströker's Husserls Werk: Zur Ausgabe der Gesammelten Schriften, Felix Meiner, Hamburg 1992

(The *Gesammelten Schriften* include only the nine books of Husserl published in his lifetime, which is a very small sample of Husserl's gigantic production. But since the proof is so overwhelming, it is unnecessary to refer here also to Husserl's posthumous writings.)

---

[53] See his book *La Théorie Physique: son Objet, sa Structure* 1914, English translation, *The Aim and Structure of Physical Theory*, Princeton University Press, Princeton 1955, 1991, as well as his paper 'Some Reflections on the Subject of Experimental Physics' in his *Essays in the History and Philosophy of Science*, edited by Roger Ariew and Peter Baker, Hackett, Indianapolis 1996, pp. 75-111.
[54] See 'Some Reflections on the Subject of Experimental Physics', pp. 90-91.
[55] See ibid., pp. 75-79.
[56] See, for example, 'Two Dogmas of Empiricism' 1951, reprinted in *From a Logical Point of View*, Harvard University Press, Cambridge, Ma. 1953, pp. 20-46.

Konstitution, begins at the bottom of p. 174 and ends at the bottom of the first column of p. 175

Konstituiren (p. 174) – *Logische Untersuchungen I*, pp. 119, 132, 244; *Logische Untersuchungen II*, pp. 169, 223, 357A, 361A, 364, 389, 390A, 397, 400, 406, 410A, 411A, 415, 417, 419, 423, 515, 517, 523, 526A, 540, 674f., 684f., 688f., 703, 705, 708f., 714f., 717, 724, 729; *Ideen I*, pp. 104, 107, 109, 114ff., 131, 182, 198, 243, 263, 274, 279, 351f., 357; *Formale und transzendentale Logik*, p. 322; *Cartesianische Meditationen*, pp. 44, 80, 82, 87, 95f., 102, 107, 110, 113, 118, 122, 127, 133, 135, 153; *Krisis*, pp. 84, 114, 170, 183, 205. (There are also extensive lists for derivatives like 'konstituierend', 'kostituiert' and konstitutiv'.)

Fundierung (p. 156) – *Philosophie der Arithmetik*, p. 79; *Logische Untersuchungen II*, pp. 268, 270, 282, 286, 290, 292, 418, 432, 515, 519, 675, 708; *Ideen I*, pp. 38, 117, 237, 266, 275, 300; *Erste Philosophie*, pp. 109, 118; *Cartesianische Meditationen*, p. 85; with the adjective 'mittelbare' in *Logische Untersuchungen II*, p. 272; with the adjective 'psychologische' in *Philosophie der Arithmetik*, p. 51; with the adjective 'unmittelbare' in *Logische Untersuchungen II*, p. 272.

Fundiert (p. 156) – *Ideen I*, pp. 38, 77ff., 90, 267, 293.

Fundierungsordnung (p. 156) – *Cartesianische Meditationen*, p. 127.

Fundierungsverhältnis (p. 156) – *Logische Untersuchungen II*, pp. 268, 271, 292, 295, 300A.

Erlebnis and its derivatives (almost the whole p. 150) – Includes, among others, references to *Logische Untersuchungen I & II*, *Ideen I*, *Cartesianische Meditationen* and *Erste Philosophie*, in all of which Husserl uses the word as a technical term.

Erlebnisstrom (p. 151) – Includes references to *Ideen I*, pp. 67, 70, 73f., 78ff., 94, 96f., 104, 119, 123, 128, 164f., 168, 181f., 184, 186f., 191f., 195, 214, 265 and 273; to *Cartesianische Meditationen*, pp. 69, 104, 106f., 130, 137; with the adjective 'absoluter' in *Ideen I*, p. 118; with the adjective 'reiner' in *Logische Untersuchungen II, U. VI*, p. 765; with the adjective 'transzendentaler' in *Ideen I*, p. 204.

Abschattung (p. 121) – *Logische Untersuchungen II, U. VI*, pp. 584, 590ff., 613f., 647; *Ideen I*, pp. 14, 85f., 88, 91, 173, 226, 230f., 92ff.,

103, 105, 117; with the adjective 'perzeptive': *Logische Untersuchungen II, U VI*, p. 646
Wahrnehmungsabschattung (p. 123) – *Logische Untersuchungen II, U. VI*, p. 770; *Ideen I*, p. 91.
Abschattungsmannigfaltigkeit (p. 121) – *Ideen I*, pp. 85 and 230.
Abschattungsreihe (p. 121) – *Ideen I*, p. 91.
Abschattungssystem (p. 121) – *Ideen I*, p. 85.
Abschattungsweise (p.121) – *Ideen I*, p. 94.

Appendix II

The Refutation of Carnap's Principle of Tolerance

Probably the central thesis of Carnap's *Logische Syntax der Sprache* is the well-known Principle of Tolerance, which in a style that pervades the whole of Carnap's work, tries to avoid controversies in the philosophy of logic and mathematics by postulating a sort of neutrality between intuitionism, formalism and logicism, nominalism and Platonism, first-order logic and higher-order logic. However, as happened with Carnap's criteria of empirical significance, the logic that he so eagerly propounded serves to show that the principle of tolerance is false. We will show that first-order model theory shows the falsity of nominalism and, hence, that of the Principle of Tolerance.

Let us suppose that we are working in first-order logic, since as Quine has argued and others admitted, higher-order logic commits its user explicitly to the acceptance of mathematical objects like sets. Consider a first-order language £ and an existential sentence φ in £ that purports to speak about mathematical entities. Let us suppose, however, that nominalism is true and that no mathematical entities exist. In such a case both φ and any other existential statement purporting to talk about mathematical entities is false, whereas any universal statement about mathematical entities is vacuously true.

However, in virtue of Robinson's Model-Completeness Test, a first-order theory T is model complete –that is, for any two models M and M^*, if M is a substructure of M^*, then M is an elementary substructure of M^*- if and only, if for any existential statement in the language of the theory, there exists a universal statement in the same language that is logically equivalent to it. Hence, there exists a universal statement ψ logically equivalent to φ and, hence, false. Thus, not all universal statements of the language are true. Moreover, since the negation of φ is equivalent to a universal statement and the negation of ψ is equivalent to an existential one, and they are logically equivalent, there are true existential statements in the language £. Hence, there are existential true and existential false statements, as well as universal true and universal false statements in £. Therefore, nominalism has been refuted. Moreover, it follows that one cannot arbitrarily make all existential (universal) statements of £ true or all of them false. Hence, conventionalism in the philosophy of mathematics has also been refuted. *A fortiori*, the Principle of Tolerance has also been refuted. If you want to construct a first-order language including its semantics, that is, the well-rounded, extensively developed and powerful classical model theory, you cannot consistently defend either nominalism or conventionalism, and have to accept Platonism. Nominalism and conventionalism are not tolerated, and the Principle of Tolerance itself is not tolerated by first-order classical model theory.

References

Awodey, Steve and Klein, Carsten (eds.) – *Carnap Brought Home*, Open Court, Chicago et al. 2004

Beaney, Michael – 'Carnap's Conception of Explication: from Frege to Husserl', in Steve Awodey and Carsten Klein (eds.), *Carnap Brought Home*, Open Court, Chicago et al. 2004, pp. 117-150

Bell, David & Vossenkuhl, Wilhelm (eds.) – *Wissenschaft und Subjektivität*, Akademie Verlag, Berlin 1992

Bonk, Thomas (ed.) – *Language, Truth and Logic*, Kluwer, Dordrecht 2003

Carnap, Rudolf – *Der Raum*, Kant-Studien (Ergänzungsheft 56) 1922, reprint, Topos Verlag, Vaduz 1991

Carnap, Rudolf – *Der logische Aufbau der Welt* 1928, second edition, F. Meiner, Hamburg 1961

Carnap, Rudolf – 'Überwindung der Metaphysik durch logische Analyse der Sprache' 1932, reprint in Rudolf Carnap, *Scheinprobleme*

in der Philosophie und andere metaphysikkritische Schriften, F. Meiner, Hamburg 2004, pp. 81-109
Carnap, Rudolf – *Logische Syntax der Sprache* 1934, English revised edition, Routledge, London 1937
Carnap, Rudolf – *Logical Foundations of Probability*, University of Chicago Press 1950
Carnap, Rudolf – 'Intellectual Autobiography', in Paul A. Schilpp (ed.), *The Philosophy of Rudolf Carnap*, pp. 3-84
Carnap, Rudolf – 'Replies and Systematic Expositions', in Paul A. Schilpp (ed.), *The Philosophy of Rudolf Carnap*, pp. 859-1013
Carnap, Rudolf – *Tagebücher 1908-1935*, http://homepage.univie.ac.at/christian.damboeck/carnap_diaries2015-2018/diaries_1908-1935_transcriptions_2015.pdf
Cohen, Robert – 'Dialectical Materialism and Carnap's Logical Empiricism', in Paul A. Schilpp (ed.), *The Philosophy of Rudolf Carnap*, pp. 99-158
Dathe, Uwe – 'Eine Ergänzung zur Biographie Edmund Husserls', in Werner Stelzner (ed.), *Philosophie und Logik*, Walter de Gruyter, Berlin 1993, pp. 160-163
Duhem, Pierre – 'Some Reflections on the Subject of Experimental Physics' 1894, reprinted in the English translation of his papers in Roger Ariew and Peter Baker (eds.), *Essays in the History and Philosophy of Science*, Hackett, Indianapolis 1996, pp. 75-111
Duhem, Pierre – *La Théorie Physique: son Objet, sa Structure* 1914, English Translation, *The Aim and Structure of Physical Theory*, Princeton University Press, Princeton 1955, 1991
Friedman, Michael – 'Carnap and Weyl on the Foundations of Geometry', *Erkenntnis 42*, 1995, pp. 247-260, reprint of the whole number in U. Majer and H. J. Schmidt (eds.), *Reflections on Spacetime*, Kluwer, Dordrecht et al. 1995
Grünbaum, Adolf – 'Carnap's Views on the Foundations of Geometry', in Paul A. Schilpp (ed.), *The Philosophy of Rudolf Carnap*, pp. 599-684
Husserl, Edmund – *Logische Untersuchungen* (2 vols.) 1900-1901, Husserliana XVIII & XIX, M. Nijhoff, Den Haag 1975 & 1984
Husserl, Edmund – *Ideen zu einer reinen Phänomenologie und phänomenologischen Philosophie I* 1913, Hua III 1950, revised edition, M. Nijhoff, Den Haag 1976

Husserl, Edmund – *Cartesianische Meditationen* 1928 (French version), Hua I, M. Nijhoff, Den Haag 1950
Husserl, Edmund – *Formale und transzendentale Logik* 1929, Hua XVII, M. Nijhoff, Den Haag 1974
Husserl, Edmund – *Ideen zu einer reinen Phänomenologie und phänomenologischen Philosophie II*, Hua IV M. Nijhoff, Den Haag 1952
Husserl, Edmund – *Zur Phänomenologie der Intersubjektivität* (three vols.), Hua XIII-XV, M. Nijhoff, Den Haag 1973
Husserl, Edmund – *Briefwechsel* (ten vols.), Kluwer, Dordrecht 1994
Mayer, Verena – 'Die Konstruktion der Erfahrungswelt: Carnap und Husserl', in W. Spohn (ed.), *Erkenntnis Orientated* 1991, pp. 287-303
Mayer, Verena – 'Carnap und Husserl' in D. Bell and W. Vossenkuhl (eds.), *Wissenschaft und Subjektivität* 1992, pp. 181-205
Mayer, Verena – 'Der *Logische Aufbau* als Plagiat', in Guillermo E. Rosado Haddock (ed.), *Husserl and Analytic Philosophy*, Walter de Gruyter, Berlin et al. 2016, pp.175-260
Mormann, Thomas – *Rudolf Carnap*, C. H. Beck, München 2000
Rosado Haddock, Guillermo E. – *The Young Carnap's Unknown Master*, Ashgate, Aldershot 2008
Rosado Haddock, Guillermo E. – 'On the Interpretation of the Young Carnap's Philosophy', in Guillermo E. Rosado Haddock, *Against the Current*, Ontos Verlag, Frankfurt 2012, pp. 261-284
Russell, Bertrand – *Our Knowledge of the External World* 1914, revised edition, 1926, fifth printing, Allen and Unwin, London 1969
Sarkar, Sahotra – 'Husserl's Role in Carnap's *Der Raum*', in Thomas Bonk (ed.), *Language, Truth and Logic*, Kluwer, Dordrecht 2003, pp. 179-190
Schilpp, Paul A. – *The Philosophy of Rudolf Carnap*, Open Court, La Salle et al. 1963
Spohn, Wolfgang (ed.) – *Erkenntnis Orientated*, Kluwer, Dordrecht 1991
Ströker, Elizabeth – *Husserls Werk: Zur Ausgabe der Gesammelten Schriften: Register*, published with the *Gesammelte Schriften Edmund Husserls*, Felix Meiner, Hamburg 1992

Husserl and Riemann
(and Bolzano and Leibniz but not Frege)

Abstract

After briefly showing that, contrary to the received view in analytic circles, Frege's influence on the evolution of Husserl's views on logic and mathematics, as well as on the distinction between sense and referent are either insignificant or, as in the last case, totally inexistent, and that Husserl's account of Leibniz and Bolzano's influence in *Logische Untersuchungen* is correct, we turn to Riemann, whose influence is certainly non-negligible. Husserl's conception of mathematics as a theory of manifolds (or structures) is a generalization of Riemann's notion of manifold –in fact, a sort of bridge between Riemann and the Bourbaki group. Moreover, Husserl's conception –since 1892- of physical geometry as empirical is also strongly influenced by Riemann.

§1 Introduction: Husserl's Place in the History of Philosophy[1]

It is said that Kurt Gödel considered Edmund Husserl as the greatest philosopher since Leibniz. Though such a statement could be questioned in at least two senses, e.g., whether Husserl was a greater philosopher than Kant, and whether Leibniz was a greater philosopher than Husserl, there should be little doubt that Husserl not only is one of the most influential recent philosophers, but also that he is one of the really great philosophers. His influence extends not only to the so-called phenomenological school, second in importance only to analytic philosophy during the twentieth century, to analytic philosophy itself, especially through Carnap, to logic and linguistics through Lesniewski's mereology and his and Ajdukiewicz' theory of semantic categories, and to existential philosophy, even though Husserl would probably not feel comfortable with the latter influence. Moreover, as pointed out by Stefania Centrone, Husserl already in his youth work *Philosophie der Arithmetik*[2] seems to have anticipated the theory of general recursive functions, and as pointed out by the present author,

---

[1] All translations in this paper are mine.
[2] *Philosophie der Arithmetik* 1891, Hua XII, M. Nijhoff, Den Haag 1970. See Centrone's paper 'Husserl on the 'totality of all conceivable operations', *History and Philosophy of Logic 27 (3)*, 2006, pp. 211-228.

he anticipated the Bourbakian conception of mathematics[3], and a possible at least indirect influence on the Bourbaki school should not be excluded. Husserl's *Logische Untersuchungen*[4] is one of the seminal works in the history of philosophy, but at least *Ideen I*[5], *Formale und transzendentale Logik*[6] and *Erfahrung und Urteil*[7] could have been the *opus magnum* of many other prominent philosophers. In fact, Husserl's greatness as a philosopher can still not be completely measured, since about half of his manuscripts have still not been published. But in any case, in his *opus magnum Logische Untersuchungen* one finds, among other things: (1) the most thorough and decisive refutation of psychologism in logic[8]; (2) the distinction between nonsense and countersense and the corresponding introduction of what later Carnap will call 'rules of formation'[9] in contrast to the rules of logic in the strict sense or, what Carnap later called, 'rules of transformation'[10]; (3) a conception of mathematics as a theory of structures, in which each mathematical theory is either a fundamental one –like set theory or the formal theory of parts and wholes-, a specialization of a fundamental structure, a combination of at least two structures, or a combination of specializations[11]; (4) a very modern conception of physical theories as explanatory theories, including the anticipation of the deductive-nomological scheme both for statements of facts and for laws; (5) related with this last case, an analysis of the role of what Husserl called *hypotheses cum fundamento in re*, of the empirical equivalence of different alternative such

---

[3] See my 'Husserl's Philosophy of Mathematics: its Origin and Relevance' 2006, reprinted in *Against the Current*, Ontos Verlag, Frankfurt 2012, pp. 145-181.
[4] *Logische Untersuchungen* (2 vols.) 1900-1901, Hua XVIII & XIX, M. Nijhoff, Den Haag 1975 & 1984.
[5] *Ideen zu einer reinen Phänomenologie und phänomenologischen Philosophie I* 1913, Hua III, M. Nijhoff, Den Haag 1950, revised edition 1976.
[6] *Formale und transzendentale Logik* 1929, Hua XVII, M. Nijhoff, Den Haag 1974.
[7] *Erfahrung und Urteil* 1939, sixth edition, F. Meiner, Hamburg 1985.
[8] *Logische Untersuchungen I*, Chapters I-VIII.
[9] Ibid. Chapter XI. Compare with Carnap's *Die logische Syntax der* Sprache 1934, revised English edition 1937, where the distinction between the two sorts of rules is introduced in p. 4 and then used throughout the whole book.
[10] *Logische Untersuchungen I*, Chapter XI. For Carnap, see preceding footnote.
[11] Ibid.

hypotheses of higher level and the acknowledgement of the ensuing subdetermination of physical theories by its empirical content[12]; (6) a theory of the ideality of meanings and a thorough analysis of so-called 'indexicals'[13]; (7) a theory of general objects[14]; (8) a theory of wholes and parts in general, and the ensuing characterizations of analytic statements and synthetic *a priori* statements[15]; (9) a theory of formal universal grammar[16]; (10) the beginning of what was going to be the most thorough analysis of all intentional acts[17]; and (11) the most serious attempt –at least since Plato- of explaining our categorial and, particularly, mathematical knowledge[18].

§2 The Myth of the Fregean Influence

What probably has been more difficult to assess are the influences Husserl suffered from earlier or contemporary authors. In analytic circles -that are not very distinguished in their historic studies of philosophy- it has been at least tacitly accepted that the mature Husserl of *Logische Untersuchungen* was influenced by Frege's unfriendly review of Husserl's *Philosophie der Arithmetik*[19] and by his now so popular distinction between sense and referent. In particular, the logician and historian of logic Evert W. Beth[20] and the analytic philosopher Dagfinn Føllesdal[21] have been the most influential proponents of that interpretation. And certainly Husserl in his youth

---

[12] Ibid.
[13] *Logische Untersuchungen II*, U. I.
[14] Ibid., U. II.
[15] Ibid., U. III.
[16] Ibid., U. IV.
[17] Ibid., U. V.
[18] Ibid., U. VI.
[19] 'Rezension von E. G. Husserl: *Philosophie der Arithmetik I*, 1894, reprinted in G. Frege, *Kleine Schriften* 1967, revised edition, Georg Olms 1990, pp. 179-192.
[20] See Evert W. Beth, *The Foundations of Mathematics*, North Holland, Amsterdam 1965, p. 353.
[21] See, e.g. Dagfinn Føllesdal's Master thesis *Husserl und Frege, ein Beitrag zur Beleuchtung der phänomenologischen Philosophie* 1964, translation in L. Haaparanta (ed.), *Mind, Meaning and Mathematics*, Kluwer, Dordrecht 1994, pp. 3-47, as well as his 'Husserl's Concept of Noema', *Journal of Philosophy 66 (20)*, 1969, pp. 680-697.

work, *Philosophie der Arithmetik*, held a mild form of Brentanian psychologism. Nonetheless, that work, though published in 1891, was an expansion of his professorship's thesis *Über den Begriff der Zahl* of 1887, and reflects Husserl's views probably up to 1889 or the first half of 1890. In fact, the published *Philosophie der Arithmetik* was supposed to be the first volume of a two volume work, the first one concerned with psychological foundations, whereas the never published second volume was to be concerned exclusively with logical foundations. But Husserl never wrote the second volume, what certainly attests to the evolution of Husserl's thought during those years. By the way, that constant evolution is also attested by Husserl's *Studien zur Arithmetik und Geometrie*[22], a posthumously published collection of manuscripts from 1886 to 1901 with which we will be concerned later in this paper.

In any case, it is in his paper 'Funktion und Begriff'[23], published in January 1891 that Frege presented for the first time his distinction between what he called 'Sinn' and 'Bedeutung', and that we will render as 'sense and referent'. But not only was Husserl's review of Ernst Schröder's book on the algebra of logic[24], in which Husserl makes the same distinction, already written and in press, since it appeared, together with the *Philosophie der Arithmetik* in March of the same 1891, but there is a posthumously published paper by Husserl titled 'Zur Logik der Zeichen (Semiotik)'[25] written in 1890, in which Husserl clearly makes the distinction between sense and referent. Immediately after publishing both works Husserl sent copies to Frege, who in return sent Husserl a copy of 'Funktion und Begriff'. It seems

---

[22] *Studien zur Arithmetik und Geometrie*, Hua XXII, M. Nijhoff, Den Haag 1983
[23] 'Funktion und Begriff' 1891, reprinted in Gottlob Frege, *Kleine Schriften*, pp. 125-142. The distinction is the central theme of his famous 'Über Sinn und Bedeutung' 1892, reprinted also in *Kleine Schriften*, pp. 143-162. See also Frege's paper written in the early 1890s, though only posthumously published, 'Ausführungen über Sinn und Bedeutung' in *Nachgelassene Schriften*, F. Meiner, Hamburg 1969, revised edition 1983, pp. 128-136.
[24] 'Besprechung von E. Schröders *Vorlesungen über die Algebra der Logik I*' 1891, reprinted in *Aufsätze und Rezensionen (1890-1910)*, Hua XXII, pp. 3-43.
[25] 'Zur Logik der Zeichen', written in 1890, but published for the first time as Appendix B (I) to *Philosophie der Arithmetik*, Hua XII, pp. 340-373.

pertinent to include here some passages of both of Husserl's papers, beginning with the review of Schröder's book.[26]

> Meanwhile... the author identifies the meaning of a name with the representation of the objects named by the name....Moreover, he uses the term meaning equivocally, and [does] this in an already unacceptable level. In the above quotation, the incompatible and confusing explanations aside, what is pointed out to is the usual sense. But in another occasion what is really meant is the object named by the name, [Besprechung von E. Schröders *Vorlesungen über die Algebra der Logik I*, p. 11]
>
> With the unclearness about the concept of meaning is, moreover, connected [the fact] that Schröder puts names of the sort of "round square" as "senseless" side by side with those with one or more meanings. Obviously, he confuses here two different questions, namely, 1) whether a name has a meaning (a "sense"); and 2) whether an object corresponding to a name exists or does not exist. Senseless names in a strict sense are names without meaning, pseudonames, like Abracadabra. "Round square", however, is a univocal general name to which, nonetheless, nothing really corresponds. [Besprechung von E. Schröders *Vorlesungen über die Algebra der Logik I*, p. 12]
>
> That is why Schröder's distinction between "logical" and "psychological" content of a judgement, or more exactly, of a statement, is unacceptable. The truly logical content of a statement is the judgement content, hence, that what it means. [Besprechung von E. Schröders Vorlesungen *über die Algebra der Logik I*, p. 25]

Those three quotations from a paper published at the beginning of 1891, but most surely written in 1890, are decisive evidence that Husserl obtained the distinction between sense and referent independently of Frege. Moreover, the last of the three quotations also serves to show that already at the time he wrote the review of Schröder's work Husserl had clearly distinguished the logical content of statements from the so-called psychological content, and

---

[26] See footnote 24.

acknowledged that only the logical content (or meaning) is genuinely the content of a statement, thus, that he had already put aside any sort of psychologism present in his *Philosophie der Arithmetik*. Hence, it seems pertinent to say that when Husserl published *Philosophie der Arithmetik* he had already surpassed some of the views present in that book, thus, that Husserl's first book was a dead born child. Concerning the sense-referent distinction, it seems appropriate to quote also some passages from Husserl's posthumous 'Zur Logik der Zeichen (Semiotik)'.

> In the case of indirect signs it is necessary to distinguish that which the sign means from that which it designates. In the case of a direct sign the two are the same. The meaning of a proper name, for example, consists precisely in that it names this determinate object. In the case of indirect signs, however, there are intermediaries between sign and thing, and the sign designates exactly by means of these intermediaries, and precisely because of this [fact] they constitute the meaning. ['Zur Logik der Zeichen (Semiotik)', p. 343]
>
> That is why, for example, the meaning of a general name consists in designating an object whatsoever on the basis and by means of some conceptual traits that it possesses. ['Zur Logik der Zeichen (Semiotik)', pp. 343-344]
>
> Two signs are identical when they designate in the same manner the same object or objects of one and the same contour. One of them is the mere repetition of the other, for example, horse and horse, five and five. ['Zur Logik der Zeichen (Semiotik)', p. 344]
>
> Two signs are equivalent in case they designate in different manner the same objects of the same contour, be it by different external or conceptual means, for example, a pair of names with the same meaning, like king and rex; Whilhelm II = present German emperor; $2+3=5=7-2=\sqrt{25}$. ['Zur Logik der Zeichen (Semiotik)', p. 344]

Finally, it should be mentioned that Frege himself in his letter to Husserl of 24 May 1891[27], in which he acknowledged the receipt of

---

[27] *Wissenschatlicher Briefwechsel*, F. Meiner, Hamburg 1976, pp. 94-98.

both *Philosophie der Arithmetik* and the review of Schröder's book, clearly accepts the fact that Husserl had also made the distinction between sense and referent and points to a difference between the two with respect to the referent of conceptual words. Thus, Frege says:
> I just want to point out here that there seems to exist a difference of opinion between us with respect to how the conceptual word (general name) relates to the objects. [*Wissenschaftlicher Briefwechsel*, p.96]

After sketching his now famous sense-referent scheme, Frege goes on to sketch what he rightly believes is Husserl's sense-referent distinction for conceptual words. Of course, he is clearly acknowledging that Husserl had also made the distinction. Frege says:
> Now, it seems to me that in your case the scheme would look like this:
>
> Conceptual Word
> ↓
> Sense of the Conceptual Word
> (Concept)
> ↓
> Object that falls under the concept,

so that in your case there would be as many steps from the proper name as from the conceptual word to the object. [*Wissenschaftlicher Briefwechsel*, p. 98]

Moreover, in 'Ausführungen über Sinn und Bedeutung Frege also acknowledges Husserl's independent discovery of the famous distinction. Thus, Frege says[28]:
> Husserl says (p. 250) "Evidently he confuses here two very different questions, namely, 1) whether a name has a meaning (a sense); and 2) whether there exists or not some object corresponding to the name".

Hence, it is clear that Frege and Husserl arrived at the sense-referent distinction independently of each other and at the same time, though differed in some concrete details of the scheme. In fact, when Husserl finally completed the details of his scheme, there is a still a more important difference, namely, though the sense of a statement is as in

---

[28] 'Ausführungen über Sinn und Bedeutung', p. 135. See also p. 134.

Frege a thought (or proposition), the referent of a statement is a state of affairs, which is based on what Husserl called a "situation of affairs". Therefore, Husserl's scheme for statements has two additional steps between the statement and the truth-value.

Thus, there should not exist the least doubt that Husserl obtained the distinction between sense and referent with complete independence of Frege. Hence, Føllesdal's and others' contention that Husserl obtained that distinction from Frege is plainly false, and should rest in peace for all eternity. Moreover, as pointed out above, Husserl arrived at the clear separation of the genuine logical content of statements from their so-called psychological content at least four years before Frege's review of *Philosophie der Arithmetik*. Furthermore, Husserl's mature views on the nature of logic and mathematics, to which he seems to have arrived precisely in 1894, that is, in the year of the publication of Frege's review, are certainly different from Frege's at least in the following points: (1) Husserl rejected logicism, set-theoreticism and any such reduction of mathematics to a single fundamental area, rejecting also the current view that there is a fundamental mathematical notion, be it that of set or whatsoever; (2) hence, because of his rejection of logicism, Husserl did not need to postulate the existence of logical objects and, thus, logic was not ontologically committed, like mathematics, being a sort of syntactic (and in *Formale und transzendentale Logik* also semantic) discipline parallel to mathematics; (3) mathematics was ontologically committed and, thus, Husserl defended mathematical Platonism, though Husserl's mathematical Platonism was not one of objects, like Frege's, but one of structures based on different equally fundamental mathematical notions.[29]

In fact, with respect to logic there is no ground to doubt what Husserl wrote in Chapter X of the first volume of *Logische Untersuchungen*[30] and in his *Introduction to the Logical*

---

[29] On Husserl's philosophy of mathematics see *Logische Untersuchungen I*, Chapter XI, §§69-70, *Formale und transzendentale Logik*, 1929, Husserliana XVII, 1974, especially Chapters 2 and 3, and *Einleitung in die Logik und Erkenntnistheorie*, Husserliana XXIV, 1984, especially Chapter 2.
[30] See *Logische Untersuchungen I*, Chapter X, §§59-61 and Appendix.

Investigations[31] about his affinities with and influences from the views of Leibniz, Bolzano and Lotze, as well as the influence of Hume. It should also be clear that Husserl's conception of a fusion of the syntactical-semantic discipline of pure logic with the ontologically fat sister discipline of mathematics in a sort of *mathesis universalis* is a Leibnizian heritage. In fact, one can very well say that with respect to the relation between logic and mathematics Leibniz was the intellectual grandfather of Husserl, as he also was of Frege and of Hilbert. As Leibniz, the three intellectual cousins considered logic and mathematics intimately related, but differed with respect to the sort of relation.

As already mentioned, Husserl conceived mathematics as a doctrine of structures, some more general, others more concrete obtained from the former, some simpler, some more complex, obtained by combining different simpler structures. To refer to mathematics Husserl did not use the word 'structure' (*Struktur* in German), but the word manifold (*Mannigfaltigkeit* in German), thus, mathematics was for Husserl essentially a doctrine of manifolds (*Mannigfaltigkeitslehre*). His friend Cantor had also used the word 'Mannigfaltigkeit', but to refer to what is now currently called 'set'. Husserl, however, meant by 'Mannigfaltigkeit' not a set but a structure and, thus, the originator of that usage is not Cantor. In fact, it is Riemann.

§3 Riemann's Notion of Manifold

It is well known that in the nineteenth century mathematics probably experienced the most radical changes in its whole history, among them the rigourization and arithmetization of analysis, the origin of abstract algebraic systems, the origin of algebraic and set-theoretical topology, as well as that of set theory and, what is more relevant here, the birth of non-Euclidean geometries. As is also very well known, around 1830 János Bolyai and Nikolai Lovachevsky discovered the first sort of Non-Euclidean geometry, namely, one in which in a plane, given a line *l* and a point *P* not on *l*, there exist more

---

[31] *Introduction to the Logical Investigations*, M. Nijhoff, Den Haag 1975, pp. 36-38

than one line through P, in fact, infinitely many, not intersecting l. In current geometric parlance, one says that Bolyai-Lovachevskyan geometry has negative curvature. In fact, the great Carl Friedrich Gauss had anticipated by about a quarter of a century the results of Bolyai and Lovaschevsky, but fearing the power of the Kantians in German academic life, opted not to publish his results. In his extraordinary monograph *Über die Hypothesen, welche der Geometrie zugrunde liegen*[32], in which, by the way, another sort of Non-Euclidean geometry was considered, namely, one in which, given a line l and a point P not in l, there are no lines through P parallel to l, briefly a geometry with positive curvature, one of Gauss' last students, Bernhard Riemann considered physical space and the different geometries as special cases of a much more general concept. He first introduced the notion of an n-fold extended magnitude, for n any natural number. Euclidean three-dimensional geometry, as well as its two three-dimensional rivals are simply particular cases, for n=3, of the general concept of an n-fold extended magnitude. Physical space is also a special case in which n=3, but, contrary to what the old Kant had taught, Riemann thought that it cannot be decided *a priori*, but only through experience, whether physical space has zero curvature (is Euclidean), negative curvature or positive curvature. Moreover, Riemann subsumed n-extended magnitudes under a still more general concept of a manifold. Riemann divided manifolds in two different classes, namely, discrete and continuous manifolds. In discrete manifolds one compares quantities by counting, whereas in continuous manifolds one compares them by means of a unit of measure. Whereas the manifold of natural numbers would be a good example of a discrete manifold, all sorts of geometric manifolds are examples of continuous ones. As one can see, in all this construction there is no reference to any sort of intuition, something Kant had considered an essential component of our mathematical knowledge. Thus, in particular, Riemann rejected Kant's *a priori* conception of physical space and, in general, any essential role of intuition –be it *a priori* or *a posteriori*- in our mathematical knowledge.

---

[32] 'Über die Hypothesen, welche der Geometrie zugrunde liegen' 1867, third edition, Berlin 1923, reprint, Chelsea, New York 1973.

§4 Brief Notes on Husserl's Conception of Mathematics

Husserl conceived mathematics as a formal ontology, that is, as a sort of theory of formal structures running parallel to its sister discipline logic. Husserl conceived both disciplines as based on fundamental concepts. In the case of mathematics, notions like those of set, cardinal number, relation, and whole and part gave rise to a variety of fundamental mathematical theories, whereas the whole edifice of mathematical theories was obtained either by specialization of those, in Bourbakian terminology, sorts of mother structures, combination of them or combination of their specializations. And the development of mathematics after 1900 –when Husserl made public his views on logic and mathematics in the last chapter of the *Prolegomena*-, has proven that Husserl was, in principle, right. Thus, for example, topological groups are mathematical structures that combine topological and algebraic structures, whereas more concrete mathematical structures, like that of real numbers or Banach spaces are much richer combinations of specializations of abstract structures.

Husserl called abstract mathematical theories 'manifolds'[33], clearly referring to Riemann's conception of manifold and his generalization of geometrical theory, and considered his notion of manifold as a generalization of that of Riemann. Moreover, Husserl considered the possibility of a sort of meta-mathematical treatment of mathematics in which one is not concerned with concrete mathematical theories, that is, with concrete manifolds, but with their abstract mathematical forms and their *a priori* relations, thus, mathematical theories are now the object of study, not the more concrete mathematical objects that constitute the manifold. On this very abstract level, Husserl discusses the possibility of different relatively more concrete mathematical theories having essentially the same form. In *Einleitung in die Logik und Erkenntnistheorie* Husserl makes this point more explicit by considering three different interpretations of an abstract commutative law, '$a+b=b+a$', where the symbol '+' can be

---

[33] See *Logische Untersuchungen I*, p. 252, and *Formale und transzendentale Logik*, p. 97 for references to Riemann in this context.

interpreted either (i) in the familiar arithmetical way of addition of numbers, or (ii) as set-theoretical union, or (iii) as the juxtaposition of straight lines in a geometrical system. Thus, one can obtain a result for a mathematical form at the most abstract level and the result is immediately true also in any specialization of that manifold.

But Riemann's influence on Husserl is not limited to the notion of mathematical manifold. In fact, as attested by a posthumously published book of Husserl containing mostly material from the transition period of 1889 to 1893, namely his already mentioned *Studien zur Arithmetik und Geometrie*[34], in which Riemann is referred to in more than twenty different pages, Riemann's influence was not limited to his views on pure mathematics. In fact, it also concerns the relation between geometry and physical space, an issue very little known both to Husserlian scholars and to analytic philosophers.

§5 Husserl's Views on the Geometric Structure of Physical Space

From 1886 to 1893 Husserl worked intensively both on the philosophy of arithmetic and on the philosophy of geometry, as attested by the already mentioned *Studien zur Arithmetik und Geometrie*, and his views were in continuous evolution. In particular, around 1892 Husserl finally accepted Riemann's views on the nature of geometry, and he remained firmly convinced of the correctness of those views. In fact, in the manuscripts on space up to 1892 Husserl seems to have some discrepancies with Riemann's and Helmholtz' views. But, as attested by his correspondence, already at the end of that year Husserl had embraced both the Riemannian conception of the nature of physical space and the latter's conception of the abstract analytic treatment of geometric manifolds. Nonetheless, before quoting from his letters it should be mentioned that already in a course of 1889-1890 titled "Geschichtlicher Überblick über die Grundlagen der Geometrie"[35], after discussing the impact of both Bolyai-

---

[34] *Studien zur Arithmetik und Geometrie*, Husserliana XXI, M. Nijhoff, Den Haag 1983.
[35] Ibid., pp. 312-347.

Lovachevskyan non-Euclidean geometry and Riemann's more general analytic approach to the nature of geometry, Husserl stressed that the parallel Axiom distinctive of Euclidean geometry is not a logical necessity. Such an isolated point should not be given too much weight. In fact, though Frege was a staunch defender of Euclidean geometry and of the non-intuitiveness of the non-Euclidean ones, he had already acknowledged in *Die Grundlagen der Arithmetik*[36] that the geometrical axioms are not logical necessities. Nonetheless, Frege was so convinced of the validity of Euclidean geometry that he never seriously discussed, as Husserl did in that course, the impact both of Bolyai-Lobachevskyan geometry and of Riemann's more general and profound views.

In any case, there is clear evidence that at the end of 1892 Husserl had embraced Riemann's conception of both physical space and of geometric manifolds. Thus, in a letter to his teacher Franz Brentano dated 29 December 1892 Husserl lets Brentano know his basic commitment to Riemann's views on geometry, and in letters to the Neo-Kantian philosopher Paul Natorp dated 29 March 1897 and 7 September 1901 Husserl reiterates that commitment. Thus, Husserl accepted that there exists a diversity of geometric manifolds of n dimensions, for any natural number n, of a purely mathematical nature, and, on the other hand, physical space, whose structure –basically, curvature and dimensionality- should be empirically established, contrary to Kant's views. Hence, Husserl was far more receptive to a revision of traditional conceptions of geometry than other philosophers of that period, including the great mathematician and also important philosopher and physicist Henri Poincaré, and certainly by far much more receptive than his rival Frege, who in a posthumous paper at the turn of the twentieth century compared non-Euclidean geometries with alchemy and astrology.[37] Before referring to some of Husserl's manuscripts of that period, it should be pointed out that, contrary to Riemann, Husserl acknowledged a sort of intermediate area of a non-Kantian synthetic *a priori*. We are not going to discuss that still very obscure point here. It suffices to say that Carnap, in his dissertation,

---

[36] *Die Grundlagen der Arithmetik*, §14.
[37] 'Über Euklidische Geometrie', in *Nachgelassene Schriften*, pp. 182-184.

Der Raum, in which he was very strongly influenced by Husserl, assigns this synthetic apriorism to the topological level of space. There are, however, passages of Husserl that attest to a sort of not only topological but also even metric synthetic *a priori*. But let us now return to our main point.

In his letter to Brentano of 29 December 1892 Husserl states on p. 10[38]:

> Recently I have been working on the philosophical-geometrical problems. Some [things] that I formerly considered secure have now become very doubtful for me. I formerly believed that a continuum in which any 2 points are connected by a straight line, should *eo ipso* be characterized as plane (Euclidean). This was not correct. One cannot prove that with respect to any straight line one can trace through each point only one [straight line] not intersecting [it]; or that parallel segments between parallels are equal; that, thus, a rigid segment can be parallelwise displaced (i.e. without changing its length). Briefly, the parallel axiom is not true.
>
> Also my judgement about the Riemann-Helmholtz theories of space has changed.... the general theories that they build, following a strike of genius, conceal a valuable content that, philosophically elucidated, would be interesting even for a theory of geometrical knowledge.

In the letters of 29 March 1897 and 7 September 1901 to Natorp Husserl is even more explicit[39]:

> Without doubt, as you say, Euclidean space is an "unfounded", i.e. a by the natural scientists unfounded hypothesis. That has its roots in the origin of science in natural thinking.... The missing foundation can only be...an empirical one; it will, thus, be of an inductive nature, though could have an enormous probabilistic foundation.
>
> But when proceeding purely scientifically it is not allowed to take anything whatever from "intuition" except in the worst of cases what is already established in the Axioms.... The

---

[38] *Briefwechsel I*, 1994, p. 10.
[39] *Briefwechsel V*, pp. 62, 63 and 83-84, respectively.

enormous significance of the intuitive procedure is thoroughly a methodical one; but the pure system of mathematics has to disown intuition completely.

I would in general not expect that no matter what beneficial preference will be obtained for the 3-dimensional as against the n-dimensional Euclidean multiplicity. Thus, my conception about aprioricity in geometry is different from yours. The pure aprioristic in space is the system of fixed relation forms, which can be obtained by means of idealization of the empirical space intuitions and by going back to their categorial forms (abstracting from everything sensible...), i.e. reaching the categorial forms of their primitive (idealized) fundamental relations. What is pure in space is the Euclidean manifold of 3rd level. I acknowledge (against my former views) the possibility of other space intuitions, which give rise to different idealized geometric spaces and whose logical structuring could be exhibited in other pure manifolds. But what is completely certain for me, is that all in general existing possibilities are rigidly demarcated by aprioristic laws: ideal possibilities, Platonic ideas. Within this frame operates the mathematical "arbitrariness", with its "conventions", by means of which determined sorts of manifolds are selected from the totality of valid [ones], are "defined", but, of course, not created.... *A priori*=pure categorial lawfulness, in virtue of its extension[,]=the mathesis in its most general sense.

The last passage is especially important as a synthesis of Husserl's views on geometry. First of all, he reiterates his view that three-dimensional Euclidean geometry does not deserve any privileged status, because of two different reasons. There are no *a priori* grounds to prefer three-dimensionality instead of n-dimensionality, for n any positive integer. On the other hand, we can very well imagine other sorts of spatial intuition besides the three-dimensional Euclidean one, for example, n-dimensional or non-Euclidean. Moreover, each of those possibilities, be it three-dimensional or n-dimensional, Euclidean or non-Euclidean, is grounded on *a priori* laws. The mathematician simply selects some of those structures for study, though from a purely mathematical standpoint there is no ground to attribute any of them a preferred status. And Husserl stresses the non-constructive character of mathematics by emphasising that the structures selected for study by the mathematician are in no way his creation or construction.

In *Studien zur Arithmetik und Geometrie* there are many passages that expand the views expressed in the three already quoted letters. We will quote only two passages from 1893 already quoted in our paper 'Husserl's Conception of Physical Theories and Physical Geometry in the Time of the *Prolegomena*: A Comparison with Duhem's and Poincaré's Views'. The first one is concerned with Hermann Lotze's argument on the logical necessity of Euclidean geometry. Husserl says:

> Lotze's and others' doctrine that there exists a logical necessity for the three-dimensionality and for the plane nature [Euclidicity GERH], then excludes the possibility of a non-three-dimensional and of a curved space. But that doctrine is false. The three-dimensionality, etc. is an empirical factuality, though a general fact (a law) like the law of gravitation. There is only an enormous improbability for space not being Euclidean, though we have to leave open its possibility. The probability [that space be Euclidean GERH] is not infinite.... Infinite is only the probability that space harmonizes with the Euclidean continuum in the limits traced by our capabilities of observation.[40] [*Studien zur Arithmetik und Geometrie*, p. 269]

After that brilliant refutation, clearly based on Riemann's views, of Lotze's and others' argument, Husserl goes on to question the requirement of intuitiveness of geometry and the ensuing attempt to disqualify non-Euclidean geometries on the basis of their lack of intuitiveness. But Husserl also criticizes Helmholtz for giving too much emphasis to a defence of the intuitiveness of non-Euclidean geometries. On this point it is clear that Husserl, the mathematician turned philosopher, feels rightly more comfortable with the mathematician Riemann's genial insights than with the natural scientist Helmholtz' observations. Thus, Husserl says:

---

[40] In more modern parlance, one would say that the probability of space been Euclidean is less than 1, since the probability of any hypothesis or theory ranges from 0 to 1. See also the acknowledgement of the Riemannian restriction of local Euclidicity.

Here lies a complete misunderstanding of the significance of the theory of curvature.... Whether intuition fails or not is irrelevant. Intuitiveness is something completely inessential. Is it then what is decisive that we can intuitively represent other spaces besides Euclid's? Does a representation have to be carried out in order for it to be epistemologically useful? Big numbers. It is a fundamental misunderstanding of those opposing metageometrical research when they believe that by showing the non-intuitiveness of the metageometrical concepts they would also have refuted their epistemological contents. In any case, the representatives of metageometry, especially Helmholtz have committed the great error of giving too much weight to the intuitive representability that they presumably establish. Riemann, however, did not do that. [*Studien zur Arithmetik und Geometrie*, p. 411.

Many other passages of *Studien zur Arithmetik und Geometrie* also attest to the influence of Riemann on Husserl's views on geometric manifolds and physical space. For example, in a passage of the same year 1893 Husserl stresses that, contrary to the geometry of physical space: "Pure geometry is a pure aprioristic science".

§6 Husserl and Riemann: a Brief Retrospect

By means of quotations from two writings of Husserl presumably written in 1890, we have shown the falsity of Føllesdal's contention, accepted by the whole analytic family, that Husserl borrowed the distinction between sense and referent from Frege. Moreover, in a letter of Frege to Husserl of May 1891 and in his 'Ausführungen über Sinn und Bedeutung' Frege acknowledges that Husserl had made the distinction independently of him. In fact, after Bolzano, the sense-referent distinction was there to be taken, as happens with a ripe fruit. Only the obsession of some analytic philosophers trying either to ignore or to diminish Husserl's stature as a philosopher can explain their philosophical-historical aberration of giving credit to Frege alone.[41] Moreover, there is no reason to doubt Husserl's recognition of the importance for the evolution of his views on logic of Leibniz, Bolzano, Lotze and Hume. If Frege had played a major role in the evolution of Husserl's views, the latter would have stated it. But in any case, as a matter of fact, Husserl's mature views on logic and its relation to mathematics are clearly different from Frege's.

That does not mean that Frege did not exert any, even indirect, influence on Husserl, or Husserl or Frege. Certainly, Frege's level of rigour most surely elevated the level of discourse and, thus, indirectly influenced the most capable of his younger contemporaries, like Husserl and Hilbert.[42] Most probably, without Frege's pioneering work, Husserl would not have arrived in his refutation of psychologism in logic in the first eight chapters of the Prolegomena to such a level of philosophical analysis that clearly surpassed Frege's previous refutation of psychologism. But Frege also would probably had not felt compelled to discuss the problem of the indexicals in 'Der Gedanke'[43], were it not for the fact that Husserl had discussed it in more detail in the First Logical Investigation[44] and arrived at a similar, but once more finer conception.

Furthermore, Husserl's views on mathematics are not only different from Frege's, but much more modern, resembling the views of the Bourbaki group of French mathematicians. Husserl used the term 'manifold', as did his friend Cantor. But for Cantor 'manifold' meant essentially what we now call 'set', that is, a finite or infinite collection of objects, without taking into account any relations between those objects. For Husserl, manifolds are structures, and mathematics as a theory of manifolds is simply a theory of formal structures. On this point, one can clearly see the affinities with Riemann. Husserl's

---

[41] The above remark does not include Føllesdal, who certainly has tried to make Husserl known in analytic circles. In fact, it should be pointed out that when he wrote his MA thesis and the paper referred to above, neither Husserl's 'Zur Logik der Zeichen' nor Frege's *Briefwechsel* had been published.

[42] In this more general and sounder sense, Hume exerted an important influence on Kant, and Quine has exerted an influence on many recent rigorous philosophers, even those like the present author, who disagree with Quine in almost any concrete philosophical issue. But that is precisely the way in which philosophy is made.

[43] 'Der Gedanke' 1918, reprinted in *Kleine Schriften*, pp. 342-362.

[44] *Logische Untersuchungen II*, U. I, Chapter 3, §§24-26.

conception of mathematics as a theory of manifolds is a generalization and development of Riemann's views.

But Husserl not only obtained from Riemann the germ of his view of mathematics as a whole, but also had accepted by the end of 1892, thus, earlier than other important philosophers of his time, Riemann's conception of physical space as being such that both its curvature and dimensionality should be determined by experience.

References

Beth, Evert W. – *The Foundations of Mathematics*, North Holland, Amsterdam 1965

Carnap, Rudolf – *Die logische Syntax der Sprache* 1934, expanded English edition, *The Logical Syntax of Language* Routledge, London 1937, reprint, Chicago et al. 2003

Centrone, Stefania – 'Husserl on the 'Totality of all conceivable arithmetical operations'', *History and Philosophy of Logic 27 (3)*, 2006, pp. 211-228

Føllesdal, Dagfinn – *Husserl und Frege, ein Beitrag zur Beleuchtung der phänomenologischen Philosophie*, translation in L. Haaparanta (ed.), *Mind, Meaning and Mathematics*, Kluwer, Dordrecht 1994, pp. 3-47

Føllesdal, Dagfinn – 'Husserl's Concept of Noema', in *Journal of Philosophy 66 (20)*, 1969, pp. 680-697

Frege, Gottlob – *Die Grundlagen der Arithmetik* 1884, Centenary Edition, edited by Christian Thiel, F. Meiner, Hamburg 1986

Frege, Gottlob – 'Funktion und Begriff' 1891, reprinted in *Kleine Schriften*, pp. 125-142

Frege, Gottlob – 'Über Sinn und Bedeutung' 1892, reprinted in *Kleine Schriften*, pp. 143-162

Frege, Gottlob – 'Rezension von E. G. Husserl: *Philosophie der Arithmetik I* 1894, reprinted in *Kleine Schriften*, pp. 179-192

Frege, Gottlob – 'Der Gedanke' 1918, reprinted in *Kleine Schriften*, pp. 342-362

Frege, Gottlob – *Kleine Schriften* 1967, revised edition, G. Olms, Hildesheim 1990

Frege, Gottlob – *Nachgelassene Schriften*, 1969, revised edition, F. Meiner, Hamburg 1983
Frege, Gottlob – 'Ausführungen über Sinn und Bedeutung', in *Nachgelassene Schriften*, pp. 128-136
Frege, Gottlob – 'Über Euklidische Geometrie', in *Nachgelassene Schriften*, pp. 182-184
Frege, Gottlob – *Wissenschaftlicher Briefwechsel*, F. Meiner, Hamburg 1974
Husserl, Edmund – *Philosophie der Arithmetik* 1891, Hua XII, M. Nijhoff, Den Haag 1970
Husserl, Edmund – 'Besprechung von E. Schröders *Vorlesungen über die Algebra der Logik I*' 1891, reprinted in *Aufsätze und Rezensionen (1890-1910)*, Hua XXII, pp. 3-43
Husserl, Edmund – *Logische Untersuchungen* (2 vols.) 1900-1901, Hua XVIII & XIX, M. Nijhoff 1975 & 1984
Husserl, Edmund – *Ideen zu einer reinen Phänomenologie und phänomenologischen Philosophie I* 1913, Hua III, 1950, revised edition, M. Nijhoff, Den Haag 1976
Husserl, Edmund – *Formale und transzendentale Logik* 1929, Hua XVII, M. Nijhoff, Den Haag 1974
Husserl, Edmund – *Erfahrung und Urteil* 1939, sixth edition, F. Meiner, Hamburg 1985
Husserl, Edmund – 'Zur Logik der Zeichen (Semiotik)', in *Philosophie der Arithmetik*, Hua XII, pp. 340-373
Husserl, Edmund – *Introduction to the Logical Investigations*, M. Nijhoff, Den Haag 1975
Husserl, Edmund – *Aufsätze und Rezensionen*, Hua XXII, M. Nijhoff, Den Haag 1979
Husserl, Edmund – *Studien zur Arithmetik und Geometrie*, Hua XXI, M. Nijhoff, Den Haag 1983
Husserl, Edmund – *Einleitung in die Logik und Erkenntnistheorie* Hua XXIV, M. Nijhoff, Den Haag 1984
Husserl, Edmund – *Briefwechsel* (10 vols.), Kluwer, Dordrecht 1994
Riemann, Bernhard – 'Über die Hypothesen, welche der Geometrie zugrunde liegen' 1867, third edition, Berlin 1923, reprint, Chelsea, New York 1973

Rosado Haddock, Guillermo E. – 'Husserl's Philosophy of Mathematics: its Origin and Relevance', *Husserl Studies 22*, 2006, reprinted as Chapter 5 of *Against the Current*, pp. 145-181

Rosado Haddock, Guillermo E. – 'Husserl's Conception of Physical Theories and Physical Geometry in the Time of the Prolegomena: a Comparison with Duhem's and Poincaré's Views', *Axiomathes 22*, 2012, reprinted as Chapter 6 of *Against the Current*, pp. 183-214

Rosado Haddock, Guillermo E. – *Against the Current*, Ontos Verlag, Frankfurt 2012

Idealization in Mathematics:
Husserl and Beyond

Abstract
Husserl's contributions to the nature of mathematical knowledge are opposed to the naturalist, empiricist and pragmatist tendencies that are nowadays dominant. It is claimed that mainstream tendencies fail to distinguish the historical problem of the origin and evolution of mathematical knowledge from the epistemological problem of how is it that we have access to mathematical knowledge.

§1. Introduction

The problem of our acquisition of mathematical knowledge has fascinated and puzzled philosophers since antiquity and throughout most of the history of philosophy. From Plato and Aristotle to Descartes, Leibniz and Kant most of the major philosophers have been impressed in one way or another both by the certainty of mathematics - in contrast to other disciplines, including philosophy - and by its methodology. Since the mid-nineteenth century, with the discovery of non-Euclidean geometry, the increasing rigor of analysis and, especially, the development of mathematical logic, the interest both in the nature of mathematics and of mathematical knowledge has incessantly grown among philosophers. But although much more has been written by philosophers on mathematics and mathematical knowledge in the last hundred years than in the whole history of philosophy up to that point, very few steps forward, if any, have been made in the mainstream of contemporary research.

In particular, the naturalism, empiricism and pragmatism that are dominant nowadays in Anglo-American philosophical circles have done very little to clarify the nature of mathematical knowledge. Moreover, a presupposition of any clarification of mathematical knowledge is a sharp distinction, totally ignored by many philosophers in that tradition, between the historical problem of the origin and evolution of mathematical knowledge and the completely different foundational-epistemological problem of how we gain access to mathematical knowledge, i.e. to knowledge of some presumed mathematical entities, their properties and relations. The first problem belongs to the history of science, the second to the epistemology of mathematics. These disciplines can complement each other, but cannot substitute for each other. For the epistemological problem there is no empirical-genetic answer. To blur this distinction is even more confusing than the blurring by some "historians" of science of the distinction between history of science and the construction of scientific theories.

Hence, we cannot search for anything but confusion in the writings of the predominant naturalistically minded philosophers. On the other hand, very little is to be found in classical Fregean Platonism, whereas both constructivisms and nominalisms are epistemologically deficient and could at best account for a meagre part of mathematics. This does not mean, however, that nothing has been written that represents an important step forward in the clarification of the epistemology of mathematics. Edmund Husserl, in the very little known Sixth Logical Investigation of his opus magnum *Logische Untersuchungen*[1], made a decisive contribution to this problem that should not be ignored by any serious scholar working in this area. Husserl's epistemology of mathematics - which is our main concern here - together with his philosophy of mathematics and logic[2] and his semantics seem capable of solving a problem that we consider a touchstone for any philosophical clarification of the nature of mathematics and which puts in a predicament all above mentioned sorts of philosophies of mathematics, namely, the problem of the philosophical assessment of the mathematical "fact" that there exist seemingly unrelated interderivable mathematical statements like Zorn's Lemma and Tychonoff's Theorem or the Ultrafilter Theorem and Tychonoff's Theorem for Hausdorff spaces. By the way, nominalisms in particular are incompatible with a classical result in model theory, namely, with Robinson's test for model-completeness. For if there are no mathematical entities, all existential mathematical statements are false and universal statements all vacuously true. But according to Robinson's test for model-completeness, a theory T in the first order

---

[1] See his *Logische Untersuchungen II*, U. VI.

[2] See *Logische Untersuchungen I*, Chapter XI.

language L(T) is model-complete if and only if for every existential sentence σ in L(T), there is a universal sentence π in L(T) such that σ and π are interderivable in T. But, if nominalism were true[3], since π qua universal is true and σ qua existential is false, they could not be interderivable in T, if T is consistent[4].

§2. Preliminaries

There is a sense in which mathematics - as any other human endeavor – is "empirical", but that sense does not shed any light on the nature of mathematics and mathematical knowledge. Besides being a corpus of theoretical knowledge purportedly referring to some abstract entities, their properties and relations, mathematics is a cultural and social phenomenon like art and music. Historically, our knowledge of mathematics has evolved from the primitive mathematical knowledge bounded to practical applications of ancient civilizations to the beautiful abstract theories developed in the last two centuries. In individual human beings, mathematical knowledge also seems to have evolved empirically from the rudimentary ways of counting in early childhood to the abstract theories examined nowadays by professional pure mathematicians. Even logic has its empirical history, both a socio-cultural and an individual one.

However, those historical-empirical aspects of mathematics and mathematical knowledge are unable to explain the presumed necessity of mathematical propositions, its unrestricted validity and the seemingly abstract, objective and objectual nature of the referents of mathematical propositions. Empiricists and naturalists of all sorts are in a quandary when they try to assess these familiar purported facts about mathematics and mathematical knowledge. Thus, they either try to propound an argument for mathematical realism that they think is compatible with their naturalism - like the so-called "indispensability

---

[3] Footnote added for clarity in the present version of the paper.

[4] See our 'On the Semantics of Mathematical Statements', Appendix I?.

argument" so dear to Quine[5], Putnam[6] and Maddy[7] (1980, 1990) - while ignoring any other argument on behalf of mathematical realism that does not fit their empiricist or naturalist prejudices, or they resort, like Field[8] (1980, 1989), to an unwarranted rejection of the truth of the most trivial mathematical statements - e.g. existential statements like the one that asserts that there exists a number n in the natural number series such that n + n=n×n- and argue on behalf of the most counterintuitive views on mathematics. What is common to all such conceptions, as we argued elsewhere[9], are some well established dogmas and prejudices, particularly, the belief that to recur to a so-called mathematical intuition in our assessment of mathematical knowledge is to enter the realm of mysticism and esoterism. Of course, this prejudice against mathematical intuition could be traced back to a philosopher that cannot be accused of empiricism, namely to Kant and his rejection of intellectual intuition. But the fact is that if you have such a primitive view of experience as Anglo-American naturalists usually have, then it is understandable that you cannot conceive of any knowledge that transcends sense data. Thus, you are obliged either to reject it as metaphysical or even mystical, or to introduce it as hypothesis or convention, blurring, by the way, the distinction between mathematics and physical science.

§3. Husserl's Notion of Categorial Intuition

The first and decisive step towards the "objectifying" of mathematical entities in Husserl's philosophy is done by categorial intuition. But categorial intuition is nothing mysterious or esoteric, as

---

[5] See Quine's 'On what there is' in *From a Logical point of View*, pp. 1-19.

[6] See Putnam's 'What is Mathematical Truth' in *Philosophical Papers I*, pp. 60-78.

[7] See her 'Phisicalistic Platonism' of 1990 and her book *Realism in Mathematics*.

[8] See his very influential *Science without Numbers*, as well as his Collection of papers *Realism, Mathematics and Modality*.

[9] See our 'On Antiplatonism and its Dogmas'.

naturalists and empiricists would like us to believe. On the contrary, it is built immediately on sensory intuition. Let us consider as empirical statements as there are, e.g., "The cat is under the table", "John is taller than Joe", "Mary and Elisabeth are at the door", or "The red of this book is more intense that the red of the notebook". Almost everyone would assert that those statements are empirical ones. However, if you are consistent with your empiricism, you would have to acknowledge that what is given in sense perception are the cat and the table, John and Joe, Mary, Elisabeth and the door, the red book and the red notebook. Nothing in sense perception corresponds to the "under", to the "is taller than", to the "and", to the "at" or to the "is more intense". Moreover, nothing in sense perception corresponds to the "on" or to the "at the side of, to the "or" or to the "not". Nonetheless, we clearly understand the difference in truth conditions between "The cat is under the table" and "The cat is on the table" and between "Mary and Elisabeth are at the door" and "Mary or Elisabeth is at the door", and acknowledge that some experiences can confirm one of the members of the pair but not necessarily the other. If only Mary is at the door, only the statement "Mary or Elisabeth is at the door" can be confirmed by sense perception, whereas the statement "Mary and Elisabeth are at the door" is disconfirmed by that same experience. Hence, even with respect to the confirmation of the simplest empirical statements, there are formal constituents of statements without any sensible correlate but which play a decisive role with regard to the possible empirical confirmation or disconfirmation of the statements in which they occur. Thus, there are nonsensible constituents of experience that build on the sensible ones and that account for the truth or falsehood of statements. Those correlates of the formal constituents of statements form categorial objectualities. Statements refer, according to Husserl's semantics of (in the more popular Fregean terminology) sense and reference, to states of affairs, and states of affairs are among the most fundamental categorial objectualities. In particular, the referents of empirical statements like those mentioned above are states of affairs immediately founded on sensible objectualities.

Sets are also categorial objectualities. We do not perceive sets sensibly. We see Mary and Elisabeth, John and Joe, the cat, the door and the table. But we do not sensibly perceive the set of those seven objects. The set of those seven objects —like the states of affairs referred to by the above mentioned statements— builds on those sensible objectualities but is not reduced to them. States of affairs and sets are categorial objectualities and are the correlates of corresponding founded acts, acts of categorial perception. But even if the objects are not really given in sense perception, but only imagined in our sensory imagination, states of affairs and sets can be constituted —which does not mean created or constructed— on the basis of the imagined sensible objects in founded acts of categorial imagination. For our purposes here sensory imagination can play the same role as sense perception, and categorial imagination the same as categorial perception. We follow Husserl in our use of the word intuition as a generic term for both perception and imagination, and from now on will prefer the terms "sensory intuition" and "categorial intuition".

Categorial objectualities do not need to be immediately founded on sensible objectualities. The connection could be much more mediate. Relations between sets of sensible objects and sets of relations between sensible objects are categorial objectualities of the second level. A set of relations between sets of sensible objects and a relation between sets of sets of sensible objects are categorial objectualities of the third level, whereas relations between (and sets of) such categorial objectualities of the third level are categorial objectualities of the fourth level The hierarchy of categorial objectualities continues indefinitely upwards through all the finite levels, obtaining, thus, a hierarchy of categorial objectualities of any finite level. By the way, it is completely irrelevant if the categorial objectualities of the first level were built on objects sensibly perceived or sensibly imagined. Finally, it should be clear that the transit to the transfinite does not create any difficulty, and that in this hierarchy of categorial objectualities paradoxical sets such as Cantor's set of all sets and Russell's set of all sets that do not contain themselves as members cannot appear[10]. In Husserl's terminology, those paradoxical sets can never be constituted in the hierarchy, where, as mentioned before,

---

[10] See Appendix II to our 'Husserl's Epistemology of Mathematics and the Foundation of Platonism in Mathematics'.

"constituted" does not mean constructed or created, but simply made the objectuality of a categorial intuition.

We have, however, still not shown how mathematical objectualities are constituted. We have not shown how they free themselves from any dependence on the sensible objects that lie at the zero level of the hierarchy of categorial objectualities described above. For mathematical objectualities, in contrast to other categorial objectualities that are mixed with sensibility, are pure categorial objectualities. The act of purification of categorial objectualities is called by Husserl in Logische Untersuchungen "categorial abstraction", and it can occur at any level of the hierarchy of categorial objectualities, including the first level. Categorial abstraction is simply a process of formalization that is very common in mathematics, whose iteration is at least partly responsible for the abstract structures of contemporary mathematics. The members of a concrete set M are replaced by indeterminates, and the terms of a concrete relation are also replaced by indeterminates. Although Husserl was not explicit about it, it is clear that the process of abstraction can be iterated to some extent. Thus, we can also replace the relation under discussion by the "form" of the relation, e.g. the relation "is taller than" by a transitive, irreflexive and asymmetric relation. This process of formalization can take us from sensible objects through arithmetic, algebra, abstract algebra to universal algebra, and although historically it has required such a long development, from the point of view of the epistemology of mathematics it is the iteration of the process of formalization that Husserl called "categorial abstraction" and that purifies mathematics from any residue of sensibility. Thus, one can paraphrase Kant and say that although all our knowledge has its origin in experience, it is not necessarily founded on experience. Mathematical knowledge does not have any trace of sensibility in its foundation. It is, thus, a priori. But since it admits formalization preserving only the logical structure, it is also analytic in Husserl's precise use of the term expounded in the "Third Logical Investigation"[11].

---

[11] See *Logische Untersuchungen II*, U. III, §12.

Finally, it should be underscored that both categorial intuition and categorial abstraction are different from the better-known eidetic intuition. This is a very important distinction that still most of the better-known Husserlian scholars fail to see. It is not true that categorial intuition and categorial abstraction are, if anything, special cases of eidetic intuition. In the Sixth Logical Investigation Husserl saw the relation between categorial and eidetic intuition the other way around, and considered eidetic intuition as a peculiar special case of categorial intuition[12]. In *Erfahrung und Urteil*[13] however, he clearly distinguished these two sorts of intuition. Moreover, eidetic intuition is clearly different from categorial abstraction, which is simply a process of formalization, and Husserl clearly distinguishes formalization from the process of obtaining the so-called "essences". The final products of eidetic intuition are usually mixed categorial objectualities like redness or triangularity, and its epistemological domain that of the synthetic *a priori*, not that of the analytic a priori, which is the realm of mathematics (physical geometry excluded).

§4. On the shoulders of Husserl

Once the most basic mathematical objectualities, like those of set and relation, are constituted by means of the combined efforts of categorial intuition and categorial abstraction, other more complex mathematical objectualities follow. First of all, via the repeated hierarchic process of subsequent intuitions, a whole hierarchy of pure categorial, i.e. mathematical objectualities of ever higher level but of the same "structure" as the basic ones can be constituted, e.g. relations or sets of any finite level. Moreover, as we mentioned above, we can obtain new mathematical objectualities by further formalization, e.g. by replacing a relation by any relation with the same formal properties. But mathematical objectualities can also be obtained by many other means. One can, e.g. consider the addition of further structure. Linear

---

[12] See ibid., U. IV, §52.

[13] See *Erfahrung und Urteil*, §64.

orders are obtained in this way from partial orders, as can also Abelian groups from groups or integral domains and fields from rings, or Hausdorff spaces and compact spaces from topological spaces. Mathematical objectualities can also be obtained from other mathematical objectualities by the process of constituting equivalence classes module a determinate congruence relation between the elements of an already constituted mathematical objectuality - as in Frege's famous discussion of the concept of (cardinal) number in his *Die Grundlagen der Arithmetik*[14]. By similar means a so-called quotient structure can be constituted as a new mathematical objectuality. Thus, quotient groups are obtained from groups, quotient topological spaces from topological spaces and quotient differentiable manifolds from differentiable manifolds. Products and powers of mathematical objectualities are also clearly constituted on the basis of already constituted mathematical objectualites by another very common method of obtaining new mathematical entities. Last but not least, as Husserl already envisaged, structures of quite different sorts serve as basis for new mathematical objectualities obtained by connecting already constituted mathematical objectualities[15]. Thus, ordered groups, topological groups and ordered topological groups are examples of such complex mathematical objectualites. In some cases there is a sort of compatibility requirement for the successful meshing of the two or more structures, e.g. in the case of topological groups, the requirement that homomorphisms between those entities be continuous. We do not intend to exhaust all the possible processes of constitution of mathematical objectualities, but only show how the above mentioned and possibly other methods of obtaining mathematical objectualities, when combined and iterated, can serve to constitute an enormous variety of mathematical entities maybe only a small part of which is familiar to actual mathematicians.

---

[14] See Frege's *Die Grundlagen der Arithmetik*, §§62-67.

[15] For Husserl's conception of a "Mannigfaltigkeitslehre" see, for example, *Logische Untersuchungen I*, Chapter XI, §§69-70, *Formale und transzendentale Logik* §§28-36 and *Einleitung in die Logik und Erkenntnistheorie*, §19.

References

Benacerraf, P. & Putnam, H. (eds.) - *Philosophy of Mathematics*, second edition, Cambridge University Press, Cambridge 1983

Bourbaki, N. - 'The Architecture of Mathematics'. American Mathematical Monthly 57, 1950, pp. 221-32

Field, H. - *Science without Numbers*, Princeton University Press, Princeton 1980

Field, H. - *Realism, Mathematics and Modality* B. H. Blackwell, Oxford 1989

Frege, G. - *Die Grundlagen der Arithmetik* 1884, Centenarausgabe, Felix Meiner, Hamburg 1986.

Frege, G. - *Kleine Schriften*, 1967,, second edition, Georg Olms, Hildesheim et al. 1990.

Husserl, E. – *Logische Untersuchungen* 1900-1901, Husserliana XVIII & XIX, Martinus Nijhoff, Den Haag 1975 & 1984

Husserl, E. - *Formale und Transzendentale Logik* 1929, Husserliana edition, Vol. XVII, Martinus Nijhoff, Den Haag 1974.

Husserl, E. - *Erfahrung und Urteil* 1939, fifth edition, Felix Meiner, Hamburg 1976.

Husserl, E. - *Einleitung in die Logik und Erkenntnistheorie*, Husserliana XXIV, Martinus Nijhoff, Den Haag 1984

Irvine, A. D. (ed.) - *Physicalism in Mathematics*, KluwerDordrecht 1980

Maddy, P. - Physicalistic Platonism, in Irvine *Physicalism in Mathematics*, pp. 259-289.

Maddy, P. - *Realism in Mathematics*, Clarendon Press, Oxford 1990.

Putnam, H. - 'What is Mathematical Truth?' In: *Philosophical Papers*, Vol. I., Cambridge University Press, Cambridge 1975, pp. 60-78.

Quine, W. O. – 'On what there is', in *From a Logical Point of View*. Harvard University Press, Cambridge, Ma. 1953, pp. 1-19.

Resnik, M. D. (ed.) - *Mathematical Objects and Mathematical Knowledge*, Dartmouth, Aldershot et al. 1985

Rosado Haddock, G. E. - *Edmund Husserls Philosophie der Logik und Mathematik im Lichte der gegenwartigen Logik und*

Grundlagenforschung (Diss.), Bonn 1973.

Rosado Haddock, G. E. - 'Husserl's Epistemology of Mathematics and the Foundation of Platonism in Mathematics'. *Husserl Studies 4*, 1987, pp. 121-134.

Rosado Haddock, G. E. - 'On Husserl's Distinction between State of Affairs (Sachverhalt) and Situation of Affairs (Sachlage)', in: D. Føllesdal, J. N. Mohanty & Th. M. Seebohm, (eds.), *Phenomenology and the Formal Sciences*, Kluwer, Dordrecht 1991, pp. 31-48.

Rosado Haddock, G. E. - 'Interdenvability of Seemingly Unrelated Mathematical Statements and the Philosophy of Mathematics' Dialogos 59, 1992, pp. 121-134.

Rosado Haddock, G. E. - 'On Antiplatonism and its Dogmas'. Dialogos 67, 1996, pp. 7-38.

Rosado Haddock, G. E. - 'On the Semantics of Mathematical Statements' *Manuscrito XIX (1)*, 1996, pp. 149-175.

Rosado Haddock, G. E. - 'To be a Fregean or to be a Husserlian: that is the Question for Platonists', in Walter A. Carnielli. & M. L. D. d'Ottaviano, (eds.) *Advances in Contemporary Logic and Computer Science*, American Mathematical Society Series *Contemporary Mathematics*, Vol. 235, Providence, Rhode Island, 1999, pp. 295-312

III

Doing Rigorous Philosophy: Critical Studies and Critical Reviews

Critical Review of Matthias Schirn (ed.), *Studies on Frege*, Stuttgart-Bad Canstatt, Fromann-Holzboog, 1976 (3 vols.)[*]

This collection of papers edited by Matthias Schirn is in our opinion the most complete and at the same time the most profound study to this date of the philosophical and scientific work of Gottlob Frege.[1] Schirn collects in three volumes – approximately 815 pages- 36 papers (20 of them in English and 16 in German)- discussing the most diverse aspects of Frege's philosophical thought. Among the authors represented therein are some of the best-known Fregean scholars (as, e.g., Thiel, Dummett, Angelelli and Gabriel), authors (like Richard M. Martin and David Wiggins) who have contributed significantly to areas of philosophy that were of prime concern to Frege, and less known authors (like Shwayder and Schirn himself), whose papers here included are the best testimony of their solid knowledge of Frege's writings.

---

[*] The footnotes have been added to the present edition.
[1] That assertion, made some thirty-five years ago is most probably still completely valid nowadays. Even the four volumes collection *The Philosophy of Gottlob Frege*, edited by Hans Sluga, which in fact, reproduces many of the papers published in the present collection, in general, is not as good a collection and lacks anything comparable to the thorough and profound fourteen page Introduction by Schirn, whereas Schirn's other outstanding collection, *Frege: Importance and Legacy* has not the wide scope of the present one. Of the much more recent *Cambridge Companion to Frege* –as happens with other books in the series, for example, those concerned with Carnap and with Logical Positivism-, there is almost nothing positive that could be said, being only the occasion to publish for a group of friends with very similar renderings. It is a shame that Matthias Schirn and Christian Thiel were neither invited to publish in that collection nor are they even mentioned in the bibliography or the index.

Each of the three volumes has a subtitle that more or less delimits the research area of the papers it contains. The first volume has the subtitle 'Logic and Philosophy of Mathematics', and is preceded by an important introduction by the editor on the connection between logic, mathematics and philosophy of language in Frege. This is followed by a paper of a general character by Hans D. Sluga in which the author tries to insert Frege in the history of western philosophical thought. The second paper is an extensive and detailed study by Albert Veraart of the history of the scientific-philosophical writings of Frege not published during his lifetime, many of which –as we know- were published for the first time under the title *Nachgelassene Schriften* in 1969. Beginning with the third paper and until the thirteenth and last of this first volume the papers are concerned with different aspects of the general theme 'Logic and Philosophy of Mathematics'. Victor H. Dudman compares some aspects of Frege's logic with that of Boole. Robert Sternfeld analyses the logicist thesis from the standpoint of developments both in logic and in the philosophy of mathematics after Frege. Hart's paper is the only one in the whole collection, which is barely concerned with Frege. In his strange paper that author tries to analyze the possibility of developing –what he calls- an epistemology of modality in mathematics. In their respective papers, Resnik and Kambartel examine the polemic between Frege and Hilbert on the axiomatic method. In his paper, Dummett discusses Frege's views on the consistency of a theory. The first of Thiel's two papers examines the role of abstraction in Frege's philosophy of arithmetic. The papers by Parsons and Bynum are concerned with the evolution of Frege's views on the relation between logic and mathematics. In his second paper, Thiel analyzes Frege's reasoning in §10 of *Grundgesetze der Arithmetik I*. Finally von Kutschera discusses in great detail the original foundation of mathematical analysis given by Frege in that work. As in the case of the two remaining volumes, this first volume ends with a list of abbreviations and some brief biographical notes on each of the authors.

The second volume, whose subtitle is 'Logic and Philosophy of Language', contains fourteen papers devoted to different problems in the philosophy of logic and the philosophy of language, followed by a list of abbreviations and short biographical notes on the authors. The volume begins with a paper of Reinhardt Grossmann on structures, functions and forms. As happened with the paper by Hart, the paper cannot be properly considered a study about Frege, though its link to that philosopher is greater than that of Hart's paper. Wolfgang Carl examines in his paper the interesting problem of the grounding given by Frege for his sharp distinction between concept and object. Eike-Henner W. Kluge discusses the important issue of the logically simple in Frege. The well-known Fregean scholar Gottfried Gabriel presents us with a valuable critical study of Frege, in which he tries to emphasize the one-sidedness of some of Frege's views, the origin of which seems to have its roots in his battle against psychologism. Hans-Ulrich Hoche's paper examines the change that occurred in Frege's rendering of what he called in *Begriffsschrift* 'the content line'. Leslie Stevenson also discusses in his paper a change in Frege's thought from *Begriffsschrift* to *Grundgesetze der Arithmetk*, however, not that of the rendering of the 'content line', but of the definition of quantification. Sternfeld is also present in the second volume. His paper is concerned with the mathematization of logic. In an interesting paper Angelelli examines the different standpoints held by many important philosophers on the issue of the substitutivity of identicals. The papers of Caton, Schirn, Kienzle, Wiggins, Suter and Khatchadourian all discuss the interesting problem of identity statements. Caton, Schirn and Kienzle examine this issue exclusively in Frege's works, whereas Suter and Khatchadourian compare what they believe are Frege's views with the views of Russell and Kripke, respectively. On the other hand, Wiggins gives us a somewhat more general treatment of the same problem. These six papers are a sample of the great prevailing confusion on how to interpret both Frege's view from 1879 and especially his view of 1892.

The third volume, whose subtitle is 'Logic and Semantics', is much shorter than the two previous ones. It consists of nine papers, eight of them in its main part and one in the appendix. The first eight papers are concerned with the general theme, 'Logic and Semantics', whereas the appendix is concerned with Frege's only writing on the philosophy of physics. The book ends with an impressive bibliography –the most complete we know of- on Frege's writings, a list of abbreviations (in fact, it is the same in the three volumes) and some short biographical notes of the authors. The first paper of this volume is a comparative study by Fred Sommers of some views on logic of Frege and Leibniz. Sommers ardently defends Leibniz against Frege, though we sincerely doubt that he is going to attract many followers. In his second paper in this anthology Michael Resnik examines the role played in Frege's work by the so-called 'context principle' –so dear to many followers of Wittgenstein. Ernst Tugendhat gives us an analysis of the concept of 'Bedeutung' in Frege. (Tugendhat rejects both the translation of 'Bedeutung" as 'denotation' and the more frequent one as 'reference'.) In his second paper in this collection Dudman examines the problem of the reference of predicates. In one of the conceptually finest papers of the whole collection David S. Shwayder discusses the issue of the determination of reference by sense. In his paper –which is essentially the second chapter of his book *Names and Descriptions*- Linsky compares the treatments given by Frege and Russell to empty singular terms. Howard Jackson and Malcolm Acock are concerned with the most important aspects of the strange task of relating Frege's concept of 'sense' with sense data, whereas Richard M. Martin examines some pragmatic considerations of Frege. Finally, Peter Janich discusses in the appendix Frege's critical study of Lange's treatment of Newton's first law. (That paper, together with that of Kambartel, was originally published in 1975 in the collection edited by Christian Thiel *Frege und die Grundlagenforschung.*)

We have chosen to examine –sometimes critically- some ten of the thirty-six papers. The choice is based exclusively on our own preferences, and in no way should be rendered as meaning that the selected papers are the most valuable ones.

(I)   Hans D. Sluga - Frege as a Rationalist

At the beginning of his paper Sluga observes that the two main objectives of Frege's criticism were psychologism and formalism, and that both are products of the philosophical naturalism that flourished in the mid nineteenth century. On the other hand, the German idealists, referred to by Dummett in his monumental study *Frege:*

Philosophy of Language are never mentioned by name in Frege's writings.

According to Sluga, Frege's theory of the objectivity of numbers, value ranges, functions, etc. never pretended to be an ontological thesis. It should be compared with Lotze's theory of validity, of which it is an apparent heir. Lotze affirms that ideal objects have validity, without therefore being real. According to him, such a distinction preserves what is true in the Platonic theory of ideas, while avoiding both realism and nominalism.

In Sluga's opinion, to approach Frege's thought from an ontological standpoint is to approach it in a completely unhistorical way. Frege is interested in the problem, popular since Leibniz and Kant, of the power of reason and of the ultimate foundation justifying arithmetical propositions. Frege did not ask whether numbers exist or not, but whether the laws of numbers are or are not principles of reason.

Dummett has argued in his already mentioned book that Frege was the first philosopher of the present era, on the grounds that he rejected the epistemological problems that flourished in the period of modern philosophy, since he did not consider them of primary importance, and replaced them by problems related to logic. According to Sluga, such a rendering is mistaken. Instead of rejecting epistemological issues, Frege tried to delimit the spheres of both disciplines. Both are concerned with truth, but in different, though strictly related, manners. Moreover, Frege's concern for the foundation of geometrical and arithmetical propositions is of an epistemological nature. The theses on the reducibility of arithmetic to logic and of geometry to intuition are, according to Sluga, epistemological theses. Furthermore, the whole discussion about logic is, for Frege, epistemological, since it is not concerned with the derivation of truths from other truths. Even the formal language used in *Begriffsschrift* is, for Frege, a tool for resolving some epistemological problems concerning the nature and status of arithmetical and geometrical propositions.

Sluga sketches (pp. 34-35) a parallelism between the epistemological concerns of Frege and those of Kant. According to Sluga, both Frege and Kant were interested in some epistemological problems, and both of them differentiated such problems from genetic ones. Now, if one were to accept that genetic problems are epistemological, it would be correct to say that Frege did not consider some sorts of epistemological problems. But such sorts of problems were the same that Kant avoided in his parallel study.

We think that the parallelism sketched by Sluga between Frege and Kant does not take into account fundamental differences between the two thinkers. If it is correct that Frege is mostly concerned with problems that we could call 'epistemological', it is also true that they are always very specific epistemological problems, which are more appropriately classified as belonging to the philosophy of mathematics, the philosophy of logic, or semantics. Epistemological problems of a more general nature, like that of the foundation for the evidence had by the axioms, are usually avoided by Frege, and fundamental epistemological problems, like the one that is probably the central problem of Kantian epistemology, namely, the problem of the conditions of possibility of knowledge, are not even considered by Frege. Certainly, if we consider as epistemological problems (in a strict sense) the sort of problems that are in the centre of the philosophical reflections of Descartes, Hume and Kant, and, later, of Husserl, then Dummett is right. His fear of committing the 'sin' of psychologism did not allow Frege to consider such problems face to face –though, as can be seen in 'Der Gedanke', he could not avoid them completely-, nor see the difference between studies on the psychology of knowledge and studies about the conditions of possibility of knowledge.

Sluga considers Frege (p. 36) a rationalist, and tries to sketch (pp. 37-41) a bridge from Frege to Leibniz, going through Trendelenburg, Lotze and Bolzano, and ending with an interesting comparison between the rationalisms of Frege and Leibniz.

Sluga ends his paper pointing out –in our opinion, correctly- that Frege's work does not represent any answer to a predominant idealism, but an answer to an array of philosophies that had originated after the collapse of German idealism.

(II) W. D. Hart - Imagination, Necessity and Abstract Objects

At the beginning of his paper Hart points out that the distinction between absolutely necessary truths and merely contingent ones is metaphysical in nature, neither epistemological nor semantic, and that probably because of that Frege did not take it into account in *Die Grundlagen der Arithmetik*. (Certainly Frege excludes the modalities from his logic, but not because he believed that the distinctions expressed by them are metaphysical, since he seems to believe –in our opinion, erroneously- that they are epistemological or, maybe, even psychological. As a matter of fact, in §4 of *Begriffsschrift* Frege makes an epistemological distinction between apodictic and assertoric judgements, which serves him as grounding for excluding apodictic judgements from any particular consideration in his system of logic.)

According to Hart, Frege seems to presuppose that mathematical truths are necessary truths and mathematical falsities necessarily false, without any attempt at justifying such assumptions. Now, Hart asks whether it is feasible to construct an epistemology for modality in pure mathematics. He will begin by considering epistemological problems for modality in general, and then will consider the special case of pure mathematics, taking into account especially the opinion that all mathematical truths are necessary.

Hart will maintain: (i) that abstract entities can be imagined and (ii) that we can base our knowledge of the necessity of truths in pure mathematics on the possibility of imagining such abstract entities. Now, Hart will assume the existence of some abstract mathematical objects, what does not mean that he is committed to the existence of any abstract object that someone considers as existent. Hart will, rather, trust the capacity of the reader to recognize examples of abstract mathematical entities.

As Kripke, Hart distinguishes between *a priori* knowledge and necessary truth. He maintains that neither all necessary truths are known *a priori* nor everything that is known *a priori* to be true is necessarily true.

According to Hart, in order to show that something, let us say p, is possible, it is enough to show that it is possible that someone imagines that it is the case that p, and for the latter it is sufficient to imagine that it is the case that p. On the other hand, if it is the case that p, then in order to show that p is necessary it is sufficient to show that there could not exist a being endowed with imagination that could imagine that p is not the case. Moreover, some evidence that there could not exist such a being is given by our continuous failures in imagining that it is not the case that p, in case the failures exemplify a coherent and lawful pattern that explains them by remitting to the nature of the subject matter of p. Now, there could certainly be contingent truths, whose negations could be so complex that they would exceed the capabilities of any human imagination. However, Hart does not maintain that the failures in imagining that the negation of a truth is the case is conclusive evidence for the necessity of that truth, since he acknowledges that there could exist more imaginative beings than us that could very well imagine it.

Later (p. 171) Hart maintains that in the same way in which we do not perceive natural numbers, since they are abstract objects, in the same way we cannot imagine natural numbers. We cannot imagine too abstract objects clearly and distinctly. On the other hand, Hart considers that in the same way in which perception is the faculty we use when examining the actual world, imagination is the faculty we use when examining other possible worlds. (The last two theses of Hart are not easily reconcilable. If imagination is the faculty by means of which possible worlds and (at least) some abstract objects are imaginable, though some of them are not imaginable, one can ask how is it that we can maintain that such objects exist. We will try to clarify the relation between those two theses somewhat later.)

Even more problematic is Hart's argumentation, considered by him as his synthesis of Russell, Plato and Hume, and which has a weak version (for necessary truths) and a strong version (for all truths). Hart argues (in the weak version) as follows: Let us consider a necessary truth, all of whose referential parts refer to very abstract objects. Since we cannot imagine them, we cannot imagine them connected in any other way as that in which the necessary truth states that they are connected. From this we inductively infer that it is unimaginable that they are connected in another way as that stated in the necessary truth.

On the basis of such an argumentation Hart will infer a view about some truths of set theory that he calls 'the reverse of Gödel's view'. According to Gödel, since the truth of some axioms of set theory imposes itself on us, we should have something similar to a perception of sets. According to Hart, the known truths of set theory impose themselves on us, that is, -according to him-, we know that they are necessary truths, precisely because we do not have anything remotely similar to a perception of sets, nor have we the capability to imagine them.

The strong version of Hart's 'synthesis' can be obtained from the weak version essentially by replacing 'necessary truth' with 'truth' in all occurrences of that expression in the weak version. In our opinion, however, both the weak and the strong version of Hart's synthesis are built on a really grave confusion –as the following remarks will show. If in the weak version we begin not with a necessary truth about abstract entities -let us call it S-, but with a necessarily false statement about abstract entities, for example, ¬S, we could argue in a similar fashion to Hart's argumentation and conclude that the falsity of ¬S is unimaginable and, hence, it would be unimaginable that S –which is necessarily true- be true. Thus: Let S be a necessarily true statement, all of whose referring expressions refer to very abstract objects. Let us now consider the necessarily false statement ¬S –or any other statement that contradicts S-, all of whose referential expressions refer to very abstract objects. Since they are very abstract, we cannot imagine them clearly and distinctly. Since we do not imagine them, we cannot imagine them in any other way than in that in which they are related in ¬S. Therefore, we inductively infer that it is unimaginable that they be related in any other way different from that in ¬S. Hence, S is unimaginable.

From our argumentation one can infer that, under the hypothesis that very abstract entities are unimaginable, there are necessary truths, that is, truths in any possible world (or at least in any possible world in which the objects referred to by referring expressions occurring in the statements that expresses the necessary truths exist) that are unimaginable. Hence, it is false –under the assumption mentioned above- that imagination is an adequate tool for examining possible worlds. Expressed with more rigour: Either it is possible to imagine very abstract entities, or there are no necessary truths about very abstract entities, or imagination is not an adequate tool to examine possible worlds. Thus, under the Platonist hypotheses -accepted by Hart- that there are very abstract entities and necessary truths about such entities, Hart's two theses mentioned above, namely, (1) that very abstract entities are unimaginable, and (2) that imagination is the faculty that serve us to examine possible worlds, are incompatible. Hart's objective, expressed in (i) and (ii) at the beginning of our discussion of his paper, is simply absurd. (On the other hand, the induction made in Hart's argumentation does not have any justification.) The 'synthesis' between Russell, Plato and Hume seems more entanglement than synthesis. As a matter of fact, we suspect that we have not understood Hart's paper, since we have not been able to find in it anything worthy.

(III) Christian Thiel – Gottlob Frege: Die Abstraktion

Thiel considers the following question as the central theme of Frege's whole work: How do we apprehend logical objects and, in particular, numbers? This question is clearly of an epistemological nature. Frege answers that question, according to Thiel, as follows: We apprehend logical objects by means of abstraction. Thiel considers that Frege deserves special credit for having made the objects of philosophical reflection, and having helped to clarify them, the following questions: how do these abstraction processes occur?, how do they manifest themselves, although irreflexively, as artificial linguistic instruments?, and how can they be introduced, no less artificially but reflexively, in the sciences?

According to Thiel, that which is fundamental for Frege's view of numbers is that in a statement about natural numbers they are attributed to a concept –under which fall things belonging to the totality determined by that concept- a property of second level, which is the property of including under itself exactly so many things. In this way it becomes clear to what sort of entity is a natural number assigned to, namely, to a concept. But it is not clarified of what sort is what is attributed in such a numerical statement to that concept. In *Die Grundlagen der Arithmetik* Frege makes three different attempts to answer the question about the nature of a natural number. In his paper Thiel discusses those three attempts with considerable detail.

It would take us too much space if we tried to follow Thiel in his exposition of the three attempts to define 'natural number'. Nonetheless, it is pertinent to mention the following essential points referred to by Thiel in his discussion of the second and third attempts —which are undoubtedly the most important. On the basis of the second attempt, the definition of natural number would look as follows: The natural number that corresponds to the concept P is the same natural number that corresponds to the concept Q. As Thiel correctly mentions, Frege rejects such a definition. Thiel points out that Frege's objective (i) in part consisted in making recognizable the natural number that corresponds to the concept P when it appears as the natural number that corresponds to a concept Q equinumerous with P; but that (ii) Frege also wanted to logically clarify the concept of natural number, and that could not be reached by merely stipulating that in the statement obtained, for example, $\chi(P)=\chi(Q)$, the expression "$\chi(P)$" would play the role of a proper name of the natural number that corresponds to the concept P, since that is rather always assumed. The definition offered by Frege in his third and final attempt is the following: The natural number corresponding to the concept P = The extension of the concept "equinumerous to the concept P".

Thiel considers the question, whether Frege could have had any answer from his standpoint in *Die Grundlagen der Arithmetik* to a direct question concerning the extensions of concepts. (On this point we should remember that in that book Frege evades that question, while presupposing that the extension of a concept can be determined in a purely logical fashion.) Thiel observes that in that book Frege says nothing about the nature of extensions of concepts, and, thus, it seems incomprehensible that Frege, on the one hand, stresses the importance of the extensions of concepts, especially for the higher sorts of numbers, while at the same time says that he does not concede any decisive importance to the predominant role of the extensions of concepts, since precisely on that role is grounded the logicist programme. (As a matter of fact, Frege adds something more in his extensive footnote of §68. He says that instead of the extension of a concept one could have used the concept itself to define the notion of natural number. Nonetheless, we do not remember any writing in which Frege attempted to give such a definition.)[2]

In *Grundgesetze der Arithmetik* Frege did not take as primitive the statements about extensions of concepts, but rather requires that they be grounded. Thiel reminds us on this issue that Frege introduces extensions of concepts by means of a transition rule in which, according to Thiel, the left side expresses the equality of two extensions of concepts, whereas the right side states that for any permissible argument 'c' the statements 'P(c)' and 'Q(c)' are either both true or both false. In symbols:

$$\varepsilon_x P(x) = \varepsilon_x Q(x) \leftrightarrow (\forall x)(P(x) \leftrightarrow Q(x)).$$

We think that these last assertions of Thiel are not completely correct –neither are those of Frege on this issue. Firstly, one should point out that Frege offers the transition rule for value ranges, not for extensions, although he thinks that extensions are special cases of value ranges. Secondly, in Frege's formal presentation –in contrast to what happens with Thiel's formulation displayed above- there is no distinction between the symbol expressing equivalence and the identity sign. Frege's formalization of the transition rule looks more or less as follows: (Law V) $\vdash (\grave{\varepsilon} f(\varepsilon) = \grave{\alpha} g(\alpha)) = (\forall x)(f(x) = g(x))$. (See on this issue *Grundgesetze der Arithmetik I*, §§20 and 47.) Thirdly, Frege's assertion –which seems to be accepted by Thiel- that extensions of concepts are special cases of value ranges of functions, namely, the special case in which the function has one argument and its value is always a truth-value, is false. Value ranges are sets of pairs, and in the special case of the value ranges of functions of one argument whose value is always a truth-value, as second member of such a pair can very well occur 'the false' and as first member of the

---

[2] A possible explanation of such an assertion could be that Frege has here an inkling of the later difficulties with expressions like 'the concept', which refer not to a concept but to an object related to a concept, which most surely is not a mysterious entity –as some Fregean scholars believe- but simply the extension of the concept. Nonetheless, there is precisely no inkling in *Die Grundlagen der Arithmetik* that Frege had already arrived at the sense-referent distinction, a distinction to which he will later assign so much importance.

pair can very well occur objects for which the concept is defined though they do not fall under the concept. On the other hand, extensions of concepts (i) are not sets of pairs, and (ii) it does not have as members the objects for which the concept has 'the False' as value. Therefore, even if we were to define the extension as a set of pairs, neither the second member of such a pair could be the false nor could the first one be an object for which the concept is defined but that does not fall under the concept, that is, is not a member of its extension.

Later in the paper Thiel remarks that the manner in which extensions are introduced in *Grundgesetze der Arithmetik* is interestingly the same that Frege had developed in his second attempt to define 'natural number' in *Die Grundlagen der Arithmetik* and later rejected as unsatisfactory.

We cannot dwell longer in Thiel's paper, but would like to stress that both this and Thiel's other paper in the same first volume are especially interesting and profound, what cannot surprise us, since Thiel is without doubt one of the very best Fregean scholars.

(IV) Gottfried Gabriel – Einige Einseitigkeiten des Fregeschen Logikbegriffs

Gabriel's paper is one of the most interesting in the whole collection. Its author combines a solid knowledge of Frege's writings with a healthy critical stance that we sometimes miss in many Fregean scholars.

At the beginning of his paper Gabriel points out that Frege's philosophy of language is the product of a working up of logic from the grammar and semantics of colloquial language. According to Gabriel, for Frege psychologism begins with an orientation towards the language of life. Gabriel points out that in his attempts to dissociate logic from psychology Frege was from the beginning too prone to ascribe psychologists everything that could be connected, even in the most indirect way, with psychology. One could even state that Frege assigned to psychology everything that he did not consider logically interesting, for example, grammatical distinctions. Thus, Frege's concept of psychologism was, according to Gabriel, too wide; what certainly affects the understanding of the term 'logic'.

Gabriel's research plan is as follows: He will attempt to show that in his battle to eradicate psychologism, Frege goes too far, extending considerably his concept of psychologism at the expense of a corresponding narrowing of his concept of logic. As examples, Gabriel will discuss Frege's conception of the so-called "colouring of senses", as well as his attitude towards what is known today as "strict implication".

Concerning coloration, Gabriel points out that in "Über Sinn und Bedeutung" Frege not only distinguishes between sense and reference, but also delimits the region of sense, that is, the objective content of linguistic expressions, from the region of colouring. Under the "colouring of sense" (and, especially, under the "colouring of thought") Frege understands the subjective contribution to the linguistic expression. Frege attempts to establish that the differences he considers as logically irrelevant are merely differences in the colouring of thoughts.

Gabriel makes explicit the criterion that seems to be used by Frege to determine whether the contents of two expressions α_1 and α_2 (sentences or not) differ only in their colouring or concern also their senses. The criterion reads as follows: Let us consider pairs of expressions of thoughts, that is, of statements, differing in each case because α_2 replaces α_1 (or the other way around). If it is not possible to find a pair $<S(\alpha_1), S(\alpha_2)>$ such that $S(\alpha_1)$ expresses a true thought and $S(\alpha_2)$ a false one (or the other way around), α_1 and α_2 differ at most in the colouration and not in their sense. This criterion is, thus, also a criterion for the equality of senses of expressions. According to Gabriel, Frege himself gave three different versions of this criterion, namely, one in *Logik*, one in "Kurze Übersicht meiner logischen Lehren", and one in a letter to Husserl of 9 December 1906.[3]

Although we cannot expound here Gabriel's rich and detailed analysis of Frege's notions of colouring and sense, we would like to mention an especially strong criticism of Gabriel, by means of a

---

[3] In that letter what Frege attempts to give is a criterion for logical equivalence in terms of identity of sense, and he is, by the way, wrong. See on this issue Husserl's criticism in his recently published *Vorlesungen über alte und neue Logik: 1908/09* and our review reprinted in this collection.

counterexample, of Frege's demarcation criterion between sense and colouring expounded in the paragraph immediately above.

Gabriel points out that though the statement "All horses in the tournament are horses" is clearly a tautology, the statement "All horses in the tournament are jades" expresses much more. The difference between the two statements is not merely subjective in Frege's usage. One can consider the first statement true and the second false. Thus, by means of Frege's criterion one can show that – in contrast to what Frege thought- expressions like "horse" and "jade" do not differ merely in the colouring. Gabriel concludes that Frege's criterion does not fulfil Frege's expectations, but, on the contrary, shows that the frontier between logic and psychology (in Frege's usage) has to be moved in the direction of psychology.

With respect to Frege's attitude towards modal logic and, especially, towards strict implication, Gabriel offers the following comments: Frege thinks that in order to express a necessary connection one requires besides an expression for conditionality also one for generality. He differentiates between material implication, in usual formalisation: p→q, and formal implication: $(\forall x)(f(x) \to g(x))$. According to Frege, possibility and necessity either can be reduced by means of a partial explanation to the particular affirmative judgement or to the general affirmative one, respectively, or are assigned to the region of the dispositions of the speaker. Frege excludes in principle modal logic from the sphere of logic. Hence, he does not acknowledge strict implication as a connective between statements. According to Frege, the logical component of any statement expressing a necessary connection can be expressed in the form of a formal implication.

In order to illustrate Frege's rejection of modalities, Gabriel comments (pp. 83-85) on the controversy between Frege and Husserl of 1906 with regard to strict implication. Although that issue is certainly very interesting and, as a matter of fact, we have compared Frege's and Husserl's views on other issues (beginning with our doctoral dissertation, *Edmund Husserls Philosophie der Logik und Mathematik im Lichte der gegenwärtigen Logik und Grundlagenforschung*, and especially in our paper "Some Remarks on

Sense and Referent in Frege and Husserl"[4]), we prefer to conclude here our discussion of this interesting paper, since we still want to comment on other six also very interesting papers, some of which will generate some criticisms from us.

(V) Matthias Schirn – Identität und Identitätsaussage bei Frege

At the beginning of his paper Schirn states that if one compares the semantic foundation of the augmenting character of (informative) knowledge of "a=b" in "Über Sinn und Bedeutung" with the corresponding foundation in *Begriffsschrift*, then one will confirm without difficulty that, leaving aside the context of the identity theory, the two foundations differ only terminologically, but not thematically. On this issue Schirn attempts to establish (pp. 181-182) a parallelism between both Fregean conceptions.

In his paper Schirn will mainly consider three aspects of the identity problem in Frege, namely: (1) He will critically consider the question about the essence of equality and will try to show that the equality that one has in mind in the case of a true statement of the form "a=b" neither in the train of thoughts of "Über Sinn und Bedeutung" nor in the frame of the Fregean theory of functions, concepts and relations can be characterized with convincing arguments as a relation of an object with itself. (2) He will consider some questionable consequences concerning identity statements of Frege's subsuming assertive indicative statements under the category of proper names and his conception, immediately related to the former, of taking truth-values to be objects. (3) He will attempt to show that the conception Frege developed, on the basis of his theory of sense and referent, of identity statements expanding our knowledge

---

[4] Although published a year later in *Kant-Studien*, it was already accepted for publication when the present critical review was published. For other papers comparing Husserl's and Frege's views, see the collection of papers of Claire O. Hill and the present author, *Husserl or Frege?: Meaning, Objectivity and Mathematics*, Open Court, La Salle et alia, where the above mentioned paper is also included.

makes possible a conception of identity that does not entail a hypostasis of a predicative non-differentiation, but takes into account the constitutive aspect of identity for an authentic understanding of identity.

Schirn points out that since for Frege the connection of two expressions with the same object is arbitrary, the plausible explanation for the determination of equality of the difference in cognitive value of "a=a" and "a=b", for "a" and "b" two expressions for the same object, as a relation between signs is excluded. On the other hand, as Schirn correctly states, if in "Über Sinn und Bedeutung" Frege rejects on the basis of epistemological considerations the conception of identity given in "Begriffsschrift", he does not maintain there –as Dummett believes- that identity is a relation of an object with itself. On the contrary, Frege argues that if one wanted to see in identity a relation between the referents of "a" and "b", the cognitive value of "a=a" and "a=b" would seem to be the same. Now, Schirn points out that Frege himself encourages interpretations like Dummett's when he carelessly states in "Ausführungen über Sinn und Bedeutung" that identity is a relation between objects and in *Grundgesetze der Arithmetik I* that it is a relation of an object with itself.

However, Schirn points out that in "Über Sinn und Bedeutung" identity cannot be either a relation of an object with itself, or between two signs, or a relation between two objects. Furthermore, if identity were a relation of an object with itself, one could ask whether it is really a relation and not a concept. It also does not seem clear how can we justify that we talk about two equal objects (that is, objects that coincide in everything) on the Leibnizian basis of Frege, according to which two objects cannot differ only numerically. If two objects are predicatively indistinguishable, they are the same object. If Frege were to define identity as a relation between two objects, he would be exposed to that paradoxical situation.

Schirn concludes that his arguments (pp. 192-196) show that identity cannot be introduced in the frame of Frege's theory of functions, concepts and relations either as a relation between objects or as a relation of an object with itself.

In the last part of his paper Schirn will offer as solution a relativist conception of identity. On this issue, he argues that, for example, with the statement "The Morning Star is the same as the Evening Star" one does not assess that the morning star and the evening star are absolutely the same star, but only that they are relatively the same. The morning star and the evening star do not coincide in all their properties, they are not indistinguishable.

We completely agree with the sharp remarks made by Schirn against those views on identity statements that conceive them as expressing either a relation between two objects or a relation of an object with itself (views between which Dummett fluctuates in his rendering of Frege, as pointed above). We also coincide with Schirn's rendering of the reasons why Frege had to reject the view that identity statements express a relation between signs. Schirn's remarks on the interpretations of identity statements in "Ausführungen über Sinn und Bedeutung" and *Grundgesetze der Arithmetik I* seem also appropriate.[5] However, Schirn's solution, namely, that what is expressed in "a=b", in case that is a true statement, is a relative identity between the referent of "a" and the referent of "b", is by no means convincing. In our opinion, Schirn's rendering of Frege's views is as confusing as the renderings he criticized. The referent of "the Morning Star" is exactly identical to the referent of "the Evening Star". What happens is that in a semantic theory of sense and reference –as Frege's- the relation expressed in identity statements is a congruence relation between the senses of proper names, in which the congruence relation is determined by the identity of reference. Thus, an identity statement is true exactly when both senses belong to the same equivalence class determined by their reference, that is, when they have the same referent. This referent, of course, is exactly identical to itself.[6]

---

[5] Nonetheless, such expressions of Frege seem more like slips of the tongue, since both writings belong to the period begun with "Funktion und Begriff" in 1891, where the sense-reference distinction appeared for the first time. In fact, in §2 of *Grundgesetze der Arithmetik I*, the sense-reference distinction is introduced in a similar fashion as in "Über Sinn und Bedeutung".

[6] See our paper "Identity Statements in the Semantics of Sense and Reference" in *Logique et Analyse 25 (100)*, December 1982, pp. 399-411, reprinted in Claire O. Hill and Guillermo E. Rosado Haddock, *Husserl or Frege?*, 2000, reprint 2003, pp. 41-51.

(VI) Bertram Kienzle – Notiz zu Freges Theorien der Identität

This very brief paper (three pages long) of the youngest contributor to this collection is a small jewel of philosophical analysis.

At the beginning of his paper Kienzle points out that one should not identify "augmenting knowledge" with "being synthetic". Now, according to Kienzle, in *Begriffsschrift* the judgements of content identity, at least when two different names are connected with different ways of fixing the reference, all are synthetic. The grounds for that are given by the arbitrariness of the connection between a name and what is named.

According to Kienzle, the treatment of identity statements in "Über Sinn und Bedeutung" originates in the incompatibility between the interpretation of the content identity in *Begriffsschrift* and Frege's logicist views.

Now, if one renders identity as a relation in the realm of objects, one would have to consider analytic all true identity statements –including the geometric ones. Kienzle does not develop sufficiently that issue. On the basis of Frege's definition of analyticity, a statement is analytic if and only if it is a logical principle or can be derived exclusively from logical principles (and definitions). A possible explanation of Kienzle's assertion is that on the basis of such a conception of identity statements, all true identity statements would be instantiations of some logical law of identity expressing the identity of an object with itself. This explanation of Kienzle's assertion is not satisfying, but we do not know of any other explanation –under the supposition that Kienzle understands under 'analytic' the same as Frege does. On the other hand, what is perfectly clear is that if we render identity statements as expressing a relation of identity of an object with itself, then all true identity statements –even the empirical ones- would be necessary. (See on this issue our critical remarks of Kripke in our discussion of Khatchadourian's paper below.)

Kienzle does not try to solve the problem of identity statements in Frege, but simply concludes that in "Über Sinn und Bedeutung Frege has the task of explaining the nature of identity statements, since identity cannot be a relation between objects –since then all true identity statements would be analytic- or a relation between names or signs –since in such case all identity statements would be synthetic.

(VII) Haig Khatchadourian – Kripke and Frege on Identity Statements

Khatchadourian begins his paper with a brief exposition of Kripke's views on identity statements, which he will later critically assess. Khatchadourian coincides with Kripke in considering necessary all true identity statements between proper names as usually understood (not in Frege's usage) –or at least those that refer to existent objects. For Khatchadourian, as for Kripke, proper names are rigid designators and all true identity statements between rigid designators are necessary. According to Khatchadourian (a) the rigidity of its subject and predicate terms in a true identity statement and (b) the necessary identity of something with itself, are a logically sufficient condition for a statement to be necessarily true. But (a) is not a logically necessary condition for it. Khatchadourian considers that since Kripke tends to ignore it, he fails in localizing the logical origin of the necessity of true identity statements between rigid designators that are necessarily true and, especially, the necessity of identity statements between rigid designators.

According to Khatchadourian, the truth of Kripke's thesis on the necessity of identity statements between proper names partially depends on the assumption that proper names that refer to non-existent things (more exactly: to merely possible ones), refer to the same objects in all possible situations, as do proper names that refer to existent objects in the actual world.

Although Khatchadourian coincides with Kripke in maintaining that "Cicero is Tully" is a necessarily true identity statement, he accuses Kripke of confusing (i) the fact that "Cicero" and Tully" are rigid designators with (ii) the problem of personal identity and, hence, of essentialism. Kripke needed to establish (i), since (ii) is not under discussion when considering the necessity or contingency of true identity statements between proper names referring to persons. According to Khatchadourian, the most important reason for the rigidity of proper names in any counterfactual statement is that it is a condition of its intelligibility.

On this last issue it should be pointed out that in any discourse we usually presuppose and, as a matter of fact, take it as a condition of its intelligibility that we use not only proper names but also (definite) descriptions to refer always to the same object. When we say "Tully could had not been a senator" and "The man who denounced Catiline could had not been a senator" in both cases the intelligibility of the sentences presupposes that the proper names and descriptions in such statements refer to the objects that are their referents in the actual world. In this sense proper names in the strict sense are not more rigid than (definite) descriptions. Now, there certainly are unusual situations in which with a statement like "The man who denounced Catiline could have not been a senator' one wants to express not that the man Cicero could not have been a senator (usual situation), but that a person different from the man Cicero and also not a senator –for example, an accomplice of Catilina- would have been the person who denounced Catiline. In such a situation the statement would be expressing the possibility that the (definite) description could have had a different referent from the one it has in the actual world. But also the statements "Tully could have not been a senator" and even "Tully could have not been Cicero" admit similar renderings. The first statement could be expressing the possibility that the word "Tully" could have had a different referent than the one it has in the actual world, that is, the man Cicero. The second statement could be expressing the possibility that the proper names 'Tully" and "Cicero" could have had different referents, though in the actual world they have the same one.[7] Thus, there is no difference of rigidity between proper names and (definite) descriptions.)

On the other hand, we agree with Khatchadourian's contention that Kripke confounds the presumed rigidity of proper names with

---

[7] Imagine the situation in which the names "Tully" and "Cicero" referred not to the same person but to identical twins, one of which was a senator and the other a writer. In such minimal variant of the actual world, the statement "Tully is Cicero" would be false, whereas "Tully is a senator" would be true, and "Cicero is a senator" would be false.

personal identity. In fact, Kripke himself accepts that the names "Hesperus" and "Phosphorus" could have referred to different celestial bodies. However, he alleges that those two proper names are rigid designators, and argues on its behalf that the referent of "Hesperus" and of "Phosphorus", that is, the planet Venus, is identical to itself in every possible world. But that has nothing to do with the rigidity of proper names. On the other hand, the fact that Kripke can maintain that the statement "Hesperus is Phosphorus" is necessarily true, while the statement "The Morning Star is the Evening Star" is only contingently true is based not on any difference of rigidity between strict proper names and (definite) descriptions, but on what follows: (i) For Kripke proper names do not have a (Fregean) sense, while definite descriptions do have it. (ii) He interprets the identity between definite descriptions as Frege does, namely, as a congruence relation between senses having the same referent (or, at least, does not interpret it as an identity of their referents). (iii) He interprets the identity between two proper names as an identity between their referents. Now, if he were to interpret the identity between descriptions as identity of their referents, or if he were to presuppose that proper names have senses and were to interpret the identity between proper names as a congruence between senses with the same referent, the same 'arguments' on behalf (or against) the rigidity of proper names (respectively, the non-rigidity of descriptions) could be applied in the case of descriptions (respectively, of proper names). On the other hand, on the basis of the two diverging interpretations of identity statements mentioned in (ii) and (iii), an identity statement between a proper name in the strict sense and a definite description would be a logical monstrosity, since it would be expressing an identity relation between an object, for example, Cicero, and a sense, for example, the sense of the expression "the man who denounced Catiline". Thus, in brief: Kripke's conception, according to which, true identity statements between proper names are necessary, whereas true identity statements between definite descriptions are usually contingent, is based on (i) the confusion between the problem of the presumed rigidity of some expressions with the identity of an object with itself, and (ii) the diverging renderings on which the identity between proper names and that between definite descriptions are based. Once such confusions are set aside, it is clear that (i) there is no difference with respect to necessity or contingency between those two sorts of statements, and (ii) as stated already at the end of the last paragraph: there is no difference in rigidity between proper names and definite descriptions.

In the second part of his paper Khatchadourian expounds what he considers is Frege's conception of identity statements. We are not going to offer a detailed assessment of that discussion, since we have already extended us more than enough with this paper. Nonetheless, it seems convenient to insert a few remarks: (i) On p. 283 Khatchadourian identifies, on the one hand "*a priori*" and "analytic" in Frege, and, on the other hand, "*a posteriori*" and "synthetic". That is completely unwarranted. On this point it seems pertinent to remind the reader that for Frege geometrical theorems are both synthetic and *a priori*. Moreover, it seems convenient to reread §3 of *Die Grundlagen der Arithmetik*. (ii) On p. 284 Khatchadourian states that Frege's distinction between *a priori* and *a posteriori* coincides with that of Kripke. On this issue it should be pointed out that Kripke does not have a clear idea of the distinction between *a priori* and *a posteriori*, and that precisely the presumed examples given by Kripke of mathematical examples of necessities *a posteriori* (for example, Goldbach's conjecture) are based on notions of *a priori* and *a posteriori* completely alien to the tradition of Leibniz, Kant, Frege and Husserl. Not even after he abandoned logicism at the end of his life did Frege dare to maintain that there were statements that were necessarily true but *a posteriori*. With regard to the unacceptability of such a rendering of Frege, we refer the reader to the relevant arguments given by Schirn and Kienzle in the papers discussed above.

(VIII) Michael D. Resnik – Frege's Context Principle Revisited

In an earlier paper Resnik had argued that Frege's acceptance of the Context Principle -according to which words have meaning only in the context of sentences- was limited to the period in which he wrote *Die Grundlagen der Arithmetik*. Sluga submitted Resnik's thesis to criticism, and in the paper under discussion Resnik reaffirms his thesis, arguing that Frege used the Context Principle to solve a series of problems, but that he later abandoned it and offered other solutions. Moreover, almost at the beginning of the paper Resnik points out that if it were true that Frege never abandoned the Context Principle, then one would have to ask whether in that principle, once the distinction between sense and referent was made, the word "meaning" should be rendered as "sense", or as "referent", or as an amalgamation of both, or as something different from any of those possible renderings.

According to Resnik, in *Die Grundlagen der Arithmetik* the meanings of statements are judgeable contents, though Frege does not say anything explicit about them. Judgeable contents have to be abstract entities, that is, objective entities that are neither in space nor in time. Frege's writings do not offer an unequivocal answer to the question whether already in 1884 Frege acknowledged the existence of unities of meaning smaller than judgeable contents, though the most plausible rendering of Frege's theory of meaning in *Die Grundlagen der Arithmetik* is that only sentences but not single words had meaning.

Resnik states that only later, while considering the problem of how we are capable of understanding sentences that we had never heard before, did Frege have to acknowledge the independent meanings of words.

Later (pp. 43-45) Resnik comments on Dummett's rendering of the Context Principle in its relation to the abstract entities. According to Resnik and contrary to Dummett's assessment, the Context Principle is not used by Frege to establish the existence of numbers or classes, but rather as a methodological principle in order to assess their nature. Whereas Dummett's rendering, according to Resnik, considers that there is a problem with the existence of abstract entities, he considers that Frege presupposes the existence of abstract entities as a basic unquestionable premise and never questions the objectivity and truth of mathematics.

According to Resnik, after 1884 Frege abandoned the Context Principle. Moreover, such a principle not only is not present in his later writings, but is explicitly contradicted by Frege, and where it had been applied, Frege applied different methods. For example, in *Die Grundlagen der Arithmetik* he applies it in his criticism of psychologism, objecting to it for asking about the meaning of isolated words. But after 1884 Frege continued his battle against psychologism, though without making use of that objection.

Resnik argues that Frege was seriously concerned with the problem of explaining how we can understand sentences we had never heard before, and -in order to solve that problem- in his later writings he assigned independent senses to single words and postulated an isomorphism between the construction of senses and the construction of thoughts. The meaning of sentences, instead of conferring meaning to the words, was a function of the meanings of the words. (Resnik uses the relatively neutral word "meaning", since what he maintains applies in "Über Sinn und Bedeutung" both to the senses and to the referents. However, in the case of the referents of atomic sentences the issue is by no means as clear as Frege seemed to believe.) The Context Principle does not explain how compound thoughts –compound of thoughts with independent existence- build unities. Frege's work in the semantics of propositional logic led him to formulate that question, and as he did it, according to Resnik, he introduced unsaturated truth-functions to resolve the problem.

(IX) Ernst Tugendhat – Die Bedeutung des Ausdrucks 'Bedeutung' bei Frege

Tugendhat begins his paper by observing that the translations of 'Bedeutung' in Frege either as 'reference', 'denotation' or 'nominatum' tend to generate confusions, since all such translations lead us to think that Frege understood under the 'Bedeutung' of an expression the object designed by it. According to Tugendhat, however, this cannot be the case, since Frege speaks of the 'Bedeutung' not only of proper names, but also of predicates.[8]

---

[8] As a matter of fact, Frege also speaks of the 'Bedeutung' of statements, namely 'the True' or 'the False", which in *Grundgesetze der Arithmetik I* are acknowledged as the foremost logical objects. Tugendhat seems to forget that Frege was a Platonist and rationalist, with no qualms for acknowledging the existence of properties and relations also as sorts of abstract entities, though incomplete or unsaturated ones.

Tugendhat suggests that we translate 'Bedeutung' into English as 'significance'.

In this paper Tugendhat will discuss the problem of the 'Bedeutung' both of statements and predicates. (We prefer not to translate 'Bedeutung' in the context of our commentaries of Tugendhat's paper, since we consider Tugendhat's translation as 'significance' by far less adequate than those he rejects.)

With regard to the doctrine of the 'Bedeutung' of statements, according to Tugendhat, there are two parties, namely, that of the Kneale's, which reject it because it ignores important semantic distinctions, and that of Church, who accepts it on the basis of some analogies between the reference (Tugendhat uses the word 'Referenz') of a name and the truth-value of a statement. According to Tugendhat, the observations of both parties are correct, but he considers that neither of them builds a sufficient base either to reject or to accept Frege's doctrine.

According to Tugendhat, recent semantics has a technical term for the word 'Bedeutung', not already compromised with the name relation, namely, 'extension'. We cannot agree with Tugendhat on this point. The German term for the English word 'extension' is 'Umfang', and this one is used by Frege as a technical term to: (i) designate that object, which is the collection of those objects that fall under a given concept; and (ii) contrast it with the concept, which is for Frege the referent of the conceptual word, whereas the extension, precisely because of being an object, cannot be, according to Frege, the 'Bedeutung' of a conceptual word.[9] Moreover, we think that the translation of 'Bedeutung' as either 'denotation' or 'reference' seems to imply that the 'Bedeutung' of any expression is an object only to someone who ignores Frege's fundamental ontological distinction between objects and concepts, and the corresponding linguistic distinction between proper names and conceptual words. Certainly, for

---

[9] On this issue it is especially pertinent to look at Frege's letter to Husserl of the 24th of May 1891, in which he objects to Husserl's taking the extension and not the concept as the referent of conceptual words in the latter's similar semantic distinction between sense and referent. For Husserl, the concept is the sense of, in Fregean terminology, conceptual words.

Frege concepts are (abstract) entities, but not objects (neither concrete nor abstract).

Later Tugendhat argues that since Frege considers that we are interested in the 'Bedeutung' of a part of a sentence only when we are interested in the truth-value of the sentence, we can conclude that the 'Bedeutung' of the parts of a sentence and, very especially, of proper names consists in its contribution to the truth-value of sentences. On that basis, Tugendhat suggests that we have to invert the order and ask first for the 'Bedeutung' of sentences and later try to define the 'Bedeutung' of proper names by means of that concept used to define the 'Bedeutung' of sentences. With this objective, Tugendhat introduces his notion of a 'potential of truth-value'. According to him, two expressions Φ and Ψ have exactly the same potential of truth-value when each time that they are extended (or complemented) by the same expression in order to build sentences, let us say, $S(\Phi)$ and $S(\Psi)$, respectively, these sentences have the same truth-value. In the special case in which Φ and Ψ are sentences, the phrase 'when they are extended by the same expression in order to build sentences' is, according to Tugendhat, superfluous, and the definition reduces to the following: two sentences 'p' and 'q' have exactly the same potential of truth-value when they have the same truth-value. Tugendhat renders 'Bedeutung' as potential of truth-value.

In order to back his rendering of 'Bedeutung', Tugendhat makes use of the so-called Context Principle –according to which (as seeing above) an expression has a meaning only in the context of a sentence- and to a sort of modification of what he calls 'Frege's Substitutivity Principle' –according to which the 'Bedeutung of a sentence needs to remain invariant when you replace some of its constituent expressions with other expressions with different senses but the same 'Bedeutung'. The 'modification' consists in the fact that Tugendahat begins by identifying the truth-value of sentences with their 'Bedeutung' and then stipulates that the property of names that will remain invariant when we interchange them in sentences that remain equal in everything else without affecting the truth-value, is going to be called the 'Bedeutung' of the names.

It should be pointed out, however, that neither Frege in "Über Sinn und Bedeutung", nor Frege in 'Einleitung in die Logik' or

Church in his *Introduction to Mathematical Logic* were able to show by means of what Tugendhat called the 'Principle of Substitutivity' (nor by any other means) that the 'Bedeutung' of a sentence is a truth-value. (See on this point our already mentioned paper "Some Remarks on Sense and Reference in Frege and Husserl", in which we consider other possible candidates for the 'Bedeutung' of sentences.[10]) On the other hand, with regard to the Context Principle we coincide with the analyses of both Resnik and Shwayder – whose paper we will assess below. More exactly, we think that: (i) There does not seem to be any evidence of Frege endorsing the Context Principle after 1890. (ii) If one argues –contrary to (i)- that Frege continued believing in that principle, one should ask whether it applies to the senses, to the 'Bedeutungen', to both or to what. (iii) The Context Principle does not seem to be compatible with Frege's conception from 1891 on about the sense and the 'Bedeutung', according to which the sense of a compound expression is a function of the senses of its constituent expressions, and the 'Bedeutung' of a compound expression is a function (or, at least, pretends to be) of the 'Bedeutungen' of the constituent expressions. Now, none of these two functions has an inverse function. It is by no means clear how we would obtain the 'Bedeutungen' of the constituent expressions from the 'Bedeutung' of an atomic sentence, even if one presupposes –since it cannot be proved- that the 'Bedeutung' of that sentence is a truth-value. Therefore, Tugendhat's modification of Frege's Principle of Substitutivity does not seem to have the least plausibility of success. According to Frege, sentences (atomic or compound) have only two possible referents: the True and the False. To try to obtain from those two the referents of the constituent expressions of each and every sentence of a language is simply crazy. As can be seen by examining Church's discussion mentioned above, it is possible to make the most varied substitutions of constituent expressions without affecting the truth-value. On the other hand, an expression can occur in denumerably many different sentences of a language (that is, in as

---

[10] On this point one should consult Oswaldo Chateaubriand's criticism of the many variants of the so-called 'Slingshot Argument' in the first volume of his outstanding book *Logical Forms* (2 vols.).

many as there are natural numbers), and, thus, following Tugendhat's method we could never exhaust them and conclude that two expressions Φ and Ψ have the same 'Bedeutung' no matter how big is the (necessarily finite) sample of sentences in which we have replaced Φ with Ψ or the other way around, leaving the rest of the sentence concerned untouched and without affecting the truth-value of the sentence. Moreover, in order to know the 'Bedeutung' of a sentence in a non-arbitrary way –be it a truth-value or not- it seems that we need to know first the 'Bedeutung' of the constituent expressions.

With regard to the potential of truth-value of expressions, it should be stressed that it is not a good *'explicans'* for Frege's 'Bedeutung'. Let us consider the conceptual words 'least even number' and 'even prime number'. These two conceptual words would have, according to Frege, different 'Bedeutungen', namely, the concept "least even number" and the concept "even prime number". Now, let Φ be the conceptual word 'least even number' and Ψ the conceptual word 'even prime number'. Then (in extensional contexts), given a sentence S(Φ) in which Φ occurs, one can replace one or more occurrences of Φ in S(Φ) with Ψ -and, thus, obtaining as sentence S(Ψ)- without affecting the truth-value. On the basis of Tugendhat's definition of potential of truth-value, Φ and Ψ have the same potential of truth-value, but on the basis of Frege's conception Φ and Ψ have different 'Bedeutungen'. Thus, the potential of truth-value is not a good *'explicans'* and precisely in the case of conceptual words, for Frege's 'Bedeutung'.

In the remaining part of his paper Tugendhat discusses the problem of the 'Bedeutung' of conceptual words and applies his conception of the potential of truth-value to the analysis of the indirect 'Bedeutung'. Since we have already shown by means of a counterexample the inadequacy of Tugendhat's *'explicans'* for 'Bedeutung', it seems uninteresting to dwell on that remaining part of the paper.

(X) David S. Shwayder – On the Determination of Reference by Sense

At the beginning of his paper Shwayder points out that Frege did not sufficiently worked out his views on sense in their relation to his theories of logic and language. Frege was very little explicit and somewhat imprecise on that issue. Shwayder goes on to expound more systematically Frege's views on sense.

Shwayder extracts twelve principles from 'Über Sinn und Bedeutung' and *Grundgesetze der Arithmetik* that characterize Frege's notions of sense and reference and their relation. They are the following:

(i) Every (meaningful) expression has a sense and should have only one sense. We can, thus, stipulate the existence of a function, let us call it Σ, from the expressions to their senses.

(ii) The sense of a complex expression is determined by the senses of its constituent expressions. There should be rules of semantic concatenation, and we can then stipulate the existence of a concatenation function, K_1, according to which $\Sigma(A_1 \frown A_2) = K_1(\Sigma(A_1), \Sigma(A_2))$.

(iii) Anything can be a referent, be they objects or functions, and even senses. On the other hand, many things are not senses, for example, the sun or the True.

(iv) Expressions can very well lack a referent.

(v) Expressions with referent have only one referent.

(vi) The rules of an adequate concept script guarantee us that any (meaningful) expression in that notation has a unique referent. If we have such a concept script, this allows us to stipulate the existence of a reference function R from the expressions to entities (that is, either functions or objects).

(vii) The referent of a complex expression is completely determined by the referents of its constituent parts. Thus, we have here another concatenation function, K_2, such that $R(A_1 \frown A_2) = K_2(R(A_1), R(A_2))$.

(viii) If an expression A does not have a referent, then any complex expression having A as a constituent part is also devoid of referent. If $RS(A_j)$ is not defined, then neither are $R(A_i \frown A_j)$ nor $R(A_j \frown A_k)$ are defined.

(ix) Each sense determines at most a unique referent, for any expression with sense. In an adequate concept script it is our objective that to any sense expressible in the concept script there is assigned a value. More precisely, that for any sense s, there is a referent r such that S(s)=r, where S is a function from senses to referents.

(x) Since different senses can determine the same referent, there is no inverse function S^{-1} from referents to senses.

(xi) Since both the sense and the referent assigned to an expression could have been constituted in a different way, neither K_1 nor K_2 has an inverse. This is clearly required by Frege's comments on the reference and seems to be also true for the senses, which sometimes are also referents.

(xii) The referents of statements are truth-values.

Shwayder considers questionable that both the referents of the constituent expressions, as well as their senses determine the referent of complex expressions —especially, the truth-value of statements. Thus, for him the following equation —let us call it 'Δ'- is by no means clear: $K_2(S*\Sigma(A_1)),S*\Sigma(A_2)) = S(K_1(\Sigma(A_1),\Sigma(A_2)))$. (Shwayder's query is certainly justified, since both the assignment of a truth-value as referent to a simple thought —that is, a thought without constituent parts that are also thoughts- as well as the stipulation that, for example, when A_1 is a proper name and A_2 a conceptual word, r_1 is the object that is the referent of A_1 and r_2 is the referent of A_2, then $r_2(r_1)$ is a truth-value, are completely arbitrary. More precisely: The assignment of truth-values as referents of statements is arbitrary, since there are other candidates that fulfil Frege's invariance requirement. Hence, it seems that the lack of intuitiveness does not concern so much the commutativity of the diagram corresponding to the equation Δ, but to the arbitrariness of the last vertex of the diagram.)

Later in the paper Shwayder considers the problem discussed by Resnik, namely, of the permanence of the Context Principle in Frege's work after 1890, and arrives essentially at the same conclusions. According to him, in *Die Grundlagen der Arithmetik* Frege invokes only once the Context Principle announced at the beginning of that work. (We think that Frege invokes it twice, once in §60 and once in §66.) Moreover, Frege never mentions it in later writings published during his lifetime. When Frege introduced his distinction between sense and referent, it became unclear whether the Context Principle would apply to senses, to referents or to a combination of both. But Shwayder does not think that such was the reason to abandon the principle. He rather believes that Frege abandoned it on the following grounds: (i) because he could not accept both the Context Principle in all its generality and his new semantics; (ii) because he did not need it anymore. He could not accept it on the basis of his semantics because there is no inverse function from the sense or from the referent of a statement to the referents of its constituent expressions. Moreover, Shwayder points out that in *Die Grundlagen der Arithmetik* Frege denied the Context Principle any application to conceptual words. Such a principle was introduced as a sort of protective means against psychologism, but precisely the critique of psychologism made unnecessary the defence against it.

At the end of his paper Shwayder sketches a theory of his about statements, which is part of a broader project of constructing a system of intensional logic. We think, however, that what has been said about this paper is more than sufficient to convince the reader of its importance. In our opinion, this is one of the very best papers in this collection. Both because of the lucidity of its exposition as of the correctness and pertinence of his critical remarks, Shwayder's paper should be studied by anyone interested in Frege's semantics.

Essay Review of Matthias Schirn (ed.), *Frege: Importance and Legacy*, Berlin, Walter De Gruyter, 1996, viii + 466 pp.

As happened two decades ago with his three volume collection of papers *Studies on Frege's Logic* (Frommann-Holzboog 1976), the present collection of papers on Frege edited by Matthias Schirn is exemplary both for the high quality of the papers and for the detailed and careful introduction that the editor has contributed. We are convinced that the present collection, mostly on Frege's philosophy of mathematics but including also papers on other Fregean issues, will be regarded as an irreplaceable reading for years to come for everyone who wants to acquire a profound understanding of Frege's contributions to philosophy, its strengths and some of its weaknesses. The book, which originates in a conference organized by the editor in Munich in 1991, consists of a long introduction by the editor followed by sixteen papers written by as many distinguished Fregean scholars.

The introduction, more than forty pages long, is an excellent introductory essay to Frege's philosophy of mathematics. It easily divides into three parts, namely, Frege's philosophy of arithmetic, his conception of real numbers and his views on geometry. The most detailed treatment by Schirn corresponds to the most detailed treatment by Frege, i.e. that of Frege's conception of arithmetic as a branch of logic and, especially, of numbers as logical objects. In his excellent exposition Schirn tries to throw light on some unclear areas both of Die Grundlagen der Arithmetik (briefly: GlA) and Grundgesetze der Arithmetik (GgA), acknowledging in some cases that Frege's remarks at different places are not easy to reconcile. This is the case (e.g. see p. 10) with the issue of whether truth-values and courses-of-values are the only members of the domain of first-order quantifiers in GgA or whether Frege is operating with an all encompassing domain. On the one hand, as Schirn correctly puts it (pp. 11, 12), Frege's axioms in GgA do not require the existence of any objects other than truth-values and courses-of-values, but a restriction to those objects seems to be at odds with several Fregean remarks. Concerning Frege's conception of real numbers, Schirn observes (p. 15) that Frege passes over in silence

Cantor's proof that the cardinality of the power set of any given set S is greater than that of S.

A similar remark is made by Schirn when discussing Frege's views on geometry (pp. 26, 27). Schirn is somewhat surprised that no reference is made to the work of Riemann and Helmholtz. We, on the other hand, are surprised that a scholar who has dealt for such a long time with Frege's writings is still surprised himself when acknowledging that Frege prefers to ignore an important author—in case he does not distort his views. With respect to Frege's views on geometry (pp. 19, 20) Schirn offers a detailed list of Frege's theses on geometry, only one of which, according to Schirn, was later abandoned when at the end of his life Frege replaced logicism by a geometrical foundation of arithmetic.

In the rest of this part of his essay Schirn tries to show that, even though Frege's views on geometry were similar to Kant's, the grounds for such views were different. Particularly, there is in Frege no transcendental idealism in the background. There is some tension, however, between some of Schirn's comments on Frege's views on spatial intuition, for on p. 26 he adduces that spatial intuition is for Frege subjective and incommunicable, whereas on p. 28 he mentions that Frege was convinced that everything geometrical must be (spatially) intuitable, and, of course, Euclidean (intuitable) geometry was for Frege objective. In the rest of the introduction Schirn offers a brief survey of the papers in the collection. We will now follow Schirn's footsteps and briefly survey most of the papers with some longer surveys of half a dozen.

(1) Michael D. Resnik's paper 'On positing mathematical objects 'is also a critical paper on Frege, especially, on Frege's mishandling of other important researchers' views, and an attempt to offer alternative views. Nothing less could be expected of one of the foremost Fregean scholars in the world who happens to be also a philosopher of mathematics holding views clearly distinct from those of Frege. At the beginning of his interesting paper Resnik states something that should by now be common knowledge for all non-dogmatic Fregean scholars, namely, that Frege tried to focus on the lack of precision and rigour in the writings of thinkers as important as

Cantor, Dedekind or Hilbert—one could also very well add the young Husserl and probably others to that list—discrediting them and overlooking the importance and originality of their writings. Resnik expounds some of Dedekind's and Hilbert's views—of Cantor he says very little—not only on their own right but also in order to introduce his own views. Before properly commenting on the bulk of Resnik's paper, we should like to mention that he, more emphatically than Schirn in the introductory essay, states as an example of Frege's lack of appreciation of other mathematicians' writings, that in GgA Frege rejected the definitions of real numbers given by Weierstrass, Dedekind and Cantor, although later in the same work he propounded a view of the reals which from a mathematical point of view was very similar to theirs (p. 47).

Concerning Dedekind, Resnik observes (p. 50) that he was not a reductionist, since he did not try, e.g. to reduce the natural numbers to sets of systems. We rather create them by starting with a simply infinite system and abstracting from the particular features both of its elements and of its generation. Moreover, Dedekind does not identify the real numbers with his famous cuts, but rather a real number is created to correspond to each cut and is uniquely associated with it. Resnik states (p. 52) that contrary to Frege and Dedekind, Hilbert was not interested in any a priori foundations of mathematics. As is well known, Hilbert conceived axioms as devices for introducing and specifying mathematical concepts. For Resnik, Hilbert's postulationism was a way of avoiding Cantor's and Dedekind's psychologically flavoured talk about creation and abstraction (pp. 45, 52). More specifically, Hilbert wanted, according to Resnik, to substitute his thesis that we recognize new structures by way of axiom systems that postulate them, for Dedekind's creationist thesis. Resnik calls Hilbert's thesis 'epistemological' and Dedekind's 'ontological', but we are not sure whether such a terminology is more enlightening than confusing.

Although Resnik acknowledges (pp. 45-46) that at first sight postulationism does not seem easy to reconcile with mathematical realism, that is precisely the path that he is going to follow. He propounds a sort of mathematical structuralist realism and at the same time adheres to what he calls (p. 56) a postulational epistemology. Of course, he is conscious that, as Frege has argued and almost every philosopher of mathematics knows (or so we hope), we cannot create mathematical objects simply by postulating them (pp. 56, 57). This is the reason why Resnik claims that he is no ontological postulationist but an epistemological one, who regards positing mathematical objects just as a way to recognize something—in Resnik's case, mathematical structures—that already exist independently of us and of our postulating them. It is in this sense that Resnik is a mathematical structuralist realist, one might say, of a postulationist flavour. Resnik takes from Dedekind, as he acknowledges (p. 58), the view that mathematical objects are just positions in structures with no other purely mathematical features than those derived from their relationships to other positions in the structure that contains them.

From Hilbert Resnik takes not only his postulationism but also his views on mathematical existence and truth as related to the consistency of axiom systems. Resnik claims (p. 60) that his postulationist epistemology commits him to acknowledge the independent existence of mathematical objects—in the sense of being a postulationism of independently existing mathematical structures. One could very well think, however, that his postulationism is perfectly compatible with fictionalism. Conscious of this possible objection, Resnik tries to distance himself from fictionalism arguing that, contrary to fictional objects, mathematical posits must answer to a clear mathematical need, e.g. they could help us 'answer questions that were independent of our previous mathematics' or could help us 'systematize and extend a body of previous results' (pp. 61, 62). Moreover, Resnik adds that, contrary to fictional objects, mathematical posits 'are hypotheses that we are prepared to modify or withdraw in the face of evidence that they are inconsistent, have unwanted models, fail to yield the consequences we seek or poorly fit our broader mathematical and scientific programs' (p. 62).

We agree with Resnik that mathematical entities are clearly distinct from fictional objects, but are not convinced that his postulationism is a sufficient antidote against fictionalism, and think that his arguments can at best be seen as a first step towards a differentiation from fictionalism, certainly not doing justice to some mathematical facts. As a realist alternative to fictionalisms, nominalisms and constructivisms, Resnik's feeble Platonism seems not enough. Stronger arguments and a less timid stance seem to be required. However, this is not the place for a lengthy discussion of these issues. Incidentally Resnik very correctly argues (pp. 65, 66), as we have also argued elsewhere, not only that, by their very nature, mathematical objects cannot occur in causal chains, but that some entities posited by physicists cannot be causally connected to us.

(2) W. W. Tait's paper ' Frege versus Cantor and Dedekind: On the Concept of Number' is the most critical of Frege of all papers here and one of the most interesting. By the way, it is perhaps the most congenial to the present author's views on Frege's importance and legacy, to use the pompous words of the title. Tait begins his paper with a quotation from Michael Dummett, who at the end of his Frege: Philosophy of Mathematics wrote that Frege was the greatest philosopher of mathematics ever. On this matter, Tait remarks 'that one has to have a rather circumscribed view of what constitutes philosophy to subscribe to such a statement—or indeed to any ranking in philosophy of mathematics' (p. 71). Moreover, Tait criticizes the sharp distinction between what is philosophical and what is technical—and, thus, non-philosophical.

Concerning some of the most important foundational and philosophical problems of mathematics in the second half of the nineteenth century, Tait claims (p. 71) that Frege showed a particular incapacity to contribute to their solution and sometimes even to assess them. Thus, e.g. he seriously misunderstood, and contributed nothing, to the clarification of the transfinite initiated by Bolzano (who was never mentioned explicitly by Frege in his published writings) and to which Cantor made such extraordinary contributions. Likewise, Frege seems not to have fully assessed either Cantor's distinction between cardinal and ordinal numbers—a distinction, as is well known, essentially relevant for the transfinite—or Dedekind's characterization of the system of finite numbers up to isomorphism as a simply infinite system. Moreover, as Tait correctly asserts (p. 72), even Frege's analysis of the arithmetical continuum came thirty years after those of Weierstrass, Dedekind and Cantor, and was incomplete, although it could be the case that its completion was included in a never published (and, if written, now lost) third volume of GgA. And with regard to the too often praised presumed ' superior clarity of thought and powers of conceptual analysis' of Frege in comparison with his confused predecessors and contemporaries, Tait also correctly points out that 'Frege's discussions of other writers are often characterized less by clarity than by misinterpretation and lack of charity, and, on many matters, both of criticism of other scholars and of substance, his analysis is defective' (p. 72).

On this issue, it should also be mentioned that often Frege's certainly well-structured analyses are built on unacknowledged dogmas. For example, the whole discussion surrounding the so-called paradox of the concept ' horse' presupposes a pre-established harmony between the realm of expressions (that of their senses) and the realm of their referents, which is totally unwarranted. Moreover, it should be added that Frege not only misinterpreted others' views, but usually avoided having to publicly acknowledge any coincidence with other thinkers. Thus, e.g. although in a letter to Husserl of May 1891 he acknowledges that Husserl had also obtained the sense-reference distinction independently of him, and even uses a Husserlian example to illustrate the distinction in a letter to Paul F. Linke of 1919, of all his writings (after 1891) only in the posthumous 'Ausfuhrungen über Sinn und Bedeutung' and in his review of Schroder of 1895 is there a brief and confusing mention of this fact. And this omission has caused such blindness among Fregeans that more than one hundred years later almost all of them, most of whom seem not to have read Husserl, and even some Husserlians (like Fellesdal) believe that Husserl obtained the distinction from Frege.

On these issues, Tait cites (pp. 76, 77) a passage of Frege's review of a paper of Cantor of 1890, which Tait considers as one of the most impertinent passages in the history of philosophy. We agree with Tait that Frege's incapacity to recognize the merits of other thinkers was particularly acute in the case of Cantor. With regard to Cantor, Tait remarks (p. 78) that in 1883, a year before G1A, Cantor stated that two sets have the same power when they are equipollent and, thus, is just a step from the cardinality of a set M as 'the general concept under which fall precisely those sets equipollent to M'. Moreover, the definition of equinumerosity in terms of equipollence, as applied to sets in general and not only to finite ones, is Cantor's and not, of course,

Hume's. Moreover, Tait adds (p. 78) that already in 1883, and more explicitly in his review of G1A, Cantor warned about the mistake of identifying the notion of a set with the extension of a concept. Contrary to Frege, who learnt it the hard way in 1902, Cantor knew what he was talking about. As Tait puts it (p. 78), Frege 'was unaware of the difficulties involved in treating the infinite'. Furthermore, Tait argues (p. 82) that the abstractionism of neither Cantor nor Dedekind is subject to the criticism that it is psychologistic. For neither of them are the laws of numbers subjective nor are numbers psychological entities. Something similar could be said (but is not said by Tait) of Frege's distortion of the young Husserl's views in his review of Philosophie der Arithmetik. The young Husserl was clearly influenced by a Brentanian brand of psychologism, but he never considered numbers psychological entities nor took the laws of arithmetic (or of any other branch of mathematics) to be subjective.

We cannot discuss all points treated in Tait's challenging paper. For example, we cannot dwell on his interesting analysis of Dedekind's and, especially, Cantor's views, which serve him to argue (pp. 95, 96) that when in G1A Frege tried to refute Cantor's views, he completely misunderstood him. That does not mean, however, that Tait overlooks possible difficulties in some of Dedekind's or Cantor's views, as attested by his argumentation (pp. 96, 97) to show that Cantor's conception of cardinal numbers as sets of pure unities is ill-conceived, although perfectly coherent—even on Frege's presumably incorrect interpretation and contrary to what Frege thought. Moreover, Tait once more underscores at the end of his paper (pp. 105ff.) Cantor's incomparably superior understanding than Frege's on matters concerning infinity and related concepts, from equinumerosity of infinite sets, through the distinction between cardinals and ordinals, to the difficulties of Frege's assumption in his two major works that every concept has an extension. On this issue, there is little to add or comment (since it should be clear to all but the most dogmatic Fregeans) except maybe that Frege should have learnt from Cantor, as no lesser lights with lesser egos probably did.

(3) Matthias Schirn's 'On Frege's introduction of cardinal numbers as logical objects' is the longest and most thoroughgoing, and

one of the most interesting papers in the present collection. It is without doubt a solid, well-documented and exemplarily well-argued paper on very difficult issues in Fregean exegesis, and written by one of the very best Fregean scholars in the world. It is impossible here to do justice to all issues discussed in Schirn's paper, even though we will deal with this paper more extensively than with any other in the collection. And we will also deal more critically with it, both because we consider some of his renderings of Frege at least questionable and because, although Schirn sometimes tries to distance himself a little from Frege, he is still too much of a Fregean to be critical enough.

Schirn's paper concerns Frege's failed attempt (as we now know) in G1A and GgA to conceive numbers as logical objects, a very important step in the latter's programme of establishing (his brand of) logicism. Thus, at the start, Schirn states (p. 114) both that Frege argued that in view of their universal applicability, arithmetical laws should be of a purely logical nature, and that Frege's conception of objects is almost entirely based on syntactical considerations. On this last issue, it should be said, however, that (i) Frege is very selective in using grammatical considerations of ordinary German when they fit his purposes, while repeatedly stating that philosophy has to free itself from the chains of the very unreliable ordinary language, and (ii) that, as we already mentioned, the ontological relevance of some syntactical (or better: grammatical) considerations of Frege presuppose a pre-established harmony between the realm of expressions and the realm of their referents. With regard to the last point, it is convenient to look at Frege's argumentation at the beginning of' Ausfuhrungen über Sinn und Bedeutung' on behalf of his thesis that the referent of a conceptual word is a concept. What his actual argumentation leads to is to the conclusion that the extension is the referent of the conceptual word (and concepts are just their senses). But then the pre-established harmony enters the scene and he concludes, not on rational grounds but on the harmony dogma, that it cannot be the extension, since extensions of concepts are objects, and must be the concept. Schirn overlooks such issues.

Schirn asserts that Frege took the concept as the bearer of number to avoid the possibility of having to regard numbers as perceptible or intuitible objects and also to try to offer a plausible explanation for their universal applicability (p. 116). Moreover, he was interested in rejecting both the psychological and the physicalistic conceptions of numbers. We wonder whether Schirn believes that this was the only avenue open to Frege. The whole of set-theoretical foundation from Cantor onwards shows that other approaches were available. And even from a purely philosophical standpoint he could very well have argued on behalf of the non-psychologistic and non-physicalistic view of numbers as he later argued in 'Der Gedanke' (briefly: DG) in the case of thoughts. Very clear and rigorous is Schirn's discussion of Frege's introduction of logical objects in G1A by transforming an equivalence relation into an identity (p. 117). Thus, 'we apprehend cardinal numbers by converting an equinumerosity holding between first-level concepts into a numerical identity, relying on the identification of cardinal numbers with equivalence classes of equinumerosity'. In more general terms, Schirn says (p. 117) 'we conceive logical objects by making the transition from an equality holding between the values of two functions to an identity of courses-of-values'. This is, of course, the content of Frege's notorious Axiom V of GgA. Moreover, Schirn adds, in this way 'our grasp of the sense of the new sentence, i.e. the identity statement, is mediated by our recognition of its equivalence with the old one, i.e. the equivalence statement' (p. 118). Schirn correctly claims (p. 119) that Frege was not only a logicist, but an ontological Platonist. For him numbers are logical objects, which exist with complete independence from the human mind. Thus, Schirn very aptly rejects the recent 'Kantianization' of Frege by Sluga, Kitcher, Curry and others. We totally agree with Schirn on this issue, as well as with his distancing Frege from the creationism of his fellow logicist Richard Dedekind.

On p. 120 Schirn begins to discuss Frege's path from the syntactical considerations to his ontological distinctions. And a footnote on p. 121 brings to the surface Schirn's limitations as a Fregean. We will not dwell on that footnote, but for now will only mention that Schirn almost identifies Frege's Begriffsschrift (briefly: BS) notion of judgeable content, his vague use of the term ' content' in G1A and (presumably) his post-1890 notion of thought, i.e., the sense of a statement. (For the qualification see below.) Before continuing, it should be mentioned that on p. 122 Schirn acknowledges somewhat timidly that Frege's argumentation from syntactical considerations to ontological distinctions is highly dubious. On pp. 123,124 Schirn introduces some material that we should bear in mind to understand the rest of the paper. First, he considers (p. 123) the following three numerical statements:

(1) The number 4 belongs to the concept Jupiter's moons.
(1*) $N_x^4 F(x)$
(2) There are four moons of Jupiter.
(2*) $\exists_4 x F(x)$
(3) The number belonging to the concept Jupiter's moons = 4.
(3*) $N_x F(x) = 4$

Moreover, he states (pp. 123,124) the following four syntactic-semantic theses, presumably Fregean:
(A) Different sentences can express the same thought.
(B) A sentence and the thought which it expresses may be analysed (or decomposed) in different ways.
(C) A thought is built out of parts, which correspond to the parts out of which the sentence can serve as a picture of the structure of the thought.
(D) We start out from judgements and their contents, and not from concepts. We only allow the formation of concepts to proceed from judgements.

On (pp. 123,124) footnote 18, after citing Dummett, Schirn argues that Dummett's rendering of Frege's notion of sense 'is incompatible with thesis A if it applies'—as Schirn believes—'to sentences which under the standard interpretation have significantly different logical structures such as sentences (2) and (3) above' and is in sharp contrast with thesis (B). Moreover, he accuses Dummett of confusing Frege's notion of sense with Carnap's notion of intensional isomorphism and adds, presumably contra Dummett and as if it were somehow illuminating, that 'to maintain that one and the same thought can be seen as put together out of parts in different ways' is in perfect accordance with theses (A) and (B). (The issue here for Schirn is Dummett's distinction between analysis and decomposition, but that does not concern us here. By the way, like Schirn, Dummett also fails to make Frege coherent.) On p. 124, Schirn claims that sentences (1)-(3) (respectively, (1*)-(3*)) confirm thesis (A) and, according to Frege, they all express the same thought. Furthermore, on pp. 133,134 Schirn states that in §64 of G1A—when discussing the transition from (A1) 'a is parallel to b' to (A2) 'the direction of A = the direction of b' and of (B1) 'F(x) is equinumerous to G(x)' to (B2) 'the number of F(x) = the number of G(x)'—Frege 'maintains that one and the same judgeable content can be carved up in distinct ways and so emerge in sentences of significantly different logical form'. Although immediately afterwards Schirn asserts in a somewhat unclear way that the transition from (A1) to (A2) (or from (B1) to (B2)) is only in part linguistic, being also in part contentual, as a Fregean he does not have the semantical tools to deal with this mess.

On this whole issue, it must first be said that it is unwarranted and bad scholarship to identify Frege's loose use of the word 'content' in G1A, as applied to sentences, with Frege's notion of judgeable content introduced in BS. This is especially important since in the latter Frege introduced another more technical notion, namely, that of conceptual content, which according to one of its not easily reconcilable characterizations, would perfectly fit the transition from (A1) to (A2) and from (B1) to (B2), being the same for any two interderivable statements. Of course, Schirn and the Fregeans do not differentiate between judgeable content and conceptual content, but Frege introduced those notions in §§2-3 of BS without any mention of their coincidence. Moreoever, Frege would clearly reject characterizing the same notion twice in the same work and use two different names for it (without later establishing their coincidence). Thus one can be confident that what Frege meant in BS by 'judgeable content' is different from what he meant by 'conceptual content', and also different from what he meant by 'content' in the passage of §64 of G1A referred to by Schirn.

Moreover, although we agree with Schirn that Frege's notion of judgeable content comes closer to his official notion of thought in 'Uber Sinn und Bedeutung' (briefly: SB)—and thus, Frege's assertions in GgA and in a letter to Husserl of 1891 that he split the notion of judgeable content into those of thought and truth value could be somewhat misleading—the fact is that Frege's characterization of thoughts in a passage of DG and especially in his letters to Husserl of 1906 coincide with his characterization of conceptual content in BS. Hence, Schirn's confusions (as well as those of most Frege interpreters on this and related issues) originate in Frege himself. (In some sense this confusion of two different Fregean notions of sense, one originating in the notion of judgeable content and the other essentially coinciding with the notion of conceptual content, can be considered the original sin of Fregean exegesis, and accounts for the surprising elasticity of Frege's notion of thought so dear to Schirn and others.) Thus, if you consider what Frege says about his notion of sense in SB and GgA, Dummett's reading of Frege's notion of the sense of statements is probably correct, or at least very near to the truth. In §2 of GgA Frege states that '2 + 2' and '2x2' have different senses, and, thus, '2 + 2 = 4' and '2x2 = 4" express different thoughts. But if '2 + 2 = 4' and '2x2 = 4' express different thoughts, a fortiori (Al) and (A2) (as well as (Bl) and (B2))—which, as Schirn acknowledges, differ not only linguistically—express different thoughts. Moreover, on the basis of Frege's brief characterization of the notion of judgeable content in BS, —which, as mentioned above, approximates it to precisely this official notion of thought—(Al) and (A2) (as well as (Bl) and (B2)) do not have the same judgeable content. What the members of each pair presumably would have in common is the same conceptual content.

But, as briefly mentioned above, Frege's remarks on the notion of conceptual content in BS are in part used to characterize the sense of statements (i.e. the thought) in two letters to Husserl of 1906 contending that two equipollent statements (precisely like '2 + 2 = 4' and '2x2 = 4') express the same sense, whereas the other components of his characterization of conceptual content in BS reappear in DG and in his posthumously published 'Logik' of 1897. Thus, Frege really had two notions of sense, which he and his recent disciples like Dummett and Schirn are not able to differentiate. As we shall see below, Schirn's confusions on these matters are even more serious.

Another delicate issue discussed by Schirn is Frege's context principle introduced in G1A. According to Schirn (p. 136), although in G1A Frege had not drawn the distinction between sense and reference, the context principle was supposed to apply to the reference and not to the sense of words. The principle, on Schirn's reading, 'embodies the primacy of sentence-reference over word-reference' and expresses that 'the reference of a subsentential expression consists exclusively in its contribution to determining the reference of any sentence in which it may occur.' Schirn claims (p. 137) that in G1A the context principle serves the following purposes: (i) rejecting a psychological conception of word-reference in general, (ii) avoiding a physical view of number in particular without slipping into a psychological view, (iii) serving as a guideline for the logical analysis of numerical statements, and (iv) defending the legitimacy of ascribing determinate references to abstract singular terms.

But Schirn also considers the reading of the context principle as bearing on the sense of words. In that case the principle states, according to Schirn (pp. 137,138), that the sense of a word consists in its contribution to the sense of any sentence in which it may occur. In this case, the context principle would embody the primacy of the sense of a sentence over the senses of the words, which are its constituents. Schirn claims that 'while after 1892 Frege constantly subscribed to the rationale that the senses of the parts of a sentence are parts of the thought expressed by the sentence', he rejected the analogue in the realm of reference: 'the references of sentence constituents cannot be reasonably conceived of as constituents of the reference (i.e. truth value) of the whole sentence' (p. 138).

Moreover, Schirn claims that the context principle is perfectly compatible with Frege's thesis (C) mentioned above, according to which we build a thought out of its constituents. As Schirn underscores here, thesis (C) conveys that 'we grasp the sense of a sentence on the strength of our prior knowledge of its constituent expressions and the manner these are structurally combined to form a sentence'. Schirn makes great efforts to try to show that (C) is compatible both with the context principle and with thesis (D). He even argues (p. 139), against Hodes that 'thesis (C) and the context principle, construed as a principle concerning sense, work hand in hand'.

We cannot dwell here on the issue of the context principle, but would want merely to mention that, although Schirn's is the official reading on which orthodox Fregeans more or less coincide both with neo-Kantian Fregeans and Dummettians, we respectfully disagree. First of all, it should be underscored that the context principle, one of Frege's three guiding principles in G1A, is not explicitly mentioned in GgA (although it is probably implicit in Frege's precisely misguided circular attempt to prove referentiality) and, in general, is barely mentioned after 1892. Moreover, probably the most important services rendered by the context principle, namely, (i) and (ii) are taken care of, from 1891 onwards, by the distinction between sense, reference and representation. Furthermore, contrary to Schirn's claim, the context principle is not easy to reconcile with Frege's theses in 'Über Sinn und Bedeutung' that the sense of a sentence is determined by the senses of its constituent words. By the way, Schirn's claim that Frege never conceived the referents of the sentence's constituents as constituents of the referent of the whole sentence, is falsified by Frege's remarks in a letter to Russell of 28 July 1902. Nonetheless, it should be said with regard to the context principle, as applied to the reference, that both in 'Über Sinn und Bedeutung' and in §66 of GgA(II) Frege clearly maintains that the referent of the whole, even together with the referent of all its parts but one, cannot determine the referent of this remaining part. And, if the whole is a sentence and its Fregean referent a truth-value, any attempt at determining the referent of a constituent word from the referent of the whole would be devoid of any reasonable possibility of being successful. There are some tensions here, but they are Frege's and our task is not to conceal them or to try to show that after all Frege was incapable of incoherence.

With respect to Frege's attempt at defining the concept of number, Schirn claims (pp. 147, 148) that for Frege any methodologically sound introduction of abstract objects presupposes that we can state an adequate criterion of identity for them that would allow us 'to recognize them as the same, and to distinguish them from other objects'. Moreoever, according to Schirn (p. 150), if we take into account that Axiom V of GgA, namely, $\varepsilon^{\smile}F(\varepsilon) = \alpha^{\smile}G(\alpha) \equiv \forall x(F(x) = G(x))$ and (T) $N_xF(x) = N_xG(x) \equiv Eq_x(F(x),G(x))$ of G1A are clearly formal analogues, it should be clear that in his two main works Frege remained convinced that the transformation of an equivalence relation into an identity was the way to be followed for the introduction of logical objects. As is well known and Schirn stresses (p. 150), neither Axiom V nor (T) fulfills the expectations of uniquely fixing the referents of abstract singular terms. A further point made by Schirn (p. 150) is that, contrary to what happens with the direction of a line, the introduction of the numerical operator presupposes that the domain of the first-order variables is infinite. Moreover, Schirn adds (p. 150) that the contextual definition 'fails to supply any means of eliminating the operator $N_x\varphi(x)$' from an expression of the form '$N_xF(x) = x$'.

With respect to Frege's explicit definition of number in G1A, Schirn argues (pp. 152, 153) that Frege's assertion in a footnote to §68 of G1A that in the definition of number one could very well replace the words 'extension of the concept' by 'concept' do not seem convincing and would generate insurmountable difficulties. But it is Schirn's remarks on this issue that are not very convincing (pp. 154, 155). If one presupposes Frege's syntactical criteria for establishing the reference of expressions, the expression 'the concept' cannot refer to a concept and must refer to an object that is a substitute for the concept. Although Frege is not totally explicit on this issue, the object by far more naturally connected to the concept—and more so in Frege—and, thus the clear candidate to replace the concept in such a context is the extension of the concept—and not any mysterious object of a quite special kind, as Schirn seems to believe. Thus, if in the explicit definition of number you replace the words 'the extension of the concept' by 'the concept', since both refer to the same extension, you are just replacing a name by another name with the same reference (and, by the way, contrary to Frege's assertion, would not have avoided talking about extensions). Schirn's attempt to show p. 157 that Frege's proposed replacement would generate an infinite regress is totally unwarranted since extensions do not have extensions, nor could such a replacement have affected, contrary to what Schirn states (pp. 155, 156), the possible derivation of the laws of arithmetic. Of course, Schirn also points out (p. 157) that 'Frege's analysis of our use of the expression 'the concept F' gives rise to an unsolvable conflict between what we mean with our words and what we actually say with them'. This, however, is not exactly the problem under discussion, namely, the replacement of the expression 'the extension of the concept' by 'the concept', but in some sense a converse problem created by Frege's belief in a pre-established harmony between grammar and ontology. By the way, in GgA Frege did not follow the path mentioned in the famous footnote of G1A, since he became convinced that extensions, as presumed special cases of courses-of-values, were perfectly legitimate logical objects.

On pp. 160ff. Schirn discusses, following Wright and Boolos, the possibility of taking (T) as an axiom and, with the help of second-order logic, trying to derive the axioms and theorems of arithmetic. In his discussion, Schirn asserts that 'for Frege, both halves of (T) have the same judgeable content, i.e. express the same thought' (p. 162). We have already dealt with such unwarranted assertions of Schirn. It is false that both halves of (T) have the same judgeable content, or the same thought in Frege's later official use of the term 'thought'. What is the same is what Frege in BS called 'conceptual content'. To Frege's imprecisions and confusions Schirn adds some of his own. For example, after correctly pointing to a confusion by Boolos between self-evidence and analyticity (p. 163), Schirn reaches the peak of his confusions when he claims once more that both halves of (T) have the same sense, since Frege had claimed that they had the same judgeable content ('judgeable' is, of course, added by Schirn), but presumably 'neither claims nor denies that the two sides of Axiom V express the same sense' (pp. 163,164). In other recent writings, however, Schirn has explicitly said that the two halves of Axiom V, similarities with (T) notwithstanding, do not express the same sense, but only have the same reference. Frege himself was far from clear on this issue. In GgA he says that the two halves of Axiom V only have the same reference in common—which, according to Frege's official notion of the reference of sentences, had to be a truth value—whereas in 'Funktion und Begriff (briefly: FB) he claimed that the two halves of Axiom V expressed the same sense, i.e. the same thought. (A similar incoherence occurs in Frege's stipulations about definitions: sometimes he says that the definiendum and the definiens need to have both the same sense and the same referent in common, whereas in other occasions he says that they need to have only the same referent and even emphatically denies in his review of Husserl's Philosophic der Arithmetik that they need to have the same sense.) Thus, it is clear that Frege was very confused on this issue, and such a confusion has been inherited by his putative sons, including scholars as different as Dummett and Sluga, and assumes considerable proportions in Schirn's claims about the two halves of (T) versus the two halves of Axiom V. Such a different rendering of (T) and Axiom V is totally unwarranted. Of course, all such confusions of Frege and the Fregeans disappear if one acknowledges that what both halves of Axiom V (as of (T)) have in common is what Frege tried to apprehend somewhat unclearly in BS with the notion of conceptual content.

Following Boolos, Schirn states (p. 166) that the equivalence (T) is not a logical truth, since it can only be true in an infinite domain. Thus, in a footnote on the same page he says that what threatens logicism are not the set-theoretical paradoxes, but arithmetic's commitment to the existence of infinitely many objects. Also following Boolos, Schirn claims (p. 167) that the equation '$N_x(x = x) = N_xFN(x)$' where 'FN' is an abbreviation for 'finite number', is an undecidable sentence of what has recently been baptized as 'Frege's arithmetic', namely, a second-order theory in which (T) is the only non-logical axiom. There are models of Frege's arithmetic in which that equation is true and models in which its negation is true. Finally, Schirn stresses (p. 169) that (T) does not uniquely fix the reference of numerical terms and, in particular, does not allow us to decide whether either of the two truth values is a cardinal number. Although these last issues, especially the problems of the threats to logicism and the importance of Boolos's programme, merit some discussion, we have already dwelled long enough on Schirn's paper.

(4) Bob Hale's and Crispin Wright's paper 'Nominalism and the Contingency of Abstract Objects' is one of many papers by the two distinguished philosophers in Scotland who deal critically with Hartry Field's philosophy of mathematics and propound a sort of Platonism anchored in Fregean syntactic (or grammatical) considerations. Hale and Wright are especially concerned with Field's assertion that although it is false that there are mathematical entities, it is logically possible that there are mathematical entities. Thus, the non-existence of mathematical entities, is for Field, a contingency. As usual Hale and Wright's paper is well-argued and structured. We are, however, not sure that they will decisively refute Field. We think that stronger arguments, not based on Frege's syntactic considerations, need to be used against Field's queer philosophy of mathematics. For example, as we have argued elsewhere, it can be shown that an immediate consequence of Field's views, namely, that existential mathematical statements are false and universal mathematical statements vacuously true, and, thus, on the assumption of consistency, not equivalent, is logically inconsistent with Robinson's test for model-completeness, according to which a theory T is model-complete if and only if for any existential sentence in the language of T there is a universal sentence in the language of T interderivable with it. Since there are model-complete theories, on the basis of classical model theory, Field's philosophy of mathematics is inconsistent.

(5) Richard G. Heck's paper' Definition by Induction in Frege's Grundgesetze der Arithmetik is also one of many related papers by this Fregean scholar. However, it is perhaps unfortunate that it has already appeared in William Demopoulos's collection Frege's Philosophy of Mathematics (Harvard University Press, 1995). We are not going to discuss this paper, although we note some discomfort when we read on p. 227 that although Frege never formulated a sort of Isomorphism Theorem for what Heck calls 'Frege's axioms for arithmetic' (p. 225), he not only established it, but was also well aware of its great significance. Moroever, Heck states (p. 227) that one should not put too much weight on the distinction between what Frege writes down and what he leaves for the reader to infer. We wonder how is it that such a meticulous writer as Frege would not explicitly mention a result which he believed was so significant and which was so similar to Dedekind's previous result.

(6) George Boolos' 'Whence the Contradiction?' is a critical assessment of some theses of Dummett in his controverial Frege: Philosophy of Mathematics of 1991. Boolos is especially concerned with two different Dummettian assertions in that book about the grounds for the derivation of Russell's (better: the Zermelo-Russell) Paradox in GgA. As Boolos correctly observes (p. 234), in Chapter 17 of his work Dummett claims that Frege's insouciance in his use of the second-order quantifier was the main reason for the contradiction, whereas in Chapter 2 he had stated that the contradiction is due primarily to Frege's assumption that there is a totality containing the extension of every concept defined over it. Boolos maintains (pp. 234, 235) that Dummett's explanation of the paradox rests on two mathematical facts, namely, the consistency of the first-order fragment of GgA and the non-existence of a bijection between a given set and its power set. Moreover, Boolos adds that when second-order quantifiers are admitted, 'no domain is large enough to contain all extensions of concepts defined on that domain' (p. 235). For Boolos Dummett's explanation is unnecessarily complicated. He prefers to adhere to the now classical explanation that the reason for the contradiction was the notorious Axiom V of GgA.

According to Boolos (p. 239), one of the difficulties with Dummett's assessment of the contradiciton in Chapter 17 is that Dummett argues that if we examine the so-called proof of referentiality of §31 of GgA and see why it fails, we will also see that the reason is Frege's carelessness with the second-order quantifier, whereas the argument really fails also for the first-order portion of GgA. On this issue, we totally agree with Boolos. Moreover, Boolos states (p. 239) that Dummett considers to be the cause of the contradiction what really is a sort of background condition. Another concern of Boolos is Dummett's claim that Frege's explanation of the second-order quantifier in GgA is substitutional rather than objectual. Such a reading of Frege is for Boolos unwarranted. For the objectual interpretation, Boolos refers to §§20, 24, 25, 34 and 45 of that work. According to Boolos (pp. 241, 242), Frege probably expressed himself imprecisely because he lacked Tarski's notion of satisfaction, and he believes that 'Frege would have accepted the natural Tarski-style definition' of the notion of satisfaction 'as a friendly amendment to his views'. We consider this last claim of Boolos as totally unjustified. Firstly, if we take into account Frege's rejection and argumentation against the correspondence theory of truth in DG and Tarski's intuitive motivation for his theory in 'The concept of truth in formalized languages', in 'Truth and Proof and in 'The semantic conception of truth' in which he avails himself of a version of the correspondence theory of truth, it is very improbable that Frege would have seen Tarski's definition as a friendly amendment to his semantics. Moreover, Boolos seems to ignore Frege's eagerness to exaggerate any weakness in the works of others—even of people like Cantor, Dedekind, Hilbert, Husserl and Weierstrass—in order to avoid having to publicly grant them merit.

On p. 245, Boolos observes with regard to the possible replacement of Axiom V of GgA by the so-called Hume's Principle (essentially Schirn's (T)) that in such a case even elementary questions would not be settled, especially those containing cardinality issues.

Thus, e.g. each of the following four sentences is consistent with Hume's Principle:
(1) The number of natural numbers is identical (or non-identical) with the number of numbers.
(2) The number of numbers is identical (or non-identical) with the number of
objects.

We already mentioned (l)'s independence from the so-called Frege's arithmetic at the end of our discussion of Schirn's paper. With regard to (2), we do not even know if it can be made sense of and admit a mathematical answer, since it looks too much like the 'problem' of deciding if there are as many angels as real numbers.

Boolos argues (p. 245) that it was Frege's 'adoption of a theory about a function from second-order to first-order objects that could not be true', facilitated by a belief that 'contextual definitions', as he calls Hume's Principle and Axiom V, are 'if not logically true, then near enough as could make no difference', that was responsible for the contradiction. Of course, in a strict sense Hume's Principle and Axiom V are not intended as definitions by Frege, but are clearly very similar in their form to Frege's attempted contextual definition of number in G1A. It should be mentioned that Boolos does not explain what he understands by 'logically true' nor by 'near enough [to logically true] as could make no difference'. On p. 249, Boolos tries to explain how Frege arrived at Axiom V of GgA. At the root of this story lies, according to Boolos (p. 249), Frege's incapacity to solve the so-called Julius Caesar problem, and the necessity to introduce extensions and adhere to the principle that extensions of concepts coincide exactly when the same objects fall under the concepts. Moreover, Boolos states (p. 250) that Frege tried to inject the power set of a set into that set, which is certainly impossible. Of course, if Frege had not disqualified Cantor's works with accusations of imprecision and had taken the advice of the clearly superior mathematician, he would probably had avoided the contradiciton—although he would also not have proved his logicist thesis. But as a matter of fact, no one has done it: neither Frege nor Whitehead, nor, of course, Russell, nor any of the new Fregeans like Boolos, Heck or Schirn.

(7) Michael Dummett's 'Reply to Boolos' is just a response to Boolos criticisms, and a not very satisfactory one. We note a few salient points. First, it should be mentioned that Dummett retracts his attribution of a substitutional interpretation of second-order quantification to Frege in GgA (pp. 254, 255) and argues that Frege does not seem to have been conscious of the distinction. This is probably correct, since in BS the interpretation of quantification is substitutional, whereas in GgA it is (at least predominantly) objectual, without there being any remark in this work on such a change. On the basis of an objectual interpretation of second-order quantification, Dummett concedes that Boolos's assessment of the paradox is the only explanation needed. But there is nothing in the theory, according to Dummett that would compel us to adopt an objectual rather than a substitutional interpretation (pp. 224, 225). Moreover, Dummett claims that in his book he has tried to show that Frege's inductive reasoning is grossly ill-founded and that it is the circularity of Frege's stipulations that leads to the inconsistency. Dummett acknowledges (pp. 255, 256) with Boolos that Frege's proof of referentiality was not successful even for the first-order fragment of his theory, presumably since he 'attempted to specify simultaneously the domain and the reference within it of course-of-value terms'.

(8) Christian Thiel's ' On the Structure of Frege's System of Logic' also deals with the issue of the grounds for the inconsistency of Frege's GgA. As with Dummett's paper, we mention only some salient features of it. Thiel states (p. 262) that on the inconsistency issue two devices of GgA are under suspicion, namely, courses-of-values and the horizontal. With regard to courses-of-values and their introduction in §3 of GgA, Thiel claims (p. 262) 'contra Dummett'—although he should better had said 'contra Schirn', since in his Frege: Philosophy of Mathematics Dummett has changed his reading of Axiom V—that Frege's stipulation is not of merely having the same reference but also the same sense. Thus, on this issue, the editor of the centenary edition of GlA coincides with Sluga. On p. 265, Thiel maintains that the inconsistency in Frege's system is due not only to Axiom V but also to an insufficient delimitation of the function names admissible in it. Thus, Thiel absolves the horizontal, since if the horizontal were to be

blamed for the inconsistency, then the equality sign would also have to be blamed for it, since the horizontal is definable by means of the equality sign (pp. 264, 265). Thiel believes that it is not necessary to completely abandon Axiom V, since one could retain it while restricting the function names admitted (p. 265). He claims that although Axiom V may be false, this could be due not so much to its formal structure as to an excessive liberality in admitting some courses-of-values, like the extension of the Russell set in the Zermelo-Russell Paradox, together with the function names out of which they were formed (p. 275). Thus, Thiel thinks that 'the exclusion of such expressions might prove to be an alternative solution to Frege's inconsistency problem'. Thiel's assertions, however, remain speculative at best. His paper, which includes much more than we have mentioned here, is full of interesting remarks, but does not elaborate enough its main theses. For example, one could very well ask Thiel if the restrictions to Axiom V needed to avoid the paradox do not essentially hamper its deductive capabilities to the point that in the new system obtained we cannot derive the arithmetical laws. Of course, Boolos and Heck have followed another path, namely, abandoning Axiom V completely, adding Hume's Principle to second-order logic, and deriving arithmetic. But since the logicality of Hume's Principle is hardly defensible, Frege's logicist programme remains unfulfilled. Either way the prospects do not look very attractive for Fregeanism.

(9) Peter Simons's paper' The horizontal' deals with the transformation of Frege's logic from BS to GgA due to the reinterpretation of the sign called by Frege in GGA 'the horizontal'. As is well-known, apart from the introduction of courses-of-values, the sense-reference distinction, the identification of the reference of statements with truth values and the ensuing modification in the understanding of concepts and relations, the only other major change from BS to GgA is the reinterpretation of the horizontal stroke. But, as Simons remarks (pp. 285, 286), from the new interpretation of the horizontal stroke in GgA it follows that every formula that contains it (thus, essentially, every formula) has a new interpretation, as has also every compound of symbols incorporating the horizontal stroke, i.e. almost every (compound) symbol in Frege's system. Thus, Simons

prefers to speak of 'Frege's logics' in the plural instead of 'Frege's logic' (p. 285). We cannot dwell on this interesting paper, since we need space for a discussion of the papers dealing with epistemological issues.

(10) Franz von Kutschera's short paper' Frege and Natural Deduction' is the last of the papers dealing with Frege's logic and philosophy of mathematics. Von Kutschera claims (p. 301) that in the first volume of GgA Frege developed a system of deduction closely related to Gentzen's calculus of sequents, introduced some forty years later for formalizing natural deduction. Von Kutschera sketches a treatment of the first-order portion of GgA as a system of natural deduction.

(11) Eva Picardi's paper 'Frege's Epistemology' is one of three interesting papers on this matter. Frege's conception of truth 'produces the link between his antipsychologism in logic and his antipsychologism in the account of meaning'. Moreover, she attributes to Frege the thesis that 'nothing short of the classical notion of truth can give us a correct account of the meaning we attach to our utterances' (p. 309). We agree with Picardi that this attribution is a strong and controversial one, and it is so especially if one takes into account Frege's arguments against the correspondence theory of truth in DG and his surely not classical identification of truth and falsehood with the referents of statements. Of course, there is a very wide sense of the word 'classical'—as used, e.g. in 'classical logic' as opposed to 'intuitionist logic'—in which Frege's conception of truth could be called 'classical'. But that sense of 'classical', as applied to truth, is not very informative.

Picardi correctly rejects (pp. 313, 314) Sluga's, Kitcher's and others' attempts to make a Kantian of Frege. Thus, she claims that Sluga's attempt to show that Frege was not a realist is unsuccessful, and argues that Kitcher's opinion that Kantianism is at the root of Frege's foundational programme is not evidenced by Fregean texts. Moreover, Picardi points out (pp. 315, 316) that Frege recasts epistemological issues in semantical terms. The originality of Frege's Platonism lies 'in his view that the sense and reference of mathematical statements are determined once their truth conditions have been laid down' (p. 318). Thus, she considers misleading Sluga's and Kitcher's claim that for Frege Kantian transcendentalism would be enough to avoid psychologism and to ground objectivity. She acknowledges, on the other hand, that in DG the answer to psychologism seems to rest not so much on semantic grounds as on what she calls 'a metaphysical postulation' (p. 320). This fact presents problems of interpretation for Fregean scholars, as Picardi states (p. 321), namely, whether by 1918 Frege believed that only through an explicit recourse to a third realm could one secure the objectivity of thoughts and prevent a possible fall into psychologism. On this issue, her rendering of a somewhat obscure passage of DG could generate discussion among Fregean scholars (pp. 321, 322).

(12) Gottfried Gabriel's 'Frege's "Epistemology in Disguise"' is a paper in the tradition of Sluga and his followers, contrary to Picardi's, which has a Dummettian imprint. For Gabriel the entire programme of logicism is an attempt at clarifying the epistemological nature of arithmetic (p. 331). Gabriel claims that 'Frege had an immediate interest in logical and epistemological questions, but only a mediate interest in the philosophy of language'. Thus, he adds that 'Frege becomes a philosopher of language out of necessity and not of his own free will', and 'the philosopher-of language reading [of his work by the Dummettians] tries to make a virtue out of Frege's necessity' (p. 332). On this issue of the philosophy of language we totally agree with Gabriel, although we most radically disagree from his rendering of Frege as an epistemologist. Frege's interest in semantics (no matter how important are his achievements in this area) are of a subsidiary interest and originate in a necessity arising from his primary interest in the philosophy of mathematics.

It is somewhat odd that Gabriel argues on behalf of his rendering of Frege as an epistemologist, but at the same time asserts that Frege lumps together theory of knowledge, psychology of knowledge and traditional modal logic, avoiding any distinctions between them (p. 335). Moreover, he adds that Frege is primarily interested in distinguishing logic from epistemology 'in order to protect logic from intrusions from psychology', and that 'distinguishing sharply between epistemology and the psychology of knowledge does not seem to have been particularly important to Frege' (p. 336). In his attempt to make an epistemologist of Frege, Gabriel tries to assimilate some of Frege's views to Kantian epistemology (pp. 342, 343). In general, on pp. 342-346 Gabriel tries to force an epistemological rendering of Frege, which is based on a very convenient reading of him. Thus, e.g. he pretends (pp. 345, 346) that Frege clearly distinguished epistemology as an argumentative basic discipline from the psychology of knowledge. We most emphatically disagree. Although there are epistemological components in Frege's writings (e.g. the classification of statements in BS and G1A), he was so horrified by psychologism and so afraid of falling into it that he tries to avoid as much as possible in most of his works, and even in his letters, the discussion of general epistemological matters. Among the writings published during his lifetime, it is in DG that he for the first time openly discussed general epistemological problems—although DG seems to be a polished version of his 'Logik' of 1897, published only posthumously—, and only in the 1924-25 papers (also published posthumously) does he consider the most general epistemological matters. As a philosopher, Frege was primarily a philosopher of mathematics, who soon became convinced that the clarification of some issues in what is now called 'philosophy of logic' and—with probably greater reluctance—in the philosophy of language was vital for his investigations in the philosophy of mathematics, and only very gradually and with uneasiness did he venture openly late in his life in questions of a clear epistemological nature.

(13) Tyler Burge's 'Frege on knowing the third realm' is probably the most sophisticated of this epistemological trio. Burge is neither inclined to reject—as have Dummettians and others—that Frege was an epistemologist nor does he try to render Frege—as Sluga, Kitcher and their followers have done—as a follower of Kantian (or Neo-Kantian) epistemology. According to Burge, 'Frege accepted the traditional rationalist account of knowledge of the truths of logic and geometry, for which the most basic truths in these areas are self-evident' (p. 347).

Burge approvingly mentions that, contrary to contemporary

Benacerrafians, Frege did not think that 'mathematical or logical knowledge is questionable because it apparently lacks causal-perceptual relations to its subject matter' (p. 350). Frege combined a rationalist theory of knowledge with his Platonism about logical objects, functions and thoughts; he did not discuss some epistemological issues in detail because he thought that he had little to add to the traditional rationalist answer. But he adds that Frege's epistemological views 'involve not only Platonic elements, but elements not at all associated with Platonism' (p. 351). Moreover, Burge claims (p. 352) that Frege's arguments on behalf of the objectivity and lawfulness of logic, and the imperceptibility, causal inertness, non-spatiality, and atemporality of extensions, functions and thoughts might be maintained by Non-Platonists, and, thus, that 'Platonism has no monopoly on claims to lawlike or intersubjective objectivity about non-spatial, atemporal entities'. On p. 353, however, Burge emphasizes that Platonism is incompatible with a Kantian view. He correctly states (p. 354) that Frege considers extensions, functions and thoughts as genuinely existent and clearly independent of our minds, and nowhere does Frege imply that he defends any sort of idealism, be it Kantian or not. Thus, Burge argues (p. 355) against Sluga and his followers that 'it is dubious historical methodology to attribute to a philosopher with writings that stretch over decades, a large, controversial doctrine, if he nowhere states it in his writings'. However, although Burge acknowledges that Frege ignores epistemological questions in most of his work, he thinks that 'it would be a serious misunderstanding to believe that he [Frege] thought that the questions were off-limits' (p. 362). On this issue, Burge claims that Frege made a three-fold distinction between (i) the psychological explanation of belief or judgement, (ii) the (epistemological) justification for our belief or judgement, and (iii) the grounding for logical truth. Not only in his attribution to Frege of such a three-fold distinction, but also in the claim that Frege repeatedly discusses the epistemological question of the justification of our belief, does Burge coincide with Gabriel (p. 363). His is just a more cautious epistemological reading of Frege somewhat free of Kantian overtones. Moreover, he incorrectly claims (p. 365) that 'in GgA Frege characterized the laws of logic not only as laws of truth' but as laws that 'prescribe the way in which we ought to think, as laws of thought'. This is a clear misunderstanding of Frege, although a very common one. Frege considered the laws of logic in GgA and elsewhere as laws of truth, although they admit (as do the laws of other theoretical sciences) a prescriptive use as laws of how one ought to think. But, as Frege adds at the very beginning of DG, such a normative use originates the misunderstanding of logical laws as (natural) laws of thought, which for Frege is not an epistemological but a psychological understanding of the laws of logic.

(14) Terence Parsons' 'Fregean theories of truth and meaning' is the first of three papers on Frege's philosophy of language and the first of two dealing with indirect senses. We shall not deal with any of them in detail. A point in Parsons' paper, however, that deserves special mention is his remark on p. 371 that the attribution to Frege by Kripke, Searle and others of the thesis that the sense of a proper name is constituted by the descriptions associated with it by the speaker is an unwarranted extrapolation from a footnote in SB, and is not easy to reconcile with passages in other writings, especially in DG. According to Parsons, 'Frege's semantical views form a framework that encapsulates much of what everybody agrees in the semantics of simple English' (p. 371). Parsons does not elaborate such a claim, but we are convinced that at least the Fregean thesis that truth-values are the referents of statements is not part of what everybody agrees in the semantics not only of simple English, but also of German, or Spanish, or French, or Russian, or Italian, or Portuguese, or, probably, any other Indo-European language. Parsons states his goal as that of focusing on Fregean accounts of the semantics of natural language, and developing a precise rendering of certain semantical theories inspired by Frege. According to Parsons, 'the principal complication in Frege's theory [of indirect senses] is the issue of whether there is a hierarchy of senses and references associated with each meaningful piece of language', a hierarchy that Parsons considers ill-motivated and not necessary for formulating an adequate semantics for natural language (p. 372).

(15) Richard L. Mendelsohn's 'Frege's treatment of indirect reference' is thematically a near relative of Parsons' paper. At the

beginning of his paper Mendelsohn observes that most philosophers regard the prospect of an infinite hierarchy of indirect senses as a *reductio ad absurdum* of Frege's theory of indirect sense (pp. 411, 412). Against this possibility, Mendelsohn states that some philosophers have developed the notion of a rigid hierarchy in which customary sense uniquely determines indirect sense, which avoids the charge of absurdity (p. 413). The smallest rigid hierarchy is Dummett's, in which customary sense and indirect sense coincide, and all levels of the hierarchy of senses collapse into the first level. Mendelsohn argues in this paper against the rigid hierarchy and, especially, against Dummett's version. According to Mendelsohn (pp. 414-415), in Dummett's version of Frege's theory, the sense-reference distinction collapses. Since the indirect sense is just the customary sense, in a simply indirect context, the indirect sense and the indirect reference, i.e. its customary sense—coincide. Thus, for indirect contexts, the sense-reference distinction disappears. This does not mean, however, that the distinction itself disappears, since in customary contexts the distinction is maintained.

(16) Bob Hale's 'Singular Terms (1)' deals with the problem of distinguishing singular terms syntactically from other expressions. As Hale mentions, 'semantically, a singular term is an expression the function of which is to convey a reference to a particular object' (p. 438). But a syntactical (or logical-grammatical) characterization cannot presuppose such a semantical role. Hale's task consists of (i) excluding the various kinds of non-substantial expressions as lying outside the category of singular terms, and (ii) developing tests, which will allow us to exclude, within the class of substantival expressions in general, those that, like the quantifiers and restricted quantifier phrases, are not singular terms (p. 442). Dummett introduced some criteria to fix the delimitation, but Hale argues (p. 448) that they cannot be relied upon to exclude predicates and other incomplete expressions, although they fare well with regard to the exclusion of substantival expressions that are not singular terms. Hale introduces an Aristotelian distinction between qualities and primary substances, namely, that qualities have a contrary, whereas (primary) substances do not (pp. 448, 449). Syntactically transposed, the distinction would be between predicates and singular terms, namely, that for each predicate there is a complementary predicate applying to any given object to which the original predicate does not apply, whereas that is not the case for singular terms (or substantival expressions in general). Hale, however, does not explain on what grounds such a transposition is legitimate, whereas one from semantics to syntax is not. According to Hale (p. 452), the Aristotelian criterion is required 'as a means of excluding various types of nonsubstantival expressions which Dummett's tests fail to exclude from the category of singular terms'. Hale concludes his paper with a proposal, which combines the Dummettian with the Aristotelian criteria. At first sight, this proposal seems too good to be true, and requires further development. Thus, we will have to wait for' Singular Terms (2)', or so we hope.

Critical Study of Oswaldo Chateaubriand's *Logical Forms I* and *Logical Forms II*, CLE, Unicamp, Campinas, Brasil 2001, 442pp., 2005, 521pp.

Abstract

In this critical study I try to highlight some of the most important issues discussed in Chateaubriand's excellent book. In particular, I discuss in some detail Chateaubriand's criticism of one of the icons of analytic philosophy, namely, Quine, as well as some of his own valuable contributions to philosophy in this book - for example, his refutation of the various forms of the slingshot argument and his characterization of logical truth.

Oswaldo Chateaubriand's book *Logical Forms* is a seminal and monumental book – amounting to 963pp.- on most of the central issues of analytic philosophy. It discusses in depth the most important problems in philosophy of logic and philosophy of language, as well as issues in the philosophy of mathematics and epistemology. However, it is not so much the wide scope of problems discussed in the book what makes it outstanding, but the depth of the analyses and the independence and originality of Chateaubriand's views. In some sense, this book represents, probably like no other book, the maturation of analytic and, in general, rigorous philosophy in Latin America. The whole book consists of a long introduction, twenty-five chapters and an Epilogue. The first volume consists of the introduction and twelve chapters, under the general heading *Truth and Description*, whereas the second consists of the remaining chapters and the Epilogue, under the general heading *Logic, Language and Knowledge*. To give the reader of this critical study a brief idea of the contents of this exceptional book, before commenting on single issues, I will enumerate the chapter headings:

Chapter 1: Truth, description, and identification
Chapter 2: The True and the False

Chapter 3: Use, mention, and Russell's theory of descriptions
Chapter 4: Arguments for Frege's thesis
Chapter 5: Objections to facts
Chapter 6: Truth, denotation and, interpretation
Chapter 7: Tarski's semantic conception of truth
Chapter 8: The True and the False revisited: Frege's logic
Chapter 9: Structuring reality: properties, sets and states of affairs
Chapter 10: Identity and extensionality
Chapter 11: Senses
Chapter 12: Truth and correspondence
Chapter 13: Language meaning and reference
Chapter 14: Syntax and Semantics
Chapter 15: Grammar and logical form
Chapter 16: Propositional logic
Chapter 17: Predicate logic
Chapter 18: Grammar and logical truth
Chapter 19: Proof and logical deduction
Chapter 20: Proof and Proving
Chapter 21: Proof and truth
Chapter 22: The tyranny of belief
Chapter 23: Ockam's razor
Chapter 24: Knowledge and justification
Chapter 25: Logic and Knowledge
Epilogue: Plato, Zeno, Parmenides, and Frege

    Since I have dealt with the first volume of Chateaubriand's book in a critical essay precisely in this journal[1] I will try to comment on the first volume rather briefly. Already in the Introduction, p. 16, Chateaubriand makes it clear that he conceives logic as metaphysical and epistemological, thus, as inserted both in a general theory of what exists and in a general theory of knowledge. In fact, on p. 26 Chateaubriand underscores that he, as Frege did, believes in the existence of logical objects, though, as will be seen later, he seems to be using the word 'object' in a wider sense than Frege's – much more similar to Husserl's usage and to Carnap's in *Der logische Aufbau der*

---

[1] 'Chateaubriand on Logical Forms and Semantics', *Manuscrito XXVII*, no. 1, 2004, pp. 115-128.

Welt[2] -, and referring specifically to properties and states of affairs. Hence, he vehemently rejects the proof-theoretic and syntactic views of logic current nowadays. Chateaubriand conceives logic as essentially concerned with truth, and since truth is not a syntactical notion, then – as pointed out on p. 19 - proof, which is supposed to preserve truth, cannot be purely syntactic either. Hence, Chateaubriand objects – see p. 24 – to Quine's disqualification of second-order logic because its semantics cannot be completely mirrored by its syntax. This basic disagreement with Quine marks the beginning of one of the most complete and decisive criticisms of Quine's views throughout the whole book, with which the present author completely agrees, and which constitutes a thorough dismantling of the influential philosopher's misdirection of research in rigorous philosophy. Chateaubriand correctly points out – see also p. 24 –, that the restriction of logic to first-order logic, which goes back to Skolem and Hilbert, and has been championed by Quine, has helped to sediment the identification of logic and proof with syntax. Nonetheless, as will be seen below when commenting on the second volume, Quine's definition of logical truth in his *Philosophy of Logic* is by no means totally unrelated to Chateaubriand's own definition, being a sort of failed attempt, aborted by his views on logic and grammar, to conceive logical truth as linked to logical form. On this issue of logical truths and logical properties Chateaubriand makes already on pp. 27-28 an important distinction between a logical law and its instantiations, a distinction to which I will return when discussing the second volume. In any case, it should already be mentioned that Husserl made essentially the same distinction in the Third Logical Investigation using the expression 'analytic necessity' for the instantiations in contradistinction to what he called 'analytic laws'. In fact, as will be seen throughout this critical study, though Chateaubriand seems not to be acquainted with Husserl's *Logische Untersuchungen* or any other of Husserl's writings, there are many affinities between some of his views on logical and semantic issues and those of the great philosopher.

---

[2] *Der logische Aufbau der Welt* 1928, fourth edition, Hamburg 1974.

Already in Chapter 1, p. 47, comes to the fore another coincidence of Chateaubriand with Husserl's views. As Chateaubriand and every Fregean scholar should remember, but usually forgets, in a letter to Husserl of May 1891 Frege acknowledges that Husserl had independently obtained the distinction between sense and reference, and correctly comments that probably the two points in which they disagree are about the referent (and sense) of what he called 'conceptual words' and about the referent of statements, which for him are the truth values. As is clear from Husserl's *Logische Untersuchungen* and other related writings, for Husserl the referents of statements are states of affairs. For Chateaubriand also the referents of statements are states of affairs, and though he relates such a view to Russell, one should not forget that Russell more than once confused the notion of state of affairs with that of proposition. Husserl, as well as Chateaubriand, did not commit such an elementary sin.[3] Continuing with Chateaubriand, he mentions the possibility – see p. 47 – that to adequately deal with states of affairs, one would have to take into account not only actual states of affairs, but also factually non-actual states of affairs – like that referred to by the statement 'My personal computer is made of chocolate' – and impossible states of affairs – like that referred to by the statement '2+2=5'. However, Chateaubriand rejects such a possibility, opting for an ontologically more economic but also intuitively less clear alternative, namely, that both true and false statements "state something of an identifying character about the world, but true statements identify something whereas false statements do not". As Chateaubriand points out on p. 48, such a rendering is similar to that given to a definite description, which fails to refer.

But Chateaubriand does not want to distance himself too much from Frege, and on p. 53 states that "...one can combine Frege's views on truth as denotation with Russell's views on truth in terms of facts or states of affairs". Chateaubriand rejects Russell's view of proper names as abbreviations of descriptions – see pp. 54-55 -, and, in fact, does not accept either Russell's or Frege's theories of

---

[3] In Husserl there is a further distinction between states of affairs and situations of affairs, but it is unnecessary for the present purposes to discuss such a distinction, which I have treated at length in many of my writings.

description. For him there is a strong analogy between descriptions and statements. Statements serve to identify states of affairs, as descriptions serve to identify objects. In fact, a statement is true for Chateaubriand – see p. 57 - when it identifies a state of affairs. It is unnecessary to underscore that Chateaubriand views favourably the correspondence theory of truth – see p. 58 – and that, as many others before him, he rejects Frege's argumentation to try to establish his thesis that the referents of statements are truth values.[4] On pp. 60-61, Chateaubriand's affinity with Husserl's conception of states of affairs as the referents of statements, while propositions are the senses of statements, reaches its maximum expression when he states: "Propositions are senses which purport to individuate states of affairs - this is an analogue of Frege's thoughts -, for propositions in this sense are non-linguistic modes of presentation". Sentences similar to the last quoted sentence can be found in the First Logical Investigation. In fact, for Husserl, propositions are the senses of statements, are what Frege called 'thoughts', and are non-linguistic entities, since they are ideal entities similar to Frege's thoughts, as propounded in 'Der Gedanke'. Indeed, it should be stressed here that for Husserl the ideality of meanings and of abstract objectualities (e.g., mathematical objects or states of affairs) has nothing to do with idealism in its usual sense, but is essentially concerned with what Frege tried to express later less clearly as 'belonging to the third realm'.

In Chapter 3 Chateaubriand is especially concerned with Russell's and Frege's theories of descriptions. As already mentioned, he does not accept either of them, but will develop a new theory of descriptions which combines features of both Russell's and Frege's theories. Chateaubriand is perfectly conscious of Russell's well-known confusions between use and mention and, in general, his sloppy way of philosophizing, in comparison to Frege's clarity.

---

[4] On this issue, see the present authors papers (2) and (11) in Claire O. Hill and Guillermo E. Rosado Haddock, *Husserl or Frege: Meaning, Objectivity and Mathematics*, Chicago et al., Open Court 2000, 2003, as well as Hermann Weidemann's paper 'Aussagesatz und Sachverhalt: ein Verusch zur Neubegründung ihres Verhältnisses', *Grazer Philosophische Studien* 18, 1982, pp. 75-99, and Jon Barwise and John Perry's paper 'Semantic Innocence and Uncompromising Situations', in Peter A. French (ed.), *The Foundations of Analytic Philosophy*, Minneapolis 1981, pp. 387-403.

Paraphrasing Quine, Chateaubriand states on p. 97 that 'Russell's theory of descriptions was conceived in sin'. Chateaubriand compares the strong and the weak points of Frege's and Russell's theories of description, and basically concludes – see p. 100 – that, though both Frege's and Russell's theories did not offer a correct analysis of sentences involving descriptions, he will try to combine some aspects of those theories. In synthesis, Chateaubriand's view – see pp. 104 and 105 - is that when in a sentence a description appears in subject position, Frege's referential analysis is correct and Russell's wrong; but when the description appears in predicate position, it is Russell's theory which is essentially correct, whereas Frege's is wrong. Though I cannot dwell longer on this issue, I think that this third intermediate way of Chateaubriand deserves serious consideration.

Another interesting issue discussed in Chapter 3 is that of existence. The received view, adopted since Frege, does not conceive existence as a usual predicate of objects but as a second-order predicate, on the basis that if it were a predicate of objects, all objects would have that property and existence would become trivial. However, such an objection, as correctly argued by Chateaubriand on p. 111, would also apply to self-identity and, moreover, existence seems to be definable in terms of the first-order predicate of self-identity. Though I will not dwell much here on this interesting issue, I have mentioned it as an example of Chateaubriand's independence from the logical and analytic tradition in which he was schooled and in which he is, on the other hand, so deeply immersed. There is, however, a point brought by Chateaubriand on p. 113 that does not sound convincing, namely, that, as happens with self-identity and self-subordination, existence could never be truly denied. Once more, the difficulty seems to be grounded on the issue of the inclusion or non-inclusion of non-actual states of affairs. For example, let us consider the statement 'Frege exists', which seems to refer to a non-actual state of affairs. Intuitively, I do not understand why, if existence is a first-order property, I cannot truly deny such a false statement. Moreover, if existence is a first-order property, there is also no reason why I cannot truly deny the existence of a square root of -1 in the real number system. Indeed, to say that the equation '$\sqrt{-1}=x$' does not have a solution in the real number system is just another way of denying the existence of a square root of −1 in that number system. Furthermore, the mathematical fact that such a number exists in the complex number system adds to the unclearness of Chateaubriand's views on existence. In a similar fashion, the statement 'Frege exists' is false in the temporal segment of the actual world in which Chateaubriand and I live, but true in any temporal segment that intersects the year 1900. Nonetheless, I acknowledge that trying to avoid the intuitively very attractive notion of non-actual worlds – as Chateaubriand does - is a healthy idea, since I am perfectly conscious that the notions of existence of objects and possible worlds do not add up to a happy marriage.[5] Thus, contrary both to my intuitions and those of Chateaubriand, perhaps Frege was right, after all, in considering existence as a second order property.

Chapter 4 is without doubt an exceptionally important one. Already in Chapter 2 Chateaubriand had correctly observed that Frege's argument on behalf of the truth values as the referents of statements was by no means compelling, something that already had been argued by many, including among others, Hermann Weidemann, John Barwise and John Perry, and the present author, as already mentioned in footnote 3. However, in Chapter 4 Chateaubriand shows that all the best-known versions of what has being called in the specialized literature 'the slingshot argument' are not compelling. Thus, Church's two different argumentations on behalf of Frege's thesis, Davidson version and Gödel's version are fully discussed and rejected. The slingshot argument had hindered the acceptance of alternatives to Frege's choice for the referents of statements, and though intuitively the different versions of the argument seemed somewhat fishy, so far as I know, a general refutation of the various versions of the argument had not been given. Certainly, the fact that even a logician of the towering stature of Gödel had offered a version of the slingshot argument – indeed, the most detailed and solid version – stymied any critical stance against such an argument. Once more, by taking care of refuting even Gödel's version of the argument, Chateaubriand shows an independence of thought not frequently seen

---

[5] See on this issue my short paper 'On Necessity and Existence', *Diálogos* 68, July 1996, pp. 57-62, reprinted in my book *Against the Current*, Ontos Verlag 2012, pp. 419-424.

nowadays in analytic circles. It should be obvious that it is not possible in this review to discuss Chateaubriand's refutation of the different versions of the slingshot argument. Thus, I can only urge the reader to go directly to the source. Nonetheless, since I had already argued that Church's version of the slingshot argument in his *Introduction to Mathematical Logic* is fallacious, and identified the same Achille's heel as Chateaubriand does – see pp. 140-142 -, namely that the two middle statements of the four sentence argument do not have the same Fregean sense, if Fregean sense is understood as in 'Über Sinn und Bedeutung' and in *Grundgesetze der Arithmetik*, a brief remark seems pertinent. In fact, it should be pointed out that in his refutation of Church, Chateaubriand misses the fact that Frege had a second notion of sense, which is essentially his old notion of conceptual content of his *Begriffsschrift* and which he used in his letters to Husserl of 1906. Interestingly, Church is guilty of the same confusion as Frege and makes use of this second unofficial notion of sense in the transition from the second to the third statement of his fallacious argument.

In Chapter 5 Chateaubriand answers Quine's objections to the notions of fact and state of affairs, namely - see p. 163 -, that they lack a criterion of identity, that they are unnecessary intermediaries between sentences and the world, and that they originate from a confusion between use and mention. The second and third objections arise from basing the discussion on Russell's confusions, though the second objection also attests to a confusion of Quine himself, since facts or states of affairs are not intermediaries between language and the world, but are part of the world. To paraphrase a triviality in Wittgenstein's Tractatus Logico-Philosophicus, the world is a structuring of states of affairs. Propositions, on the other hand, are senses, and could be interpreted as intermediaries between sentences and states of affairs, but they are not states of affairs. With respect to the first and most serious objection, Chateaubriand correctly observes on p. 165 that propositions, properties and states of affairs would in any case be – if Quine were right – in a similar situation as physical objects. Indeed, I would add that it is immensely more difficult to provide criteria of identity for electrons or any other elementary particles than to provide similar criteria for propositions, properties or states of affairs, and nonetheless research in microphysics has flourished in the last hundred years. Hence, there is no reasonable ground to reject the existence and investigation of propositions, properties and states of affairs because they presumably lack a criterion of identity. Chateaubriand's argumentation against Quine on this issue is different from and more detailed than the above, though not unrelated to it. It is concerned with physical objects, though more exactly with ordinary physical objects like a table or a rock, about which Quine thought that a criterion of identity in terms of molecular structure could be given. As Chateaubriand states – see pp. 168-169 -, even under the very dubious assumption that one could associate in a clear way a molecular description of a physical object to an ordinary description, such a molecular description "…would necessarily be vague and would neither identify a specific aggregate of molecules or would allow for a specific description of such an aggregate to be extracted from them".

I would like to comment rather extensively on one more issue treated in the first volume of Chateaubriand's book, namely, his criticism of Tarski's semantic theory of truth. Chateaubriand's objection is that Tarski's definition of truth is not really semantic but belongs to the morphology of language. There are two passages on p. 230, which contain the nucleus of Chateaubriand's objection and deserve to be quoted:

> Even the idea that when we do semantics with interpretations we are relating syntax to something non-syntactic that is somewhat like the world is basically an illusion, because the interpretations are part of our informal metatheory for which we assume a notion of 'true' whose fundamental characteristic is to obey the principles of classical logic as usually formulated. The sort of "reality" that is involved here is more like a syntactic feature of the metalanguage, and semantic interpretations may be better viewed as syntactic translations.
>
> It seems to me, therefore, that Tarski's semantic conception of truth is really a syntactic conception of truth....Tarski manages to recover the syntactic idea through the appeal to an indefinite sequence of metalanguages within each of which the definition is purely syntactic.

Chateaubriand's objections to Tarski's theory of truth are bold and interesting. Once more, Chateaubriand has no qualms in criticizing one of the icons of analytic philosophy. On this point, however, I have some disagreements with Chateaubriand, and I think that they are more deeply anchored in our respective conceptions of logic. In contrast to Chateaubriand's views, for the present author there are probably no logical objects, not only if by 'logical object' is understood something similar to what Frege conceived under that expression, but even if one includes states of affairs and properties. The postulation of logical objects was indispensable for Frege because of his logicist thesis, since it was for him unquestionable that mathematics deals with mathematical objects. Thus, not only did he need to obtain mathematical axioms as theorems from logical axioms and by means of logical rules of inference, and define mathematical concepts by purely logical means, but had also to show that mathematical entities are reducible to logical ones. However, since I am not a logicist, I can very well accept with Husserl that mathematics is ontological, in fact, a formal ontology, but consider logic an essentially syntactic and semantic enterprise. Such a conception of logic does not isolate it from ontological matters, first of all, because logic and mathematics are very near relatives, not mother and daughter like the logicists wanted, but sister disciplines: mathematics is the ontologically fat sister of logic. On the other hand, I am perfectly conscious that logic has also to be relevant to reality. Although logic is not directly and exclusively concerned with reality, as physics or biology are – but also with every possible, though non-actual reality -, it is certainly not a simple play with formulas and languages, but should serve (as mathematics does) as a valuable instrument in discovering how things in the world are.

In the case of Tarski's defintion of truth, one should not forget that he very emphatically underscores in 'The Concept of Truth in Formalized Languages' and related writings that he is trying to make precise and define the classical notion of truth as correspondence with reality. Of course, since his attempt at a definition of such a concept for natural language, under some reasonable assumptions, failed, he opted to offer a definition for a concrete formalized language: the calculus of classes. If Tarski had limited himself to such an enterprise, up to this point, Chateaubriand's contentions would be perfectly right, since such a result would be language bounded, more specifically, bounded to a particular object language and to a particular metalanguage. However, Tarski immediately generalized his result to any language of finite order and then in the Epilogue even to languages that did not fulfil the requirements of the Husserl-Lesniewski theory of semantic categories. That is already a partial, though not a complete emancipation of the results from language. Of course, in Tarski's construction there is no explicit mention of states of affairs, which both for Chateaubriand and for the present author are the referents of statements. However, one could very well understand the result of the assignments of values to all the free variables of a sentential function as assignments of states of affairs. Clearly, those 'states of affairs' would not be the concrete states of affairs which we encounter everyday in the real world, but to ask that from Tarski's results would be beside the point. In fact, if one has followed the discussion about the concept of truth in natural language from Tarski's negative result to Kripke, to the revision theory of Herzberger, Gupta, Belnap, Yaqûb and others, to Yablo's agonistic theory of truth, one can very well understand the role of logical devices and languages in their application to traditional philosophical problems. You have first to isolate the problem, as the physicist does, and then construct those sophisticated models in the traditional sense of the empirical sciences. For such models, you use all the logico-linguistic devices required. Without them, you cannot even attempt to tackle the problem. However, and on this point I suppose that there is complete agreement with Chateaubriand, you need to free your result from any bond to any particular language or logical system being used. To paraphrase once more Wittgenstein's *Tractatus Logico-Philosophicus*, once has to throw the ladder away after you have reached your result. But without the logico-linguistic ladder there is no climbing.

With respect to the remaining chapters of the first volume of Chateaubriand's book, I just want to make two brief and isolated comments without any elaboration. In Chapter 8 – see, for example, pp. 261-262 and 270 – Chateaubriand tends to confuse Frege's official notion of thought with Frege's old notion of conceptual content (his unofficial second notion of thought) as Church did in his fallacious argumentation discussed above. Frege's official notion of thought derives from his old notion of judgeable content, which he introduced in *Begriffsschrift* in § 2, and immediately after introduced the notion of conceptual content in § 3. Although Fregean scholars have had the tendency to ignore the distinction between the two notions – and Chateaubriand is on this point in very good company – it would be completely anti-Fregean to introduce two names for the same notion one after the other, with very different characterizations, but without saying that the notions so introduced coincide. In Chapter 9, p. 330, Chateaubriand points out that Frege's argumentation for the undefinability of truth on the basis of being circular could easily be applied to his definition of identity. Interestingly enough, once more Husserl has anticipated Chateaubriand, this time for 110 years, since already in his *Philosophie der Arithmetik* of 1891 he argued that, besides having confused identity and equality, Frege's definition of identity was circular.[6]

At the end of Chapter 13, thus, at the beginning of the second volume, Chateaubriand continues his critical dialogue with Quine's views. Thus, on p. 37 he reminds the reader that at present it is widely accepted that there are some innate components in learning – some of which could very well be of a logical nature - and, moreover, that Quine's views on language learning – see p. 38 - can be proven false on empirical grounds, as can, in particular, Quine's belief in the primacy of one word sentences in our acquisition of language. Furthermore, on p. 39, Chateaubriand stresses that Quine's indeterminacy of translation argument is not compelling, even if taken as a loose plausibility argument.

In Chapter 14, there is a long discussion on the Löwenheim-Skolem theorems and the so-called Skolem Paradox. Chateaubriand renders the Löwenheim-Skolem theorems in the same fashion as he rendered Tarski's theory of truth, namely, as a syntactic, not a semantic, result. In this case, however, Chateaubriand's rendering is more plausible, since the Löwenheim-Skolem theorems are language bounded. They are valid for first-order languages and for some of its less natural extensions, but false for second- and higher order logic in

---

[6] *Philosophie der Arithmetik* 1891, 1970, Den Haag, p. 119.

their usual non-Henkian rendering. As is well known, the nucleus of the Löwenheim-Skolem theorems states that any set of first-order sentences that has an infinite model has a countable model. In its stronger Tarkian version, the theorem states that any infinite model of a set of first-order sentences has an elementary substructure, which is also a model of the set of first-order sentences. On the other hand, the so-called Skolem Paradox arises when we axiomatize set theory in a first-order language. Clearly, the intended model of the axioms is a non-denumerable totality. But in virtue of the Löwenheim-Skolem theorem, the set of axioms has a denumerable model. Thus, in virtue of a well-known theorem of Cantor, one cannot establish a bijective correspondence between the two models. According to Skolem's questionable rendering, though there is no bijective correspondence inside the model, one could establish the correspondence from outside the model. Hence, the notion of cardinality is not an absolute, but a relative notion.

Continuing with Chateaubriand – see pp. 70-71 -, since the notion of an elementary submodel is a first-order notion, the Löwenheim-Skolem theorem is not semantic, but syntactic. Moreover, as is also very well-known, the nowadays most usual proof of the Completeness theorem, of which the Löwenheim-Skolem theorem is a corollary, proceeds by building a syntactic model, or more picturesquely, by extracting a rib from the enriched syntax of the first-order language. Thus, as Chateaubriand puts it on p. 71, "…what this shows is that the completeness theorem itself has a purely syntactic formulation…". With respect to the so-called Skolem Paradox, Chateaubriand rejects – see p. 72 – the contention of the supporters of first-order logic that on the basis of that so-called paradox they could in some sense reduce to absurdity the absolutist view of a reality not moulded by language.

Although I cannot dwell on this issue here – which I have discussed more thoroughly in a paper of 1996 -,[7] the lesson that in my opinion can be extracted from the so-called Skolem Paradox is that first-order logic is inadequate as a language for set theory, that set

---

[7] See Hill, Claire O.& Rosado Haddock, Guillermo E., *Husserl or Frege?: Meaning, Objectivity and Mathematics*, Chapter 15.

theory needs a second-order axiomatization. I suspect that on this point – as on many others -, Chateaubriand and I coincide.

Continuing with the exposition, after countering Skolem's relativism, Chateaubriand goes on to argue against other propounders of a syntactic view. Thus, on p. 75, he criticizes constructivists, who stress so much the importance of rules over abstract properties, but, on the other hand, are very timid when it comes to the formulation of such rules. Since constructivism is not one of the central issues of the book, and I am not especially concerned with it here, it seems pertinent to refer now to another critique made by Chateaubriand much later, in fact, in the Epilogue of the best-known constructivist school, namely, intuitionism. Thus, on p. 468, Chateaubriand correctly observes that one could ask mathematical intuitionists and other related brands of constructivists, who give so much importance to their constructions occurring in time, what happens with such constructions as beings in time. This is a very serious objection, very similar in fact to that usually offered against historicist views by asking whether their views are also to be seen as historically bound to a determinate period of time. In the case of intuitionists, one may certainly wonder whether the mathematical objects being constructed in time will also disappear after a determined extension of time – like any of our physical constructions - or whether they will exist in time forever. Probably only the *hybris* of a Brouwer could make someone opt for the second possibility.

Continuing with the order of the book, on p. 78, Chateaubriand observes that the syntactic point of view is usually defended by nominalists, physicalists and empiricists, because of their rejection of everything abstract, since such a syntactic rendering of logic and mathematics would maintain alive their belief in a world exclusively of particulars. I perfectly agree with Chateaubriand on this and the foregoing points. However, when Chateaubriand refers on p. 79 to the Gestalt psychologists as having established the falsity of such a view by showing that there are abstract components in perception, I must once more refer Chateaubriand to Husserl, who said it first and who most surely influenced Gestalt psychology on that point. Already on p. 79 and once more on p. 89, Chateaubriand stresses that all efforts to formulate the fundamental logical notions as purely syntactic have failed, even though the notion of syntax taken as base is essentially as strong as the structure of the natural numbers. Moreover, interestingly enough, as Chateaubriand observes on the same p. 89, to fully characterize first-order logic and also the structure of natural numbers one has to recur to second-order logic. A somewhat isolated point deserves being briefly mentioned here, namely, that on p. 92, Chateaubriand states that intentionality is "a very interesting and fundamental feature of humans and animals". Once more, Chateaubriand does not mention that it is Husserl who offered the most thorough theory of intentionality.

It is precisely in Chapter 14 where Chateaubriand offers his most decisive criticism of Quine's views. In an extensive footnote on pp.101-102, Chateaubriand contrasts Gödel's detailed procedure in his famous paper of 1931 with Quine's vague holistic thesis. It is best to quote this devastating criticism here.

> If Gödel had argued loosely in terms of Richard's paradox that somehow syntax can be arithmetized by proxy functions in some unspecified way, nobody would have accepted the incompleteness results....Gödel did the arithmetization of syntax very carefully, and this was an absolutely essential part of his proof. Moreover, while Gödel was only talking about the specific formal system of *Principia Mathematica*, and similar well-defined systems, Quine is talking about the whole of science, and without any rigorous formulation and development he wants us to accept an "arithmetization" of (an alleged interpretation of) that, and some kind of impossibility result.

I completely agree with such a criticism of Quine, having more than once expressed similar views.[8] Nonetheless, what is astonishing is that very few analytic philosophers, especially in North America, have dared to criticize Quine on this and other issues.

---

[8] See the paper referred to in the preceding footnote, as well as my recent paper 'Kritische Fußnoten zu Bernulf Kanitscheiders Naturalismus Aufsatz', in *Erwägen, Wissen, Ethik* 17, no. 3, 2006 as well as Chapter 4 of my *The Young Carnap's Unknown Master*, Ashgate 2008.

There is a passage on p. 110, already in Chapter 15 that once more reminds us of Husserl's *Logische Untersuchungen*. Chateaubriand says:

> If logic is indeed universal in the sense of not being language specific, then it would seem that the object of logical analysis must be something that is common to the various specific languages, and that, perhaps, manifests itself in each language in specific ways.

Precisely the study of that logical nucleus common to all languages is the task of Husserl's pure logical grammar, expounded in the Fourth Logical Investigation. Husserl's theory of meaning categories is clearly an attempt in such a direction. Of course, Chateaubriand can always try to distance himself from Husserl by underscoring that he understands by logic something essentially non-syntactic. But the fact of the matter is that such a logical nucleus was conceived by Husserl as being present in each language and, thus, as not bounded to any particular language, and the quotation of Chateaubriand immediately above approaches him once more to a Husserlian conception.

On pp. 114-116 Chateaubriand once more criticizes the syntactic view of logic. For him – see p. 115 -, it is the concept of truth which anchors the whole of classical logic. Moreover, the syntactic attempt to avoid logical and mathematical abstract objects by reducing logic to formal languages does not take into account the fact that formal languages are themselves infinite mathematical structures of significant complexity - see pp. 115-116 -, and, thus, nothing is gained by those allergic to abstract entities and infinities by proceeding in that direction.

Chateaubriand returns to Quine and his grammatical view of logical truth. Thus, he reminds us that for Quine two expressions are interchangeable if they can be replaced for each other in a grammatically well-formed sentence so as to obtain a new grammatically well-formed sentence. Chateaubriand correctly observes – see pp. 127 and 128 -, that Quine wanted to have the benefits of not remaining completely anchored in language without having to acknowledge abstract entities like properties or attributes in his ontology, or having to acknowledge that he is speaking about truth and reality.

On p. 131, Chateaubriand discusses an interesting issue, also discussed by Husserl in the Sixth Logical Investigation and even ten years earlier in the posthumously published 'Zur Logik der Zeichen (Semiotik)'.[9] It is the problem of the role of symbolism in mathematics (and logic), without which the astonishing progress in those disciplines would be unattainable, but which, on the other hand, seems also to make some believe that symbolism is all what there is to mathematics and logic. Chateaubriand correctly observes – see p. 131 –, that sometimes the symbolism used is so adequate that mathematicians get accustomed to reason over the symbols and in some sense forget about the mathematical structures underlying the symbolism. Moreover, he considers that the fact that the syntax of first-order logic is so adequate to its semantics has played a decisive role both in the frequent restriction of logic to first-order logic successfully championed by Skolem and Quine, and in taking logic to be essentially syntax. Chateaubriand, of course, underscores once more his rejection of both contentions.

On pp. 132-133, Chateaubriand states that the logical forms are the logical properties, and that in different systems of notation – depending on the strength of the logical system - different logical properties can be expressed. Thus, as Chateaubriand puts it on p. 133, it is not the structure of reality that depends on language but the structure of language that is dependent on reality. A less powerful language cannot represent as many logical properties or features of reality as a more powerful one.

In Chapter 16, p. 162, there is an interesting assertion of Chateaubriand, which deserves being mentioned. He says that in the same way in which the simple theory of types blurred the definability distinctions made by Russell in his ramified theory, two-valued extensional logic blurred the distinctions of sense made by Frege and, presumably, incorporated into his logical system. On the first point, I just want to mention that since the simple theory of types, together with the distinction between object language and metalanguage can protect against the semantic paradoxes as effectively as the ramified theory but in a more natural and uncomplicated fashion, it seems

---

[9] That paper of 1890 was published only in 1970 as an Appendix to his *Philosophie der Arithmetik*, Den Haag, M. Nijhoff 1970, pp. 340-373.

perfectly natural to avoid the unnecessary complications of the ramified theory. On the second point, one should not forget that it was Frege himself who blurred many of the distinctions of his (and Husserl's) theory of sense. First of all, Frege's logic is a two-valued extensional logic. Furthermore, it was Frege who blurred the most basic sense distinction when he, as made perfectly clear in his letters to Husserl of 1906, identified sameness of meaning with interderivability, that is, with sameness of conceptual content. Thus, for the Frege of the letters to Husserl of 1906 and for his uncritical followers the Axiom of Choice, Zorn's Lemma and Tychonoff's Theorem in general topology should be considered as expressing the same sense.

At the beginning of Chapter 17 Chateaubriand makes some important remarks on his conception of logic. On p. 211, he asserts that for him the theory of types is the core of logic, though he does not make it clear whether he means the ramified or the simple theory. Although in view of his prior assertion on p. 162 mentioned above, one could be inclined to render Chateaubriand as referring on p. 211 also to the ramified theory, a charitable rendering of that passage as referring to the simple theory of types is also possible. In fact, I am inclined to think that it is the simple theory, not the ramified, which forms the core of logic. On p. 212, Chateaubriand states that a fundamental feature of logic is its universality and, thus, "…should be formulated in terms of the broadest possible categorization of reality". Those remarks of Chateaubriand are especially important, since as he points out on p. 213, logical properties require a logic somehow structured in types or levels. The universality of logical properties consists, for Chateaubriand – see p. 213 -, in the fact that "…once a logical property appears at a certain level, there will be "analogous properties" appearing at all higher levels". As Chateaubriand puts it more explicitly, when a property appears at a certain level, its range of application is certainly fixed by its type, but, nonetheless, at any higher level there will appear similar properties. Take, for example, the logical property of subordination – which together with identity, universality, existence and duality is one of the examples of logical properties given in the book. Subordination between concepts appears already at the level of first-order concepts, but from then on there occurs at each higher level a similar relation of subordination between concepts of that level. Such a feature of logical properties, as Chateaubriand underscores on p. 213, is not shared by non-logical properties.

Another remark of Chateaubriand in Chapter 17, which deserves being mentioned, since it also serves as preparation for the fundamental Chapter 18, occurs on p. 129. On that page, he observes that whereas propositional logic is essentially concerned with analyzing truth, predicate logic – in the wide sense of a theory of types, as used by Chateaubriand – offers an analysis of the structure of states of affairs.

Chapter 18 is probably the most important single chapter of the whole book. After some additional comments on what he calls – see p. 250 - Quine's linguistic view of logic, Chateaubriand expounds some of his most interesting views. Thus, on p. 251, he characterizes logical states of affairs as consisting exclusively of combinations of logical properties. Moreover, Chateaubriand correctly assumes that such logical properties either combine necessarily or do not combine necessarily. Furthermore, in the same extremely important paragraph Chateaubriand characterizes logical truths as propositions that denote logical states of affairs. The above, however, is not a definition, but a first approach, since as Chateaubriand observes on p. 252, there can very well be statements that contingently denote a logical state of affairs. To make clear this distinction, Chateaubriand reminds the reader – on the same p. 252 - of Frege's definition of the number 0 in *Die Grundlagen der Arithmetik*, where he opted to define it as the extension of a concept that had an empty extension on logical grounds, in contrast to other concepts contingently having an empty extension. Thus, Chateaubriand adds to his characterization of logical truth that in order for a proposition to be a logical truth it is necessary that it be "…a logical proposition, that is, a proposition that consists exclusively of logical properties". Here Chateaubriand incurs in the confusion between sense and reference. He had already said on the previous page that logical states of affairs, which are the referents of propositions, are combinations of logical properties, whereas now he says that the logical propositions are the ones that are exclusively formed by logical properties. I am not going to dwell on this slip of

Chateaubriand, since it is nothing more than a slip. Thus, precisely on p. 253, he makes perfectly clear the correct ontological status of logical properties. The passage, which contains Chateaubriand's definitions of logical truth and logical falsity, is so important that deserves being quoted.

> Given that logical properties either combine necessarily or do not combine, it seems reasonable to say that logical propositions whose parts denote logical properties that combine necessarily into a logical state of affairs, are logically true, and to say that logical propositions whose parts denote logical properties that necessarily do not combine, are logically false.

On p. 254, Chateaubriand reintroduces the important distinction already made in the Introduction between logical truths and its applications, which has not always been grasped by analytic philosophers. Chateaubriand considers three examples of instantiations of logical truths, namely, (i) Frege=Frege, (ii) $(\forall x)$ (Human $(x) \rightarrow$ Human (x)), and (iii) Human (Russell)$\vee \neg$ Human (Russell). All those three statements refer to existing states of affairs, but those states of affairs are not logical states of affairs. They depend on contingent circumstances, like the existence of the individuals Frege or Russell, or the non-logical property of being human. As Chateaubriand puts it on the same p. 254, "...they attribute logical properties to certain non-logical entities, and...these logical properties apply universally to any entities of the appropriate type". As Chateaubriand puts it on p. 255, such statements are simply applied logical truths. In each of the three cases, the universal applicability of a logical property to a non-logical entity is contingent on the existence of that entity. It seems convenient to quote here two important passages, the first from p. 262 and the second from pp. 262-263.

> A logical truth must be true simply in virtue of the logical features of the world, but an applied logical truth may just happen to be true because of certain contingencies... given Frege's existence [a contingent fact: GERH], his self-identity is not only a necessary truth, but a logically necessary truth.
> An applied logical truth such as Frege's self-identity is contingent in the sense that the existence of the state of affairs

> in question is contingent, depending on Frege's existence. But given Frege's existence, the state of affairs necessarily exists; it is a necessary combination between a logical property and Frege....If an entity necessarily exists, but is not a logical entity [for example, presumably the God of Christianity: GERH], the self-identity of that entity would be an applied logical truth that is not contingent. This would not make it a logical truth, however, because, as I characterized them, logical truths must denote states of affairs that consist exclusively of logical entities.

As Chateaubriand mentions immediately afterwards, he is using the following complex combination of parameters in his classification of states of affairs: (i) the contingency or necessity of the existence of the state of affairs, (ii) the contingency or necessity of the entities that combine to form the state of affairs, (iii) the logical or non-logical nature of such entities, and (iv) the necessity or contingency of the combination.

It is unnecessary to underscore the extreme subtlety of Chateaubriand's analysis, which seems to have few counterparts in analytic philosophy. Once more, the point of comparison is neither Frege nor Russell, nor Wittgenstein, Carnap or Quine, but Husserl, who in the Third Logical Investigation made a distinction similar to Chateaubriand's fundamental distinction between logical truths and their applications. Husserl was not trying to define logical truth but analyticity – in a very different manner than either Carnap or Frege, in fact, in a non-Kantian but Bolzanian way - and offered a definition of analyticity in terms of logical form, while distinguishing analytic laws, which are true in virtue of their purely categorial form, from their applications, which he called 'analytic necessities'. It seems appropriate to quote here Husserl somewhat extensively, since neither Chateaubriand nor most of his potential readers are used to reading Husserl.

> Analytic laws are unconditionally general laws (and, thus, free from any explicit or implicit postulation of individual existence), which contain no other concepts except formal[ones], [and] thus, when we go back to the primitives, nothing other than formal properties. In comparison with the analytic

laws, are their particularizations, which originate by means of the introduction of material concepts and eventually of thoughts postulating individual existence.... As in general particularizations of laws produce necessities, so particularizations of analytic laws [produce] analytic necessities. What one calls "analytic propositions" are usually analytic necessities. *[Logische Untersuchungen II*, U. III, § 12.]

Analytically necessary propositions, so we can define them, are such propositions, which are completely independent from the material peculiarity of their objectualities (determined or conceived in undetermined generality) and from the eventual factuality of the case, from the validity of the eventual postulation of existence, thus, propositions that allow being completely formalized and [being] considered as special cases or empirical applications of the formal or analytic laws obtained by means of such a formalization. In an analytic proposition it must be possible to replace any material content with the void form something, while completely preserving the logical form of the proposition, and eliminate each postulation of existence by means of passing to the corresponding form of judgment of "unconditional generality" or lawfulness. [*Logische Untersuchungen II*, U. III, § 12]

Thus, Husserl's definitions of analytic law and analytic necessity, as well as their contrast, are very similar to Chateaubriand's definitions of logical truths and their instances, and their contrast. In particular, statements like "Frege=Frege" or the other examples given by Chateaubriand and reproduced above would be considered by Husserl not as analytic laws but as analytic necessities. Hence, Husserl's definitions should be rendered as forerunners of the corresponding definitions of Chateaubriand. Nonetheless, though Husserl's definition of analyticity is not liable to the objections offered against Frege's or against Carnap's completely different definitions, I think that such a sort of definition is more adequate for logical truth than for analyticity, since this last notion was meant by Husserl to include mathematical truths (with the exception of non-formal geometry). However, I suspect that not all mathematical truths (for example, number-theoretic statements) could be considered analytic in Husserl's sense. Therefore, I agree with Chateaubriand in considering such a notion as one of logical truth instead of analyticity.

However, though I am inclined to accept Chateaubriand's definition of logical truth (or one very similar to it), there is a non-negligible difficulty. Chateaubriand in some sense presupposes that logic is type theory - be it ramified or simple type theory -, with some additional features. (I have acknowledged my subjective preference for simple type theory together with the distinction between object language and metalanguage, in order to deal with the semantic paradoxes without having to deal with the complications of ramified type theory.) Nonetheless, as a matter of fact, there exists a great diversity of logics, most of which can be considered as extensions of first-order logic in one or another sense. Thus, for example, there is a variety of what one could call 'the vertical extensions of first-order logic', with which generalized model theory is concerned, and which includes not only higher-order logics, but also infinitary logics and logics with additional numerical quantifiers. There is no guarantee that the logical forms or properties, if not invariant to a change of logic, then at least are preserved in Chateaubriand's sense – that is, there is a similar logical property in the new logic, for example, when one goes from ramified type theory to a more powerful logic without type-theoretic distinctions -, and in any case that would have to be proved. Moreover, philosophical logicians are concerned with what one could call 'the horizontal extensions of first-order logic', for example, first-order modal logics, as well as other less central varieties, like epistemic or temporal logics. Once more, the logical forms or properties present in all these logics do not need to coincide with those of the logic preferred by Chateaubriand. Furthermore, many logicians of the constructivist schools would understand by logic not an extension but a restriction of classical first-order logic. Therefore, though I would certainly prefer, like Chateaubriand, that our logic would capture exactly all the logical properties (or logical forms) there are, the prospects seem rather cloudy.

There is an additional point made by Chateaubriand in Chapter 18 that deserves some brief comment. On p. 270, Chateaubriand goes back to second-order logic, and mentions its two usual interpretations, namely, the absolute interpretation, in which in each model there are as many possible n-adic relations, for any natural number n, as there can be on the basis of the cardinality of the individual domain, and the so-called general interpretations, or Henkin interpretations, for which the above requirement is not necessarily fulfilled. Chateaubriand states that one should prefer the interpretation via general models and not the absolute one via full models, on the ground that the latter "...involve general metaphysical principles that strictly speaking go beyond the scope of logic". This sounds very strange, coming from the pen of a philosopher who conceives logic as essentially ontological and gives more weight to the semantic than to the syntactic side of logic. But in any case, the requirement is more set-theoretical than metaphysical. However, the by far most important objection to Chateaubriand's choice of general models over full models represents Per Lindström's famous theorem, according to which an extension of first-order logic for which both the Löwenhein-Skolem theorem and the compactness theorem are valid, is essentially a first-order logic. As is well-known, the interpretation of second-order logic via general models makes possible a Weak Completeness theorem for second-order logic, from which the Löwenhein-Skolem and compactness theorems easily follow. Hence, second-order logic with general models is essentially a first-order logic. Moreover, originally Henkin proved the Weak Completeness theorem for simple type theory, that is, for the whole higher-order logic. Therefore, simple type theory with general models collapses to first-order logic. Thus, the features making second- and higher-order logic much more powerful than first-order logic are neutralized. In fact, Chateaubriand's remark on p. 270 is not easy to reconcile with his stance through the whole book on the pressing issue of first-order versus second- and higher order logic. I think that we should acknowledge second- and higher-order logic with full models and its semantic incompleteness as full citizens in the realm of logic with equal rights as first-order logic or propositional logic, and not be satisfied with first-order logic in second-order clothes – to paraphrase Quine -, which is to what second-order logic with general models amounts to.

Interestingly enough, in Chapter 19, p. 295, Chateaubriand, while arguing against the usual restrictions in logic textbooks of logical deduction, points out to the fact that in second-order logic we cannot syntactically characterize completeness. However, as already stressed, semantic incompleteness, to which Chateaubriand alludes, is - as he very well knows - a feature of second-order logic with full models, not of second-order logic with so-called general models.

In Chapters 21 and 22, Chateaubriand underscores the intuitive relation between proof, truth and knowledge. Thus, he says in Chapter 21, p. 340, that proof is designed to reach truth and to reach it with understanding. In this sense, as Chateaubriand correctly observes, proof is essentially different from other possible ways to try to obtain truth, for example, by means of oracles or revelations. In Chapter 22, p. 355, Chateaubriand modifies the well-known characterization of knowledge as justified true belief, and defines it as "...truth justified beyond a reasonable doubt". As he points out: "If there is enough doubt or if there is no truth, then we may have theoretical belief but no knowledge".

In Chapter 23 there are some interesting remarks on the so-called Ockham's razor, which has been used widely, be it explicitly or implicitly, by analytic philosophers in the Anglo American empiricist and pragmatist tradition from Russell to Quine, Benacerraf, Field and others. Thus, on p. 376, Chateaubriand in a memorable phrase states that as an absolute principle, "...Ockham's razor is the expression of a philosophical castration complex". Nonetheless, on p. 377, Chateaubriand acknowledges some value to Ockham's razor. Thus, given a theory with strong ontological commitments, it is interesting to examine what could still be obtained if we were to apply such a restricting criterion as Ockham's razor. I think that a similar role can be played by constructivist restrictions in mathematics. Constructivist mathematics is not going to replace classical Platonist mathematics. It would be a tragedy for mathematics and for science if such a replacement were to occur. Nonetheless, it is always interesting to see how much could still be obtained of classical mathematical results if we were to put some more stringent or less stringent constructivist restrictions.

Chapter 25 is one of the most interesting of the whole book. It is so rich in philosophical insights that any choice of some of the issues treated would do some injustice to it. Nonetheless, a choice is unavoidable. A general theme present along the whole chapter is Aristotle's conception of the role of the axiomatic method and its difficulties. Chateaubriand correctly conceives – see p. 423 - the attempts made in the last century to make empirical science and philosophy more logical and mathematical as an example of this honest quest for justification and foundation of truths. However, Chateaubriand argues – see p. 426 - that Gödel's incompleteness theorems represent a blow not only to Russell's logicism and to Hilbert's program, but in a more general way, also to Aristotle's views.

As is well known, Hilbert's new axiomatics had already challenged Aristotle's conception of the axiomatic method, and tried to separate it from truth and foundation. Moreover, as Chateaubriand correctly states – p. 429 -, the logical positivists reinterpreted Hilbert's axiomatic method as the hypothetico-deductive method. In some sense, as Chateaubriand puts it on p. 429, what they did was to transpose Hilbert's conception of the axiomatization of the logical-mathematical to the natural world and bring it together with their empiricism. On this point, I think, the emphasis should be on the last component, namely, empiricism, since Hilbert had already tried to axiomatize parts of theoretical physics a decade before the advent of the second Vienna Circle, that is, that of Schlick and Carnap - since Hahn and Neurath had already had, together with Philip Frank, a sort of first Vienna Circle years before the arrival of Schlick in Vienna.

Gödel reacted very differently, and on pp. 429-431 Chateaubriand discusses Gödel's reactions both as a logician and as a philosopher to the consequences of his own celebrated incompleteness results. I have only one objection to Chateaubriand's exposition, namely, that he does not even mention Husserl, though it is already usually acknowledged – one can consult the writings on Gödel of Wang, Føllesdal, Tieszen, van Atten and Kennedy, and most recently and foremost of Hauser – that Husserl's philosophy had a non-negligible impact on Gödel's philosophical views – even though some of those scholars may have failed to adequately assess the core of that impact.[10] (I have used the word 'impact' and not 'influence', since it

---

[10] See the corresponding writings in the references.

seems that Gödel arrived at his views before he ever read Husserl. However, after learning from Husserl's congenial but more developed views, he reached a clearer and deeper insight into the philosophical issues of mathematical intuition and our knowledge of abstract entities. Indeed, Chateaubriand, who also has arrived to similar views about abstract entities, semantics and other related issues, could also profit from a systematic study of Husserl's writings.)

Another very important issue discussed in Chapter 25 – and already in previous chapters – is the inadequacy of the official syntactic notion of proof found in logic textbooks. Chateaubriand has a much wider conception of proof. Thus, on p. 433, he rejects the current view of proof as being linear and finite. Moreover, he correctly observes that proofs of infinite length are current in mathematics, though due to our own limitations, they are coded in a finite way. Chateaubriand offers two decisive examples, firstly, proofs involving the Axiom of Choice and, secondly, the many Induction Principles used in mathematics, including the induction schema of first-order arithmetic and the induction principle of second-order arithmetic. Hence, Chateaubriand concludes – see p. 433 – that "...there is no reason not to introduce explicitly into logic infinitary principles of proof, as long as we can describe them effectively (or in some reasonable way)." Furthermore, Chateaubriand propounds an additional liberalization of the notion of proof in another direction. He considers that in some proofs analogies and insights can play a decisive role, and even states – see p. 434 – that we cannot even exclude the possibility of a new revolutionary proof, which would not fit the current standards but would have to be accepted as correct. Moreover, Chateaubriand makes the point – see pp. 434-435 - that the attempts to analyze philosophical (and other non-logical-mathematical) arguments in terms of propositional and first-order logic have been very unsuccessful, having served to support the view (so dear to all sorts of irrationalism) of the irrelevance of logic to philosophy and to life. On p. 439, Chateaubriand suggests that we have not only to broaden the concept of proof and the relation between premises and conclusion, but also try to better understand the structuring of the reality about which speak our propositions and their connections. I suspect that on this last point we are already transcending the limits even of a non-syntactic logic.

On the same p. 439, Chateaubriand brings to the fore a very interesting issue. He vehemently rejects the usually accepted thesis of Hume about the non-existence of necessary connections in the realm of facts – contrary to what occurs in the realm of the relations of ideas. Chateaubriand had already argued that there are logical connections between matters of fact – for example, in the statement: Frege=Frege - , and such a connection is, of course, a necessary one. But Chateaubriand is not concerned here so much with such statements as the above, but with statements like: "All humans are mortal". On p. 440, Chateaubriand states that the truth of such statements is not a matter of probabilities but of evidence. Moreover, he underscores – see p. 440 – the futility of trying to argue on behalf of such a statement by taking particular cases of humans that have died. As Chateaubriand puts it on the same page 440: "The character of the properties (or predicates) is quite essential for the proof". Moreover, he adds also on the same page: "In the case of the mortality of humans, what we suppose is that there is a necessary connection between the fact of being human and the fact of being mortal". Once more, without knowing it, Chateaubriand comes close to Husserl, this time, however, not exclusively to the Husserl of *Logische Untersuchungen* and related writings, but to Husserl's better-known intuition of essences. For Chateaubriand, the relation between humanity and mortality is clearly neither purely logical nor a matter of fact, but is a necessary relation concerned with the nature or character (or as Husserl would say: essence) of the properties involved. Hence, as I already said, Chateaubriand would profit immensely by looking into Husserl's writings, where, as happened with Gödel, he could find congenial particular views and a general stance certainly much nearer to his than the naturalism of Quine, and on many issues even much nearer than Frege's corresponding views

I want, finally, to reiterate part of what I said at the beginning of this critical review. I consider *Logical Forms* an outstanding book, a book that deserves to have a much wider audience than it has had up to now. Chateaubriand's knowledge both of logic and of analytic philosophy is impressive. However, much more valuable are his excellent capability to see the weak points in the views of many of the most important analytic philosophers, as well as his independence of thought, which contrasts with blind acceptance by most Anglo American analytic philosophers of the post-positivistic new dogmas of empiricism and naturalism. I have little doubt that if *Logical Forms* reaches a much wider audience, Oswaldo Chateaubriand would have to be considered as one of the most important living analytic philosophers. That does not mean that one should agree with everything that he says or that he cannot still polish more his philosophical views, and my criticism of some of his views, as well as my frequent comparison of some of his views with Husserl's have had the objective of opening new paths of fruitful philosophical discussion.[11]

References

Barwise, Jon & Perry, John – 'Semantic Innocence and Uncompromising Situations', in Peter A. French et al. (eds.), *Midwest Studies in Philosophy*, Vol. 6, *The Foundations of Analytic Philosophy*, University of Minnesota Press, Minneapolis 1981, 387-403

Carnap, Rudolf – *Der logische Aufbau der Welt* 1928, fourth edition, Felix Meiner, Hamburg 1974

Føllesdal, Dagfinn – 'Gödel and Husserl', in Jaakko Hintikka (ed.), *From Dedekind to Gödel*, Kluwer, Dordrecht 1995, pp. 427-446

Hauser, Kai – 'Gödel's Program Revisited: Part I: The Turn to Phenomenology', *The Bulletin of Symbolic Logic 12 (4)*, December 2006, pp. 529-590

Hill, Claire O. & Rosado Haddock, Guillermo E. – *Husserl or Frege?: Meaning, Objectivity and Mathematics*, Open Court, Chicago et al. 2000, paperback edition, 2003

Husserl, Edmund – *Philosophie der Arithmetik* 1891, mit ergänzenden Texten (1890-1901), M. Nijhoff, Den Haag 1970

Husserl, Edmund – *Logische Untersuchungen* 1900-1901, M. Nijhoff, Den Haag 1975 (I) and 1984 (II)

---

[11] I would like to thank Prof. Chateaubriand for correcting a few misinterpretations of his views.

Husserl, Edmund – *Ideen zu einer reinen Phänomenologie und einer phänomenologischen Philosophie I*, 1913, M. Nijhoff, Den Haag 1976

Rosado Haddock, Guillermo E. – 'On Necessity and Existence', *Diálogos* 68, July 1996, pp. 57-62

Rosado Haddock, Guillermo E. – 'Kritische Fußnoten zu Bernulf Kanitscheiders Naturalismus Aufsatz', *Erwägen, Wissen, Ethik 17 (3)*, 2006, pp. 351-353

Rosado Haddock, Guillermo E. – *The Young Carnaps Unknown Master*, Ashgate, Aldershot 2008

Tieszen, Richard – 'Gödel's Path from the Incompleteness Theorems (1931) to Phenomenology (1961)', *The Bulletin of Symbolic Logic 4(2)*, June 1998, pp. 181-203

Van Atten, Mark & Kennedy, Juliette – 'On the Philosophical Development of Kurt Gödel', *The Bulletin of Symbolic Logic 9(4)*, December 2003, pp. 425-476

Wang, Hao – *From Mathematics to Philosophy*, Routledge, London 1974

Wang, Hao – *Reflections on Kurt Gödel*, MIT Press, Cambridge, Ma. 1987

Wang, Hao – *A Logical Journey: From Gödel to Philosophy*, MIT Press, Cambridge, Ma. 1996

Weidemann, Hermann – 'Aussagesatz und Sachverhalt: ein Versuch zur Neubestimmung ihres Verhältnisses', *Grazer Philosophische Studien 18*, 1982, pp. 75-99

Rereading the Young Carnap: Critical Study of *Der Raum*[*] 1922, reprint Topos Verlag, Vaduz, Liechtenstein 1991

Abstract
This study is concerned with Rudolf Carnap's doctoral dissertation, *Der Raum*. It offers a brief exposition of this, so often ignored, youth work of Carnap, and tries to correct some misleading renderings of that work. It is convincingly shown that the main philosophical influence in *Der Raum* is neither Kant nor the Neo-Kantians, but Edmund Husserl, and that Carnap's defence in this work of the synthetic *a priori* is clearly non-Kantian, but much nearer to what Carnap correctly interpreted that were Husserl's views on the synthetic *a priori*.

In recent years a profound interest has surged among the researchers in analytic philosophy to examine the origins of logical empiricism and, very especially, the relatively early but classical work of Rudolf Carnap *Der logische Aufbau der Welt*[1], published in 1928. Some of those recent scholars have been made conscious that that work possesses a variety of philosophical influences that contrasts with Carnap's most popular works, most of them written in his forced exile in the United States of America. However, very few scholars have carefully examined Carnap's dissertation, *Der Raum*, published six

---

[*] I am grateful to Prof. Sebastian Luft, then working at the Husserl Archives in Leuwen, and currently professor at Marquette University, to Prof. Hans-Rainer Sepp and to Prof. Karl Schuhmann –who died before the original Spanish version of this study appeared- for their valuable help trying to bring some light to the relation between Husserl and Carnap, a relation that had intrigued me for almost four decades. I am very thankful to Prof. Thomas Mormann for having sent me some of his writings, even some that were still unpublished at that moment, and for having pointed out to Carnap's confusion between affine spaces and projective spaces. Finally I am especially grateful to Prof. Werner Diederich for his also very valuable help of having bought for me and given as a present a copy of *Der Raum*. Without it I would have had to postpone even more my research on Husserl's influence on Carnap, as well as the pleasure derived from reading this short but extremely interesting book.
[1] Carnap (1928).

years before the publication, but only three before having basically completed the manuscript of the *Aufbau*, as this important book of Carnap is referred to. A dozen years ago the little known Topos Verlag in Vaduz, Liechtenstein reprinted Carnap's dissertation, originally published in a special number of Kant-Studien in 1922, but that reprinting has not received the desired consideration. It is our objective in this sort of late critical commentary to examine this important small book, in order to somehow illuminate the present flourishing debate on the origins and influences lurking in the *Aufbau*.

As other important philosophers of the XXth century, like Bertrand Russell, Moritz Schlick and Hans Reichenbach, Rudolf Carnap began his philosophical endeavours with the examination of philosophical problems intimately attached to the revolutionary developments had by our conception of space during the end of the XIXth century and the beginnings of the XXth. In contrast to Bertrand Russell, whose *Foundations of Geometry*[2] of 1897 precedes the revolution in physics and does not take into account the developments in logic made by Frege, Peano and others –and to which he would later contribute so decisively-, Rudolf Carnap nourishes his views both with the revolution that had occurred in physics and with that in logic, as well as with the development and expansion of mathematics towards generalization, which culminated at the beginning of the XXth century. Thus, while in his well-known book Russell contrasts the metrical properties of space with the more general projective properties, but ignores the even greater generality of the topological spaces, and is unable to assess the extremely important contributions of Riemann to the elucidation of the nature of space, Carnap is perfectly conscious of the importance of the topological properties of space for its adequate understanding, and, in view of the rise of general relativity theory, was in a better position to appreciate Riemann's views.

As Carnap puts it in the Introduction to his valuable dissertation, he is going to offer in this work a general view of the different sorts of space corresponding to the different meanings of the word "space" both in philosophy and in science. Specifically, he distinguishes three different meanings of the word "space", namely,

---

[2] Russell (1897).

formal space, intuitive space and physical space. With respect to the first meaning, Carnap says (pp. 5-6) that formal space is a structure of relations, whose members remain completely undetermined, and about which one only knows that on the basis of some connections of a given sort one can conclude about connections of some other different sorts in the same region. On the other hand, with respect to intuitive space, Carnap says the following:

> Under intuitive space, on the other hand, one should have in mind the structures of relations between [spatial] figures in the usual sense..., whose specific particularity we apprehend by means of perception or also by pure representation. Therein actual spatial facts of our empirical reality are not being considered, but only the >>essence<< of precisely those figures, which can be recognized in any representative of the species.

Any scholar moderately familiarized with Edmund Husserl's writings would detect in the two sentences of the Introduction of *Der Raum* we have quoted three clear reminiscences of Husserl's thought. Firstly, there is the indistinctness for the phenomenological study of essences between perception and imaginative representation. Secondly, one should obviously point out the interest for the essences of spatial figures, not for empirical facts. Finally, it should be emphasized that such essences are recognized in any representative of the species.

Finally, Carnap tells us (p. 6) that the spatial facts form the structure of physical space, and adds that its knowledge presupposes that of intuitive space, while that of the latter presupposes formal space. That is the reason why Carnap will first examine what is understood by formal space, then what is understood by intuitive space, and finally what is understood by physical space. In each of the three classes of space Carnap will acknowledge two sorts of subdivisions. The first subdivision is concerned with dimensions, and here Carnap will consider the specific case in which the space has three dimensions and the general case in which it has n dimensions, being n any positive whole number. On the other hand, Carnap distinguishes, in descending order of abstractness, three sorts of spatial abstraction, namely, topological space, projective space and metric space. Thus, Carnap will consider eighteen sorts of space, six formal ones, R_{3T}, R_{3P}, R_{3M}, R_{nT}, R_{nP}, and R_{nM}, six intuitive ones, namely, R_{3T}^*, R_{3P}^*, R_{3M}^*, R_{nT}^*, R_{nP}^* and R_{nM}^*, and six physical spaces, namely, R_{3T}^{**}, R_{3P}^{**}, R_{3M}^{**}, R_{nT}^{**}, R_{nP}^{**} and R_{nM}^{**}.

In Chapter I Carnap is concerned with formal space. It is obtained, as Carnap point out (p. 7), using the tools of the new logic, especially those of the theory of classes and the theory of relations. In this way one obtains ordered series and, especially, continuous series. Formal topological spaces of two or more dimensions are obtained as continuous series of continuous series –thus, the three dimensional ones as continuous series of the third level[3], whereas the corresponding formal projective spaces are obtained from them by means of specific particularizations. Finally, the corresponding formal metric spaces are obtained from the latter also by means of specific particularizations. Carnap maintains (p. 9) that only in this way can one obtain for formal space the complete generality required in order to comprise all possible subspecies. Thus, a continuous series of the third level – a continuous series of continuous series of continuous series- is called by Carnap (see pp. 13-14)- a formal topological space of three dimensions, in symbols: R_{3T}. In this sort of abstract space, be it of three or more dimensions, it does not have sense to talk about spatial figures. On the other hand, the specializations that can be obtained from the formal topological spaces, namely, the formal projective spaces of three dimensions and of n dimensions, and the corresponding metric spaces of three and of n dimensions, are justified, according to Carnap (p. 14) only when they are applied to special figures properly. Since, as Carnap states (p. 14) "… we still are concerned here with mere formal relations, without presupposing what sort of objects are in those relations". Carnap stresses (p. 14) that the relation between the formal topological space of three or, more generally, of n dimensions and the corresponding formal projective space of three, respectively, n dimensions in symbols, R_{3P} and R_{nP}, respectively-, is not that between a species and an individual object that belongs to the species, but that between a genus and a species, whereas formal metric space of three dimensions, respectively, of n dimensions (in symbols: R_{3M},

---

[3] On this point, Carnap seems to be influenced by Russell (1903), what would falsify Roberto Torretti's assertion (1977, p. 319) that Russell's characterization of geometry in that work as the study of series of two or more dimensions was completely ignored by philosophers and mathematicians. By the way, in his valuable well-documented book Torretti does not even include Carnap's dissertation in the bibliography.

respectively, R_{nM}) is a subspecies of R_{3P}, respectively, of R_{nP}. Once more, both the terminology and the distinctions, remind us, in the philosophical context in which *Der Raum* was written, of Husserl, who very frequently made use of this Aristotelian terminology.

In Chapter II Carnap examines intuitive space, which is not concerned with formal relations, but with intuitive spatial figures and relations, thus, as Carnap points out (p. 22), with points, lines, surfaces, spaces, points lying on a line, the intersection of lines, etc. Carnap is not in the least interested in the psychological origin of our representation of intuitive space, but only in the logical foundation of our knowledge of intuitive space, especially in the axioms that serve as logical-formal basis for the remaining statements that constitute that knowledge. On this issue Carnap refers us to Driesch when pointing out that the axioms of intuitive space are independent of experience, in the sense that "contrary to empirical statements, their knowledge does not turn more and more secure by means of the constant repetition of the experience" (p. 22). When explaining the reason for the latter, Carnap refers expressly to Husserl. On this point, Carnap says:

> Thus, here we are not concerned, as Husserl has pointed out, with facts in the sense of our empirical reality, but with the essence (Eidos) of certain given objectualities [Gegebenheiten], that, being so as they are [sosein], can be apprehended by means of their being given [Gegebensein] only once.

Moreover, Carnap adds:

> Since we are here not concerned with the isolated fact..., but only with the non-temporal essence, its >>essence<<, it seems important to distinguish this mode of experience from intuition in the strict sense, which is directed to the fact itself, by means of the expression >>contemplation of essences [Wesenserschauung]<< (Husserl), in case there could be [some] confusion. But, in general, it can be that the expression 'intuition' also includes the contemplation of essences, since in this broad sense it is also used since Kant. (pp. 22-23)

The reference to Kant in the latter quoted sentence could have the purpose of appeasing his dissertation's director [in German: Doktorvater] Bruno Bauch, who not only was a Neo-Kantian, but had obtained his professorship in Jena after the faculty, for still unknown reasons, changed its decision of giving the professorship to Husserl.

As Carnap underscores (p. 23), only the axioms of intuitive space need be obtained by intuitive means. However, our intuition, as Carnap correctly points out (p. 23), is only of a limited region of space, and thus from it "... we can also extract knowledge about spatial figures of [clearly] limited size. On the other hand, we are free with respect to the total structuring that we build from those basic figures." Thus, e.g., we obtain the concept of an unlimited straight line from a straight line in our intuitively limited region by means of iterated addition of similar straight lines. "But", as Carnap correctly stresses (p. 23), "to the concept so obtained [of an unlimited straight line] corresponds not only the indefinite straight line, but also the finite but unlimited, closed straight line of elliptic [Riemannian] space". Hence, adds Carnap (p. 23), neither intuition properly nor the requirement of iteration of the intuitively given would allow us to decide between the two possible extensions of the finite straight line.

In the case of intuitive space, Carnap proceeds in the inverse order to the one he followed with formal space. Thus, he first examines the most determined metric space, considering then the projective and finally the topological one. In fact, following David Hilbert[4], instead of fixing the meaning of fundamental concepts and relations of intuitive space by means of explicit definitions, Carnap offers (pp. 24-26) an extensive list of eighteen axioms that constitute implicit definitions of the concepts occurring in them. Axioms 1-12 are connection axioms, whereas the remaining ones, with the exception of the last two, are axioms of congruence. The axioms should be valid in the limited region of the intuitive metric space of three dimensions, in symbols: R_{3M}^*. In fact, axioms 17 and 18 differ from the corresponding Hilbertian axioms by limiting the congruence of triangles and the parallelism between straight lines to the immediately intuitive region. The next step clearly consists in extending the validity of the axioms to the whole intuitive metric space of three dimensions. Carnap introduces (p. 26) six requirements for the extension of the validity of the axioms to the whole R_{3M}^*. The first requirement states that the eighteen axioms are to be valid in any delimited region, while the remaining requirements allow Carnap to extend his considerations to the whole space. Thus, e.g., axioms 1-4 and 13-16 are going to be valid for the whole space, while in the case of axioms 17 and 18 to the equality (i.e. congruence or parallelism, respectively) valid in the

---

[4] David Hilbert (1899).

intuitively delimited region, there corresponds in the extended region of space a relation that approximates to equality. In this way, as Carnap stresses (p. 27), the whole space will have the property, brought to the fore for the first time by Riemann[5], of Euclidicity in its smallest parts. Carnap reminds us (p. 27) that Riemann exhibited the diverse possible structures of intuitive metric space of three dimensions R_{3M}^* compatible with what can be called "local Euclidicity", being decisive for each of these sorts of intuitive spaces that an ordered triple (the measure of curvature) is assigned to each point of space, where each number corresponds to one of the three dimensions. As already mentioned and emphasized by Carnap (p. 27), his requirements have the objective of allowing the extension to the whole of R_{3M}^* of the intuitive properties of the limited region to which we have intuitive access, and which are expressed in the eighteen axioms. Now, in order to obtain the properties of that three-dimensional space, instead of examining the diverse curved surfaces and determine for each point in them an exact analogue of the Gaussian curvature –which Gauss applied only to cases of two dimensions-, Carnap proceeds to examine the diverse planes in such a space. The diversity of the planes is certainly not less than that of curved surfaces, and the spatial relations in those planes is as varied as those in curved surfaces.[6] The examination of the spatial relations in those planes is done by assigning an ordered triple to each point of a given surface, obtaining in this way the Riemannian curvature of the given point in the plane. Now, if the ordered triples assigned to a region of a plane coincide with the ordered triples assigned to the points in a given curved surface, then in the plane and in the curved surface the same spatial relations are present. In this way, the direct examination of the structure of the diverse curved surfaces in intuitive metric space of three dimensions is replaced by an examination of the structure of the diverse planes. Of course, as Carnap stresses (p. 28), when he speaks

---

[5] "Über die Hypothesen, welche der Geometrie zu Grunde liegen" (1867). Local Euclidicity is one of the defining traits of the concept of multiplicity derived from Riemann. See on this point the book by Moritz W. Hirsch (1976, p. 1).
[6] A relatively clear exposition of the notions of Gaussian curvature and of the more general Riemannian curvature, and of the relation between them can be found in Lawrence Sklar's valuable book (1974, pp. 27ff. and 42ff.), respectively.

about planes he does not have in mind our Euclidean notion of plane, but that of a surface such that any two distinct points of which can be connected by a straight line lying completely in the plane. At the same time, under "straight line" is meant any line such that any segment connecting any two points P_1 and P_2 is the shortest line between the two points. This is perfectly compatible with the fact that to each point of a straight line a measure of curvature be assigned – precisely, the corresponding ordered triple-, and that the ordered triples assigned to the different points of a straight line do not coincide with <0.0.0>.

Before continuing our exposition of fundamental components of *Der Raum*, it seems convenient to contrast what Carnap does with Russell's Foundations of Geometry. Whereas Russell does not take into account spaces of variable curvature, that is, spaces such that to its different points could be assigned different measures of curvature, a possibility already pointed out by Riemann –though not by Helmholtz[7]-, for Carnap such spaces are perfectly legitimate. Of course, one can point out that Carnap, contrary to Russell, wrote his dissertation after the advent of general relativity theory, according to which the structure of physical space-time of four dimensions is of variable curvature. Nonetheless, the treatment in Carnap's dissertation is so general that it could have been essentially conceived even if no one had discovered general relativity theory.

Precisely in the following pages of *Der Raum*, and after having stressed that R_{3M}^* is totally fixed in its metrical relations once one assigns to each point its ordered triple of numbers corresponding to the three different directions, Carnap goes on to consider spaces of constant curvature. Hence, he introduces the well-known definitions of homogeneity and isotropy, which we are going to quote, since we cannot express them in a more clearly and concise fashion:

> Now, if for each point of space the same three numbers are valid, then in any part of space the same spatial relations are present as in any other. Space is called in this case homogeneous. Every plane of this space has then in all its points the same measure of curvature (>>planes of constant curvature<<), but it does not need to be the same for all planes. (p. 28)

---

[7] See Helmholtz' "Über die Tatsachen, die der Geometrie zum Grunde liegen" (1868). It is clear that Russell followed Helmholtz on this point, not Riemann.

Thus, two planes of constant curvature perpendicular to each other in space do not need to have the same curvature. Let us consider the other definition:

> If, on the other hand, on each point in space the three valid numbers are equal, then there all spatial directions are equivalent [gleichartig]. Space is then called isotropic. If both conditions are met, then all points and all directions are equivalent [gleichartig]; all distinctive numbers of this homogeneous and isotropic space are equal: the measure of curvature of >>space of constant curvature<<. In this case, all planes in space are not only planes of constant curvature, but all are equivalent [gleichartig]; the curvature is for all the same and, certainly, that of the space. (pp. 28-29)

Obviously, if space is isotropic but not homogeneous, its curvature can arbitrarily vary, even from point to point, though in each point the variation in the three directions is the same.

Immediately, Carnap goes on to consider (p. 29) the diverse sorts of planes determined by their curvature. Thus, as is well known, if the curvature is negative, we have a hyperbolic plane; if it is equal to zero, a parabolic (or Euclidean) plane; and if it is positive, an elliptic plane. Carnap then enumerates some distinctive properties of the three sorts of planes and, in general, of geometries. Thus, e.g., as is well known, in the first case the sum of the angles of a triangle is less than 180 degrees, and through a point not lying on a determined straight line can pass more than one –in fact, infinitely many- straight lines parallel to the first straight line; in the second case the sum of the angles of a triangle is 180 degrees, and through a point not lying on a determined straight line passes exactly one straight line parallel to the first one; in the third case the sum of the angles of a triangle is more than 180 degrees, and through a point not lying on a determined straight line cannot pass any straight line parallel to the first one. Finally, Carnap stresses (p. 29) that whereas in the first two cases the plane –and total space- is infinite, in the case of elliptic geometry the plane –and the whole space- is finite, though unlimited, since it closes on itself. Carnap sums up his discussion of R_{3M}^* as follows:

> On the basis of facts, given us by intuition of a delimited spatial region, we have encountered, with the help of the formulation of some requirements, the varied sorts of complete spatial structures, in all of whose delimited regions those intuitive facts are present. (p 29)

Carnap's next step consists in obtaining more general intuitive spaces. Such generalizations can occur in two different senses. Firstly, we can generalize the dimensions of space, obtaining in this way the spaces R_{4M}^*, R_{5M}^* and, in general, for any natural number n, the space R_{nM}^*. Clearly, the subdivision in hyperbolic, parabolic and elliptic subspecies made for intuitive space of three dimensions can be made for such generalizations obtained by indefinitely increasing the dimensions, which makes the subspecies of R_{3M}^* parts of the corresponding subspecies of the R_{nM}^*, for any natural number n>3. On the other hand, Carnap makes it clear (p. 30) that even in the case of intuitive metric space of four dimensions intuition requires conceptual help. In fact, we have already seen that in the case of R_{3M}^* we have intuitive access only to delimited regions and not to the whole space, what did not hinder that we considered the whole space. Analogously, although we cannot have intuitive access to four-dimensional figures even in a delimited region, Carnap stresses (p. 30) that we can make use of three-dimensional intuitive figures and, by means of conceptual relations, in some way we can represent four-dimensional figures, although such a possibility will not be purely intuitive, but intuitive-conceptual.[8]

The other sort of generalization consists in leaving aside the properties of space that depend on its metric relations, considering only the genera under which they are subsumed. On this issue Carnap states:

> A spatial structure built on the basis of the fundamental concepts of point, straight line and plane, together with the relation of lying on, without making use of the equality of segments or angles, can be so structured that such differences [between the three subspecies of R_{3M}^*] disappear. Such a space is called [intuitive] projective space R_{3P}^*. (pp. 30-31)[9]

Carnap adds (p. 31) that if we leave aside the concepts of straight line and plane, and consider only the concept of point, as well as those of

---

[8] On the issue of the presumed non-intuitiveness of spaces different from three-dimensional Euclidean space, we suggest to read Henri Poincaré (1902, pp. 63-76), as well as Albert Einstein's paper "Geometrie und Erfahrung" (1918).

[9] As has been observed by Thomas Mormann in an electronic correspondence, Carnap mistakes projective space with affine space. For an especially detailed treatment of affine spaces, see Hermann Weyl's classic book (1918, pp. 17-26, especially 21-22). See also Lawrence Sklar's also classic book (1974, pp. 50-51). For a clear comparison between affine and projective spaces, see the extremely long paper (or better: monograph) of Robert Coleman and Herbert Korté (2001, pp. 203-208) in Scholz (ed.) (2001, pp. 161-386).

line and surface, then we obtain the intuitive topological space of three dimensions R_{3T}^*. Be it by combining the two generalizations, thus, applying to the spaces R_{nM}^*, for any natural number n, the procedure used to obtain R_{3P}^* and then R_{3T}^* from R_{3M}^*, or beginning with formal projective space R_{nP} and formal topological space R_{nT} of n dimensions, and then introducing in them intuitive spatial figures, we obtain intuitive projective and topological spaces of n dimensions R_{nP}^* and R_{nT}^*, respectively. Clearly, as Carnap stresses (p. 31), intuitive topological space of n dimensions is the most general intuitive space, and contains all others, be it as parts –e.g., R_{3T}^* - or as particularization or specialization –e.g., R_{nM}^* -, or as a combination of both –e.g., R_{3M}^*, which can be seen either as a specialization of R_{3T}^* or as a part of R_{nM}^*.

By the way, it should be stressed that Carnap's constant use of the terminology of genera, species and subspecies, as well as the distinction between particularization or specification and singularization is very frequent in Husserl's two most important works published before 1922, namely, *Logische Untersuchungen*[10] and, especially, *Ideen zue einer reinen Phänomenologie und phänomenologischen Philosophie*[11], what does not seem to be a mere coincidence, especially if we take into account not only the inclusion of both books in the references, but even more Carnap's adhesion to the contemplation of essences on pp. 22-23.

In the third chapter Carnap goes on to examine the sorts of physical space. He is interested here in considering the spatial relations in nature, thus, the relations that he calls physical-spatial. As Carnap points out (p. 32): "The doctrine of physical space has... the task of determining which of those [spatial] relations are true for the concrete things present in experience". Before properly beginning the discussion of physical space, Carnap wants to rule out a possible misunderstanding, especially since he is going to assert that there is very little to be said of the physical-spatial relations on the basis of experience. Carnap makes it clear (p. 32) that in this study of physical space he is not interested in the frequent opinion that physical-spatial figures cannot be determined with complete precision, an opinion that

---

[10] Husserl (1900-1901).
[11] Husserl (1913, §§ 9 and 10).

would be based, according to Carnap (p. 32) both on the irregular form of bodies in nature and on the limits of precision of our measuring devices.

Firstly, Carnap is concerned with the determination of what is going to be understood by a straight line in physical space. With that objective in mind, Carnap tells us (p. 33) that we have to presuppose be it the straightness of the light rays or of a ruler. However, Carnap stresses the following:

> It is in principle impossible to establish it, if one considers only what originates exclusively in experience, without fixing [treffen] freely selected stipulations... that are formulated as requirements, without they being ever confirmed or refuted by experience.... (p. 33)

Thus, pure experience does not univocally determine what a straight line in physical space is, and, hence, we are in need of stipulations, that is, of conventions, in order to determine what one is going to understand under straight line. Another possible procedure would consist, says Carnap (pp. 33-34), in fixing not what a straight line is, but what a rigid body is. Usually one selects a body and fixes two points on it. Then one assigns a numerical measure to the distance between those two points, e.g. the unity, in determined physical circumstances, like temperature, direction and location in physical space, etc. Then there are different ways to examine the presumed straightness of a physical line. It is not necessary to expound here the two variants of this procedure suggested by Carnap, in order to determine the straightness of a line by means of the notion of rigid body, or rigid rod –as is usually called in specialized literature. Clearly, the objective is to obtain the simplest stipulation (or fixation) of the measure [Maßsetzung]. With that in mind, Carnap says (p. 35), one frequently proceeds according to certain principles of scientific procedure tacitly assumed, even when the stipulation of measure is perfectly conscious. On the other hand, the selection present in the measure stipulation, says Carnap (p. 36), is not independent of those principles, and, thus, has to take into account empirical facts, since it has to be consistent with them. Now, what is decisive in this issue, as Carnap stresses (p. 37), is that the determination of what is a straight line in physical space is not obtained only from empirical facts, but requires a stipulation, be it direct, by means of the fixation of what is going to be interpreted by a straight line, or indirectly, by means of fixing first a measure and with its help then determine what a straight line is. As Carnap points out (p. 37), the latter procedure has the advantage of not only allowing us to determine whether a particular line segment is a straight line, but also of establishing quantitative relations.

Carnap goes on to consider the different sorts of physical space. On pp. 37-38 Carnap stresses that physical topological space of three dimensions, R_{3T}^{**}, as happens with R_{3T}^{*}, is concerned neither with straight lines nor with relations of magnitude, and, thus, is not concerned with straight lines or stipulations of measure; but only with the relations of incidence of points, lines, surfaces and parts of space in physical space, since they are the only ones required for the ordering of the empirically given figures in such a space. Hence, as Carnap stresses (p. 38), for R_{3T}^{**} are relevant only those relations between physical-spatial figures that do not involve any convention or stipulation. In view of the fact that our experience up to now has not required physical spaces of more than three dimensions, Carnap opts (p. 38) not to examine its generalization to an arbitrary number of dimensions. Nonetheless, R_{nT}^{**} remains always as a possibility, and Carnap makes it clear (p. 38) that three-dimensionality is not a condition of possibility of an empirical object in general, since one could in principle indicate what sorts of empirical facts would have to be present in order to conceive them as four-dimensional figures. On the other hand, Carnap states (p. 38) that whereas topological physical space of three dimensions reproduces everything empirically given in space without needing any sort of convention or stipulation, both projective (really, affine) physical space of three dimensions, R_{3P}^{**}, which can be obtained by requiring the stipulation of what is going to be considered a straight line, and metric physical space of three dimensions, R_{3M}^{**}, which requires a stipulation of measure, are not uniquely determined by empirical facts, but require a selection between various possibilities determined by the corresponding stipulations, be it of 'straight line" or of measure.

On pp. 38-40 Carnap makes precise the important above-mentioned distinction. He first defines as "factual content" (Tatbestand) the matter of experience that has not suffered any transformation. In order to determine whether an empirical statement is only about this factual content and, in general, to be able to distinguish what in the statement is concerned only with the fact from what is concerned with the particular form selected, one would have to examine whether the statement is valid for all [different] sorts of spatial structures. This can be made precise with the mathematical notion of the invariance under bijective continuous transformations, usually called "homeomorphisms" by mathematicians. Now, the topological properties of space are precisely those that remain invariant under homeomorphisms. On the other hand, the projective (or affine) and metric properties of space are not invariant under continuous bijections. The statements about such properties of physical space are not statements only about the factual content of experience, but involve stipulations. Specifically, statements that state something about straight lines and planes are statements about projective (better, affine) physical space of three dimensions, whereas those concerned with equality (or congruence) of segments or angles are statements about metric physical space of three dimensions. In this so elegant way, Carnap tries to isolate what in physical space belongs to the factual content, given in experience without adulteration by means of some sort of stipulation.[12]

As Carnap states (p. 40), the notion of factual content, which includes the whole factual content of statements, purports to capture exactly what is given in experience. Precisely that content is what shows up in topological physical space of three dimensions, R_{3T}^{**}. Nonetheless, from the standpoint of our knowledge of physical nature, the space that interests us is metric physical space of three dimensions, R_{3M}^{**}, for which measuring is specifically relevant. In order to obtain it, Carnap points out (p. 40) one can, e.g. stipulate that the distance between two determined points on an iron rod is going to be used for measuring. It must be perfectly clear that, as Carnap stresses (p. 40), in order to be used as scale (Maßstab) the distance

---

[12] The possibility of this isolation of the topological properties of physical space from its metric properties has been questioned from different angles. The most serious objection is based on mathematical results. See on this point p. 54 of the book by Lawrence Sklar already mentioned, as well as the more detailed treatment by Thomas Mormann in his "Carnap's Metrical Conventionalism versus Differential Geometry" (2005).

between those two points has to be taken as rigid, that is, as not changing, as invariant both under temporal change and spatial displacements. On the basis of the factual content and the stipulation of measure, and, as Carnap stresses (p. 40), only on such a basis, would the nature of R_{3M}^{**} be determined. Before proceeding to obtain R_{3M}^{**}, Carnap reminds the reader (pp. 40-41) that in the whole discussion of physical space, be it topological, projective or metric, we work with a three-dimensional projection of the four-dimensional spatial-temporal multiplicity that constitutes, according to (special and general) relativity theory, the world in which we live. Such a projection, points out Carnap (p. 41), is obtained by the selection of three coordinates in Minkowski space-time –the space-time of special relativity-, with the peculiarity that none of them lies in the double temporal cone of past and future. Clearly, there is still some margin for different selections of that three-dimensional projection. Carnap reduces such non-determination by stressing (p. 41) that we can limit our considerations to those spatial relations that are independent of the fixation of simultaneity, what could be obtained if we limit the attempts to measure the distance between two points to those in which both figures are in a state of rest.

After those observations, Carnap goes on to define the notion of "rigidity" in the usual manner. Thus, Carnap says:

> We want to call >>rigid<< a set of points, a line, a piece of surface or a body with regard to a given measure stipulation, when the distance between any two points of the set remains indefinitely the same [dauernd gleich bleibt] with respect to it. (p. 42)

Obviously, the definition of rigidity depends, on the other hand, on the presupposition of the rigidity of the rod in which the scale is specified. The determination of the curvature in a region of a plane in physical space is obtained by examining the usual properties of geometric figures in that plane, e.g., the sum of the angles of a triangle. A less popular way [of obtaining it] mentioned (p. 43) by Carnap consists in fixing a point in a plane and constructing six equilateral triangles around it. If they cover the whole immediate region around the point without intersecting and without gaps, the plane is parabolic (or Euclidean); if they do not leave gaps but intersect, the plane is elliptic; and finally, if they do not cover the region completely but leave some angles uncovered, the plane is hyperbolic. If one wants to specifically determine the curvature, stresses Carnap (p. 43), one has to obtain from the fixing of the measure, with the help of the scale, a procedure to measure segments. Carnap states (p. 44) that only the topological properties of the plane, thus, those that constitute the factual content, e.g., the relation of a point lying on a line, can be established by such a procedure. Once the curvature is fixed in a piece of the plane, one can do the same with other points of the plane, and in this way be able to determine the metric relations in the whole region. The number of points to be considered will depend, Carnap says (p. 45), on the major or minor divergences between the curvatures obtained in the different parts of the plane. Obviously, if the differences are more noticeable, the number of points to be considered will augment. What is important, however, is that by proceeding in this way we can fix the curvature in the whole region and, on the basis of this result, in principle, that of the whole physical space. Even more important for Carnap is:

> ... firstly, that establishing the metric relations of physical space has sense only when a freely selected measure stipulation is available and, secondly, that such establishing takes from experience only the factual content, that is, only considers and evaluates topological properties of physical spatial figures, without presupposing the straightness of no matter what physical lines.... (p. 45)

Up to now Carnap's procedure has shown that the sort of physical space is a mathematical function of the empirical component, which consists of the factual content and the conventional component of the measure stipulation. Carnap will try to show that one could very well had started with the factual content and the metrical relations of space, and obtain the measure stipulation as a function of them. It seems unnecessary to enter here in a detailed discussion of what follows. Nonetheless, it is convenient to mention that he rejects a superficially simple measure stipulation, since it requires of later complications. Such is the case of a measure stipulation according to which the earth would not only be plane but would have 0 curvature in any of its points. In such a case the earth's surface would have to be conceived as infinitely large. Moreover, such a metric stipulation would have the inconvenience of requiring a privileged place in the plane. But that is at odds with highly desirable properties of physical space. Thus, Carnap states (p. 48) that one ought to select the simplest spatial structure compatible with the homogeneity and isotropy of space, thus, space ought to have in all its points and all directions of the surface the same curvature. Once spatial structure has been fixed, one has to try to obtain the measure stipulation corresponding to this space and compatible with the factual content of physical experience, which, as Carnap points out (p. 48), includes all spatial measurements both astronomical and terrestrial.[13]

In the next pages Carnap compares two possible measure stipulations, M_1 and M_0, applied to the earth (in German: Erde), to which Carnap refers with an "E". The first one is the usual one, which considers the earth to be a sphere, while the second considers the earth to be a plane, though one with positive curvature in all its points. M_0 will coincide with M_1 with respect to the metric relations on E. This means, among other things, as Carnap tells us (p. 48), that the equality of lines made in usual physics making use of M_1 remains when one uses M_0 instead. Similarly, since on the basis of M_1 the great circles of the terrestrial sphere are the shortest lines, on the basis of M_0, according to which the earth is a plane, the lines that correspond to the great circles are straight lines, and the property of being the shortest lines between two points is preserved. Moreover, in both cases, any two points of E determine a unique straight line, except in the poles, through which pass infinitely many straight lines. Thus, in this sort of "spherical plane' that is the earth according to M_0 and that, on the basis of the presupposition of homogeneity, Carnap calls "spherical space", the same physical measure scales are valid as in the usual terrestrial physics on the basis of the usual measure stipulation M_1. Of particular interest is the following difference stressed by Carnap (pp. 50-51) between the (ordered) pairs <E,M_1> and <E,M_0>. If we could connect two points on E by means of a tunnel through the interior of the earth, according to M_1 the distance between the two points would be shorter than the distance between the same two points connected by a straight

---

[13] The requirement of isotropy and homogeneity does not seem completely clear, that is, the limitation to structures of constant curvature, since, firstly, Carnap had already considered the possibility that one or both of these properties were not satisfied and, secondly, because Carnap should very well know that the physical space of general relativity theory is neither homogeneous nor isotropic, since the gravitational field of matter causes curvatures in the adjacent space, what clearly falsifies the thesis of the homogeneity of space and, at least, makes extremely improbable the isotropy thesis.

line on the earth's surface. On the other hand, in the case of M_0 the result is the complete opposite, namely, the distance between the two points connected by a sort of tunnel in the interior of the earth is longer that the distance of a straight line between the same two points on the surface of E. Seen from the standpoint of M_0, the divergence would be caused by the fact that, contrary to M_0, on the basis of the usual M_1, bodies expand with heat and, thus, the rod used to measure would expand in the interior of the earth. Hence, points out Carnap (p. 51), the tunnel is only presumably shorter, as measured by M_1, since the measure scales in M_1 have suffered an expansion in the interior of E. In <E,M_0>, however, any interior or exterior line between two points is longer than the straight line determined on E by those two points. In this sense, stresses Carnap (p. 51), E behaves completely as a plane.

Carnap concludes (pp. 51-53) that the above mentioned coincidences between M_1 and M_0 with respect to E notwithstanding, the adoption of M_0 would require changes in the interpretation of some physical facts and, hence, changes in the physical laws. Thus, e.g., on the basis of M_0, light rays would have to be interpreted as curved. The comparative examination of (E, M_1) and (E, M_0) induces Carnap to conclude (p. 54) that the factual content (T), the structure of space (R) and the metric stipulation (M) are so related that once any two of them are established, the third one is uniquely determined. We, thus, have the following three functions of two arguments: $R=f_1(M,T)$, $M=f_2(R,T)$ and $T=f_3(M,R)$. Concerning this last function, Carnap stresses (p. 54) that although when M and R are given, T is uniquely determined, one should not forget that, in contrast to M and R, which can be freely stipulated, T is uniquely given. It is not necessary to emphasize that it would be highly questionable that a physicist would opt to freely stipulate M and R, in order to obtain a given T without having to make empirical observations.

Somewhat later Carnap discusses the important issue of simplicity. On this point he stresses (p. 55) that although one can obtain a spatial structure simpler than others –the Euclidean spatial structure- without taking into account the other two components, and also a simpler metric stipulation –M_0-, the requirement of simplicity concerns the totality of the ordered triple (T,M,R), not M or R with independence of T. In fact, as Carnap correctly points out (pp. 55-56), neither R nor M should be selected with independence of T, even tough it is theoretically possible, and, thus, what one can look for is the greatest simplicity of the ordered pair (M, R), given T, what does not even imply that M or R will be the most simple possible. Nonetheless, Carnap adds (p. 56) that T, together with the methodological simplicity requirement, determine the most simple R. Hence, although R is independent from T and can be chosen freely, the requirement of simplicity adds a requisite to T that allows us to determine R uniquely.

On the basis of the above discussion, Carnap concludes (p. 56) that it now seems clear why physics –that is, general relativity theory- rejects the, taken apart, simplest R –Euclidean space- and why one has never adopted M_0. Physics maintains the stipulation M_1, which, as Carnap stresses (p. 57), is such that the length of any rod is independent of the place in space and of the direction of the gravitational field, though not of temperature, magnetism or elasticity. Carnap sums up the results of his examination of physical space as follows:

In the factual content of experience is given [physical] three-dimensional topological space R_{3T}^{**}, but not a metric space. Such [a space] is obtained only on the basis of a measure stipulation, by means of which we can freely select the same or another metric structure of space, though it is better to proceed in such a way that we do not do either of them, but determine the measure stipulation and its corresponding spatial structure in such a way that on that basis the factual content can be presented in the most simple form possible. (p. 59)

This brief exposition of the nucleus of the discussion about physical space in *Der Raum* expresses with utmost clarity the two fundamental points of the whole chapter. Firstly, it should be clear that in the case of physical space Carnap defends a sort of conventionalism with respect to the fixation of the metric. Only the topological structure of physical space is empirically determined. Neither its projective (or affine) structure nor its metric structure is empirically determined. But since what is of interest to physics is the metric structure of space, such a metric structure has to be freely chosen. In fact, there are two components that admit a free selection, namely, the spatial structure R and the fixation of the metric M. Once one of the two has been freely chosen, it and the factual content uniquely determine the remaining component. Now, if we take into consideration not only the factual content T, but also the methodological requirement of simplicity, the free selection of R or M disappears, since, given T and in virtue of that requirement, there is only one simplest R and one simplest M. Thus, we have in this work of Carnap a defence of a moderate form of conventionalism with regard to the non-topological aspects of physical space, mitigated by the methodological requirement of simplicity. Although in the bibliography of this work there are references to conventionalists like Dingler and Poincaré, the moderate conventionalism of *Der Raum* distances itself both from the radical conventionalism of the first author and from the less radical one of the second author, who believed that he could defend no matter how the Euclidicity of physical space, without adequately assessing the unnecessary complications in our physical theory that it would convey.

At the beginning of the very short Chapter IV on the relation between the three conceptions (or levels) of space, Carnap introduces by means of an example two notions that he is interested in maintaining apart. He is concerned with the notion of substitution, which consists in the replacement of indeterminate partial expressions (or variables) in a general expression with determinates (constants) - e.g., when from the equation n+m=m+n we obtain the equation 5+3=3+5; and the notion of subsumption, by means of which we subsume an empirical real case under the general rule –e.g., when from 5+3=3+5 we obtain the concrete case that five apples + three apples = three apples + five apples. Carnap states (p. 60) that by means of such notions we can make precise the relation between the three basic conceptions of geometry, thus, the formal, the intuitive and the physical. Intuitive geometry is obtained from formal geometry by the process of substitution, whereas physical geometry is obtained from intuitive geometry by the process of subsumption. In order to characterize in a general way the distinction between the three conceptions –better: the three levels- of geometry, Carnap refers us to an important distinction made by Husserl. Carnap says:

> It [the relation] corresponds (in Husserl's terminology) to the gradual transit [der stufenweise Fortgang]: formal ontology (Leibniz' >>*mathesis universalis*<<), regional ontology, factual science; in Ostwald's doctrine of science to the first three levels of the pyramid of science. (p. 61)

Carnap states (p. 61) that the relation between the three conceptions of geometry is the same present among their objects, namely, R, R* and R**. He points out (p. 61), using once more terminology of frequent usage by Husserl, that both the relation between R and R*, as well as that between R* and R** are relations of a genus to a singular case, though they are such in different senses. Moreover, Carnap says:

> The relation between R and R* is that of a genus of structures of determined order relations but undetermined objects to a structure with the same properties, but determined objects, namely the intuitive spatial figures. The relation between R* and R** is that of a form of intuition to a structure of such a form of empirical-real objects. (p. 61)

Carnap stresses (p. 61) that the primordial interest of his work is R** and, in particular, bringing together in a consistent way in a determined physical space the spatial relations of experience. Nonetheless, he justifies the importance of dealing with intuitive and formal spaces, in order to better understand physical space. On this issue, writes Carnap:

> Now, since for R** there are various possible sorts of R_{3M}^{**}, depending on the selection made in the fixation of the measure, then the corresponding sorts of R* have to be formed, which are then [generalized] in the way already explained either to the structure R_{nM}^{*} or to R_{3T}^{*}, and finally generalized and at the same time reunited in R_{nT}^{*}. And for these structures are built the formal frameworks of the corresponding R up to the most general R_{nT}. (p. 61)

The fifth and last chapter —on our knowledge of space and experience- is especially important to understand the philosophical and scientific influences present in Carnap's dissertation. In the first three chapters the distinct conceptions of space were under consideration, while the fourth chapter was concerned with the relation between such three conceptions. In the last chapter Carnap explores a little more the three conceptions of space. Thus, he begins this final part by pointing out (p. 62) that formal space is nothing other than the study of a particular region of the theory of relations. Moreover, he stresses (p. 62) that, as happens with number theory, the theory of relations and, in particular, the theory of formal space is not only completely independent of experience, but derivable from logic. Obviously, here is present the influence of Russell's and Whitehead's version of logicism, presented in *Principles of Mathematics* of the former author and *Principia Mathematica*, of both important logicians and philosophers.

It should be pointed out here that Frege's logicism does not extend to geometry, about which the father of contemporary logic had a conception similar to that of Kant.

Of special importance is what Carnap says about intuitive space, since it has been either ignored or misinterpreted. Contrary to what some commentators have expressed, here the decisive influence is without much doubt Husserl. On this point, the best way to proceed is to quote a long passage from *Der Raum*.

> Here [in intuitive space] we have distinguished between principles in the strict sense and requirements. Those are the result [Befund] of a determined sort of >>intuition of essences<< [Wesenserschauung] (in Husserl's sense) and, thus, as all knowledge coming from that source, do not require the accumulation of empirical facts, [and] thus, are not to be conceived as empirical knowledge, though they are not independent of the totality of experience, since they are obtained from any representative of the sort of object concerned. The requirements, on the other hand, are not knowledge but stipulations that one has to do in order to obtain a total structure >>space<< on the basis of that knowledge that, because of their very nature [ihrem Wesen nach] seemed limited to an incomplete region. For these extensions to a full structure various possibilities were considered. Topological space exhibits [darstellt] what is common to all and for that reason should be seen as the spatial form apprehensible in the intuition of essences. Intuitive metric spaces, on the other hand, are also dependent on the choice of those stipulations; [and] thus, they lack the property of unrestricted validity had by intuitive topological space and all knowledge originating in that source. (pp.62-63)

The last quotation leaves no doubt that Carnap considered the principles of intuitive space to be known by means of the Husserlian intuition of essences, and that they determine completely intuitive topological space. Here Carnap does not refer either to Kant or to Helmholtz[14], or to any other author besides Husserl.

With regard to physical space, Carnap observes (p. 63), without needing much elaboration that our knowledge of it is empirical, based on the factual content of experience and obtained by induction. Hence, it [our knowledge of physical space] can never have absolute certainty, even though absolute certainty will play the role of an unattainable

---

[14] In his excellent dissertation, Diederich (1974, p. 99), Werner Diederich links without much argumentation Carnap's position on the synthetic *a priori* in geometry to Helmholtz' conception, but there does not seem to be any basis for such a statement of the distinguished and highly appreciated scholar.

goal, to which it tries to approximate. Once more, Carnap emphasizes (p. 63) that only physical topological space is uniquely determined by the factual content of experience, while in order to consider physical metric space freely selected measure fixations are required.

On pp. 63-64, Carnap evaluates the knowledge obtained in the three levels of space, making use of the usual epistemological distinctions <analytic-synthetic> and <*a priori-a posteriori*>[*]. With regard to principles and theorems of formal space, Carnap underscores (p. 63) that they are *a priori* and analytic, since derivable from logical principles. On the other hand, the principles of intuitive space are *a priori* though not analytic, but synthetic. It is pertinent to insert here another long quotation of Carnap:

> The principles of intuitive space are also *a priori*. According to Kant's well known distinction between >>having its origin in experience<< and >>begin with experience<<, that does not mean that they are apprehensible without experience, but >>independent of the content of experience<< (Driesch) and because of that it does not contradict that for the intuition of essences one requires what is given in experience, be it immediately in perception or mediately in intuition. In the principles of intuitive space we have before us the synthetic *a priori* propositions asserted [behauptet] by Kant. But the same is not valid for the theorems derived from them, but only for such concerned only with topological space; since those that refer to one of the metric spaces depend not only on the principles, but also on the requirements, on whose basis one obtains the complete structure of intuitive space, thus, not only knowledge, but [also] stipulations. Kant's assertion is, thus, certainly correct, but is not valid for the whole realm of those propositions he was concerned with. (pp. 63-64)

Although in the preceding quotation Kant is repeatedly mentioned, a careful examination of the text shows that the Carnapian scholars trying to relate the young Carnap to Kant and the Neo-Kantians do not find much support in it. Certainly Carnap talks about Kant's famous distinction between having its grounding in experience and merely using experience as starting point. He also mentions Kant's thesis that geometrical statements are synthetic *a priori*. But besides that and the defence of the existence of synthetic *a priori* statements, thus, of a general frame of discussion, there are no specific coincidences with

---

[*] [Note added in the translation: In a strict sense only the second distinction is epistemological. See on this issue our paper 'On Analytic *a posteriori* Statements: are they possible?']

Kant. In fact, Kant was not the only philosopher that had maintained that there exists synthetic *a priori* knowledge: at least Frege and Husserl, had done it. Now, when we examine the content of Carnap's expressions we learn that he considered that we obtain synthetic *a priori* statements in the topological layer of intuitive space -and only there, not in the metric layer (about the projective (or affine) one he is not explicit-, and that in virtue of Husserl's method of the intuition of essences. The other philosopher mentioned in the extensive passage quoted is the presently very little studied Hans Driesch, who, as correctly pointed out by Carlos Ulises Moulines[15], seems to have influenced Carnap or, at least, was very respected by the latter. Finally, the case of propositions about physical space is perfectly clear: they are synthetic *a posteriori* and obtained by induction.

On pp. 64-65, Carnap offers another especially interesting classification of our geometrical knowledge. He is going to classify our knowledge of the distinct sorts of space as follows. Letters 'W', 'S' and 'T' are to function as abbreviations of "intuition of essences", "freely selected stipulation" and "factual content", respectively. Such letters will always be accompanied by a subscript, be it "1", which will express the presence of that source of knowledge, or "0", which will express its absence. Thus, we have the following classification: W_1 applies to all spaces, and thus there is no space R such that $W_0(R)$; to R_{3T} does not apply either S or T, and thus $S_0(R_{3T})$ and $T_0(R_{3T})$ and, in general, $S_0(R_{nT})$ and $T_0(R_{nT})$ are valid; to R_{3M} does not apply T, and thus $T_0(R_{3M})$ is valid, whereas S applies to R_{3M}, since its principles provide us with the formal conditions of a relational structure based on freely chosen stipulations. Obviously, T does not apply to any intuitive space, whereas S does not apply either to R_{nT}^* or to R_{3T}^*, but applies to R_{3M}^*. Finally, in the case of physical space we do not need to consider R_{nT}^{**}, and S does not apply to three-dimensional physical topological space, but applies to R_{3M}^{**}. Carnap observes, (p. 65) that although W applies in all cases, in the case of formal topological space, be it n-dimensional or three-dimensional, the application is sort of formal. Here once again Carnap mentions Husserl explicitly. Thus, Carnap

---

[15] "Las Raíces Epistemológicas del Aufbau de Carnap" (1982), reprinted in Ramón Cirera, Andoni Ibarra & Thomas Mormann (eds.) (1996, pp. 45-74).

says: "W is present in all cases, but only in the latter cases is purely >>spatial<<, in the first two only in a formal way (Husserl: >>formal ontology<<)." Here Carnap seems to have in mind the distinction present in *Ideen zu einer reinen Phänomenologie und phänomenologischen Philosophie I*[16] between material essences –the usual ones- and formal essences, by which Husserl referred in a somewhat schematic way to what in other writings he called "objects of the understanding". In the case of three-dimensional intuitive topological space, Carnap makes it clear (p. 65) that though in order to complete it one would be in need of some freely selected requirements, R_{3T}^* does not depend on any particular choice of a freely selected stipulation, since it contains only those spatial determinations common to all possible stipulations. This last point deserves special emphasis, since such freely selected stipulations should not be confounded with conventions, like those intervening in the fixation of the metric in physical space, by means of which one chooses exactly one particular metric, though one could very well have selected one incompatible with it.

Carnap goes on to examine in detail what happens with the conditions of possibility of experience. On this issue Carnap stresses (p. 65) that, since in experience the only thing present in univocal form, without the intervention of freely selected stipulations, is the factual content, only such spatial determinations contained in the factual content, thus the topological conditions –not the projective (or affine) or metrical- are conditions of possibility of experience. It is, thus, concerned, as Carnap emphasizes (pp. 65-66), with the mere topological form of space, which is invariant under topological (bicontinuous) transformations. Now, underscores Carnap (p. 66), the topological relations of space that constitute the condition of possibility of any object of experience are those of intuitive topological space and those of formal topological space, not those of physical topological space, since the latter is concerned with topological relations of empirically given objects and, thus, is not independent of the factual content of experience. In fact, according to Carnap, physical

---

[16] See footnote 11 above.

topological space apprehends exactly the factual content of experience. On this issue, says Carnap:

> The determinations of intuitive topological space, in its independence from experience, and in the universal validity [*Allgemeingültigkeit*] assigned to them on the basis of its source of knowledge and, hence, those of the formal topological space as well, that general structure of indeterminate things, of which intuitive topological space constitutes a singular case, are the only ones that can have such a founding validity of experience. (p. 66)

On the other hand, Carnap rejects (pp. 66-67) the possibility that the number of dimensions, specifically, three-dimensionality, could be considered as a condition of possibility of experience. Even though we –human beings- could only intuit in the small region of space to which we have access spatial figures of up to three dimensions that is correctly seen by Carnap as something accidental and irrelevant for the conditions of possibility of experience. As a matter of fact, as Carnap points out (pp. 66-67), from the fact that we have spatial figures of up to three –or k- dimensions, we cannot infer an upper limit for the number of dimensions, but only that space has at least 3 dimensions –respectively, k dimensions. Obviously, stresses Carnap (pp. 66-67), neither physical topological space, which depends on the factual content of experience, nor formal space, which treats all dimensions in the same way, can help determine *a priori* a particular dimension of space or an upper limit for the number of dimensions. Moreover, Carnap rejects the argument that the three-dimensionality of space guarantees the uniqueness of empirical determination. On the contrary, Carnap considers that the stipulation of an upper limit to the dimensions of space would open the door to the ambiguity of empirical determination, originated precisely in the plurality of possible upper limits. Therefore, Carnap concludes (p. 67), we have to admit an unlimited number of dimensions. Thus, it is intuitive topological space of n dimensions –that also includes the determinations of formal topological space of n dimensions-, which contains the totality of spatial conditions of possibility of experience. In this way, Carnap concludes his excellent dissertation, on the one hand, stressing (p. 67) the correction of Kant's thesis that space contained the conditions of possibility of experience, but, on the other hand, pointing out that such a space is not what Kant had in mind –three-dimensional Euclidean intuitive metric space, in the terminology here used-, but n-dimensional intuitive topological space.

Carnap's conclusion deserves some commentary. Carnap's thesis advisor [Doktorvater] at the University of Jena was Bruno Bauch, a confessed Neo-Kantian. After the surge of special and, more importantly, general relativity, Neo-Kantians felt the necessity of defending the Kantian doctrine of space against the new conception of physical space and, wherever possible, to show its compatibility with the latter. However, besides the above mentioned courtesy to Kant at the end of his writing, which essentially consisted in the general coincidence with Kant in that there is something in intuitive space that is *a priori* and condition of possibility of experience, the whole discussion of that last chapter and its conclusion rather show that the specific theses about the aprioricity of space as conceived by Kant were false. Moreover, when Carnap examines the grounds for the aprioricity of intuitive topological space and the source of its knowledge, he does not refer us to Kant, but to Husserl. In this whole discussion, besides those that contributed to forge our present conception of physical space, namely, Riemann, Einstein and other mathematicians and physicists, the most important philosophical influence, especially with respect to intuitive space, but also in part with respect to formal space –though concerning the latter the influence of Riemann and of Russell and Whitehead is equally important- is that of Edmund Husserl. In fact, we want to conclude our exposition by mentioning that in Appendices II-VI of the dissertation, in which bibliographical suggestions are included, there are references to Husserl on p. 78 (two references to p. 7), p. 79 (one reference to pp. 8-9 and one to p. 12), p. 80 (one reference to p. 22 and one to p. 24), p. 85 (two references to p. 60, in one of which one reads: The doctrine of R, of R*, of R** as a [special] case of the more general scientific relation: >>formal ontology, regional ontology, factual science<<...", and one to p. 62), and on p. 86 (one reference to pp. 63ff.). Furthermore, both in the reference on p. 80 to p. 22 as in that of p. 85 to p. 62, Carnap refers us to pp. 10ff. of *Ideen zu einer reinen Phänomenologie und phänomenologischen Philosophie* for the intuition of essences.

But besides those references, it should be pointed out that the relation between Carnap and Husserl is one of the most enigmatic in the history of philosophy. Carnap begins his university studies in Jena in 1910, hence, approximately one year before Husserl was supposed to be named full professor of philosophy at that university.[17] As already mentioned, for some unknown reason, Husserl is not appointed, and instead of him Bruno Bauch is appointed. Carnap writes his dissertation with Bruno Bauch, but writes it not in Jena, but in the small town of Buchenbach at the outskirts of Freiburg, where Husserl taught since 1916. Carnap stays from 1919 to 1921 in that small town writing a thesis in which Husserl's writings have such a visible influence. There does not seem to be any clear documentation, but only the strong suspicion that during those two years Carnap visited Husserl's seminars. There is only a photo of the participants (without being identified [though two of them seem to be Martin Heidegger and Oskar Becker]) in a seminar of Husserl's, in which three positions to the left of Husserl there is a young man very similar to the Carnap of those days.[18] Now, independently of whether the person in the photo was Carnap or not, the suspicion [that Carnap met Husserl during those years] is supported by the fact that, according to the *Husserl-Chronik*[19], Carnap visited during three semesters Husserl's seminars during the years 1924-1925[**], thus, the period in which he was writing *Der*

---

[17] See Lothar Kreiser's book (2001, p.581).

[18] The photo was included in Hans-Rainer Sepp's book (1988, p. 294). It should be mentioned, nonetheless, that the person in the photo seemed to have been shorter than Carnap. However, the terrain in which the photo was taken is slanting – seemingly mountainous-, which together with lack of clarity of the photo, do not allow for a definitive answer. In Sepp's book there is also a photo on p. 90 of Carnap in 1923, which could help for a comparison.

[19] Karl Schuhmann (ed.) (1977, p. 281). On that page Schuhmann mentions a letter sent to him by Ludwig Landgrebe, dated 6 August 1976 on that issue. Moreover, in a letter of Ludwig Landgrebe to Husserl himself, the former remembers a meeting in one of Husserl's seminars, in which Carnap participated. See on this issue, Edmund Husserl (1994, IV, p. 298).

[**] According to Carnap's diaries, see entry for 21 November 1923, Carnap asked Husserl for permission to visit his seminar already then; hence, he visited Husserl's seminars during four semesters from the winter semester of 1923 to the summer semester of 1925. Moreover, two days later, most surely during Carnap's second appearance at the seminar -and as attested by Carnap's diaries, entry for 25

logische Aufbau der Welt, a book in which –as has been pointed out in two valuable essays by Verena Mayer[20]- there is an important influence of Husserl, though not so visible and free of tensions as in *Der Raum*. In such a period Carnap lived once more in that small town near Freiburg. It does not seem clear why Carnap returned to Buchenbach after completing his studies and visited Husserl's seminars, in a period in which Husserl's influence was [presumably] less evident than when writing his dissertation, while earlier, when Husserl's influence was more visible, he had not succumbed to the temptation of visiting the latter's seminars.[***] The situation is even more complicated by the fact that Carnap never admitted having studied with Husserl, though it is now known that he did it between 1923 and 1925.[21]

In any case, it is certainly interesting that Carnap somehow suspected what is not said explicitly either in *Logische Untersuchungen* or in *Ideen zu einer reinen Phänomenologie und phänomenologischen Philosophie* on Husserl's attitude towards Kant's

---

November 1923-, Husserl invited him and other participants in the seminar to his house to drink tee. This is certainly remarkable. At German universities, full professors traditionally had almost no contact with students, even with young doctors, and though Husserl was certainly a very atypical, unconventional professor, the invitation seems to strengthen the suspicion that Husserl and Carnap had already met before 1923. By the way, there are too many entries in the diaries in the years in which Carnap was writing his dissertation –on which Husserl's influence was so visible- of visits to the library of the University of Freiburg. It is very improbable that he did not have the temptation of at least meeting Husserl.

[20] See on this issue her papers "Die Konstruktion der Erfahrungswelt: Carnap und Husserl", in Spohn (ed.) (1991, pp. 287-303); and "Carnap und Husserl", in Bell & Vossenkul (eds.) (1992, pp. 185-201), as well as her definitive 'Der *Logische Aufbau* als Plagiat'.

[***] Most surely, the influence was still very visible in the first version of *Aufbau*, which most probably was destroyed by Carnap after he lost any hope of Husserl's support and hurried to "reform" the manuscript, in order to present it to Schlick, who certainly had no sympathy for Husserl.

[21] After having written [the Spanish original of] this critical study, I got acquainted with Sahotra Sarkar's paper "Husserl's Role in Carnap's Der Raum", in Thomas Bonk (ed.) (2003, pp. 179-190), in which the author arrives to similar conclusions as those of the present work. In a future critical study of Bonk's book I will examine Sarkar's paper. [The announced critical study was never written.]

conception of space. As can be seen from his posthumous work[22], Husserl rejected at least since the early 1890s Kant's conception of the aprioricity both of the three-dimensionality of intuitive space and of its presumed Euclidicity, criticizing, in particular, the argument of incongruent counterparts in a letter to Brentano of 1892. It seems pertinent to finish this study with a question that does not seem to have an answer: Did Carnap discuss this issue with Husserl during the years 1919 to 1921?

References[+]

Bell, David. & Vossenkuhl, Wolfgang. (eds.) – *Wissenschaft und Subjektivität*, Akademie Verlag, Akademie Verlag, Berlin 1992
Bonk, Thomas. (ed.) – *Language, Truth and Knowledge*, Kluwer, Dordrecht, 2003
Carnap, Rudolf. – *Der Raum, Kant Studien*, special number, 1922, reprint, Topos Verlag, Vaduz 1991
Carnap, R. – *Der logische Aufbau der Welt*, second edition, Felix Meiner, Hamburg 1961
Carnap, Rudolf – *Tagebücher 1908-1935*, in http://homepage.univie.ac.at/ christian.daemboeck/carnap_diaries
Cirera, Ramón, Ibarra, Andoni & Mormann, Thomas (eds.) – El Programa de Carnap, C.E.L.C., Barcelona 1996
Coleman, Robert & Korté, Herbert. – 'Hermann Weyl: Mathematician, Physicist, Philosopher', in E. Scholz (ed.), *Hermann Weyls Raum-Zeit-Materie*, pp. 161-386
Diederich, Werner. – *Konventionalität in der Physik*, Dunckner & Humboldt, Berlin 1974
Einstein, Albert. – 'Geometrie und Erfahrung', *Preussische Akademie der Wissenschaften*, Sitzungsberichte I, 1918, translation in Albert Einstein, *Sidelights of Relativity*, Dover, New York 1921

---

[22] See Husserl (1994, I, pp. 10-11, as well as the letter written a decade later [and already one from 1897] to Natorp in V, pp. 80-86. See also the second part of Husserl (1983).
[+] Items (5), (10), (20), (23) and (26) have been added to the references in this translation, while item (20) was updated.

Helmholtz, Hermann von – 'Über die Tatsachen, die der Geometrie zum Grunde liegen' 1868, translation in Peter Pesic (ed.), *Beyond Geometry*, pp. 47-52

Hilbert, David. – *Die Grundlagen der Geometrie* 1899, tenth edition, Teubner, Stuttgart 1968

Hirsch, Moritz W. – *Differential Topology*, Springer, New York et al. 1976

Husserl, Edmund. – *Logische Untersuchungen* 1900-1901 (2 vols.), M. Nijhoff, Den Haag (I) 1975, (II) 1984

Husserl, Edmund. – *Ideen zu einer reinen Phänomenologie und phänomenologischen Philosophie I*, 1913, M. Nijhoff, Den Haag 1950

Husserl, Edmund. – *Studien zur Arithmetik und Geometrie*, M. Nijhoff, Den Haag 1983

Husserl, Edmund. – *Briefwechsel* (10 vols.), edited by Karl Schuhmann and Elisabeth Schuhmann, Kluwer, Dordrecht 1994

Kreiser, Lothar – *Gottlob Frege: Leben-Werk-Zeit*, F. Meiner, Hamburg 2001

Mayer, Verena. – 'Die Konstruktion der Erfahrungswelt: Carnap und Husserl', in Wolfgang Spohn (ed.), *Erkenntnis Orientated: a Centennial Volume for Rudolf Carnap und Hans Reichenbach*, pp. 287-303

Mayer, Verena. – 'Carnap und Husserl', in David Bell & Wolfgang Vossenkuhl (eds.), *Wissenschaft und Subjektivität*, pp. 185-201

Mayer, Verena – 'Der *Logische Aufbau* als Plagiat', in Guillermo E. Rosado Haddock (ed.), *Husserl and Analytic Philosophy*, pp. 175-260

Mormann, Thomas ' "Carnap's Metrical Conventionalism versus Differential Geometry', Proceedings of the 2004 Biennial Meeting of the Philosophy of Science Association, vol. 1, pp. 814-825

Moulines, Carlos Ulises – Las Raíces Epistemológicas del Aufbau de Carnap', in Ramón Cirera, Andoni Ibarra & Thomas Mormann (eds.), *El Programa de Carnap*, pp. 45-74

Pesic, Peter – *Beyond Geometry*, Dover, New York 2007

Poincaré, Henri – *La Science et l'Hypothese* 1902, reprint, Flammarion, Paris 1968

Riemann, Bernhard – *Über die Hypothesen, welche der Geometrie zu Grunde liegen* 1867, third edition 1923, reprint, Chelsea, New York 1960

Rosado Haddock, Guillermo E. – 'On Analytic *a posteriori* Statements: are they Possible?' *Logique et Analyse 229*, 2015, pp. 25-33

Russell, Bertrand – *Foundations of Geometry* 1897, reprint, Dover, New York 1956

Russell, Bertrand – *Principles of Mathematics* 1903, second edition, Allen & Unwin, London 1937

Sarkar, Sahotra – 'Husserl's Role in Carnap's Der Raum', in Thomas Bonk (ed.), *Language, Truth and Knowledge*, pp. 179-190

Scholz, Erhard (ed.) – *Hermann Weyls Raum-Zeit-Materie and a General Introduction to his Scientific Work*, Birkhäuser, Basel et al. 2001

Schuhmann, Karl – *Husserl-Chronik*, M. Nijhoff, Den Haag 1977

Sepp, Hans Rainer – *Edmund Husserl und die phänomenologische Bewegung*, second edition, K. Alber, Freiburg 1988

Sklar, Lawrence – *Space, Time and Spacetime*, University of California Press, Berkeley 1974

Spohn, Wolfgang – *Erkenntnis Orientated: a Centennial Volume for Rudolf Carnap and Hans Reichenbach*, Kluwer, Dordrecht 1991

Torretti, Roberto – *Philosophy of Geometry from Riemann to Poincaré*, Reidel, Dordrecht 1977,

Weyl, Hermann – *Raum-Zeit-Materie* 1918, translation of the fourth edition, Dover, New York 1952

Critical Study of Ramón Cirera, Andoni Ibarra and Thomas Mormann (eds.), *El Programa de Carnap*, C.E.L.C., Barcelona 1996, 324pp.

Abstract

In this critical study of the valuable collection of essays edited by Cirera, Ibarra and Mormann, the present author not only critically assesses the different renderings of Carnap's writings propounded by the different authors therein represented, but also sketches his own interpretation and subjects to criticism some of the presumed consequences of the demise of logical empiricism

As attested by the extensive recent literature, in the last two decades, thus, beginning after a temporal interval similar to that foregone after the demise of logical empiricism that had been consolidated in North America after the exile, interest in this important philosophical school of the last century has reawakened, though this time from a quite different perspective. It is an attempt both to examine the varied and somehow entangled origin of the writings of the most important authors of that philosophical current, as well as to evaluate the immense richness of ideas and their permanent flux present in logical empiricism, with its roots in Austria and Germany, previous to their ankylosis and posterior demise in the Anglosaxon exile. The present book –though mostly concerned with the writings of Rudolf Carnap- is without doubt an important contribution to this new bibliography on logical empiricism. The three distinguished editors have been able to put together in the book we are concerned with eleven papers that, with the exception of Rudolf Carnap's own paper 'Sobre el Carácter de los Problemas Filosóficos' and Carlos Ulises Moulines' 'Las Raíces Epistemológicas del *Aufbau* de Carnap', which are older, and the papers by Thomas Uebel, 'El Fisicalismo en Wittgenstein y Carnap', and by Andrés Rivaduella, 'Probabilidad Bayesiana, Probabilidad Frecuencial y la Teoría Carnapiana de la Inferencia Estadística', that were added later, have their origin in a conference organized by the Department of Logic and Philosophy of Science of the University of the Basque Country in the centenary of the

author of *Aufbau* –as is known *Der logische Aufbau der Welt* (Carnap 1928). Those seven papers presented in the conference are the following:
(1) C. Ulises Moulines – 'Un Modelo Operacional del *Aufbau* de Carnap'
(2) Javier Echeverría – 'Teoría de los Signos en Carnap'
(3) Rainer Hegselmann – 'La Concepción Científica del Mundo, El Círculo de Viena: un Balance'
(4) Josep-María Terricabras – 'La Lógica del Tractatus y la Construcción Lógica de Carnap'
(5) Ramón Cirera – 'El Análisis Lógico del Lenguaje Científico, según Carnap'
(6) Thomas Mormann – 'El Lenguaje en Neurath y Carnap'
(7) Dirk Koppelberg – 'Empirismo y Pragmatismo en Carnap y Quine'

In the present study we will be concerned in a very unequal manner with the eleven papers included in the book. In fact, we will completely ignore Carnap's paper –dating from 1934, the year in which he published his *Logische Syntax der Sprache* (Carnap 1934)- and will merely mention the theme of five of the papers. On the other hand, we will extensively discuss the first of the two papers by the distinguished Latinamerican philosopher Carlos Ulises Moulines, the paper by Rainer Hegselmann and the paper of the well-known Quinean scholar Dirk Koppelberg, and somewhat more briefly the papers of Ramón Cirera, one of the most distinguished Carnapian scholars, and of another co-editor, the important scholar Thomas Mormann.

Before discussing Moulines' important paper on the epistemological roots of the *Aufbau*, it seems pertinent to mention what the editors say (p. 16) about that work, namely, that it is considered as the most important work of the phenomenalist tradition, and that it had as objective (see p. 17) the reconstruction of our knowledge of the world on the basis of immediate experience. Of course, as the editors emphasize (p. 18), the *Aufbau* is not concerned with the psychological origin of scientific concepts, but with its epistemological constitution – making extensive use of the logical tools made available especially by Russell and Whitehead- on the basis of immediate experience. But, in the best of cases, up to this point will reach the agreement between specialists in the *Aufbau*. A somewhat quick interpretation has seen some similarities between that work and older attempts by Russell in that direction. Other scholars have emphasized the influence of Mach, Avenarius and authors of the phenomenalist tradition of the second half of the nineteenth century. Some scholars –for example, Edmund Rungaldier in his *Carnap's Early Conventionalism* (Rungaldier 1984)- have underscored the importance of the influence of Poincaré's and Dingler's conventionalism. On the other hand, Michael Friedman (see, for example, his book Friedman 1999), his former student Alan Richardson (see his book Richardson 1998) and other scholars have pointed out to the influence of Kant and the Neo-Kantians in the young Carnap. Finally, Verena Mayer, in two important papers –'Die Konstitution der Erfahrungswelt: Carnap und Husserl' (Mayer 1991) and 'Carnap und Husserl' (Mayer 1992)-, has emphasized Husserl's influence on the *Aufbau*.[1]

At the beginning of his stimulating paper 'Las Raíces Epistemológicas del *Aufabu* de Carnap', Moulines underscores (p. 45) that though the *Aufbau* was published in 1928, the manuscript was essentially completed by 1925, thus, before Carnap's arrival in Vienna. In order to adequately appreciate the place occupied by the *Aufbau* in twentieth century philosophy, Moulines will examine (see p. 46) the philosophical context in which it originates. Moulines observes (p. 47) that the *Aufbau* has a double objective, namely, "to obtain a logically unobjectionable conceptual unification of knowledge and establish a firm basis for testing empirical propositions, by means of which the latter will be systematically testable". Moulines correctly points out (p. 48) that in the hierarchical constitution of concepts and statements of empirical nature that interest Carnap, he models them after the systems of logic and set theory developed at the beginning of the twentieth century in order to systematize mathematical knowledge. According to Moulines (see p. 48), the objective of the *Aufbau* is a logical reconstruction of the theory of knowledge.

Moulines rejects (see pp. 53-55) the empiricist interpretation of the *Aufbau*, be it in Kambartel's line of thought, which tries to connect

---

[1] [Added in this edition] See also the present author's recent *The Young Carnap's Unknown Master*, Ashgate, Aldershot 2008, as well as Mayer's recent excellent 'Der Logische Aufbau als Plagiat' in Guillermo E. Rosado Haddock (ed.), *Husserl and Analytic Philosophy*, de Gruyter, Berlin 2016, pp. 175-260.

Carnap with Locke, or in Krauth's, who sees the *Aufbau* as inserted in a chain originating in Bacon, Hobbes and Locke, which goes through Hume, Comte, Mill and, finally, Mach. Against such empiricist renderings, Moulines points out (p. 54) that with the exception of Mach, Carnap does not mention such authors in the *Aufbau*. On the other hand, Moulines repeatedly underscores (see pp. 54 and 56) that in that book both Kant and the Neo-Kantians, especially Natorp, are frequently mentioned. In fact, in order to understand the influences on Carnap in the years in which he wrote the *Aufbau*, Moulines will mostly take into account the frequency in which the different authors are mentioned in that work. On this point it should be mentioned that though that elementary exegetical method can be fruitful, in Carnap's special case one has to be careful. When one examines the immense diversity of authors frequently referred to by Carnap in the *Aufbau* as his predecessors in one or other aspect, one could believe that Carnap is a sort of uncontrolled eclectic, what could serve more to hide than to clarify the most important influences present in that work. Continuing with Moulines, he emphasizes (p. 57) that Frege, Russell and Whitehead are the authors most referred to in the *Aufbau*. But such authors are not so intriguing for Moulines as a group of authors mentioned less frequently than the above-mentioned, but more frequently than others. Moulines observes (p. 56) that to that group belong authors like Dingler, Driesch, Jacoby, Mach, Natorp, Schlick, Weyl and Ziehen, which, as Moulines underscores (p. 56), are authors of the same generation as Carnap or of the immediately before him, and German speaking authors.

Before continuing the exposition, it seems important to insert some brief commentaries. Besides the delicate issue that results of the application to Carnap of the exegetical method used by Moulines, it should be pointed out here that though most of the authors mentioned by Moulines are referred by Carnap some six to eight times, thus, less than Frege, Russell and Whitehead, and more than other authors not mentioned by Moulines, there are two notable exceptions going in opposite directions. Driesch is referred to eleven times, thus, two more than Frege, whereas Dingler was mentioned five times, thus, so many times as Husserl was, though Husserl was ignored by Moulines. Moreover, Moulines does not take into account what one can call the 'relevance' of the references, thus, the qualitative difference between some references and others, especially in a book like the *Aufbau*, which on the basis of the diversity of authors referred to, could –as already observed- make us believe that it is somewhat eclectic. More specifically, one could point out that a reference to Husserl's phenomenological reduction, like that made by Carnap in the *Aufbau* (§64, p. 86), when introducing his methodological solipsism, should weight more than vague and general references to authors that have discussed the same issues as Carnap discusses in some part of the *Aufbau*. For the time being, however, we will postpone the remaining criticisms to the methodology used by the highly esteemed scholar.

On pp. 57-58 Moulines correctly emphasizes the limitations of the actual influence of Frege, Russell and Whitehead on the *Aufbau*, an influence basically restricted to the attempt by such authors of giving a logical foundation to arithmetic (Frege) or to mathematics in general (Whitehead and Russell), though in Whitehead's and Russell's case the influence was not so sharply circumscribed. Nonetheless, Moulines observes (pp. 57-58) that though Carnap acknowledged that his book had a similar objective to that of Russell's *Our Knowledge of the External World*[2] of " building with the help of logical means the most fundamental empirical concepts on a phenomenalist basis…", he also criticized in that book both the assumptions and even the execution of Russell's program. On the other hand, Moulines underscores (p. 58) the approval of the epistemological projects of Dingler, Driesch, Jacoby and Ziehen. Moulines states (p. 59) that one could render Carnap's objective in the *Aufbau* as an attempt to carry out, with the help of logical and set-theoretical tools, the programs sketched by those authors. Moulines asserts (p. 60) that all those authors, together with others less referred to by Carnap, such as Avenarius, Poincaré, Schubert-Soldern and Volkelt, are related by a sort of "family bond", since all of them were interested (see p. 61) in establishing a solid foundation of all our empirical knowledge on the basis of some *a priori* principles "applied to an epistemologically primary basis of

---

[2] (Russell 1914) With regard to the empiricism usually attributed to Russell, see the criticism by the editor, Nicholas Griffin, in the Introduction to *The Cambridge Companion to Russell*, pp. 38-41.

phenomenalist unities". However, Moulines underscores (p. 62), only in Carnap can one neatly differentiate the logic of scientific knowledge from the empirical psychology of knowledge. On this issue, one could ask Moulines if there were no other equally strong influences in Carnap –besides the logical and set-theoretical ones- that were responsible for that important difference between the *Aufbau* and its predecessors. The response that Moulines would give if asked such a question seems to have been negative, since he concludes his paper emphasizing (pp. 72-73) that Carnap had a greater affinity of purpose with the epistemologists and psychophysiologists already mentioned than with any other group of philosophers. With respect to the possible answer to that question we differ radically from the distinguished scholar. It is precisely the recourse to the phenomenological reduction on §64 of the *Aufbau* the other component that distinguishes Carnap's project from those of his predecessors mentioned by Moulines, and which, together with the constitution of concepts by means of logical and set-theoretical tools, intends to guarantee that the fruits of Carnap's efforts are not simply another contribution to the empirical psychology of knowledge. On this point, it should be stressed that in the same way in which in order to guarantee the logical nature of a theorem it is not enough to use logical rules of inference, since you need to begin only with logical axioms –remember the failure of Russell's and Whitehead's logicism,-, the logical-set-theoretical constitution of the concepts of an epistemological system is not enough to guarantee their non-empirical character, since you also need to begin with a non-empirical basis. This last function was supposed to be accomplished by Husserl's phenomenological reduction.

    The last assertion forces us to conclude the discussion of this important paper of Carlos Ulises Moulines with some general observations on the relation between Husserl and Carnap. Let us return firstly to the beginning of the paper, namely, to the correct observation made by Moulines that the *Aufbau* was essentially completed in 1925, thus, before Carnap moved to Vienna. On this point it seems pertinent to emphasize two additional deficiencies of Moulines exegesis. Firstly, since the book was finished four years after the completion of his doctoral studies and three years after the publication of his doctoral thesis, *Der Raum* (Carnap 1922), and being the *Aufbau* the next work of a sufficient extension written by Carnap in that period, it would seem reasonable to examine that doctoral thesis in order to better understand the origin of the *Aufbau*. An examination of that work shows, firstly, that neither Jacoby, nor Avenarius, Volkelt or Schubert-Soldern are even mentioned in the secondary literature. Of the rest of Moulines chosen ones, of course, Weyl, Poincaré, Dingler and Schlick are frequently mentioned, since they had investigated the same problem –of physical space- with which Carnap is concerned in *Der Raum*, whereas Mach and Driesch are also mentioned, both in the references and elsewhere [bibliographical commentaries; Literatur-Hinweise]. But what is most surprising is that Husserl, who had not published specifically on the problem of physical space-time, was referred to so frequently, not only in the references, but in the main text and notes, and always with great respect. In fact, much more clearly than in the *Aufbau*, the references to Husserl seem to have had much more weight than those made to some of the authors chosen by Moulines.

An even more important point is the following. From 1919 up to 1925 Carnap mostly lived in Buchenbach, a town in the outskirts of Freiburg, in whose university Husserl was professor. Though there is no definitive evidence, but only a grounded suspicion, it is very probable that Carnap visited some of Husserl's seminars between 1919 and 1921, that is, when he was working on *Der Raum*, in which Husserl's influence is more obvious than in the *Aufbau*. In any case, Carnap returned to Buchenbach in 1924, while he was working on the *Aufbau* and took part in three of Husserl's advanced seminars [*Oberseminare*] (from the second semester of academic year 1923-1924 to the second semester of academic year 1924-1925), as mentioned in the very valuable *Husserl-Chronik* of Karl Schuhmann (Schuhmann 1977).[3] The reasons why Carnap did not acknowledge having been Husserl's student most probably could have a psychological explanation –he feared being rejected by Moritz Schlick

---

[3] [Added in this edition] More correctly, Carnap returned to Buchenbach in 1923 and took part in four of Husserl's advanced seminars, beginning in the first semester of academic year 1923-1924. For more information, see on this point the present author's 'The Old Husserl and the Young Carnap', included in this book, as well as Verena Mayer's recent 'Der *Logische Aufbau* als Plagiat'.

and Otto Neurath[4]-, though we are not concerned here with such explanations. What is interesting is that if Carnap is considered a student of Frege, since he attended two or three of his lecture courses – that in Germany do not involve any sort of personal contact with the professor-, there is much more reason to consider him a student of Husserl, for having taken part in (at least) three *Oberseminare* that, being restricted to doctoral students and young doctors, allow for a by far more personal contact between the participants and the professor. By the way, there is an intriguing photo of an *Oberseminar* of 1920 – not at the university but in the mountains-, which appears on p. 294 of the book edited by Hans Rainer Sepp *Edmund Husserl und die phänomenologische Bewegung* (Sepp 1988). In such a photo, not at all clear and without any identification of the participants, three places to the left of Husserl there is a young man that resembles the Carnap of 1923 that appears in the same book on p. 290. Certainly, if one could confirm that the intriguing person is Carnap Michael Friedmann's assertion in his book *A Parting of the Ways* (Friedman 2000) according to which Carnap and Heidegger met for the first time in the famous colloquium between Cassirer and Heidegger a decade later would be falsified, since Heidegger appears at the extreme right of the photo with Oskar Becker. But even if the person in the photo were not Carnap –and I am inclined to think that he was not[5]- that in no way would debilitate our suspicion that Carnap also visited Husserl's courses while working on his dissertation and most probably also met

---

[4] One should not forget that in the first edition of his *Allgemeine Erkenntnislehre* Schlick had criticized Husserl's *Logische Untersuchungen*, although such criticisms disappeared in the 1925 second edition of that book, possibly as a result of Hermann Weyl's review of Schlick's book in the *Jahrbuch über die Fortschritte der Mathematik* 46, 1923-1924, pp. 59-62. (I have not had direct access to that review, and have obtained the information about it from Paolo Mancosu's and Thomas A. Ryckman's 'Mathematics and Phenomenology: The Correspondence between O. Becker and H. Weyl' (Mancosu and Ryckman 2002). With respect to Neurath, it is enough to mention his conception of the Vienna Circle as a sort of sect or political group, his radical physicalism, and his strong and polemic personality.
[5] Notwithstanding the resemblance with the young Carnap, the person in the intriguing photo seems to have been shorter than Carnap, and, thus, probably was not Carnap. Nonetheless, the terrain was not plane but had a noticeable slope, and the presumed Carnap was at the lower part of the slope.

Heidegger during those days. In fact, it is extremely improbable that Carnap did not meet Husserl between 1919 and 1921.[6]

On Moulines' second paper, 'Un Modelo Operacional del Aufabau de Carnap', we will say very little. Moulines' objective in that paper is to propose a sort of 'operational model' of the *Aufbau* (see p. 75). Moulines will reinterpret Carnap's theory of constitution as "a formal elucidation of the notion of an ideal observer... stocked with...'an ideal observational language', which would allow him to test any empirical statement made in theoretical science" (p. 76), with the understanding that the definitions that serve to introduce the higher levels of the constitutional system –the physical, the heteropsychological and the spiritual- are rules of correspondence. In this way Moulines reinterprets Carnap's theory of constitution by means of the conceptual tools usually associated with Carnap's last phase as a philosopher of science, what would make us think that Carnap's philosophical trajectory, going through the first two sorts of criteria of empirical significance, had been, in some clearly determined aspect, circular.

The only other point that we would like to mention with respect to Moulines' second paper is concerned with a passage on p. 79, in which Moulines observes that Carnap's thesis that "the primary basis of knowledge should be conceived as a total experience of consciousness (= *Erlebnis*) or, even better, as an experiential flux (= *Erlebnisstrom*)..." originates in Gestalt theory. It is much more probable that the true origin of such notions in Carnap is Husserl, in whose phenomenological descriptions of subjectivity *Erlebnis* and *Erlebnisstrom* are basic terminology, and with whom Carnap studied while he was writing the *Aufbau* Even the central term 'constitution' is a fundamental term in Husserl, and though the term was used much earlier by Kant, Carnap's usage of the term is much nearer to Husserl's

---

[6] [Added in this edition] Consider, for example, the fictitious improbable case of someone living on the outskirts of Boston in the 1960s while writing a dissertation in which Quine is frequently and approvingly referred to, but not having being tempted to meet Quine. And then, three years after finishing his doctoral studies the young doctor returns to the outskirts of Boston and during three semesters visits regularly Quine's seminars.

than to Kant's.[7] In fact, both for Husserl and for Carnap constitution means epistemological grounding. Of course, such an epistemological grounding is done in different ways by Carnap and Husserl, being in Carnap's case an attempt at a logical reduction of the different concepts of empirical science to a fundamental relation between elementary experiences of consciousness [*elementare Erlebnisse*] in a flux of such experiences [*Erlebnisstrom*]. In Husserl, from 1907 on, there is also such a flux of experiences of consciousness [*Erlebnisstrom*], though the process of epistemological grounding is somewhat different.[8] Nonetheless, both coincide in distancing themselves radically both from empiricism and subjectivism, as well as from specific relativism, in particular from the anthropologism that Husserl so severely criticized in the first volume of *Logische Untersuchungen* (Husserl 1900-1901), to which Kant fell victim.

Javier Echeverría's paper 'Teoría de Signos en Carnap' seems to be one of the lesser papers of the book and we will say very little about it. In any case, two questionable assertions of Echeverría deserve some comment. According to Echeverría (p. 102) "... Carnap has developed a Theory of Signs that clearly plays a foundational role for Frege's theory of meaning". On this issue it seems sufficient to point out that Carnap does not seem to have been always loyal to Frege's version of the distinction between sense and referent, obtained – with independence of each other- by Husserl in 1890 and by Frege approximately at the same time. Thus, whereas in §44 Carnap asserts that the referent of a statement is a truth-value (Frege), in §147 he mentions that statements refer to states of affairs (Husserl). Thus, in one part of the book Frege's official version of the distinction is adopted, whereas later Husserl's version is unofficially used. The other assertion of Echeverría that deserves some comment is the following: "The Carnapian extensional method... is epistemologically dependent from the distinction between sign, sense and referent, and hence... of

---

[7] For a more thorough discussion of this issue, see the present author's book *The Young Carnap's Unknown Master* (Rosado Haddock 2008).

[8] [Added in this edition] Though the epistemological basis is the same and the hierarchical order of constitution is exactly the same, in Husserl the epistemological grounding does not proceed by means of definitions and is not embedded in a logical and set-theoretical dressing.

the parallel distinction between cultural, psychic and physical objects" (pp. 102-103). Leaving aside the questionable generalization present in the last phrase –certainly when Echeverría refers to the number denoted by the numeral '2' or to the Pythagorean Theorem he does not refer to something physical-, the distinction made by Frege and Husserl between sign, sense and referent (or denotation) not only does not imply that the sense belongs to the realm of the psychic but, moreover, both great philosophers explicitly rejected such an interpretation.

Rainer Hegselmann's paper 'La Concepción Científica del Mundo, El Círculo de Viena: un Balance" deserves because of multiple reasons to be thoroughly examined. It is not only a very well written paper, but one that though specifically examining Max Horkheimer's criticisms of logical empiricism in his 1937 paper 'Der neueste Angriff auf die Metaphysik' not only makes justice to logical empiricism but also to any philosophical trend guided by rationality and scientific rigour, and that acknowledges the importance and value of the most exact sciences. And though Horkheimer's or other philosophers' criticisms, no matter whether those philosophers are neo-Marxists, like those of the Frankfurt school[9], Marxists, or followers of any other sort of philosophical obscurantism or pseudoscience, would seem something foregone, one should not forget that once in a while surges one or other dinosaur trying to interpret some philosopher from a historical-materialist perspective in order to show the "limitations" and the "historical indexing" of such a philosopher.

Hegselmann begins his paper by referring (p. 111) to an assertion of Horkheimer's, in which logical empiricists are accused of being intellectual pioneers and accomplices of Nationalsocialism. Hegselmann will offer a definitive answer to such unfounded and irresponsible accusation by means of a detailed examination of the different aspects of what was the most important philosophical school

---

[9] Not only Horkheimer, but also Adorno and Marcuse have made similar accusations, which have been criticized by Marxist scholars with more theoretical sophistication. On this issue, see the criticisms of Horkheimer and Adorno on pp. 377-379 and of Marcuse on pp. 397-401 in the third volume of Leszek Kolakowski's *Main Currents of Marxism* (Kolakowski 1978). See also Lucio Colletti's *Il Marxismo e Hegel* (Coletti 1973), pp. 332-334.

of the twentieth century. We shall begin our exposition by quoting a passage of Hegselmann's paper in which it is expressed in a concise and insuperable form the origins and objectives of logical empiricism.

> From a historical-philosophical standpoint, logical empiricism can be understood as an attempt to extract philosophical consequences from the cognitive revolutions produced in the natural sciences, mathematics and logic. Logical empiricism is, above all, a reaction in front of the difficulties that, in view of the progress made at the beginning of the century in physics, mathematics and logic, faced the philosophical conception that could reasonably be considered as one of the best modern foundations of the sciences, that is, Kantian transcendental philosophy.

But as Hegselmann points out on pp. 115-116, this crisis in the three most rigorous sciences –logic, mathematics and physics- could only be appreciated by those philosophers with the knowledge and conceptual tools enabling them to become conscious of it, together with the concern about the epistemological analysis of the new (scientific) theories. On this issue it should be mentioned that three of the most important logical empiricists, namely, Moritz Schlick, Rudolf Carnap and Hans Reichenbach wrote books on the foundations of relativity theory. Hans Reichenbach, in particular, wrote four books on that theme and one on the philosophical foundations of quantum mechanics. Moreover, as is well known, both Carnap and Reichenbach wrote logic texts, Carnap even wrote two.

As Hegselmann clearly points out (p. 116), an important component of logical empiricism is the interest in the classification of concepts and arguments by means of a logical-linguistic analysis, as well as the interest in conceptual reconstruction, in the transparency both of thought and verbal expression, and the intersubjective testability of assertions. Thus, it is perfectly clear why, as Hegselmann stresses (p. 117), logical empiricists give so much credit to contemporary logic and why they argue that synthetic *a priori* knowledge does not exist, and that knowledge can be achieved only by means of experience. It seems convenient to mention here that Reichenbach, who did not belong to the Vienna circle, but must be considered a logical empiricist, propounded –as has been correctly pointed out by Michael Friedmann in his *Dynamics of Reason* (Friedmann 2001)- a sort of *a priori* principles in science in his 1920 book *Relativitätstheorie und Erkenntnis a priori* (Reichenbach 1920). Nonetheless, such principles resemble more to Kuhn's notion of paradigm in the sense of disciplinary matrix used by Kuhn in the 1970 Appendix to his *The Structure of Scientific Revolutions* (Kuhn 1970) than to the Kantian *a priori*.

Moreover, as Hegselmann correctly observes (p. 119), the distinction so basic for logical empiricism between sense and nonsense, together with the logical analysis of concepts on which it is based, oppose logical empiricism to traditional philosophy –and one could add, including those critics like Horkheimer that did not understand logical empiricism. In fact, Hegselmann correctly asserts (p. 119) that the logical empiricists of the Vienna Circle attempted (at least during a short period) to replace traditional philosophy with their project of a unified science. In such a project moulded by Carnap, Hahn and Neurath in the programmatic manifesto of the Vienna Circle, *The Scientific Conception of the World* (1929), it is made clear, as Hegselmann correctly stresses (pp. 120-121) that at least these three prominent members of the Vienna Circle intended their program of the scientific conception of the world as intimately related to the socialist transformation of society. In particular, they underscore that "the scientific conception of the world offers the necessary instruments for rational action". In fact, as Hegselmann correctly states (p. 138), Carnap, Philip Frank, Hahn and Neurath were all socialists. It should be added to what Hegselmann stated that both Reichenbach and Edgar Zilzel, the latter of which occasionally differed from Carnap's and Neurath's views in the Vienna Circle, were also socialists. However, as Hegselmann once more correctly says (p. 131) the exile and the consequent disintegration of the Vienna Circle disconnected its members from the political and cultural frame of Austromarxism.

In the final part of his important paper, Hegselmann will make perfectly clear that the scientific conception of the world and the logical analysis of concepts and statements is incompatible with a doctrine like that of national-socialism. On this issue says Hegselmann (p. 136):

> ...a critical ear or eye with respect to language and its significance are part of the scientific conception of the world.... A sensible and critical ear with language and its significance will not be very receptive in front of a void pathos, in front of the great words and the suggestive formulations.

A little bit later, Hegselmann adds (p. 137):

The logical eye allows us to recognize sophisms, naturalists or of other sort, as, for example, that known with the name "*post hoc ergo propter hoc*", extensively common in political contexts. The sense of consistency and of logic is inherent to the scientific conception of the world in the same measure in which it brings bad consequences for the national-socialist ideology, what by the way explains the strong antilogical resentment that it [the latter: GERH] manifests.

But the above remarks apply not only to national-socialism, but also to those Marxists or neo-Marxists that have coincided with the national-socialists in criticizing not so much the theoretical content of the theses defended at a particular moment by (some) logical positivists, but the logical analysis of concepts, the enlightening function of the philosopher and the high esteem in which logical empiricism had the sciences, and which also characterize many of us that are not logical empiricists. Finally, with respect to socialism It should be briefly stressed that it will be constructed on the basis of rationality, scientificality and the enlightening that liberates from prejudices and dogmas offered by the logical-conceptual analysis, and human solidarity based on universal education and the development of a critical attitude; or it will not be constructed at all. Certainly, it will not be constructed on the basis of the dogmas that, in the majority of cases have ended in new forms of class systems[10], nor on the basis of presumed historical-materialist (or dialectical-materialist) so-called analyses be it of science or philosophy that have never been enough self-critical to apply to themselves and see their own historical nature, embedded in the cultural medium of the nineteenth century reductionisms –like Freudianism, psychologism and Comte's positivism-, of its own methodology.

The preceding assertions are not meant as a denial of the obvious fact that philosophy, the empirical sciences and even the deductive ones have a history. However, that historical analysis has nothing to do with historical or dialectical materialisms –or with any presumed national-socialists or whatever racial superiorities-, but has its proper internal dynamic, which is different in each case. Thus, the history of physics shows the frequent demise of hypotheses that even

---

[10] See on this issue Claude Lefort's *Éléments d'une Critique de la Bureaucratie* (1971), and the two volumes of papers by Cornelius Castoriadis *La Societé Bureaucratique* (1973).

the most optimistic Lakatosian cannot defend, either because of an overwhelming falsifying data or because of empirical sterility; whereas in other cases the falsifying data is more questionable and, thus, admits some redeeming reinterpretation or even a revision of the data itself. On the other hand, in the history of mathematics the abandonment of research in a given area is not based either on the indefensibility or falsifiability either of the content of theorems in that area or, even less, of some of its applications –what would not touch their theoretical content, but only its applicability to certain objects of study of empirical science-, but, for example, to the impossibility of the further obtainment of significant results in that area, to the fact that the area has been subsumed under a more general theory that allows the obtainment of results that are both broader and deeper, or even some times, when the importance of the area is based mostly on the applications of the theory, if applications, let us say, to physics, loose interest in the eyes of scientists working in them. That does not mean that it is impossible to falsify a mathematical theorem, but that does not occur on the basis of experience. It can very well occur –and has occurred- that a mathematician shows that mathematical statements that had been considered true by various generations of mathematicians, are not true, since the proofs that had been given of them were fallacious, or that they were not true with the generality in which they were formulated, but only in a much more restricted area. Nonetheless, not only is such a refutation not a case of an empirical refutation of mathematical statements, nor does it mean that a statement was originally true and later false, but only shows that human intelligence has clear limitations and is fallible. Now, even such internal historical dynamics of the various exact sciences can only be a complement, never a replacement, of the theoretical investigation of the sciences and their foundations. Particularly, the whole historical investigation of the physical sciences made by Kuhn, his followers and opponents in no way would make obsolete or invalid the theoretical investigation of science, as is done, among others, by some of the contributors to the book under discussion, belonging to the so-called structuralist school in the philosophy of science, of Sneed, Stegmüller, Moulines, Balzer and others.

Josep-María Terricabras' paper 'La Lógica del Tractatus y la Construcción Lógica de Carnap' is not especially illuminating, since it stresses perfectly clear differences between the theses and objectives of Wittgenstein's *Logisch-philosopische Abhandlung* (1921) better known as the *Tractatus* and Carnap's *Aufbau*. There is little doubt that, though Wittgenstein exerted some influence on members of the Vienna Circle, that influence has been exaggerated, even by the members themselves. In particular, the *Aufbau* refers only thrice to the *Tractatus* in the bibliographical commentaries of §§43, 180 and 183 –the second of which simply refers to the third-, and was completed before Wittgenstein's contact with the Vienna Circle. Moreover, it is well known that the brief personal contact between Wittgenstein and Carnap was not the best possible, whereas the influence of Wittgenstein was mostly on Moritz Schlick and Friedrich Waismann, who were extremely captivated by the aura of the author of the *Tractatus*. It is unnecessary to discuss here Terricabras' paper in order to comment the obvious –for example, that the *Aufbau* was an epistemological treatise but the *Tractatus* was not (p. 161). The only important point that seems questionable is Terricabras' assertion that Carnap's extensionality thesis is linked to the thesis of physicalism (whereas Wittgenstein's extensionality thesis does not have any such link). It should be pointed out that in the *Aufbau*, which precedes Carnap's adoption of physicalism, and whose epistemic basis is usually considered phenomenalist –though it is really phenomenological[11]-, Carnap defends the extensionality thesis and, hence, the referred link is highly questionable.

Interestingly, the next paper after that of Terricabras is Thomas Uebel's 'El Fisicalismo en Wittgenstein y Carnap'. This paper is concerned with a claim of priority made by Wittgenstein against Carnap after the latter's publication of his paper 'Die physikalische Sprache als Universalsprache der Wissenschaft', in which in a footnote Carnap ascribes to Neurath the thesis of physicalism. Uebel will argue in his paper (see p. 171) that Wittgenstein and Carnap did not have in mind the same thing when they spoke about 'physicalism'. According

---

[11] See Chapters 2 and 3 of my book *The Young Carnap's Unknown Master*. (The book was published in 2008, thus, after the original publication of this study.)

to Uebel (p. 173), for Carnap the thesis of physicalism is precisely that expressed in the title of the paper, namely, that the physicalist language is the universal language of science. But that does not exclude that he allowed at the side of the physicalist language, and in opposition to Wittgenstein (see pp. 182-183), a second phenomenalist protocol language, that would be the language to be used for epistemological purposes, what could be seen as a residue of the *Aufbau*. Though Uebel's paper is interesting, we will not consider it further.

The paper by Ramón Cirera –one of the most remarkable Carnapian scholars- 'El Análisis Lógico del Lenguaje Científico, según Carnap' begins in some sense where the former paper ended, namely, describing physicalism (p. 195) as "a version of materialism not metaphysically committed", and ascribing its acceptance by Carnap to Neurath's influence. Moreover, Cirera asserts (p. 195) that Neurath and Popper convinced Carnap to abandon the epistemological foundationalist perspective of the *Aufbau*. Cirera adds (p. 195) that what Neurath was not able to do is to convince Carnap to accept his radical empiricism, which anticipated Quine's views by trying to erase any fundamental epistemological difference between logic and mathematics, on one side, and the empirical sciences. However, as Cirera correctly points out (p. 196), physicalism complicates the situation for Carnap, since from a physicalist point of view language is a physical entity and, thus, its study is the study of something empirical. Therefore, logical truths, if they were the result of the rules of language use, would be of an empirical nature, a conclusion accepted by Neurath (p. 196).

Now, as Cirera correctly states (p. 197), Carnap considered languages as calculus completely determined by their vocabulary, and their rules of formation and of transformation. Cirera asserts (pp. 197 and 198) that Carnap obtained that conception of languages from Poincaré's conventionalism in physics (which he also extends to Duhem), according to which we are free to choose the geometry for the description of physical events. Moreover, Cirera adds (p. 199) that a significant role was also played by an important distinction that he incorrectly ascribes to Moritz Schlick between formal geometry and physical geometry -, but that contrary to Cirera's opinion, was clearly made by Riemann in his classic monograph *Über die Hypothesen*, *welche der Geometrie zugrunde liegen.*[12] It seems pertinent to point out that –contrary to Cirera's assertion– Carnap did not obtain the distinction between rules of formation and rules of transformation either from Schlick, or from Poincaré or from Duhem, but once more from Husserl. On this issue, the reader could examine both Chapter XI of the first volume and the Fourth Logical Investigation of the second volume of *Logische Untersuchungen,* as well as the first part of *Formale und transzendentale Logik* (Husserl 1929). What could have been obtained from Poincaré's and others' –not precisely Duhem- geometrical conventionalism is the Principle of Tolerance of *Logische Syntax der Sprache,* which though strictly connected in that book to the conception of language as a calculus and to the plurality of languages that such a conception gives birth to, should not be mixed with the constitutive aspects of that conception of language as are the rules of formation and transformation.

According to Cirera (p. 202), the peculiar manner in which Carnap resolves the tension between his acquired physicalism and his conception of language and logic is the important distinction between a formal and a material mode of discourse. Cirera stresses (p. 202) that though the correct form of expression is the formal mode of discourse, frequently the material mode is tolerable, if one does not forget that it is an improper form of expression. As Cirera correctly asserts (pp. 202-203), that conception of Carnap, that even rescued statements not easily classifiable either as *analytic a priori* or as *synthetic a posteriori,* separates Carnap's thought from traditional empiricism – including Neurath and Quine- and, of course, from Wittgenstein. Thus, adds Cirera (p. 203)

> ...the distinction between material and formal discourse leaves a place for philosophy, since on its basis one can understand Carnap's assertion that philosophy is nothing else than logic of the sciences, logical syntax of the language of science. Philosophical statements are expressions in the material mode of the logic of science.

Before finalizing our exposition of Cirera's excellent paper, it seems appropriate to insert two additional quotations. "Philosophy is for

---

[12] Riemann (1867). By the way, Riemann's distinction is accepted by Husserl as early as December 1892 in a letter to Brentano. Moreover, Cirera does not refer here to Carnap's *Der Raum,* a book in which the distinction is omnipresent.

Carnap a theoretical, though not a scientific enterprise..." (p. 204). "Logical syntax does not terminate philosophy, but represents the awakening of its linguistic conscience" (p. 205). On pp. 206-207 Cirera points out that for Carnap philosophy has two tasks, namely, (i) the description of a language without taking into account its possible factual actualization, and (ii) the task of proposing the adoption of a specific language for scientific purposes. In none of the two cases would one make an assertion with factual content and, thus, one could conclude (p. 207) that philosophy, as a theoretical enterprise, is completely analytic.

At the end of his paper (p. 208), but not only there (see pp. 202-203) Cirera underscores that the notorious verification principle of meaning, which had the objective of declaring nonsensical metaphysical statements, has no place in his interpretation of Carnap's thought. Regardless of the fact that Cirera's interpretation is without doubt an interesting one, we think that he would feel very uncomfortable when trying to assess from his perspective Carnap's 'Überwindung der Metaphysik durch logische Analyse der Sprache'.

Thomas Mormann's paper 'El Lenguaje en Neurath y Carnap' is also thematically related to the preceding three papers. At the beginning of his very interesting paper (p. 216), Mormann reminds the reader that in *Logische Syntax der Sprache* Carnap maintains the following chain of equations: philosophy=philosophy of science=logic of science=syntax of scientific language. Mormann will make use (see. p. 216) of a distinction made by Jean van Heijenoort and Jaakko Hintikka –and that would go across the distinction between analytic philosophy and continental philosophy- between language as a calculus and language as a universal medium. A fundamental difference between Carnap and Neurath is that Carnap, together with Husserl (one should add here Tarski and Gödel), considered language as a calculus, whereas Neurath would coincide with Heidegger, Frege, Russell, Wittgenstein and Quine (see also p. 219) in considering language as a universal medium. Though we are not enthused by such classifications, it should be pointed out that those that conceive language as a calculus have no problems with admitting the possibility of various languages and, especially, the possibility of speaking about language, whereas those that conceive language as a universal medium reject those two possibilities and maintain that, in some sense, we are prisoners of language. The fact that Carnap and Neurath had so radically different views about language induces Mormann to question (p. 216) both the uniformity of logical empiricism and the conception current in some circles about logical empiricism being a sort of "antiphilosophy" radically opposed to the continental tradition. We agree with Mormann on both issues.

Mormann stresses (p. 217) that Carnap's version of logical empiricism prevailed as the official or orthodox theory of science of that philosophical current, whereas Neurath's version was forgotten until recently when one acknowledged that Neurath had anticipated what some people now refer to (p. 217) as "the new philosophy of science". In fact, according to Mormann (p. 235), Neurath anticipated Quine's conception of a naturalized epistemology, though his rejection of Carnap's views was more radical than that of Quine and one should consider him more as a precursor of Rorty's views.

Mormann will examine (see p. 218) two controversies between Carnap and Neurath that are linked to their different conceptions of language. The first one concerns unified science, the second semantics. With respect to the latter, the author reminds us that shortly after completing his *Logische Syntax der Sprache*, Carnap was convinced by Tarski of the necessity of semantics, of which the former almost immediately became one of its most important standard-bearers. Neurath, on the contrary, due to his perspective of language as a universal medium, could not accept the distinction between object language and metalanguage (see p. 221), essential to Tarskian semantics in order to avoid the paradoxes, and considered semantics a sort of metaphysics.

On the other hand, Neurath –who was originally a sociologist and economist- considered an exaggeration (see p. 222) the systematization of the whole science as conceived by Carnap, since for him only some parts of science admit such systematization. On this point, Mormann adds (p. 222):
> Everything else is for Neurath pseudo-rationalism, that is, metaphysics: the aspiration of control of a rationalist reason that, with the excuse of empiricism, hopes to put scientific knowledge once more under its control.

As Mormann underscores (p. 225), for Neurath vagueness is an indispensable component of the language of science.

On pp. 228 and 229 Mormann characterizes the conception of language as calculus as "constructivist", especially in Carnap's semantic period. Such a characterization –as happens with the unfortunate translation into English of the technical terms "Konstitution" and "konstituieren' as "construction" and "to construct"- can only serve to confuse and even distort Carnap's thought, linking it to some conceptions in the philosophy of mathematics with which Carnap had little to do during his whole academic career from *Der Raum* to *Philosophical Foundations of Physics* (Carnap 1966). Another point in Mormann's excellent paper we need to correct is that when he discusses Carnap's semantic turn (see p. 230) he mentions the growing influence of conventionalism and the gradual assimilation of Gödel's First Incompleteness Theorem, but quite ignores the most decisive and direct influence, namely, that of Tarski, with whom Carnap discussed the necessity of studying semantic aspects of formalized languages in the early 1930s. Although his conversion to semantics was not manifest in *Logische Syntax der Sprache*, already in 1935, that is, a year later, in a conference in Paris Carnap joined forces with Tarski on behalf of semantics.[13]

Finally, Mormann stresses (see p. 234) that he coincides with Neurath in that "some Carnapian views on language are not easily reconcilable with usual empiricism". We also consider correct Neurath's appreciation, but differ radically from the consequence he extracts. Without doubt, Carnap was not an authentic empiricist, but a philosopher of great complexities, in whose thought there is an attempt to harmonize various trends of thought currents. However, if the cost to be an empiricist is to reject semantics and the theory of models, then one has precisely to reject empiricism, since – remembering a *dictum* by David Hilbert- nobody will let us out of the paradise that Tarski created (on the shoulders of that created by Cantor).

Dirk Koppelberg's paper 'Empiricism and Pragmatism in Carnap and Quine' discusses Quine's criticism of Carnap, which has been considered by the majority of scholars working on analytic philosophy as one of the main reasons –together with Kuhn's book *The Structure of Scientific Revolutions*- for the demise of logical

---

[13] See on this issue Schilpp 1963, pp. 30-31.

empiricism. Koppelberg begins his study of Quine (see p. 243) considering two well-known dichotomies defended by Carnap, between analytic truths and empirical truths, and between internal and external questions. As Koppelberg correctly asserts (p. 243):
> According to Carnap, these two dichotomies resolve the main difficulties present in all versions of classical empiricism: allow a satisfactory epistemological explanation of the existence of logical and mathematical truths, and also provide a theoretical clarification of the interrelationship between philosophy and science.

On the contrary, for Quine (see p. 243) "... no satisfactory form of empiricism can be obtained by means of those two distinctions". With respect to the distinction between analytic truths and empirical truths, Koppelberg tells us (p. 245) that Carnap thought it represented a clear advantage over classical empiricism –maybe one should add: with the exception of Hume, who distinguished between truths about matters of fact and relations of ideas-, since it can satisfactorily account for logical and mathematical truths. With respect to the distinction between internal and external questions, it served Carnap (see p. 250) to stress their different epistemological status, in which case only the former ones would be regulated.

Quine's basic objection against Carnap's distinction between internal and external questions is, according to Koppelberg (pp. 250-251), that the strategy of Carnap's argumentation to make the distinction, on the basis of a distinction between regulated and non-regulated actions, is a *petitio principii*. On the other hand, the principal objection of Quine against the distinction between analytic truths and empirical truths, and against the notion of analyticity is that, as Koppelberg puts it (p. 252), "...that in our holistic scientific system the concept of analyticity cannot fulfil the elucidating function that Carnap ascribes it with respect to logic and mathematics'. Moreover, Koppelberg adds (p. 254), "the concept of analyticity becomes superfluous, since its explanatory function is assumed by holism". The preceding formulations of Quine's main objection to Carnap's notion of analyticity do not seem correct, since in "Two Dogmas of Empiricism" (Quine 1951) the main argument consists in that an elucidation of the notion of analyticity as conceived by Carnap is irremediably circular. The transit to holism in the same paper occurs later and, in fact, does not follow from it.

Continuing with Koppelberg's exposition, he maintains (p. 255) that the rejection of the famous distinction "undermines the methodological basis of Carnap's conception of the meaning and purpose of a philosophical analysis of science". Quine would consider (see p. 255) such a methodological basis as a residue of traditional theory of knowledge, which would distort the interrelation between philosophy and science. The correct interrelation between philosophy and science, according to Quine, would be that of his notorious epistemology naturalized.

Before making some critical comments of Quine, we want to quote a passage from Koppelberg' paper with which we completely agree, even though the purpose that its author had for writing it is different from the one we have to quote it. Koppelberg says (p. 257):

> Philosophical progress frequently consists in introducing distinctions where before one did not see differences; but it can also consist in invalidating distinctions traditionally established when, after a more precise observation, they seem unnecessary, without grounding or even harmful.

Clearly, for Quine and Koppelberg the distinction between analytic truths and empirical truths is a distinction without a difference.

With respect to Quine's critique of Carnap's notion of analyticity, the first thing one should have in mind is that Carnap includes among analytic truths not only logical and mathematical truths, but also truths like "No bachelor is married", which clearly depend on the concepts of "bachelor" and "married". Quine's critique of Carnap in the famous paper is concentrated on this last sort of statement, whose presumed analyticity would depend on the notion of synonymy. This notion of synonymy is totally absent from logical or arithmetic elementary statements –for example, $\neg(p \wedge \neg p)$ or $3+2<7$-, as also from more complicated logical or mathematical statements, for example, the Chang-Los-Suszko Theorem in model theory, which says that a first order theory is preserved under unions of chains if and only, if it is axiomatizable by a system of universal-existential axioms, or Tychonoff's Theorem in general topology, which says that the product of a family of compact topological spaces is a compact topological space, or even metatheorems like that which establishes that Tychonoff's Theorem is equivalent to the Axiom of Choice. In Quine's argumentation there are two *non sequitur*. The first one consists in trying to extend his argumentation against statements whose analyticity would essentially depend on the notion of synonymy and on the presumed obscurity that Quine ascribes the notion of meaning - presumption that could be a matter of discussion- to logical and mathematical statements. The second *non sequitur* –as we already mentioned- concerns holism. That is a totally gratuitous assumption of Quine's argumentation, which has never received any grounding, as also the presumed gradual difference between empirical statements of everyday life and logical or mathematical statements. By the way, neither Quine nor any of his followers has ever explained under what circumstances would it be plausible and convenient to consider falsified any of the five examples of logical or mathematical statements mentioned above, or any similar statements. Even the presumed refutation of the Principle of Excluded Middle by quantum mechanics –the only example referred to by Quine, Putnam and their followers- is based on a confusion.

It seems pertinent to make some brief commentaries on the last issue. There exists a vast array of mathematical structures (or theories). Some of them have applications in one empirical science, others in a different one and some in none. That in the mathematical structure that best serves to model quantum mechanical events, e.g., the law of distributivity is not valid, does not teach us anything about logic, in the same way in which the existence of non-commutative algebras does not tell us anything about the validity or invalidity of the law of commutativity in propositional logic. The existence of a variety of non-classical logics, obtained either by rejecting some theorems or rules of inference –e.g. intuitionist logic or the so-called logic of relevance-, or adding new symbols and axioms –as, e.g., modal logics-, is not essentially different to the acquisition of more general or less general structures from a given mathematical structure by means of the elimination, respectively, the addition of some axiom or of some operation with its corresponding axioms. That is, in principle, usually possible, but does not need to disturb classical logicians. In fact, those two manners of obtaining non-classical logics from classical logics are perfectly similar to the acquisition of a semigroup or a monoid from a group, respectively, of a ring from an Abelian group. Now, the issue becomes much more serious when one tries to revise logic in order to adjust it to some theory in empirical science. It should be pointed out that those pretending to implement such revision of logic are going too fast, but it also seems that they have not liberated themselves from the archaic anthropocentric view of the universe, according to which human beings are the preferred creatures of the deity that presumably created them. Such authors –Quine and Putnam among them- go too fast because there is absolutely no reason to believe that current scientific theories are the ones that adequately describe the universe, its laws and those of its components. The blind faith in classical mechanics was crushed irremediably by the special and general theories of relativity, and quantum mechanics. Only such blind faith in empirical science –that is something different from the acknowledgement of the importance of science for any rational discussion- can lead someone to believe that one has to revise logic in order to adapt it to what presumably teaches some current scientific theory. In fact, if we were to follow Quine and Putnam, and at the same time reasonably thought that the successive scientific theories come closer and closer to knowing the truths about the universe without possibly reaching it, we would probably have to make successive revisions of logic, as required by the dominant theories of the empirical sciences in different periods of time. In this way we would have not only a naturalized epistemology but also a naturalized logic –that, as in the case of the former, one should better call "denaturalized". Moreover, the presumption to revise logic – a discipline that is not concerned properly with the world of experiences, though being relevant to it- in order to adjust it to the current theories in empirical science is based on the anthropocentric assumption that the human species, notwithstanding its evidently limited intelligence, has not only the actual capability to get to know the laws that govern the universe, but also has the right –as if it were its own creation- to decide about the validity of the laws of a science that does not presuppose the existence either of human beings or of the universe that is the object of study of the empirical sciences, nor even the existence of a deity. As in mathematics, revision in logic is possible, but not on the basis of what empirical science teaches, but on the basis of the limitations of human intelligence, which makes perfectly possible that logicians or mathematicians could be sure that they had proved a theorem or believed in the evident truth of an axiom, and later acknowledge that the presumed theorem is not valid or that the axiom generates contradictions, or that it can very well be consistently replaced by another axiom incompatible with it. The history of mathematics –especially, e.g., set theory- contains multiple examples illustrating the first sort of situation. The second one occurred precisely with the notorious Principle V of Frege,s *Grundgesetze der Arithmetik* (Frege 1893, 1903); the third one with Euclid's Axiom of Parallels.

Quine's holism is simply an unfounded assumption, and its (deliberate) confusion with Duhem's very reasonable thesis of the impossibility of isolating hypotheses in physics –and, hence, the impossibility of crucial experiments-, since the same instruments used in the experiment presuppose the validity of physical laws that could very well turn out to be false, does a great injustice to Duhem (and a great favour to Quine).[14] That does not mean that there do not exist thematically seemingly unrelated statements, whose truths are after all intimately related. That is the case of statements like the already mentioned Tychonoff's Theorem and Tarski's Ultrafilter Theorem, which states that any filter can be extended to an ultrafilter. This theorem is equivalent to a version of Tychonoff's Theorem restricted to Hausdorff spaces. Of course, such a version follows from the more general version valid for all compact topological spaces. Applying Husserl's semantic distinction between states of affairs and situations of affairs to mathematical statements, the present author has maintained in various of his writings that though the states of affairs referred to by Tarski's Ultrafilter Theorem and by Tychonoff's Theorem restricted to Hausdorff spaces are different, the underlying situation of affairs is the same, whereas that situation of affairs is properly included in the situation of affairs of Tychonoff's Theorem in its most general form. In his *Vorlesungen über Bedeutungslehre* (1987, pp. 101-102) Husserl already maintained that his distinction between states of affairs and situations of affairs could be applied to laws or formalisms in physics that though seem to talk about different issues, are equivalent. A very good example of such equivalences in physics

---

[14] See on this issue the collection of translations of papers by Duhem in *Essays on the History and Philosophy of Science* (1996), especially the papers "Some Reflections on the Subject of Experimental Physics", pp. 1-28, and "Logical Examination of Physical Theory", pp. 232-238. See also the third chapter of Gillies 1993.

was offered by the equivalence established in 1926 by Dirac and Jordan between Heisenberg's and Schrödinger's formalisms of quantum mechanics.[15] However, leaving aside such clear, specific and demonstrable cases, Quine's discourse about the interrelation of all our beliefs –which sometimes are opposed even among the researchers in the same scientific specialty- is pure speculation, as unfounded as astrology and has nothing to do with science or philosophy as rational enterprises. It is not casual that those who have extracted the most radical consequences of Quine's conception of philosophy have ended in extreme relativism, irrationality and lack of scientificality.

Finally, we would like to mention another very questionable component of Quine's philosophy, namely, the issue of the empirical basis of science. Quine assumes as correct in *Word and Object* (Quine 1960) and other writings a conception of our experience that is simply false. Our experience is not one of sense data (or stimulations of our senses). We obtain the notion of sense data by a sort of dissection or abstraction from experience. Our experience is a structured one, an experience of states of affairs –I perceive the glass at the side of the dish, the cup of coffee on the small dish, Peter and David in the corridor-, not isolated objects and much less isolated sense data. In such a perception there are –as Husserl pointed out in the Sixth Logical Investigation[16] - even components irreducible to sense perception, categorial components, to which I refer by particles like 'and', 'at the side of', 'on' in the preceding examples, though such particles have no sensible referent. Thus, even in such a primitive level like that of the sensible perception of objects of our entourage one transcends mere experience by the presence of categorial elements.

---

[15] See on that issue Kragh 1999, p. 167 in that book there is a reference (see p. 335) to a similar demonstration by Freeman Dyson of the equivalence of two renormalization procedures in quantum electrodynamics, one of Schwinger and Tomonaga, the other of Feynman, equivalence to which one could probably apply the same semantic distinction made by Husserl. This issue, however, transcends by far the competence of the present author. Nonetheless, it should be clear that the application of the Husserlian distinction to mathematical or physical contexts is a task of the philosopher, not of the physicist or mathematician, for whom the distinction falls outside of their respective disciplines.

[16] See on this issue the second part of the Sixth Logical Investigation, titled 'Sensibility and Understanding'.

Because of the above stated reasons, a naturalized (or better: denaturalized) epistemology, which makes philosophy an appendix of empirical science, and logic and mathematics in empirical sciences, though –following Mill– more inveterate and enthroned in our web of belief than, for example, biology, lacks any grounding. There is space for philosophy, as Carnap thought, at the side of both deductive (non-empirical) and empirical sciences. If one is going to take philosophy seriously, one cannot ignore either the deductive or the empirical sciences, but it cannot dissolve in them or form a sort of mere appendix to them.

The last paper of this interesting collection of Cirera, Ibarra and Mormann is Andrés Rivadulla's paper 'Probabilidad Bayesiana, Probabilidad Frecuencial y la Teoría Carnapiana de la Inferencia Estadística'. We are not going to discuss this paper, since we have already extended this study too much. Nonetheless, it should be mentioned that Rivadulla offers a lucid and concise exposition of Carnap's project of an inductive logic, including his attempt to explain the differences between the notions of probability as a degree of confirmation (probability$_1$) and probability as relative frequency (probability$_2$). Equally clear is the exposition of the difficulties encountered by this project of Carnap.[17]

References

Carnap, R. – *Der Raum* 1922, reprint, Topos Verlag, Vaduz 1991
Carnap, R. – *Der logische Aufbau der Welt* 1928, fourth edition, F. Meiner, Hamburg 1974
Carnap, R. – *Logische Syntax der Sprache* 1934, expanded English edition, *The Logical Syntax of Language* 1937, reprint, Open Court, Chicago et al 2002
Carnap, Rudolf – *Philosophical Foundations of Physics*, Basic Books, New York 1966

---

[17] Professors Anastasio Alemán and Ivette Fred read a first version of this critical study, and made suggestions in order to facilitate its comprehension. I am very grateful to both of them, and feel sorry that I could not profit from all their suggestions.

Castoriadis, C. – *La Societé Bureaucratique*, two volumes, Union Générale d'Éditions, Paris 1973
Colletti, Lucio – *Il Marxismo e Hegel*, Laterza, Roma 1973
Duhem, Pierre – *Essays in the History and Philosophy of Science*, Hackett, Indianapolis 1996
Frege, G. – *Grundgesetze der Arithmetik I* 1893 & *II* 1903, reprint in one volume, Georg Olms, Hildesheim 1962
Friedman, M. – *Reconsidering Logical Positivism*, Cambridge University Press 1999
Friedman, M. – *A Parting of the Ways*, Open Court, Chicago et al. 2000
Friedman, M. – *Dynamics of Reason*, University of Chicago Press, Chicago 2001
Gillies, Donald – *Philosophy of Science in the Twentieth Century*, Blackwell, Oxford 1993
Griffin, N. - Editor's Introduction to *The Cambridge Companion to Russell*, Cambridge University Press, Cambridge 2003
Hahn, H., Neurath, O. and Carnap, R. – *Wissenschaftliche Weltauffassung: Der Wienerkreis*, Arthur Wolf, Wien 1929
Husserl, E. – *Logische Untersuchungen* 1900-1901, Husserliana Edition, M. Nijhoff, Den Haag XVIII 1975 & XIX 1984
Husserl, E. – *Formale und transzendentale Logik* 1929, Husserliana Edition XVII, M. Nijhoff, Den Haag 1974
Husserl, E. – *Vorlesungen über Bedeutungslehre*, Husserliana XXVI, Kluwer, Dordrecht 1987
Kolakowski, L. – *Main Currents of Marxism*, vol. 3, Oxford University Press, Oxford 1978
Kragh, H. – *Quantum Generations*, Princeton University Press, Princeton 1999
Kuhn, T. – *The Structure of Scientific Revolutions*, University of Chicago Press, Chicago 1962, expanded second edition 1970
Lefort, C. *Éléments d'une Critique de la Bureaucratie*, Librairie Droz, Genève & Paris 1971
Mancosu, P. & Ryckman, T. A. - 'Mathematics and Phenomenology: The Correspondence between O. Becker and H. Weyl', *Philosophia Mathematica 10(2)*, 2002, pp. 130-202

Mayer, Verena – 'Die Konstruktion der Erfahrungswelt: Carnap und Husserl', in Wolfgang Spohn (ed.), *Erkenntnis Orientated: a Centennial Volume dedicated to Rudolf Carnap and Hans Reichenbach*, Kluwer, Dordrecht 1991, pp. 287-303

Mayer, Verena – 'Carnap und Husserl', in David Bell & Wilhelm Vossenkuhl (eds.), *Wissenschaft und Subjektivität*, Akademie Verlag, Berlin 1992

Quine, W. O. – 'Two Dogmas of Empiricism' 1951, reprinted in W. O. Quine, *From a Logical Point of View*, Harvard University Press, Cambridge, Ma. 1953, second edition 1953

Quine, W. O. – *Word and Object*, MIT Press, Cambridge, Ma. 1960

Reichenbach, H. – *Relativitätstheorie und Erkenntnis a priori* 1920, English translation, *The Theory of Relativity and a priori Knowledge*, University of California Press, Berkeley 1965

Richardson, Alan – *Carnap's Construction of the World*, Cambridge University Press, Cambridge 1998

Riemann, B. – *Über die Hypothesen, welche der Geometrie zugrunde liegen*, 1867, reprint of the third edition, Chelsea, New York 1960

Rosado Haddock, G. E. – *The Young Carnap's Unknown Master*, Ashgate, England 2008

Rungaldier, Edmund – *Carnap's Early Conventionalism*, Rodopi, Amsterdam 1984

Russell, B. – *Our Knowledge of the External World* 1914, fifth reprint, George Allen & Unwin, London 1969

Schilpp, P. A. – *The Philosophy of Rudolf Carnap*, Open Court, La Salle 1963

Schlick, Moritz – *Allgemeine Erkenntnislehre* 1916, third revised edition 1925, English translation of the third edition, Open Court, La Salle 1985

Schuhmann, K. – *Husserl-Chronik*, M. Nijhoff, Den Haag 1977

Sepp, H. R. – *Edmund Husserl und die Phänomenologische Bewegung*, Karl Alber, Freiburg 1988

Wittgenstein, Ludwig – *Logisch-philosophische Abhandlung* 1921, English translation, *Tractatus Logico-Philosophicus* 1922, third bilingual edition, Routledge, London 1966

Additional References for this Edition

Mayer, V. – 'Der *Logische Aufbau* als Plagiat', in G. E. Rosado Haddock (ed.), *Husserl and Analytic Philosophy*, pp. 175-260

Rosado Haddock, G. E. – 'The Old Husserl and the Young Carnap', in G. E. Rosado Haddock (ed.), *Husserl and Analytic Philosophy*, pp. 261-286

Rosado Haddock (ed.) – *Husserl and Analytic Philosophy*, de Gruyter, Berlin 2016

Review of Elisabeth Schuhmann (ed.), Edmund Husserl, Alte und Neue Logik

In recent years several volumes of Husserl's lecture notes and courses from the years before the publication of his Ideen zu einer reinen Phänomenologie und phänomenologischen Philosophic (Hua III) in 1913 have been published under the excellent editorship of Elisabeth Schuhmann, who, together with her husband, the late Karl Schuhmann have made invaluable contributions to the better understanding of Husserl's views. The present book, namely, Husserl's course on logic of 1908-09 is especially important, since it belongs to the first years of the transcendental phenomenological period, inaugurated by Husserl's 1907 lectures under the title Die Idee der Phänomenolgie (Hua II). Thus, as happens with his already published course of 1907-1908, Einleitung in die Logik und Erkenntnistheorie (Hua XXIV), it can serve to assess the impact, if any, of Husserl's transcendental turn in his views on logic and mathematics. In fact, both books show very clearly, as does his Logik und allgemeine Wissenschaftstheorie (Hua XXX), based on later lectures and manuscripts, and his Formale und transzendentale Logik of 1929 (Hua XVII) that Husserl's views on logic and mathematics during the transcendental phenomenological period remain essentially the same as those of the first volume of Logische Untersuchungen (Hua XVIII) first published in 1900-1901.There are, of course, a pair of passages that seem to be distinctive of the transcendental phenomenological period, for example, on pp. 175-176, where Husserl distinguishes between a more restricted and a wider notion of sense, which includes, besides the sense in the strict usage of that term, also its mode of apprehension as really existing or as merely given without any postulation of reality. Here both the notion of suspension of judgement and the distinction between the full "noema" and its nucleus are present.

Indeed, Husserl's logic course of 1908-1909 discusses many of the issues already considered in his opus magnum, especially in its first volume and in the first, third and fourth "Logical Investigations" of the second volume (Hua XIX). There is, however, a change of emphasis, as well as some important reflections not paralleled in Logische Untersuchungen. The change of emphasis consists basically in the fact that whereas in his opus magnum some 250 pages are concerned with the most thorough, well balanced and compelling refutation of psychologism ever made, discussing his views on logic and mathematics mostly in Chapter XI of the Prolegomena and introducing his definitions of analytic laws and necessities, and related concepts very briefly in the Third Logical Investigation, in the lecture course the situation is almost exactly the opposite. Most probably, Husserl is presupposing that it is unnecessary to present the refutation of psychologism in a detailed fashion (see, however, for example, pp. 13f., 32 and 277) and opts to concentrate on issues more lightly discussed in his opus magnum. However, for readers familiar with Formale und transzendentale Logik, Einleitung in die Logik und Erkenntnistheorie and Logik und allgemeine Wissenschaftstheorie the discussion of his views on logic and mathematics in the book that concerns us does not add much. Another related issue discussed here in more detail than in Logische Untersuchungen, and which received its definitive treatment in Formale und transzendentale Logik is that of form and matter at the propositional and, especially, subpropositional level (see, for example, the extensive discussion on pp. 66-67 and 72-82). Of course, issues like those of the ideality of meanings (see, for example, pp. 20 and 45-46), the semantic distinction between sense and referent (or meaning and objectuality), obtained almost simultaneously and independently from each other by Husserl and Frege around 1890 (see, for example, pp. 43, 45-46, 49-50, 222-223), meaning categories and laws that govern the formation of statements in contrast to the laws of logic proper, namely, those concerned with derivability and the avoidance of formal contradiction (see, for example, pp. 48-51, 54, 61-63, 224, 243 and 251-253), and the distinction between logic as theory of the proposition, based on the meaning categories, and mathematics as formal ontology (see, for example, pp. 249 and 252-253) are also discussed in the logic lectures. Incidentally, and somewhat ironically, on p. 249 Husserl stresses that he was the first to acknowledge the existence of a proto-logical region of the forms of meanings, the region that is concerned with the distinction between sense and nonsense and forms for Husserl the most basic part of logic. But up to the present date, most logicians ignore the fact that this nowadays generally accepted level of the rules of formation of a logical language originates in Husserl, not in his student Carnap, who took the idea from the former but never acknowledged it.[1] Of not negligible importance for scholars interested in the relation between Husserl and analytic philosophy is a passage on p. 3 of the logic lectures, in which he states that philosophical logic, as he conceives it, is the first or most basic philosophical discipline, and he goes on to call it "first philosophy in the strictest and most appropriate sense" of the word. Moreover, he conceives his task in a not dissimilar fashion to that of analytic philosophers when he asserts on p. 8 that he will proceed in a purely analytic way, and latter adds on p. 40 that his way of proceeding, being analytic, goes from the composite and nearer to our eyes to the simple.

Indeed, in this review I will concentrate on a few issues that need to be emphasized in order to better understand Husserl's relation to so-called analytic philosophy. First of all, it should be pointed out that in the logic lectures of 1908-09 Husserl is not content with general considerations on logical issues, but discusses specific forms of propositions, namely, conjunctions, disjunctions and conditionals, as well as rules of inference, for example, Modus Ponens and Modus Tollens see p. 29-, as well as conjunction elimination—see p. 254— and three other rules of inference on pp. 255-257, the distinction between material and formal implication see, for example, pp. 207 and 215-, formalization—see, for example, pp. 30-31, 88 and 213- and the relation between logical laws and rules of inference—see, for example, p. 253, where he stresses that not all logical laws correspond to a rule of inference. Moreover, Husserl not only mentions, as he already did in Logische Untersuchungen, that logic should be extended to include an objective theory of probability—see p. 230-, but also stresses that it should be extended to include the concepts of possibility and necessity, that is, that it should be extended to a modal logic—see pp. 230-232. Indeed, on the issue of the relevance of modal notions for logic—as occurs with the relation between logic and mathematics—Husserl's views seem more in touch than Frege's with more recent developments.

---

[1] See Carnap' *Logische Syntax der Sprache* §2.

Furthermore, the problem of mathematical existence is also touched—see, for example, p. 231-, as is the problem of axiomatisation—see p. 276. Finally, the extremely important semantic distinction between state of affairs (Sachverhalt) and situation of affairs (Sachlage), barely made in the Sixth Logical Investigation, is clearly made—see p. 273.

  The last point brings us to one of the two issues that I would like to discuss here in more detail. In 1906 Husserl and Frege interchanged letters for the second time, having already done it in 1891.[2] Regrettably, almost none of Husserl's letters to Frege—and certainly none of 1906—survived the Second World War. Frege's letters to Husserl survived and, thus, up to now scholars have had access only to one of the two parties involved in the discussion. Now, in Frege's letters to Husserl of 1906 he argued that sameness of sense should be identified with logical equivalence. Fregean scholars—with the exception of the present author—seem not to have noticed the incongruity between such a thesis of Frege and his assertions on sense both in "Uber Sinn und Bedeutung"[3] and in Grundgesetze der Arithmetik.[4] In this last work he asserts that the expressions "2 + 2" and "2×2" express different senses and, thus, "2 + 2 = 4" and "2×2 = 4" also have different senses, that is, express different thoughts. Nonetheless, they are mathematically equivalent and, in virtue of Frege's logicist thesis, also logically equivalent. That conclusion clearly contradicts Frege's assertion in the letters to Husserl that logical equivalence coincides with sameness of sense. In fact, as I have argued more than once[5], Frege's assertion in the letters to Husserl is the result of a confusion of Frege between his official notion of sense and his old notion of conceptual content of Begriffsschrift.[6] In the logic lectures of

---

[2] See Frege's *Wissenschaftlicher Briefwechsel*, pp. 94-107.

[3] See Frege's "Über Sinn und Bedeutung", in *Kleine Schriften*, pp. 143-162.

[4] See Frege, *Grundgesetze der Arithmetik I*, §2.

[5] See, for example, my articles in Hill and Rosado Haddock, *Husserl or Frege?: Meaning, Objectivity and Mathematics*.

[6] Frege, *Begriffsschrift*, §2

Critical Review of *Alte und Neue Logik: Vorlesung 1908/09*

1908-09 Husserl answers Frege—or most surely simply elaborates what he replied to Frege in the missing letters. Let us now see what Husserl answered.

On p. 111 of his 1908-09 logic lectures, Husserl says that it is an error to consider as identical two judgements, whose contents, that is, whose senses (or meanings) are equivalent in the sense that the statements expressing them are immediately derivable from each other. Moreover, he adds that one should not consider as having identical sense what should simply be taken as being equally valid, that is, valid in the same circumstances. On this point, Husserl is clearly more faithful to the Frege-Husserl distinction between sense and referent than Frege in the 1906 letters to Husserl. In the same way in which Frege stresses in "Über Sinn und Bedeutung" that an identity statement being true does not entail that the senses of the expressions connected by the identity sign be the same, but just their referents, Husserl observes that, in general, two statements can be interderivable without being required to have the same sense. On p. 116, Husserl stresses once more that it is an error to confuse equivalence with sameness of sense (or meaning). On p. 163, Husserl once more stresses that one should not confuse the equivalence of two thoughts—here Husserl uses the usual Fregean terminology—with their having the same sense. The same issue reappears once more at the end of the lectures on pp. 272-274. Thus, on p. 272, Husserl characterizes logical equivalence in a similar fashion to one of Frege's not easily compatible three characterizations of the notion of 'conceptual content' in Begriffsschrift, while at the same time stressing that logical equivalence does not coincide with sameness of sense. Husserl says p. 272):

> Also mit Beziehung auf denselben Inbegriff von Grundwahrheiten und dieselben Termini soll M aus N und N aus M folgen bzw. beweisbar sein. Naturlich brauchen dabei M und N nicht dieselben Termini zu haben.

In English the above passage reads:

> Thus, with respect to the same collection of fundamental truths [axioms: GERH] and the same terms M ought to follow, that is, be demonstrable, from N and N from M. Of course, M and N do not need to have the same terms.

In symbols, Husserl's characterization can be rendered:

$$M \equiv N =_{Df} \forall \Sigma \subseteq Ax[\Sigma \cup \{M\} \vdash N \leftrightarrow \Sigma \cup \{N\} \vdash M]$$

Husserl goes on (pp. 273-274) to distinguish a narrower and a broader concept of equivalence. The first one—see p. 273-, which he calls 'specifically logical equivalence' concerns statements with different sense but referring to the same state of affairs, and, thus, excludes the pair of inequalities 'a > b' and 'b < a'. The second one, which he calls 'content equivalence', includes such inequalities, which are rendered—as usual in Husserl's writings on logic—as sameness of the situation of affairs, though they have different categorial objectual content, briefly, they refer to different states of affairs.

With respect to Frege, some additional remarks seem pertinent. On pp. 71-72 Husserl distances himself from his usual terminology—according to which "Sinn" and "Bedeutung" are used mostly interchangeably as are "bedeuten" and "ausdrücken", whereas "Gegenstand" and "Gegenständlichkeit" are used for the referent—replacing it with the Fregean terminology—for which "bedeuten" is rendered as "to refer" and "Bedeutung" as "referent", "reference" or "denotation". Thus, Husserl says that a sentence refers to ["bedeutet"] a state of affairs ["Sachverhalt"]. Husserl then goes on to discuss the compositionality of senses and that of referents, but though on p. 60 he had stated that in a strict sense only sentences have an independent meaning, he makes it clear that the primary bearers of reference are the components of the sentence, whereas the sentence refers only derivatively. Thus, says Husserl (p. 72):

> ... der ganze Satz, dem sie [die gegenständliche Beziehung: GERH] angehort, erwachst als ein Bedeutungsganzes, das einen einheitlichen Sachverhalt bedeutet. Es ist aber klar, dass diese Sachbezüglichkeit der Formen eine sekundäre ist, namlich eine solche, welche schon die Sachbezüglichkeit der Glieder voraussetzt.

In English the above reads:

> ... the whole sentence, to which it [the objectual reference: GERH] belongs, forms a totality of meaning, that refers to a unique state of affairs. But it is clear that this objectual reference of the forms is a secondary one, namely, one that already presupposes the objectual reference of the constituent parts.

This is a clear rejection of the notorious context principle with respect to the referents.

The remaining issue that I want to comment on in this review pervades the whole lectures, though it obtains prominence in the second half. It is the problem of the analytic-synthetic distinction and the corresponding definitions. This issue was already discussed in the Third Logical Investigation, though more briefly. Nowadays that both

Carnap's definition of analyticity and that of Frege are, for different reasons, in almost complete philosophical disgrace, it seems pertinent to consider a very different sort of notion of analyticity, namely, that of Husserl, which does not have its roots in Kant, like those very different, nonetheless, of Carnap and Frege, but in Bolzano. It is impossible, however, to take into account in this review all passages of Husserl's 1908-09 lectures on logic, in which Husserl discusses the notions of analyticity and syntheticity a priori, and the reader is simply referred to the book for a more thorough treatment.

Interestingly, Husserl does not proceed directly to a characterization of the notions of analyticity and syntheticity a priori, but considers first presumed synthetic a priori inferences and contrasts them with logical or analytic inferences. Thus, on p. 30 and elsewhere—see pp. 33, 261-262- Husserl considers presumed synthetic a priori inferences. His examples are, on the one hand, arguments based on the relation of congruence in geometry, as well as some arguments about tonalities, like the transitivity of the relation of being a lower (or deeper) tone. Those presumed arguments are, according to Husserl, not capable of complete formalization and are, thus, contrasted by Husserl on pp. 30-32 with what he calls 'analytic-logical' or 'formal-logical' arguments, which are valid in virtue only of their forms and, thus, are capable of complete formalization. Indeed, as Husserl makes it perfectly clear on pp. 244-245, for him the notions of 'analytic' and 'formal' are extensionally equivalent. In concordance with this extensional identification of the formal and the analytic, he characterizes pure concepts already on p. 233 as free from any relation to individual objectualities. Mathematical—see p. 233- and, of course, logical concepts are for Husserl pure concepts. Moreover, Husserl characterizes purely conceptual truths as apodictic laws, whereas the particularizations of those apodictic laws are apodictic necessities. This runs parallel to Husserl's definition of analytic laws and analytic necessities in the Third Logical Investigation, but does not coincide with it. Such apodictic laws and necessities are contrasted by Husserl on p. 234 with natural laws, which contrary to the first are not true in any possible world and do not intend to be so, but just true in our physical world. Moreover, as Husserl asserts on the same page, pure geometrical laws that do not refer to the actual or physical space are also apodictically valid. Husserl stresses on p. 236 that the unrestricted generality of laws excludes any sort of existential postulation of individual objects. This, of course, brings to the fore, as Husserl stresses on p. 237, the fundamental difference between conceptual (rational) truths and factual truths, and, thus—see p. 238-, between a priori truths and a posteriori truths. As Husserl observes on p. 238, the last distinction is not logical but epistemological, since it concerns the different grounds on which truths are ultimately founded. Thus, a priori truths are for Husserl—see p., 230- ultimately founded on what he calls in his logic lectures "conceptual intuition", a term he probably meant to include both material essential and categorial intuition. Finally, on pp. 242ff. Husserl arrives at the characterizations of analytic law and analytic necessity, as well as to their distinction. He first observes on p. 242 that analytic laws and necessities are only a (proper) part of the conceptual laws and necessities, and on p. 243 he offers examples of both analytic and presumably synthetic a priori truths. Analytic laws are laws founded exclusively on their form and are also called by Husserl 'categorial laws' -see p. 245-, whereas analytic necessities are particularizations or individualizations of analytic laws, and could be transformed in analytic laws by replacement of their determined terms by undetermined terms (or variables). Husserl also contrasts analytic laws with synthetic a priori laws and analytic necessities with synthetic a priori necessities. In particular, the transposition of geometrical truths to particular objects, like crystals—see p. 246- are, for Husserl, synthetic a priori necessities. The same distinction is made on p. 248, whereas on pp. 246-247, Husserl sums up his distinction between analytic and synthetic truths. It is not possible to expound here those passages in more detail.

I will finish this review with some brief remarks concerning some issues related to Husserl's assertions on the synthetic a priori. As already mentioned, in his logic lectures, Husserl not only argues for the existence of synthetic a priori laws, but also of synthetic a priori inferences. Independently of the correctness or incorrectness of that thesis and of the adequacy or inadequacy of his examples, such a thesis remind the reader of Poincare's similar thesis about mathematical induction. In the case of Husserl, however, his examples are not arithmetical, since for him arithmetic was purely analytic. Indeed, the most interesting of Husserl's examples of presumed synthetic a priori inference concerns the geometric congruence relation. My main interest here, however, is not in presumed synthetic a priori inferences, or even in the synthetic a priori per se, but in Husserl's views on geometry. At first sight, on the basis of what has already being said, it would seem that geometrical statements not presupposing real physical space are simply synthetic a priori. However, Husserl's views on geometry are more nuanced. Thus, under the influence of Riemann and others, Husserl stated very clearly in Logische Untersuchungen[7], that n-dimensional multiplicities, of which Euclidean and non-Euclidean spaces are singularizations, are not only a priori but also analytic. Hence, those properties of Euclidean spaces had only in virtue of being singularizations of an n-dimensional multiplicity are analytic. On the other hand, as can be seen from a letter of Husserl to Brentano of 1892 and one to Natorp of 1901—see his Briefwechsel—[8], both the Euclidean or non-Euclidean nature of physical space and the number of dimensions are for him—once again following Riemann—empirical, thus, neither analytic nor synthetic a priori. More succinctly, the particular metric of real physical space is not given a priori, but empirically. Nonetheless, when Husserl considers arguments concerning congruence as examples of synthetic a priori arguments, he is presupposing the synthetic a priori nature of the notion of congruence. Thus, Husserl's views on space are, like those of Carnap in Der Raum[9] three-headed. There is a purely formal, analytic treatment of space, directly influenced in the case of Husserl by Riemann's theory of manifolds. There is also the study of such properties of space, like congruence, which is non-analytic, but still a priori, thus, synthetic a priori. Finally, as soon as we consider the metric of real physical space, we enter the realm of experience. The similarity with Carnap's trichotomy between formal space, intuitive space and physical space is,

---

[7] See Hua XVIII, Chapter XI, §70, pp. 252-253.

[8] *Briefwechsel*, vol. II, pp.10-11 and vol. V, pp. 80-86 and Textkritischer Anhang, pp. 233-236.

[9] See *Der Raum* 1922.

however, not complete, since for Husserl the synthetic a priori components of physical space extend far beyond the topological ones, since congruence is not a general topological notion, not even an affine notion, but already presupposes the notion of isometry, that is, of an affine transformation that preserves distance. Thus, not only affine (and projective)
features, but also some general features of the metric seem to be synthetic a priori for Husserl, though the particular metric of real physical space is not.[10]

It is pertinent to end this review with a brief comparison of Husserl's views with those of Kant[11] and Frege.[12] Firstly, it is clear that not only Husserl's notion of a mathematical synthetic a priori is much more restricted than Kant's—since for Husserl non-geometrical mathematics was analytic—, but also his very notion of the geometrical synthetic a priori—though, of course, the distinction between topological, affine and metric features of space was not known to Kant. Moreover, Husserl's geometrical synthetic a priori was more restricted than Frege's, for whom the Euclidean structure of physical space was synthetic a priori. On the other hand, it is clear that Husserl's notion of a synthetic (also called by him 'material') a priori was much wider than Kant's or Frege's in another important aspect, since for Husserl there were synthetic a priori statements in the foundations of any regional ontology. But that issue transcends by far the boundaries of this review.

References

Carnap, R. - *Der Raum* 1922, reprint, Vaduz, Liechtenstein: Topos Verlag, 1991.

---

[10] For the geometrical notion of 'congruence', see, for example, Cederberg's *A Course in ModernGeometry*. For Hilbert's Axioms of Congruence, see Hilbert's classic *Grundlagen der Geometrie*.

[11] See Kant's *Kritik der reinen Vernunft*.

[12] See Frege's *Die Grundlagen der Arithmetik*.

Carnap, R. - *Logische Syntax der Sprache* 1934, English revised edition 1937, reprint, Open Court, Chicago et al.2003.

Cederberg, J. - *A Course in Modern Geometries* 1989, reprint, Springer, New York et al. 2001

Frege, G. - *Wissenschaftlicher Briefwechsel*, F. Meiner, Hamburg 1976

Frege, G. - *Begriffsschrift* 1879, reprint, Georg Olms, Hildesheim 1964.

Frege, G. - *Die Grundlagen der Arithmetik* 1884, Centenarausgabe, F. Meiner, 1986.

Frege, G. – 'Über Sinn und Bedeutung' 1892, reprinted in I. Angelleli (ed.), *Kleine Schriften*, Georg Olms, Hildesheim 1967, 1990.

Frege, G. - *Grundgesetze der Arithmetik I* (1893) & *II (1903)*, reprinted in one volume, Georg Olms, Hildesheim 1962.

Hill, C, O. & Rosado Haddock G. E. - *Husserl or Frege?: Meaning, Objectivity and Mathematics*, Open Court, Chicago et al. 2000, paperback edition, 2003.

Hilbert, D. - *Grundlagen der Geometrie* 1899, tenth edition, B. G. Teubner, Stuttgart 1968.

Husserl, E. - *Logische Untersuchungen 1900 (I) & 1901 (II)*, Husserliana XVIII & XIX, M. Nijhoff, Den Haag 1975 & 1984.

Husserl, E. - *Formale und transzendentale Logik* 1929, Husserliana XVII, M. Nijhoff, Den Haag 1974

Husserl, E. - *Einleitung in die Logik und Erkenntnistheorie*, Husserliana XXIV, M. Nijhoff, Den Haag 1984

Husserl, E. - *Briefwechsel* (10 Vols.), Kluwer, Dordrecht 1994

Husserl, E. - *Logik und allgemeine Wissenschaftstheorie*, Husserliana XXX, Kluwer, Dordrecht 1996

Kant, I. - *Kritik der reinen Vernunft* 1781, second revised edition 1787, reprint of both editions, Felix Meiner, Hamburg 1930, third edition 1990

Critical Review of Anastasio Alemán's Lógica, Matemáticas y Realidad

This book is a collection of nine papers, originally published in different Spanish journals, on current issues in philosophy of mathematics, philosophy of logic and other areas of contemporary analytic philosophy, and preceded by a detailed introduction (pp. 15-45). Each of the papers contains an abstract in Spanish followed by a (sometimes rough) English translation. The titles of the papers are the following:
(1) Matemática y Experiencia (Mathematics and Experience);
(2) El Realismo en Matemáticas (Realism in Mathematics);
(3) El Argumento de Indispensabilidad en Matemáticas (The Indispensability Argument in Mathematics);
(4) La Nocion de Convención en Wittgenstein (The Notion of Convention in Wittgenstein);
(5) Wittgenstein: Lógica, Matemáticas y Convención (Wittgenstein: Logic, Mathematics, and Convention);
(6) El Debate Carnap-Quine en torno a la Naturaleza de la Lógica (The Carnap-Quine Controversy on the Nature of Logic);
(7) La Definición de Analitico para Enunciados Teóricos en Carnap (The Definition of Analyticity for Theoretical Concepts in Carnap);
(8) Los Enunciados de Observación en Quine (Observation Sentences in Quine);
(9) Objetos y Propiedades (Objects and Properties).

In the present review, we will be mainly concerned with the papers more directly related to the philosophy of mathematics, thus, papers 1-3 and 5. Some few words, however, should be said about the Introduction and the remaining papers. In the lengthy Introduction, Alemán offers (pp. 15-20) a general description of some of the most popular trends in the philosophy of mathematics, dividing them in two groups, namely, the descriptive trends, Platonism and empiricism, and the (in a very wide sense) constructivist trends, namely, intuitionism and conventionalism. Formalism is simply considered by Alemán as a forerunner of conventionalism. With respect to empiricism, he distinguishes (p. 20) a radical variety—represented not only by Tymoczko and Kitcher, but also by Maddy—and a moderate Quinean holistic variety. The rest of the Introduction is a brief but accurate compendium of the book.

Already in the Introduction (see, e.g., p. 44), Alemán makes it clear that for him logic and mathematics are creations of human activity, more specifically, the results of conventions. His—as he calls it—moderate conventionalism is inspired by Wittgenstein and somewhat also by Quine. Thus, e.g., the rules of logic completely determine the meaning of the logical connectives (see p. 27), and those rules are purely conventional. Hence, the task of Alemán in the papers concerned with the philosophy of mathematics is twofold, namely, to argue against empiricism and Platonism—about intuitionism he says almost nothing—and to argue on behalf of conventionalism. Interestingly enough, in the case of Platonism, he agrees with Hartry Field in considering the indispensability argument as the best argument on behalf of the existence of mathematical entities, even though very few Platonists would agree with them. Thus, in papers 1-3 Alemán argues against the rival realist philosophies of mathematics and, after a brief introduction to conventionalism in Chapter 4, in Chapter 5 he argues on behalf of conventionalism in logic and mathematics.

Chapter 1. Mathematics and Experience

At the beginning of this paper, Alemán distinguishes the radical empiricism of Kitcher, Tymoczko and—pace Maddy—Penelope Maddy, which he correctly associates (pp. 47-48) with John Stuart Mill's crude empiricism, from Quine's holistic empiricism, according to which there are not two separate domains of truths, logico-mathematical truths and empirical truths, but only one domain of interconnected truths, which face experience as a whole and not isolated. As is well known, according to Quine, in case of any discrepancy with the facts, although the scientist usually gives up some more peripheral statements, it is in principle possible to give up some logical or mathematical statements. Alemán correctly considers (pp. 49-50) that the revitalization of radical empiricism can be seen in some sense as a natural evolution of the more moderate holistic empiricism. According to Alemán (see pp. 50, 51), radical empiricism, in any of its variants, maintains that our knowledge of logical and mathematical truths is based on sense perception, thus, that there is no essential difference between the way we obtain logico-mathematical knowledge and the way we obtain our usual empirical knowledge. However, the arguments offered in this paper are directed against the most crude sort of radical empiricism of the John Stuart Mill and Philip Kitcher type, not so much against Maddy's version.

Alemán offers some five arguments against radical empiricism. Firstly, he observes that if mathematical statements are based on sense perception and obtain their confirmation from experience, each new relevant observation would augment the degree of confirmation, probability, corroboration or whatever of the mathematical statement concerned. But in that case—contrary to what is tacitly accepted by mathematicians—some mathematical statements would be better established than others, depending on the number and quality of its confirmation instances. One could add to Alemán's argument that precisely the more abstract statements that usually serve as foundation of more concrete ones would be the less established by such empirical procedures. Secondly, Alemán argues (pp. 52-53), that some mathematical statements would remain totally unintelligible for the mathematical empiricists, e.g., (i) that for any natural number, there is a larger one, or (ii) that between any two points on a line there are infinitely many other points.[1] On this issue one could mention as many statements as one wishes, e.g., (iii) that there exist infinitely many prime numbers, or, on a much more sophisticated level and also unintelligible for any non-Platonist—not only empiricist—conception of mathematics, (iv) that the Axiom of Choice is mathematically equivalent to Tychonoff s Theorem. Even many mathematical and logical concepts would be completely unintelligible for the mathematical empiricist. E.g., one could simply ask a mathematical empiricist to trace the notion of ultraproduct to our sense perception.

Alemán's third argument against radical mathematical

---

[1] Alemán offers two other examples, one of which is incorrect: 7 is the cube root of 343, not of 362, as is stated on p. 52. (362 is not even divisible by 7.)

empiricism consists (see p. 54) in observing that if such a view were correct, mathematicians would not be acting rationally, since mathematicians do not refer us to any sense perceptions or spatio-temporal regions in which such sense perceptions relevant to their mathematical statements could be. The fourth argument (see pp. 55-56) appeals to a sort of symmetry between confirmation and disconfirmation by experience. If mathematical statements are based on our sense perception and in some sense obtain their confirmation from observation, then they could also be disconfirmed by observation. However, no empirical observation has ever disconfirmed (or can disconfirm) a single mathematical statement. Hence, they cannot be confirmed by observation. Finally, Alemán refers us (pp. 58-59) to the well-known fact that some mathematical theories have remained without any application for long periods of time. Although the applicability of a theory can add to its interest, especially for non-mathematicians, as a mathematical theory it is not affected by such applications. Thus, contrary to what happens with physical theories, which physicists would even reject if they had no empirical applications, the non-applicability of a mathematical theory does not detract from its mathematical character. We are in complete agreement with Alemán on this point.

Alemán correctly considers (p. 62) that moderate holistic empiricism represents a much more subtle and complex rejection of the boundaries between mathematical and empirical statements. According to holistic empiricism, statements do not face experience in isolation, but as a complete system of statements to which single statements belong. The first argument of Alemán against holistic empiricism is an extension of the fourth argument against radical empiricism. No matter if we accept a sort of holism, the fact of the matter is that if a mathematical theory is disconfirmable by experience, at least one mathematical statement would have to be disconfirmable. This is, however, not possible. The second argument of Alemán against holistic empiricism is an argument, which seems to originate in Elliot Sober. Consider two empirical theories, namely T and T*, both based on a common mathematical formalism Q, e.g., that of arithmetic or that of differential equations. Suppose also that they have incompatible consequences, e.g., that $T+Q \vdash S$ and $T^*+Q \vdash \neg S$.

Alemán argues that S offers empirical evidence favorable to T and, according to empiricism, to Q, but that it also disconfirms T*, and according to empiricism, should also disconfirm Q. On this point it should be said that Alemán forgets the difference between the two sorts of empiricism, when trying to apply this argument to holistic empiricism. What faces the tribunal of experience is T + Q + P and T* + Q + P', where P and P' represent the remaining part of the scientific system that faces experience. P and P' can be identical, but do not have to be so. Let us first assume that they coincide. In such a case, no matter how holistic the scientists are, they would almost surely abandon T* and would not touch either Q or P. On the other hand, if P ≠ P', then the scientists would abandon either T' or P', but surely not Q. Thus, Alemán's argument does not apply—at least so directly—to holistic empiricism. The related difficulty that faces such a view is to offer any situation, historical or imaginary, in which observations have forced (or would force) scientists to consider a mathematical statement as false. It is perfectly possible that the scientists decide to abandon the use of a mathematical theory and replace it by another, but that does not falsify a single statement of the abandoned mathematical theory. Such a situation would simply mean that the mathematical theory cannot be adequately applied

Chapter 2. Maddy's Realism

As is well known, Penelope Maddy has defended a sort of realism in mathematics, i.e., that mathematical entities exist and have their properties independently of the knowing subjects. What is peculiar to Maddy's realism is that, contrary to the more common Platonist realism, she propounds a sort of empirical direct acquaintance with at least some mathematical entities. According to Maddy, for example, we perceive elementary sets directly in experience. Thus, we not only perceive the chair with our senses but also the unit set of the chair, and we do not only perceive the chair and the book with our senses but also perceive the (unordered) set, whose members are the chair and the book. Of course, as Alemán acknowledges (see p. 74), Maddy is not so naive as to believe that all statements of set theory are simply based on sense perception. Other criteria, similar to those of the empirical sciences, like simplicity, explanatory power, and theoretical interconnections serve to justify the Axiom of Choice and similar statements.

Alemán's first argument against Maddy's realism (see pp. 78-82) consists in showing that there is an alternative explanation of our supposed perception of sets at least as plausible as Maddy's empirical realism. This plausible alternative is a Kantian one. Thus, in the same way as a Kantian argues that all objects are perceived in space and time, he could argue that they are perceived in some set. However, this argument, as it stands, is not very convincing. If sets were to be conceived as constitutive of objects in a Kantian sense, the analogy would probably be with the categories of the understanding and not with the forms of intuition, namely, space and time. But although, according to Kant, the categories are constitutive, they do not constitute each and every object, as do the forms of intuition. Of course, a Kantian would say that we think the objects always by means of some category. Nonetheless, we do not apply each and every category to each and every object or event. For Alemán's argument, however, it is not so much the plausibility of such an interpretation, but its simple possibility that weakens Maddy's contention. Thus, if there is a consistent alternative to Maddy's rendering of our knowledge of sets, then Maddy's contention is far from being established. Of course, a much more plausible analysis of the constitution of sets was given by Husserl in the Sixth Logical Investigation, but both Maddy and Alemán seem to be totally ignorant of it. (It would take us too far to expound here Husserl's almost totally ignored theory of categorial intuition—ignored even by the specialists, who usually confound it with eidetic intuition.)

A much more decisive argument against Maddy is the second one offered by Alemán. Since for Maddy sets are no longer abstract entities, but the objects of sense perception, they must occupy some region of space, and that region of space is precisely the same as occupied by its elements. Thus, although a set of two eggs is an entity different from any of its members, and has properties different from theirs, it presumably occupies the same region of space as they do. This, however, contradicts a basic principle of individuation for spatiotemporal entities, namely, that different entities cannot occupy the same spatiotemporal region. Alemán's argument is clearly related to the critique of Maddy's views, which contends that Maddy cannot differentiate a unit set from its unique member, nor can she differentiate a set from a whole. This last argument together with the problem posed by the empty set—which, of course, could not be perceived—constitute two of the most basic objections to Maddy's conception.

Before discussing the famous indispensability argument, Alemán repeats (see p. 83) against Maddy some of the critiques he had directed against radical empiricism in the first paper. With respect to the indispensability argument—which will be the main issue of the third paper—Alemán mentions (p. 86) that the decisive point in the argument is the transition from the truth of the theory to the existence of the entities assumed by the theory. In this way, the problem of establishing the existence of the mathematical entities postulated by the mathematical theories used by a physical theory is established when this physical theory is proved to be true. On pp. 89-90 Alemán repeats—this time directed against the indispensability argument—the argument that if mathematics receives some sort of empirical confirmation, it could also receive empirical disconfirmation, which really is not the case. Moreover Alemán adds (p. 91) that false physical theories also use mathematical theories as correctly as true ones, but we do not consider their refutation as a refutation of the postulates of the mathematical theory used. Here once more Sober's argument is tacitly present. Alemán concludes (p. 92) that even if we accept the indispensability of mathematics in physics, the confirmation of the physical theories does not establish either the mathematical theories or the existence of the mathematical entities postulated in the latter. On this point, and before discussing the third paper, it should be noted that—contrary to what Alemán seems to believe—no physical theory has ever been established in a definitive manner. Thus, even if the indispensability argument were correct, we could only establish the existence of mathematical entities in a hypothetical way, namely, so: if this presently accepted physical theory is really true, then the mathematical entities postulated by the underlying mathematical theory exist. In the case that the physical theory is later falsified, the mathematical entities would cease to exist. But if a new physical theory is later accepted, which uses more or less the same mathematical apparatus, the mathematical entities would resurrect. This consequence of the indispensability argument is simply dialectical nonsense. Of course, many other objections could be offered against an argument, whose fame is inversely proportional to its weight.

Chapter 3. The Indispensability Argument in Mathematics

Like many other antiplatonists—the best-known case is Hartry Field—Alemán seems convinced that the indispensability argument is the best argument for Platonism. Thus, its refutation would pave the way for his Wittgensteinian conventionalism. Alemán begins his refutatation of the indispensability argument by referring once more to Sober's argument of two incompatible physical theories with the same underlying mathematical theory, which combined with the symmetry requirement between confirmation and disconfirmation, would allow us to extract from the indispensability argument the conclusion that the entities postulated by the mathematical theory exist and do not exist at the same time. We are here somewhat more explicit than Alemán. In any case, the premise of the symmetry could be questioned. The indispensabilists could counterargue that the falsity of a physical theory only allows us to conclude that the existence of the mathematical entities has not been established. In the case of the Sober argument, they would say that the false theory was not able to guarantee the existence of the mathematical entities, but the true one was.

With respect to a very careful version of the indispensability argument offered by Michael Resnik, namely, that our justification in considering mathematical theories as true—and the mathematical entities postulated by such theories as existent—is a necessary condition for being justified in extracting conclusions in physical science, Alemán argues (pp. 103-104) that to extract such conclusions justifiably we need only a much weaker requirement, namely, that the logic or mathematics used preserves truth. Moreover, he adds (pp.

107-108) that an antirealist could very well accept such a role of mathematics in science without having to acknowledge the existence of mathematical entities as independent of the constructive capabilities of our mind.

After such a mixture of some strong and some weak arguments against radical empiricism, holistic empiricism, and what he believes is the strongest argument for Platonism in the first three chapters, the terrain is now prepared for Alemán to expound his conventionalist conception of mathematics and logic.

Chapter 4. The Notion of Convention in Wittgenstein

In this essay, on which we will comment very briefly, Alemán refers us to Wittgenstein's conventionalism on grammatical and arithmetical rules as the basis of his views. According to Wittgenstein, a rule is conventional if it cannot be justified by an appeal to its coincidence with reality. Thus, for him not only the rules of chess, but also the rules of grammar (see p. 123) are conventional. Of course, one could add that under such a criterion for conventionality and a definition of reality as physical reality, one does not have any option but to render the rules (and statements) of logic and mathematics as conventional. But this is precisely the theme of the next paper.

Chapter 5. Wittgenstein: Logic, Mathematics, and Convention

At the beginning of this paper, Alemán states (pp. 134-135) that the indispensability argument is the strongest argument on behalf of realism. Having shown its weaknesses, as well as those of radical empiricism and, he contends, also of Platonism, he will examine the conventionalist alternative, which he considers to be one of the most important and original contributions of the second philosophy of Wittgenstein. According to this conventionalism, mathematical propositions are really only (grammatical) rules for the use of signs. Thus (see pp. 136-137), mathematical equations are merely rules of substitution for the interchange of expressions appearing on the left and right sides of the identity symbol. On the other hand, logical inference rules are also essentially grammatical rules for the use of connectives. Although mathematical theorems usually appear in the form of declarative statements, such a rendering is simply an abbreviation of rules of substitution, which are essentially grammatical rules. Thus, we write '2 + 2 = 4' as an abbreviation of the longer sentence 'The expression ((2 + 2)) is interchangeable with the expression ((4))'. For Wittgenstein and Alemán (see pp. 144-145), in the same way in which the rules of chess completely determine the nature of the chess pieces, so also the meaning of mathematical expressions is completely fixed by such grammatical-mathematical rules. Moreover (see pp. 150-151), logical and mathematical rules are, like the rules of chess, constitutive of meanings, and cannot be checked for their correctness against any independently established meanings. Alemán underscores (pp. 159 and 162-163) that for Wittgenstein's conventionalism mathematical statements are either the result of conventions or consequences of such conventions. Hence, not every mathematical statement requires a specific convention but could very well be derived from other statements, which obtained their meaning and truth by means of conventions.

Before continuing our exposition, a few words should be said on Alemán's and any other sort of conventionalism, as well as on the presumed refutation of Platonism. The plausibility of conventionalism derives from the consideration of the most elementary, almost trivial, parts of logic and mathematics, e.g., arithmetical propositions or the rules of natural deduction. But for a philosophical account of mathematics to be taken seriously, it must be capable of assessing the whole of mathematics. As soon as we abandon such trivialities, all rivals of Platonism encounter difficulties. In the case of any sort of constructivism—which for many, due to the Kantian and Brouwerian traditions, has been the most serious rival of Platonism—it has been known for many years that it is not able, under any of its varieties, to give an account of the whole of mathematics, not even of the mathematics with known applications to physics. By the way, no philosophical account of any empirical science would be taken seriously—as constructivism in mathematics is—if it yielded the exclusion of parts of the discipline. For example, a philosophical assessment of physics, which would exclude quantum mechanics (or general relativity or quantum field theory), would be rejected without further consideration. Other philosophies of mathematics, like Field's nominalism, do not acknowledge explicitly their limitations to give an account of the whole of mathematics, but in fact they are unable to do it. In an earlier paper, we have shown that the trivial consequence of Field's nominalism that all existential statements are false and all universal statements are vacuously true is incompatible with Robinson's Model-Completeness Test, according to which a first-order theory T is model-complete—i.e., for any two models M and M* of T, if M is a substructure of M*, then M is an elementary substructure of M*—if and only if for any existential sentence in the language of T, there is a universal sentence in the same language interderivable with it. Of course, since they are interderivable, they also have the same truth-value. Moreover, since model-complete theories exist, by modus tollens the above mentioned consequence of Field's nominalism is false and, thus, Field's nominalism is also false. Hence Field's nominalism is not compatible with our whole system of logico-mathematical statements. Furthermore, the Model-Completeness Test—like model theory in general—is hardly compatible with a conventional view of mathematics. If there exist (first-order) model-complete theories—and there exist theories of that sort—then for any existential sentence in the language of the theory, there exists a universal sentence in the same language interderivable with it and, thus, with the same truth-value. That the two sentences have the same truth-value is not a matter of convention but of logical necessity. Moreover, their negations would also be interderivable and have the opposite truth value, and since the negation of an existential sentence is logically equivalent to a universal one and the negation of a universal sentence is logically equivalent to an existential one, there are logically equivalent universal and existential sentences of the opposite truth-value. Hence, the existence of model-complete theories implies the existence of both true universal and existential sentences, and of false universal and existential sentences. This also is not a matter of convention. The thesis that all logico-mathematical truths are conventional is, thus, hardly compatible with the Model-Completeness Test, since on the basis of such a theorem, we could not possibly arbitrarily decide to make all universal sentences false and all existential sentences true, or all universal sentences true and all existential sentences false. Moreover, if the Model-Completeness Test is true, there are true logico-mathematical existential sentences, and, hence, the entities about which they talk must exist. Thus, the existence of mathematical entities would not be a matter of convention either.

Concerning more general arguments on behalf of Platonism, besides the indispensability argument, at least three others should be mentioned. The best-known—and also the weakest—is the Frege-Wright argument, which tries to base Platonism on syntactical considerations. Thus, since numbers are referred to by proper names, they are objects, i.e., saturated entities, like dogs, books and human beings, only that they are logical objects. The greatest weakness of this argument is that it presupposes a pre-established harmony between grammar (of at least some privileged languages) and ontology. The other related difficulty would be either to show that all natural languages are in this sense similar or to try to 'justify' the superiority of such languages like German—Frege's language—or English—that of Wright—whose grammar 'reflects the ontology of the world', in face of other underprivileged languages of people deprived of such a direct contact with what there is.

A more compelling argument has been used by Godel in a paper of 1951 titled 'Some Basic Theorems on the Foundations of Mathematics and their Implications' and published only recently in 1995 in his Collected Works, Volume 3. The argument extracts philosophical conclusions from his famous incompleteness results, and although directed against constructivism, is also applicable to conventionalism and other sorts of rivals of Platonism. Thus, if mathematics were constructible or conventional, how is it possible that there are essentially undecidable statements? If the mathematicians were to construct mathematical entities and their properties (or by decree or convention decide the meaning and truth of logical and mathematical basic rules and statements), then such incompleteness phenomena would not have occurred, since the mathematician would have complete control of his constructions (or the meaning and truth of all mathematical statements would be completely determined by the conventions previously established).

A related argument was offered by the present author in a small conference in Mexico in 1988 and later published in 1992. In mathematics there are many cases of interderivable statements, which do not even belong to the same area of mathematics. The best-known examples are the Axiom of Choice, which is interderivable with an impressive number of mathematical statements in the most varied areas of mathematics, and the weaker Ultrafilter Theorem. Thus, e.g., the Axiom of Choice is interderivable with Tychonoff's Theorem in general topology, according to which the product of compact topological spaces is also a compact topological space. A similar situation occurs between the Ultrafilter Theorem and the theorem, which asserts that the product of compact Hausdorff spaces is a compact Hausdorff space. Interderivability phenomena of seemingly unrelated mathematical statements are 'brute mathematical facts' of a metamathematical flavour, and totally unintelligible for non-Platonists. If we were to construct mathematical entities with their properties, the construction of families of sets and the choice set would produce entities very different from compact topological spaces and their products. Similarly, if we were to construct mathematical entities, the result of the construction of filters and ultrafilters would be very different from the result of the construction of compact Hausdorff spaces and their products. How it is that such mathematical equivalences are possible would remain totally unintelligible. The situation for conventionalists and formalists is even worse, since it is simply grotesque to try to render the interderivability between, e.g., the Ultrafilter Theorem, namely, 'Every filter can be extended to a maximal filter (i.e., an ultrafilter)' and the statement 'The product of a family of compact Hausdorff spaces is a compact Hausdorff space' as a matter of any sort of convention (no matter how indirect) or as a simple manipulation of symbols. It should be clear that nominalisms of any sort as well as fictionalisms would face similar difficulties. The argument, of course, also applies to all sorts of empiricism, which are very far from being capable of giving an account even of entities like ultrafilters and topological spaces. Finally, on account of the insufficient differentiations made in Fregean semantics, Fregean Platonism is also not able to give an adequate account of the interderivability phenomena. The Husserlian distinction between states of affairs, as the references of statements, and situations of affairs—or some similar distinction—is required to assess such phenomena adequately, since it is, on the one hand, clear that the Axiom of Choice and Tychonoff's Theorem speak about very different states of affairs, and, on the other hand, it is also clear that they have much more in common than the truth value -which they also have in common with '2 + 2=4' and with 'Paris is the capital of France in 2002'.

With respect to the remaining chapters of Alemán's book, we will limit our presentation to just two or three sentences.

Chapter 6. The Carnap-Quine Controversy on the Nature of Logic

In this paper Alemán discusses the famous controversy between Carnap and Quine on the linguistic doctrine of logical truth, according to which logically true statements are true in virtue of the rules that govern the use of logical words occurring in them and that determine the statement's meaning. In this controversy Alemán favors Carnap, whose refutation of Quine's triviality objection is discussed in detail.

Chapter 7. Analyticity for Theoretical Statements in Carnap

This paper on the notion of analyticity for theoretical statements in Carnap's late philosophy of science belongs in some sense to the frontier between philosophy of logic and philosophy of science. There is nothing essentially new in this paper. It is simply an exposition of Carnap's position in his late book Philosophical Foundations of Physics with its usual critiques.

Critical Review of *Lógica, Matemáticas y Realidad*

Chapter 8. Observation Sentences in Quine

This paper expounds Quine's well-known conception of occasional sentences and observation sentences introduced in his discussion of the indeterminacy of translation around 1960 and maintained with little modifications the rest of his life. In this paper also there is nothing essentially new.

Chapter 9. Objects and Properties

Of the papers not directly related to the philosophy of mathematics, this one is probably the most interesting for the present author. It deals with the existence of properties, thus, with an interesting issue in what can be called analytical ontology. As made clear by Quine, properties are suspicious entities, since they lack a criterion of individuation—contrary to what happens with physical objects and classes. Alemán argues—against Quine—that the existence of properties is implied by the truth of some statements formalizable in first-order logic. On this issue he introduces the following two postulates: (PS) If property P does not exist, then $(((\exists x)P(x)))$ is false; and (CPS): If property P exists, then $(((\exists x)P(x)))$ is true. If we accept both (PS) and (CPS), then Alemán argues (p. 236) that to say that property P exists is the same as to say that the corresponding existential statement that asserts that there are objects x with the property P is true. Thus, properties would be (see p. 241) what makes some predicates true or false of some objects, and what helps us identify an object and distinguish it from other objects. We cannot dwell any longer on this very interesting paper on behalf of the existence of properties, but urge the reader able to read Spanish to take account of it.

References

Frege, Gottlob - *Die Grundlagen der Arithmetik* 1884, Centenarausgabe, Felix Meiner, Hamburg 1986
Godel, Kurt - *Collected Works III* 1995, Oxford University Press, Oxford 1995
Hill, Claire Ortiz, and Guillermo E. Rosado Haddock - *Husserl or Frege?: Meaning, Objectivity and Mathematics*, Open Court, Chicago et al 2000, paperback edition 2003
Husserl, Edmund - *Logische Untersuchungen*, (2 vols.) 1900-1901. Husserliana Vol. XVIII (1975) and Vol. XIX (1984).
Wright, Crispin - *Frege's Conception of Numbers as Objects*, Aberdeen University Press, Aberdeen

Critical Review
of Jaakko Hintikka (ed.),
The Other Philosophers
of Mathematics: *From Dedekind to Gödel*

The present collection of papers is mostly based on a conference on the philosophy of mathematics held at Boston University in 1992 and organized by the Boston Colloquium for the History and Philosophy of Science. Contrary to most collections of papers on the philosophy of mathematics, which usually give too little or no space to currents other than Frege's and Russell's logicism, Hilbert's formalism, Brouwer's intuitionism and, more recently, Benacerraf s critique of Fregean Platonism, the present book allows not so well known voices to take center stage. This produces a particularly interesting - but also unbalanced- combination of contributions towards a reinterpretation of the history of the philosophy of mathematics. None of the papers studies Hilbert's formalism, Russell's logicism or Brouwer's intuitionism specifically, although there are many references to their undoubtedly important contributions to the philosophy and foundations of mathematics. On the other hand, important philosophers of mathematics whose writings in this field have not received the due attention in similar works - e.g., Husserl, Gödel, Weyl and Dedekind - and other authors whose contributions to the philosophy of mathematics are perhaps more questionable, are well represented in this book. The papers included in the present collection, of which we will examine in detail only a few, are the following:

(1) Judson Webb - Tracking Contradictions in Geometry: The Idea of a Model from Kant to Hilbert
(2) Jaakko Hintikka - Standard vs. Non-Standard Distinction
(3) Harold M. Edwards - Kronecker on the Foundations of Mathematics
(4) David Charles Mc Carty - The Mysteries of Richard Dedekind
(5) Claire Ortiz Hill - Frege's Letters
(6) Richard G. Heck, Jr. - Frege's Principle
(7) Claire Ortiz Hill - Husserl and Hilbert on Completeness

(8) Philip Ehrlich - Hahn's Über die nichtarchimedischen Grössensysteme and the Development of the Modern Theory of Magnitudes and Numbers to Measure them
(9) Gregory H. Moore - The Origins of Russell's Paradox
(10) Akihiro Kanamori - The Emergence of Descriptive Set Theory
(11) Jan von Plato - Chance Against Constructibility
(12) William Boos - Thoralf Skolem, Hermann Weyl and "Das Gefuhl der Welt als begrenztes Ganzes"
(13) Jan Wolenski - On Tarski's Background
(14) Mathieu Marion - Wittgenstein and Ramsey on Identity
(15) Juliet Floyd - On Saying What You Really Want to Say: Wittgenstein,
Gödel and the Trisection of the Angle
(16) Dagfinn Føllesdal - Gödel and Husserl

(1) Webb's paper "Tracking Contradictions in Geometry: The Idea of a Model from Kant to Hilbert" is a contribution to the historiography of Non-Euclidean geometries. The paper traces the idea of Non-euclidean models to Kant's friend Lambert, who already discovered the sense of being true in a structure for elliptic and hyperbolic geometries - see pp. 5-6. Interestingly, however, Webb claims - see pp. 2 and 7 - that when in Kritik der reinen Vernunft Kant talks about the consistency of a biangle, he means simply what he says and is not relying on any familiarity with his friend's discovery (which appeared in a memoir of 1786, i.e., five years after the publication of Kant's book). In the rest of the paper Webb discusses the maturation of the idea of Non-Euclidean geometries, their models and, thus, their consistency in the writings of Lobachevsky, Beltrami, Klein and others. This very clearly written and well-documented paper contains, however, many typographical errors, e.g., on p. 11 (line 11) it should read 'projective' instead of 'productive,' and on p. 16 (line 28) it should read 'equanimity' instead of 'equinimity.'

(2) Jaakko Hintikka's paper "Standard vs Non-standard Distinction" is one of the most interesting papers included in this collection and one on which we will comment somewhat extensively. It concerns the distinction made famous by Leon Henkin between standard and non-standard interpretations of higher-order logics and, especially, of second-order logic. As is well-known, higher-order logics with the standard interpretation are semantically incomplete, but Leon Henkin managed to establish a completeness theorem for them via a nonstandard interpretation. Most philosophers of mathematics have taken lightly the decisive distinction between the standard and the non-standard interpretations of higher-order logic. It is the purpose of Hintikka's paper to address this issue and examine its importance for the philosophy and foundations of mathematics.

At the beginning of his paper Hintikka remarks (p. 21) that Henkin's terminology of 'standard' and 'non-standard' is confusing in many ways. Firstly, it is not clear at all which interpretation should, from a historical perspective, be considered the standard and which the non-standard. Secondly, one can conceive more than one non-standard interpretation of higher-order logics. Thirdly, the distinction between standard and non-standard interpretations does not have to be restricted to higher-order logics. Finally, it is not clear how is Henkin's use of the term 'standard' related to the logicians' use of a notion of standard model to mean the same as 'intended model.'

Hintikka very aptly relates (p. 25) the notion of a standard interpretation of higher-order quantifiers –in which, e.g., the monadic second-order variables range over the entire power set of the domain of individuals of the structure- with the notion of a completely arbitrary function. He, thus, suggests (p. 25) that we can at least partially follow the maturation of the notion of standard interpretation by examining the history of the notion of a completely arbitrary function.

Hintikka emphasizes (p. 29) the importance of the standard vs non-standard distinction for the philosophy and ontology of mathematics. As is well known by philosophers of mathematics and logicians, quantification over all reals is nothing else than standard quantification over sets of integers (i.e., quantification over all sets of integers). Thus, as Hintikka remarks (p. 29), rejection of all standard interpretations of higher-order quantifiers amounts to a rejection of unrestricted quantification over the reals.

A very important related issue, namely, the first- vs second-order logic discussion also has its due place in this paper. Hintikka's position - which is very congenial with the present author's - is that of the minority, which sides with second-order logic. Thus, Hintikka asserts (p. 32) that second-order logic – in contrast with first-order logic - is clearly sufficient for the purposes of mathematicians, but only if we endow it with its standard interpretation. As is well-known, the capacity of second-order logic for expressing mathematical notions and, as Hintikka emphasizes (p. 32), virtually all major unsolved mathematical problems, is a great advantage over first-order logic. On the other hand, as he also points out (p. 32), second-order logic has the tremendous advantage over set theory as a foundation of mathematics that in it mathematical problems become well-defined problems concerning the model-theoretical properties of specific second-order formulas, e.g., their validity or satisfiability.

On this last point, we would like to add that, contrary to the usual interpretation of the so-called Skolem's Paradox both in current logic textbooks and in philosophical discussions (like Putnam's), what this so-called paradox shows is precisely that usual first-order set theory is insufficient to adequately grasp basic set-theoretic notions and distinctions (especially cardinality distinctions). But since set theory axiomatized in first-order logic admits denumerable models, first-order logic is not an adequate frame for set theory and, thus, for mathematics. As we have argued elsewhere, only philosophical prejudices have prevented such a conclusion.

Hintikka continues his argumentation on behalf of second-order logic stressing (p. 33) that under non-standard interpretations of second-order logic we cannot express some of the most important notions of mathematics, like the principle of mathematical induction or the notion of cardinality, nor can we define the cardinality of a set in terms of bijections between the elements of two classes, since it could be the case that two classes are equinumerous in the usual sense of the word, without there being, under a non-standard interpretation, any bijection between them.

A very interesting analysis of Whitehead and Russell's Principia Mathematica follows. Hintikka argues (p. 33) that Russell - as well as Frege - believed in a non-standard interpretation of his logical system. But only under the standard interpretation can second-order logic (or even type theory) serve as a foundation of mathematics.

Thus, the Whitehead-Russell project, as well as Frege's, was, as Hintikka remarks (pp. 33-34), doomed to failure even before it started. As is well known, classes enter into the system of Principia Mathematica only as extensions of propositional functions. But the ramified hierarchy of types makes it impossible to speak of all propositional functions. Any variable for propositional functions can take as values only propositional functions occurring lower in the hierarchy. But if you cannot speak of all propositional functions, you cannot speak of all functions. Hintikka underscores (p. 34) that Russell and Whitehead's axiom of reducibility does not help to guarantee a standard interpretation, but only serves to restrict the kind of nonstandard interpretation Russell and Whitehead are assuming. Moreover, he adds (p. 34) that if Whitehead and Russell had assumed the standard interpretation for quantifiers ranging over elementary functions, there would be no need to introduce the axiom of reducibility, since for any class apprehended by a function of higher ramified type, there would exist a class apprehended by an elementary function. Hence, Hintikka maintains (p. 34) that the need for an axiom of reducibility really shows that Whitehead's and Russell's system assumes a non-standard interpretation. Hintikka concludes his interesting comments on Principia Mathematica with the claim - see p. 35 - that Ramsey saw the problem under discussion very clearly when he argued that any attempt to restrict the classes under consideration to those capable of being apprehended by predicates - or given by propositional functions - will inevitably alter the interpretation of higher-order quantifiers to produce a non-standard interpretation. Thus, "all classes" would mean not what it is supposed to mean under the standard interpretation, but all extensions of predicates expressed in the language.

Hintikka correctly underscores (p. 36) that if the standard interpretation of second-order logic is not adopted, the entire contrast between first- and second-order logic (and, in general, higher-order logic) remains a distinction without a difference. Moreover, if we adopt a non-standard interpretation of higher-order logic, one can treat this logic simply as a many-sorted first-order logic. For Hintikka, Henkin's proof of the semantic completeness of higher-order logic under a non-standard interpretation is an instance of this strategy.

On this last issue - on which we totally agree with Hintikka - we would like to add that Henkin's proof is really a reduction of second-order (and higher-order) logic to first-order logic. In fact, that is precisely what such non-standard interpretations as Henkin's do. Henkin's semantic completeness result has as corollaries - as in first-order logic - both the Compactness theorem and the Lowenheim-Skolem theorem. But there is a famous theorem of Per Lindstrom, which establishes that any extension of first-order logic for which both the Compactness theorem and the Lowenheim-Skolem theorem are valid is equivalent to first-order logic and, thus, not a proper extension of it. Second-order logic under the standard interpretation is clearly a proper extension of first-order logic, but under Henkin's non-standard interpretation it collapses into it. Hence, in that case the distinction between first- and second-order logic is a distinction without a difference. However, anyone acquainted with second-order logic under its standard interpretation knows that this logic is much more powerful in its expressive and deductive capabilities than first-order logic. Thus, he should also know how much is lost by this sort of Henkian transformation into first-order logic.

It should, however, be mentioned that Hintikka acknowledges (p. 38) interesting uses of non-standard interpretations. On this point, he mentions a strategy first used by Gödel to obtain a constructive interpretation of a first-order theory T. Firstly, the theory receives a sort of syntactical interpretation in a second-order theory T*. Then T* receives a non-standard interpretation, and from this a constructive interpretation of the original first-order theory is obtained.

Finally, Hintikka sees the possibility (pp. 40-42) of viewing the distinction between standard and non-standard interpretation as an epistemological, and not as an ontological distinction. We are not going to dwell on this interesting issue, but simply recommend this highly stimulating paper by one of the foremost analytic philosophers.

(3) Harold M. Edwards' paper "Kronecker on the Foundations of Mathematics" is an attempt to vindicate the great nineteenth century mathematician in face of Georg Cantor's accusations of persecution and use of his politico-academic influence to stymie his former student's career. Edwards' defense of Kronecker is, in our

opinion, very weak. He acknowledges that there is evidence that Kronecker strongly opposed Cantor's revolutionary ideas, and that he publicly referred to those ideas -in a course offered during the summer period of 1891- as mathematical sophistry. Edwards seems to believe that, nonetheless, Cantor exaggerated, and that Kronecker really did not persecute him. We are not going to enter in this discussion mostly of interest to historians of mathematics. However, anyone that has lived enough time in the academy- and is not particularly naive- knows very well that academic life, even in the case of philosophers and mathematicians, is full of personal tensions, rivalries and intrigues, and in cases in which one of the professors involved has enough influence in the philosophical or mathematical community, sometimes even of persecution. Frege's intellectual relation with both Cantor and Husserl was full of tensions and rivalries, as also was Hilbert's relation with Brouwer and at some point even with Weyl. Husserl's relation with Leonard Nelson -who was Hilbert's protégé - was full of tensions, as was his relation with Heidegger after the latter's publication of Sein und Zeit. And when the Nazis arrived to power and Heidegger had the political support, he wasted no time in isolating his former Jewish mentor. (In fact, it was a result of a heroic deed that Husserl's unpublished work survived the war, contrary to what happened - see Claire Ortiz Hill's first paper - with Frege's.)

(4) David Charles Mc Carty's paper "The Mysteries of Richard Dedekind" is one of the philosophically most interesting papers in this collection. Dedekind's views on mathematics have begun to draw serious attention relatively recently, and since they were not systematically expounded as those of Frege and others, they have created some puzzlement. There has even been an attempt a decade ago by Philip Kitcher to approach Dedekind's views to those of empiricism. Mc Carty's well-argued paper is a good antidote against such excesses.

As is relatively well known, in Was sind und was sollen die Zahlen? Dedekind offers a 'proof' of the existence of infinite systems that has puzzled many readers. Dedekind's proof consists in establishing that the world of his own thoughts constitutes an infinite system. As Mc Carty puts it (pp. 54-55), Dedekind maintains that there is a transformation φ, which maps his thought-world S into itself, φ takes each object of thought s into the distinct object φ(s), namely, the thought that s can be an object of his thinking. Dedekind then asserts that φ is a one-to-one map, but that the range of φ is a proper part of S, his own 'I' belongs to S but is different from every φ(s). But according to a definition of infinite system he had previously introduced, a system that admits a one-to-one but not onto transformation into itself is infinite. Thus, he concludes that his thought-world is infinite. Mc Carty claims (pp. 59-60) that the thought-world proof is a keystone to Dedekind's enterprise, laying out the ground on which his foundation of mathematics is to be constructed. On that ground are, according to Mc Carty - see p. 60 – Dedekind's answers to the title questions to be found.

As is also relatively well known, in Stetigkeit und Irrationalzahlen Dedekind introduces a crucial test for being the domain of real numbers, namely, being an ordered extension of the rationals satisfying the Continuity Principle. "A suitably ordered domain," recalls Mc Carty (p. 61), "satisfies the Continuity Principle when any of its cuts into disjoint upper and lower halves has a single domain element as its point of division." Mc Carty remarks (p. 61) that although Dedekind showed how to construct a domain which passes the test, he does not establish that there is a unique domain so picked out and, thus, Dedekind's main claim in the monograph, namely, that continuity captures the essence of the reals, remained unproven. Moreover, Mc Carty comments (p. 61) that it is somewhat puzzling that Dedekind did not seem pressured to compare his construction of the reals with the approaches of Weierstrass and Cantor, with which he was well acquainted, and that in his monograph, apart from his 'arithmetical' continuum, there is a geometrical continuum consisting of the points of a straight line.

Mc Carty underscores (p. 63) that although Dedekind is considered a classical logicist, he does not make any definitional identification between mathematical and logical objects. Thus, the reals fail to be identified with cuts, and natural numbers fail to be the same as elements of simply infinite systems. Instead, we have creation. E.g., the reals are created from cuts and then produce their corresponding cuts in turn. In the preface to Was sind und was sollen die Zahlen? Dedekind explicitly mentions, as Mc Carty recalls (pp. 63-64), that numbers are free creations of the human mind. Mc Carty stresses (pp. 65-67), however, that contrary to what could be expected of a thinker who considered numbers as creations of our (mathematical) mind, Dedekind was firmly on the anticonstructivist side. E.g., he favored Dirichlet's concept of a completely arbitrary function, and disagreed publicly with Kronecker over the admissibility of non-constructive definitions. Contrary to constructivist renderings of Dedekind and to Kitcher's peculiar rendering, Mc Carty remarks (p. 66) that for Dedekind not only inner experience but indeed any experience was, to say the least, mathematically otiose. He even seems to have considered intuition, Mc Carty claims (p. 66), a Cartesian demon for mathematics. Moreover, Mc Carty adds (p. 67), in insisting on absolute free creation, Dedekind was rejecting the epistemological views of mathematical thought to be found in 19th and early 20th century constructivists.

To solve this puzzling apparent combination of views present in Dedekind, Mc Carty very aptly points to a Kantian source. First of all, however, he underscores (p. 70) that Dedekind's logicism - as happens with Frege's - opposes Kant's doctrines in the Transcendental Aesthetic with respect to arithmetic. Nonetheless, he considers that to solve the mysteries of Richard Dedekind we have to recur to the doctrines of Kant's Transcendental Dialectic. Mc Carty claims (p. 71) that the frame in which Dedekind chooses to place his mathematical work is Kant's "facultative model of transcendental mind."

However, Kant was a constructivist. The "logical heart of his mathematics" resides in pure intuition and, thus, in presentation and particularity. But Dedekind was a logicist, and his mathematics is "the project of reason alone." Hence, Mc Carty argues (p. 71), although Dedekind can accept Kant's whole inventory of the mental mechanisms of the faculties, he cannot go along with Kant in the way the epistemological tasks are assigned by Kant to the different faculties, and decides to shift the burden of mathematics from intuition to reason.

But according to Mc Carty (p. 71), besides the general inventory of the transcendental mind, Dedekind also took from Kant the enumeration of the ideas of reason in the Transcendental Dialectic.

Mc Carty claims (p. 71) that Dedekind's seemingly mysterious ontological requirements in his proof of the existence of an infinite system and elsewhere can be explained using notions in Kant's Dialectic, especially, that the mathematical objects of Dedekind are among the pure ideas of Kant.

Although Mc Carty's interpretation is not only challenging but probably on the right track, the details are not sufficiently argued for. Thus, he assumes (p. 72) that Dedekind's thought-world is at the same time the whole domain of pure mathematics and that of Kant's ideas of reason. If this is so, he argues (p. 72). Dedekind's "eigenes Ich" and Kant's "Ich" may well be akin - and, thus, available for use in Dedekind's existence proof of an infinite system. On this point, we would like to underscore that although the conclusion of Mc Carty's argument is probably correct, the hypothesis does not seem to have been sufficiently justified.

Mc Carty claims (p. 73) that Section 2 of Book I of the Transcendental Dialectic contains the necessary tools for an argumentation on behalf of the existence of an infinite system. Kant's task in that section is to prepare the ground for the antinomies by showing that the realm of reason may itself be infinite. Mc Carty correctly argues (p. 73) that for Kant - as, by the way, for Dedekind - reason is the faculty of inference, the top level organizer that imposes on the judgments of the understanding an organization into inferential chains. On the other hand, Mc Carty also correctly observes (p. 75) a certain similarity between the elements of Dedekind's existence proof of an infinite system and the conceptual material on which Kant relies - this time in the Transcendental Analytic - for his discussion of the unity of apperception in the famous Transcendental Deduction. Moreover, Mc Carty also says (p. 75) that Dedekind's assumption that the T is different from every thought is perfectly congenial with the assumption that Dedekind's T coincides with Kant's psychological idea in the Transcendental Dialectic. Here, however, Mc Carty tacitly identifies the transcendental unity of apperception of the Transcendental Analytic with the psychological idea, an identification that probably not many Kantian scholars would be eager to endorse. (By the way, this identification is in some sense similar to Descartes' identification of his cogito with a res cogitans.)

Moreover, Mc Carty claims (p. 79) that the inferential difficulties in Dedekind's existence proof of an infinite system can be overcome with the help of Kant, as can also be explained - see p. 80 - Dedekind's misgivings about logistic treatments of the natural numbers as cardinal numbers. Furthermore, Dedekind's conception of the geometrical continuum as neither a mathematical object nor a possible object of strict mathematical determination can be explained, according to Mc Carty (p. 81), if one sees that geometrical continuum as a manifold of objects of Kantian intuition. And since for Kant there is no determinable correspondence between objects of reason and objects of intuition, the geometrical continuum is very different from the arithmetical continuum, which, for Dedekind, as every mathematical object, is an idea of reason.

According to Mc Carty (p. 82), Dedekind's 'free creation' is an expression for the transcendental mental acts by which mathematical definitions originate mathematical entities. Mc Carty thinks - see p. 82 - that there are various avenues in Kant's writings that we could follow to find support for the characterization of mathematical objects as free creations, i.e., creations of reason, and free in the sense of being completely divorced from the natural world and its causal necessity. Moreover, Mc Carty claims (p. 83) that creation, understood as Kant did, is not a process that occurs in time, and in this aspect Dedekind has to be distinguished from constructivists like Brouwer, who also spoke of the genesis of mathematical objects as acts of free creation, but who conceived that creation as a mental process taking place in time.

Mc Carty states (p. 85) that the immediate goal of Dedekind's systematization was - as he himself put it in the Preface to the First Edition of Was sind and was sollen die Zahlen? - to overthrow Kant's constructivist epistemology of mathematics. Dedekind hoped to show that mathematics lies neither within the province of intuition nor within the province of the understanding, but is essentially a function of the faculty of reason. But to attain his goal he needed to offer a new explanation of mathematical thought in transcendental terms, but superior to Kant's. That is why, according to Mc Carty (p. 85), "the ultimate terms of Dedekind's explanation cannot find completion" - as in Frege - "in a list of axioms and rules, but must go beneath them to find the mental acts by which those forms are filled by which axioms and rules are themselves grasped."

Mc Carty ends his extremely interesting paper with some general comments on a sense of psychologism under which Dedekind's views can be surmised and which differs from the psychologism criticized by Frege. He also points out (p. 90) that one can refuse Kant's ideas a place in mathematics without having to reject Dedekind's type of argument for the existence of an infinite system as inherently flawed, since a reasonable version of Dedekind's argument can be formulated in Quine's New Foundations.

We hope that Mc Carty's challenging interpretation of Dedekind's views will receive its due attention and will stimulate research on Dedekind. And we also hope that Mc Carty will take care of those points in his rendering of Dedekind's views, which require further elaboration and clarification.

(5) Claire Ortiz Hill's first paper concerns Frege's letters, but not in the sense of examining the available letters for their philosophical value. On the contrary, as she puts it (p. 100), she is going "to engage in the 'unphilosophical' task of systematically trying to piece together what we actually can know about the philosophical content of the letters that have been lost." And, as she mentions (p. 102), more than three-fourths of Frege's correspondence, as gathered by Scholz, together with any copies that he might have made of them, were lost. Moreover, she claims (pp. 110-111) that almost all the material from 1906 on concerning authors like Schoenflies and Korselt and issues like extensions, identity and Russell's Paradox (really, Zermelo-Russell Paradox) disappeared presumably during the war, as also did earlier unpublished writings on more or less the same subjects. In the rest of the paper Ortiz Hill mentions some of the most important losses, e.g., some twenty letters between Frege and Leopold Löwenheim. We miss, however, a special reference to Husserl's letters to Frege of 1906, particularly since Ortiz Hill is one of the foremost Husserlian scholars in the world. It would have been interesting to know directly from Husserl what he thought of the great logician's identification in two letters to Husserl of that same year of the equipollency of statements with the sameness of the thoughts expressed by them. Someone acquainted with Husserl's Vorlesungen über Bedeutungslehre -the content of which dates from 1907- can, nonetheless, be pretty sure that for Husserl such an identification was really a confusion.

(6) Of all more or less established Fregean scholars, Richard G. Heck is without much doubt the one that has dealt more thoroughly with the technical issues of Frege's logic. He has followed the path traveled by his mentor, the late George Boolos, but has penetrated even farther in the details of Frege's logical system of Grundgesetze der Arithmetik (briefly: GgA). In 'Frege's Principle' Heck is especially concerned with two principles that are now usually called 'Frege's Principle' and 'Hume's Principle.' This last principle, which is obtained in Die Grundlagen der Arithmetik (briefly: G1A) from Frege's definition of number reads: the number belonging to the concept F is identical with the number belonging to the concept G if and only if the concept F is equinumerous with the concept G.

Heck claims (p. 120), following Boolos, that one can divide Frege's proof (better: sketch of proof) in G1A of the arithmetical axioms in two parts, namely, the proof of the so-called Hume's Principle from the explicit definition and that of the arithmetical axioms from Hume's Principle, since in this last part the explicit definition does not play any role (and even the extensions of concepts play no role). That the arithmetical axioms follow in second-order logic from the so-called Hume's Principle without any appeal to the explicit use of the definition or of the notion of an extension is what Boolos has labeled as 'Frege's Theorem.' Heck underscores (p. 121) that the situation in GgA is very similar to that encountered in G1A. The so-called Hume's Principle is derived from the infamous Axiom V, but then no other use of Axiom V (nor even of courses of values) is made. All proofs of arithmetical properties are carried on in second-order logic plus Hume's Principle, which has proven to be a consistent subtheory of the formal theory of GgA. (Although the ascription to Hume of such a principle could be questioned, for brevity's sake we will omit from now on the prefix 'the so-called.') Thus, Heck asserts (p. 121) that Frege proved Frege's Theorem, and considers this fact of the utmost importance to understand Frege's philosophy of mathematics.

In Heck's opinion - see p. 121 - the importance of the infamous Axiom V does not lie in its formal role, since presumably Frege knew very well, even after Russell's discovery of the inconsistency, that there was no real obstacle to the logicist programme. He even contends (p. 121) that we can only understand Frege's attitude towards Axiom V once we understand its meager role in GgA. On these last two points, he mentions (p. 122) Crispin Wright's suggestion to abandon the explicit definition of number and operate from the outset with Hume's Principle. It is not mentioned, however, that without an explicit definition of number in logical terms and a convincing argument to the effect of showing that Hume's Principle is a logical principle, one could not have saved logicism. Moreover, to claim that Frege knew very well that there was no real obstacle to the logicist programme even after he learnt of the inconsistency is doubly questionable. First of all, Frege not only thought that there was such an obstacle - see the Epilogue to GgA - but after his first failed attempts to amend his system, began to doubt about the possibility of his programme and finally abandoned it altogether. Secondly, there was such an obstacle to the logicist programme that to this day no one - not even Heck - has succeeded to establish it.

According to Heck (p. 122), Frege introduced extensions to solve the indeterminacy problem recently baptized as 'Caesar's Problem.' (Mainstream Fregean Scholars have a somewhat strange jargon, e.g., 'Frege's Theorem' -never explicitly formulated by Frege- 'Hume's Principle' -never formulated by Hume in such a general form as to apply to the transfinite- and 'Caesar's Problem' -of course, never formulated by Caesar.) Heck claims (p. 122) that the issue that concerned Frege in the central sections of G1A is whether Hume's Principle on its own could be taken as a complete explanation of the senses of identity statements between numbers. But Hume's Principle did not provide such a general explanation, serving only for cases in which on both sides of the identity sign occur what are recognizably names of numbers. Without entering in the details of Heck's interpretation, it should at least be mentioned that since Frege in G1A had still not made the distinction between sense and reference, one should be careful when using terminology that could bias our rendering.

Moreover, Heck maintains (p. 123) that the so-called Caesar's Problem obstructs any attempt to explain statements of numerical identity using only Hume's Principle. Nonetheless, Heck contends (p. 123) that the explanation of the senses of such statements must yield the referred principle, a task done by the explicit definition. Hence, Heck argues (p. 124) that extensions of concepts and the explicit definition of number are introduced by Frege to resolve the so-called Caesar's Problem, which is, after all, a philosophical problem. Thus, in the analogous case of GgA, if Frege could not abandon Axiom V, it would have been because he could not abandon the explicit definition and, thus, because he could not solve the so-called Caesar's Problem without it.

According to Heck (p. 126), an explicit definition of number has to yield immediately Hume's Principle, since it is in its terms that the senses of identity statements connecting numerical terms are to be explained. In this way, Heck contends (p. 126), the immediate derivation of Hume's Principle serves as a constraint for the explicit definition of number. Moreover, Heck asserts (p. 126) that not all theorems of a particular theory of arithmetic are analytic of the concept of number, since an explicit definition of number has always an arbitrary character, but only those that follow from Hume's Principle and, hence, do not depend upon arbitrary features of the explicit definition. According to Heck (p. 126), it is, thus, essential to Frege's philosophical project that such an irremediably arbitrary definition does not figure in the proofs of any of the axioms of arithmetic.

Heck asserts (p. 130) that in G1A Frege tacitly appealed to a sort of analogue of Axiom V, an axiom governing names of extensions of second-order concepts, in order to transform the statement expressing the identity of the extensions of the concepts "equinumerous with the concept F" and "equinumerous with the concept G" into the statement expressing that the concepts falling under the one are exactly the concepts falling under the other. In fact, Heck underscores (p. 130) that the proof of Hume's Principle in GgA is very similar to the sketch of a proof given in G1A. On pp. 131-132, Heck argues that in GgA Hume's Principle is derived from a principle that he calls 'Frege's Principle' - which should not be confused with

'Frege's Theorem' mentioned above. (Frege's Theorem states that Second-order logic + Hume's Principle $\vdash$ Arithmetic, whereas Frege's Principle says that Num(F) = Num(G) $\dashv\vdash \forall H(Eq(F,H) = Eq(G,H))$, i.e., that the number of F and the number of G coincide if and only if the extensions of the concepts 'equinumerous with F' and 'equinumerous with G' also coincide.) Axiom V and the explicit definition serve only the purpose, according to Heck (p. 132), of first deriving Frege's Principle and then Hume's Principle from it.

Heck argues (pp. 133-134) that since the so-called Caesar's Problem is not a formal problem, it could be solved, and was solved by Frege in G1A, in the metatheory. Moreover, he adds (p. 134), that Frege's Principle could be justified informally in terms of the explicit definition given in the metatheory, and taken as the fundamental axiom of the formal theory of arithmetic. However, Heck correctly rejects this way out and contends (p. 134) that to show arithmetic to be a branch of logic, the derivation of Frege's Principle from the explicit definition should be carried out formally and not informally in the metatheory.

On pp. 135-136, Heck discusses the differences in the 'resolutions' of the so-called Caesar's Problem in G1A and GgA. In G1A Frege offers an explicit definition of number from which Hume's Principle follows, whereas in GgA Frege stipulates the references of certain terms and tries to show the consistency of such stipulations. Moreover, Heck considers the possibility of adapting the strategy of GgA to G1A. We are not going to dwell on this issue, except to mention that on pp. 136-137 Heck claims that the GgA version of Caesar's Problem is formal, although metatheoretical, whereas the G1A version is philosophical, and so Frege would very probably have refused to solve the latter by stipulation as he tried to do in GgA.

According to Heck (p. 137), if Frege had been confronted with Russell's Paradox when he wrote G1A, he would have probably renounced appealing to extensions and to the explicit definition, and install Hume's Principle as an axiom. On the other hand, he claims (p. 138) that in GgA the abandonment of Axiom V was not an option because the identification of numbers with the extensions of certain concepts gave him the only way to answer the epistemological question raised in G1A of how we apprehend numbers with the aid neither of intuition nor perception. Moreover, according to Heck (p. 138), Frege's logicist programme did not fail - even by his own lights! - because he could not derive the axioms of arithmetic from principles which have some claim to be logical in character, but because he could not explain how we can apprehend the objects of arithmetic as logical objects or, what for Heck seems to be the same, because he failed to solve the so-called Caesar's Problem.

On these last issues, we would like to make a few remarks. First of all, Heck has not sufficiently justified the contention that if Russell's Paradox had been discovered when he wrote G1A, Frege would simply have let extensions and the explicit definition go. Such a move would have meant that he would have to abandon his logicist programme or would have to be convinced that what Fregean scholars have recently baptized 'Hume's Principle' is a logical principle. But there is no evidence that he ever maintained such a conviction. In G1A Frege certainly seemed to feel uncomfortable with extensions of concepts, and if he had seen a way of giving a definition of number in terms of other logical notion - see footnote to § 68 of G1A - he would probably have done it. But to avoid an explicit definition of number altogether seems to have been no option to Frege when he wrote G1A. On the other hand, precisely by deriving arithmetical theorems from logical principles and defining the notion of number in logical terms, Frege would have explained how we apprehend arithmetical objects as logical objects. Moreover, since the logicality of Hume's Principle is, to say the least, questionable, to put it as an axiom would probably only have had the advantage - to use Russell's words - of theft over honest toil.

Finally, it should be mentioned that on note 2 of p. 158, Heck reads Axiom V as expressing that its two sides have the same referent, i.e., the same truth-value (since both sides are statements and the referents of statements are for Frege truth values). This reading, which is that of Schirn and was -but is no more- that of Dummett, differs essentially from Sluga's and Thiel's reading of Axiom V as expressing an identity of sense between its sides. As we have argued elsewhere, both readings are based on two different readings by Frege himself - one in "Funktion und Begriff' and one in GgA - and both are open to serious objections. Specifically, Heck's reading leaves Axiom V and, thus, the identity of courses of values - and, hence, also that of numbers – completely undetermined. Even on the assumption of Axiom V's consistency, denumerably many sentences expressible in the formal system of GgA and having the same truth value as $(\forall x)(F(x)=G(x))$ could replace this statement in Axiom V without affecting the truth value of the whole.

(7) Claire Ortiz Hill's second paper "Husserl and Hilbert on Completeness" is one of the two very interesting contributions to the present collection, which deal with Husserl's too often neglected views on mathematics. The other, with which we will be concerned in a more detailed manner, is Dagfinn Føllesdal's paper "Gödel and Husserl." Ortiz Hill's paper, which considers Husserl's views on mathematics more thoroughly, discusses particularly Husserl's analysis of the completeness of axiom systems. As Ortiz Hill underscores (p. 146), but many - as Føllesdal - have refused to completely assimilate, the turning point in Husserl's views on mathematics and his consequent abandonment of the Brentanian brand of psychologism present in his Philosophic der Arithmetik of 1891 occurred already between 1890 and 1891. In those years, while preparing material for his planned second volume of that work, Husserl studied intensively the foundations of mathematics and began to develop his mature views on mathematics, logic and their relation, essentially completed by the mid-1890's. Thus, Frege's critique, as both Ortiz Hill and the present author have emphasized more than once, came too late. By the end of the 1890s Husserl was especially concerned with the completeness of axiom systems, and some of this material appeared much later in abbreviated form in his Formale und transzendentale Logik of 1929. That does not mean that Husserl had arrived at the fine differentiations known to us thanks to Gödel and Tarski. Husserl had already conceived axiom systems as complete both in the semantic sense - see p. 155 - and in the deductive (or syntactic) sense –see p. 151- but seems not to have known that the two notions are not equivalent. (We miss a remark of Ortiz Hill on this point.) However, since most working logicians before Gödel and Tarski also missed that distinction, not much weight should be put on this issue. Probably of equal interest are Husserl's qualms against an axiom of completeness in Hilbert's sense. There is much more on the philosophy of mathematics in Husserl's writings than what is said in Ortiz Hill's paper, which, by the way, has no pretension to be exhaustive. We hope, nonetheless, that this paper can serve the important task of awakening interest in Husserl among analytic philosophers. When this finally occurs, the excellent (and valiant) scholarly work of Ortiz Hill's writings will without doubt be partly responsible for it.

(8) Philip Ehrlich's paper "Hahn's Über nichtarchimidischen Grössensysteme and the Development of the Modern Theory of Magnitudes and Numbers to Measure them" is really a paper on the (recent) history of mathematics. As most of the readers of this collection surely know, Hans Hahn was Gödel's dissertation advisor and a prominent member - even founder - of the Vienna Circle. But what most readers did not know - the present author included - were Hahn's contributions to the theory of Archimedean complete ordered number fields and his more general Archimedean complete generalizations of R as an ordered Abelian group. We are not going to discuss this paper - as will be the case of most of the remaining papers - but, so far as we can judge, it seems to be a serious contribution to the historiography of mathematics.

(9) Gregory H. Moore's "The Origins of Russell's Paradox" is also a paper of a historiographical nature, although on a very well known issue. An important point already mentioned by Moore in his excellent scholarly work Zermelo's Axiom of Choice is that Ernst Zermelo discovered Russell's Paradox -really the Zermelo-Russell Paradox- around 1899 and communicated it to Hilbert and Husserl.

(10) Akihiro Kanamori's paper "The Emergence of Descriptive Set Theory" is also of a historiographical nature. It does not seem to offer anything particularly interesting to the philosopher of mathematics, although on its behalf it should be said that the author is a distinguished researcher in the area of his concern.

(11) Jan von Plato's "Chance Against Constructibility" is another paper addressed more to the history of mathematics than to its philosophy, although it is philosophically more pretentious. As Ehrlich's, Moore's and Kanamori's papers, it concerns the period between the end of the nineteenth century and the first decades of the twentieth. But instead of dealing with problems related to set theory - like the last two mentioned - it deals with constructibility and mathematical probabilty. After mentioning (p. 263) that the notion of mathematical existence radically changed at the end of the nineteenth century, mainly in Hilbert's hands, from a conception of existence as something constructed to a conception of existence as consistency, he goes on to virtually identify - see p. 264 - constructivism in mathematics with determinism in physics. This is a bold contention and a very questionable one, especially since when constructivists have tried to make precise their notion of constructivism, they have arrived at very different notions, whereas the notion of determinism in the physical sciences is certainly much more intersubjective. Moreover, all sorts of constructivisms require the abandonment of ("non-constructive") parts of classical mathematics, whereas even if determinism is incompatible with some areas of current physical science, its propounders can still argue that behind the apparent indeterminism of current physical theory, there is a more profound deteministic reality. (And even if that is not the case, it is very improbable that determinists would opt to reject, e.g., quantum mechanics in a similar fashion to that in which constructivists reject, e.g., higher set theory.) We are not going to dwell, however, on this issue. The rest of von Plato's paper deals mainly with the contributions of the French semi-intuitionists, especially Borel, to the theory of denumerable probability.

(12) William Boos' paper "Thoralf Skolem, Hermann Weyl and 'Das Gefühl der Welt als begrenztes Ganzes'" is in our opinion one of the more ambitious, but also probably the worst structured of the papers in the present collection. Boos' aims in this paper are - see p. 287 - the following: (i) to mediate between Skolem's pleas for metalogical relativism and Weyl's tendency towards a "predicative variant of transcendental idealism"; (ii) to reconcile Skolem's cautious metalogical justification of his views with Weyl's attempts to ground his views in "traditional European metaphysics"; (iii) to articulate an independent alternative to a complex of mathematical realist assumptions, which both Skolem and Weyl (for different reasons) rejected. We are not going to discuss this paper in any detail, but we suspect that Boos would have been more productive if he had concentrated his efforts on either of the two distinguished mathematicians instead of offering us this half-cooked and peripheral philosophical paper.

(13) Jan Wolenski's "On Tarski's Background" is also one of the weakest papers in the present collection, but, contrary to Boos' paper, its aims are much more modest. Wolenski wants to throw some light - see p. 331 - on the presumed conflict between Tarski's nominalistic and empiricist sympathies and his Platonistic mathematical practice. Thus, he intends to address -see p. 334- the following issues: (i) the development of Tarski's research in logic and foundations in the 1920s; (ii) his general philosophical views; (iii) some of his particular views; (iv) his general attitude towards logic; and (v) his attitude towards set theoretical methods. However, in our opinion, Wolenski's paper does not say anything especially illuminating or new for the reader familiar with Tarski's work and the history of contemporary logic. Particularly, there is not much new with respect to other papers by Wolenski and by Peter Simons on related issues. But that is one of the consequences of the publish or perish dictum, under whose spell most people in our profession fall - the present author being probably no exception.

(14) Mathieu Marion's paper "Wittgenstein and Ramsey on Identity" is one of two papers in the present collection concerned with issues in Wittgenstein's philosophy of mathematics, the other being Juliet Floyd's "On Saying What You Really Want to Say: Wittgenstein, Gödel and the Trisection of the Angle". Although Wittgenstein's contributions to the philosophy of mathematics seem questionable for many of us, both excellent scholars' papers offer interesting discussions on important issues related to Wittgenstein's views on mathematics. Marion's particularly stimulating paper deals with Wittgenstein's and Ramsey's critique of the logic of Principia Mathematica, especially of its treatment of identity, and their very different positions evolving from this critique. Marion's paper also complements Hintikka's paper discussed above in its approach to the standard versus non-standard distinction from a more specific angle, although arriving at similar conclusions. On this issue Marion claims (pp. 364-365) that while Ramsey tried to establish the standard interpretation - and reform Principia Mathematica in this direction - Wittgenstein adopted a non-standard and constructivist interpretation, and their feud can only be understood if we bear that difference in mind. We cannot extend further our discussion of this interesting paper, which we hope will receive the due attention by scholars in our field.

(15) Juliet Floyd's "On Saying What You Want to Say: Wittgenstein, Gödel and the Trisection of the Angle" is the second paper on Wittgenstein – and written also by an excellent young scholar. However, her task is more difficult, since she intends to argue against those who have claimed that Wittgenstein did not appreciate the import of Gödel's incompleteness results. As Floyd repeatedly mentions - see pp. 374-375, 380, 386, 399-400 - according to Wittgenstein, Gödel's incompleteness theorems do not have more significance for mathematics than any other impossibility proof. Moreover, she adds (p. 409) that Gödel's own assessment of the importance for mathematics of his incompleteness results was similar to Wittgenstein's. Although we are not going to dwell on this paper, we recognize that there is some truth in Wittgenstein's assertion, in case we consider only Gödel's first incompleteness theorem. For the working mathematician, the undecidable sentence obtained by Gödel – and even others obtained later - could be seen as too detached from the nucleus of mathematical research. However, the limitations to consistency proofs imposed by Gödel's second incompleteness theorem are of a much wider scope, which includes essentially all of mathematics. Moreover, what is at issue when people have argued that Wittgenstein did not appreciate the import of Gödel's results is whether he understood the general import of those results which, as

everyone well acquainted learnt long before Wittgenstein's death, is immense. We suspect that the grounds for Wittgenstein's assessment are not the same as those of an able mathematician working in functional analysis, differential topology or any branch of mathematics presumably unrelated to the incompleteness results. (And we underscore the word "presumably," since in mathematics sometimes seemingly unrelated statements are proven to be related by implication or even equivalence, as has occurred with the Axiom of Choice and many of its equivalents.)

(16) Dagfinn Føllesdal's "Gödel and Husserl" is the last paper in the collection and the second paper on Gödel's philosophical views published in 1995 by one of the major exponents of mainstream analytic philosophy. The other one is Charles Parsons' "Platonism and Mathematical Intuition in Kurt Gödel's Thought" (the Bulletin of Symbolic Logic, Vol. 1, No. 1, March 1995, pp. 44-73). Whereas Parsons' paper describes in a very clear manner the maturation of Gödel's philosophical views by examining Gödel's relevant texts, he dismisses the relation with Husserl's views with a brief remark on p. 67 and an immediate reference to a presumably more direct connection with Kant and Leibniz than with Husserl. Such a remark seems strange to someone acquainted both with Gödel's relevant papers, Wang's multiple references to the affinity between Gödel and Husserl, and Husserl's views on the epistemology of mathematics. Føllesdal's paper (previous versions of which were read at many places, including some not mentioned in the long list of acknowledgements) addresses, as its title anticipates, such an issue.

Føllesdal begins his paper with general comments on Gödel's knowledge of Husserl's philosophy. He mentions (p. 427) -as others before him– that Gödel's Nachlass gives testimony of Gödel's interest in Husserl, whose philosophy he began to study with great care and sympathy in 1959. As Føllesdal correctly points out (pp. 427-428), Gödel had already expressed before 1959 views on the philosophy of mathematics, which had clear affinities with Husserl's. Thus, one has to be careful in attributing Husserl an influence in the formation of Gödel's philosophical views. Nonetheless, Føllesdal also correctly states (p. 428) that before reading Husserl, Gödel's philosophical views on mathematics, e.g., his Platonism with regard to mathematical entities and concepts, and his belief in a sort of mathematical intuition, are not systematically worked out in his writings. Føllesdal is also probably on the right track when he claims (pp. 427-428) that Husserl's philosophy was so attractive to Gödel because it produced a systematic framework for his own views on the foundations of mathematics. That does not exclude, however, that the most explicit remarks on mathematical intuition of the 1964 revised version of his paper on Cantor could have been stimulated by his acquaintance with Husserl's related views.

On pp. 430-431, Føllesdal tries to explain to his analytical audience what Husserl understood by intuition. In some aspects, however, his exposition simplifies too much and is, thus, inaccurate. E.g., on p. 430, when he explains how we get acquainted with 'essences' he obviates the distinction between 'material essences,' constitutive of the material ontologies, and pure mathematical entities, which belong to what Husserl calls 'formal ontology.' Moreover, Føllesdal seems to completely assimilate categorial intuition -which, as Husserl asserts in his Sixth Logical Investigation, combines with the process of categorial abstraction to produce pure mathematical objects- to the intuition of essences (or Wesensschau). Also his remark on p. 431, according to which Husserl's notion of intuition divides into perceptions (of physical objects) and Wesensschau is very inaccurate. Intuitions, in Husserl's sense, divide, first of all, in perceptions, in which the object is really present, and imaginations. Sense perception and sense imagination concern physical objects, whereas categorial perception and categorial imagination -or, briefly, categorial intuition- concern categorial objectualities. Some of these categorial objectualities are pure and are, thus, mathematical objectualities, whereas others -like 'shape,' 'redness' and 'triangularity'- are mixed categorial objectualities. In the Sixth Logical Investigation, what Husserl later called 'Wesensschau' is just a special sort of categorial intuition, which will let us obtain mixed categorial objectualities, whereas mathematical objects are obtained through a combination of another sort of categorial intuition with categorial abstraction. In his late Erfahrung und Urteil (first published a year after his death) the separation between (material) essences and what he now called "objects of the understanding," is sharpened. (See also his Einführung in die Logik und Erkenntnistheorie, pp. 108-109.)

Continuing with Føllesdal's paper, on pp. 434-435, he tries to explain that both in Husserl and in Gödel there is a combination of a sort of Platonism concerning mathematical entities and a sort of Kantian streak. He contrasts his rendering of this combination with the Platonism of Frege, Bolzano and Cantor, all of which, according to Føllesdal (p. 435), inspired Husserl. On this issue, we would like to point out once more our disagreement with Føllesdal. Bolzano was certainly an important influence on Husserl's views on mathematics and logic. Cantor was very probably the greatest[1] single influence on Husserl's views on mathematics. They were colleagues and friends for some decisive years at Halle. Moreover, if you examine Husserl's writings on mathematics from the early 1890s, you will surely find Cantor's and others' - like Riemann's or Klein's - presence in the background. What you will not find is Frege's influence. When in 1894 Frege published his review of Husserl's early book, Philosophie der Arithmetik, Husserl had already abandoned the Brentanian brand of psychologism present in that book and was developing his mature views expounded in Chapter XI of the first volume of his Logische Untersuchungen, which must have been finished by 1895, since it was the first part of that volume to be written and the volume was completed in 1896. Moreover, as attested by his review of Schroder's *Vorlesungen über die Algebra der Logik I* in 1891 and by his 1890 paper published only posthumously "Zur Logik der Zeichen," and acknowledged by Frege in a letter to Husserl of May 1891 and timidly in his posthumous "Ausfuhrungen über Sinn und Bedeutung," Husserl arrived at the distinction between sense and reference at least as early as Frege and with complete independence of the latter. This case is very similar to what happened just recently with Herzberger and Gupta developing, with complete independence of each other, the so-called revision theory of truth. The much publicized influence of Frege on Husserl -publicized by Føllesdal, Beth and others, and

---

[1] I now do not agree with that assertion. Though Cantor's influence is undeniable and was the most direct one, I think that Riemann's influence was at least as decisive.

accepted as a dogma of faith by Fregeans- is nothing other than a historiographical myth, and a myth that has stymied the study of Husserl's views in analytic circles. Furthermore, an acquaintance with precisely Chapter XI of the first volume of Logische Untersuchungen, with Formale und transzendentale Logik and the only recently published Einführung in die Logik und Erkenntnistheorie will convince the reader that the Platonist Husserl's views on mathematics had very little to do with those of the Platonist and Logicist Frege. It is with the ontological and epistemological Platonism of Husserl that the Platonist Gödel had a profound affinity. By the way, with regard to the presumed combination of Platonist and constructivist elements in Husserl's philosophy of mathematics, we should not get confused by the latter's transcendental phenomenology. We should see the so-called transcendental turn from a methodological standpoint, which did not force in Husserl any essential modification in his views on mathematics and logic. Finally, in Gödel's case, it also does not seem appropriate to attribute him such a combination. Of course, Gödel was interested in epistemological problems, as attested by his interest in Kant and, especially, in Husserl. But his argumentation against constructivism in his lecture "Some basic theorems on the foundations of mathematics and its implications" should preclude any rendering like Føllesdal's -in case the multiple explicit advocacies of Platonism are not sufficient.

With all the mentioned limitations of Føllesdal's paper, we hope that it will serve the purpose of motivating analytic philosophers to study Husserl's relevant work. At least the high regard that both Cantor, Hilbert and Weyl had of their friend Husserl, and the equally high regard shown by Gödel will finally prevail over the prejudices entrenched in analytic circles against the former assistant of Karl Weierstrass.

Frege and the Fregean's "Frege"
Critical Study of Dirk Greimann (ed.), *Essays on Frege's Conception of Truth*

In the last two decades the research on Frege's philosophical views has suffered a double-headed turnaround. On the one hand, books and papers on Frege's philosophy have flourished like mushrooms. On the other hand, the rationalist philosopher of mathematics, who propounded both logicism and a Platonist conception of logic and mathematics has suffered a reinterpretation in the hands of interpreters, mostly in the Anglo-American countries that have turned him in an epistemologist of a Kantian or neo-Kantian flavour, more palatable to the empiricist background of most of those interpreters.[1] Some of the papers in the book *Essays on Frege's Conception of Truth*, edited by Dirk Greimann, can serve as perfect examples of the reinterpretation of Frege's views. The collection of essays is basically a reprint of a special number of *Grazer Philosophische Studien* on Frege's conception of truth. One can wonder how is it possible to publish a collection of papers exclusively on Frege's views on truth, since Frege wrote relatively little on that issue. Nonetheless, the editor had already published in his native German a whole book on that issue, namely, *Frege's Konzeption der Wahrheit*. Moreover, one should not forget that Fregean scholars, especially in North America and England, have been extremely prolific in some sort of exegetical, usually very selective and imaginative studies that have attempted to reinterpret the Platonist and rationalist Frege, who not only believed in the existence of abstract mathematical objects but – consistent with his logicism - in logical objects, as a sort of Kantian or Neo-Kantian epistemologist, and are probably on the verge of "discovering" that Frege was after all an empiricist. Of course, the Kantianization of Frege is not the only

---

[1] Other Kantianizers of Frege not represented in Greimann's book include most notably Philip Kitcher, Gregory Currie and Joan Weiner.

recent 'revolutionary' rendering of Frege, and some other confused reinterpretations are also represented in this book.[2]

The present collection consists of nine papers, some of which are only marginally concerned with Frege's views about truth, and are divided into four general issues, namely: (i) Truth in Frege's Formal System (three papers), (ii) Truth and the Truth-Values (two papers), (iii) Truth and Judgment (two papers), and (iv) The nature of the Truth-Bearers (two papers). In general, this collection of papers is not especially illuminating. I have opted to say very little about some of the papers, in order to concentrate my efforts on pointing to some weaknesses of a few of the most questionable ones.

(1) Hans Sluga's main interest in 'Truth and the Imperfection of Language' –see p. 1- is to examine the compatibility or incompatibility of two assertions of Frege about truth, namely, (i) that his conception of logic 'gives pre-eminence to the content of the word "true"', and (ii) that the word "true" seems devoid of content. Without entering in a detailed discussion of Sluga's paper, I would like to point out that it could certainly serve as an example of the artificial problems discussed in recent Anglo-American Fregean studies. The fact of the matter is simply that, on the one hand, Frege's conception of logic, in contrast to the conception of logic had by psychologism, is not concerned with judgements, beliefs or other similar entities admitting a psychological rendering, but with truth. On the other hand, since in usual parlance, declarative sentences, when stated, already are being asserted as true, the addition either of the words "It is true that" before the sentence or of the predicate "is true" does not add any more content to the mere stating the declarative sentence. Thus, it seems as if the word "true" were devoid of content.

On p. 6, Sluga correctly emphasizes that for Frege logic is concerned with what is, not with any sort of prescription or norm. On this point, I would like to refer the reader to a passage in the Preface to *Grundgesetze der Arithmetik* - p. XV - and one in 'Der Gedanke' – p. 342, since there are still some Fregean scholars that miss this basic point. On the other hand, Sluga's treatment of Frege's views on

---

[2] However, the most 'revolutionary' rendering of Frege to this day, namely, Tappenden's Riemannization of Frege, is not represented in this collection.

thoughts and facts on p. 8, according to which thoughts are identified with facts, and, thus, constitute the actual world and, hence, do not belong to any third realm, is simply an empiricist distortion of Frege's views. The fact of the matter is that for Frege thoughts belonged to a third realm – as attested by numerous passages of 'Der Gedanke' conveniently ignored by Sluga. This third realm is different both from the world of consciousness and from the world of facts, and thoughts do not need to be actualized in order to exist. The Principle of Non-contradiction and the equation "5+3=3+5" do not need to be actualized for Frege in order to exist, or even in order to be true. Of course, other thoughts, as that of Paris being the capital of France in 2010, though not requiring of the actual world to exist, correspond to facts in the actual world, and are true or false, depending on whether in the actual world Paris is the capital of France in 2010 or not. What Frege meant in 'Der Gedanke' when he stated that facts are true thoughts is simply that facts are actualizations of some thoughts and that in virtue of such actualizations those particular thoughts are true (in the actual world). There is no place in 'Der Gedanke' or in any of Frege's writings for Sluga's rendering of that passage.

On the basis of that misinterpretation, Sluga goes on – see pp. 12-13 - to try to distance Frege's views from those of Bolzano. I just want to point out that contrary to what Sluga asserts on p. 13, and independently of whether Bolzano influenced Frege directly – probably not - or indirectly via Lotze – almost surely yes -, Bolzano and Frege are on the same bank of the great divide. It is precisely Sluga and many other Fregean scholars, especially in the Anglo-American world, who are on the other bank of the same divide. Still more questionable are Sluga's remarks on p. 23, in which he tries to establish a connection, based on their supposed interest in truth, between Frege, Tarski and Russell, on the one hand, and, on the other hand, Nietzsche, Heidegger and Foucault. With respect to such a philosophical salad of Sluga, in my view, comparing such different philosophers only increases confusion, and does not help to clarify the issues.

(2) Richard Heck's paper 'Frege and Semantics' attempts to establish – see pp. 27-28 - that Frege used semantic notions for making semantic claims, for example, that he argued that all the axioms of *Grundgesetze der Arithmetik* were true, that its rules of inference preserve truth and that every well-formed expression has a reference. Heck's paper is a sound and well-rounded paper, with a very interesting discussion – see pp. 55-58 - on Frege's attempt to prove the referentiality of all well-formed expressions of his logic system in *Grundgesetze der Arithmetik*, but it would take me too far to examine it adequately. In fact, I just want to point out that Heck sometimes emphasizes too much the obvious. This attests not so much to any weakness in Heck's paper but to the level of discussion of the audience he has in mind. An example of this is the following. On p. 33, Heck needs to underscore the triviality that in order for the basic arithmetical laws to be logical truths, they have to be derived from logical truths by means of logically valid inference rules. That remark of Heck is as deep as the assertion that if Bobby is a dog, his parents must also be dogs. Well, maybe some Fregean scholars are not convinced of this either.

(3) With respect to Danielle Macbeth's paper 'Striving for Truth in the Practice of Mathematics' I have almost nothing positive to say. I suppose that I did not understand her well. In any case, I will make a few critical comments. On p. 66, Macbeth states: "This answer [Kant's: GERH] is unacceptable philosophically insofar as it entails transcendental idealism...". I am certainly very critical of Kant's conception of mathematical knowledge, but to argue like Macbeth does in the passage quoted is to "argue" on the basis of prejudices, to reject a thesis because it entails a philosophical doctrine that you do not like. As a matter of fact, independently of Macbeth's sympathies, Kant was a transcendental idealist, as were Frege and Gödel Platonists and rationalists.

However, what I find less convincing is Macbeth's general scheme of the three "levels of articulation" – exactly three, neither two, nor four or five - that in her opinion permeate the whole of mathematics. According to Macbeth – see p. 68 -, Kant identifies such three levels of articulation, which are present also in Frege's conceptography (Begriffsschrift) – see p. 77. Moreover, according to Macbeth, what she calls – see p. 74 - 'the standard model-theoretic conception of language' lacks such a three level articulation, having only a two level one and is, thus, clearly inferior to Frege's conceptography – see pp. 88 and 91. Nonetheless, in spite of Macbeth's views, the fact of the matter is that mathematics developed in a gigantic way after Kant, and logic has also developed immensely after Frege, notwithstanding the fact that Macbeth's general scheme of the three levels of articulation has not been taken into account in those developments.

Finally, I want to point out to two errors committed by Macbeth, one conceptual and one historical. Thus, in footnote 13, pp. 76-77, Macbeth asserts that the expression "2/0=5", though having no referent, expresses a thought, that is, has a sense. However, as Frege stressed, since the component expression "2/0" does not have any sense, the compound expression "2/0=5" cannot have any sense either.

Moreover, on pp. 89-90, Macbeth considers some material inferences, like 'if something is red, it is coloured' and 'something red is not blue', and states that Wilfrid Sellars in 1953 and Robert B. Brandom in 1994 argued on behalf of those inferences. Macbeth seems completely ignorant of the fact that Husserl discussed those and other examples of presumed synthetic *a priori* statements in the Third Logical Investigation of his 1900-01 *Logische Untersuchungen*. I suppose Macbeth, like most analytic philosophers, is not acquainted with Husserl, though analytic philosophers, especially those working on Frege and on Carnap, would profit at least as much from reading Husserl's most important writings as from reading Kant's.

(4) Michael Beaney's paper 'Frege's Use of Function-Argument Analysis and his Introduction of Truth-Values as Objects' attempts to trace Frege's function-argument analysis from *Begriffsschrift* to the introduction of truth-values as objects in the early 1890s. In this review, however, I will be concerned exclusively with some misinterpretations originated by Beaney's effort to force Fregean texts into his conceptual analysis. In particular, I will restrict my discussion to Frege's important, though evasive and unclear notion of conceptual content, and especially to Beaney's even more confused treatment of that notion.

On p. 96, Beaney refers for the first time to Frege's notion of conceptual content, introduced by Frege in §3 of *Begriffsschrift*, and mentions the most important of the three components of Frege's characterization of conceptual content, namely, that two statements S and S* have the same conceptual content when they have the same logical consequences or, in other words, when they are logically equivalent. More precisely, S and S* have the same conceptual content if and only if for any set of statements Σ and any statement φ: $\Sigma \cup \{S\} \models \varphi \Leftrightarrow \Sigma \cup \{S^*\} \models \varphi$. Frege immediately observes that a statement in the active mode and its corresponding statement in the passive mode ought to have the same conceptual content. More generally, all statements of the form aRb and their converses should also have the same conceptual content. Thus, Beaney is right when he considers on p. 97 that 'Hydrogen is lighter than carbon dioxide' and 'Carbon dioxide is heavier than hydrogen' have the same conceptual content. Beaney uses *ad nauseam* this example to try to argue on behalf of his thesis that in *Begriffsschrift* the conceptual content is simply the common value of different functions, one of the argument 'hydrogen' and the other of the argument 'carbon dioxide'. However, it should be pointed out against Beaney that other cases of logically equivalent statements do not allow such a simple treatment as his. Thus, in propositional logic the statements '$\varphi \rightarrow \psi$' and '$\neg \varphi \vee \psi$' are logically equivalent and, hence, have the same conceptual content, but do not allow for Beaney's treatment. Moreover, the first-order statements '$(\exists x)\Phi(x)$' and '$\neg(\forall x)\neg\Phi(x)$' and many more not so trivial examples are logically equivalent, thus, have the same conceptual content, but do not allow for Beaney's treatment. Furthermore, if we replace Σ in the above schema by ZF (Zermelo-Fraenkel Set Theory without Choice), it follows that the Axiom of Choice, Zorn's Lemma, Tychonoff's Theorem and about a hundred other mathematical statements in different areas of mathematics have the same conceptual content, though they do not admit of Beaney's treatment.

Before continuing, it should be pointed out that Frege did not have a crystal clear notion of conceptual content. Thus, besides stating that two statements with the same conceptual content have the same logical consequences and, hence, that a statement in the active mode and its passive counterpart have the same conceptual content, he also stated that his concept script (Begriffsschrift) does not need to distinguish between statements having the same conceptual content.

Beaney completely ignores this troublesome partial characterization of conceptual content. In fact, this component of Frege's characterization of conceptual content is hardly compatible with the first one, and would not allow for different notations for logically (or mathematically) equivalent statements as those listed above, in particular, for the Axiom of Choice and Tychonoff's Theorem. This fundamental confusion is Frege's, not Beaney's, though the later will add some confusions of his own vintage.

On pp. 98-99, Beaney refers to §2 of *Begriffsschrift*, where Frege introduces the notion of a judgeable content, as well as to 'Boole's rechnende Logik und die Begriffsschrift', where Frege also refers to judgeable contents, and he takes the completely unwarranted step of identifying the notions of conceptual content and of judgeable content. However, it seems completely unreasonable to render a philosopher and logician so conceptually rigorous and so conscious in his use of language as having introduced in successive sections (§§2 and 3) of a logical treatise the same notion twice, but using different terminology, different characterizations and, moreover, without explicitly stating that the two notions are after all one and the same. Beaney simply completely misinterprets Frege on this fundamental issue. A judgeable content is in Frege's *Begriffsschrift* a content to which one can prefix the judgement stroke. That means – in *Begriffsschrift*, not in *Grundgesetze der Arithmetik* - that the symbol whose content is a judgeable one is a symbol for a statement, not for a proper name, a predicate or a function. As the etymology of the word clearly shows, a judgeable (in German: beurteilbar) content is one about which it is possible to judge. Since in *Begriffsschrift* Frege had not distinguished between sense (Sinn) and referent (Bedeutung), he characterizes a judgeable content both as 'the proposition that" and "the circumstance that" - although such characterizations are hardly equivalent. It should be stressed that though in *Grundgesetze der Arithmetik* Frege stated that he split his old notion of judgeable content – not that of conceptual content – in those of thought and truth-value, his notion of judgeable content was much closer to that of thought than to that of truth-value. In any case, it does not matter how we render the notion of judgeable content, be it as proposition (or thought) or as circumstance (or state of affairs), it is unwarranted to identify it with the conceptual content. It should be at least clear that in virtue of Frege's characterizations of the two notions, many judgeable contents would correspond to the same conceptual content, namely, those judgeable contents that are logically equivalent. Thus, conceptual contents are some sort of equivalence classes of judgeable contents.

But there are still more fundamental confusions in Beaney's paper. Thus, on p. 100, he says that in his later work Frege replaced the claim that two different propositions have the same conceptual content with the claim that two propositions – better: two statements – have the same thought. However, those two claims are of a very different level, since on the basis of Frege's official notion of sense, expounded in 'Über Sinn und Bedeutung' and *Grundgesetze der Arithmetik* – see §2, p. 7 – '2+2' and '2^2' have different senses, and, hence, '2+2>3' and '2^2>3', though logically equivalent, express different thoughts. Beginning on pp. 100-101, Beaney adds another confusion to his salad of confusions. Now he also identifies the vague notion of content with that of conceptual content and, on the basis of Frege's analysis of identity statements in §8, goes on to attribute conceptual content to names, whereas Frege talks simply about content, not conceptual content. In fact, neither in *Begriffsschrift* nor in *Die Grundlagen der Arithmetik*, where Frege uses frequently and loosely the word "content", does he attempt to define it or somehow characterize it with some precision. In fact, Frege uses the word "content" with the same ambiguity as many of his contemporaries.

As a result of Beaney's identification of Frege's notion of conceptual content both with the latter's notion of judgeable content and with his multiply ambiguous uses of the word "content', other confusions follow, which I cannot consider here. There is, however, a fundamental point – see p. 105 - in which I agree with Beaney, namely, that Frege meant 'conceptual content' when in the second (and also in the third) attempt at defining the notion of number in *Die Grundlagen der Arithmetik* he stated that pairs of statements like (1) "Straight line a is parallel to straight line b" and (2) "The direction of straight line a is identical with the direction of straight line b", have the same content. In fact, there is no possibility of interpreting the equivalence of such statements as that of having the same judgeable content, be it rendered as the same proposition (thought) or as the same circumstance (state of affairs). Moreover, there is no possibility of adequately interpreting that equivalence using Frege's semantic tools of 'Über Sinn und Bedeutung' and *Grundgesetze der Arithmetik*, as expressing either identity of thought – which is clearly not present – nor identity of truth-value – which they certainly have in common either with "Paris is the capital of France at the end of 2010" or with its negation.

On pp. 118-119, Beaney discusses, among other things, the notorious Axiom V of *Grundgesetze der Arithmetik*, and the many confusions of his paper come to the fore when trying to render the equivalence of its two sides: (i) $\acute{a}\Phi(\hat{a})=\hat{e}\Psi(\hat{e})$ and (ii) $(\forall x)(\Phi(x)\Leftrightarrow\Psi(x))$. Once more, however, some of the confusions originate in Frege. As is well known, in §3 of *Grundgesetze der Arithmetik* Frege stated that (i) and (ii) have the same referent (sind bedeutungsgleich). But since (i) and (ii) are statements, Frege's assertion amounts to saying that (i) and (ii) have the same truth-value. However, that is too little, since they have the same truth-value either with all true statements or with all false ones. On the other hand, in 'Funktion und Begriff' Frege states that what (i) and (ii) have in common is their sense. However, if we understand by sense the notion of sense of 'Über Sinn und Bedeutung' and *Grundgesetze der Arithmetik*, (i) and (ii) do not express the same sense. The solution to this apparent puzzle is once more the conceptual content. What (i) and (ii) presumably would have in common – in case Axiom V were true – is, as in the examples used by Frege in his second and third attempts at defining the concept of 'number' in *Die Grundlagen der Arithmetik*, the conceptual content. In fact, the conceptual content did not disappear completely from Frege's conceptual framework after the distinction between sense and referent – as Beaney and most Fregean scholars believe -, but subsisted as a second (unofficial) notion of the sense of statements. Thus, in 'Der Gedanke' – see p. 348 - Frege uses the example of a statement in the active mode and its counterpart in the passive mode, as well as a similar example using the verbs 'to give' and 'to receive', and states that the corresponding statements have the same sense. Moreover, in his letters of 1906 to Husserl, Frege identifies identity of sense of statements with their logical equivalence. However - as argued above -, if 'sense' is understood as in 'Über Sinn und Bedeutung' and *Grundgesetze der Arithmetik*, Frege's assertion is evidently false, since neither '4+4>7' and '2^3>7' nor 'p→q' and '¬p∨q' express the same sense. Of course, if 'sense of a statement' is understood not as thought but as conceptual content, the pieces come perfectly into place and Frege's assertion would be true in case Axiom V had been true. Since Husserl's letters to Frege of 1906 are lost, I urge Beaney to examine Husserl's response to Frege in his *Alte und Neue Logik* –especially pp. 111, 116, 163 and 272-274-, since Husserl was by far much clearer than Frege on this issue (and also on many others).

(5) Dirk Greimann's paper 'Did Frege Really Consider Truth as an Object?' is an interesting attempt to clarify Frege's notion of truth by disentangling it from the notion of the truth-value 'the true'. According to Greimann – see p. 126 -, Frege did not consider truth as an object, but for him truth is what is expressed by the "form of the assertoric sentence". Of what I would call the 'free-exegetical papers' in this collection (Sluga's, Macbeth's, Beaney's, Greimann's and Reck's) Greimann's is probably the most successful. Certainly, Frege did not explicitly separate his discussion on the addition or suppression of the predicate 'is true' and the assertive force of declarative sentences in 'Über Sinn und Bedeutung' and 'Der Gedanke', from his introduction of 'the true' and 'the false' as courses of values in *Grundgesetze der Arithmetik* and as referents of statements in 'Über Sinn und Bedeutung', but it seems at least plausible to avoid mixing them up. By radically separating those notions, Greimann is able to arrive to a cogent and persuasive rendering of Frege's notion of truth. However, since I have already extended this review too much, I will not deal with particular issues of Greimann's paper. It is enough to mention that I have minor disagreements with some of his renderings of Frege's views, for example – see pp. 129-130 – with the postulation of a special kind of objects as denotations of expressions like 'the concept horse'.

(6) Erich H. Reck's paper 'Frege on Truth, Judgment and Objectivity' is one of the several papers in this collection, in which, on the basis of philosophical prejudices, the author tries to find some

isolated passage in Frege's writings, which he can somehow reinterpret in order to avoid the obvious conclusion that Frege was a rationalist and a mathematical as well as a logical Platonist. I am not going to dwell much on this paper except to point out to Reck's prejudice. Thus, on p.153, after having acknowledged that for Frege numbers are self-subsisting objects and thoughts inhabit a third realm – he could also have pointed out to the postulation of courses of values (including the truth-values) as objects in *Grundgesetze der Arithmetik* -, which clearly make Frege a full-blown Platonist, Reck states that Platonism is a problematic position, especially because of the impossibility of having any causal contact with abstract objects. Moreover, on p. 154 Reck refers to Platonism as 'a heavy-handed and objectionable view' – I would add: especially for empiricists of any sort. Hence, Reck attempts at giving the notion of judgement a central stage in his reinterpretation – better: misinterpretation – of Frege. The fact of the matter, however, is that judgements have only a derived role – not a central one - in Frege's philosophy. They are simply recognitions of the truth of thoughts: to judge is to recognize the truth or falsity of a thought. Moreover, a thought exists, and is true or false independently of its being judged as true or as false.

(**7**) Verena Mayer's paper 'Evidence, Judgment and Truth' is certainly on the right track. The comparison of Frege's philosophical views with those of Husserl – especially with those of his *opus magnum*, *Logische Untersuchungen* and related works – is extremely fruitful. As Frege, Husserl was a mathematician turned philosopher via the philosophy of mathematics, and though the scope of his philosophical interests widened by far more than Frege's, the comparison of their views on many issues examined by Frege is very rewarding. Nonetheless, although I agree with Mayer's general perspective, as well as with most of her analyses, I will mention here briefly a few points of disagreement. For example, on pp 176-177, Mayer states that for Frege, in contrast to Husserl, logic was a normative discipline. Such an interpretation, though popular, is incorrect. As mentioned above, in the Preface to *Grundgesetze der Arithmetik* and in 'Der Gedanke' Frege stated that logic is a theoretical science, though it admits of a normative application, as also do other theoretical disciplines. Certainly, Husserl had much clearer views than

Frege both of the theoretical nature of logic (and mathematics) – see, for example, Chapter XI of *Logische Untersuchungen I* –, as well as of the nature of normative disciplines and of the relation of logic as a theoretical discipline to its normative applications, but that does not mean that Frege did not acknowledge the theoretical nature of logic.

On pp. 181-182, Mayer is concerned with Frege's identification in his letters to Husserl of 1906 of the logical equivalence of two statements with their having the same sense. She states – see p. 182 – that Husserl was of the same opinion and refers to a passage of *Logische Untersuchungen* in which Husserl speaks of two judgements being essentially the same judgement (or statement). That is, however, a completely different matter from what Frege asserts in his letters to Husserl of 1906. In fact, as already stressed above, Husserl did not agree with Frege at all – if under 'sense of a statement' one understands the thought or proposition expressed by the statement. I refer Mayer also to Husserl's *Alte und Neue Logik*, where Husserl responds to Frege's view with a much more subtle distinction in perfect agreement with his more sophisticated semantics of sense and referent than the latter's.

Finally, on pp. 189-190, Mayer comments on a letter of Frege to Husserl of 24 May 1891 and states that in it Frege refers to a sketch of the sense-referent distinction for conceptual words in Husserl's *Philosophie der Arithmetik*. As a matter of fact, however, Frege is not referring to Husserl's youth book, where the distinction is not explicitly made, though such a distinction is unmistakably present in Husserl's review of the first volume of Ernst Schröder's *Vorlesungen über die Algebra der Logik*, which also appeared in 1891 and was sent by Husserl to Frege together with the book. Moreover, an even clearer acknowledgement of the fact that Husserl already had the distinction in the review of Schröder's book appears in Frege's 'Ausführungen über Sinn und Bedeutung' - see p. 135. Interestingly enough, Mayer misses the opportunity of making two important points: (i) that contrary to the myth accepted as a dogma of faith by almost all analytic philosophers that have never studied Husserl (nor understood Frege!), Frege himself admits in that letter that Husserl had made the distinction between sense and referent independently of him; (ii) that with respect to statements, Husserl's later distinctions in *Logische*

Untersuchungen and elsewhere were much more nuanced than Frege's. For Husserl, though the senses of statements were thoughts (or propositions), the referents were states of affairs, which had a sort of abstract referential basis, called by Husserl 'situations of affairs' (Sachlagen). Hence, for Husserl the relation of statements to their truth-values has two additional intermediate stages. More importantly, situations of affairs can be seen as a refinement of Frege's conceptual contents. Thus, all pieces now fall into their respective places.

(8) Oswaldo Chateaubriand's paper 'The Truth of Thoughts: Variations on Fregean Themes' purports to offer – see p. 199 – an abstract theory of senses, thoughts and truths based on Frege, but without the objective of merely expounding Frege's views. Interestingly enough, however, Chateaubriand has a much sounder understanding of Frege's views than most of the authors represented in this collection of papers, in particular, much sounder than all those authors that, in view of the empiricist and naturalistic philosophical views prevailing in the Anglo-American world, make all sorts of mental circus acts in order to reinterpret whom they consider their intellectual grandfather as less a rationalist and less a Platonist as possible. Moreover, Chateaubriand is not only an excellent Fregean scholar but also by far the most original author represented in the present collection. Thus, already on p. 204, Chateaubriand introduces his new theory of descriptions, which coincides with Frege's with respect to singular terms, but coincides with Russell's with respect to descriptive predicates. Since I agree with Chateaubriand on most points discussed in his excellent and refreshing paper, and have already dealt with our minor disagreements elsewhere, I will not comment further on it.

(9) Marco Ruffino's paper 'Fregean Propositions, Belief Preservation and Cognitive Value' is a sober paper, basically dealing with one issue: the problem of indexicals in Frege, Kaplan and Perry. Although I disagree from Ruffino's Slugian general interpretation of Frege as being especially concerned with epistemological issues, his comparison of Frege's views on indexicality with those of Kaplan and Perry, and his support of Frege's views are sound and interesting. I will not discuss Ruffino's paper any further, but would also urge him to compare Frege's views on indexicals with those of Husserl, expounded in the First Logical Investigation, almost two decades before the publication of 'Der Gedanke'.

References

Chateaubriand, Oswaldo - *Logical Forms* (two vols.) 2001 & 2005, CLE, Campinas

Frege, Gottlob - *Begriffsschrift* 1879, reprint, Georg Olms, Hildesheim

Frege, Gottlob - *Die Grundlagen der Arithmetik* 1884, reprint, Georg Olms, Hildesheim 1961

Frege, Gottlob - 'Funktion und Begriff', 1891, reprinted in I. Angelelli (ed.), *Gottlob Frege; Kleine Schriften*, pp. 125-142

Frege, Gottlob – 'Über Sinn und Bedeutung' 1892, reprinted in I. Angelelli (ed.), *Gottlob Frege: Kleine Schriften*, pp. 143-162 Hildesheim, Georg Olms 1967/1990)

Frege, Gottlob - *Grundgesetze der Arithmetik* (2 vols.) 1893 & 1903, reprint, Georg Olms, Hildesheim 1962

Frege, Gottlob – 'Der Gedanke' 1918, reprinted in I. Angelleli (ed.), Gottlob Frege: *Kleine Schriften*, Georg Olms, Hildesheim 1967, second edition1990, pp. 342-361

Frege, Gottlob - 'Ausführungen über Sinn und Bedeutung', in H. Hermes et al. (eds), *Nachgelassene Schriften*, Felix Meiner, Hamburg 1969, second edition 1983, pp. 128-136

Frege, Gottlob - *Wissenschaftlicher Briefwechsel* (Gottfried Gabriel et al. (eds.), Hamburg, Felix Meiner 1976

Greimann, Dirk - Freges *Konzeption der Wahrheit*, Georg Olms, Hildesheim 2003

Hill, Claire O. & Rosado Haddock, Guillermo E. - *Husserl or Frege?: Meaning, Objectivity and Mathematics*, Open Court, Chicagoet al 2000, paperback edition 2003

Husserl, Edmund -. *Philosophie der Arithmetik* 1891, Husserliana XII, M. Nijhoff, Den Haag 1970

Husserl, Edmund - *Logische Untersuchungen* (2 vols.) 1900 & 1901, Husserliana XVIII & XIX M. Nijhoff, Den Haag 1975 & 1984

Husserl, Edmund - *Alte und Neue Logik: Vorlesungen 1908/09* Kluwer, Dordrecht 2003

Rosado Haddock, Guillermo E. - *A Critical Introduction to the Philosophy of Gottlob Frege* Ashgate, Aldershot 2006

Rosado Haddock, Guillermo E. 'Critical Study of Oswaldo Chateaubriand's *Logical Forms I* and *Logical Forms II*' *Manuscrito*, *30*, 2007, pp. 185-218

Critical Footnotes to Bernulf Kanitscheider's Paper on Naturalism

§1 General Considerations

In his paper 'Naturalismus und logisch-mathematische Grundlagenprobleme'[1] Kanitscheider intends to defend a sort of "Platonism" that should be compatible with the naturalism of the natural sciences. Kanitscheider opts for the sort of "realism" in mathematics propounded by Quine, which originates in his criticism of Carnap's peculiar distinction between analytic and synthetic statements, as well as in Quine's "holist" and naturalist theses.

Kanitscheider does not distinguish between three different senses of the word "naturalism" that ought to be sharply differentiated, namely: (i) the naturalism of natural scientists, (ii) the naturalism of philosophers of natural science –to which Kanitscheider belongs-, and (iii) the so-called "naturalism" of Quine and his followers. The first very healthy sort of naturalism is both the most natural and most reasonable stance a natural scientist can take with regard to his research object. He should try to offer a systematic and theoretical explanation of nature grounded on experience, without any hypothesis transcending the natural bounds, as, e.g. the existence of God. Such naturalism does not exclude that in the development of the cosmos and of life there could be some points in which the development process seems to have made jumps and that the product is not completely reducible to the former stages of development.[2]

A very different sort of naturalism is that of the philosophers or philosophers of nature, which has also appeared in the history of philosophy under the names of materialism or physicalism, and which Kanitscheider –see §§3 and 4 of his essay- calls "methodological naturalism". This sort of naturalism is essentially an ideological naturalism. Usually such naturalism tries to ground itself on the

---

[1] 'Naturalismus und logisch-mathematische Grundlagenprobleme', in *Erwägen Wissen Ethik 17 (3)*, 2006, pp. 325-338.
[2] By the way, such naturalism does not exclude natural scientists from being believers, but only that they mix their scientific activity with their religious beliefs.

naturalism of natural scientists but also demands the complete reduction of all worldly phenomena on the basis of physical events. For such an ideological naturalism any possible jump in the development of the cosmos would be suspicious of preparing the ground for the introduction of metaphysics in the scientific explanation of nature –see §7. A good example of an ideological naturalism is Otto Neurath's physicalism, according to which Tarski's brilliant analysis of the semantic problem of truth was suspicious of containing metaphysical traits. The downfall of all versions of logical empiricism from 1930 on should be a warning for such philosophers that demand a complete reduction either to simple experience or to the physical events. We postpone the discussion of Quine's so-called "naturalism" for later. Nonetheless, it is clear that Kanitscheider is taking for granted Quine's philosophical standpoints both on naturalized epistemology and on ontology.

§2 A Pair of Footnotes to Kanitscheider's Naturalism

That Kanitscheider's naturalism is an ideological naturalism is evidenced by his adhesion to Vollmer's naturalist program, to which he refers in §6. In §14 Kanitscheider arrives at a precise determination of the concept of his naturalist conception, a naturalism for which the unity of nature can be considered as the guiding idea. We will not be concerned so much with the peculiarities of Kanitscheider's concept of naturalism, but will be concerned with another issue, from which he tries to extract not permissible conclusions.

In §18 he discusses the standpoint of creationists, which try to make use of a probabilistic consideration in order to give support to their thesis of creation. According to Kanitscheider –see §18-, the creationists argue that life is such an improbable event that it could not be an accident, but has to be somehow planned. But Kanitscheider argues that precisely the improbability and complexity of life could be used as argument against the creationists, since the more improbable and complex is an event –as is life- the more incredible it is that it would have been produced by God or similar supernatural forces. It is, however, exactly the opposite, namely, that the more improbable is an event, the more space there is for the introduction of such big hypotheses –like the existence of a God that creates-, especially when one presupposes a concept of God like the almighty Christian one. Moreover, it should here be stressed that what the development of our knowledge in the natural sciences has shown is the possibility of offering a consistent, free of holes and probable description of the development of the cosmos, which can serve as an explanation free of godlike intervention of the present state of life on earth and possibly somewhere else –and that independently of whether there are jumps in such development or not. Hence, natural science has shown that one can dispense of the big hypothesis of the existence of a God creator in order to explain the development of the cosmos and the origin of life. What natural science has not shown and cannot show is that there is no such God.

In §22 Kanitscheider underscores that the arguments on behalf of a Platonist rendering of mathematics are the strongest ones against naturalism, since such mathematical entities would have an existence independent of the order of nature. In the third and last part of his paper Kanitscheider will propose a realist conception of mathematical entities that, in his opinion, ought to be compatible with his ideological naturalism. In the second part of his paper Kanitscheider offers a brief summary of research in the foundations of mathematics. We do not need to say here anything about this part of Kanitscheider's paper.

§3 Naturalism in Mathematics

The most important part of the paper we are here concerned with is the last one, in which Kanitscheider considers uncritically the mathematical naturalism of Quine and his school. Kanitscheider bases his discussion of mathematical Platonism in §36 on a description of set-theoretic Platonism given by Penelope Maddy. By the way, it should be emphasized that mathematical Platonism is not only independent of Frege's logicism but also of the reducibility of the whole of mathematics to set theory, thus, does not need to be a set-theoretical Platonism. In §37 Kanitscheider first discusses the opposition between mathematical Platonism and naturalism, sees, however, immediately some hope in what he calls "the newest development in mathematical physics". Kanitscheider appropriates an observation of Gödel on an analogy between mathematical intuition and ordinary perception, and renders it in a way that does not do justice to Gödel.[3] The reference to Gödel notwithstanding, at the end of §38 appears once more the ideological naturalism of Kanitscheider, when he asserts that somehow the abstract entities ought to be brought in connection with the neuronal system that thinks them.

In §41 Kanitscheider finally comes to Quine, whose philosophical opinions he uncritically accepts as a third dogma of empiricism. According to Kanitscheider, Quine has shown the indefensibility of the analytic-synthetic dichotomy, thus, that the radical separation of the mathematical part of a theory from its physicalist part is unsustainable, since only the whole theory can be empirically examined. According to this Quinean methodological holism, there is no qualitative difference between mathematical and empirical statements, and any statement of a theory is in principle revisable.

That Kanitscheider uncritically accepts Quine's so-called "naturalism", while seeing only the few advantages but not the many disadvantages of such a conception, can be seen with complete clarity from many assertions in §§ 42-43. According to him, "the Quine-Putnam version of mathematical ontology is the most economic and the only rendering compatible with naturalism". At the end of §42 Kanitscheider's uncritical acceptance of the present "received view" becomes evident when he speaks about the Duhem-Quine thesis.

In §44 Kanitscheider criticizes some philosophers of mathematics, criticisms with which we essentially coincide. At the end of the paragraph he quotes a letter from John Smart, in order to emphasize the great "discovery" of Quine that mathematical entities are not spiritual but physicalist objects. His ideological war against everything that could not be reduced to the natural sciences is especially evident in the first sentence of §45, which is based on

---

[3] There is a remark similar to Gödel's in Frege's 'Der Gedanke' 1918, in *Kleine Schriften*, edited by I. Angelleli, Georg Olms, Hildesheim 1967, 1990, pp. 342-362 – see p.360- though no one, as far as we know, has considered it related to naturalism.

Smart's remark, according to which, with the aid of Quine's conception "one can free the Platonic forms from their ghostly existence and put them in a respectable ontology" Similar observations are present in §47 and in §48.

§4 Critique of Quine's and Kanitscheider's Naturalism

Kanitscheider's whole discussion about mathematics presupposes an argument that the whole tradition from Quine, Putnam, Benacerraf, Field and Maddy considers as the only acceptable argument on behalf of mathematical realism, namely, the so-called "indispensability argument". According to this argument, mathematical objects ought somehow to exist, since the theories about them are applicable to physics and other natural sciences. We have offered a detailed critique of that argument in a 1996 paper[4] and will briefly say here only that such "foundation" of mathematical existence does not confirm the existence of mathematical entities that do not belong to the applicable parts of mathematics, for example, the existence of mathematical entities about which model theory or universal algebra purport to talk about. On the other hand, mathematical existence would be dependent on the development of the natural sciences. By the way, Kanitscheider himself acknowledges –see §46- that for the application to physics only the first two (or three) infinite cardinal numbers are necessary. Thus, the existence of an infinitely immense hierarchy of infinite cardinal numbers and the infinitely many mathematical structures with universes of such big cardinalities, with which model theory is concerned, could not prove their existence on the basis of their application to physics. In general: a mathematical object about which a mathematical theory speaks and whose existence it purports to prove –existence understood as mathematicians and Platonists understand it- could remain hundreds of years without "genuine

---

[4] See our 'On Antiplatonism and its Dogmas' 1996, reprint in Claire O. Hill and Guillermo E. Rosado Haddock, *Husserl or Frege?: Meaning, Objectivity and Mathematics*, Open Court, Chicago et al. 2000, 2003, pp. 163-189.

existence", until a physicist casually finds an application of such a mathematical theory. Then and only then would the mathematical entity be born. But even worse, it could also die, namely, in case a part of mathematics were applied in the past to the natural sciences, but beginning today would not be applicable anymore, the mathematical objects would "lose their mathematical lives". Such and similar nonsensical conclusions can be inferred from the only argument for mathematical realism that is acceptable to Quine and his followers.

I would like to point out here to the metamathematical fact that in mathematics there are statements, for example the Axiom of Choice or Tarski's Ultrafilter Theorem, which are mathematically equivalent with theorems from other parts of mathematics. In particular, the Axiom of Choice is equivalent to Tychonoff's Theorem on the product of compact topological spaces, and to almost one hundred statements in different areas of mathematics, whereas Tarski's Ultrafilter Theorem is equivalent, among others, to Tychonoff's Theorem applied to Hausdorff's spaces. Such mathematical results are completely inexplicable on the basis of mathematical naturalism, as also on the basis of any non-Platonist philosophy of mathematics –and even inexplicable on the basis of Frege's Platonism. In case Mr. Kanitscheider thinks otherwise, I would be glad to see a naturalist philosophical explanation of such metamathematical hard facts. Since a philosophy of mathematics that cannot philosophically explain such mathematical results does not deserve to be taken seriously.[5]

With respect to Quine's views there is a lot to be said. First of all, it should be pointed out that even in case his criticism of Carnap's distinction between analytic and synthetic statements is correct, it would be true only of Carnap's concept of "analyticity".[6] But Carnap's concept of "analyticity", even though it is presupposed by the whole tradition in Anglo American philosophy, is not the only one. As is well known, Frege defines analytically true statements in *Die Grundlagen*

---

[5] See our 'Interderivability of Seemingly unrelated Mathematical Statements and the Philosophy of Mathematics' 1992, reprint in Claire O. Hill and Guillermo E. Rosado Haddock, *Husserl or Frege?: Meaning, Objectivity and Mathematics*, pp. 141-152.
[6] See Quine's 'Two Dogmas of Empiricism' 1951, in W. O. Quine, *From a Logical Point of View*, Harvard University Press, Cambridge, Ma. 1953, pp. 20-46.

der Arithmetik as derivable from the logical laws.[7] Although Frege's concept of "analyticity" is a refinement of a proposal of Kant and Carnap's linguistic concept of "analyticity" has also a Kantian origin, the two determinations of "analyticity" in Kant are not equivalent and their heirs in Frege and Carnap have little in common. In particular, Frege would never consider analytic statements like "All unmarried men are bachelors". The connection between analytic, synonymy and meaning, which plays such an important role in Carnap, is non-existent in Frege. Of course, the collapse of Frege's logicism has disappeared Frege's concept of "analyticity". But besides Frege's there is at least another concept of "analyticity" deserving consideration that does not have any connection to the concepts of "synonymy" and "meaning", namely, Husserl's concept of "analyticity"[8], a concept not having roots in Kant but in Bolzano, and according to which analytically true statements are such that remain true when they are deprived of all their material content. Clearly, Husserl would not consider analytic statements like "All unmarried men are bachelors". Therefore, it should be stressed that Quine's critique is concerned only with a particular concept of "analyticity" and, hence, on its basis only Carnap's concept of "analyticity" could, in the best of cases, be shown to be incorrect.

With respect to Quine's holism, it should first be pointed out that it was introduced by Quine as an unfounded dogmatic "solution" to the difficulties in Carnap's views. Secondly, one should underscore that Quine's holism has little to do with Duhem's thesis.[9] Duhem's thesis is a very reasonable thesis applied only to physics, namely, that

---

[7] *Die Grundlagen der Arithmetik* 1884, Centenary Edition, edited by Christian Thiel, Felix Meiner, Hamburg 1986, §3, p. 15.

[8] *Logische Untersuchungen I & II*, 1900-1901, Hua XVII 1975 and XIX 1984, Martinus Nijhoff, Den Haag, U. III, §12, pp. 258-260,

[9] For Duhem's thesis see his *La Théorie Physique, son Objet, sa Structure* 1906, English translation, *The Aim and Structure of Physical Theory*, Princeton University Press, Princeton 1954, 1990, as also his papers 'Quelques réflexions au sujet de la physique expérimentale' 1894, and 'Examen logique de la théorie physique' 1913, translated into English in the collection of his papers *Essays on the History and Philosophy of Science*, edited by Roger Ariew and Peter Baker, Hackett, Indianapolis et al. 1996, pp. 75-111 and 232-238. See also Chapter Five of Donald Gillies *Philosophy of Science in the Twentieth Century*, Oxford, Blackwell 1993.

in physics one cannot isolate hypotheses in order to examine its empirical content, since in order to produce the experiment one has to make use of other physical hypotheses and laws, which are at the basis of the construction of the instruments used in the experiment. Such a Duhemian thesis is not concerned with other natural sciences and certainly not with the whole web of belief. In particular, Duhem does not say anything about a connection of logical and mathematical statements with those of biology or of ordinary life.[10] On the contrary, Quine's holism –according to which our statements, from those of ordinary life to those of logic, are all interconnected in a web, all on the same level, only some nearer to the center of the web of belief-, is a metaphysical thesis on the same level as historical materialism and astrology. In fact, Quine's holism contradicts the multi-secular procedure in the natural sciences. As Mr. Kanitscheider, who is a natural philosopher, very well knows, in physics one proceeds by isolating some systems –for example, the solar system- and studies its laws with complete independence of what happens away from the system, let us say, on other stars. One should very especially point out here to the fact, very well known by Mr. Kanitscheider, that the successful development of the two presently most important physical theories, general relativity and quantum mechanics has been possible because they have ignored each other.

Quine's holism has very little to do with the sound naturalism of the natural scientist. On the contrary, it can be correctly considered as a support for postmodernism and other sorts of irrationalism and relativism. Kanitscheider's uncritical adhesion to such a questionable conception in order to give support to his ideological naturalism is an attempt to base a serious, though not necessarily correct interpretation of the results of the natural sciences, on a theoretical swamp. It is much more reasonable to let the natural sciences, but also the deductive sciences, speak for themselves. It is classical mathematics the one that tells us what is mathematically existent, not the ideologies of a natural philosopher, but also not the possible applications to no matter which

---

[10] In the first of the two papers mentioned above there is an isolated paragraph, which could possibly give some support to Quine's rendering, though it is not easily reconcilable with the rest of the paper. See pp. 84-85.

natural science. That ultraproducts and inaccessible cardinal numbers exist –as existence is understood by classical mathematics- has nothing to do with ghosts or Gods. And in such sense ultraproducts exist, independently of whether human beings with their theories, the cosmos or a God exist.

Bibliography

Awodey, Steve & Klein, Carsten (eds.) – *Carnap Brought Home*, Open Court, Chicago et al. 2004
Barwise, Jon & Perry, John – 'Semantic Innocence and Uncompromising Situations', in Peter A. French et al. (eds.), *The Foundations of Analytic* Philosophy, Vol 6 of *Midwest Studies in Philosophy*, University of Minnesota Press, Minneapolis 1981, pp. 387-403
Beaney, Michael – 'Carnap's Conception of Explication: from Frege to Husserl', In Steve Awoodey and Carsten Klein (eds.), pp. 117-150
Bell, David & Vossenkuhl, Wilhelm (eds.) – *Wissenschaft und Subjektivität*, Akademie Verlag, Berlin 1992
Benacerraf, Paul & Putnam, Hilary (eds.) – *Philosophy of Mathematics*, revised edition, Cambridge University Press, Cambridge 1983
Beth, E. W. – *The Foundations of Mathematics*, North Holland, Amsterdam 1965
Bolzano, Bernard – *Grundlegung der Logik*, selected sections from volumes 1 and 2 of his *Wissenschaftslehre*, Felix Meiner, Hamburg 1963, revised edition 1978
Bonk, Thomas (ed.) – *Language, Truth and Logic*, Kluwer, Dordrecht 2003
Bourbaki, Nicholas – 'Foundations of Mathematics for the Working Mathematician', *Journal of Symbolic Logic 14 (4)*, 1949, pp. 1-8
Bourbaki, Nicholas – 'The Architecture of Mathematics', *American Mathematical Monthly 57*, 1950, pp. 221-232
Cantor, Georg – *Abhandlungen mathematischen und philosophischen Inhalts*, Georg Olms, Hildesheim 1966
Carnap, Rudolf – *Der Raum*, *Kant-Studien* (Ergänzungsheft 56) 1922, reprint, Topos Verlag, Vaduz 1991
Carnap, Rudolf – *Der logische Aufbau der Welt* 1928, second edition, Felix Meiner, Hamburg 1961, fourth edition 1974
Carnap, Rudolf – 'Überwindung der Metaphysik durch logische Analyse der Sprache' 1932, reprinted in *Scheinprobleme in der Philosophie und andere metaphysikkritische Aufsätze*, Felix Meiner, Hamburg 2004, pp. 81-109

Carnap, Rudolf – *Logische Syntax der Sprache* 1934, enlarged English edition, *The Logical Syntax of Language*, Routledge, London 1937
Carnap, Rudolf – *Meaning and Necessity*, The University of Chicago Press, Chicago 1947, enlarged edition 1956
Carnap, Rudolf – 'Meaning Postulates' 1952, reprinted as Appendix 2 in the enlarged edition of *Meaning and Necessity*, pp. 222-229
Carnap, Rudolf – *Logical Foundations of Probability*, University of Chicago Press 1950
Carnap, Rudolf – 'Intellectual Autobiography', in Paul A. Schilpp (ed.), *The Philosophy of Rudolf Carnap*, pp. 3-84
Carnap, Rudolf – 'Replies and Systematic Expositions', in Paul A. Schilpp (ed.), *The Philosophy of Rudolf Carnap*, pp. 859-1013
Carnap, Rudolf – *Philosophical Foundations of Physics*, Basic Books, New York 1966
Carnap, Rudolf – *Tagebücher 1908-1935*, http://homepage.univie.ac.at/christian.damboeck/carnap_diaries2015-2018/diaries_1908-1935_transcriptions_2015.pdf
Castoriadis, Cornelius – *La Societé Bureaucratique* (2 vols.), Union Générale d'Éditions, Paris 1973
Cederberg, J. – *A Course in Modern Geometries* 1989, reprint, Springer, New York et al. 2001
Centrone, Stefania – 'Husserl on the 'Totality of all conceivable arithmetical operations'', *History and Philosophy of Logic 27 (3)*, 2006, pp. 211-228
Centrone, Stefania – *Logic and Philosophy of Mathematics in the Early Husserl*, Springer 2010
Chang, C. C. & Keisler, H. J. – *Model Theory* 1974, revised edition, North Holland, Amsterdam 1990
Chateaubriand, Oswaldo – *Logical Forms* (2 vols.), Centro de Lógica, Epistemologia e Historia da Ciencia, Campinas, 2001 (I) and 2005 (II)
Church, Alonzo – *Introduction to Mathematical Logic*, Princeton University Press, Princeton 1944, enlarged edition 1956
Cirera, Ramón, Ibarra, Andoni & Mormann, Thomas (eds.) – *El Programa de Carnap*, C. E. L. C., Barcelona 1996
Cohen, Robert – 'Dialectical Materialism and Carnap's Logical Empiricism', in Paul A. Schilpp (ed.), *The Philosopohy of Rudolf Carnap*, pp. 99-158

Bibliography

Coleman, Robert & Korté, Herbert – 'Hermann Weyl: Mathematician, Physicist, Philosopher', in Erhard Scholz (ed.), *Hermann Weyls Raum-Zeit-Materie and a General Introduction to his Scientific Work*, pp. 161-386

Coletti, Lucio – *Il Marxismo e Hegel*, Laterza, Roma 1973

Confort, W. W. & Negrepontis, S. – *The Theory of Ultrafilters*, Springer, New York et al. 1978

da Silva, Jairo J. – 'The Many Senses of Completeness', *Manuscrito 23 (2)*, 2000, pp. 41-60, reprinted in Hill & da Silva, *The Road Not Taken*, pp. 137-150

da Silva, Jairo J. – 'Husserl's Two Notions of Completeness, Husserl and Hilbert on Completeness and Imaginary Elements', *Synthese 120*, 2010, pp. 417-438, reprinted in Hill & da Silva, *The Road Not Taken*, pp. 115-136

Dathe, Uwe – 'Eine Ergänzung zur Biographie Edmund Husserls', in Werner Stelzner (ed.), *Philosophie und Logik*, Walter de Gruyter, Berlin 1993, pp. 160-163

Descartes, René – *Meditationes de prima philosophia* 1641, reprint with parallel German translation, Felix Meiner, Hamburg 1959, English translation, Hackett, Indianapolis 1951

Diederich, Werner – *Konventionalität in der Physik*, Druckner & Humboldt, Berlin 1974

Dugundji, James – *Topology*, Allyn and Bacon, Boston 1966, ninth printing 1974

Duhem, Pierre – *La Théorie Physique, son Objet, sa Structure* 1914, English translation, *The Aim and Structure of Physical Theory*, Princeton University Press, Princeton 1955, 1991

Duhem, Pierre – 'Some Reflections on the Subject of Experimental Physics', French original, 1894, translated in his *Essays in the History and Philosophy of Science*, pp. 75-111

Duhem, Pierre – *Essays in the History and Philosophy of Science*, edited by Roger Ariew and Peter Baker, Hackett, Indianapolis 1996

Einstein, Albert – 'Geometrie und Erfahrung', *Preussische Akademie der Wissenschaften*, Sitzungsberichte I, 1918, translation in Albert Einstein, *Sidelights of Relativity*, Dover, New York 1921

Field, Hartry – *Science without Numbers*, B. H. Blackwell, Oxford 1980

Field, Hartry – 'Realism and Antirealism about Mathematics', in H. Field, *Realism, Mathematics and Modality*, B. H. Blackwell, Oxford 1989

Føllesdal, Dagfinn – *Husserl und Frege, ein Beitrag zur Beleuchtung der phänomenologischen Philosophie* 1958, English translation in L. Haaparanta (ed.), *Mind, Meaning and Mathematics*, Kluwer, Dordrecht 1994, pp. 3-47

Follesdal, Dagfinn – 'Husserl's Concept of Noema', *Journal of Philosophy 66 (20)*, 1969, pp. 680-697

Føllesdal, Dagfinn – 'Gödel and Husserl', in Jaakko Hintikka (ed.), *From Dedekind to Gödel*, Dordrecht, Kluwer 1995, pp. 427-446

Føllesdal, Dagfinn, Mohanty, J. N. and Seebohm, Thomas (eds.) – *Phenomenology and the Formal Sciences*, Kluwer, Dordrecht 1991

Frege, Gottlob – *Begriffsschrift* 1879, reprint, Georg Olms, Hildesheim 1964

Frege, Gottlob – *Die Grundlagen der Arithmetik* 1884, Centenarausgabe, with an Introduction by Christian Thiel, Felix Meiner, Hamburg 1986

Frege, Gottlob – 'Funktion und Begriff' 1891, reprinted in *Kleine Schriften*, pp. 125-142

Frege, Gottlob – 'Über Sinn und Bedeutung' 1892, reprint in Gottlob Frege, *Kleine Schriften*, pp. 143-162

Frege, Gottlob – *Grundgesetze der Arithmetik I* 1893, *II* 1903, reprinted in one volume, Georg Olms, Hildesheim 1962

Frege, Gottlob – 'Rezension von E. G. Husserl, *Philosophie der Arithmetik I*', 1894, reprinted in *Kleine Schriften*, pp. 179-192

Frege, Gottlob – 'Kritische Beleuchtung einiger Punkte in E. Schröders *Vorlesungen über die Algebra der Logik*', 1895, reprinted in *Kleine Schriften*, pp. 193-210

Frege, Gottlob – 'Der Gedanke' 1918, reprinted in *Kleine Schriften*, pp. 342-362

Frege, Gottlob – *Kleine Schriften*, edited by Ignacio Angelelli, 1967, revised edition, Georg Olms, Hildesheim 1990

Frege, Gottlob – *Nachgelassene Schriften* 1969, revised edition, Felix Meiner, Hamburg 1983

Frege, Gottlob – 'Ausführungen über Sinn und Bedeutung', in *Nachgelassene Schriften*, pp. 128-136

Frege, Gottlob – 'Über euklidische Geometrie', in *Nachgelassene Schriften*, pp. 182-184
Frege, Gottlob – *Wissenschaftlicher Briefwechsel*, Felix Meiner, Hamburg 1974
Frege, Gottlob – 'Brief an Husserl vom 24ten Mai 1891', in *Wissenschftlicher Briefwechsel*, pp. 94-98
French, Peter A., Uehling, Theodore E. & Wettstein, Howard (ed.) – *the Foundations of Analytic Philosophy*, Vol. 6 of *Midwest Studies in Philosophy*, University of Minnesota Press, Minneapolis 1981
Friedman, Michael – *Kant and the Exact Sciences*, Harvard University Press, Cambridge, Ma. 1992
Friedman, Michael – 'Carnap and Weyl on the Foundations of Geometry', *Erkenntnis 42*, 1995, pp. 247-260, reprint of the whole number in U. Majer and H.J. Schmidt (eds.) – *Reflections on Spacetime*, Kluwer, Dordrecht et al 1995
Friedman, Michael – *Reconsidering Logical Positivism*, Cambridge University Press, Cambridge 1999
Friedman, Michael – *A Parting of the Ways*, Open Court, Chicago et al. 2000
Friedman, Michael – *Dynamics of Reason*, University of Chicago Press, Chicago 2001
Gabbay, D & Guenther, F. (eds.) – *Handbook of Philosophical Logic I*, Kluwer, Dordrecht 1983
Gillies, Donald – *Philosophy of Science in the Twentieth Century*, Blackwell, Oxford 1993
Gödel, Kurt – 'Über formal unentscheidbare Sätze der *Principia Mathematica* und verwandter Systeme' 1931, reprinted with English translation in Kurt Gödel, *Collected Works I*, Oxford University Press, Oxford 1986, pp. 144-195
Gödel, Kurt – 'Russell's mathematical logic', in Kurt Gödel, *Collected Works II*, pp. 119-141
Gödel, Kurt – 'Some basic theorems on the foundations of mathematics and its implications', in Kurt Gödel, *Collected Works III*, pp. 304-323
Gödel, Kurt – 'Is mathematics syntax of language?', in Kurt Gödel, *Collected Works III*, pp. 334-356 (version III), 356-362 (version V)

Gödel, Kurt – *Collected Works* (5 vols.), Oxford University Press, Oxford 1986-2003

Grätzer, George – *Universal Algebra* 1968, revised edition, Springer, New York et al. 1978

Greenberg, Marvin Jay – *Euclidean and Non-Euclidean geometries*, W. H. Freeman, San Francisco 1973

Greimann, Dirk – *Freges Konzeption der Wahrheit*, Georg Olms, Hildesheim 2003

Griffin, N. – Editor's Introduction to *The Cambridge Companion to Russell*, Cambridge University Press, Cambridge 2003

Gruber, Monika – *Alfred Tarski and the 'Concept of Truth in Formalized Languages'*, Springer, Switzerland 2016

Grünbaum, Adolf – 'Carnap's Views on the Foundations of Geometry', in Paul A. Schilpp (ed.), *The Philosophy of Rudolf Carnap*, pp. 599-684

Hahn, Hans, Neurath Otto & Carnap, Rudolf – *Wissenschftliche Weltauffassung: Der Wienerkreis*, Arthur Wolf, Wien 1929

Halmos Paul – *Measure Theory* 1950, reprint, Springer, New York et al. 1974

Hartimo, Mirja (ed.) - *Phenomenology and Mathematics*, Springer, Heidelberg et al. 2010

Hauser, Kai – 'Gödel's Program Revisited: Part I: The Turn to Phenomenology', *The Bulletin of Symbolic Logic 12 (4)*, December 2006, pp. 529-590

Hegel, Georg W. F. – *Wissenschaft der Logik I* 1812, *II* 1813, second edition 1834, reprint, Felix Meiner Hamburg 1967 (*I*) and 1969 (*II*)

Hilbert, David – *Die Grundlagen der Geometrie* 1899, tenth edition, Teubner, Stuttgart 1968

Hill, Claire O. & Rosado Haddock, Guillermo E. – *Husserl or Frege: Meaning, Objectivity and Mathematics*, Open Court, Chicago et al. 2000, 2003

Hill, Claire O. & da Silva, Jairo J. – *The Road Not Taken*, College Publications 2013

Hirsch, Moritz – *Differential Topology*, Springer, New York et al. 1976

Hodges, Wilfrid – 'Elementary Logic', in D. Gabbay & F. Guenther (eds.), *Handbook of Philosophical Logic I*, Kluwer, Dordrecht 1983, pp. 1-131

Husserl, Edmund – *Über den Begriff der Zahl* 1887, reprinted as Appendix A in Hua XII, pp. 289-339

Husserl, Edmund – *Philosophie der Arithmetik* 1891, Hua XII 1970, Martinus Nijhoff, Den Haag

Husserl, Edmund – 'Zur Logik der Zeichen' (1890), Appendix B.(I) to *Philosophie der Arithmetik*, Hua XII, 1970, pp. 340-373

Husserl, Edmund – 'Besprechung von E. Schröders *Vorlesungen über die Algebra der Logik I*' 1891, reprinted in Edmund Husserl, *Aufsätze und Rezensionen 1890-1910*, Hua XXII 1979, pp. 3-43

Husserl, Edmund – *Logische Untersuchungen I* 1900 & *II* 1901, Hua XVIII 1975 & XIX 1984, Martinus Nijhoff, Den Haag

Husserl, Edmund – *Ideen zu einer reinen Phänomenologie und phänomenologischen Philosophie I* 1913, Hua III, 1950, revised edition, Martinus Nijhoff, Den Haag 1976

Husserl, Edmund – *Cartesianische Meditationen* 1928, Hua I, Martinus Nijhoff, Den Haag 1950

Husserl, Edmund – *Formale und transzendentale Logik* 1929, Hua XVII, Martinus Nijhoff, Den Haag 1974

Husserl, Edmund – *Erfahrung und Urteil* 1939, sixth edition, Felix Meiner, Hamburg 1985

Husserl, Edmund – *Ideen zu einer reinen Phänomenologie und phänomenologischen Philosophie II*, Hua IV, Martinus Nijhoff, Den Haag 1952

Husserl, Edmund – *Zur Phänomenologie der Intersubjektivität* (three vols.), Hua XIII-XV, Martinus Nijhoff, Den Haag 1973

Husserl, Edmund – *Introduction to the Logical Investigations*, Martinus Nijhoff, Den Haag 1975

Husserl, Edmund – *Aufsätze und Rezensionen 1890-1910*, Hua XXII, Martinus Nijhoff, Den Haag 1979

Husserl, Edmund – *Studien zur Arithmetik und Geometrie*, Hua XXI, Martinus Nijhoff, Den Haag 1983

Husserl, Edmund – *Einleitung in die Logik und Erkenntnistheorie*, Hua XXIV, Martinus Nijhoff, Den Haag 1984

Husserl, Edmund – *Vorlesungen über Bedeutungslehre*, Hua XXVI, Martinus Nijhoff, Den Haag 1987
Husserl, Edmund – *Briefwechsel* (10 vols.), Kluwer, Dordrecht 1994
Husserl, Edmund – *Logik und allgemeine Wissenschaftstheorie*, Hua XXX, Kluwer, Dordrecht 1996
Husserl, Edmund – *Logik Vorlesung 1896*, edited by Elisabeth Schuhmann, Kluwer, Dordrecht 2001
Husserl, Edmund – *Alte und Neue Logik: Vorlesungen 1908/09*, edited by Elisabeth Schuhmann, Kluwer, Dordrecht 2003
Husserl, Edmund – *Gesammelte Schriften Edmund Husserls* (8 vols.), Felix Meiner, Hamburg 1992
Iovino, José – *Applications of Model Theory to Functional Analysis*, Dover, Mineola, New York 2014
Irvine, A. D. (ed.) – *Physicalism in Mathematics*, Dordrecht, Kluwer 1980
Kant, Immanuel – *Kritik der reinen Vernunft* 1781, revised edition 1787, reprint of both editions, Felix Meiner, Hamburg 1930, third edition 1990
Kelley, John L. – *General Topology*, D. van Nostrand, Princeton, New Jersey 1955
Kolakowski, L. – *Main Currents of Marxism*, vol. 3, Oxford University Press, Oxford 1978
Kragh, H. – *Quantum Generations*, Princeton University Press, Princeton 1999
Kreiser, Lothar – *Gottlob Frege: Leben, Werk, Zeit*, Felix Meiner, Hamburg 2001
Kripke, Saul – 'Naming and Necessity', in D. Davidson and G. H. Harman (eds.), *Semantics of Natural Language*, Reidel, Dordrecht 1972, enlarged edition, Blackwell, Oxford 1980
Kripke, Saul – 'Identity and Necessity', in Stephen P. Schwartz (ed.), *Naming, Necessity and Natural Kinds*, Cornell University Press 1977, pp. 66-101
Kuhn, Thomas – *The Structure of Scientific Revolutions*, University of Chicago Press 1962, expanded second edition 1970
Lefort, Claude – *Éléments d'une Critique de la Bureaucratie*, Librairie Droz, Genève and Paris 1971

Leibniz, Gottfried W. – *Allgemeine Untersuchungen über die Analyse der Begriffe und Wahrheiten*, bilingual edition Latin-German, edited by Franz Schupp, Felix Meiner, Hamburg 1982
Lesniewski, Stanislaw – *Collected Works I*, Kluwer, Dordrecht et al. 1992
Lindström, Per – 'On Characterizing Elementary Logic', in Sören Stenlund (ed.), *Logical Theory and Semantic Analysis*, Reidel, Dordrecht 1974, pp. 129-146
Maddy, Penelope – 'Physicalistic Platonism', in Irvine (ed.), *Physicalism in Mathematics*, pp. 259-289
Maddy, Penelope – *Realism in Mathematics*, Oxford University Press, Oxford
Majer, Ulrich – 'Husserl and Hilbert on Completeness: A Neglected Chapter in Early Twentieth Century Foundations of Mathematics', *Synthese 110*, 1997, pp. 37-56
Majer, Ulrich & Schmidt, H. J. (eds.) – *Reflections on Spacetime*, Kluwer, Dordrecht et al. 1995
Mancosu, P. & Ryckman, T. A. – 'Mathematics and Phenomenology: The Correspondence between O. Becker and H. Weyl', *Philosophia Mathematica 10 (2)*, 2002, pp. 130-202
Manzano, María – *Extensions of First Order Logic*, Cambridge University Press, Cambridge 1996
Mayer, Verena – 'Die Konstruktion der Erfahrungswelt: Carnap und Husserl', in W. Spohn (ed.), *Erkenntnis Orientated 1991, pp. 287-303*
Mayer, Verena – *'Carnap und Husserl'*, in D. Bell and W. Vossenkuhl (eds.), *Wissenschaft und Subjektivität* 1992, pp. 181-205
Mayer, Verena – 'Der Logische Aufbau als Plagiat', in Guillermo E. Rosado Haddock (ed.), *Husserl and Analytic Philosophy*, pp. 175-260
Mohanty, J. N. – *The Philosophy of Edmund Husserl* (2 vols.), Yale University Press, New Haven 2008 (I) and 2011 (II)
Morman, Thomas – *Rudolf Carnap*, C. H. Beck, München 2000
Mormann, Thomas – 'Carnap's Metrical Conventionalism versus Differential Geometry', Proceedings of the 2004 Biennial meeting of the Philosophy of Science Association, vol. 1, pp. 814-825
Moulines, Carlos Ulises – 'Las Raíces Epistemológicas del Aufbau de Carnap', in Ramón Cirera, Andoni Ibarra and Thomas Mormann (eds.), *El Programa de Carnap*, pp. 45-74

Paton, Herbert J. – *Kant's Metaphysics of Experience* (2 vols.), Allen and Unwin, London 1936
Pesic, Peter – *Beyond Geometry*, Dover, New York 2007
Pierce, Richard S. – *Introduction to the Theory of Abstract Algebras* 1968, reprint, Dover, New York 2014
Poincaré, Henri – *La Science et l'Hypothèse* 1902, reprint, Flammarion, Paris 1968
Potter, Michael & Ricketts, Tom (eds.) – *The Cambridge Companion to Frege*, Cambridge University Press, Cambridge 2010
Putnam, Hilary – 'Models and Reality', in *Journal of Symbolic Logic 45*, 1980, reprinted in P. Benacerraf & H. Putnam (eds.), *Philosophy of Mathematics*, revised edition, Cambridge University Press 1983, pp. 421-444
Quine, Willard van Orman – 'On what there is' 1948, reprinted in *From a Logical Point of View*, pp. 1-19
Quine, Willard van Orman – 'Two Dogmas of Empiricism' 1951, reprinted in *From a Logical Point of View*, pp. 20-46
Quine, Willard van Orman – *From a Logical Point of View*, Harvard University Press, Cambridge, Ma. 1953
Quine, Willard van Orman – *Word and Object*, MIT Press, Cambridge, Ma. 1960
Reichenbach, Hans – *Relativitätstheorie und Erkenntnis a priori* 1920, English translation, *The Theory of Relativity and a priori Knowledge*, University of California Press, Berkeley 1965
Resnik, Michael D. (ed.) – *Mathematical Objects and Mathematical Knowledge*, Dartmouth Publishing Co., Aldershot et al.
Richardson, Alan – *Carnap's Construction of the World*, Cambridge University Press, Cambridge 1998
Riemann, Bernhard – *Über die Hypothesen welche der Geometrie zugrunde liegen* 1867, third edition, Berlin 1923, reprint, Chelsea, New York 1960
Rosado Haddock, Guillermo E. – *Edmund Husserls Philosophie der Logik und Mathematik im Lichte der gegenwärtigen Logik und Grundlagenforschung* (Diss.), Bonn 1973
Rosado Haddock, Guillermo E. – 'Necessità *a posteriori* e Contingenze *a priori*: alcune Note Critiche', *Nominazione 2* 1981 (in Italian), revised English version in *Against the Current*, pp. 285-301

Rosado Haddock, Guillermo E. 'Remarks on Sense and Reference in Frege and Husserl' *Kant Studien 73 (4)* 1982, reprinted in Claire O. Hill and Guillermo E. Rosado Haddock, *Husserl or Frege*, pp. 23-40
Rosado Haddock, Guillermo E. – 'Identity Statements in the Semantics of Sense and Reference', *Logique et Analyse 25 (100)* 1982, reprinted in Hill and Rosado Haddock, pp. 41-51
Rosado Haddock, Guillermo E. – 'On Frege's Two Notions of Sense', *History and Philosophy of Logic 7 (1)* 1986, reprinted in Claire O. Hill and Guillermo E. Rosado Haddock, *Husserl or Frege,* pp. 53-66
Rosado Haddock, Guillermo E. – 'Husserl's Epistemology of Mathematics and the Foundation of Platonism in Mathematics', *Husserl Studies 4 (2)* 1987, reprinted in Claire O. Hill and Guillermo E. Rosado Haddock, pp. 121-139
Rosado Haddock, Guillermo E. – 'On Husserl's Distinction between State of Affairs (Sachverhalt) and Situation of Affairs (Sachlage)', in D. Føllesdal, J. N. Mohanty Th. M. & Seebohm (eds.), *Phenomenology and the Formal Sciences*, pp. 35-48, reprinted in Claire O. Hill and Guillermo E. Rosado Haddock, *Husserl or Frege*, pp. 253-262
Rosado Haddock, Guillermo E. – 'Interderivability of Seemingly Unrelated Mathematical Statements and the Philosophy of Mathematics' *Diálogos 59* 1992, reprinted in Claire O. Hill and Guillermo E. Rosado Haddock, *Husserl or Frege*, pp. 241-252
Rosado Haddock, Guillermo E. – 'On Antiplatonism and its Dogmas' *Diálogos 67* 1996, reprinted in Claire O. Hill and Guillermo E. Rosado Haddock, *Husserl or Frege*, pp. 263-289
Rosado Haddock, Guillermo E. – 'On the Semantics of Mathematical Statements', *Manuscrito XIX (1)* 1996, reprinted in *Manuscrito XXX (2)* 2007 and in *Against the Current*, pp. 399-418
Rosado Haddock, Guillermo E. – 'To be a Fregean or to be a Husserlian: that is the Question for Platonists', in Walter A. Carnielli and M. L. D. d'Ottaviano (ed.), *Advances in Contemporary Logic and Computer Science*, American Mathematical Society series *Contemporary Mathematics*, Vol. 235, Providence, Rhode Island 1999, reprinted in Claire O. Hill and Guillermo E. Rosado Haddock, pp. 199-220 and in D. Moran and L. Embree (eds.), *Phenomenology*, Vol. 3, Routledge 2004

Rosado Haddock, Guillermo E. – *A Critical Introduction to the Philosophy of Gottlob Frege*, Ashgate, Aldershot 2006
Rosado Haddock, Guillermo E. – 'Husserl's Philosophy of Mathematics: its Origin and Relevance', *Husserl Studies 22*, 2006, reprinted in *Against the Current*, pp. 145-181
Rosado Haddock, Guillermo E. – 'Kritische Fußnoten zu Bernulf Kanitscheiders Naturalismus Aufsatz', *Erwägen, Wissen, Ethik 17 (3)*, 2006, reprinted in this volume
Rosado Haddock, Guillermo E. – 'Why and How Platonism?', in *Journal of the Interest Group in Pure and Applied Logic 15 (5/6)*, 2007, reprinted in *Against the Current*, pp. 341-364
Rosado Haddock, Guillermo E. – 'Issues in the Philosophy of Logic: a Heterodox Approach', in *Principia 11 (1)*, 2007, reprinted in *Against the Current*, pp. 305-325
Rosado Haddock, Guillermo E. – 'Critical Study of Oswaldo Chateaubriand's *Logical Forms I* and *Logical Forms II*, in *Manuscrito 30*, pp. 185-218, reprinted in this volume
Rosado Haddock, Guillermo E. – *The Young Carnap's Unknown Master*, Ashgate, Aldershot 2008
Rosado Haddock, Guillermo E. – 'Husserl on Analyticity and Beyond', *Husserl Studies 24*, 2008, reprinted in *Against the Current*, pp. 327-339
Rosado Haddock, Guillermo E. – 'Platonsism, Phenomenology and Interderivability', in Mirja Hartimo (ed.), *Phenomenology and Mathematics*, pp. 23-46, reprinted in *Against the Current*, pp. 235-259
Rosado Haddock, Guillermo E. – 'Some Uses of Logic in Rigorous Philosophy', *Axiomathes 20 (2-3)* 2010, reprinted in *Against the Current*, pp. 365-383
Rosado Haddock, Guillermo E. – 'Husserl's Conception of Physical Theories and Physical Geometry in the Time of the Prolegomena', *Axiomathes 22* 2012, reprinted in *Against the Current*, pp. 183-214
Rosado Haddock, Guillermo E. – *Against the Current*, Ontos Verlag, Frankfurt 2012
Rosado Haddock, Guillermo E. 'On the Interpretation of Frege's Philosophy', in *Against the Current*, pp. 21-62
Rosado Haddock, Guillermo E. – 'On the Interpretation of the Young Carnap's Philosophy', in *Against the Current*, pp. 261-284

Rosado Haddock, Guillermo E. – 'On First- and Second-Order Logic', in *Against the Current*, pp. 385-398
Rosado Haddock, Guillermo E. (ed.) – *Husserl and Analytic Philosophy*, Walter de Gruyter, Berlin 2016
Rosado Haddock, Guillermo E. – 'The Old Husserl and the Young Carnap', first published in Guillermo E. Rosado Haddock (ed.), *Husserl and Analytic Philosophy*, pp. 261-286, and reprinted in this volume
Rungaldier, Edmund – *Carnap's Early Conventionalism*, Rodopi, Amsterdam 1984
Russell, Bertrand – *Foundations of Geometry* 1897, reprint, Dover, New York 1956
Russell, Bertrand – *Principles of Mathematics* 1903, second edition, Allen & Unwin, London 1937
Russell, Bertrand – *Our Knowledge of the External World* 1914, revised edition, 1926, fifth printing, Allen and Unwin, London 1969
Sarkar, Sahotra – 'Husserl's Role in Carnap's *Der Raum*', in Thomas Bonk (ed.), *Language, Truth and Logic*, pp. 179-190
Schilpp, Paul A. (ed.) – *The Philosophy of Rudolf Carnap*, Open Court, la Salle et al. 1963
Schirn, Matthias (ed.) – *Studien zu Frege* (3 vols.), Fromann-Bad Canstatt 1976
Schirn, Matthias (ed.) – *Frege: Importance and Legacy*, Walter de Gruyter, Berlin 1996
Schlick, Moritz – *Allgemeine Erkenntnislehre* 1916, third revised edition 1925, English translation of the third edition, Open Court, La Salle 1985
Scholz, Erhard (ed.) – *Hermann Weyls Raum-Zeit-Materie and a General Introduction to his Scientific Work*, Birkhäuser, Basel et al. 2001
Schuhmann, Karl – *Husserl-Chronik*, Martinus Nijhoff, Den Haag 1977
Sepp, Hans Rainer – *Edmund Husserl und die phänomenologische Bewegung*, second edition, Karl Alber 1988
Simpson, Stephen G. – 'The Gödel Hierarchy and Reverse Mathematics', in Charles Parsons, Solomon Feferman and Stephen G.

Simpson (eds.), *Kurt Gödel: Essays for his Centennial*, Cambridge University Press, Cambridge 2010, pp. 109-127

Sklar, Lawrence – *Space, Time and Spacetime*, University of California Press, Berkeley 1974

Sluga, Hans – *Gottlob Frege*, Routledge, London 1980

Smith, David W. – *Husserl*, Routledge, London 2007

Spohn, Wolfgang (ed.) – *Erkenntnis Orientated*, Kluwer, Dordrecht 1991

Stenlund, Sören (ed.) – *Logical Theory and Semantic Analysis*, Reidel Dordrecht 1974

Ströker, Elizabeth – *Husserls Werk: Zur Ausgabe der Gesammelten Schriften: Register*, published with the *Gesammelte Schriften Edmund Husserls*, Felix Meiner, Hamburg 1992

Tappenden, Jamie – 'Geometry and Generality in Frege's Philosophy of Arithmetic', *Synthese 102 (3)*, 1995, pp. 319-361

Tappenden, Jamie – 'The Riemannian Background of Frege's Philosophy', in José Ferreiros and Jeremy Gray (eds.), *The Architecture of Modern Mathematics*, Oxford University Press, Oxford 2006, pp. 97-132

Tarski, Alfred – 'Der Wahrheitsbegriff in den formalisierten Sprachen' (expanded version of the Polish 1933 original), English translation from the German version, 'The Concept of Truth in Formalized Languages', in Alfred Tarski, *Logic, Semantics, Metamathematics* 1956, second edition, Hackett, Indianapolis 1983

Thron, Wolfgang J. - *Topological Structures*, Holt, Rinehart and Winston, New York et al. 1966

Tieszen, Richard – 'Gödel's Path from the Incompleteness Theorems (1931) to Phenomenology (1961)', *The Bulletin of Symbolic Logic 4 (2)*, June 1998, pp. 181-203

Torretti, Roberto – *Philosophy of Geometry from Riemann to Poincaré*, Reidel, Dordrecht 1977

van Atten, Mark & Kennedy, Juliette – 'On the Philosophical Development of Kurt Gödel', *The Bulletin of Symbolic Logic 9 (4)*, December 2003, pp. 425-476,

von Helmholtz, Hermann – 'Über die Tatsachen, die der Geometrie zum Grunde liegen' 1868, translation in Pesic (ed.), *Beyond Geometry*, pp. 47-52

Wang, Hao – *Reflections on Kurt Gödel*, MIT Press, Cambridge, Ma. 1987

Wang, Hao – *A Logical Journey*, MIT Press, Cambridge, Ma. 1996

Weidemann, Hermann – 'Aussagesatz und Sachverhalt: ein Versuch zur Neubegründung ihres Verhältnisses', *Grazer Philosophische Studien 18*, 1982, pp. 75-99

Weyl, Hermann – *Raum-Zeit-Materie* 1918, English translation of the fourth edition, Dover, New York 1952

Wittgenstein, Ludwig – *Logisch-philosophische Abhandlung* 1921, English translation, *Tractatus Logico-Philosophicus* 1922, third bilingual edition, Routledge, London 1966

Wolenski, Jan – 'Analytic vs Synthetic and a Priori vs A Posteriori', in I. Niniluoto, M. Sintonen and J. Wolenski (eds.), Handbook of Epistemology, Kluwer, Dordrecht 2004, pp. 781-839

Wright, Crispin – *Frege's Conception of Numbers as Objects*, Aberdeen, Aberdeen University Press 1983

Name Index

Acock, Malcolm 238
Adjukiewicz, Kasimierz 130, 199
Adorno, Theodor W. 369
Alemán, Anastasio 9, 386, 403-412, 416-417
Angelelli, Ignacio 15, 28-29, 145, 148, 160, 163-64, 235, 237, 458
Ariew, Roger 84, 95, 101, 193, 197, 467
Aristotle 116, 221, 321-322
Avenarius, Richard 91, 167-168, 180-181, 361, 363, 365
Awodey, Steve 192, 196
Baker, Peter 84, 95, 101, 193, 197, 467
Balzer, Wolfgang 373
Barwise, Jon 301, 303, 325
Bauch, Bruno 91, 171-172, 175, 183, 189, 331, 353-354
Beaney, Michael 192, 196, 449-454
Becker, Oskar 178, 354, 366, 387
Bell, David 179, 196, 198, 355-357, 388
Bell, Winthrop Pickard 178
Belnap, Nuel 307
Beltrami, Eugenio 420
Benacerraf, Paul 24, 29, 230, 321, 413, 465
Berkeley, George 116
Bernard, Claude 95
Beth, Evert W. 85-86, 100, 126, 138, 201, 217, 443

Bishop, E. 21, 124
Bolyai, János 207, 208
Bolzano, Bernard 31, 54, 71, 116, 125, 127, 132, 145, 162-163, 199, 207, 215-216, 240, 271, 397, 443, 447, 467
Bonk, Thomas 169, 196, 198, 348, 355-356, 358
Boole, George 107, 236
Boolos, George, 281-287, 431
Boos, William 420, 438-439
Born, Max 3, 173
Brentano, Franz 3, 8, 90, 125-126, 211-212, 376, 399
Brouwer, L. E. J. 21, 122, 302, 419, 425, 429
Bourbaki, Nicholas 4, 47, 54, 87-88, 100, 131, 133, 138, 152, 158, 163, 199-200, 216, 230
Bunge, Mario 5, 10
Burge, Tyler 291-292
Bynum, Terrell Ward 236
Cantor, Georg 3, 89, 109, 111, 132, 207, 216, 226, 268-269, 271-273, 275, 285-286, 309, 379, 424-426, 442-444
Carl, Wolfgang 237
Carnap, Rudolf 7-9, 23, 25-26, 28, 59, 68, 71, 78, 83, 85, 90-95, 98, 100-103, 117, 123-124, 127-129, 138, 141, 155-158, 162-163, 165, 167-170, 172, 174-184, 186, 188-193, 195-198, 199-200, 211, 217, 235, 276, 298, 325-326, 327-358, 359-368, 370-371, 374-381,

386-389, 393, 397, 399-401, 409-410, 449, 461, 466-467
Cartan, Henri 131
Cassirer, Ernst 90-91, 167, 169, 177, 188-189, 366
Castoriadis, Cornelius 372, 387
Caton, Charles E. 237
Cavaillès, Jean 158
Centrone, Stefania 159, 162-163, 199, 217
Chateaubriand, Oswaldo 5, 9, 60, 62, 68, 297-325, 457-459
Church, Alonzo 6, 99, 101, 260, 262, 303-304, 307
Cirera, Ramón 359-360, 375-377, 386
Cohen, Hermann 188
Cohen, Robert 91, 101, 168, 197
Coleman, Robert 336, 356
Colletti, Lucio 369, 387
Comte, Auguste 362, 372
Currie, Gregory 445
da Silva, Jairo 13, 61, 67, 134, 139, 159, 163-164
Dathe, Uwe 171, 197
Dauben, Johannes 177
Davidson, Donald 303
Dedekind, Richard 5,10, 27, 50, 73, 132, 269-271, 273, 275, 284-285, 325, 419, 425-430
Demopoulos, William 284
Descartes, René 93, 116-118, 123, 127, 139, 189, 428
Diederich, Werner 327, 348, 356
Dieudonné, Jean 47, 131

Dingler, Hugo 178, 346, 361-363, 365
Driesch, Hans 169-170, 173, 331, 349-350, 362-363, 365
Dudman, Victor H. 236, 238
Duhem, Pierre 1, 84, 95-96, 101, 153-154, 192-193, 197, 214, 219, 375-376, 384, 387, 464, 467-468
Dummett, Michael 10, 235-236, 238-240, 251-252, 258, 271, 276, 278, 282, 284-285, 287, 294-295
Dyson, Freeman 385
Echeverría, Javier 360, 368-369
Edwards, Harold M. 419, 424-425
Ehrlich, Philip 420, 437-438
Einstein, Albert 3, 98, 336, 353, 356
Eucken, Rudolph 171
Feferman, Solomon 48, 55
Fernández, Max 67
Ferreiros, José 67
Feynman, Richard P. 385
Field, Hartry 101, 224, 230, 283-284, 321, 404, 410, 413, 465
Floyd, Juliet 420, 439-440
Føllesdal, Dagfinn 6, 30, 86, 101, 201, 206, 215-217, 231, 322, 325, 420, 436, 441-444
Fraenkel, A. 38, 48, 450
Frank, Philip 371
Fred, Ivette 386

Name Index

Frege, Gottlob 2-4, 6-7, 9-10, 15-16, 21, 28-30, 31-32, 35-36, 54-55, 58-59, 65, 68, 71-72, 78, 81, 83, 85-89, 91, 94, 101-104, 107, 110-111, 125, 128-129, 131-133, 139, 143-145, 147-151, 156-157, 159-166, 167, 171, 176-177, 188, 196, 199, 201-207, 211, 215-218, 229-230, 235-241, 244-254, 256-266, 267-269, 271-294, 298, 300-304, 306-308, 313, 315-318, 324-325, 328, 347, 349, 357, 362-363, 366, 368-369, 377, 384, 387, 388-391, 392-397, 400-401, 414-415, 418, 419, 423, 425, 427, 429-436, 443-444, 445-459, 463-467
French, Peter A. 301, 325
Friedman, Michael 93, 102, 123-124, 139, 169, 197, 361, 366, 370, 387
Gabbay, D. 24, 29, 51, 54-55
Gabriel, Gottfried 5, 235, 237, 247-249, 290-292, 458
Gauß, Carl Friedrich 89
Geiger, Moritz 178
Gillies, Donald 384, 387, 467
Gochet, Paul 72
Gödel, Kurt 8, 10, 48, 55, 129, 137-139, 159, 199, 243, 303, 311, 322-326, 377, 379, 419-420, 424, 436-437, 439-444, 448, 464
Greenberg, Marvin Jay 68

Greimann, Dirk 10, 445, 454, 458
Griffin, Nicholas 357, 381
Griss, G. F. C. 21
Grossmann, Reinhardt 237
Gruber, Monika 129, 140
Grünbaum, Adolf 90, 102, 168-169, 197
Guenthner, F. 24, 29, 51, 54-55
Gupta, Anil 307
Hahn, Hans 371, 387
Hale, Bob 5, 283, 294-295
Hart, W. D. 236-237, 240-244
Hauser, Kai 322, 325
Heck, Richard G. 284, 286, 288
Hegel, Georg Wilhelm Friedrich 9, 14, 29
Hegselmann, Rainer 360, 369-371
Heidegger, Martin 85, 178, 366-367, 377
Hempel, Carl G. 96, 154
Henkin, Leon 27-28, 99-100, 320, 420-421, 423-424
Herzberger, Hans G. 307
Hilbert, David 2-3, 13, 21, 98, 128, 133, 159, 163, 165, 207, 216, 236, 269-270, 285, 299, 322, 332, 357, 379, 400-401, 413-414, 419, 436-438, 444
Hill, Claire O. 7, 13, 29-30, 35, 55, 150, 152, 159-160, 163-165, 249, 252, 293, 301, 309, 325, 394, 401, 419, 425, 430, 436-437, 458, 465-466

Hintikka, Jaakko 5, 10, 325, 377, 419-424, 440
Hoche, Hans-Ulrich 237
Hodes, Harold 279
Hodges, Wilfrid 24, 29, 51, 55
Horkheimer, Max 369, 371
Hume, David 116, 118, 127, 140, 207, 216, 240, 242, 244, 273, 285-286, 288, 324, 362, 380, 431-435
Husserl, Malvine 178
Ibarra, Andoni 350, 356-357, 359, 386
Ingarden, Roman 178
Iovino, José 20, 29
Jacoby, Günther, 362-363, 365
Jackson, Howard 238
Janich, Peter 238
Kambartel, Friedrich 236, 238
Kanamori, Akihiro 420, 437-438
Kanitscheider, Bernulf 8, 10, 461-466, 468
Kant, Immanuel 3, 6-7, 9, 13, 21-23, 53, 57-59, 65, 68, 71, 73, 78, 81, 88, 90-91, 93, 103, 105-108, 111-112, 115-126, 133-135, 139, 141, 150, 152, 162, 165, 167-174, 176-177, 179, 188-189, 199, 208, 211, 221, 224, 227, 239-240, 257, 268, 327, 331, 347-349, 352-353, 355-356, 361-362, 367-368, 397, 400-401, 408, 419-420, 427-430, 441, 444, 448-449, 467
Kaplan, David 457
Kaufmann, Felix 167
Kelley, John L. 63, 68
Kennedy, Juliette 322, 326
Khatchadourian, Haig 237, 253-255, 257
Kienzle, Bertram, 237, 253, 257,
Kitcher, Philip 275, 289-291 398-399, 419, 421, 440
Klein, Carsten 192, 196
Klein, Felix 3, 133, 420, 443
Kluge, Eike-Henner W. 237
Kneale, Martha 260
Kneale, William 260
Kolakowski, Leszek 369, 387
Koppelberg, Dirk 360, 379-381
Korselt, Reinhold Alwin 430
Korté, Herbert 336, 356
Köhler, Wolfgang 167-168
Kragh, H. 385, 387
Kripke, Saul 57-58, 68, 75, 78, 80, 237, 241, 253-257, 293, 307
Krivine, Jean Louis 20
Kronecker, Leopold 3, 89, 124, 419, 424-425, 427
Kuhn, Thomas S. 370-371, 373, 379, 387
Landgrebe, Ludwig 3, 156, 176, 178, 180
Langford, C. H. 192
Lasalle Casanave, Abel 67
Lefort, Claude 372, 387
Leibniz, Georg Wilhelm 63, 118, 127, 128, 131, 141, 199, 207, 216, 222, 238-240, 257, 346, 441

Name Index

Lesniewski, Stanislaw 5, 110, 112, 130, 199, 307
Lindström, Per 28-29, 37, 55, 100, 103, 3120
Linke, Paul F. 272
Linsky, Leonard 238
Locke, John 116, 352
Lotze, Hermann 116, 127-128, 207, 214, 216, 239-240, 447
Löwenheim, Leopold 9, 24, 27-28, 37, 50-51, 53, 97, 100, 308-309, 430
Luft, Sebastian 327
Mach, Ernst 91, 93, 167-168, 175, 180-181, 189, 361-362, 365
Maddy, Penelope 224, 230, 403-405, 407-409, 463, 465
Majer, Ulrich 159, 165, 169, 197
Mancosu, Paolo 366, 387
Manzano, María 100, 103
Marcuse, Herbert 369
Marion, Mathieu 420, 439-440
Markov, A. A. 21, 124
Martin, Richard M. 235, 238
Mayer, Verena 179, 198, 355, 357, 361, 365, 388-389, 455-456
Macbeth, Danielle 442-443, 448
Mc Carty, David Charles 419, 425-430
Mendelsohn, Richard L. 293-294
Mill, John Stuart 362, 386, 404-405

Miller, David 67
Minkowski, Hermann 89
Mohanty, J. N. 134, 141, 231
Moore, Gregory H. 45, 47, 55
Morley, Michael 24, 44, 49, 51, 53
Mormann, Thomas 163, 191, 198, 327, 336, 340, 350, 356-357, 359-360, 377-379, 386
Moulines, Carlos Ulises 350, 357, 359-365, 367, 373
Natorp, Paul 8, 87-88, 123, 163, 165, 173, 184
Neurath, Otto 179, 191, 360, 366, 371, 374-379, 387
Newton, Isaac 85, 96, 153, 193
Nietzsche, Friedrich 85
Niniluoto, I. 59, 69
Parsons, Charles 48, 55, 441
Parsons, Terence 236, 293
Paton, Herbert J.
Peano, Giuseppe 27, 49, 73, 320
Perry, John 301, 303, 325
Picardi, Eva 289-290
Plato 201, 221, 242, 244, 298
Poincaré, Henri 125, 153, 211, 214, 219, 336, 346, 357-358, 361, 363, 365, 375-376
Poli, Roberto 5
Popper, Karl 1, 5, 96, 154, 375
Putnam, Hilary 24, 29, 49, 52, 224, 230, 382-383, 422, 464-465
Quine, Willard O. 1, 23, 25-26, 30, 49-50, 52-53, 59, 68, 71, 83-85, 97-98, 135, 141, 173,

193, 195, 216, 224, 230, 297, 299, 302, 304-305, 308, 311-313 315, 317, 320-321, 324, 360, 375-385, 388, 403-404, 416-417, 430, 461-468
Ramsey, Frank 420, 423, 439-440
Reck, Erich H. 454-455
Reichenbach, Hans 328, 357-358, 370-371, 388
Resnik, Michael 236, 238, 257-259, 262, 265, 268-271
Richardson, Alan 93, 103, 361, 388
Rickert, Heinrich 91, 175, 183, 188-189
Riemann, Bernhard 3, 7-8, 13-14, 22, 30, 65, 68, 73, 77-78, 88-89, 105, 107-109, 112, 125, 127, 130, 132, 138, 141, 151, 165, 199, 207-212, 214-217, 268, 328, 333-334, 353, 357-358, 375-376, 388, 399, 443
Rivaduella, Andrés 359
Robinson, Abraham 7, 19, 25-26, 42, 49-50, 98, 222, 413
Rorty, Richard 372
Ruffino, Marco 67
Rungaldier, Edmund 361, 388
Russell, Bertrand 4, 83, 91, 93, 129, 132, 139, 167-169, 175, 183, 198, 226, 237-238, 242, 244, 280, 284, 286, 288, 298, 300-302, 304, 313, 316-317, 321-322, 328, 334, 347, 353, 358, 355-358, 360-364, 377, 387-388, 419-420, 422-423,

430, 432, 434-435, 437, 447, 457
Ryckman, Thomas A. 366, 387
Sanz, Wagner 67
Sarkar, Sahotra 90, 169, 198, 355, 358
Schilpp, Paul A. 90-91, 101-102, 167-168, 197-198, 379, 388
Schirn, Matthias 9, 235, 237, 250-252, 257, 267-269, 273-283, 285-287
Schlick, Moritz 179, 191, 328, 362, 365, 370, 374-376, 388
Schmidt, H. J. 165, 169, 197
Schoenflies, A. 430
Scholz, Erhard 336, 356, 358
Scholz, Heinrich 178, 430
Schröder, Ernst 6, 86, 102, 110-111, 125, 140, 145-147, 164, 202-203, 205, 218
Schuhmann, Elisabeth 9, 141, 148, 165, 391
Schuhmann, Karl 94, 103, 128, 141, 155-156, 166, 176, 391
Schuppe, Wilhelm 91, 167
Schwartz, Stephen P. 57, 68, 78
Schwinger, Julian 385
Searle, John 293
Sepp, Hans-Reiner 327, 354, 358, 366, 388
Shwayder, David S. 235, 238, 262-266
Simons, Peter 439
Simpson, Stephen G. 48, 55
Sintonen, M. 69

Name Index

Sklar, Lawrence 333, 336, 340, 358
Skolem, Thoralf 24, 27-28, 37, 50-53, 97, 100, 299, 308-310, 313, 320
Sluga, Hans 235-236, 238-240, 257
Smith, David Woodruff 134, 141
Sneed, Joseph D. 373
Sober, Elliot 406, 409-410
Sommers, Fred 238
Spinoza, ? 118
Spohn, Wolfgang 179, 198, 355, 357-358, 388
Stegmüller, Wolfgang 373
Stenlund, Sören 28-29, 37, 55-56, 100, 103
Sternfeld, Robert 236-237
Stevenson, Leslie 237
Ströker, Elisabeth 193, 198
Suter, Ronald 237
Tait, W. W. 271-273
Tappenden, Jamie 89, 104
Tarski, Alfred 24, 41, 50-51, 53, 73, 97, 129-130, 140-141, 159, 285, 298, 305-308, 377-379, 384, 420, 436, 439, 447, 462, 466
Terricabras, Josep-María 360, 374
Thiel, Christian 235-236, 238, 244-247, 287-288, 435
Thron, Wolfgang J. 56, 63, 69
Tieszen, Richard 322, 326
Tomonaga, Si-Itiro 385
Torretti, Roberto 330, 358
Tugendhat, Ernst 238, 259-263
Tymoczko, Thomas 403-404
Uebel, Thomas 359, 374-375
van Atten, Mark 322, 326
Veraart, Albert 236
Volkelt, Johannes 363, 365
von Helmholtz, Hermann 210, 214-215, 334, 348
von Kutschera, Franz 236, 289
von Plato, Jan 420, 437-438
von Schubert-Soldern, Richard 167
Vossenkuhl, Wilhelm 179, 196, 198, 356-357, 388
Wang, Hao 138, 141, 322, 326, 441
Webb, Judson 419-420
Weidemann, Hermann 303, 326
Weierstrass, Karl 3, 5, 124, 426, 444
Weil, André 131
Weiner, Joan 445
Wertheimer, Max 167-168
Weyl, Helene 178
Weyl, Hermann 3, 133, 169, 178, 197, 336, 356, 358, 362, 365, 387, 419-420, 425, 438-439, 444
Whitehead, Alfred North 4-6, 129, 286, 360, 362-364, 422-423
Wiggins, David 235, 237
Wittgenstein, Ludwig 8-9, 238, 304, 307, 317, 359, 374-377, 388, 403-404, 410-412, 420, 439-441

Wolenski, Jan 59, 69, 420, 439
Wright, Crispin 281, 283
Yablo, Stephen 307
Yaqûb, Aladdin M. 307
Zermelo, Ernst 3-4, 38, 47-48, 55, 133, 284, 288, 430, 437, 450
Ziehen, Theodor 362-363
Zilzel, Edgar 371

Subject Index

abstract object 240-243, 280, 283, 312, 455
abstract objectuality 301
$\aleph_0$-categorical 74
α-categorical ($\aleph_1$-, β-categorical, etc.) 24, 44, 52
$\aleph_0$-categoricity
α-categoricity ($\aleph_1$-, β-categoricity, etc.) 52
amalgamation property 43
analytic *a posteriori* 57-60, 62-68, 72, 74-75, 79, 357
analyticity 57, 71-77, 79-81, 152, 162
analytic law 57, 62, 65- 67, 76-77, 299, 317-318, 392, 397-398
analytic judgement 120
analytic necessity 62, 299, 318, 398
analytic statement 58-65, 72-73, 76-78, 162, 201, 247, 467
analytic truth 380-381
apodictic 241
apodictic laws 397
apodictic necessities 397
apodictically valid 398
a posteriori 57, 59, 65-68, 71-72, 74-79, 208, 257, 349-350, 357, 376, 398
aposterioricity 57-58, 65, 75-76
a priori 57, 59, 65, 67-69, 75, 77-78, 85, 105-107, 118-120, 122, 134, 159, 173-174, 208-209, 213, 227, 241, 257, 269, 349, 352-353
aprioricity 57-58, 65, 75, 90, 126, 213, 353, 356
autopsychological 181, 189
autopsychological basis 180-181, 181, 186, 189-191
Axiom of Choice 20, 45-48, 55, 437, 441
Axiom V 275, 280, 282, 285-288
Banach space 131, 209
Benacerrafian 292
Brouwerian 412
Bourbakian 108, 154, 196, 204
Cantorian 14
Carnapian 85, 91, 93, 96, 123, 169, 359-360, 368, 375, 379, 386
cardinal number 45, 52, 130, 209, 273, 275, 283, 429, 465, 469
cardinality 21, 24, 52, 121, 268, 272, 285, 309, 320, 422
cardinality, infinite 14, 24, 50-51, 53, 99
categorial 149, 187, 201, 213-209, 396, 398
categorial abstraction 137, 227-228, 442
categorial component 136-137
categorial form 213, 317
categorial imagination 226, 442

categorical intuition 134, 136-137, 148, 224, 226-228, 398, 442
categorial objectuality 137, 225-228, 442
categorial perception 226, 442
categorical 27, 73, 99
categoricity 27, 51-52, 99
closed formula 25, 42-43
closed formula, existential 42
closed formula, universal 42
Compactness Theorem 28, 100, 320
complete, semantically 27, 436
complete, syntactically (or deductively) 24, 42, 44, 52, 436
completeness, semantic 26, 28, 96, 159, 423-424
completeness, syntactical 159
Completeness Theorem 46, 309
conceptual word 260, 263, 265-266, 274, 456
constitution 92-93, 179, 179-180, 184, 186-188, 191, 229
constitutional 93, 184
constitutional system 92, 168, 179, 181-182, 184, 186
constructibility 105, 420, 437-438
construction 52, 103, 105, 108, 122, 124, 151, 191, 208, 214, 222, 307, 310, 379, 388, 414-415, 426, 468
constructivism 21-24, 51, 88, 108, 222, 438, 444

constructivist 21, 49, 51-52, 124, 310, 319, 321, 379, 427, 429, 438, 440, 444
content, conceptual 277-278, 282-283, 449-447, 450-454, 457
content, judgeable 258, 275, 277-278, 282, 451-452
content line 237
context principle 238, 257-259, 261-262, 265-266, 278-280
contingency 57-58, 75
contingent *a priori* 57
conventionalism 24-26, 51-52, 98, 196, 345-346, 357, 361, 375-376, 379, 388, 403-404, 410-412, 414
conventionalist 49-50, 346, 411, 4015
countersense 87, 129, 156-157, 200
curvature 22, 52, 65, 67, 77, 90, 125, 208, 211, 215, 217, 333-335, 341-343
curvature, constant 334
curvature, variable 52, 334-335
decidability 26, 99
decidable 99
Dedekind-Peano arithmetic 27, 50
Downward Löwenheim-Skolem Theorem 47, 100
dualism 40-41, 44
Duhemian 468
Dummettian 279, 284, 290-291, 295
eidetic variation 134-135, 137

Eklof-Sabbagh Theorem 43
Elementarerlebnisse 168, 181-182
elementary equivalence 64
empiricism 49, 71, 83, 85, 97, 101, 118-119, 144, 175, 191-193, 368, 375-376, 378-380 388, 403-407, 409, 411, 415
empiricism, logical 178, 197, 359, 369-372, 378
empiricism, mathematical 405-406
empiricist 83-84, 96-99, 116, 118, 144, 191, 193, 221, 223-225, 361-362, 379, 405
empiricist, logical 97, 118, 154, 192, 369-372
empiricists, mathematical 405
empiricist-positivist 93, 95, 167, 191
equinumerous 422, 431, 433-434
Erlebnisse 168, 180, 186, 190, 194
Erlebnisstrom 168, 194
essence 170-171, 174, 185
essence, contemplation (or intuition) of 152, 170-174
Euclidean 214, 333, 335, 341, 344, 400
Euclidean-geometric 132
Euclidean geometry 22, 122, 204, 211, 213-214
Euclidean multiplicity 213
Euclidean space 91, 169, 212, 336, 345, 352, 399
expansion, language 42

expansion, model 42
explanatory science 96, 153-154
εποχη 184
First Characterization Theorem 28, 100
first philosophy 116-118, 126-127
formalization 137-138, 152, 227-228, 246, 318, 393, 397
formation rules 94, 128, 155-156
form of intuition 122, 347
Fregean 88, 118, 151, 160, 201, 222, 225, 235, 237, 247, 250, 256, 267-268, 272-280 282-284, 286, 289-290, 293, 300, 304, 308, 394-396, 415, 419, 431-432, 435, 443, 445-449, 453, 457
Fregean group 16
Fregeanism 288
Fregean semantics 18, 33, 35-36, 415
functions 21, 27, 38, 51, 124, 199, 237, 239, 246, 250-251, 259, 262, 264, 275, 292, 311, 423, 450
functions, propositional 423
Fundierung 92, 194
Gestalt psychology 167
Gestalt psychologists 168
Gödel's incompleteness results (or theorems) 133, 159, 311, 322, 326, 440-441
grounding 88, 92, 143, 157, 168, 186-187, 190

group 15-16, 23, 30, 36, 39, 43, 49, 53, 107, 121, 132, 136, 229
group, Abelian 229
group of transformations 17-18, 35-36, 48
group, topological 131, 209, 229
Hausdorff space 40, 46, 222, 229, 384, 415
Henkin's semantics 27-28, 99-100
heteropsychological 92-93, 180 189-191
heteropsychologicality 93
homeomorphism 340
Hume's Principle 285-286, 288
Husserlian group I 18
Husserlian group II 18
Husserlian semantics 34, 49
hypotheses cum fundamento in re 96, 154
imagination 119, 135, 226, 442
imagination, categorical 226, 442
imagination, sensory (or sense) 226, 442
incomplete, semantically 26, 421
incompleteness, semantic 320
indispensabilism 52
indispensabilist 49, 52-53
indispensability argument 97, 223-224
interderivable 161, 222-223
interderivability 30, 48
intersubjectivity 92-93, 189-190

intuition 21-22, 88, 105-107, 108, 119-122, 124, 127, 135, 171, 189, 208, 212-213, 215, 225, 228, 239, 268, 303, 331-332, 335-336, 349, 408, 427, 429, 435, 442
intuition, categorial 134, 136-137, 152, 224, 226-228, 398, 408, 442
intuition, conceptual 398
intuition, eidetic (or of essence) 134-135, 152, 221-222, 228, 324, 348-350, 353, 398, 408, 442
intuition, forms of 14, 122-120, 347, 408
intuition, intellectual 122, 124, 134, 224
intuition, mathematical 137-138, 152, 224, 314, 441-442, 464
intuition, sensible 107, 122, 124, 133, 135
intuition, sensory 225-226
intuitionism 108, 195, 310, 403, 419
intuitionist 289, 310, 382, 432, 434
isomorphic 27, 43-44, 46, 50, 60-64, 66-67, 72-74, 76-77, 79-80
isomorphism 39, 60, 64, 67, 74-77, 79, 259, 271, 276, 284
Kantian 14, 21, 73, 88, 123-124, 133, 159, 167, 172, 188-190, 208, 211, 240, 289-292,

Subject Index

353, 370-371, 408, 412, 427-429, 443, 445, 467
Kantianism 289
Keisler-Shelah Theorem 43, 51
logicism 128, 131-133, 160, 195, 206, 257, 274, 268, 283, 290, 322, 347, 364, 419, 427, 432, 445, 463, 467
logicist 20, 88, 157-158, 236, 245, 253, 275, 286, 288, 306, 394, 426-427, 444
logicist programme 432, 435
Löwenheim-Skolem Theorem 28, 308-309, 320
Löwenheim-Skolem-Tarski Theorem 47, 50-51, 53
manifold 22, 89, 107-108, 125, 127, 130, 151, 158-159, 199, 207-210, 213, 216-217, 429
manifold, continuous 22, 105, 108-109, 208
manifold, countable 121
manifold, differentiable 229
manifold, discrete 22, 108-109, 121, 208
manifold, Euclidean 213
manifold, geometric(al) 22, 87, 132, 138, 210-211, 206-207, 210-211, 215
mathematical necessity 62-64, 75
mathesis universalis 88, 128, 131, 133, 138, 159, 207
Maximal Ideal Theorem 44-45
metalogical 26-27, 39, 41, 48, 438-439
model companion 43

model completion 43
model-complete 25, 42-43, 50, 223, 284
model-completeness 19, 222, 283
model theory 14, 19-20, 29, 37, 41, 50, 52, 64, 98-100, 222, 319
model theory, abstract 26, 100
model theory, classical 18-20, 23-25, 27, 37, 50, 98-99
Morley's Theorem 44, 49, 51
multi-sorted semantics 27, 99
naturalism 221, 223, 461-465, 468
naturalism, ideological 461-464, 468
naturalism, mathematical 463, 466
necessary *a posteriori* 57
necessary truth 241-244, 316
necessity 57-58, 62-63, 65, 68, 72, 75, 78, 93, 110, 211, 214, 223, 240-242, 249, 254, 257, 286, 299, 317-318, 326, 353, 378-379, 393, 398
necessity, logical 413
necessity, causal 429
neighbourhood 40, 109
neighbourhood, open 40
Neo-Kantian 88, 90-91, 93, 115, 118, 123-124, 126, 167, 171-172, 176, 188-189, 211, 279, 291, 327, 331, 349, 353, 361-362, 445
nexus, objective 153
nexus, of truths 96, 153-154

nexus, ontological 153
nexus, subjective 153
noema 86, 101, 391
n-fold extended magnitude 22, 107, 208
nominalism 24-26, 49-52, 83, 97-98, 222-223, 239, 270, 283, 413, 415
nominalist 23, 25-26, 49, 97-99, 110, 144, 310
nominalistic 138, 439
non-categoricity 27
non-Euclidean 213
non-Euclidean geometries 14, 22, 89, 207, 211, 214, 420
nonsense 53, 87, 94, 128, 138, 155-157, 191, 200, 371, 392, 410
objectual 223, 396
objectualities 53, 137, 170, 187, 227, 301, 318, 392, 397
objectualities, categorial 137, 225-228, 442
objectualities, mathematical 137, 227-229, 442
objectualities, sensible 225-226
Ockam's Razor 83, 298
ontology, formal 87, 128, 130, 138, 151, 209, 306, 353, 392, 442
ontology, regional 346, 353, 400
open set 39, 107
ordinal number 130, 158, 271, 273
perception 220, 428
perception, categorial 226, 442

perception, sense (or sensory) 225-226, 442
phenomenalism 175
phenomenalist 95, 192, 360-361, 363-364, 374-375
phenomenological reduction 92, 126, 183-184
phenomenology 29, 30, 115-117, 123, 126-127, 135, 144, 151, 167-168, 171, 178, 180, 183, 231, 325-326, 366, 387, 444
philosophia prima 116-117
Platonism 19, 24, 31, 52, 55, 152, 165, 231, 270, 283, 289, 441, 443-444
Platonism, Fregean 222, 283, 419
Platonism, logical 292
Platonism, mathematical 31, 49, 206
Platonism, physicalistic 230
physicalism 374-376, 461-462
physicalist 95, 97, 123, 180, 189-190, 192, 310, 375, 464
positivism 93, 94, 372
positivism, logical 97, 229
positivist 90, 92, 135, 153, 183
positivist, logical 95-96, 322, 372
positivistic 181, 316
Prime Ideal Theorem 20
Principle of Tolerance 98, 195-196, 376
protocol sentences 95, 182
psychologism 86-87, 116, 125-126, 147, 150-151, 162, 187,

Subject Index

200, 202, 204, 216, 237-238, 240, 24-248, 259, 266, 273, 290-291, 372, 392, 430, 436, 443, 446
psychologistic 150, 273, 287
Quinean 23, 97, 192, 360, 403, 464
reason 119, 189, 427-429
reduced product 43
referent 15-17, 31-40, 49, 84, 86-87, 125, 127, 145, 147-150, 161, 199, 201-206, 215, 223, 225, 249-252, 255-256, 258-260, 262, 264-266, 272, 274, 280, 282, 285, 289, 293, 300-303, 307, 315, 368-369, 385, 392, 395-396, 435, 449, 451, 453-454, 456-457
referential basis 17, 19, 34-36, 149, 161, 457
relativity, general 14, 328, 334, 341, 345, 353, 413, 468
relativity, special 341
representation 22, 106, 121, 146, 151, 170, 173, 203, 215, 280, 329, 331
requirement 131, 172-173, 214, 229, 265, 307, 320, 332-333, 335, 338, 344-346, 349, 351, 410, 428
reverse mathematics 47-48, 55
Riemannian 89, 104, 210, 214, 332-333
Robinson's Model-Completeness Test 19, 25-26, 42, 49-50, 98, 413

sense 15-16, 31-36, 47-49, 55, 84, 86-87, 125, 127, 143, 145-149, 156, 160-161, 163, 165, 199-206, 213, 215, 238, 248-250, 252, 256, 258-259, 261-266, 272, 274-276, 278-280, 282, 287-289, 293-294, 391-392, 394-396, 449, 451-454, 456-457
senseless 146, 203
sensibility 89, 119, 122, 137, 152, 189, 227, 385
set 15, 16, 21-22, 25, 27, 35-41, 43, 45-48, 50, 108-111, 130-132, 136-137, 158, 200, 206-207, 209, 216, 225-228, 240, 262, 266, 278, 280-281, 298, 309, 341, 407-409, 415, 420-422, 416, 444
set-theoreticism
set theory 38, 46, 48, 109-110, 130, 132, 200, 207, 243, 309-310, 361, 384, 408, 420, 422, 437-438, 450, 463
set theory, Bernays-von Neumann-Gödel 38, 48
set theory, Zermelo-Fraenkel 38, 48, 450
situation of affairs 17-20, 30, 33-36, 40-41, 44, 47, 149, 160-161, 206, 231, 384, 394, 396
Skolem's model 27,
Skolem's Paradox 309, 422
Skolem's Theorem on Non-Standard Models 50-51
space 13-14, 21-22, 90, 105-109, 119-122, 125, 168, 172,

174, 210, 212-213, 215, 258, 328, 331-336, 339-340, 342-346, 348-353, 355, 399-400, 408, 463
space, affine 319, 329
space, curvature of 52, 334
space, dimensionality of 87, 352
space, formal 174-175, 328-330, 347, 349, 352, 399
space, formal metric 330
space, formal projective 330, 337
space, formal topological 174, 330, 337, 350-352
space, homogeneous 91, 169, 334
space, intuitive 90, 167-170, 172-175, 328-329, 331-333, 335-337, 348-350, 353, 356, 358, 399
space, intuitive metric 172, 324-326, 328, 332-333, 336, 340, 345-346, 352
space, intuitive projective 332, 336-337
space, intuitive topological 172, 332, 336-337, 348, 351-353
space, isotropic 335
space, metric 131, 172, 329-330, 332, 345, 348-349
space, physical 14, 89-90, 107, 126, 129, 132, 170, 174-175, 208, 210-211, 215, 217, 328-329, 337-342, 345-348, 350-351, 353, 365, 397-400,

space, physical metric 331, 333, 339-341, 349-350
space, physical projective 341
space, physical topological 339-341, 348, 350-352
space, projective 319, 329, 337
space, topological 23, 33, 39-40, 45, 53, 107, 109, 121, 172-173, 229, 328-329, 340-342, 348-349, 351, 381, 384, 415, 466
space, vector 45-46
space-time 197, 334, 341, 350, 365
species 170-171, 187, 329-330, 337, 383
state of affairs 16-18, 30, 33-34, 36-38, 136-137, 149-150, 161, 206, 231, 300-302, 304, 315-317, 394, 396, 451, 453
state of affairs, abstract 38
stipulation 338-345, 348-352
Stone's Representation Theorem 46
substitution 346
substructure 25, 41, 98, 195, 413
substructure, elementary 25, 41, 98, 195, 309, 413
subsumption 346
synthetic *a priori* 57-58, 61, 72-75, 78-79, 81, 110, 174, 201, 211, 228
syntheticity 57-58, 65, , 75
syntheticity *a priori* 71-72, 74-76, 152, 162, 397

synthetic *a priori* inferences 397-399
Tarskian 378
Tarski's Upward Löwenheim-Skolem Theorem 24, 97
theory of types, ramified 313-314
theory of types, simple 313-314
Transcendental Aesthetic 21, 107, 427
Transcendental Analytic 428
transcendental consciousness 127
transcendental deduction 428
Transcendental Dialectic 427-428
transcendental ego 190
transcendental idealism 268, 438
transcendental phenomenological 391
transcendental phenomenologist 150
transcendental phenomenology 115-117, 123, 126-127, 144, 183, 444
transcendental philosophy 115, 370
transcendental psychologism 126
transcendental reduction 117
transcendental subject 115, 122, 124
transcendental turn 117, 126-127, 134, 144, 157, 184, 391
transformation rules 94, 129, 155-156

Trichotomy of Cardinals 45
truth-value 3, 15-16, 18-19, 32-33, 36-37, 50, 148-150, 206, 246, 250, 260-263, 265, 267, 280, 293, 368, 413, 435, 446, 449, 451, 453-455, 457
Tychonoff's Theorem 20, 45, 222, 381, 384
Tychonoff's Theorem for Hausdorf Spaces 46, 222, 384
ultrafilter 41, 43, 54
Ultrafilter Theorem 20, 41, 45-47, 222
ultrapower 43
ultraproduct, 43, 53, 469
undecidable 26, 414, 440
underdetermination 96, 193
understanding 116, 119-120, 132, 152, 189, 428-429, 442
verificationism 97
Weak Semantic Completeness Theorem 28, 99, 320
well-formed sentence 128, 312
whole, 105, 109, 110-111
Zorn's Lemma 20, 222

www.ingramcontent.com/pod-product-compliance
Lightning Source LLC
Chambersburg PA
CBHW070713160426
43192CB00009B/1177